O9-BUD-292

From Jerusalem to Irian Jaya

Other Books by Ruth A. Tucker

Daughters of the Church: A History of Women and Ministry from New Testament Times to the Present, with Walter Liefeld

Private Lives of Pastors' Wives

Guardians of the Great Commission: The Story of Women in Modern Missions

Christian Speakers Treasury

Another Gospel: Alternative Religions and the New Age Movement

Stories of Faith: Inspirational Episodes from the Lives of Christians

Women in the Maze: Questions and Answers on Biblical Equality

Multiple Choices: Making Wise Decisions

Family Album: Portraits of Family Life through the Centuries

Seasons of Motherhood

Not Ashamed: The Story of Jews for Jesus

Walking Away from Faith: Unraveling the Mystery of Belief and Unbelief

Second Edition

From Jerusalem to Irian Jaya

A Biographical History of Christian Missions

Ruth A. Tucker

From Jerusalem to Irian Jaya

Requests for information should be addressed to:

Zondervan, *Grand Rapids, Michigan 49530*

Library of Congress Cataloging-in-Publication Data

Tucker, Ruth, 1945-
From Jerusalem to Irian Jaya : a biographical history of Christian missions / Ruth A. Tucker.— 2nd ed.
p. cm.
Includes bibliographical references and indexes.
ISBN 0-310-23937-0
1. Missionaries—Biography. 2. Missions—History. I. Title.
BV3700.T83 2004
266'.0092'2—dc22 2003027902

This edition printed on acid-free paper.

Interior design by Sharon VanLoozenoord

Printed in the United States of America

11 • 15 14 13

To

my cousin

Valerie Stellrecht

for

many years

of faithful missionary service

in Quito, Ecuador

Contents

Part 2: The "Great Century"

Part 3: The Expanding Involvement

Part 4: The Era of the New Millennium

List of Graphics

Pictures and Credits

Maps

Charts

Preface to the Second Edition

More than two decades have passed since the first edition of this volume was published. I was then new in the field of mission studies. Three years earlier, when I was assigned to teach a course on the history of missions, a colleague commented, "It's an important course, but it's too bad the subject matter is so boring." He was right. The texts then available on the worldwide scope of Christian missions were encyclopedic—filled with names and dates and statistics and offering a vast array of factual details about mission organizations and geographical locations. I needed a text that would engage my students. My own teaching style gravitated to content fueled by thorny issues and brutally honest biography.

In my course preparation I quickly discovered that the most interesting debates and controversies in church history have related to mission outreach and evangelism. An added bonus was the lively cast of characters. I have often wondered as I have studied missions history if there is any other field of endeavor that has been peopled by such a "crazy" lot. Many of them were, it seems to me, more eccentric and risky and individualistic and driven than other segments of the population. Often self-sacrificing to the extreme, many were also pedantic and critical and mean-spirited—unable to live in harmony with colleagues or with those to whom they sought to minister.

When I think of missionaries of past generations I am reminded of Sonny, the lead character in Robert Duvall's film *The Apostle*, and of Michael Yaconelli's book *Messy Spirituality*. Sonny was a preacher and evangelist whose commitment to ministry was unrivaled. But he had feet of clay. His sins were as big as was his heart. He was driven. Nothing could hold him back—not even the messy spirituality that shaped his entire persona. In the end, the law caught up with him, and the last scene, as the credits are rolling, shows Sonny on a chain gang—still preaching the gospel.

The fascinating story of Sonny and messy spirituality has been played out time and again in the mission setting—often with critical issues swirling in the midst of cultural misunderstanding. Here theology is raw and basic. Who is God—in light of other religions? What is the fate of those who have never heard the gospel? Is the message one of contextualization or transformation? Where does competition end and ecumenical harmony begin? The issues that troubled missionaries of the past continue to trouble us today—not just on the "mission field" but at home.

But where is "home"? Two decades ago there was a greater distinction between *home* and *foreign*. Today such distinctions are set aside as missionaries crisscross the globe. This new edition reflects this phenomenon of globalization, and it more fully represents missionaries from the whole *community* of the Christian faith—from Catholics to Pentecostals. Material has been updated where appropriate and new information has been added—all in a humble effort to tell an incredibly good story.

PREFACE

How does one write a history of Christian missions—a history that entails tens of thousands of noteworthy professionals sent out by hundreds of mission societies to every country in the world over a period of some two thousand years? It is an enormous subject that has unfortunately been almost destroyed by historians who have attempted to squeeze too many dates, events, organizations, and names into one volume. But the history of missions is not a compilation of arid facts. It is a fascinating story of human struggles and emotions, intertwined with tragedy, adventure, romance, intrigue, and sorrow.

It was only through the tireless efforts of its missionaries that Christianity became the world's largest religion, a factor that has changed the face of the globe. "World Christianity," writes Lesslie Newbigin, "is the result of the great missionary expansion of the last two centuries. That expansion, whatever one's attitude to Christianity may be, is one of the most remarkable facts of human history. One of the oddities of current affairs . . . is the way in which the event is so constantly ignored or undervalued."

But if the remarkable expansion of Christianity has been ignored and undervalued, so have the men and women who have been responsible for its expansion. They were single-minded people, wholly equal to the task they accomplished, driven by a sense of urgency that is rarely seen even within the most patriotic and militant of causes. "The early missionaries were born warriors and very great men," wrote Pearl Buck (who could hardly be termed a missionary enthusiast). "No weak or timid soul could sail the seas to foreign lands and defy death and danger unless he did carry religion as his banner, under which even death itself would be a glorious end. To go forth, to cry out, to warn, to save others—these were frightful urgencies upon the soul already saved. There was a very madness of necessity—an agony of salvation."

Who were these missionaries who sacrificed so much to carry the gospel to the ends of the earth? Were they spiritual giants who gloriously overcame the obstacles they confronted? No. They were ordinary individuals, plagued by human frailties and failures. Supersaints they were not. Like the colorful cast of biblical characters beginning with the book of Genesis and continuing on through the New Testament, they were willing to be used by God despite their human weaknesses, and it was in that sense that they were able to make such an indelible imprint on the world.

When thinking of the great missionary force that spread out over the world during the past centuries, the names that generally come to mind first are those of great men—David Brainerd, William Carey, Adoniram Judson, David Livingstone, or Hudson Taylor. But women—single and married—constituted almost two-thirds of the North American missionary force. Family life and children had a significant bearing on missionary work. "Family problems," writes Harold J. Westing, "are the number one cause on the missionary casualty list." Thus, a strong emphasis on family life is fully warranted in a historical account of Christian missions.

The most difficult challenge in developing a biographical history of the Christian missionary movement has been to limit the number of people to be dealt with. In the final analysis, the choice of the individuals covered and the issues and incidents in their lives that are emphasized is a subjective decision of the author. A number of great missionaries and mission societies have been left out; others with fewer credits to their names have been included. Hopefully, this account covers a representative and significant cross section of those who so valiantly served in the front lines of the Christian advance.

That biography should be the element that binds a history of Christian missions together is only fitting. Ralph Waldo Emerson once said there is "properly no history, only biography," an insight that is essentially true of any field of history. But biography is especially suitable for portraying the history of missions. The Christian missionary movement through the centuries has been perpetuated by missionary biography. In fact, writes Geoffrey Moorhouse, it "became the most fruitful . . . stimuli" to the vocation during the nineteenth century. It is hoped, then, that this book will not only inform and instruct but also inspire readers to be willing to be used of God in this, the greatest cause in all human history.

PART 1

The Irresistible Advance

PART 1

The Irresistible Advance

The urgency of the Great Commission that Jesus gave to his disciples was probably not well understood by many New Testament believers, nor was it even the primary impetus for the rapid church growth during the early centuries. Persecution scattered believers throughout the Mediterranean world and Christianity quickly took root, at first mainly where Gentile seekers had gotten a head start in synagogues. By the end of the first century the church was beginning to move into Europe, Africa, and Asia. "Had the church been wiped off the face of the earth at the end of the first century," writes Ramsay MacMullen, "its disappearance would have caused no dislocation in the empire, just as its presence was hardly noticed at the time. . . . Three centuries later it had successfully displaced or suppressed the other religions of the empire's population."[1]

While evangelism and church planting took priority in the New Testament church, theological issues soon came to the fore in the era of Emperor Constantine, and Christian leaders found themselves consumed not only with heretical influences from without, but also with doctrinal controversies from within. Theologians hammered out creeds, and church councils argued about everything from the deity of Christ to the date of Easter. In the process, the New Testament missionary fervor declined. Missionary outreach would continue in the centuries following Constantine largely through monastic ministries—some more polite and proper than others. For example, one of the most celebrated evangelists of the fifth century was the peculiar saint known as Symeon Stylites. He made his home high on a pillar near Antioch, where he stood "day after broiling day . . . drawing to him by his great repute the most various visitors from the most distant places."[2] Bishop Theodoret, who spent time in a small enclosure at the base of Symeon's pillar, wrote about the evangelistic appeal that radiated from this remote outpost:

> [Even the bedouins] in many thousands, enslaved to the darkness of impiety, were enlightened by the station upon the pillar. . . . They arrived in companies, 200 in one, 300 in another, occasionally a thousand. They renounced with their shouts their traditional errors; they broke up their venerated idols in the presence of that great light; and they forswore the ecstatic rites of Aphrodite, the demon whose service they had long accepted. They enjoyed divine religious initiation and received their law instead spoken by that holy tongue [of Symeon]. . . . And I myself was witness to these things and heard them, as they renounced ancestral impiety and submitted to evangelic instruction.[3]

With the invasion of the barbarians and the subsequent fall of the Roman Empire, Western Europe was in chaos, and it required the talent and ability of a man like Gregory the Great, bishop of Rome (590–604), to stabilize the church and revitalize its missionary activity. He saw the necessity of political alliances, and he established a pattern of church-state cooperation that continued for centuries—convinced that the church could not maintain its presence among hostile peoples without the military support of temporal rulers.

Charlemagne (742–814), the great king of the Franks, ranks above all other kings as a military supporter of Christianity. No other ruler before or after gave as much attention to the copying and transmission of the Bible. Charlemagne brought nominal Christianity to vast portions of Europe and was the prime mover in the Carolingian Renaissance that fostered learning and a wide variety of Christian activity.

But while the Christian movement seemed to be making headway with the barbarians in middle Europe, it was rapidly losing ground to the mighty force of Islam as that religion spread out from east to west through Palestine, across Africa, and on into Spain. The Muslims were stopped by military might at the Battle of Tours in 732, and during this period force was seen by most leaders as the only viable response to this all-encompassing threat. The Crusades (1095–1291), described by Ralph Winter as "the most massive, tragic misconstrual of Christian mission in all history,"[4] were launched to reclaim lost territories. They eventually failed in that effort, while at the same time diverting vast resources of Christendom from any true missionary endeavor.

This is not to suggest that there were no sincere missionary enterprises during the Middle Ages. Celtic and Arian missionaries conducted noteworthy evangelistic ventures, bringing vast numbers of barbarians into the church. In many cases, the Roman Catholic monks actively evangelized the barbarians. The Benedictines were particularly influential through their founding of mission compounds in remote areas; but gradual accumulation of wealth eventually brought about their decline, diverting the monks' attention from spiritual matters and making their monasteries prime targets for Viking raids.

The attacks of the Goths, the Visigoths, and the Vandals that brought down the Roman Empire were almost mild in comparison to the later raids by the

Vikings. These seafaring warriors "were the scourge of England and the continent," according to Herbert Kane. "So devastating were their raids on the monasteries and churches that for a time they threatened to terminate the missionary outreach of the English Church."[5] The "Irish volcano which had poured forth a passionate fire of evangelism for three centuries," writes Winter, "cooled almost to extinction." The destruction of the monasteries, though, did not erase the gospel witness. "The phenomenal power of Christianity," as Winter points out, could not be destroyed: "The conquerors became conquered by the faith of the captives. Usually it was the monks sold as slaves or the Christian girls forced to be their wives and mistresses which eventually won these savages of the north."[6] Nevertheless, the Viking attacks were a devastating blow to the stability of both the Celtic and Roman traditions in the British Isles and in central Europe.

The destruction of biblical manuscripts along with monasteries and churches had a negative effect on missions, but there were other factors that were no doubt an even greater deterrent to evangelism during the Middle Ages. Church leadership during much of the medieval period was in a sad state of affairs. The power of the papacy had long invited abuses, and in the tenth century the decadence representing that office had reached an all-time low. Some of the popes were among the worst scoundrels in society. Pope Stephen IV (d. 772) brought his deceased predecessor to trial (propping his corpse up in a chair to face the synod), and he himself was thrown in prison, where, after serving less than a year, he was murdered at the orders of an opponent. Other popes openly committed immoral and criminal acts while in office. The Great Schism of the fourteenth and fifteenth centuries that resulted in two popes, and for a time three, did nothing to improve the image of the office or spirituality of the church leadership.

But if this politicized form of Christianity was too preoccupied with other matters to be concerned about missions, so was the academic tradition. The speculative and philosophically-oriented theology of the Middle Ages known as Scholasticism occupied the best minds of the church. Education turned away from practical pursuits and instead was concentrated on reconciling dogma with reason. "With intrepid confidence," writes Philip Schaff, "these busy thinkers ventured upon the loftiest speculations, raised and answered all sorts of doubts and ran every accepted dogma through a fiery ordeal to show its invulnerable nature. They were knights of theology. . . . Philosophy . . . was their handmaid" and "dialectics their sword and lance."[7]

On the positive side, there were many movements that sought to purify the church. A number of efforts were aimed at reforming the papacy, some more successful than others, and there were significant monastic reforms—ones that usually resulted in a greater evangelistic outreach. The Cluniac reform that began in 910 at the monastery of Cluny in central France was the beginning of a spiritual renewal in monasticism. It was followed by the inspirational ministry of Bernard of Clairvaux (1090–1153) and the founding of the Cistercians that brought an even greater resurgence of evangelistic activity in Europe. The greatest mission development in Roman Catholic religious orders, however, came with the rise of the friars—the preaching monks who in the late medieval period stimulated mission outreach. The Franciscans (founded 1209) and Dominicans (founded 1216) and later the Jesuits (founded 1534) planted churches and monasteries in Europe and all over the world.

For many Christians these reform efforts were not carried far enough, and throughout the Middle Ages there were movements to purify the body of Christ that were in direct opposition to the Roman Catholic Church. The Waldensians are a prime example. Though they were branded as heretics, they sought to reflect New Testament Christianity more closely than did most Roman Catholics. They emphasized evangelism, Bible study, and personal commitment to Christ, and from the twelfth through the fifteenth centuries they made their presence known in central and eastern Europe. Beginning in the fourteenth century, the followers of Wycliffe and Hus instituted similar reforms, paving the way for the Protestant Reformation.

The sixteenth-century Protestant Reformation stirred hearts and shook the very foundations of Christendom but contributed little to evangelism outside areas that were already deemed Christian. This spiritual renewal in Europe brought a meaningful faith to large segments of the population, but the urgency to reach out to others was not seen as a top priority. Protestants were consumed in fighting for their own survival (and among themselves), and in some cases the Great Commission was all but forgotten.

The Protestant Reformation, as with all other reform movements throughout church history, had difficulty maintaining its spiritual vitality. The enthusiasm generated by Luther, Calvin, Melanchthon, and Zwingli soon began to wane and many Protestant churches became appendages of the state. But as had been the case in centuries past, no matter how low the established church sank there were always those who sought a deeper spiritual meaning in life. The Anabaptist movement that spawned the Brethren and Mennonite churches reached out in evangelistic zeal, and during the seventeenth and eighteenth centuries evangelical revivals furthered the mission advance. Pietism on the continent and the evangelical movements in Britain and America led to a revitalization of Christianity from which a passion for missions arose. Pietists and their Moravian successors fanned out all over the world, and Christians in Britain and America were moved to action by a spiritual concern for the native American Indians. The dawning of the modern missionary movement had begun, but only after generations of uncertainty.

1

The Early Centuries: Evangelizing the Roman Empire

The world today—not just the Christian church—would be very different if the zeal to evangelize had not been at the very heart of the Christian faith. Christianity and missions are inseparably linked. It is impossible to imagine Christianity as a living religion today without the vibrant missionary outreach that sprang forth after Pentecost. This missionary vision was part and parcel of the life of the church. The New Testament writers were not religious thinkers who speculated on matters of doctrine. Rather, theology was born out of necessity—the necessity of preaching the gospel. The New Testament is the result of that passion. "The gospels in particular," writes David Bosch, "are to be viewed not as writings produced by an historical impulse but as expressions of an ardent faith, written with the purpose of commending Jesus Christ to the Mediterranean world."[1]

It was the post-Pentecost generation that turned the world upside down—spreading Christianity beyond the borders of Palestine as far west as Rome and into virtually every major urban center in the entire eastern empire. "What began as a Jewish sect in A.D. 30," writes missiologist-historian J. Herbert Kane, "had grown into a world religion by A.D. 60."[2] Inspired by the leadership of such great Christians as Peter and Paul, and driven abroad by persecution (and the destruction of the temple in Jerusalem in A.D. 70), many trained and lay evangelists spread out, bringing the message of Christ with them. "Every Christian," writes Stephen Neill, "was a witness," and "nothing is more notable than the anonymity of these early missionaries."[3]

Fortunately for these early missionaries, circumstances were almost ideal for spreading the faith. In comparison to later missionaries, who would often face almost impossible odds, these early evangelists worked within a system that often paved the way for their ministry. There was great opportunity for mobility within the Roman Empire in the centuries after Christ. The amazingly well-structured Roman roads were an open invitation for people to move about, and the relative peace that prevailed made travel even more appealing. Moreover, unlike most missionaries of later centuries, the early evangelists were not forced to endure years of grueling language study. Greek was the universal language of the empire, and Christians could communicate the gospel freely wherever they went.

Another factor paving the way for a public Christian witness was the availability of synagogues. The book of Acts mentions over and over again the preaching that occurred in Jewish synagogues—public forums that allowed Christian ideas to be disseminated throughout the empire for more than a generation following the death of Christ. Though persecution was an ever-present reality, there was room for public debate in Roman society. There was a spirit of openness to new ideas—"a shifting toward a rational and moralistic monotheism," while at the same time a shifting away from "polytheistic religions with their capricious and malicious deities."[4]

Christianity stood out from other ancient religions in its exclusivist stance. While the knowledge of doctrine was often shallow for most new converts, there was no ambiguity about the uniqueness of the new religion. Christianity alone demanded that followers deny all gods but the one true God. The gospel "was presented in sharply yes-or-no, black-and-white, friend-or-foe terms. Urgency, evangelism, and the demand that the believer deny the title of god to all but one, made up the force that alternative beliefs could not match." The growth of the new faith was remarkable: "on the order of half a million in each generation from the end of the first century up to the proclaiming of toleration."[5]

Christianity penetrated the Roman world through five main avenues: the preaching and teaching of evangelists, the personal witness of believers, acts of

MISSIONARY TRADITION OF THE APOSTLES

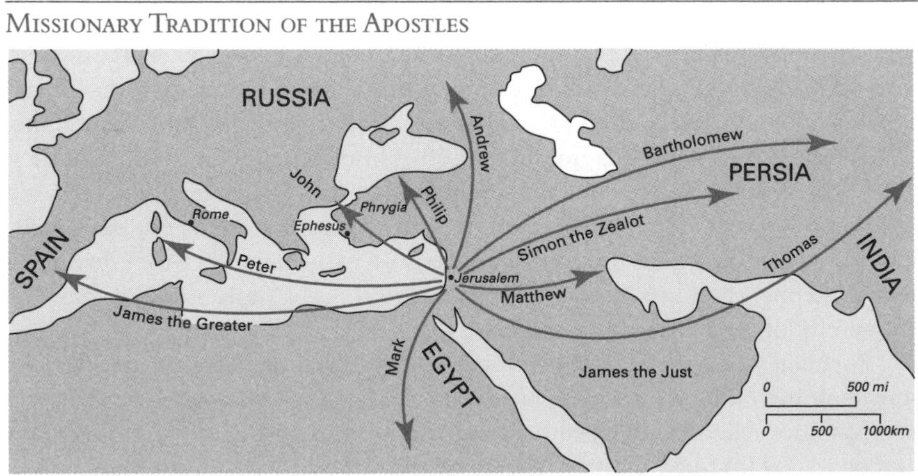

kindness and charity, the faith shown in persecution and death, and the intellectual reasoning of the early apologists.

From contemporary accounts we learn that the Christians of the early centuries were very eager to share their faith with others. When the synagogues closed their doors to them, teaching and preaching was done in private homes, usually by itinerant lay ministers. Eusebius of Caesarea tells of the dedication of some of these traveling evangelists in the early second century:

> At that time many Christians felt their souls inspired by the holy word with a passionate desire for perfection. Their first action, in obedience to the instructions of the Saviour, was to sell their goods and to distribute them to the poor. Then, leaving their homes, they set out to fulfill the work of an evangelist, making it their ambition to preach the word of the faith to those who as yet had heard nothing of it, and to commit to them the book of the divine Gospels. They were content simply to lay the foundations of the faith among these foreign peoples: they then appointed other pastors and committed to them the responsibility for building up those whom they had merely brought to the faith. Then they passed on to other countries and nations with the grace and help of God.[6]

Perhaps even more significant than the evangelism conducted by the traveling lay preachers was the informal testimony that went out through the everyday lives of the believers. "In that age every Christian was a missionary," wrote John Foxe in his classic *Book of Martyrs.* "The soldier tried to win recruits . . .; the prisoner sought to bring his jailer to Christ; the slave girl whispered the gospel in the ears of her mistress; the young wife begged her husband to be baptized . . .; every one who had experienced the joys of believing tried to bring others to the faith."[7] Even the Christians' harshest critics recognized their fervent evangelistic zeal. For example, Celsus's description, though very biased, is telling:

> Their aim is to convince only worthless and contemptible people, idiots, slaves, poor women, and children. . . . They would not dare to address an audience of intelligent men . . . but if they see a group of young people or slaves or rough folk, there they push themselves in and seek to win the admiration of the crowd. It is the same in private houses. We see wool-carders, cobblers, washermen, people of the utmost ignorance and lack of education.[8]

As important as such witnessing was, the nonverbal testimony of Christian charity may have had an even greater impact. Christians were known by their love and concern for others, and again, some of the most telling evidence of this comes, not from the mouths of Christians themselves, but from the critics of Christianity. Emperor Julian was concerned that Christians not outshine those of his own religion. He was chagrined that Christianity had "advanced through the loving service rendered to strangers, and through their care for the burial of the dead." He found it scandalous that the "godless Galileans care not only for their own poor but for ours as well; while those who belong to us look in vain for the help that we should render them."[9]

The testimony that the early Christians displayed in life was also evident in death. Until the fourth century, when Emperor Constantine publicly professed Christianity, persecution was a real threat for believers who openly confessed their faith. Though the total number of martyrs was not unusually high in proportion to the population, and though outbreaks of persecution occurred only sporadically and even then were generally local in nature, no Christian could ever feel entirely safe from official retribution. Beginning with the stoning of Stephen, they faced the grim reality that such might also be their fate—a sobering thought that served to exclude nominal Christians from their numbers. The fire of persecution purified the church, and the courage displayed by the innocent victims was a spectacle unbelievers could not fail to notice. There are many "well-authenticated cases of conversion of pagans," writes Neill, "in the very moment of witnessing the condemnation and death of Christians."[10] The second-century apologist Tertullian perhaps said it best: "The blood of the martyrs is the seed of the church."

> *While persecution drew many unbelievers to Christianity through their emotions, the reasoned arguments of the early apologists won still others through their intellects.*

While persecution and martyrdom drew many unbelievers to Christianity through their emotions, the reasoned and well-developed arguments of the early apologists won still others through their intellects. Christians, beginning with the apostle Paul in Athens, realized that this factor alone could be a drawing card in witnessing to the learned pagan philosophers. These defenders of the faith, including Origen, Tertullian, and Justin Martyr, had a powerful influence in making Christianity more reasonable to the educated, a number of whom were converted.

Even as the church was expanding through various means, however, it was facing setbacks as well. The very persecution that set the stage for testimonies of unbending faith also set the stage for denial of faith. This was the case in Asia Minor around A.D. 112. In a letter to Emperor Trajan, Pliny the Younger, who was then governor of Bithynia, outlined his actions against those people who were brought before him accused of being Christians. "So far this has been my procedure when people were charged before me with being Christians. I have asked the accused themselves if they were Christians; if they said 'Yes,' I asked them a second and third time, warning them of the penalty; if they persisted I ordered them to be led off to execution."[11]

Pliny did not specify the number of executions, but when threatened with death, many denied the faith and supported that denial by giving homage to the images of the emperor and the gods and cursing Christ. Indeed, the number that denied the faith was apparently far greater than the number who did not, because

Pliny reported to the emperor that "the temples, which had been well-nigh abandoned, are beginning to be frequented again" and "fodder for the sacrificial animals, too, is beginning to find a sale again." And he sums up his success by saying: "From all this it is easy to judge what a multitude of people can be reclaimed, if an opportunity is granted them to renounce Christianity."[12]

A similar outcome was reported in Alexandria in the mid-third century during the persecution under Emperor Decius. According to Eusebius, both women and men were brutally persecuted. Among them were Quinta, Apollonia, Metra, and Serapion, who endured terrible torture before they succumbed to death. "Much terror was now threatening us," writes Eusebius, "so that, if it were possible, the very elect would stumble." And some did stumble. They approached the pagan altars and "boldly asserted that they had never before been Christians." Others, "after a few days imprisonment abjured"; and still others, "after enduring the torture for a time, at last renounced."[13]

Another factor that impeded the growth of the early church was doctrinal controversy. "The list of major Christian doctrinal controversies during the first five centuries is long," writes Milton Rudnick. "Among the groups regarded as dangerously false were: Judaizers, Docetists, Gnostics, Marcionists, Montanists, Monarchians, Novationists, Donatists, Arians, Nestorians, and Monophysites." Besides these groups there were factions within the church that fought over such things as the date of Easter and clerical appointments. "It is impossible to measure the negative impact of these controversies," continues Rudnick. "In all likelihood it was considerable."[14]

But the vibrant evangelism that was conducted during the post-apostolic period began to wane in the early fourth century during the reign of Emperor Constantine. Christianity became a state religion, and as a result, the churches were flooded with nominal Christians who had less concern for spiritual matters than for political and social prestige. Christianity became the fashion. Elaborate structures replaced the simple house-churches, and creeds replaced the spontaneous testimonies and prayers. The need for aggressive evangelism seemed superfluous—at least within the civilized Roman world.

On the outskirts of the empire, however, barbarians threatened the very stability of the Roman state. The prospect of converting them to Christianity became a much-sought-after goal of government officials who strongly supported the work of aggressive evangelists such as Martin, Bishop of Tours. Martin was a fourth-century soldier who entered a monastery and went out from there spreading the gospel throughout the French countryside. Some of the earliest and most effective "foreign" missionaries, though, were not aligned in any way with the state or the church at Rome. Ulfilas (an Arian) and Patrick and Columba (both Celtics) had no direct ties with the Roman church or state (though their evangelistic efforts made certain areas of Europe more amenable to the Roman system). Their primary objective was evangelism, accompanied by spiritual growth—an objective that would often become secondary during the succeeding centuries.

Paul the Apostle

The starting point of Christian missions is, of course, the New Testament church. The frightened and doubting disciples who had fled during their master's anguished hours on the cross were empowered with the Holy Spirit on the day of Pentecost, and the Christian missionary movement was born. The most detailed and accurate record of this new missionary outreach is contained in the book of Acts, where the apostle Paul stands out, while Peter, Barnabas, Silas, John Mark, Philip, Apollos, and others also play important roles. Apart from Scripture, however, little is known of these biblical figures. According to tradition, some time after the death and resurrection of Jesus, the disciples met in the "upper room" or the Mount of Olives (depending on the source), and there Peter or another disciple divided up the world among them for missionary outreach.[15] By some accounts Matthew is said to have gone to Ethiopia, Andrew to Scythia, Bartholomew to Arabia and India, Thomas also to India, and the rest to other regions.

Most of these accounts, except for that of Thomas, have little or no historical support. As the story goes, Thomas disregarded the Lord's call for him to take the gospel to the East—a defiance that resulted in his being carried off as a slave to India, where he was placed in charge of building a palace for King Gundaphorus. The tradition continues that, while under the king's service, Thomas spent his time spreading the gospel rather than building the palace—an offense that quickly brought him a prison term. In the end, Thomas had the opportunity to share his faith with the king, who then became a believer himself and was baptized. Though many of the details of the story seem fanciful, the basic outline may have an element of truth. A group of "Thomas Christians" in southwest India still worship in an ancient church said to be founded by Thomas, and archaeological digs have now established that there actually was a King Gundobar who reigned in India during the first century.

Many historians discount this tradition as no more than legend, but the significance goes beyond the actual historicity of the stories themselves. The widely circulated tales of the apostles carrying the gospel to the very ends of the earth infused the early church with a missionary mind-set that has been passed down through the centuries.

The apostle Paul unquestionably ranks as the greatest missionary of the early church. He, in the words of Kenneth Scott Latourette, "has been at once the prototype, the model, and inspiration of thousands of successors."[16] Paul is viewed by many as the greatest missionary of all times—a man who conducted an extraordinary ministry of establishing Christianity on a grassroots level that insured its growth and stability in the centuries that followed. From a strictly human standpoint, however, Paul is a less awesome figure than some adulatory devotees would have him be. In many ways he was a very ordinary man facing ordinary problems that have confronted missionaries ever since.

The biblical record of Paul's life and ministry is well known. Born into a Jewish family in Tarsus, he grew up a strict Pharisee, violently opposed to the latest threat menacing Judaism, namely, the new "cult" of Jesus. He witnessed the martyrdom of Stephen and was empowered by the high priest to arrest other such heretics. He was on his way to Damascus to carry out this very commission when he was suddenly and miraculously converted. Supremely qualified for the task that lay ahead—a Jew thoroughly immersed in his Jewish heritage—he was now prepared to tell the world that the promised Messiah had indeed come. N. T. Wright sums up Paul's comprehensive mission that so profoundly bound together the old and the new:

Paul's extraordinary accomplishments have prompted missiologists to argue that his methods should be closely emulated today.

> Saul's vision on the road to Damascus thus equipped him with an entirely new perspective, though one which kept its roots firm and deep within his previous covenantal theology. Israel's destiny had been summed up and achieved in Jesus the Messiah. The Age to Come had been inaugurated. Saul himself was summoned to be its agent. He was to declare to the pagan world that YHWH, the God of Israel, was the one true God of the whole world.[17]

Paul's extraordinary accomplishments in the field of missions have prompted missiologists to argue that his methods should be closely, if not precisely, emulated today. Roland Allen in his book *Missionary Methods: St. Paul's or Ours?* makes a strong case for this—if for no other reason than the fact that Paul's methods worked:

> In little more than ten years St. Paul established the Church in four provinces of the Empire, Galatia, Macedonia, Achaia and Asia. Before A.D. 47 there were no Churches in these provinces; in A.D. 57 St. Paul could speak as if his work there was done.... this is truly an astonishing fact. That churches should be founded so rapidly, so securely, seems to us today, accustomed to the difficulties, the uncertainties, the failures, the disastrous relapses of our own missionary work, almost incredible.... Today if a man ventures to suggest that there may be something in the methods by which St. Paul attained such wonderful results worthy of our careful attention, and perhaps of our imitation, he is in danger of being accused of revolutionary tendencies.[18]

Allen points out that Paul, unlike so many missionaries since his day, concentrated his work in the strategic population centers—centers of trade and political influence from which the gospel would quickly be carried to outlying

PAUL'S MISSIONARY JOURNEYS

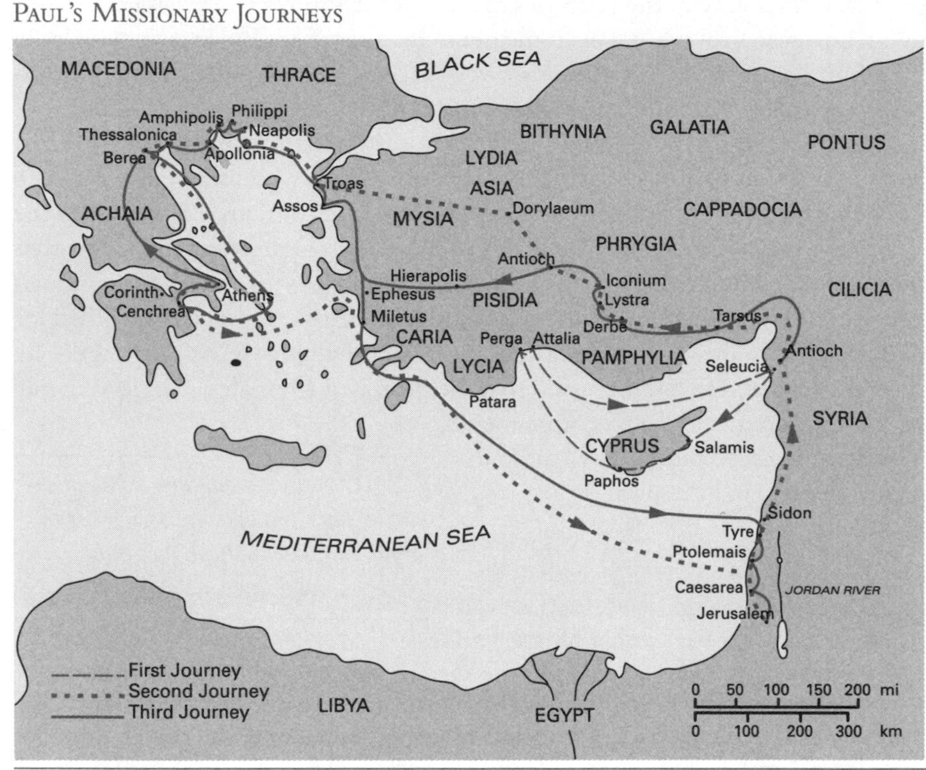

areas. Moreover, he reached people from all levels of society, providing the church with a broad base. And above all, he established independent churches, not mission stations. He "did not gather congregations, he planted churches," avoiding an "elaborate" and "foreign system of church organization."[19] In other areas as well, missiologists have seen Paul's methods as particularly applicable for today. J. Christy Wilson, in his book *Today's Tentmakers,* argues that missionaries should consider the advantages of going abroad with secular careers, supporting themselves while conducting evangelism and establishing churches even as Paul did. But Paul did more than merely become a tentmaker. He consciously pursued a course of "downward mobility," according to Ben Witherington III. "Paul deliberately stepped down the social ladder in order to reach as wide an audience for the gospel as possible."[20]

Paul also serves as a model for courage and commitment—especially for those confronting seemingly insurmountable obstacles in Christian ministry. He endured imprisonments and floggings and persecution and hardships of every description:

> Three times I was beaten with rods, once I was stoned, three times I was shipwrecked, I spent a night and a day in the open sea, I have been constantly on

> the move. I have been in danger from rivers, in danger from bandits, in danger from my own countrymen, in danger from Gentiles; in danger in the city, in danger in the country, in danger at sea; and in danger from false brothers. I have labored and toiled and have often gone without sleep; I have known hunger and thirst and have often gone without food; I have been cold and naked. Besides everything else, I face daily the pressure of my concern for all the churches. (2 Cor. 11:25–28 NIV)

There were emotional scars as well—rejection not only from Jewish leaders but also from followers of Jesus. And he confronted interpersonal conflicts, as in the dispute with Barnabas over the worthiness of John Mark as a missionary companion. The sharp disagreement that ensued resulted in a split between Paul and Barnabas, at the same time launching an additional missionary team: Barnabas went out with his nephew, John Mark; and Paul went with Silas. Dealing with cultural and religious traditions also stirred conflict. Eating meat offered to idols and the rite of circumcision were matters Paul faced forthrightly. In doing so, he established a precedent of liberty rather than law in contextualizing the gospel that set a standard for all future generations. Indeed, it is difficult to overemphasize the significance of the apostle Paul in laying a pattern for effectively reaching cross-culturally to those who have never heard the gospel.

Yet some would insist that Paul should not be viewed as a model of success. Michael Duncan, in an article entitled "The Other Side of Paul," emphasizes the failures in ministry that Paul endured: "It would almost seem as though Paul's early years produced little fruit. . . . He had an incredible ministry, yes: but we must not read the current heresy of triumphalism back into his life." In Paul's life and ministry, Duncan has derived a theology of failure: "Paul's ministry grew out of the soil of wilderness years, painful theological debate, ruptured friendships, spoiled church growth, numerous hardships and dubious project success." But despite the setbacks, "Paul could look back on all the failure, pain and hardships and still conclude that he had been running in the grandest run of all."[21]

But more than a "theology of failure," Paul set forth a theology of mission. Mission is "the mother of theology" was the bold assertion of Martin Kahler, writing in 1908. Theology in the infant church was not a luxury but a necessity. This is profoundly demonstrated in the writings of Paul. According to David Bosch, "the missionary dimension of Paul's theology has not always been recognized. For many years he was primarily regarded as the creator of a dogmatic system. . . . It is today widely acknowledged that Paul was the first Christian theologian precisely because he was the first Christian missionary."[22]

The succeeding generations of missionaries carried on Paul's legacy—both the message and the methods. From Eusebius and the *Didache* there are accounts of itinerant missionaries in the second century who followed the Pauline example. Origen, in the third century, made similar observations: "Some of them have made it their business to itinerate, not only through cities, but even villages and country houses, that they might make converts to God."[23]

In life and death Paul set the stage for the next two millennia of missions. Like many of the Christian evangelists who followed him, he met a violent end. According to tradition, he was martyred along with Peter and many other Christians during the bloodthirsty persecution under Emperor Nero in A.D. 64. Even in the example he set in death, Paul inspired future generations not to count their lives dear to themselves, for if they suffered they would also reign with Christ.

Polycarp

The unbending faith of the Christians during the first centuries of the church stood out as a shining example to the pagan world. How could anyone stand unflinching in the face of death and claim the crucified Jesus to be God, if the story was a myth? Such absolute trust in an unseen God was inexplicable to the pagan mind. What was the source of such courage? Many people began their journey of faith asking those very questions.

One of the first widely publicized martyr stories in the post-apostolic era was that of Polycarp, the much-loved bishop of Smyrna. Like all ancient figures, his story is dimmed by the centuries that separate his time from ours, and the most recent scholarly research of his life leaves the reader with more questions than answers. The traditional account is familiar. "He was a venerable figure," writes F. F. Bruce, "forming the last link with those who had seen Christ in the flesh, for he had sat at the feet of John, the beloved disciple."[24] How or when he became a Christian is unknown, but by the early second century he had a thriving ministry in Smyrna. "Slaves, local aristocrats and . . . members of the Proconsul's staff were counted among his tightly knit and well-organized congregation," according to W. H. C. Frend.[25]

So forceful was his ministry against paganism that he was denounced throughout all Asia Minor as the "atheist"—"the teacher of Asia, the destroyer of our gods."[26] In the eyes of the pagans he was glorifying a dead man, and his stirring sermons on the teachings and miracles of Jesus, of which he had been told firsthand by John, were particularly upsetting. His writings too were a source of irritation. The only extant document written by him is a letter to the Philippian church, a letter that shows Christology as the pivotal point of his message. "Of Christ it speaks in high terms as the Lord, who sits at the right hand of God to whom everything in heaven and earth is subject."[27]

But was Polycarp even a disciple of the apostle John? In *Polycarp and John,* Frederick Weidmann reviews the ancient literature and provides an English text of Coptic literary fragments on Polycarp that had not previously been available. He points out that Polycarp's writing more closely parallels Paul's than John's, and that the references to his learning at the feet of John may refer to a John other than the apostle.[28] Certainly, he revered the apostles, especially Paul, as is evident in his letter to the Philippians: "I write these things, brethren, not in arrogance, but because you have requested me. For neither I, nor any other like me, can attain the wisdom of the blessed and glorious Paul, who was among you . . . and firmly taught the word of truth."[29]

But despite such discrepancies, the sources consistently show Polycarp as a man who was deeply devoted not only to preserving the true faith passed down by the apostles but also to spreading that faith as the apostles had. Indeed, like so many "theologians" of this era, Polycarp was an evangelist and missionary who conveyed a deep sense of urgency in his interaction with the pagan culture around him. He was known in Smyrna as a teacher who could be found sitting in his special spot with believers and unbelievers, listening and debating. But he did not confine his ministry to one geographical area. He journeyed to Rome as an old man, and during that visit, according to Irenaeus, he "won many of the Gnostic heretics over to the Christian Church."[30]

Like so many "theologians" of this era, Polycarp was an evangelist and missionary who conveyed a deep sense of urgency in his interaction with the pagan culture around him.

For some fifty years Polycarp wielded powerful influence in his position as bishop. Yet in the words of Elliott Wright, "He was the gentlest . . . of men . . . a case study in humility."[31] He was remembered as a man of prayer—a man who, according to one ancient source, "prayed constantly night and day"—prayer that apparently did not interfere with his daylight hours devoted to teaching and his nights to studying the Scripture.[32]

In approximately A.D. 156 anti-Christian persecution broke out in the province of Asia. Civil authorities, for reasons not fully clear, decided to kill certain Christians. Realizing that he was a target, Polycarp, with the help of local believers, went into hiding. But after torturing a servant, as one account relates, the soldiers discovered Polycarp in a hayloft and took him into custody.

Polycarp being burned at the stake in Smyrna.

Execution was not what the authorities wanted, however. After all, Polycarp was a very old man, and what could be gained by putting him to death? What they really wanted was a denial of his faith. What a victory that would be for paganism and what a blow to the "cult" of Jesus. "Why, what harm is there in saying, 'Caesar is Lord' and offering incense and saving yourself," the officials pleaded after they had taken him into custody. "Have respect for your age," the proconsul begged; "swear by the divinity of Caesar; repent and say, 'Away with the atheists.'... Take the oath, and I will let you go." Polycarp stood firm, and then uttered the words that will forever be associated with his name: "For eighty-six years I have been his servant, and he has never done me wrong: how can I blaspheme my king who saved me?"[33]

The authorities carried out their threat, and Polycarp was burned at the stake. But the end result was a victory for the Christians. Many nonbelievers were horrified by the spectacle of burning at the stake this revered man, by some accounts 86, by other accounts 104 years old. His death served as a witness to believers and nonbelievers alike to the suffering of Christ and to the courageous commitment of Christ's followers.

Perpetua

The cessation of persecution in Asia Minor following the death of Polycarp did not apply to the whole Roman Empire. Persecution continued elsewhere, and during the early years of the third century it became widespread and well-coordinated, especially in North Africa where Perpetua and her slave girl Felicitas were executed. Before this period of intense persecution, however, there were isolated instances that were highly publicized—one in Rome just one decade following the death of Polycarp. This time it was Justin, who since his death has been referred to as Justin Martyr.

Schooled in the philosophy of Plato, Justin was converted to Christianity as a young man and soon became one of the faith's ablest defenders. He was a forceful writer who intelligently presented Christianity to his pagan readers and openly denounced the persecution of his fellow-believers. In Rome he gave instruction to believers and inquirers in private homes, and it was this crime more than any other, apparently, that led to his martyrdom. After a trial, the death sentence was pronounced by the judge, and Justin, along with five other men and one woman, was beheaded.

Some decades later, under the rule of Emperor Septimus Severus, the first widespread, intense persecution of Christians occurred. In 202 he issued an edict that forbade conversion to either Christianity or Judaism. The emperor himself worshiped Serapis, an Egyptian god of the dead, and he feared Christianity was a threat to his own religion. Although the edict was aimed mainly at prospective converts, its consequences were felt by new believers as well as mature leaders in the church.

The emperor's persecution was most bitterly felt in Carthage. Here in this great Roman city of North Africa, the growth of Christianity was alarming officials, and the emperor's edict extended to anyone "teaching or making converts."[34] Among the Christians of Carthage was Saturus, a deacon who conducted catechism classes for a group of converts. Vibia Perpetua, a twenty-two-year-old mother of an infant son and her personal slave Felicitas (who was eight months pregnant) had joined the class and were among those affected by the emperor's edict. Nothing is known of Perpetua's husband, but historians have speculated that either he was dead or he had abandoned her because of her newfound faith. The others condemned to die were Saturus, their teacher, and three other men.

Perpetua's plight has been preserved in a third-century document, *The Passion of Perpetua and Felicitas,* believed to be based on diaries and records of Perpetua and Saturus. "Some part of the story may be legendary," notes Elliott Wright, "but compared with most hagiography of third-century martyrs the account is filled with convincing human touches."[35] In this account, Perpetua tells of the distress and humiliation that her father, a respected nobleman, endured when he was informed that his only daughter had been arrested and imprisoned as a common criminal. He came immediately and pleaded with her to renounce this new faith about which she had been learning. When she refused, he became so incensed that he threatened to beat her, but she remained unmoved.

Perpetua's stolid demeanor, however, was soon broken. What her adamant father could not accomplish, her helpless infant could. She was "racked with anxiety," almost to the breaking point, when two Christians managed to have her baby brought to the prison. "I nursed my baby, who was faint from hunger. In my anxiety I spoke to my mother about the child, I tried to comfort my brother, and I gave the child in their charge. I was in pain because I saw them suffering out of pity for me. These were the trials I had to endure for many days. Then I got permission for my baby to stay with me in prison. At once I recovered my health, relieved as I was of my worry and anxiety over the child."[36]

The stoical young woman would not bend: "This will be done on the scaffold which God has willed; for I know that we have not been placed in our own power but in God's."

As the time of her execution approached, the family crisis became more acute. Her father came to the prison, and again he pleaded with her to put family considerations above her creed: "Do not cut us off entirely; for not one of us will ever hold up his head again if anything happens to you." But the stoical young woman would not bend: "This will be done on the scaffold which God has willed; for I know that we have not been placed in our own power but in God's."[37] The next day when her father heard the news that she was to be thrown into the arena with wild beasts, he sought to rescue her. Though it was a heroic act of compassion, authorities ordered that the aged man be beaten. It was a pathetic sight. "I grieved for my father's plight," wrote Perpetua, "as if I had been struck myself."[38]

Perpetua's father was persistent. Again he returned to the prison, laying the ultimate burden of guilt on her. "Then the father laid her child upon her neck, and he . . . said: 'Be merciful to us, daughter, and live with us!'" Her response is impossible to comprehend apart from her unbending faith that would testify to the reality of the Christian faith in a pagan world. An account written in the thirteenth century, drawn from early sources, describes her words and actions in blunt terms: "But she threw the child aside, and repulsed her parents, saying: 'Begone from me, enemies of God, for I know you not!'"[39]

Once the so-called trial was over, the fate of the prisoners was sealed and the remaining days before the execution were spent in personal reflection, "more concerned about their worthiness, their loyalty to Christ," according to Wright, "than about the suffering ahead of them."[40] They met for prayer, shared their last meal—their agape love feast—and witnessed their faith to the crowd outside.

On the day of the execution the prisoners were brought to the arena where, according to Roman custom, the men were taken first to be tortured for the entertainment of the crowd before their execution. Saturus stopped at the gate for one last word of testimony with Pudens, the prison governor, who later turned to Christ and became a martyr himself. The men were then sent into the arena with a bear, a leopard, and a wild boar. Saturus was so mangled and bloody after the ordeal that spectators ridiculed him, shouting, "He is well-baptized!" Perpetua and Felicitas (who had given birth to her baby in prison) were stripped and sent into the arena to face a "mad heifer." The gory torture soon became too much for the crowd, and the people began shouting, "Enough!"[41]

When this preliminary exhibition was ended and the young women were brought to the executioner, Perpetua called out to some grieving Christian friends, "Give out the Word to the brothers and sisters; stand fast in the faith, love one another, and don't let our suffering become a stumbling block to you."[42] She was then taken to the gladiator to be beheaded. Whether due to hesitancy or lack of skill, his first blow was not sufficient. Perpetua cried out in pain, took the gladiator's trembling hand and directed the sword to her throat, and it was over.

After this wave of persecution there followed fifty years of relative peace during which the church grew steadily. Many people who may themselves have never been able to pass such a test of faith were, nevertheless, attracted by the example of Perpetua and her comrades to a faith that demonstrated such serenity and courage.

Ulfilas

Following the much-publicized conversion of Emperor Constantine in 312, the Roman Empire became nominally Christianized, and the vibrant testimony of the Christians seemed to decline. No longer did they suffer for their faith, for it was in vogue to be a Christian, and as a result, there was a weakening in spiritual fervor. Martyrdom from official persecution had become a terror of the past. The church and the state became closely allied, and Christianity was being used more and more as a means of fostering imperial expansion. Missionaries were viewed in a political light in the hope that their evangelistic efforts could bring outlying areas within the scope of Roman control.

Ulfilas was one such missionary. Though he himself was motivated by his desire to spread the gospel, in the eyes of Roman policy, his mission was well-suited to territorial expansion. Ulfilas was one of the greatest cross-cultural missionaries of the early church. His ministry was to the Goths, a barbarian tribe outside the Roman Empire living in the area of present-day Romania.

Born in 311, Ufilas was raised in the pagan environment of the Goths. His mother is believed to have been Gothic and his father a Cappadocian Christian who was taken captive by Gothic raiders. When he was in his early twenties, Ulfilas was sent to Constantinople for diplomatic service. Here he spent several years and came under the influence of Bishop Eusebius of Nicomedia, who taught him the Scriptures in Greek and Latin. Under Eusebius he served as a "reader," ministering possibly to Gothic soldiers in the Roman army.

THE ROMAN EMPIRE

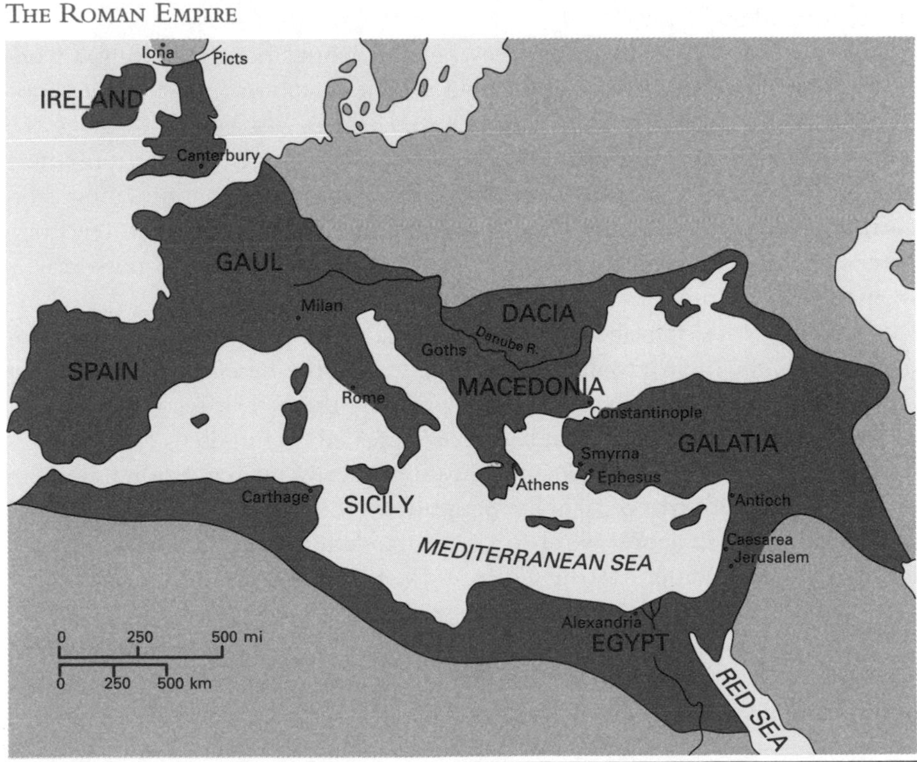

Eusebius, like most Byzantine bishops of his day, was Arian, or at least Semi-Arian, and this heretical teaching was passed on to Ulfilas. Arius, a contemporary of Ulfilas, was a popular and persuasive Christian preacher who is most remembered for his theological claims relating to the divinity of Christ. From Scripture passages that speak of Christ as "begotten of the Father" and the "first-born of all creation" he concluded that, though Christ was sinless and unchangeable and the Savior of mankind, he was essentially different from the Father and was therefore not God. Although this doctrine was overruled at the Council of Nicaea, many of the churchmen, particularly in the eastern portion of the empire, continued to hold the view—Ulfilas being one. But according to Latourette, "It was a mild form of Arianism which he professed."[43]

At the age of thirty, after spending nearly ten years in Constantinople, Ulfilas was consecrated Bishop to the Goths—those living north of the Danube outside the borders of the empire. His assignment was to evangelize the barbarians—"wild and undisciplined," a "rude and crude sort, with a relatively low standard of living, dwelling often in 'wagons' because they had no fixed abodes."[44] To such "simple people," Stephen Neill suggests, Arianism "may have presented itself as a rather attractive simplification, since it set them free from the knotty controversies about the nature and person of Christ, to follow him as a leader and to concentrate on the already sufficiently difficult task of learning to live a sober, righteous, and godly life."[45]

For forty years Ulfilas conducted evangelistic work among the Goths, a work that was highly successful, though hampered by persecution. In 348 fierce opposition from a Gothic chieftain (who believed Ulfilas was seeking to bring the Goths under Roman domination) almost decimated the entire mission enterprise. Ulfilas, with the permission of the Arian Emperor Constantius, moved his Gothic Christian community across the Danube into safer Roman territory. Later some of these Christians returned to their people to serve as missionaries themselves.

The most enduring labor of love that Ulfilas bestowed on the Goths was his translation of the Bible into their native tongue, an unwritten language for which he had to devise an alphabet. This was "probably the first or second instance," according to Latourette, "of what has since happened for hundreds of tongues—their reduction to writing by Christian missionaries and the translation into them by that medium of a part or all of the Scriptures."[46] Ulfilas was scrupulously accurate in rendering an almost word-for-word translation from the Greek without losing the Gothic idiom, and the Goths and Vandals alike carried it with them as they moved from place to place in Europe.

Though Ulfilas's translation was a monumental contribution to missions of the early centuries, even this area of his ministry has come under fire. He purposely omitted the books of Samuel and Kings from his translation because, in the words of an early church historian, "They are merely an account of military exploits, and the Gothic tribes were particularly devoted to war. They were in more need of checks on their warlike natures than spurs to urge them on to acts of war."[47]

Ulfilas died at the age of seventy while on a mission to Constantinople for the Gothic king. The longtime military rivalry between the Goths and the Roman Empire continued after his death. There were devastating attacks by the Visigoths against the empire, and the plunder continued for decades, climaxing on the night of August 24, 410, when Alaric and his army stormed Rome. But despite the military campaigns, the gospel continued to be preached to the Goths by Ulfilas's faithful successors. They accompanied the wandering Gothic tribesmen to the battlefield and wherever else their caravans took them, prompting a sarcastic comment from the anti-Arian Ambrose of Milan: "Those who had formerly used wagons for dwellings, now use a wagon for a church." But sarcasm aside, that "caustic comment," writes V. Raymond Edman, "becomes a compliment for the men of faith who, like Paul, were 'all things to all men, that they might by all means save some.' Their doctrine, perhaps, was defective; their hearts were not. They sought service, not security; comradeship in Christ, not a cathedral; discipleship, not domination."[48]

Patrick

Shrouded in legend and glorified by sainthood, Patrick, Ireland's great fifth-century missionary is one of the most misrepresented figures in church history. Popular opinion notwithstanding, Patrick was neither a Roman Catholic nor an Irishman, and his promotion to sainthood was bestowed at the Council of Whitby some two centuries after his death, most likely as an incentive for bringing the Celtic church under Roman Catholic domination.

Yet today he has become a man for all seasons. David Plotz sums up his prestige and popularity:

> The scarcity of facts about St. Patrick's life has made him a dress-up doll: Anyone can create his own St. Patrick. Ireland's Catholics and Protestants, who have long feuded over him, each have built a St. Patrick in their own image. Catholics cherish Paddy as the father of Catholic Ireland. They say that Patrick was consecrated as a bishop and that the pope himself sent him to convert the heathen Irish.... Ireland's Protestant minority, by contrast, denies that Patrick was a bishop or that he was sent by Rome. They depict him as anti-Roman Catholic and credit him with inventing a distinctly Celtic church, with its own homegrown symbols and practices.... Evangelical Protestants claim him as one of their own. After all, he read his Bible, and his faith came to him in visions.... Utah newspapers emphasize that Patrick was a missionary sent overseas to convert the ungodly, an image that resonates in Mormon country. New Age Christians revere Patrick as a virtual patron saint.... Patrick has even been

> enlisted in the gay rights cause.... He was a proto-feminist who valued women in an age when the church ignored them.... Now television has invented yet another Patrick.[49]

Because the birth date is not precisely known and scholars proffer such widely divergent death dates, some have speculated that there were actually two Patricks, Patrick and Old Patrick, the former dying in 461, and the latter in 493. Perhaps so. But one of these Patricks left behind autobiographical writings, and whether he died old or young, his legacy has loomed large over the Christian church and the history of Western civilization.[50]

Patrick was born into a Christian family in the Roman province of Britain around A.D. 389. His father was a deacon and his grandfather a priest in the Celtic church. (During the period before Roman domination, most clergy were married.) Little is known of his early childhood, but when he was in his mid-teens, his town near the west coast of Britain was invaded by a band of Irish plunderers, and many of the young boys, including Patrick, were carried away to be sold as slaves. Patrick was sold to a farmer of Slemish, where for the next six years he herded swine.

Although he had been raised in a Christian home, Patrick testifies that he "did not know the true God" at the time of his captivity. During those years, however, he began reflecting on his spiritual condition, and his life changed: "The Lord opened the understanding of my unbelief, that, late as it was, I might remember my faults and turn to the Lord my God with all my heart; and He had regard to my low estate, and pitied my youth and ignorance, and kept guard over me even before I knew Him, and before I attained wisdom to distinguish good from evil; and He strengthened and comforted me as a father does his son."[51]

From that time on, writes F. F. Bruce, "Patrick's life was marked by intense and persistent prayer, and from time to time he was conscious of... divine response to his prayers." This sense of God's leading prompted him to escape to a seaport and make his way back to his homeland. "Sure enough he found the ship of which the inner voice had forewarned him."[52] As a free man, Patrick went to an island off the coast of the French Riviera, where he found refuge in a monastery.

He later returned to his home, and it was there, he relates in his *Confession,* that God called him "in the depth of the night." It was his Macedonian call: "I saw a man named Victoricus, coming as if from Ireland, with innumerable letters; and he gave me one of these, and... while I was reading out the beginning of the letter, I thought that at that very moment I heard the voice of those who were beside the wood of Focluth, near the western sea; and this is what they called out: 'Please, holy boy, come and walk among us again.' Their cry pierced to my very heart, and I could read no more; and so I awoke."[53]

Following this call, Patrick trained for ministry at the church of Auxerre in Gaul. But there were further delays. Even after his ordination as a deacon, his superiors found him unsuited for mission work in Ireland. Palladius was chosen to go instead. But he died less than a year after he arrived, and that opened the way for Patrick, then past age forty.

When he arrived in Ireland in 432, Patrick described the region as "the very ends of the earth." He was beyond the borders of the empire. "Now he had gone out there to the very end, to the nations that are beyond the reach of everyone."[54] Truly this was an isolated area. Before he arrived, there were isolated enclaves of Christians, but the vast majority of the people were still entrenched in paganism. They worshipped the sun, moon, wind, water, fire, and rocks and believed in good and evil spirits of all kinds inhabiting the trees and hills. Magic and sacrifice—including human sacrifice—were part of the religious rites performed by the druids or priests.

It is not surprising that Patrick immediately encountered stiff opposition from the druids, but he accepted their social and political order, and eventually some of the powerful druid chieftains were converted to Christianity. It was not long before the druids as a class began to lose their power, but their magical beliefs endured through Patrick's apparent compromise with paganism. He sought to diminish their prestige, according to F. F. Bruce, "not by the power of the Christian message, but by proving himself to be a mightier druid than the pagan druids,"[55] a phenomena missiologists term "power encounter." This type of superstitious magic continued for centuries in Celtic Christianity.

Soon after he arrived in Ireland, Patrick secured an important victory when he convinced King Loigaire to grant religious toleration for Christians. Not long afterward the king's brother became a convert and granted Patrick land for a church in his domain. After establishing the church, Patrick moved on to new areas where the gospel had never been preached; and by 447, after fifteen years of preaching, much of Ireland had been evangelized. Though by this time Patrick was recognized all over Ireland as a great man of God, his popularity and prestige had not come easily. In his *Confession,* he recounted the perilous life he had

TENDING flocks was my daily work, and I would pray constantly during the daylight hours. The love of God and the fear of him surrounded me more and more—and faith grew and the Spirit was roused, so that in one day I would say as many as a hundred prayers and after dark nearly as many again, even while I remained in the woods or on the mountain. I would wake and pray before daybreak—through snow, frost, rain—nor was there any sluggishness in me (such as I experience nowadays) because then the Spirit within me was ardent."

(Patrick: quoted in Thomas Cahill, *How the Irish Saved Civilization* [New York: Doubleday, 1995], 102)

lived. Twelve times he faced life-threatening situations, including a harrowing kidnapping and a two-week captivity. Nevertheless, he continued on for more than thirty years, motivated by fear as much as anything else: "I fear to lose the labor which I began [lest God] would note me as guilty."[56]

Patrick's methods of evangelism in some ways were similar to those of so many missionaries before and after him. His first step in evangelizing a new area was to win the political leader in hopes that his subjects would fall in behind him, and he was not averse to lavishing gifts on these local rulers. Unlike so many of the Roman Catholic missionaries, however, Patrick and the Celtic missionaries who followed him placed great emphasis on spiritual growth. Converts were given intensive training in the Scriptures and were encouraged to become involved in the ministry themselves. Women played a significant role in the Celtic churches, though as a single missionary Patrick was cautious in his relationship with them, "refusing the gifts of devout women lest any breath of scandal should arise."[57]

Patrick's success as a missionary evangelist was evident in the some two hundred churches he planted and the estimated 100,000 converts he baptized. Yet he was ever aware of his own shortcomings and credited God with all his accomplishments, concluding his *Confession* with this testimony: "But I pray those who believe and fear God, whosoever has deigned to scan or accept this document, composed in Ireland by Patrick the sinner, an unlearned man to be sure, that none should ever say that it was my ignorance that accomplished any small thing which I did or showed in accordance with God's will; but judge ye, and let it be most truly believed, that it was the gift of God. And this is my confession before I die."[58]

Columba

The evangelism of Ireland by Patrick and others resulted in one of the most extraordinary missionary accomplishments of the Middle Ages. It was a missionary venture conducted largely by the Celtic church as compared with the Western Roman church. "There was a passion for foreign missions in the impetuous eagerness of the Irish believers," writes Edman, "a zeal not common in their day. Burning with love for Christ, fearing no peril, shunning no hardship, they went everywhere with the Gospel."[59] But though they spread out all over central Europe and as far north as Iceland, it was Britain, the homeland of the first great missionary to Ireland, that became their first "foreign" field. Although the church there would later become part of Roman Catholicism, it would be that land that centuries later would provide the impetus for Protestants in the global evangelism of the nineteenth century.

Celtic missionary monks, according to E. H. Broadbent, conducted "a purer form of missionary work" than that which went out from Rome:

> Their method was to visit a country and, where it seemed suitable, fund a missionary village. In the centre they built a simple wooden church, around which were clustered school-rooms and huts for the monks, who were the builders, preachers, and teachers. Outside this circle, as required, dwellings were built for the students and their families, who gradually gathered around them. The whole was enclosed by a wall, but the colony often spread beyond the original enclosure. Groups of twelve monks would go out, each under the leadership of an abbot, to open up fresh fields for the Gospel. Those who remained taught in the school, and, as soon as they had sufficiently learned the language of the people among whom they were, translated and wrote out portions of Scripture, and also hymns, which they taught to their scholars. They were free to marry or to remain single; many remained single so that they might have greater liberty for the work. When some converts were made, the missionaries chose from among them small groups of young men who had ability, trained them specially in some handicraft and in languages, and taught them the Bible and how to explain it to others, so that they might be able to work among their own people. They delayed baptism until those professing faith had received a certain amount of instruction and had given some proof of steadfastness. They avoided attacking the religions of the people, counting it more profitable to preach the truth to them than to expose their errors. They accepted the Holy Scriptures as the source of faith and life and preached justification by faith. They did not take part in politics or appeal to the State for aid. All this work, in its origin and progress, though it had developed some features alien to New Testament teaching and Apostolic example, was independent of Rome and different in important respects from the Roman Catholic system.[60]

One of the most noted of these Celtic abbot-missionaries was Columba, who was born into a noble Irish family in 521 and brought up in the Christian faith. As a young man he entered a monastery, where he was ordained a deacon and later a priest. His evangelistic zeal was evident early in his ministry, and he is credited with establishing many churches and monasteries in Ireland, including those famous ones at Derry, Durrow, and Kells.

Columba's switch from "home" missions to "foreign" missions at the age of forty-two was motivated "for the love of Christ," according to his seventh-century biographer, but there were apparently other factors involved as well. His biographer concedes that he was excommunicated by the synod but claims that it was an unjust action over a trifling matter. However, Will Durant contends that his excommunication and departure for Britain were motivated by more than a trifling matter: "He was a fighter as well as a saint, 'a man of powerful frame and mighty voice;' his hot temper drew him into many quarrels, at last into war with King Diarmuid; a battle was fought in which, we are told, 5,000 men were killed; Columba, though victorious, fled from Ireland (563), resolved to convert as many souls as had fallen in that engagement at Cooldrevna."[61]

Whatever Columba's reasons were for embarking on the foreign field, the fact remains that he went, and through his years of service he made a significant impact on Britain. With twelve clerics to serve under him, he established his headquarters just off the coast of Scotland on Iona, a small bleak, barren, foggy island battered year-round by the pounding waves of the sea. Here he established a monastery that fostered the routine monastic life of prayer, fasting, meditation, Bible study, and manual labor; but in addition, and more importantly, it provided training for evangelists who were then sent out to preach the gospel, build churches, and establish more monasteries.

Columba himself was active in missionary work, and from Iona he traveled many times into Scotland proper. He is credited with having evangelized the Picts, who lived in the Scottish highlands. Through his witness, King Brude, who reigned over the northern Picts, was converted. Brude initially refused to allow Columba to enter the gates of his city, but Columba stayed outside and prayed until the king relented. As with Patrick more than a century earlier, Columba faced fierce opposition from the druids; but like his predecessor, he challenged them to match their trickery against the power of God. Columba's theology, according to Latourette, "was as much a religion of miracles as of ethics and even more than of formal creeds."[62]

As important as Columba's missionary efforts were, many scholars today would disagree with his admiring seventh-century biographer that he and his trainees at Iona were alone responsible for the evangelism of England and Scotland. There were many other missionaries from Ireland and elsewhere doing evangelism in this area who were in no way associated with him. The issue of Columba's importance relates in part to the importance of Roman Catholic missionaries, and many later historians have attempted to give the missionaries commissioned by the pope a greater share of the credit than may have been warranted. There was strong competition between Roman Catholic and Celtic missionaries, the Catholics eventually gaining the upper hand, but the initial work of evangelizing much of Britain and central Europe was accomplished by the energetic and faithful Celtic monks.

SELECT BIBLIOGRAPHY

Allen, Roland. *Missionary Methods: St. Paul's or Ours?* Chicago: Moody Press, 1956.

Bruce, F. F. *The Spreading Flame: The Rise and Progress of Christianity from Its First Beginnings to the Conversion of the English.* Grand Rapids: Eerdmans, 1979.

Cahill, Thomas. *How the Irish Saved Civilization.* New York: Doubleday, 1995.

Frend, W. H. C. *Martyrdom and Persecution in the Early Church.* Oxford: Blackwell, 1965.

MacMullen, Ramsay. *Christianizing the Roman Empire (A.D. 100–400).* New Haven, CT: Yale University Press, 1984.

O'Loughlin, Thomas. *St. Patrick: The Man and His Works*. London: Society for Promoting Christian Knowledge, 1999.
Rudnick, Milton L. *Speaking the Gospel through the Ages: A History of Evangelism*. St. Louis: Concordia, 1984.
Salisbury, Joyce E. *Perpetua's Passion: The Death and Memory of a Young Roman Woman*. New York: Routledge, 1997.
Weidmann, Frederick W. *Polycarp and John*. Notre Dame, IN: University of Notre Dame Press, 1999.
Wright, N. T. *What Saint Paul Really Said*. Grand Rapids: Eerdmans, 1997.

2

Roman Catholic Missions: Baptizing the Masses

It is natural to think (especially from a Western linear perspective) that with the passage of time comes progress—that the Mediterranean world in A.D. 600, for example, would be far more advanced than it had been hundreds of years earlier. But that was not true. Western Europe was uncivilized in comparison with the Greco-Roman world at the time of Christ. "The new Western world which emerged, the world of the first half of the Middle Ages," writes Philip Hughes, "was to be a world where countrysides were vastly more important than towns—which indeed shrank to vanishing point." It was a world of illiterate peasants and "country-bred, fighting warrior lords" far removed from "the centuries-old urban civilization of the Hellenistic East where the Church was born and for four hundred years had its first developments."

With the fall of Rome, the world changed. Where once there was peace and where lay missionaries had traveled along the extensive network of Roman roads and the very Scriptures were carried through an almost-modern mail system, now there was violence and crime—a deteriorating infrastructure and danger at every turn. It was a world of barbarians that stretched far beyond the old borders of the Roman Empire. "Life in this vast Western backwoods—on this vast frontier—was hard and cruel."[1]

Missionary endeavors in this new world of the "Dark Ages" looked very different from those in earlier generations. Indeed, from this time forward the role of the missionary would primarily be that of a pioneer or explorer—one who ventured into the *interior* or the *backwoods* or the *regions beyond*—the *foreign* missionary venturing into faraway deserts and mountains and jungles, often in the company of soldiers or diplomats or merchants. These physical and geographical changes paralleled spiritual changes:

> It is very difficult for the modern mind to enter this world of popular Christian imagination.... It is the Christianity of a society striving against the all-pervading influence of a barbaric environment. In this twilight world it was inevitable that the Christian ascetic and saint should acquire some features of the pagan shaman and demigod: that his prestige should depend upon his power as a wonder-worker and that men should seek his decision in the same way as they had formerly resorted to the shrine of a pagan oracle.
>
> Nevertheless it was only in this world of Christian mythology—in the cult of the saints and their relics and their miracles—that the vital transfusion of the Christian faith and ethics with the barbaric tradition of the new peoples of the West could be achieved. It was obviously impossible for peoples without any tradition of philosophy or written literature to assimilate directly the subtle and profound theological metaphysics of a St. Augustine or the great teachers of the Byzantine world. The barbarians could understand and accept the spirit of the new religion only when it was manifested to them visibly in the lives and acts of men who seemed endowed with supernatural qualities. The conversion of Western Europe was achieved not so much by the teaching of a new doctrine as by the manifestation of a new power.[2]

But *power encounter* came in two forms—the most visible being that of military might. From the beginning, medieval Catholic missions were closely tied to political and military exploits, and mass forced conversions were considered a legitimate means of church growth. More often, however, diplomatic negotiations paved the way for conversion. A political leader would be lured by promises of military aid, and his subjects generally followed suit. In some instances the need for military protection was mixed with a superstitious belief that the Christian God was a better ally in battle than a pagan god or gods. Clovis, the fifth-century king of the Franks, is an example. He married a Christian princess but held on to his pagan deities until his army was on the verge of military defeat. At that moment he allegedly made a vow that he would serve the Christian God in exchange for victory. On Christmas Day of 496, the victorious king was baptized along with three thousand troops.

This mass conversion of Clovis's army was the first of many during the Middle Ages, and it was this method, writes Bruce Shelley, "that converted Europe." The concept of individual conversion was "the method used by Protestant missions under the evangelical movements of the nineteenth century, with individual change of heart," but mass conversion is what expanded the Roman Catholic Church during the Middle Ages.[3]

During this time, however, there were individuals who were truly concerned about Christian missions. Among them was Gregory the Great (540–604), one of the most able and influential popes during the whole medieval period. The story is told of how he was touched when he saw blond British boys in the slave market and said, "They are Angles, let them become angels."[4] From that point on,

Gregory made missions to faraway Britain a top priority. In 596 he dispatched Augustine of Canterbury and a company of monks to take the gospel to that remote and undeveloped part of the world.

Though sincere and pious, Augustine was not initially a strong leader. On the way to Britain, while traveling through Gaul, he turned back with his monks, claiming that "they should not be compelled to undertake so dangerous, toilsome and uncertain a journey" through such a "barbarous, fierce and unbelieving nation." Gregory was unmoved. He wrote back, insisting that they continue. They did, and Augustine and his monks were largely responsible for planting the Roman Catholic Church in England.

As Augustine and his team of monks evangelized England and baptized thousands of converts, they faced knotty problems relating to pagan traditions. Could pagan ceremonies, for example, be transformed into Christian observances? And what should be done with pagan temples? Should they be destroyed or abandoned? Gregory's response established a framework for contextualizing the gospel that served as a model for centuries to follow:

> The heathen temples of these people need not be destroyed, only the idols which are to be found in them.... If the temples are well-built, it is a good idea to detach them from the service of the devil, and to adapt them for the worship of the true God.... And since the people are accustomed, when they assemble for sacrifice, to kill many oxen in sacrifice to the devils, it seems reasonable to appoint a festival for the people by way of exchange. The people must learn to slay their cattle not in honor of the devil, but in honor of God and for their own food.... If we allow them these outward joys, they are more likely to find their way to the true inner joy.... It is doubtless impossible to cut off all abuses at once from rough hearts, just as a man who sets out to climb a high mountain does not advance by leaps and bounds, but goes upward step by step and pace by pace.

There were other monks who served the missionary cause during the early Middle Ages, most notably Boniface, known as the "Apostle to Germany." It was not until later in the medieval period, however, that large numbers of Roman Catholic clerics became involved in missions-oriented monastic orders, most notably the Franciscans, the Dominicans, the Augustinians, and the Jesuits. Through these orders, Roman Catholicism spread throughout the world and established churches that would dominate the religious scene in many regions.

Although Roman Catholics dominated Christian missions during the Middle Ages, they were not the only missionaries of the period. The Celtic church, represented by St. Patrick, Columba, and others, burned with evangelistic zeal, as did the Eastern or Nestorian church that spread out across Asia. Not to be confused with the Eastern Orthodox Church, the Nestorian church, according to historian John Stewart, was "the most mission-oriented church the world has ever seen." From their early strongholds in Asia Minor, they fled into Persia and the Arabian Peninsula to avoid persecution from Roman officials and Catholic church leaders. But there they met fierce opposition from Zoroastrians and later from Muslims, so they continued to push farther east into central Asia, India, Afghanistan, and Tibet, areas that became "centers of Christian activity." These men and women were Christians of "great faith" and "mighty in Scripture, large portions of which they knew by heart." Schools were established to train the young, and monasteries, resembling modern-day Bible institutes, thrust young adults into full-time evangelistic activity.[6]

From Central Asia the Nestorians moved farther East, and by the ninth century had reached China and from there Korea, Japan, and Southeast Asia. Their influence continued to grow, and by the thirteenth century it is estimated that there were no less than twenty-seven metropolitan patriarchs and two hundred bishops under them in China and surrounding areas. But in the centuries that followed, the church rapidly declined. The peace-conscious Nestorians were no match for militant Muslims, and even worse were the armies of Genghis Khan and other barbarians who devastated large portions of Asia, including major centers of Nestorian Christianity.

An era of Christian missions was over and mostly forgotten. Because of the early doctrinal differences between the Nestorians and the Western church over the two natures of Christ, Nestorians were viewed as heretics, and their great evangelistic endeavors were discounted. Scholars have more recently recognized that the charges of heresy were overstated and that the Nestorians were a vital part of the Christian missionary heritage.

As the Nestorians were pushing eastward, the Roman Catholic Church was pushing north—and eventually across the seas. Unencumbered by families, missionaries spread out with courage and zeal to take the one true church to the ends of the earth.

Boniface (Winfried)

The expansion of Roman Catholic missions in central Europe during the early Middle Ages was associated with Boniface more than with any other individual. He has been variously described as "the greatest of all missionaries of the Dark Ages," "one of the most remarkable missionaries in the entire history of the expansion of Christianity," and "a man who had a deeper influence on the history of Europe than any Englishman who has ever lived."[7] But he is not universally acclaimed. His career, according to V. Raymond Edman, "reflects the lowering spiritual tone of English and Continental Christianity, which had begun to emphasize Church more than Christ, Sacrament more than Scripture."[8]

Boniface was born in Devonshire, England, in the late seventh century. He entered monastic life as a youth, and at the age of thirty was ordained a priest. There were many opportunities for this young cleric with "unusual gifts" to excel in his homeland. He was a recognized leader and was "outstandingly suited to the work of teaching, preaching and oversight," but his "call" was to evangelize the pagans on the Continent.[9]

His first tour of duty to Friesland, however, was unsuccessful because of political opposition and turmoil. He returned home, tempted to stay there and accept a position as head of a monastery. But his burden for foreign missions would not go away, and in 718, three years after he left on his first venture, he went back to the Continent. This time he went to Rome first. He had learned a lesson from his first experience. Papal recognition and backing were essential, and that is what he sought and received in Rome—an endorsement that colored his entire career. He was no longer an independent missionary going out simply to evangelize the pagan world. He was an emissary of Rome, commissioned to establish papal authority over the church in central Europe.

Boniface went first to what is present-day Germany and then back to Friesland for most of three years before returning to Germany, where he served the remainder of his life. In 723 he made his second journey to Rome, at which time

MEDIEVAL EUROPE

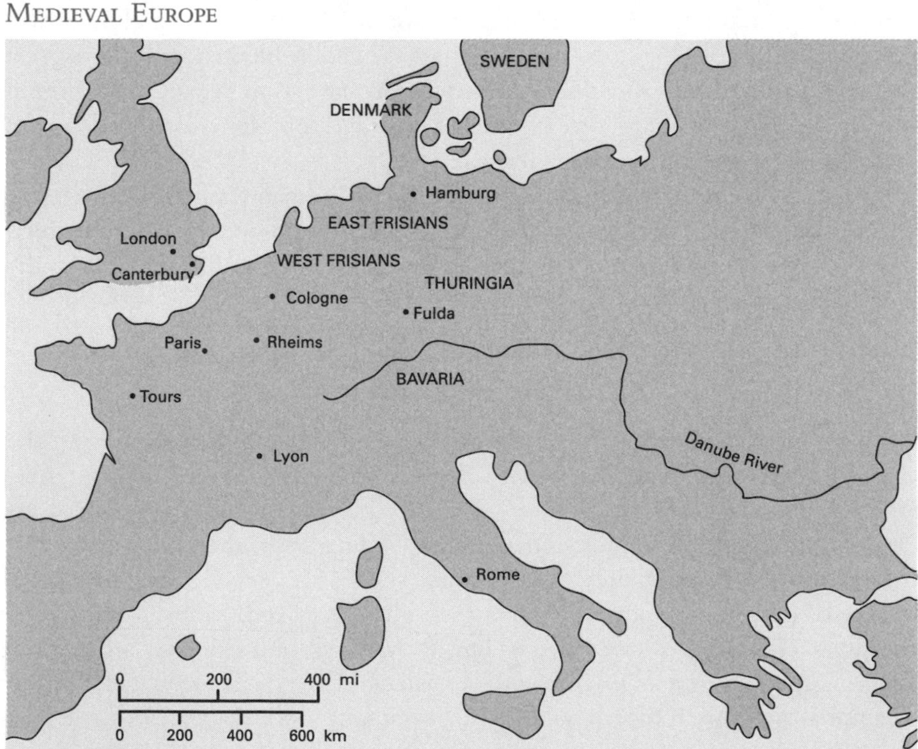

he was consecrated a missionary bishop to Germany by Pope Gregory II. Following his return to Germany, Boniface began his missionary work in earnest and won a reputation for courage throughout the Rhineland. Here he exhibited leadership skills that would be the key to his successful ministry. Indeed, he had an uncanny ability to enlist the loyal assistance of others in his ministry. Through correspondence and personal contacts, he urged others to join him in his grand calling from God. While visiting Rome, he presented his vision not only to the pope but to anyone else who would listen. He visited the shrines not just as a pilgrim but also as a recruiter. There he knew he would find potential missionaries.[10]

Back in Germany, he focused first on the upper classes, knowing the masses would likely—out of fear or respect—follow their example. He took the beliefs of the people seriously and sought to communicate with them in a way that they understood. Many of the nominal Christians of the area had reverted to pagan practices and were involved in spirit worship and magical arts. To counteract this sacrilege, Boniface was convinced, drastic measures were needed. So he boldly struck a blow to the very heart of the local pagan worship.

He assembled a large crowd at Geismar, where the sacred oak of the Thundergod was located, and with the people looking on in horror, he began chopping down the tree. It was a defiant act, but one that clearly drew attention to the fact that there was no supernatural power in either the tree or the god whom it honored. At the same time, it heightened the prestige of Boniface, and soon fanciful tales were associated with the incident, one alleging that when "the giant monster fell, its trunk burst asunder into four parts which, as they fell to the ground, miraculously shaped themselves into the arms of a cross, each arm of equal length."[11]

Boniface at Geismar after chopping down the sacred oak of the Thundergod.

It was "a master stroke of missionary policy," according to Philip Schaff, and thousands of people recognized the superiority of the Christian God and submitted to baptism.[12] Boniface was encouraged and relieved by the positive reaction and continued on in the same vein, destroying temples and shrines and smashing sacred stones into bits.

Gradually, he began to question the validity of this aggressive approach. He confided his doubts to another bishop, who advised him that such forceful methods were unwise and that a more meaningful and lasting approach was to "ask them questions about their gods, to inquire about their origins, their seemingly human attributes, their relationship with the beginning of the world, and in so doing elicit such contradictions and absurdities from their answers that they would become confused and ashamed."[13]

Whatever the impact the felling of sacred trees and smashing of shrines may have had on initial evangelistic work, it was obvious that much more was needed to build an enduring church. Like the Celtic missionaries before him, Boniface established monastic mission outposts as training centers where monks who worked with him prepared new converts for the ministry. The only truly innovative aspect of his ministry was his enthusiastic recruitment of women to serve the cause of missions. "For the first time in a number of centuries," writes Latourette, "we find women taking an active part in missions."[14]

The most noted of these women was Lioba, a cousin of Boniface who had corresponded with him and expressed interest in mission work in Germany. Through arrangements with her abbess back in Wessex, England, thirty nuns were sent abroad to join the mission work. Boniface deeded them a convent that became known as Bischofsheim, and Lioba served as the abbess. They were considered missionary nuns, but like many missionaries of this era they did not travel about conducting evangelistic outreach. They were cloistered. Their evangelism consisted of seeking to attract native women to become nuns. Lioba served faithfully for decades, long after the death of Boniface. Though confined to her convent, she had regular contact with a wide range of people—from villagers to bishops—who often came to her for counsel on church matters.[15]

In 737, following his third visit to Rome, Boniface was empowered to organize bishoprics throughout Bavaria, and in 744 he founded the famous monastery of Fulda that has remained a center for Roman Catholicism in Germany to this day. The phenomenal accomplishments credited to Boniface could not have been carried out without the powerful backing of Charles Martel, whose victory over the Muslims at the Battle of Tours in 732 marked a turning point in the struggle against Islam. "Without the protection of the prince of the Franks," wrote Boniface, "I can neither rule the people or the church nor defend the priests and clerks, monks and nuns; nor can I prevent the practice of pagan rites and sacrilegious worship of idols without his mandate and the awe inspired by his name."[16]

To the end, Boniface's ministry was to bolster the Roman Catholic Church—to "turn the hearts of the heathen Saxons to the Catholic Faith" and to "gather them among the children of Mother Church."[17] From that perspective, it is not surprising that the work of Boniface clashed with the missionary endeavors of Celtic and French monks. "He reaped the fruits of their labors," according to

Schaff, "and destroyed their further usefulness, which he might have secured by a liberal Christian policy. He hated every feature of individuality.... To him true Christianity was identical with Romanism."[18]

The fact that many Celtic missionaries had wives and defended clerical marriage was anathema to Boniface, but imbued with the Roman passion for uniformity, even such nonessential issues as the date for Easter, the right to eat certain meats, and the frequency of making the sign of the cross during mass caused him to denounce them as false prophets.

During the last years of his ministry, Boniface relinquished the administrative church work that had long consumed so much of his energy and went back to doing pioneer missionary work. "The spirit of the missionary prevailed," writes Neill, "and drove him out again into the lands where Christ had not been named."[19] In 753 he returned to Friesland, which was still largely pagan. There on the banks of the river Borne, he and some fifty assistants and followers set up their tents in preparation for a confirmation service of new converts. But the service never took place. Boniface and his companions were set upon and slain by a band of armed bandits, thus ending the ministry of medieval Europe's most energetic and outwardly successful missionary.

Boniface and his companions were set upon and slain by a band of armed bandits, thus ending the ministry of medieval Europe's most energetic and outwardly successful missionary.

In 771, less than two decades following the death of Boniface, the great Emperor Charlemagne ascended the throne, and during the nearly half-century of his reign, he was the most powerful promoter of Roman Catholic missions. Charlemagne freely mixed missions and military might to extend the boundaries of the Holy Roman Empire. "How much of his zeal for missions," writes Latourette, "arose from religious convictions and how much from political policy Charlemagne himself would probably have found it difficult to say."[20]

But even while Charlemagne was expanding the empire, there were setbacks as barbarians and marauders of every description continued to plunder the outlying regions. This havoc continued on in the generations after Charlemagne, when the strength of both the emperor and the papacy was at a low point. Raids from Scandinavia and elsewhere sometimes seemed to threaten the very future of a Christian Europe.

Anskar

The earliest Roman Catholic missions to Scandinavia, like those to Germany, were very closely tied to political and military exploits. The first knowledge of Christianity came to that part of the world through traders. Then, in 826, King Harold of Denmark, along with his wife and some four hundred court attendants and followers, submitted to baptism in hopes of obtaining Frankish military aid. Though such mass conversions gave no evidence of spiritual commitment, they opened the way for missionaries, and Anskar was summoned to begin evangelistic work in Scandinavia following the king's turn to Christianity.

Anskar, often referred to as the "Apostle of the North," was born in France in 801 and schooled from the age of five at the monastery of Corbie, founded more than two centuries earlier by Columba. Moved by visions and dreams, Anskar was a mystic whose highest ambition was to obtain a martyr's crown. Thus, he accepted his dangerous new assignment with eagerness. His hopes of converting the Danes soon dimmed when the political and military impotence of King Harold became apparent, however; and in less than three years Anskar, along with the king, was expelled from Denmark.

No sooner had he been forced out of Denmark than an invitation came from the king of Sweden requesting missionaries. Anskar and another monk immediately accepted the challenge, only to have the ship on which they were sailing attacked by pirates and all of their possessions stolen. On their arrival in Sweden, King Björn warmly welcomed them and gave them liberty to preach. There were many conversions, especially among the nobility—but as in the case of King Harold, conversions were apparently politically motivated.

So significant was Anskar's work from a political perspective that Emperor Louis the Pious struck a deal with Pope Gregory IV to appoint him Archbishop of Hamburg for the Scandinavian and Slavic states of Northern Europe. To aid him in his efforts, Louis gave him a wealthy monastery in West Flanders—a financial source that allowed him to bestow gifts on the provincial rulers. He recruited monks to assist him, and Catholicism made great strides in the next dozen years. The line between religion and politics, however, continued to be a fine one, and the gains were usually political in nature, motivated by what it was thought the Christian God and his temporal rulers could provide. Latourette relates one such incident recorded by Rimbert, Anskar's colleague and biographer:

> An army of non-Christian Swedes in besieging a town faced a discouraging outlook. They cast lots to inquire whether any of their gods would help them. The answer was unfavorable and the Swedes were much disheartened. However, some merchants who recalled Anskar's teaching suggested that lots be cast to see whether Christ, the God of the Christians, would assist them. The outcome was propitious, the beleaguered purchased peace, and the victors, returning home, honored Christ by observing fasts and giving alms to the poor.[21]

While political and military victories brought new areas under Roman Catholic influence, defeats often brought a return to paganism. Such was the case in 845 when Anskar saw fourteen years of labor destroyed by invading Danish raiders from the north. They swept down on Hamburg, sacking and burning and driving Anskar into hiding. When he sought protection from a neighboring bishop, the bishop refused to help because of political rivalry.

But after a series of political alliances and military victories, Hamburg was again under Christian control and Anskar was given expanded authority. As military threats lessened, he was able to devote more time to spiritual ministry. He was an ascetic who regarded prayer and fasting as paramount—though never to be done at the expense of useful activity. He insisted his monks be ever occupied with work, and he himself was often seen knitting while he prayed. As with most medieval spiritual leaders, he was credited with great miracles, but he personally sought to avoid all such praise, telling others that "the greatest miracle in his life would be if God ever made a thoroughly pious man out of him."[22]

Anskar died peacefully in 865 without the martyr's crown that he had longed for. But that certainly was not the greatest prize that eluded him. In spite of all his efforts, he was unable to establish a permanent base for Christianity in Scandinavia. After he died, the people reverted to paganism, and not until after the tenth century did the Catholic Church gain a sure foothold in that region.

Safeguarding the borders was a continual struggle for the successors of Charlemagne. By the time one boundary was secured, another was being invaded by the enemy. This was particularly true in central Europe, which had long been ravaged by invasions from the east—a situation further complicated by warring ethnic factions and political rivalry. "On the one side was German imperialism or Papal ambition, and on the other Byzantine imperialism."[23] Enter two brothers from Thessalonica—a city visited by Paul eight centuries earlier.

Cyril and Methodius

Like most medieval mission ventures, the work of Cyril and Methodius was tied to political maneuvering. Caught between East and West, a Moravian prince whose territory had been invaded by Western forces reached out to Constantinople—not for military might, but for missionaries. He wanted missionaries who could teach the people in their own language.

Cyril (whose given name was Constantine) and his brother Methodius were already seasoned missionaries—though for both, missions was a second career. They were raised in a Christian family, sons of a high-ranking military officer. Cyril became a philosopher and educator, whose first missionary experience was that of a Christian apologist to Muslims and later as an evangelist to the Khazars in Russia, many of whom were apparently converted through his teaching. Methodius, a civil servant, entered the monastery and then joined his brother in the mission to the Khazars.

In the early 860s Emperor Michael III of Constantinople arranged for Cyril and Methodius to begin a new mission among the nominally Christian Slavic peoples of central Europe. Like so many peoples before and after, the Christian

EIGHTEEN CENTURIES OF ADVANCE

0 100 200 300 400 500 600 700 800 900

MEDITERRANEAN WORLD

- (64) Nero persecution begins
- (67) Martyrdom of Peter and Paul
- (70) Destruction of Jerusalem
- (156) Martyrdom of Polycarp
- (303) Diocletian persecution begins
- (165) Death of Justin Martyr
- (203) Martyrdom of Perpetua
- (325) Council of Nicaea
- (638) Islam conquers Jerusalem
- (340) Ulfilas begins ministry with Goths
- (313) Constantine issues Edict of Milan
- (595) Gregory the Great commissions Augustine

NORTHERN AND WESTERN EUROPE

- (732) Battle of Tours
- (361) Martin of Tours begins missionary work
- (432) Patrick arrives in Ireland
- (496) Conversion of Clovis
- (744) Founding of
- (563) Columba arrives in Scotland
- (827) Anskar
- (716) Boniface begins
- (800) Charlemagne

ASIA AND AFRICA

- (635) Nestorians arrive in China

THE NEW WORLD

1000 1100 1200 1300 1400 1500 1600 1700 1800

- (1095) Crusades begin
- (1276) Lull opens monastery at Majorca
- (1316) Death of Raymond Lull

Fulda

arrives in Denmark
missionary work
crowned emperor

- (1212) Francis of Assisi begins mission to Syria
- (1219) Franciscans sent to North Africa
- (1216) Founding of Dominicans
- (1534) Founding of Jesuits
- (1705) Founding of Danish-Halle Mission
- (1722) Zinzendorf establishes Herrnhut
- (1622) Founding of *Propaganda*
- (1773) Jesuits suppressed by pope

- (1219) Friar John arrives in Peking
- (1542) Xavier arrives in India
- (1583) Ricci arrives in China
- (1606) de Nobili arrives in India
- (1706) Ziegenbalg arrives in India
- (1750) C. F. Schwartz arrives in India
- (1737) George Schmidt arrives in South Africa

- (1510) Dominicans arrive in Haiti
- (1523) Las Casas joins Dominicans
- (1646) John Eliot delivers first sermon to Indians
- (1675) King Philip's War
- (1555) Calvin sends colonists to Brazil
- (1722) Egede arrives in Greenland
- (1733) Christian David arrives in Greenland
- (1744) Zeisberger begins ministry to Indians
- (1743) Brainerd begins missionary work
- (1732) Moravians send missionaries to Virgin Islands
- (1625) Brèbeuf commissioned to New France

faith had seemed to them entirely foreign. Now they would have their own alphabet devised by Cyril, and the gospels and liturgy in their own language. The brothers' ministry had a profound spiritual influence in the region and also gave the Slavic peoples a sense of identity that they had not had previously. Their achievements, according to Latourette, had "lasting consequences for Slavic literature, not only in Central Europe and the Balkans, but also in Russia."[24]

> *The brothers' ministry had a profound spiritual influence in the region and also gave the Slavic peoples a sense of identity they had not had previously.*

Their missionary tenure, however, was not without controversy. Roman Catholic clerics resented the outsiders and their translations into the vernacular. To counteract the opposition, the brothers journeyed to Rome in 867 and there gained the endorsement of the pope. Before they could return to their Slavic mission, however, Cyril died. Methodius returned to the mission but found himself caught between political and religious rivalries for the remainder of his life. Yet, with the help of disciples, he continued to translate the Bible and other literature. Today the brothers are commemorated by both the Roman Catholic and Eastern Orthodox churches and are seen as precursors to the translation work of Martin Luther and of translators of the modern missions era.

Raymond Lull

The politically oriented missionary endeavors of the Roman Catholic Church during the medieval period brought many new regions into the sphere of Christian influence. But the church was losing ground at the same time—and not just *any* ground. The Holy Land—the very center of Christianity in the early centuries—was shaken to the core by the invading armies of Islam. "With lightening speed," writes J. Herbert Kane, "they conquered Damascus (635), Antioch (636), Jerusalem (638), Caesarea (640), and Alexandria (642)." Unlike the marauding barbarians that had brought down the Roman Empire more than two centuries earlier, the Muslims often brought culture with them. It was a time when "Arab civilization was at its height"—a time when "Baghdad boasted twenty-six public libraries and countless private ones."[25]

But no amount of culture or civilization could compensate for the losses, which came at a time when the West was barely holding its own against barbarian invasions. But for Charles Martel, whose army was victorious at the Battle of Tours in 722, France and all of Western Europe might have fallen to Muslim control. The Christians were clearly on the defensive. The long-delayed response to this tragic situation was itself a tragedy of monumental proportions—coming in the form of the Crusades. With no strategic planning, the Crusades had a snowball effect, the consequences of which are still being felt today. The swarms of people that set out for the Holy Land over a two-hundred-year period (1095–1291) caused unspeakable damage, and tens of thousands of lives were lost. Though the early crusades were favored with a degree of military success, those gains were lost in the end. So bitter was the animosity of Muslims toward Christians that even today the memory has not been erased.

Not all Christians of this period, however, believed that military force was the appropriate way to deal with the Muslims. During the early thirteenth century, while the crusading spirit was still at high pitch, Francis of Assisi proposed that the Muslims should be won by love instead of by hate. His first two attempts to evangelize them were completely unsuccessful, but his third attempt in 1219 brought him into the presence of the sultan of Egypt. Restricted by language barriers, Francis nevertheless made a feeble attempt at presenting the gospel. Though there is no evidence that any actual conversions resulted from his efforts, his example paved the way for others to view Muslims as potential brothers in Christ. Among them was Raymond Lull, an outstanding missionary of this period.

Lull was born in 1232 to a wealthy Roman Catholic family of Majorca, an island off the coast of Spain in the Mediterranean that had been taken back from the Muslims not long before his birth. As a young man he served in the Spanish court of the king of Aragon. Though married with children, he had mistresses on the side, and "by his own testimony lived a life of utter immorality."[26] Yet he was recognized for his scholarship and literary talent.

In his early thirties, Lull returned to Majorca, where he underwent a profound religious experience—a mystical experience marked by visions. The first vision came suddenly one evening when he was composing an erotic song. He saw "the Savior hanging on His cross, the blood trickling from His hands and feet and brow, look reproachfully at him." Though moved by the vision, he returned to his song-writing the following week. Again the vision appeared, and this time he committed his life to Christ. But immediately doubts arose: "How can I, defiled with impurity, rise and enter on a holier life?"[27] Consumed with guilt, he decided to forsake wealth and prestige and devote himself to God.

A vision convinced Lull that God was directing him to evangelize the nomadic Muslim Saracens—the most hated and feared enemies of Christendom.

Lull equated God's call with a call to monasticism. The ultimate demonstration of love for God, he believed, was living a life as a reclusive monk, wholly separated from the temptations of the world. It would take another vision to make him conscious of his responsibilities to others. In his book *The Tree of Love,* he relates the vision that became his missionary call: He is in a forest alone where he meets a pilgrim, who, on learning of Lull's chosen vocation, scolds him for his self-centeredness and challenges him to go out into the world and bring others the message of Christ. This vision convinced him that God was directing him to evangelize the nomadic Muslim Saracens—the most hated and feared enemies of Christendom. "I see many knights going to the Holy Land beyond the seas," he wrote, "and thinking that they can acquire it by force of arms, but in the end all are destroyed before they attain that which they think to have. Whence it seems to me that the conquest of the Holy Land ought . . . to be attempted . . . by love and prayers, and the pouring out of tears and blood."[28]

Following this vision, Lull studied the Arabic language—a nine-year ordeal that was marred by an unfortunate incident that almost ruined his future missionary career. To aid in his study of the language he purchased a Saracen slave, who one day lashed back at Lull by cursing Christ. Lull lost his temper and hit the slave, who grabbed a weapon and severely wounded him. For that crime the Muslim slave was imprisoned and soon afterward committed suicide, fearing his fate would be worse. It was a traumatic ordeal for Lull, but it gave him an even greater passion to reach the Muslims for Christ.

Lull was past the age of forty when his actual missionary career began, and in later life he recalled what sacrifices that decision entailed: "I had a wife and children; I was tolerably rich; I led a secular life. All these things I cheerfully resigned for the sake of promoting the common good and diffusing abroad the holy faith."[29] He set aside funds for his wife and children and gave the remainder to the poor.

Lull's missionary outreach was three-pronged: apologetical, educational, and evangelistic. "He devised a philosophical . . . system for persuading non-Christians of the truth of Christianity; he established missionary colleges; and he himself went and preached to the Moslems."[30] His achievement as a Christian apologist to the Muslims was immense—some sixty books on theology. His mission, as he perceived it, was to "experiment whether he himself could not persuade some of them [to believe in] the Incarnation of the Son of God and the three Persons of the Blessed Trinity in the Divine Unity of Essence." He sought to establish "a parliament of religions, and desired to meet the bald monotheism of Islam face to face with the revelation of the Father, the Son, and the Holy Spirit."[31]

In the area of missionary education, Lull, in the tradition of Columba, viewed monasteries as the ideal training ground for evangelists. He traveled widely, appealing to church and political leaders to support him in the cause. King James II of Spain was one of those who caught his vision; and in 1276, with his enthusiastic support and financial contributions, Lull opened a monastery on Majorca with thirteen Franciscan monks and a curriculum that included courses in the Arabic language and in the "geography of missions." His dream was to establish training centers all over Europe, but to do that he had to convince the Roman Catholic hierarchy of their value—no easy task. When he visited Rome on various occasions, his ideas were either ridiculed or ignored by a church hierarchy that was more interested in worldly pleasures and personal aggrandizement than in missions. He was successful, however, in influencing a decision at the Council of Vienna to have Arabic offered in the European universities—a step that he believed would open up dialogue between Christians and Muslims.

Lull's own missionary career did not begin with the flair that one might expect from this visionary missions enthusiast. It was one thing, he realized, to preach missions to others, but it was quite another to go forth himself. He was at the port in Genoa, ready to sail for Tunis. His belongings were on board ship. Crowds of well-wishers were preparing for a rousing send-off. Then at the last moment he was "overwhelmed with terror," as he later recalled; he was paralyzed "at the thought of what might befall him."[32] His belongings were unloaded, and the ship left port without him. Almost immediately he was overcome with remorse, and he determined to go on the next ship no matter what the consequences. Though racked by fever—probably caused by the emotional turmoil he was suffering—he was placed aboard another ship, and thus began his missionary career.

Lull's fears about conducting mission work in Tunis were certainly not unfounded. Tunis was a powerful center of Islam in North Africa that had held off repeated invasions. The crusaders were viewed with hatred and bitterness. His arrival was not greeted with as much hostility as he had expected, however. He made his presence known to the leading Muslim scholars and then called a conference to debate the relative merits of Christianity and Islam, promising that if Islam were demonstrated to be superior, he would embrace it as his faith. The Muslim leaders agreed to his terms.

The reaction to Lull's defense of Christianity was mixed. A number seemed to accept his arguments or at least showed an interest in hearing more, but the majority were stung by the verbal attack. Not surprisingly, he was thrown into prison, where he waited in terror, fully expecting the death penalty. Instead, he was stoned by a mob and ordered out of the country—an order he secretly defied. For three months he "concealed himself like a wharf-rat" in the coastal town of Goletta.[33] Frustrated by his lack of freedom, he returned to Europe, where he spent several years in Naples and then France, lecturing and writing books on his "New Method," always seeking new recruits to join his mission.

While the Muslims were the primary object of Lull's missionary passion, Jews also caught his attention. The twelfth and thirteenth centuries were marred by horror stories of anti-Semitism. Jews were blamed for almost every ill in society, and as a result were expelled from France and England—mild punishment compared with that meted out by the Spanish Inquisition. Here and there, outspoken individuals defended the Jews, and among them was Lull. He reached out to them as he had the Saracens, presenting Christ to them as their Messiah.

Lull's travel and varied activities kept him busy in Europe, but in 1307, at the age of seventy-five, after a fifteen-year absence, he returned to North Africa—this time to Bugia, east of Algiers. As in Tunis years earlier, he immediately sought a forum for public debate, and he boldly challenged the Muslims to compare their religion with Christianity. Though he claimed to reach out to the Muslims in love, his message was often very offensive and may have further embittered the Muslims toward Christianity. One of his arguments, as Samuel Zwemer relates, was to hold up the Ten Commandments "as the perfect law of God, and then [to show] from their own books that Mohammed violated every one of these precepts. Another approach was to portray the seven cardinal virtues and the seven deadly sins, only to show subsequently how bare Islam was of the former and how full of the latter!" Again, Lull's public debate did not continue long. He was sent to prison, and for six months his captors "plied him ... with all the sensual temptations of Islam."[34]

Following his imprisonment, he was sent back to Europe. His career as a foreign missionary, however, was not over. In 1314, when he was past the age of eighty, he returned to Tunis, where his age alone apparently brought him some protection. Perhaps too, he had mellowed over the years, for he was granted more liberty than before. He won some converts, though ever more conscious of the difficulty of the task. "For one Saracen who becomes a Christian," he wrote, "ten Christians and more become Mohammedans."[35]

Although Lull's stay in Tunis was rewarding, he did not win the ultimate reward—the crown of martyrdom. To die in the service of his Master would be the highest privilege. So in 1314 he returned to Bugia to see his little band of converts and to put his defense of Christianity to the final test.

> For over ten months the aged missionary dwelt in hiding, talking and praying with his converts. ... At length, weary of seclusion, and longing for martyrdom, he came forth into the open market and presented himself to the people as the same man whom they had once expelled from their town. ... Filled with fanatic fury at his boldness, and unable to reply to his arguments, the populace seized him, and dragged him out of the town; there by the command, or at least the connivance, of the king, he was stoned on the 30th of June, 1315.[36]

He died shortly thereafter.

Lull's missionary focus was primarily that of apologetics—to persuade people to accept the Christian faith because it was true. He was convinced that true understanding was built on systematic teaching and rational arguments. Other Catholic missionaries would focus on social justice and good works.

Bartholomew de Las Casas

The age of discovery that began in the late fifteenth century ushered in an era of overseas missions for the Roman Catholic Church. The New World was viewed in terms of territorial expansion, and both popes and political leaders were eager to do their part to bring it under Catholic domination. Queen

Isabella of Spain regarded the evangelism of the Indians as the most important justification for colonial expansion, and she insisted that priests and friars be among the first to settle in the New World. The Franciscans and Dominicans (and later the Jesuits) eagerly accepted the challenge. In some areas mass conversions were commonplace. In 1529 a Franciscan missionary in Mexico recorded that he and another monk baptized "upwards of 200,000 persons—so many in fact that I cannot give an accurate estimate of the number. Often baptized in a single day 14,000 people, sometimes 10,000, sometimes 8,000."[37]

The greatest obstacle to missions in the New World proved to be the colonists themselves and their cruel treatment of the native Indians. Though Queen Isabella had decreed that the freedom of the Indians was to be honored, they actually were treated inhumanely in a system that fostered their virtual slavery. Such treatment did not go unnoticed by the missionaries, and some risked their lives to protect the native people. Among them was Bartholomew de Las Casas, who though slow to recognize and admit the evil, became the greatest champion of the native Indians during the Spanish colonial period.

Las Casas was born in Spain in 1474, the son of a merchant who had sailed with Columbus on his second voyage. After receiving his law degree, he sailed to the island of Hispaniola to serve as the governor's legal advisor. He quickly settled into the affluent lifestyle of the colonists, accepting the conventional view of the native population, participating in raids against them, and enslaving them on his plantation. In 1510, in his mid-thirties, a spiritual experience prompted him to seek ordination as a priest. Yet outwardly he changed little, enjoying the lavish lifestyle that characterized most of the clergy. Gradually, however, his heart changed—particularly through the influence of Dominicans who decried the cruel enslavement of Indians.

Some missionaries risked their lives to protect the rights of the native people, among them Bartholomew de Las Casas, who became the greatest champion of the native Indians during the Spanish colonial period.

In 1514, at age forty, Las Casas, now a priest in Cuba, was preparing a sermon for Pentecost Sunday. As he read the Scripture, he suffered "pangs of conscience," realizing that there can be no true prayer and public worship without the outward exercise of justice. In that transforming moment he truly began to "consider the misery and servitude that those people suffer." After several days of meditation, he vowed that his life would take a different course. "In that Pentecost," writes Gustavo Gutierrez, "the feast that recalls the presence of the Holy Spirit, Las Casas recognized his own responsibility."[38]

Las Casas joined the Dominicans, and in the years that followed would become the New World's most vocal advocate for the Indians. In that role he traveled to and from Spain, pleading their cause with government officials and anyone who would listen, sometimes presenting a naïve and oversimplified case:

> God created these simple people without evil and without guile. They are most obedient and faithful to their natural lords, and to the Christians whom they serve. They are most submissive, patient, peaceful, and virtuous. Nor are they quarrelsome, rancorous, querulous, or vengeful. They neither possess nor desire to possess worldly wealth. Surely these people would be the most blessed in the world if only they worshipped the true God.[39]

Las Casas's ministry was more than mere humanitarianism, however. Evangelism was a priority, and for a number of years he traveled in Central America doing pioneer work. In one instance he convinced a native chief who had been terrorizing the colonists to lay down his weapons and to let all his tribe be baptized. Due to colonial opposition, however, most of his conversions did not come that easily.

At the age of seventy, Las Casas was appointed Bishop of Chiapas, an utterly impoverished area in southern Mexico that he chose above another far more prosperous diocese, even though, according to Latourette, "He must have known [it] would be one of the most trying tasks of his career."[40] Most of the Spanish planters there blamed him for the New Laws enacted by the Spanish crown that were designed to give the Indians protection and liberty. The enforcement of these laws would ruin the plantation economy—so said the Spanish landowners—and they simply ignored them. Las Casas, in turn, ordered his priests to deny absolution to any such lawbreakers, and the battle lines were drawn. Many of Las Casas's own priests defied him, and after three years he gave up his bishopric, discouraged and defeated. In 1547, at the age of seventy-three, he sailed from the New World, never to return. His battle for human rights continued on in Spain until his death almost two decades later, however, and he is still remembered as one of Christendom's greatest humanitarian missionaries.

Not all Dominicans were known for social justice and humanitarian outreach. They, along with Franciscans and other religious orders, played an active role in the Inquisition—a "mission" to keep the church free from heresy. All these were a significant part of what could be termed "*home* missions" in Europe. But the age of discovery would see the Catholic Church planted far beyond the boundaries of Europe and the New World.

Francis Xavier

The sixteenth century, which often seems dominated by the events of the Protestant Reformation, was also marked by a Catholic Reformation—a reformation to counteract the gains of the Protestants, to shore up the crumbling walls of the medieval church, and to expand the church to distant lands. This expansion was aimed not only to the West, but also toward India and the Far East, where lucrative trade routes were being established. The Catholic Church was anxious to cash in on this new wave of overseas travel, and adventurous missionary monks and friars eagerly volunteered for duty. The late-medieval religious orders, the Dominicans and Franciscans, supplied many of these courageous volunteers, but it was the Jesuits (the Society of Jesus), founded in 1535, who became the Counter-Reformation's most active participants. The founding of that organization, writes Stephen Neill, "is perhaps the most important event in the missionary history of the Roman Catholic Church."[41]

Ignatius of Loyola, a Spanish nobleman, was the founder of the Jesuits, and under his control the little band of dedicated disciples grew into a highly centralized, military-like organization that viewed loyalty to the pope and the Roman Catholic Church as its highest ideal. The order expanded rapidly: by the time of Loyola's death in 1556 there were over a thousand members, and in less than a century after its founding there were more than fifteen thousand members spread all over the globe. The most renowned of these early Jesuit missionaries was Francis Xavier, one of Loyola's inner circle of six and a charter member of the order. In 1541 he sailed for India, representing both the pope and the king of Portugal, to begin his short but extraordinary missionary career.

Xavier was born in 1506 to a Spanish noble family and grew up in a castle in the Basque countryside. As a youth he attended the University of Paris, where his interests leaned toward philosophy and theology. There he began spending time with a group of Protestants—dedicated young Christians who were risking their lives in the Catholic stronghold of Paris. But then Xavier met Loyola, a man fiercely devoted to the Roman Catholic Church, whose dynamic personal magnetism had a powerful effect on the spiritually unsettled young student. It was not long before Xavier joined with Loyola, turning his back both on the Protestants and on the lucrative career he might have had in the Catholic Church. Instead, he took a vow of poverty and celibacy, and committed himself wholly to spreading the Catholic faith.

Xavier's call to overseas missions came suddenly and without visions or voices. Two other Jesuits had been chosen to go to India as missionaries, and when one of them became ill, Xavier was assigned to take his place. With less than twenty-four hours warning, he was on his way. He arrived at the port city of Goa in 1542, where he found a morally corrupt society influenced far more by European culture than by religion. Xavier was frustrated, wondering how such people could be brought to Christ. He soon discovered that a ministry focused on children was more effective than one focused on adults. Children were more easily swayed than their parents, and it was his hope that he and the priests who would follow him could train them from early childhood to become effective Christian leaders in their own communities. This strategy was one he would follow during most of his missionary career.

Xavier did not remain in Goa long. The westernized society with its mixture of Jews and Muslims was not to his liking. When his exhortations failed to make an impact on the city, he pled with the king of Portugal to introduce the Inquisition and force the people to adhere to Catholic dogma and morality. But before that could be arranged, he left, seeking a more fruitful vineyard. "I want to be where there are . . . out-and-out pagans," he wrote, believing that in such an environment conversions would come more easily.[42]

From Goa, Xavier moved farther south in India to work among the impoverished pearl fishermen along the coast. The people were Hindus, and their response to Christianity depended largely on caste. The high-caste Brahmans were antagonistic, but the low-caste Paravas were much more open to change, realizing their status in society could not be worsened by such a move. Great crowds came out to learn and recite creeds, and baptisms were plentiful—so many that on some days Xavier was so tired from performing the sacrament that he could hardly move his arms. Yet baptism was to him the most important aspect of the ministry, and he would not deny anyone, no matter how tired he was. Appealing to Loyola for more workers, he wrote, "In these heathen places the only education necessary is to be able to teach the prayers and to go about baptizing little ones who now die in great numbers without the Sacrament because we cannot be everywhere at once to succor them."[43]

Francis Xavier, missionary to India and Japan.

Xavier's emphasis on baptism and his concentration on children went hand in hand. To a fellow worker he wrote, "I earnestly recommend to you the teaching of the children, and be very diligent about the baptism of newly born babies. Since the grownups have no hankering for Paradise, whether to escape the evils of life or to attain their happiness, at least let the little ones go there by baptizing them before they die."[44] But Xavier's emphasis on children was not just to ensure them a place in Paradise. His child converts became evangelists:

> As it was impossible for me to meet personally the ever growing volume of calls . . . I resorted to the following expedient. I told the children who memorized the Christian doctrine to betake themselves to the homes of the sick, there to collect as many of the family and neighbors as possible, and to say the

> Creed with them several times, assuring the sick persons that if they believed they would be cured.... In this way I managed to satisfy all my callers, and at the same time secured that the Creed, the Commandments, and the prayers were taught in the people's homes and abroad in the streets.[45]

Perhaps far more exciting for the youngsters than visiting the sick and reciting creeds were the other types of religious activities in which Xavier encouraged them to become involved. "They detest the idolatries of their people, and get into fights with them on the subject," he wrote with pride. "They tackle even their own parents if they find them going to the idols, and come to tell me about it. When I hear from them of some idolatrous ceremonies in the villages ... I collect all the boys I can, and off we go together.... The little fellows seize the small clay idols, smash them, grind them to dust, spit on them and trample them underfoot."[46]

Xavier's evangelism in India was superficial at best. Whether the children and adults who were baptized even knew the most fundamental truths of Christianity is doubtful. After three years of working among the pearl fishermen along the coast, he still had not begun to master the very difficult Tamil language, and even the simple prayers and creeds he taught the people were later found to be very poorly translated. Church services were ritualistic and repetitious, as Xavier's own account would indicate:

> On Sundays I assemble all the people, men and women, young and old, and get them to repeat the prayers in their language. They take much pleasure in doing so, and come to the meetings gladly.... I give out the First Commandment, which they repeat, and then we all say together, Jesus Christ, Son of God, grant us grace to love thee above all things. When we have asked for this grace, we recite the Pater Noster together, and then cry with one accord, Holy Mary, Mother of Jesus Christ, obtain for us grace from thy Son to enable us to keep the First Commandment. Next we say Ave Maria, and proceed in the same manner through each of the remaining nine Commandments. And just as we say twelve Paters and Aves in honour of the twelve articles of the Creed, so we say ten Paters and Aves in honour of the Ten Commandments, asking God to give us grace to keep them well.[47]

Xavier had not come to India to settle down in one area and establish a long-term ministry. He considered himself a trailblazer and was anxious to move on and lay the groundwork for Jesuit missions elsewhere. When he left India in 1545 for the Far East, his place was quickly filled by others, and within a few decades there were more than a dozen Christian villages.

Whether encountering children or adults, Xavier was always prepared to offer an evangelistic witness. He writes of one such incident before he left India: "I encountered a merchant who had a ship with wares. I spoke to him about the things of God, and God gave him to realize within himself that there are other wares in which he had not traded." The man left behind his ship and wares and became Xavier's companion evangelist. "He is thirty-five years old. A soldier of the world for all his life, he is now a soldier of Christ. He heartily commends himself to your prayers. His name is Joao d'Eiro."[48]

From India, Xavier went to Malacca on the Malay peninsula, where he ministered for a time; but his dream was to visit Japan and bring the gospel there. While in Goa in 1548 he met Anjiro, a Japanese man who convinced him that with proper conduct and logical reasoning a missionary could expect great results in Japan: "The king, the nobility, and all other people of discretion would become Christians, for the Japanese, he said, are entirely guided by the law of reason."[49]

Xavier arrived in Japan in 1549 and quickly realized that his ministry there would be much more difficult than the glowing predictions had indicated. The language barrier stymied any attempt at evangelism: "We are like so many statues amongst them, for they speak and talk to us about many things, whilst we, not understanding the language, hold our peace." Nevertheless, Xavier could write only months after he arrived that the people were very fond of hearing about the things of God, "chiefly when they understand them."[50] Some apparently did understand, for when Xavier left the country after two years he left behind some one hundred converts.

The freedom they encountered was a result of Japan's unstable political environment. There was no centralized government, and Buddhism was on the decline. That situation continued after Xavier departed, and the Jesuit missionaries who followed him witnessed impressive results. In the 1570s large numbers of Japanese began turning to Catholicism. Some fifty thousand in one region alone were baptized, and it is estimated that by the close of the sixteenth century there were some three hundred thousand professing Christians. This occurred despite a dramatic change in the Japanese political scene. Foreign missionaries were no longer welcome, and Japanese Christians faced severe persecution, sometimes resulting in death by crucifixion. In 1638 several thousand Christians took part in the Shimabara Rebellion, protesting persecution and exorbitant taxes. They finally took refuge in a castle where, after weeks of holding their own, they were defeated and slaughtered. But despite such setbacks, Catholicism continued to have an influence in Japan for more than two centuries.

Xavier returned to Goa following his departure from Japan, and from there he made plans to go to China, hoping to penetrate that land with the gospel. But it would be left to another Jesuit to pioneer the work there. For while Xavier was arranging entry, he contracted a fever and died on an island just off the coast of China, only ten years after his missionary career had begun.

Matthew Ricci

"Barbarians Not Welcome." This slogan, more than any other, spoke for China during much of its history. China was a proud and isolationist region that opposed the planting of Christianity on its soil. Attempts were made, but without success. Nestorians who traveled overland from Syria during the sixth century were the first known Christian missionaries to China. Their influence began to decrease by the thirteenth century when the first Roman Catholic missionary, Friar John, arrived. He found considerable freedom to preach under the protection of the Mongols who were then ruling China, and thousands were baptized. During the fourteenth century, when the Ming Dynasty came to power, however, missionaries were expelled. Not until the end of the sixteenth century did Christianity actually gain a permanent foothold in China, and it was an Italian Jesuit, Matthew Ricci, who "became and has ever remained the most respected foreign figure in Chinese literature who was most responsible for that breakthrough."[51]

Ricci was born in 1522, the year of Xavier's death. His father was an Italian aristocrat who sent him to Rome to study law. While there, however, young Ricci fell under the influence of the Jesuits, and after three years he turned away from his pursuit of a secular career and entered the Jesuit order. So distressed was his father when he heard the news that he left immediately for Rome to rescue his son. On the way, he became violently ill and was unable to go on. Fearing this was a sign of God's anger, he returned home. Ricci's acceptance into the Society of Jesus did not signal an end to his secular studies. He went on to study under a leading mathematician of his day, acquiring an education that later opened a door for him among the *literati* of China.

Accompanied by thirteen other missionaries, Ricci was assigned first to Goa, where Xavier had begun his missionary career. Like Xavier, they baptized and trained children, a ministry to which Ricci did not feel uniquely called. But after four years in India, he "received the marching orders for which he had been praying so long."[52] He was soon on his way to the Portuguese port city of Macao on the coast of China. His friend Ruggieri had gone there earlier; and even though he was depressed and hopelessly bogged down in language study, Ricci sailed for his new post with anticipation.

His arrival in China signaled the breakthrough that had long been awaited. Though missionaries had for some time resided in Macao, entering China proper had not been permitted. But when word of his expertise in such fields as mathematics, astronomy, and geography reached Wang P'an, the governor of Shiuhing, he invited Ruggieri and Ricci to come and live in his province. Though they initially feared the invitation might be a ploy to kill them, they accepted the risk and went. It was not a trick, however, and Ricci quickly demonstrated the value of his secular learning in foreign missionary work. With him he brought a supply of mechanical gadgets, including clocks, musical instruments, and astronomical and navigational devices as well as books, paintings, and maps—all of which drew widespread interest from scholars. The maps were particularly intriguing for these men who had previously refused to believe that the world consisted of more than China and her immediate neighbors.

Ricci's primary aim was not to bring Western learning, but to bring the gospel. To make that point, he and Ruggieri shaved their heads and took on the garb of Buddhist monks.

Ricci's primary aim was not to bring Western learning, but to bring the gospel. To make that point, both he and Ruggieri shaved their heads and took on the garb of Buddhist monks. After only two years there were converts, and the two missionaries dedicated a small church and private residence that they had built with the help of Chinese labor. In 1588, five years after they entered China proper, Ruggieri returned to Europe, and Ricci was left in charge of the work with several other Jesuits.

Before he left China, Father Ruggieri had become the focus of a sex scandal. A Chinese convert accused him of committing adultery with a married woman, whose husband concurred with the charge. "This was a classic case of shakedown," writes Jonathan Spence, "and Ruggieri was able to clear his name." Other priests faced similar accusations in this hostile climate where sexual promiscuity was commonplace. "Such rumors were constantly fanned by the Chinese, who staged plays on market days in the little towns, mocking the Christians and the Portuguese, who kept their swords and rosaries in action at the same time, and let their priests mix indiscriminately with local women. These plays were reinforced by comic prints attacking the Jesuits and their converts, which enjoyed a brisk sale."[53]

In the meantime Ricci changed his attire to that of a Confucian scholar. Confucianism was the religion of the Chinese intelligentsia, and Ricci was focusing his attention on that segment of the population. If the Chinese could view Confucianism as merely a philosophy, he reasoned, then they could accept Christianity as well and not be forsaking their traditional beliefs.

While he was seeking to contextualize Christianity in China, another Jesuit missionary, Robert de Nobili, was doing the same thing in India—in essence, becoming a Brahmin to reach that caste for Christ. He observed the laws and wore the clothes of the Brahmin caste, and he disassociated himself from the existing Christian church—not, however, without a barrage of criticism. Both he and Ricci were highly controversial figures within Roman Catholicism.

Ricci's effort to make Confucianism compatible with Christianity appealed to the Chinese and paved the way for conversions. But critics insisted that he was not being true to the basic tenets of Christianity. For the name for God, for instance, he used the term Lord of Heaven (*T'ien* for heaven and *Shang-Ti* for sovereign lord) from the ancient classics. Likewise, Ricci did not insist that converts abandon ceremonies honoring ancestors. He argued that such traditions only indicated a healthy respect for deceased family members.

Not surprisingly, his methods came under fire almost immediately, especially from competing orders, the Dominicans and Franciscans. Jesuits had maintained a virtual monopoly on spreading Catholicism in China for a number of years, and the other two orders were quick to find fault. By the early seventeenth century the issue had blown up into what became known as the Chinese Rites Controversy, probably the most heated debate ever to confront Roman Catholic missions. Papal pronouncements generally took the side of the Dominicans and Franciscans, forbidding Christians to sacrifice to Confucius or to their ancestors. The Chinese emperor, on the other hand, took the side of the Jesuits, threatening to expel those who opposed ancestor worship. The controversy raged for centuries without being fully resolved.

In defense of Ricci, it should be noted that he had not sought controversy, and his leniency toward Confucianists may have been influenced by the intellectuals with whom he associated. "It is conceivable," writes A. J. Broomhall, "that to them the ceremonial, civic and political aspects of these rites could have been distinct from the religious and superstitious, but not to the average Chinese with his animistic beliefs."[54]

For Ricci himself, the acceptance of Confucianist ideas came naturally. As he studied and translated the Chinese classics, he developed great respect for what this ancient culture had to offer. He dismissed the doctrine of the *tabula rasa*—the belief that non-Christian philosophies and religions must be entirely eradicated before Christianity can be effectively introduced. Such also was the conclusion of Xavier after he came in contact with the Japanese and their highly developed culture. Earlier, in India, he had sought to debunk non-Christian systems and had little success. The policy of accommodation thus became a pattern for the Jesuits, and the debates have continued to the present day. It was a pattern of contextualizing the gospel that was viewed by some as syncretism—a heretical mix of Christian and non-Christian beliefs.

Ricci's great respect for the Chinese people and his eagerness to share his scientific knowledge with them brought him unusual opportunities that have been accorded few other foreigners before or since. In 1601, at the invitation of Wan Li, he was permitted to locate in Peking and continue his mission work near the emperor's palace, while living on a stipend from the imperial government. With him he brought a large striking clock that he presented to the emperor, and he and his fellow priests became the official clock-winders of the imperial court. "When enemies tried to oust him," writes Broomhall, "the powerful palace eunuchs were afraid they could not keep it going and saw to it that Ricci was not expelled."[55] "It is a miracle of the omnipotent hand of the Most High," wrote Ricci, and "the miracle appears all the greater in that not only do we dwell in Peking, but we enjoy here an incontestable authority."[56]

Ricci ministered in Peking until he died in 1611, nearly ten years after he arrived in that city. During that time a significant number of scholars and government officials professed faith in Christ, among them Paul Hsü, one of China's leading intellectuals and a member of the Imperial Academy. His faith was real, and he passed it on to his children who kept it alive for generations. His daughter devoted her time to training professional storytellers to take the gospel out into the villages. Two other female descendants of Paul became famous through their marriages—one became Madame Sun Yat-sen, and the other, Madame Chiang Kai-shek. Though the number of Chinese converts at the time of Ricci's death (some two thousand) was miniscule in comparison to China's vast population, their influence was far greater because of their high status in society, and in the seventeenth and eighteenth centuries, Christianity continued to grow, despite periodic outbreaks of violent persecution. During the half-century following Ricci's death, the church increased a hundredfold.

Ricci was above all else a faithful Roman Catholic, as were his converts. In his journal, he writes of Paul Hsü bowing "before the statue of the Blessed Virgin" before he entered the residence of one of the Jesuit priests and how, after he was baptized, "he attended the sacrifice of the Mass every day" and "found a great consolation in going to confession."[57] Amid the ritual was the gospel message, and according to Broomhall, "much pure doctrine was taught, whatever else was added."[58]

One pamphlet on God written by a Jesuit priest during this period was widely circulated in the provinces and later used by Protestant missionaries, and it was just such literature that kept the message alive following a 1724 edict that expelled the missionaries and forced the Chinese Christians to worship in secret.

SELECT BIBLIOGRAPHY

Brodrick, James. *Saint Francis Xavier.* New York: Wicklow, 1952.

Cronin, Vincent. *The Wise Man from the West.* New York: Dutton, 1955.

Cuming, G. J., ed. *The Mission of the Church and the Propagation of the Faith.* Cambridge: Cambridge University Press, 1970.

De Vaulx, Bernard. *History of the Missions.* New York: Hawthorn, 1961.

Edman, V. Raymond. *The Light in Dark Ages.* Wheaton, IL: Van Kampen, 1949.

Greenaway, George William. *Saint Boniface.* London: Adam & Charles Black, 1955.

Gutierrez, Gustavo. *Las Casas: In Search of the Poor of Jesus Christ.* Translated by Robert R. Barr. Maryknoll, NY: Orbis, 1993.

Sladden, John Cyril. *Boniface of Devon: Apostle of Germany.* Exeter, England: Paternoster Press, 1980.

Spence, Jonathan. *The Memory Palace of Matteo Ricci.* New York: Viking, 1984.

Xavier, Francis. *The Letters and Instructions of Francis Xavier.* Translated and introduced by M. Joseph Costelloe. St. Louis: Institute of Jesuit Sources, 1992.

Zwemer, Samuel M. *Raymond Lull: First Missionary to the Moslems.* New York: Funk & Wagnalls, 1902.

3

American Indian Missions: Seeking the "Noble Savage"

"Redskins." "Aborigines." "The noble savage." "The lost tribes of Israel." No other native population of the world has been more ardently solicited and pushed around by government officials, politicians, and church leaders than the native American Indians. For centuries, Native Americans were a prime target of Christian evangelism. Both Catholics and Protestants invested heavily in this mission endeavor. The story of American Indian missions is an intriguing one—a story of deep emotion, of great courage, and of spiritual devotion, but ultimately a story of failure. How could so much concerted effort result in so little fruit? Two centuries of aggressive land grabbing, cultural clashes, and slow extermination tell the story.

The first missionaries to come to North America were Roman Catholics. In the sixteenth century, Spanish priests, mainly from the Franciscan order, began working among the Pueblos in what is now the southwest United States. A number of missions were established, and there was great interest in the new way of life that the friars introduced. They brought domestic animals, an array of food plants, metal tools, and weaponry. In exchange, many of the Pueblos were baptized and attended Mass, yet continued to practice ancient religious traditions. The Franciscan friars made little effort to translate the liturgy or the Scriptures into the native tongue, and they moved frequently from place to place and from one language group to another. Yet by 1625 they reported large numbers of converts—tens of thousands within a few short decades of mission work.[1]

Missionaries of European decent, whether Catholic or Protestant, immediately discovered major cultural differences between themselves and the Native Americans. The concept of *land* was of enormous significance. This was true of the Pueblos as with all other tribes from coast to coast. Unlike the Europeans, who viewed the land—the natural world around them—as resources for their own benefit, the natives viewed the land in spiritual terms. They saw the land as sacred and felt a oneness with the environment around them. The land was their ancestral land. It could not be bought or sold; it belonged communally to the living and the dead. And the natives themselves were a communal unit. European individualism was unknown. "Anyone setting himself apart from others was more likely to be ridiculed than honored."[2] Most of the early missionaries adjusted to the communal nature of Native American life, with the recognition that individual conversions were unlikely.

Most of the early missionaries adjusted to the communal nature of Native American life, with the recognition that individual conversions were unlikely.

A century after the Franciscans came to the Southwest, French Jesuits, under the leadership of Jean de Brèbeuf, entered the St. Lawrence Valley (present-day Ontario) and began working among the Hurons. True to Jesuit mission strategy, the worldview of the natives was studied and appreciated. The Jesuits believed that in many ways the native religion was compatible with Christianity. Both recognized a "god above" and divine forces in everyday life, gave rituals and ceremonies great importance and placed a great emphasis on supernatural experiences such as dreams and visions. "One group sprinkled tobacco on a lake and talked to fish spirits before setting traps," writes Henry Bowden, "the other venerated saints and performed novenas, but at bottom the way they conducted themselves from day to day was easily understandable to each other."[3]

To present the gospel to the natives, the Jesuits were willing to compromise in critical areas. For example, they did not refer to eating the body or drinking the blood of Christ (an essential aspect of the Mass) because to the Hurons this would have been associated with cannibalistic rituals. Rather, Brèbeuf presented the Mass as a memorial of thanksgiving. Because the natives attached positive significance to the color red, the Jesuits used red freely—especially for the cross. Likewise, the Hurons' confidence in dream interpretation was employed by Jesuits in encouraging them to see their dreams as leading them to Christianity.[4]

One of the unique aspects of the Jesuit work among the Hurons was Bible translation. Unlike early Protestant missionaries who frequently doubled as Bible translators, Catholics were usually content to translate liturgy and creeds—and perhaps a few scattered portions of actual Scripture.

Paul Le Jeune

Located some 750 miles from the nearest city, the remote mission outpost among the Hurons was primitive by European standards. By 1732, when Paul Le Jeune arrived, the Jesuits had established a school for native children, but there was little else to show for their seven years of work. Le Jeune, born in 1591, might have seemed ill-suited for the task at hand. Nearly forty, with an academic background in theology and philosophy from the University of Paris, he was wholly unprepared for the privations he would encounter. His reason for being there was simply obedience. "I thought nothing of coming to Canada when I was sent here," he confessed. "I felt no particular affection for the Savages, but the duty of obedience was binding."[5] His assignment was to translate the Scriptures.

The winters were bitterly cold and the summers hot, humid, and bug-infested, and the temptation to give up was sometimes almost overwhelming. "It is true that God does not allow himself to be conquered," he wrote, "and that the more one gives the more one gains; but God sometimes hides himself, and then the Cup is very bitter."[6] What Le Jeune was experiencing was a common lament of missionaries—ones whose setbacks were only exceeded by their sacrifices. Where was God in the midst of such hardship?

With no preparation as a linguist or translator, Le Jeune struggled to make headway in the very difficult Huron language. Complicating the situation were native helpers whose moods ranged from trickery to lethargy. Sometimes he caught them "teaching him obscene words in place of the right ones." On other occasions the work bogged down to a standstill: "I was compelled sometimes to ask twenty questions to understand one word, so changeable was my master's way of teaching." Le Jeune recognized the intelligence of the natives; the biggest problem was their lack of motivation. The solution came unexpectedly in a shipment from back home: "Oh, how grateful I am to those who sent me some tobacco last year. The Savages love it to madness. Whenever we come to a difficulty, I give my master a piece of tobacco, to make him more attentive."[7]

"I thought nothing of coming to Canada when I was sent here," Le Jeune confessed. "I felt no particular affection for the Savages, but the duty of obedience was binding." His assignment was to translate the Scriptures.

The goal of Le Jeune's arduous labor was converts. At times the situation seemed utterly hopeless, but there were moments of optimism, as he penned in his journal:

> On the 14th of November, the Savage la Nasse being with us, I instructed him about the Creation of the world, the Incarnation, and the Passion of the Son of God. We talked well into the night, everyone being asleep except him. Returning to his cabin, he said to Pierre that he was much pleased to listen to such talk.
>
> Seeing us praying to God one day after dinner, he sighed deeply, saying: "Oh, how unhappy I am that I am not able to pray to God as you do!"
>
> La Nasse often said to Pierre: "Teach that man as soon as you can," speaking of me, "in order that we may be able to understand what he says."[8]

In 1639, seven years after Le Jeune began his mission work, there were fewer than one hundred converts in this tribe of some ten thousand, with ten resident Jesuits. But within two decades and an increased missionary force, it was estimated that half the tribe had been converted. But then disaster struck. The Iroquois League launched an all-out military campaign against the Hurons, and before it was over, most of them were either killed or scattered. Jean de Brèbeuf was tortured and murdered, and an era of Jesuit missions to the Hurons was over. Work continued in Quebec and elsewhere, but not with the enthusiasm it had once had.

Later on, Roman Catholic missionaries began working among Indians on the Great Plains and in the Oregon Territory, but it was the Protestant missionary venture more than the Roman Catholic that made a lasting impact on the North American Indians.

John Eliot

From the very beginning of English exploration of the New World there was a strong impulse to win the native population to Christianity. Evangelizing the natives became a powerful rationale for colonialism, and colonial charters emphasized this. The Virginia charter of 1606 opens with the king's blessing on the colonists "in propagating the Christian religion to such people as yet live in darkness and miserable ignorance." The Massachusetts Bay charter pledged to "wynn and incite the natives of the Country to the Knowledge and obedience of the only true God and Savior of Mankinde, and the Christian fayth." And the seal of the colony testified to this need; its emblem was a figure of an Indian crying out "Come over and help us." The charter of Connecticut asserted that "evangelization" was the "onlye and principal end" for the colony's establishment. Likewise, Pennsylvania and other colonies were founded with the declared purpose of converting the Indians.

In most instances, however, these pronouncements meant nothing. As settlers staked out their land claims, the "poor savage" became a threat and hindrance. Greed overpowered the sentiments of humanitarianism and evangelism, and the work of the missionaries was openly despised. Thus, missionaries encountered not only a hostile native population but also strong opposition by their own people. There were exceptions. Massachusetts, more than any other colony, sought to fulfill its charter obligations. Ministers were charged with a dual responsibility of serving a congregation and evangelizing the Indians. Most, however, were too busy to devote time to both facets of their ministry, and the latter was neglected.

One who stood out in his determination to take both roles seriously was John Eliot, often referred to as the "Apostle to the Indians." But despite his achievements as a missionary, his primary vocation was his ministry at the Roxbury church. Eliot was born in England and educated for the ministry at Cambridge, graduating in 1622. Although he was ordained in the Anglican Church, he was a Nonconformist, thus limiting his opportunities in England. After serving for a time as a schoolteacher, he set sail for Massachusetts in 1631. Within a year, he was joined by his three brothers and three sisters as well as his fiancée.

Eliot soon became the minister of the congregation in the small frontier settlement of Roxbury, just two miles outside Boston, and there in October of 1632, he married Hanna Mumford. His early years in the ministry were filled with the needs of his congregation. There were Indians close by, but their occasional visits to Roxbury attracted little attention. They were peaceful, and the settlers accepted their presence with little thought of evangelizing them. In fact, many New Englanders, including ministers, looked on the growing death rate of Indians due to imported European diseases as God's means of "clearing the land" for "His people."

Not until 1644, when Eliot was forty years old, did he seriously begin his missionary endeavor. There was no Macedonian call. There was no solemn commission. There was simply a need, and he was available. His first step was language study—two years of mental anguish learning the Massachusetts dialect of the Algonquin tongue, an unwritten language composed of guttural sounds and voice inflections. This difficult task was aided by Cochenoe, a young Indian captured in the Pequot War. Cochenoe served as Eliot's teacher and also accompanied him as an interpreter and assistant.

John Eliot, Puritan missionary to the Algonquin Indians.

In the fall of 1646 Eliot delivered his first sermon to a group of Indians who lived nearby. This was the first crucial test of his ability to communicate effectively. Despite his best effort, his message fell on deaf ears; the Indians "regarded it not" nor gave "heed unto it, but were weary and despised what I said." A month later Eliot preached again, this time to a larger group of Indians who congregated at Waban's wigwam. This time the Indians listened for more than an hour, and when the sermon was over, they asked questions—questions Eliot later described as "curious, wonderful, and interesting." Eliot answered some of the questions, but then with perceptive missionary psychology he closed the question time and "resolved to leave them with an appetite." Before leaving the encampment, he passed out treats, including sweetmeats and apples for the children and tobacco for the men. He had his first taste of success, and he "departed with many welcomes."[9]

Two weeks after this encouraging meeting he returned, accompanied by two pastors and a layman (as he had been on his first visits). Following his opening prayer, he drilled the children in recitation of catechism, the parents learning while they listened. He then preached on the Ten Commandments and on Christ's love, to which some Indians responded with tears and weeping. Again there were questions that followed—the most difficult of which to answer was, "Why has no white man ever told us these things before?"

Eliot continued making biweekly trips to Waban's wigwam in the months that followed, always with catechism lessons and evangelistic sermons that were carefully prepared and rehearsed in the complex Algonquin language. Although he carried a heavy share of the ministry himself, he actively recruited the help of others, including neighboring pastors and his own parishioners. Their enthusiasm buoyed his spirits and kept the mission going during difficult times. Travel was always slow and cumbersome. Trudging through the rugged wilderness trails was fatiguing, but his optimism could not be dampened: "We never had a bad day to go preach to the Indians all the winter. Praised be the Lord."[10]

As the weeks and months passed, some Indians were converted and noticeable changes were seen in their lives. A report published less than a year after Eliot's first meeting documented the following progress:

> The Indians have utterly forsaken their powwows.
>
> They have set up morning and evening prayers in their wigwams.
>
> They not only keep the Sabbath themselves, but have made a law to punish those who do not.
>
> Whoever profanes it must pay twenty shillings.
>
> They begin to grow industrious and are making articles to sell all the year long. In winter, brooms, stoves, eelpots, baskets; in spring they sell cranberries, fish, strawberries.
>
> The women are learning to spin.[11]

One of Eliot's first concerns was to have an area of land specifically designated for the Christian Indians. His rationale was that new converts needed to be separated from those who had no interest in the gospel. The Indians, likewise, wanted some place to call their own. White settlers had been building homes and fences, leaving the Indians restricted in their hunting and fishing. Eliot made an appeal in their behalf to the General Court, and the Indians were granted several thousand acres eighteen miles southwest of Boston, where they established the settlement of Natick, commonly referred to as a "praying town."

Natick was not a typical Indian settlement. Streets were laid out, and each family was given a lot. Some buildings, through the encouragement of Eliot, were constructed European style, but most of the Indians chose wigwams for their own homes. A biblical form of government, based on Jethro's plan in Exodus 18:21, was set up by Eliot; the town was divided into tens, fifties, and hundreds, each division with a ruling adult male. The white man's civilization became the standard, and Christian Indians were expected to simply accept it. To Eliot, true Christianity not only changed the heart and mind but also changed the lifestyle and culture. He could not envision a truly Christian community apart from European culture, and this factor, in hindsight, is seen as the one grave weakness of his ministry.

American Indian Missions in New England

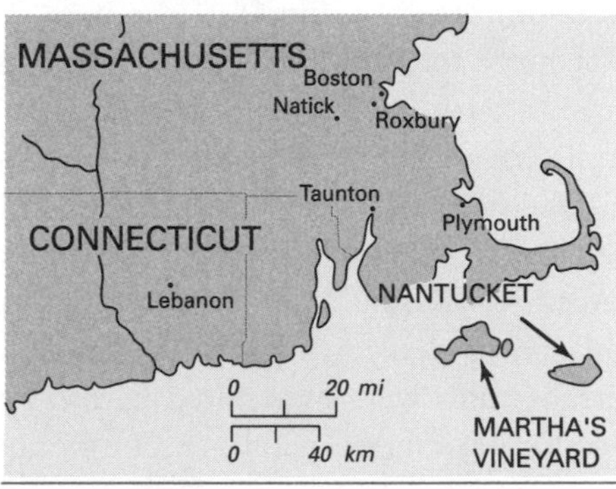

There were problems in establishing Natick, particularly from white settlers who resented the Indians' permanent residence among them, but Eliot periodically petitioned the Massachusetts General Court for more grants of land, and by 1671 he had gathered more than eleven hundred Indians into fourteen "praying towns." His ministry was scrutinized by the General Court, and he eagerly accepted all public funding they appropriated for his projects.

Although Eliot spent time and effort with temporal matters, his primary concern was the spiritual welfare of the Indians. He was slow and meticulous in his evangelism, and though he witnessed his first conversions after preaching to them only three times, he did not rush the process. In fact, he purposefully delayed baptism and church membership until he was convinced that they were committed to their new faith. The first baptisms were delayed until 1651, five years after the first conversions. Likewise, the establishment of a church was put off until he and his fellow ministers determined that the Indians were adequately prepared to assume church offices.

Eliot was interested in more than professions of faith. He sought spiritual maturity in his Indian followers, and in his view, that could be accomplished only if they could read and study the Bible in their own language.

Eliot was interested in more than professions of faith. He sought spiritual maturity in his Indian followers, and in his view, that could be accomplished only if they could read and study the Bible in their own language. Thus, in 1649, three years after his first sermon at Waban's wigwam, amid a hectic schedule, he began his translation work. His first completed project was a catechism printed in 1654. The following year the book of Genesis and the gospel of Matthew were published; and in 1661 the New Testament was completed, with the Old Testament following two years later. Despite this noteworthy accomplishment, he was harshly criticized for wasting his time in the Indian language when he could have been teaching the Indians English.

As the years passed and as the praying towns grew in numbers and the Christian Indians grew spiritually, Eliot concentrated more and more on training Indian leaders. By 1660 twenty-four Indians had been trained as evangelists to minister to their own people, and several churches had ordained Indian ministers. Schools were established in every town, and the Indians were seemingly adapting to European culture. On the surface the future looked bright, but time was running out. Decades of European encroachment on Indian lands could not go unchecked indefinitely. The land grabbing, dishonest bargaining, and ill-treatment of the Indians were bound to bring retaliation. There was unrest among the Indians of the Northeast, and even the praying Indians would not escape the horror looming on the horizon—the bloodiest war in American colonial history.

King Philip's War broke out in the summer of 1675, after three of the chief's braves were hanged for the murder of an Indian agent who had tipped off a colonial governor of the chief's plan to attack. The war was nearly lost by the settlers, and before the fighting was over more than a year after it began, thirteen towns and many more settlements had been utterly devastated. Whole families—grandparents, aunts, uncles, and little children—were obliterated from the registers of colonial record books.

The saga of the praying Indians during this bloody war was a tragic one—a story repeated again and again in American history. Although the praying Indians had complained bitterly about encroachment on their land and, in the words of Eliot, "the business about land giveth them no small matter for stumbling,"[12] they nevertheless stood by the white settlers when the Wampanoags and later other tribes attacked. In fact, they aided the colonial militia as scouts and fighters, so much so that their aid tipped the scales in favor of the settlers. But this service was ignored. Tensions were high. Hundreds of Christian Indians were exiled to a "bleake bare Island" in Boston Harbor—"harried away" before they could even gather possessions, forced to endure a harsh winter without sufficient food or supplies.

Eliot visited them during that dire winter and pleaded with officials on their behalf for more food and medicine, but he found little sympathy for his cause. Yet these exiled Indians fared better than the families they left behind. Many who remained were indiscriminately murdered by cowardly settlers. When the violence ended, most of the surviving Christian Indians trickled back to their devastated towns. Efforts were made to rebuild, but life was never the same. The

Indians had been weakened not only numerically but also spiritually. Many of those who became soldiers were enticed by the white mans' liquor.

King Philip's War was a tragedy for the many Indians and whites directly involved as well as for the seventy-two-year-old John Eliot. He had poured decades of selfless service into his missionary work, and it was difficult to view the wreckage of the war. But he was not one to give up: "I can do little, yet I am resolved through the grace of Christ, I will never give over the worke, so long as I have legs to go."[13] As the years passed, his output decreased, but he remained faithful to the work until his death in 1690 at the age of eighty-five.

Although much of Eliot's work was ravaged by the devastation of war, his example as an evangelist and Bible translator paved the way for further missionary efforts among the natives, and his influence in the founding of the Society for the Propagation of the Gospel (SPG), a missionary arm of the Anglican Church that actively worked in the American colonies, was significant.

What was the secret behind Eliot's exceptional life of service? What carried him through the years of opposition, hardship, and disappointment? Three characteristics are worth noting: his unbending optimism, his ability to enlist the help of others, and his absolute certainty that God, not he, was saving souls and was in control of the bad times as well as the good.

The Mayhews

Eliot was only one among several colonial New England pastors who was ministering effectively among the Indians. Another noteworthy mission to the native population was conducted on Martha's Vineyard by the Mayhew family. Thomas Mayhew Sr. came to America in the 1630s at about the same time that Eliot arrived. Soon after he arrived, he settled on Martha's Vineyard, where he purchased the proprietary rights and became governor. His son, Thomas Jr., studied for the ministry, was ordained in his early twenties, and then returned home to Martha's Vineyard to serve as a minister.

Although young Mayhew's primary ministry was to white settlers, like Eliot, he conducted mission outreach to the nearby Indians. His first convert, Hiacoomes, became an interpreter and evangelist, and in less than a decade there were nearly three hundred converts. Mayhew opened a school and sought support from others for the work. In 1655, in his early thirties, he set sail for England to publicize the work there. But he was lost at sea, leaving behind a wife and young children.

When it became apparent that his son would not return, Thomas Mayhew Sr., the seventy-year-old governor and landlord of Martha's Vineyard, took over the mission work. Though not a minister himself, he was respected by the Indians because he had honored their land titles and social structure. With a grave sense of responsibility, he assumed his son's duties and served as a missionary for twenty-two years until he died at the age of ninety-two. His grandson, John Mayhew, was also associated with the work. And after his death, Experience Mayhew, the fourth generation of Mayhews, took over the work for thirty-two more years.

David Brainerd

The most well-known missionary to the American Indians is David Brainerd, an heir of New England Puritanism and a product of the Great Awakening. Bringing the gospel to scattered wandering tribes of Indians was his single mission. He spent his life for that cause. However, his place in history is based largely on the inspiration his personal life has had on others. His journal, diary, and biography, published by Jonathan Edwards, are classics of Christian literature; and missionaries through the centuries, including William Carey and Henry Martyn, have been deeply influenced by his life. Brainerd's methods of evangelism, which differed markedly from those of his great missionary predecessor to the American Indians, John Eliot, have been questioned, however; and in spite of the intensity of his efforts, the results of the work were meager. At the age of twenty-nine, after a mere five years of missionary work, he died as a result of his strenuous labors.

David Brainerd was born in 1718 in Haddam, Connecticut. His father was a country squire who lived with his wife and nine children on a substantial estate overlooking the Connecticut River. When David was eight years old, his father died, and six years later his mother also died. Death was thus very real to him, and in many respects he missed the joys of a happy, carefree childhood. He was sober and studious and deeply concerned about the condition of his soul. From his youth, his spiritual journey took him from peaks of lofty spirituality to valleys of mortifying despair. At the age of twenty, after living with his sister and working on a farm for a time, he returned to Haddam to study in the home of an elderly minister, who counseled him "to stay away from youth and cultivate grave, elderly people."[14]

In 1739, at the age of twenty-one, Brainerd enrolled at Yale College at a time when the school was in transition. When he first entered the school, he was distressed by the religious indifference, but the impact of George Whitefield and the Great Awakening soon made its mark, and the atmosphere changed. Prayer and Bible study groups sprang up overnight—often at the displeasure of school authorities, who were fearful of religious "enthusiasm." It was in this atmosphere that Brainerd made an intemperate remark about one of the tutors, commenting that he had "no more grace than a chair," and judging him to be a hypocrite. The remark was carried back to the school officials, and Brainerd was expelled after he refused to make a public apology.

This was an unfortunate situation for Brainerd, causing him distress for years afterward and contributing to his melancholy disposition. Despite his own efforts and those of influential friends, he was not reinstated or allowed to graduate. During his student days, however, he had heard Ebenezer Pemberton deliver a stirring message about the opportunities for missionary work among the Indians. He never forgot that message, and in November of 1742, following his expulsion from Yale, he met with Pemberton to discuss mission opportunities. Pemberton was an American minister who also served as field secretary for the Society in Scotland for the Propagation of Christian Knowledge. Only recently had the society inaugurated its work among the Indians, and Brainerd was being considered as one of two missionary appointees whose ministry would be funded.

Although Brainerd viewed himself as unworthy of the task, the commissioners saw otherwise and enthusiastically offered him the appointment. After several months of itinerant preaching, he was assigned to work among natives of the Bay Colony. His mission outpost was a day's travel from Stockbridge, where veteran missionary John Sergeant was serving with his wife Abigail. "There was much that Brainerd could learn before taking the forest trail to his new station," writes David Wynbeek. "But he did not tarry."[15] Independent and eager for his own converts, he plunged into the task alone.

His first days as a missionary were lonely and depressing: "My heart was sunk. . . . It seemed to me I should never have any success among the Indians. My soul was weary of my life; I longed for death, beyond measure." Though he later was assisted by an Indian interpreter from Stockbridge, for several weeks he attempted to preach to the Indians without an interpreter. His efforts were fruitless and his life was miserable:

> I live in the most lonely melancholy desert. . . . I board with a poor Scotchman; his wife can talk scarce any English. My diet consists mostly of hasty-pudding, boiled corn, and bread baked in ashes. . . . My lodging is a little heap of straw laid upon some boards. My work is exceeding hard and difficult: I travel on foot a mile and a half, the worst of ways, almost daily, and back; for I live so far from my Indians.[16]

The following summer Brainerd built his own hut near the Indian settlement, but his attempt to evangelize the Indians remained unsuccessful. His first winter in the wilderness was one of hardship and sickness. On one occasion he was lost for a time in the woods, and on another he "was very much exposed and very wet by falling into a river." In March of 1744, after a year of mission work, he remained deeply discouraged. But despite offers from established churches to serve as their pastor, he "resolved to go on still with the Indian Affair."[17]

Brainerd's next assignment was in Pennsylvania, north of Philadelphia within the Forks of the Delaware River. Here he was well received by the Indians and was often allowed to speak to them in the chief's house. Progress was slow, however. His new Indian interpreter, Tattamy, had a serious drinking problem, and Brainerd viewed his own prospects for winning converts "as dark as midnight."

After several months at the Forks of the Delaware, he traveled west to reach Indians along the Susquehanna River. "We went our way into the wilderness; and found the most difficult and dangerous traveling by far, that any of us had seen; we had scarce anything else but lofty mountains, deep valleys, and hideous rocks to make our way through." To make matters worse, his horse fell and broke a leg, which left Brainerd with no alternative but to kill it and continue on to the nearest house some thirty miles away. After preaching with little success, he returned to the Forks of the Delaware where, except for frequent travels, he remained during his second year of missionary service.[18]

Illness and depression continued to plague him. His high hopes of revival among the Indians had long since dimmed. With the exception of Tattamy and his wife, who had been converted and were apparently making remarkable spiritual progress, he regarded his year at the Forks of the Delaware a loss. He was guilt-stricken, believing he had accomplished nothing for his pay, and he was tempted to quit. His "self-preoccupation was so intense," writes William Hutchinson, "that his Indian charges and their problems figured as little more than intrusions."[19]

Brainerd blamed himself for his lack of success, but he also blamed the Indians. He found them "brutishly stupid and ignorant of divine things" and given to asking "frivolous and impertinent questions." Yet, in hindsight, their questions appear astute. Why, for example, was Brainerd seeking to convert them to Christianity when the Christians behaved so much worse than did the Indians? The Indians reasoned that the whites were seeking to convert them in order to take their land and enslave them. Brainerd's private reflections were that they were "some of the most jealous people living, and extremely averse to a state of servitude" and that they regarded their own way of living as "vastly preferable to the white people." They, likewise, had no desire to go to the white man's heaven, but rather preferred "to go with their fathers when they die."[20] In summing up Brainerd's attitudes toward Native Americans, Hutchinson writes: "Modern readers may wonder . . . whether Yale College in officially expelling Brainerd for rudeness may actually have sought to rid itself of one of its dimmer scholars."[21]

In hindsight, the Indians' questions appear astute. Why, for example, was Brainerd seeking to convert them to Christianity when the Christians behaved so much worse than did the Indians?

In the summer of 1745 Brainerd's spirits brightened. He heard about a group of Indians eighty-five miles to the south, in Crossweeksung, New Jersey, who were more open to the Christian message. Once again, he pulled up stakes and moved on. But this time his fortune would improve. The Indians in New Jersey were more eager to hear the gospel. Soon Indians as well as whites were coming from miles away to hear him preach. Anxious for results, he baptized twenty-five converts within a matter of weeks, and the following winter he organized a school.

David Brainerd preaching to the Indians.

Later that summer, Brainerd witnessed a revival among the Indians. Although he still depended on an interpreter and the Indians understood only the most elementary tenets of Christianity, they responded to his preaching in the emotional and physical ways that were so characteristic of the Great Awakening. His diary shows that this was an exhilarating time for him as he witnessed the visible results of the people to whom he was preaching:

> August 6. In the morning I discoursed to the Indians at the house where we lodged. Many of them were then much affected and appeared surprisingly tender, so that a few words about their souls' concerns would cause the tears to flow freely, and produce many sobs and groans.
>
> In the afternoon, they being returned to the place where I had usually preached among them, I again discoursed to them there. There were about fifty-five persons in all, about forty that were capable of attending divine service with understanding. I insisted upon 1 John 4:10, "Herein is love." They seemed eager of hearing; but there appeared nothing very remarkable, except their attention, till near the close of my discourse. Then divine truths were attended with a surprising influence, and produced a great concern among them. There were scarce three in forty that could refrain from tears and bitter cries.
>
> They all, as one, seemed in an agony of soul to obtain an interest in Christ . . . and the more I invited them to come and partake of His love, the more their distress was aggravated, because they felt themselves unable to come. . . . It was very affecting to see the poor Indians, who the other day

were hallooing and yelling in their idolatrous feasts and drunken frolics, now crying to God.[22]

In the spring of 1746, Brainerd convinced the scattered Indians in New Jersey to settle together at nearby Cranbury, and soon thereafter a church was established. More revivals followed, and his converts numbered more than a hundred. But Brainerd's health was broken. His fourth and final journey back to the Susquehanna, though more successful than previous preaching tours, was too much for his frail constitution. He was dying of tuberculosis. His missionary work was over.

After spending the winter in the home of a friend in New Jersey, Brainerd traveled to Northampton, Massachusetts, where he spent his last months in the home of the great preacher and scholar Jonathan Edwards, whose daughter, Jerusha, he hoped to marry. This dream, however, was never realized. For nineteen weeks Jerusha tenderly nursed him, but to no avail. He died on October 9, 1747. The following Valentine's Day Jerusha joined him, dying of consumption that she apparently contracted from him.

Eleazer Wheelock

If Brainerd was disorganized and lacking direction in his ministry, there were others among his contemporaries who presented developed strategies for Native American missions. Among them was Dr. Eleazer Wheelock, a minister and educator who graduated from Yale in 1733. Ten years later, in 1743, he brought an Indian youth, Samson Occum, into his home and spent four years educating him. His success with Occum led him to develop a concept that historian R. Pierce Beaver has termed "the most original scheme of operations in the entire history of New England missions to the Indians."[23]

Wheelock's plan was to bring Indians and whites together for training in missionary service.

Wheelock's plan was to bring Indians and whites together for training in missionary service. In the process, the white students would learn the language and culture of the Indians, and the Indian youths would receive a classical education and learn the ways of whites. Both would be trained for Indian evangelism, though there would be an emphasis on recruiting natives who would not have to cross cultural barriers and who could live and work on far less financial support than their white counterparts.

Wheelock opened his school in Lebanon, Connecticut, in 1754 with two Indian students sent by John Brainerd, who had succeeded David at the New Jersey mission (and was a far more successful missionary than his famous brother). The school met in a house donated by Joshua Moor, and the institution became known as Moor's Training School. At its peak there were twenty-two students enrolled, and Wheelock's missionary work was the most extensive of any in New England. Altogether he trained nearly fifty Indian students, and approximately one-third of those returned to their home communities to serve as evangelists or teachers.

Wheelock's experiment, however, was not a shining story of success. What the project demonstrated in innovative ideas it lacked in effective leadership. Wheelock's domineering personality obstructed the path of progress. Instead of mutual sharing of culture, the school became dominated by white culture. Wheelock could never overcome his contempt for Indians and their culture. Though he trained Indian students and sent them out to minister, he was unable to work with them as equals—particularly Samson Occum, his first student, who became a highly respected missionary in his own right. As time went on, Wheelock's school declined in numbers and was eventually moved to Dresden, where it was eventually transformed into Dartmouth College.

David Zeisberger

The greatest thrust for Indian missions during the colonial period came from New England, but there was effective work going on elsewhere in the colonies, in many cases carried out by European missionaries—particularly Moravians. The most noted Moravian missionary to the Indians was David Zeisberger, who labored amid tragedy and hardship for sixty-three years. His story is just one of many that graphically illustrates the cruel injustices dealt to the Native Americans as colonists took over the land.

As a missionary to Native Americans, Zeisberger not only endured strong opposition to his calling but also faced prejudice against his faith.

Soon after Zeisberger began his ministry in 1744 in the Hudson River Valley, he and his associate were arrested and confined in jail for several weeks. As a missionary to Native Americans, he not only endured strong opposition to his calling but also faced prejudice against his faith. Moravians were "sect people," who were looked down upon by members of Protestant denominations. Despite setbacks Zeisberger persisted. In 1746 he helped establish Gnadenhuetten, a Christian Indian village in Pennsylvania that became a prosperous farming community of some five hundred Indian residents. So respected was he that the Indians made him a sachem and "keeper of the archives."

The good times did not last, however. Both whites and unfriendly Indians viewed Gnadenhuetten with suspicion, and in 1755, at the outbreak of the French and Indian War, a band of raiding Indians attacked the settlement, killed eleven people, and burned the buildings. While most of the residents fled for their lives, Zeisberger remained with a segment of Indians who did not scatter and tried without success to establish a permanent settlement in Pennsylvania. Finally, in the 1770s, he secured a tract of land in Ohio.

For several years he and the Indians lived peacefully and prospered in their new land, but again the calm was broken. The American Revolution brought unrest to the frontier, and in 1781 Zeisberger and his associates were accused by the English forces of being spies. The Indians were evacuated to the Sandusky River, where they nearly starved during the harsh winter. The following spring more than one hundred of these Christian Indians returned to their settlement in Ohio to gather unharvested corn. While they were there, ninety of their number (including thirty-four children) were brutally murdered by a company of American militia. Of this incident, Zeisberger wrote:

> Warriors came in, bringing a prisoner, from whom we now get certain news that all our Indians in Gnadenhuetten and Salem were put to death, and that none were spared; he said the militia had 96 scalps, but our Indians only numbered 86, who went away from us. The rest then must have been friends, who did not belong to us. . . .
>
> The news sank deep into our hearts, so that these our brethren, who as martyrs, had all at once gone to the Savior, were always day and night before our eyes and in our thoughts, and we could not forget them.[24]

For the next decade Zeisberger and his Christian following moved from place to place in northern Ohio and southern Michigan, and then finally settled in Ontario in 1792 when Zeisberger was past the age of seventy. There he established a mission station that survived for more than a century. In 1798 he returned to work among the Indians of Ohio, where he remained until his death a decade later.

Isaac McCoy

Protestant missions to the American Indians changed considerably during the late eighteenth century. The Great Awakening that had fanned the flames of colonial missions had died down, and for many years following the American Revolution there was a lull in Protestant missions. With the steady march of colonization westward, Indians were pushed farther and farther into the uncharted wilderness. Those who sought to evangelize them followed the wagons westward, pushing beyond the white settlements to reach the Indians.

As the Indians were pushed westward, there was a renewed interest in Indian missions—perhaps because many people found missions at a distance more compelling than missions close to home. Among the first of the Methodist missionaries of this era was John Steward, a black man from Ohio who, after his conversion at a camp meeting, felt called to preach to the Wyandot Indians at Upper Sandusky, Ohio. He was well received by the Indians when he arrived in

1816 and was surprised to learn that another black man, Jonathan Painter, a runaway slave from Kentucky, was living among them. Steward asked him to serve as an interpreter, but he declined: "How can I interpret the Gospel to the Indians when I have no religion myself?" That night he "got religion," and together he and Steward preached to the Indians. Steward was licensed as a Methodist preacher, and in 1819 the Methodist Missionary Society was formed, and missionaries were appointed to the Upper Sandusky area.

Baptist missions to the Indians began with Isaac McCoy and his wife, who opened a mission at Fort Wayne in 1820. From there they moved to southern Michigan, where they founded the Carey Mission with substantial government funding. A U.S. military officer visiting the mission only seven months after its establishment found an impressive, efficiently run mission compound that included a large mission house, a school, a blacksmith shop, and other buildings as well as well-cultivated, enclosed gardens and pastures. The school enrolled some forty children, and the mission showed every sign of success, but within two years McCoy was once again moving on, fearing the encroachments of whites and the dire consequences such encroachments would have on Indians.

McCoy's rationale for Indian removal was that Indians had to be segregated from whites to be Christianized.

McCoy was convinced that the only solution was removal of the Indians. In 1823, by his own testimony, he "formed the resolution" that "providence permitting, [he would] thenceforward keep steadily in view and endeavor to promote a plan for colonizing the natives in a country to be made forever theirs, west of the State of Missouri."[25] In 1824 he traveled to Washington to offer his plan at the annual meeting of the Baptist Board of Missions. With the board's approval, he set up a meeting with Secretary of War John C. Calhoun, who supported the proposal. From that meeting onward, McCoy was primarily a political lobbyist. He headed a commission that traveled to Kansas to select a tract of land for the resettlement of the Pottawatomies who were removed from their lands in Michigan.

Although Baptists historically fought for the separation of church and state, it is paradoxical that through McCoy's influence Baptist Indian missions became closely tied to the government—especially in the forced removal of Indians from their lands. The most notorious case in which he became embroiled was the removal of the Cherokees from Georgia. McCoy's rationale for Indian removal was that Indians had to be segregated from whites to be Christianized, and he supported the state of Georgia in its claims on Cherokee land. He had no qualms about initiating this controversial and drastic measure, and he readily accepted a government commission to explore and survey land in the West suitable for an Indian colony.

The removal of the Cherokees was one of the greatest injustices committed by the U.S. government in the nation's history. In 1837, several years after the discovery of gold on their lands, the peaceful and culturally advanced Indians of the Cherokee nation were forced, by government decree and nine thousand troops, to leave their homes in Georgia. They were herded into stockades while their property was auctioned off. Thousands of them were then transported by riverboat, while others were forced to march overland beyond the Mississippi River. It was a perilous journey.

McCoy's strong support of this removal policy was not representative of all missionaries. In fact, many missionaries valiantly fought against the measure. Four Presbyterian and two Methodist missionaries were arrested, tried, convicted, and sentenced to hard labor because of their sharp protests. Accounts of missionaries being dragged from their homes in chains were not unusual. Missionaries also accompanied the Cherokees on the "trail of tears" westward. Among them was Dr. Elizur Butler, a medical missionary with the American Board of Commissioners for Foreign Missions. "God knows, even the storms, the elements conspired to afflict this people," he observed. His estimate was that one in five of the Cherokees had died. "From the first of June," he wrote, "I felt I have been in the midst of death."[26]

Although McCoy was one of the strongest advocates of removal, he did have the courage to condemn the wanton cruelty in carrying out the government mandate. While he did not personally benefit from the Cherokee removal, many of his fellow Baptists in Georgia quickly laid claim to the native lands. In the end, this forced removal was a setback for mission work. Belatedly, McCoy "discovered that the policy which he had so earnestly and persistently advocated would not produce all the results for which he had hoped." Indeed, while they were still on the trail of tears, "white settlers followed the Indians and entered as squatters upon their land."[27]

Marcus and Narcissa Whitman

The Louisiana Purchase and the exploration into the far West gave birth to a new breed of missionaries—courageous men and women with a spirit of adventure. Among them were Marcus and Narcissa Whitman, whose mission work in the Oregon territory might be all but forgotten today but for its very sad ending.

Born in the early years of the nineteenth century, they both experienced spiritual awakenings as young people (Narcissa in New York and Marcus in Massachusetts). Narcissa, the daughter of Judge Stephen Prentiss, became a kindergarten teacher, but her sense of calling was to mission work. The missionary challenges of Reverend Samuel Parker as well as the oft-repeated story of the Nez Percé Indians pleading for someone to bring them the "Book of Life" weighed heavily on her mind. Parker traveled extensively in the East, raising funds and recruiting missionaries for the American Board of Commissioners for Foreign Missions. The need for volunteers was great, but the American Board did not accept single women.

Marcus, too, had long been interested in missions, but he could not afford the cost of seminary. Entering the field of medicine was a more realistic option, and at the age of twenty-one he began "riding with a doctor." In the years that followed he taught school part-time and took formal medical training. Then, like Narcissa, he was influenced by Samuel Parker in the direction of Indian missions. Marcus applied to the American Board as a single man, though he had heard through friends that Narcissa Prentiss was available. With the possibility of marriage in mind, he visited her to discuss mission work. He was planning an exploratory trip west, and if he found the journey to be suitable for a woman, he would return to marry her. He left with no promises. It was not a love affair or an engagement. It was a business arrangement.

Following their meeting, the thirty-two-year-old Whitman, accompanying Reverend Parker, traveled to Missouri to join up with the American Fur Com-

Statue of Marcus Whitman.

Narcissa Whitman, wife of Marcus Whitman.

pany in its expedition west in the spring of 1835. The intended destination was Oregon, but in late August Whitman turned around and returned home with a caravan of fur traders, arriving only months after he had left. He and Narcissa were married in February of 1836, and the following day they left for Missouri in order to join the expedition to Oregon in the spring.

The Whitmans were not the only American Board missionaries heading for Oregon that spring. With them were Henry and Eliza Spalding. Though Spalding was a well-trained minister, his personality was not suited for the teamwork required for the Oregon project. Moreover, he had known Narcissa years before, and her refusal of his marriage proposal caused bitterness that would surface for years to come.

Strenuous travel, illness, and personality problems combined to make the overland journey a very difficult one, but there were delightful moments along the way. Narcissa found the journey less arduous than she had anticipated, and she wrote often of the beautiful scenery. She was happy and she was in love, and somewhere under the night sky between the Elkhorn and the Loup, she conceived their first and only child.

After nearly two thouand miles of difficult travel, the expedition was approaching its destination, the missionary party being much poorer than when

WHITMAN'S TRAVELS AND MISSION IN THE OREGON TERRITORY

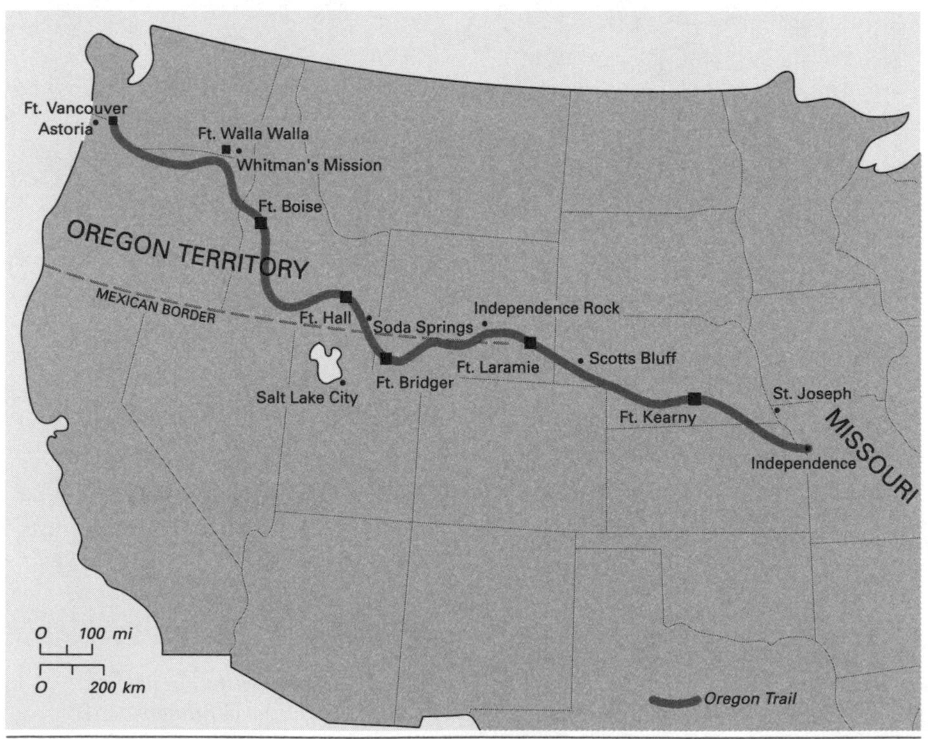

it began. Precious possessions had to be thrown out all along the way to lighten the load. "We scatter as we go," Narcissa lamented, concluding that it would be better to travel with nothing, "then you lose nothing."[28] This same conclusion could have been applied to missionary colleagues. By the time the Whitmans had reached Oregon, they had already decided to part company with the Spaldings. After nearly five months of traveling together and sleeping together in the same tent, their relationship was so strained that they could no longer work together. Contemporary reports generally placed most of the blame on Spalding and his jealousy of Whitman, though Whitman himself, by many accounts, was not easy to deal with.

More than one tribe of Indians was asking for missionaries, however, so their decision to work separately was beneficial. Whitman settled in Waiilatpu, a lush green valley, while Spalding settled at Lapwai, a bleak, dry mountainous area. Spalding may have looked at Whitman's site at Waiilatpu with envy, not realizing that ultimately his location would prove to be the superior one. His mission was to the Nez Percé Indians, who welcomed him and seemed eager to learn of his God. Whitman, on the other hand, sought to reach the Cayuse, a more hostile tribe of only a few hundred, who resented the coming of the white man.

On December 10 the Whitmans moved into their new house—a lean-to with few of the amenities of back home. Waiilatpu was a desolate and lonely place that winter, but spring brought new hope. On March 14, 1837, the eve of Narcissa's twenty-ninth birthday, a baby daughter, Alice Clarissa, was born.

Henry Spalding, missionary to the Nez Percé Indians.

The first summer in Oregon was spent in constructing buildings and fences and in planting and harvesting crops, with little time for medical work, language study, and evangelism. Unlike the Catholic missionaries, who lived simply and sometimes followed the wandering Indians, the Protestant missionaries often built compounds and in some instances maintained large farming ventures. The task was enormous, and the Whitmans pleaded for additional recruits. The fall of 1838 brought three new missionary couples, whose presence brought further conflict. In the words of one biographer, "It seemed that the 'reinforcements' had brought not help, but dissension only." Instead of fellowship and harmony, the joint planning meetings of these missionaries were often stormy and bitter. One of the wives described a typical flare-up: "It came on so sharp that I was compelled to leave. . . . It is enough to make one sick to see what is the state of things in the mission."[29]

Part of the difficulty was a much-overcrowded mission house, and Narcissa was not receiving the help she needed from the other women. But Narcissa herself was not without blame. She was often critical of the other women without explaining what she needed them to do, and sometimes she did not come out of her room for a whole day. Lack of leadership was the single most pressing problem among the missionaries—and not just with Narcissa and household management. There was no leadership designated by the American Board, and no one individual rose up with leadership qualities to guide the mission work during this troublesome time. "Without any leaders to establish clear goals and direct the mission's energies," writes Julie Roy Jeffrey, "competing interests and conflicting personalities caused ill will."[30]

There were times of unity, but they were sometimes the result of tragedy. Such was the case in the summer of 1839. Sympathy and sorrow healed the wounds of bitterness as the Whitmans suffered the pain of a heartrending tragedy. On a late June Sunday afternoon at Waiilatpu—a day of rest from the week's heavy labor—Marcus and Narcissa were engrossed in reading, and little Alice was playing close by—or so they thought. When they suddenly realized she was missing, it was too late. The little two-year-old had wandered off and drowned in a nearby stream. The Spaldings came immediately to share the sorrow at the first funeral for the Oregon missionaries. A year later a package arrived from back east with the little shoes and dresses Narcissa had requested from her mother. A weaker woman could not have endured, but Narcissa was stoical. It was God's divine purpose, and she resolutely accepted his will. Though she could see the little grave on the hill every time she stepped out of her door, she knew her dear Alice was in God's care: "My thoughts seldom wander there to find her."[31] Yet, in the years that followed, Narcissa's grief was often manifested in physical illness and bouts of depression. Though she had tried to accept the tragedy "without murmuring thought," she later wrote to her father that she suffered from "dejection considerably" and felt "desponding and cast down." Again, she lamented: "I often look up to that place of rest where my dear babe has gone and feel that I shall soon follow her."[32]

But time marched on at Waiilatpu. There was work to be done, and sorrow was not permitted to stay the progress. The Whitmans' time was consumed with more than medical missions. They were farmers—and prosperous ones at that. After only six years at Waiilatpu, their "plantation" consisted of a large whitewashed adobe mission house, a guest house, a gristmill, and a blacksmith shop, all surrounded by well-cultivated fields. Dr. Whitman was not the only Protestant missionary in Oregon to be tempted by the richness of the land. Jason Lee, a Methodist missionary, had fallen prey to materialism and spent his time in politics, immigration, and land ventures.

In the case of Whitman, the materialism was not so blatant, but the consequences were far greater. Waiilatpu became a receiving station for new missionaries and other immigrants as well as a school for Indian and white children. For that reason Whitman had to concern himself with more than subsistence farming. Soon Waiilatpu resembled an immigrant inn more than a missionary compound. The Whitmans began selling produce to immigrants as they passed through and were often accused of overcharging and exploiting their circumstances. On hearing such rumors, the American Board scolded him for the secularization of the mission, but the letters were slow in coming, and they knew little of the actual circumstances under which he worked.

The greater condemnation came from the Cayuse, the Indians the Whitmans came to serve. Though Marcus sacrificially worked among them as a minister and doctor, the Indians resented his prosperity and all the white immigrants they believed he was attracting to their land. Narcissa wrote of this resentment of the Indians who feel "we are rich and getting rich by the houses we dwell in and the clothes we wear and hang out to dry after washing from week to week and the grain we consume in our families."[33]

For Henry Spalding, the situation was different. He had less time for worldly pursuits. He was too busy with his missionary activities. He established a church among the Nez Percé, and Eliza ran a school for the children and made hand-

The Whitman mission in 1845.

painted books and translated hymns into their language. With her artistic talent, she made large brightly colored charts illustrating Bible truths. (She had heard how Father François Blanchet's famous "Catholic Ladder," depicting Bible history, had intrigued the Indians, and she was not to be outdone in visual aids.) The Spaldings faced opposition, but they also heard confessions of faith at their revival meetings.

By 1844, after less than eight years in Oregon, the Whitmans' missionary work for all practical purposes was over. Narcissa had long since lost the excitement and zeal she initially had for Indian missions. She spent her days feeding and housing immigrants and her adopted family, including the seven Sager children whose parents both died on the overland trip from the East. Marcus, too, was consumed by the needs of the white immigrants. He continued treating the Indians' physical needs, but he was discouraged by their lack of response to spiritual values, and like so many other missionaries throughout history, he could not separate salvation from civilization. If the Indians refused the white man's civilization, including his work ethic, how could they be saved?

Time was running out for Waiilatpu and the Whitmans. Despite repeated warnings, they never fully appreciated the Cayuse's reputation for treachery. It was a difficult period for the Cayuse. In 1847 the new immigrants numbered more than four thousand, bringing their diseases with them. The Cayuse villages were ravaged by a plague, and within the space of eight weeks nearly half of the four-hundred-member tribe had suffered painful deaths. Though Whit-

The massacre at Waiilatpu in 1847.

man had tried to help, the situation only grew worse, and suspicion mounted among the Indians that he was purposely poisoning them with his "medicine."

The end for Waiilatpu came suddenly. On a dreary late November afternoon in 1847, two Indians, one with a personal vendetta against Marcus, appeared at the mission house door. Others were stationed outside. Without warning, the massacre began. It was not a mass uprising with a hoard of savage Indians suddenly descending on a helpless compound. There were seventy-two people living at the mission, including more than a dozen men, and the murderers were Indians whom the Whitmans knew well. Pulling tomahawks out from under the blankets they were carrying, the small party began the slaughter, starting with Dr. Whitman. When it was over, fourteen were dead. With the exception of Narcissa, the women and children had been spared, only to be held in terrifying captivity until their release some five weeks later.

News of the Whitman massacre spread rapidly. American troops were sent in, and the missionaries in the interior were ordered out. In the spring of 1850 the five Cayuse Indians responsible for the murders were brought to trial, convicted, and sentenced to die; and on June 3 all of Oregon, it seemed, came out to watch the hangings.

For generations following the massacre, Protestants promoted the Whitmans as "noble martyrs to their faith." But in recent decades, the Native American perspective has been taken more seriously. On the last page of her biography of Narcissa Whitman, Julie Roy Jeffery quotes lines from a Mass celebrated by a Roman Catholic bishop in Brazil—lines that offer a sad perspective on mission work:

> And we missionized you,
> betrayed errors of the gospel,
> driving the Cross into your lives
> like a sword,
> the Good News ringing
> a death knell.[34]

Not until 1871, twenty-four years after he was ordered out, did Spalding return to Lapwai, without Eliza, who had long since died. There he witnessed revival among the Nez Percé and Spokane Indians and claimed to have baptized more than a thousand. After three years of service, Spalding died among the Indians that he so loved, thus ending a difficult and controversial era of Protestant missions in Oregon.

The work at Lapwai was taken over by two single sisters, Kate and Sue McBeth. A training school for Indian preachers was set up, and the Nez Percé, perhaps more than any other Indian tribe, became active in evangelizing other Indian tribes. Sue assumed the leading role in this ministry, and of her Nez Percé students she wrote: "I do not think any one could have more *interested, earnest* and *diligent* pupils. . . . They are all farmers—and busy ploughing and sowing nearly every day. But they are here every morning by 7 o'clock." Their diligence was no doubt inspired by their teacher. Robert Speer referred to Sue McBeth as a woman of "apostolic zeal" who "trained preachers, taught and preached."[35]

As the nineteenth century progressed, missionary work among the Indians decreased. The emphasis, instead, was on exotic foreign lands where the native population could not interfere with the advance of American society. Many scholars agree that Indian evangelism, as a whole, was not a story of success, the greatest reason being the intense conflict between the two cultures for supremacy over the land. But perhaps equally important was the deep-seated belief of white America that Indians were racially inferior and that their culture was not worth saving.

SELECT BIBLIOGRAPHY

Beaver, R. Pearce. *Church, State, and the American Indian*. St. Louis: Concordia, 1966.

______. *Pioneers in Mission: The Early Missionary Ordination Sermons, Charges and Instructions*. Grand Rapids: Eerdmans, 1966.

Berkhoffer, Robert F., Jr. *Salvation and the Savage: An Analysis of Protestant Missions and American Indian Response, 1787–1862*. Louisville: University of Kentucky Press, 1965.

Bowden, Henry Warner. *American Indians and Christian Missions: Studies in Cultural Conflict*. Chicago: University of Chicago Press, 1981.

Drury, Clifford M. *Marcus and Narcissa Whitman and the Opening of Old Oregon*. Two vols. Glendale, CA: Arthur H. Clark, 1973.

Edwards, Jonathan. *Life and Diary of David Brainerd*. Chicago: Moody Press, 1949.

Ehle, John. *Trail of Tears: The Rise and Fall of the Cherokee Nation*. New York: Doubleday, 1988.

Hinman, George W. *The American Indian and Christian Missions*. New York: Fleming H. Revell, 1933.

Humphreys, Mary G., ed. *Missionary Explorers among the American Indians*. New York: Scribner, 1913.

Hutchinson, William R. *Errand to the World: American Protestant Thought and Foreign Missions*. Chicago: University of Chicago Press, 1987.

Jones, Nard. *The Great Command: The Story of Marcus and Narcissa Whitman and the Oregon Country Pioneers*. Boston: Little, Brown, 1959.

Olmstead, Earl P. *David Zeisberger: A Life among the Indians*. Kent, OH: Kent State University Press, 1997.

Winslow, Ola Elizabeth. *John Eliot, "Apostle to the Indians."* Boston: Houghton Mifflin, 1968.

Wynbeek, David. *David Brainerd: Beloved Yankee*. Grand Rapids: Eerdmans, 1961.

4

The Moravian Advance: Dawn of Protestant Missions

The upsurge of Roman Catholic missions that occurred during the sixteenth-century Catholic Counter-Reformation had no parallel among the Protestants. Worldwide missions was not a primary concern of most of the Reformers. Just holding their own in the face of Roman Catholic opposition and breaking new ground in Europe were considered achievements in themselves, and there was little time or personnel for overseas ventures. The Protestants, moreover, lacked the opportunities for overseas missions that were readily available to Roman Catholics, who dominated the religious scene in most of the seafaring nations and who consequently were able to travel with and live under the military protection of explorers and commercial companies. The landlocked Swiss and German states, early strongholds of Protestantism, offered no such access to foreign lands. Furthermore, the Protestants did not have a ready-made missionary force like the Roman Catholic monastic orders.

Protestant theology was another factor that limited the vision of missionary enterprises. Martin Luther was so certain of the imminent return of Christ that he overlooked the necessity of foreign missions. He further sought to justify his position by claiming the Great Commission was binding only on the New Testament apostles, who had fulfilled their obligation by spreading the gospel throughout the known world, thus exempting succeeding generations from responsibility. Calvinists generally used the same line of reasoning, adding the doctrine of election that made missions appear extraneous if God had already chosen those he would save. Calvin himself, however, was at least outwardly the most missionary-minded of all the Reformers. He not only sent dozens of evangelists back into his homeland of France, but he also commissioned four missionaries, along with a number of French Huguenots, to establish a colony and evangelize the Native Americans in Brazil. But that short-lived venture, which began in 1555, ended shortly in failure when the renegade leader, Villegagnon, defected to the Portuguese, who then plundered the fledgling colony and left the few remaining defenseless survivors to be overpowered by the Jesuits.

The seventeenth century saw more scattered Protestant missionary efforts, but aside from the work carried on in the American colonies, none of the ventures had real staying power. The Quakers had more than a passing interest in foreign missions; in 1661 George Fox commissioned three of his followers to serve as missionaries to China, but the party never reached its destination. Some years later the first Lutheran overseas missionary, Justinian von Weltz, sailed to Surinam on the Atlantic Coast of South America, where he gave his life in an unsuccessful effort to establish a mission.

It was only in the eighteenth century that various groups of Protestants began acknowledging their responsibility to evangelize those without the gospel.

The eighteenth century witnessed the first thrust of Protestant missions, for it was only then that various groups of Protestants began acknowledging their responsibility to evangelize those without the gospel. Among the first to recognize this biblical obligation were Lutheran Pietists such as Philip Jacob Spener and August Hermann Francke, who were seeking to bring renewal to the state churches. Francke, a professor at the University at Halle, turned that school into the center of Continental Pietism and along with that a center for evangelism and foreign missions. Overseas mission, however, was not commended by most eighteenth-century church leaders, and Pietists were often ridiculed as "enthusiasts." But the biblical mandate propelled them forward.

The first significant breakthrough in Protestant missions came when King Ferdinand IV of Denmark, a Pietist himself, appealed to Halle for missionaries to evangelize the people in his overseas holdings—particularly in Tranquebar, along the southeast coast of India. Bartholomew Ziegenbalg and Henry Plütschau, Lutheran missionaries supported by the Danish-Halle mission, were the first to be commissioned. They began their ministry near the southern tip of India in Tranquebar. Though hampered by the commercial interests of the Danish East India Company, they nevertheless made progress and witnessed many converts during their years of service. After six years Plütschau returned home due to ill health, while Ziegenbalg remained to oversee the infant church and translate the New Testament and a large portion of the Old Testament into one of India's many languages. He died in 1719 after fourteen years of service.

Ziegenbalg's translation was completed by another Danish-Halle missionary, who in turn influenced Christian Frederic Schwartz to serve in India. Schwartz, also a devout Lutheran, was the most notable eighteenth-century missionary to serve with the Danish-Halle mission. He arrived in India in 1750 and served faithfully until his death forty-eight years later. Much of his missionary career was spent traveling along the coast of India, preaching the gospel and planting churches, an accomplishment that would have been impossible without his mastery of several languages and dialects. Though he remained unmarried and without children of his own (like Roman Catholics before him), he conducted an effective ministry with children, who matured in the faith and swelled the ranks of his church in Tanjore to a membership of some two thousand. During his lifetime the Danish-Halle mission had seen significant growth, with approximately sixty of its missionaries coming from Halle alone, but the enthusiastic spirit of earlier years was waning. At the time of his death there were few new volunteers to fill the vacant posts.

Other groups of Christians, however, became part of this early Protestant missionary movement. Also influenced by the Pietism at Halle were the Moravian Brethren (Unitas Fratrum)—one of the most remarkable missionary churches in Christian history. Stirred by Count Zinzendorf, who took the Great Commission to heart, the Moravians paved the way for the great era of modern missions. During the eighteenth century alone, the Moravians served in mission outposts in the Virgin Islands (1732), Greenland (1733), North America (1734), Lapland and South America (1735), South Africa (1736), and Labrador (1771). Their all-consuming purpose was to spread the gospel to the ends of the earth, a passion that was evident in their proportion of missionaries to laypeople, by some estimates a ratio of 1:60.

A unique feature of Moravian missions that made possible the large percentage of missionaries was the expectation of self-support. Moravians were primarily artisans and peasants, and it seemed natural that the missionaries should take their trades and work ethic with them as they traveled abroad. Voluntary contributions, according to Moravian mission theory, were simply inadequate to finance the task of world evangelism. The only alternative, then, was for Christians to be missionaries while pursuing their vocations.

In Labrador, Moravian missionaries supported themselves through trade, with enough money left over to provide basic necessities for needy Eskimos. They owned ships and trading posts, and through their example they interested Eskimos in productive pursuits. The effect of their ministry was not only to bring the gospel to the people but also to make an impact on the native economy and social conditions. In Surinam, the Moravians established a variety of businesses, including tailoring, watchmaking, and baking. As their economic influence grew, so did their spiritual influence, and a thriving Moravian church emerged in that country.

"The most important contribution of the Moravians," writes William Danker, "was their emphasis that every Christian is a missionary and should witness through his daily vocation. If the example of the Moravians had been studied more carefully by other Christians, it is possible that the businessman might have retained his honored place within the expanding Christian world mission, beside the preacher, teacher, and physician."[1]

Count Nicolaus Ludwig von Zinzendorf

Count Zinzendorf was one of the most influential mission leaders of the modern Protestant missionary movement. He pioneered ecumenical evangelism, founded the Moravian church, and authored scores of hymns; but above all else, he launched a worldwide missionary movement that set the stage for William Carey and the "Great Century" of missions that would follow. Yet in many respects he lacked leadership skills, and the mighty movement to which he devoted his life more than once nearly collapsed due to poor planning and decision making.

Zinzendorf was born in 1700 into wealth and nobility. The death of his father and the subsequent remarriage of his mother left him to be reared by his grandmother and aunt, whose warm evangelical Pietism turned his heart toward spiritual matters. His early teaching was reinforced by his formal education. At the age of ten he was sent away to study at Halle, where he sat under the inspiring teaching of the great Lutheran Pietist August Hermann Francke. Here Zinzendorf banded together with other dedicated youths, and out of their association came the "Order of the Grain of Mustard Seed," a Christian fraternity committed to loving "the whole human family" and to spreading the gospel.

From Halle, Zinzendorf went on to Wittenberg to study law in preparation for a career in state service—the only acceptable vocation for a nobleman. But he was unhappy with his prospects for the future. He longed to enter the Christian ministry—yet to break with family tradition would be unthinkable. The decision weighed heavily on his mind until 1719, when an incident during a tour of Europe changed the course of his life. While visiting an art gallery, he viewed a painting (Domenico Feti's *Ecce Homo*) that depicted Christ enduring the crown of thorns, with an inscription that read, "All this I did for you, what are you doing for me?"[2] That experience had a profound impact not only on his future vocation but also on his theological and spiritual formation.

A turning point in Zinzendorf's call to ministry came in 1722 when some Protestant refugees sought shelter on his estate at Berthelsdorf, later named Herrnhut, meaning "the Lord's watch." He invited the refugees to settle on the land, and Herrnhut grew rapidly as word of the count's generosity spread. Religious refugees continued to arrive, and the estate became a thriving community dotted with newly constructed houses and shops. But with the increasing numbers came problems. The diverse religious backgrounds of the residents created discord, and on more than one occasion the very existence of Herrnhut was in jeopardy.

Then in 1727, five years after the first refugees arrived, the whole atmosphere changed. A period of spiritual renewal was climaxed at a communion service on August 13 with a great revival, which, according to participants, marked the coming of the Holy Spirit to Herrnhut. Whatever may have occurred in the spiritual realm, there is no doubt that this night of revival brought a new passion for missions, which became the chief characteristic of the Moravian movement. There was a heightened sense of unity and dependence on God. At this time a prayer vigil was initiated that continued around the clock, seven days a week, without interruption for more than a hundred years.

Direct involvement in foreign missions did not come until some years after this spiritual awakening. Zinzendorf was attending the coronation of Danish King Christian VI, and during the festivities he was introduced to two native Greenlanders (converts of Hans Egede) and an African slave from the West Indies. So impressed was he with their pleas for missionaries that he invited the latter to visit Herrnhut, and he himself returned home with a sense of urgency for world evangelism. Within a year the first two Moravian missionaries were commissioned to the Virgin Islands, and in the two decades that followed, the Moravians sent out more missionaries than all Protestants had sent out in the previous two centuries.

Count Nicolaus Ludwig von Zinzendorf.

In 1738, some years after the first missionaries had arrived in the Caribbean, Zinzendorf accompanied three new recruits who were joining their colleagues. But when they reached their destination, they learned that their colleagues had been imprisoned. Zinzendorf quickly took charge, using his prestige and authority as a nobleman to secure their release. During his visit he conducted daily services for the Africans and revamped the organizational structure and territorial assignments for the missionaries. Satisfied that the mission work was on a solid footing, he returned to Europe. Two years later he sailed to the American colonies, where he observed the mission work to the native Indians.

Although Zinzendorf had renounced his life as a nobleman, he was never able to suppress his taste for the good life, and he found it difficult to lower himself to the life of a rank-and-file missionary. He did not conceal his displeasure with living in the wilderness and the drudgery of day-to-day missionary work. He viewed the Native Americans as uncivilized and crude, and he resented their invasion of his privacy. However, his inability to relate to them or even get along with them did not dim his enthusiasm for evangelizing them. Before leaving America he appointed twenty more missionaries to American Indian mission work.

As a missionary statesman, Zinzendorf spent thirty-three years as the overseer of a worldwide network of missionaries who looked to him for leadership. His methods were simple and practical and ones that endured the test of time. All of his missionaries were laypeople who were trained as evangelists, not as theologians. As self-supporting artisans and laborers, they were expected to work alongside their prospective converts, witnessing their faith by the spoken word and by their living example—always seeking to identify themselves as equals, not as superiors. Their task was solely evangelism, strictly avoiding any involvement in local political or economic affairs. Their message was the love of Christ—a very simple gospel message—with intentional disregard for doctrinal truths until after conversion; and even then, an emotional mysticism took precedence over theological teaching. Above all else, the Moravian missionaries were single-minded. Their ministry came before anything else. Wives and families were abandoned for the cause of evangelism. Young men were encouraged to remain single, and when marriage was allowed, the spouse was often chosen by lot.

The chief example of single-minded ministry was Zinzendorf himself. His wife and children were frequently left behind as he traveled through Europe and abroad, and his exile for more than a decade from his homeland further com-

THE MORAVIAN CHURCH AROUND THE WORLD

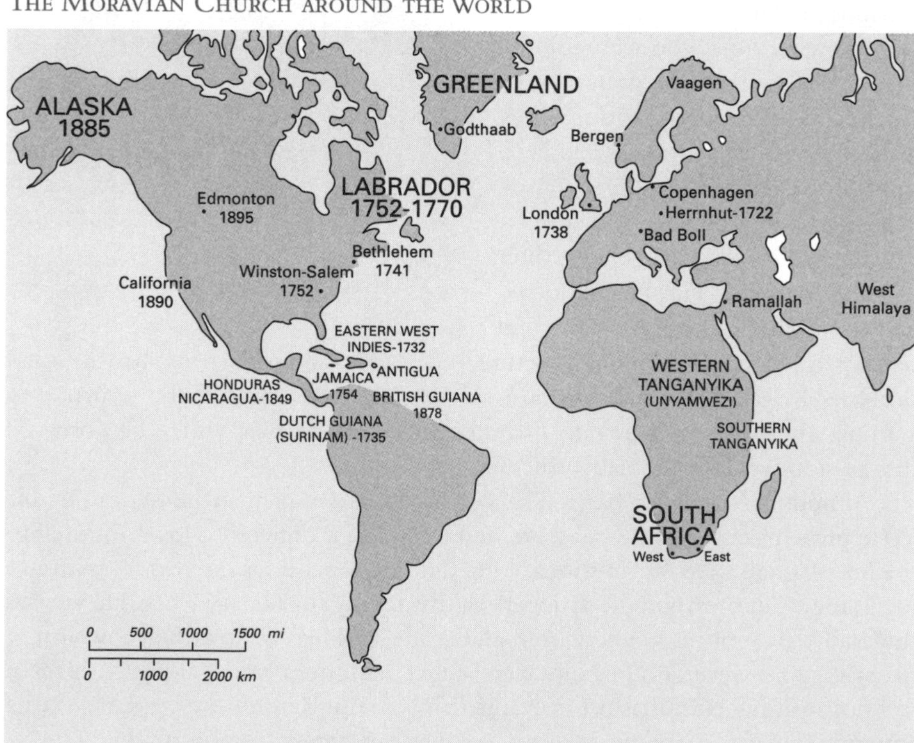

plicated his family life. While he was away, his business and legal affairs were handled by his very capable wife, Erdmuth, but she was less adept at keeping their marriage relationship intact. It was no secret that he and Erdmuth had grown cool toward each other and that the last fifteen years of their marriage was a marriage in name only. Nevertheless, her death was a difficult time for Zinzendorf. According to John Weinlick, "the count's sorrow was aggravated by remorse. He had not been fair to Erdmuth. Cynics to the contrary, he had not been unfaithful to her during their long periods of separation; but he had been extremely thoughtless. He had forgotten that she was a woman, a wife, and a mother."[3]

Erdmuth Zinzendorf, Count Zinzendorf's wife.

After a proper year of mourning, Zinzendorf married Anna Nitchmann, a peasant woman who, along with others, had been his traveling companion for many years. The marriage was kept secret for more than a year, partly to avoid a family controversy over his marrying a woman so far beneath his social rank. Anna had a strong ideological influence on Zinzendorf, particularly in the area of mysticism, and this phenomenon led to grave problems for the mission.

Under the count's leadership, the Moravian church had placed great emphasis on the death of Christ. As a child Zinzendorf had meditated on the death and agony of the Lord, and his call to ministry had been influenced by a painting depicting Christ's agony. As time passed, what once had been an emphasis turned into an obsession, and the whole church seemed to be carried away in a radical form of mysticism. Through his example, the Moravians began denigrating their own worth as they morbidly meditated on the death of Christ. In a circular letter to the churches, Anna (years before she and Zinzendorf were married) had written, "Like a poor little worm, I desire to withdraw myself into his wounds," and Zinzendorf himself spoke of the brethren as "little blood worms in the sea of grace." An "Order of Little Fools" was formed, and he encouraged the members to behave like little children and to think of themselves as "little fish swimming in the bed of blood" or "little bees who suck the wounds of Christ."[4]

This mysticism had a negative impact on missions. The more mystical and introspective the Moravians became in their identification with Christ's physical suffering, the less they focused on world evangelism and the needs of others.

Active missionaries were sometimes discredited because they had not yet reached the mystics' high plane of spirituality, and the cause of missions therefore suffered.

This turn of events might have brought a quick demise to the missionary movement, but the count recognized the problem before that occurred. Admitting that the condition of the church had "greatly degenerated" and that he himself had "probably occasioned it," Zinzendorf was able to put that "brief but fearful"[5] period behind him and to steer his following back on course again.

Other problems were soon to surface, however. By 1750 the Moravian church was deeply in debt due to Zinzendorf's lack of financial management. "Its expansion," writes J. C. S. Mason, "its land purchases, its great buildings and other initiatives—in which the cost of missions was no more than a fraction of a much greater problem—was funded mainly by loans."[6]

In Britain and on the Continent there was an "avalanche of books and pamphlets," the effect of which was "nearly ruinous." The mystical theology of previous years was not forgotten as critics took aim at the now financially strapped movement. "Herrnhutism," wrote Henry Rimius, "has debased Christianity by connecting with it the most detestable absurdities, and expresses doctrines which it has grossly corrupted." Such derision did not fade quickly. "As late as 1808 the evangelical *Christian Observer* reminded readers that Moravians, like the 'Anabaptists' in an earlier period, had more recently 'exhibited a deplorable licentiousness of practice.'"[7]

Despite his flaws and failures and his marred reputation, Zinzendorf left a legacy that continued on long after his death. Indeed, his contribution to missions is perhaps best seen in the lives of the men and women who left behind family and homeland for the cause of world missions.

Christian David and Hans Egede

Apart from Count Zinzendorf, the individual most involved in the founding of the Moravian church was Christian David, who was largely responsible for bringing refugees from all over Europe to Zinzendorf's estate. David was born in Moravia in 1690 into a Roman Catholic family. As a youth he was a devout Catholic, zealous in his observance of rituals, holidays, and in his adoration of the Virgin Mary. Later he recalled that his heart burned like a stove with religious devotion—a devotion that took the form of evangelical enthusiasm while he was serving as an apprentice and living with his master's family. But even then his exposure to Christian teachings was limited. He was twenty before he acquired a Bible, a book that he had never before laid eyes on.

In 1717, at the age of twenty-seven, David experienced an evangelical conversion, and soon after that, through the encouragement of his wife, Anna, he became a traveling lay preacher. During his travels he met hundreds of disheartened, persecuted Christians who longed for a refuge where they could worship freely. Against that backdrop David met Zinzendorf in 1722, which led to their joint efforts to establish Herrnhut. During the years that followed, David represented Herrnhut as he traveled around Europe recruiting settlers.

Although he was a carpenter by trade and had been effective in recruiting settlers, Christian David was eager to become involved more directly in evangelism, and in 1733 his opportunity came. Along with two other Moravians, he was commissioned as a missionary to Greenland to revitalize the mission work there. Two years before their departure for Greenland, Zinzendorf had heard a rumor that Lutheran missionary Hans Egede was about to abandon his work there, and it was this erroneous information that prompted Zinzendorf to come to the rescue. He immediately called for volunteers among his Moravian following to fill the gap, and David was chosen to be the leader.

The arrival of Moravian missionaries came as a surprise to Egede. He welcomed them, but almost immediately problems and misunderstandings arose. Both Egede and David were strong willed, and a language barrier further complicated matters. Egede, a native of Norway, had difficulty understanding the German spoken by the Moravian newcomers, and they could not comprehend his Norwegian tongue at all. David and his companions, however, quickly realized that Egede had no intention of forsaking his mission.

Hans Egede and his family had been in Greenland for more than a decade when the Moravians arrived, and despite setbacks, they remained wholly dedicated to the mission. Born in Norway in 1686 (four years before Christian David), Egede grew up in a devout Lutheran family and was deeply influenced by a warm spirit of pietism that had penetrated the Scandinavian countries. He studied for the ministry and then spent a stormy ten years in the pastorate. Conflict with another minister in his diocese over money matters resulted in his being fined more than once by an ecclesiastical court. He charged that he was not receiving enough money to cover even the basic needs of his family, but his manner was considered by the court to be disrespectful of authority.

Christian David, Moravian missionary to Greenland.

Since his childhood Egede had heard tales of Greenland and of the Christians who centuries before had migrated there from Scandinavia—Christians whose descendants had not been heard from for more than two hundred years. He had learned from his Norwegian tradition that the gospel had been carried to Greenland hundreds of years before by Leif the Lucky. Leif, accompanied by a priest, propagated Christianity among the Greenlanders, and by the twelfth century the church there had grown to the point where it could have its own bishop. But over time, the church fell back into the ways of paganism.

These stories, combined with pietistic missionary fervor, challenged the young Norwegian pastor to pursue the possibility of opening a mission to Greenland to these "poor people, who in former times had been Christians and enlightened in the Christian faith, but who now for lack of teachers and instruction had again fallen into heathen blindness and savagery."[8] With no mission board to sponsor him, he sent a proposal "for the conversion and enlightenment of the Greenlanders"[9] to the king of the joint kingdom of Denmark and Norway and to church authorities. A war being waged with Sweden, however, delayed action on his request for several years.

In the meantime, Egede confronted strong personal opposition to his plans. His mother-in-law was deeply distressed when she heard the news, and his wife, Giertrud (thirteen years his senior), was so taken aback that she confessed that she regretted ever marrying him. But eventually, after she and her husband talked and prayed together about the matter, she became his most faithful supporter, and they moved forward together in what would become a joint calling. When others pressured him to abandon his plans, she held firm in her support: "My dear wife gave a proof of her great faith and constancy by representing to me that it was now too late to repent of what had been done. I cannot say how much she encouraged me by speaking in this way and by the fact that she, a frail woman, showed greater faith and manliness than I."[10]

In the summer of 1718, Egede, along with his wife and four children, left his parish in the north and sailed south to the seaport at Bergen, where he hoped to secure passage to Greenland. This first leg of the journey, along the treacherous Norwegian coast, turned out to be a perilous nightmare that might have crushed a weaker commitment. At one point he fell overboard and would have perished but for a daring rescue by a fisherman. Rather than discouraging him, the mishap buoyed his faith and convinced him that his rescue was a clear sign from God that he had been spared for a divine purpose.

Finally, after more than two years of delays and uncertainty in Bergen, the Egedes obtained passage through the Bergen Company and arrived in Greenland in the summer of 1721. After hastily building a dwelling to shelter his family during the cold months ahead, Egede settled down to the very unromantic life of being a foreign missionary. The pleasant summer weather was spoiled by swarms of ever-present gnats. But even more troublesome than the gnats was the language barrier. Egede had hoped to find a language similar to his own, brought to Greenland centuries before by his own people, but his hopes were dashed. Trying to communicate even the simplest phrases turned into a lengthy ordeal, and to make matters worse, Egede failed to detect even a trace of Christian beliefs that he had hoped might have been passed down through the centuries.

Communication was not the only cultural barrier that Egede had to overcome. The lifestyle of the Eskimos was vastly different from his own. They lived in primitive dwellings four to six feet high, often overcrowded with several families in one dwelling and torturously overheated in the winter. The sickening stench of spoiled meat and fish, combined with the repugnant odor of the urine tubs (for soaking hides), made the atmosphere almost unbearable for the Norwegian preacher; but home visitation was his only effective means of contact with the Eskimos during the long winter months.

Egede's ministry to the Eskimos got off to a slow start. While his young sons, Paul and Niels, quickly picked up the difficult language as they played with their native friends, Egede struggled for years with the complexities of the grammar, and even then he found it very difficult to communicate spiritual values. He depended heavily on Paul and Niels, and they proved to be an enormous asset in his ministry. His most effective method of winning the friendship and the audience of the Eskimos during his early years in Greenland was through music. According to his biographer, Louis Bobé, "He won their hearts by singing to them."[11]

Nevertheless, the progress of evangelism was painfully slow. Egede demanded that the Eskimos forsake their pagan practices—insisting there could be no compromise between Christianity and paganism. He demanded that they abolish their sacred protective charms, their superstitious drum dances and songs, and their "devilish jugglery." With little understanding of their beliefs, he was unable to establish any common ground between their religious tradition and Christianity. This impasse prompted him to concentrate his efforts on children, who were not as enmeshed in native superstitions. With their parents' permission, he baptized them and began teaching them Christian doctrine as soon as he believed they could grasp the meaning.

Egede never abandoned his dream of finding Greenlanders whose heritage could be traced back to his own native land. Through his searching he discovered remnants of European architecture, including the foundation of a church preserved from Norse ruins, but he never was able to detect beliefs passed down from the earlier generations of Christians.

The slow progress of his mission work and the lack of commercial success of the Bergen Company combined to dim the early enthusiasm there had been for the Greenland venture back home. Then in 1730, King Frederick IV, a strong supporter of the Greenland missionary venture, died, and his successor, King Christian VI, came to power. The following year Christian VI decided to abandon the Greenland commercial enterprise, and the company officials and workers were recalled. Egede himself was permitted to stay, but even his residence there was in question. This situation led to the rumor that he was giving up his missionary work and prompted Zinzendorf to commission Christian David and his Moravian colleagues to continue the work that Egede had begun.

Problems between the newly arrived Moravians and the veteran missionary Hans Egede were virtually inevitable. Egede, with his domineering and harsh personality, offended the Moravians, who believed in a softer approach to evangelism. "What followed," according to historian Stephen Neill, "is typical of what almost always happens when a second mission enters a territory where an older mission is already established. The newcomers pick on the weaknesses of the old, with little regard for what the pioneers have endured."[12]

The conflict between the two groups focused largely on the method of evangelism. To the Moravians, Egede was a rigid and doctrinaire Lutheran who was more concerned with teaching his cold orthodoxy than with saving souls. How, they asked, could the Eskimos ever be expected to understand complex doctrine until God had given them the light of salvation? Egede, on the other hand, viewed the Moravians as preaching a deplorably sentimental religion, with little concern for Christian doctrine and the eradication of religious superstitions. Their one-sided gospel of the love of Christ, with little reference to a holy, righteous, almighty God, he maintained, failed to present Christianity as it really was.

Despite the differences, Egede and the Moravians worked side by side, at times maintaining a reasonably warm relationship. Egede shared all of his linguistic notes and material with the Moravians as they struggled to come to grips with the language (though the language barrier between them made the notes of little value); and when they were ill with scurvy, he visited them often, doing what he could to relieve their suffering. His wife, Giertrud, also showed kindness to them and was loved and respected by them. Nevertheless, the conflict was ever present, causing a contemporary observer to comment that the Greenlanders "are apt to doubt the whole of the Christian faith and to say: 'How can it be truth, which you yourselves are quarreling about?'"[13]

The first real breakthrough for Egede in his ministry to the Eskimos came in 1733, around the time of the arrival of Christian David and his coworkers. Good news arrived from Denmark that their new king had decided to continue the Greenland mission work. But with this good news came a converted Greenlander returning from a visit to Denmark, who had become a carrier of the smallpox virus. On his return he traveled from village to village, ministering with Egede and unknowingly spreading the deadly disease wherever he went. Soon the Eskimos were ravaged with sickness and fighting for their lives, and only then were the warmth and sacrificial love of this otherwise stern churchman clearly demonstrated to them. What could not be transmitted in words was shown through weeks and months of selfless service as the disease continued to rage. He was on continual call, and when he was not out in the villages nursing the sick, he was besieged at his own home. Hearing of his generosity, Eskimos came from miles around for treatment, and the sickest among them were brought into his own home, where he and his wife gave them beds and cared for them.

After the danger had passed and a calm had returned to the region, Egede noticed a greater interest in spiritual things among the people. He had endeared himself to them, and the Eskimos were now seeking him out for spiritual counsel. A dying Greenlander who had ignored the teaching of Egede when he was in good health expressed the feelings of many of his people toward their Norwegian missionary: "You have been more kind to us than we have been to one another; you have fed us, when we were famished; you have buried our dead . . . you have told us of God . . . so that we may now die gladly, in expectation of a better life hereafter."[14] The terrible epidemic of 1733 lasted less than a year, but the scars were permanent. Egede never fully regained his health, and his wife remained ill until her death in 1736.

Soon the Eskimos were ravaged with sickness and fighting for their lives, and only then were the warmth and sacrificial love of the otherwise stern churchman clearly demonstrated to them.

In the meantime, the Moravians had become established in their missionary work and soon began seeing a response to their preaching. In 1738 a revival broke out, and in the years that followed hundreds of Eskimos made professions of faith. Egede angrily accused Christian David of having "reaped what I have ploughed."[15] His charge had an element of truth, but the Moravians' simple message and method of evangelism were more suited to the Eskimos than were Egede's. Their presentation of the gospel, filled with emotional sentimentality, appealed to people whose mystical superstitions were in some ways not so far removed from the mysticism of the Moravians. Soon the little chapel at New Herrnhut was overcrowded, and a new church was constructed by the missionary-carpenter Christian David.

After the death of his wife, Hans Egede returned to Copenhagen and remarried. From there he supervised the mission work in Greenland and trained young men for missionary service, but he saw very little fruit from his labors. His greatest joy was seeing his sons continue in the work of the mission. His son Paul, in particular, carried out a very effective ministry in the area of Disko Bay, where religious revival broke out and people came from great distances to hear him preach. His ministry, though, was cut short due to failing eyesight. He returned to Copenhagen, where he continued his Bible translation work and collaborated with his father in developing a doctrinal guide for the Greenlanders. Hans Egede died in 1758 at the age of seventy-two. His son Paul lived another thirty years, supporting the cause of missions in Greenland to the very end.

George Schmidt

At the very time that Christianity was being planted in Greenland, it was also being introduced in other remote areas of the world by dedicated Moravian missionaries. In South Africa, George Schmidt, an unmarried Moravian brother, was struggling against almost overwhelming odds to bring the gospel to the native population there. Born in Moravia in 1709, Schmidt was converted at the age of sixteen during a revival among the Moravian brethren. Soon after that he journeyed to Herrnhut and was there at the time of the great revival on August 13, 1727.

At Herrnhut, Schmidt was commissioned to go back to his homeland of Moravia with two other "brethren." It was a region of deep religious animosity, where the Protestant minority faced severe persecution from Catholic authorities. Soon after they arrived, their meetings were detected, and he and his companions were imprisoned. After their release, the three young Moravians returned to Herrnhut, but soon Schmidt was again sent out to preach—this time to Austria, an even harsher environment. Once again he and his traveling companion sought to elude the authorities and conduct secret religious meetings, and once again arrests were made and he found himself in prison.

For three years he languished in a dungeon cell. Conditions were deplorable, and after less than a year his comrade died, leaving him to suffer alone. Had his suffering been only physical, Schmidt's trials would not have been so unbearable, but he also suffered mental anguish. Daily he was pressured to recant by the Jesuits who were holding him, but he steadfastly refused. After three years of misery and torment, he was sentenced to hard labor, which lasted for another three years until finally he broke down and signed a revocation of his beliefs to satisfy the authorities.

Having endured so much suffering and humiliation, Schmidt returned to Herrnhut, expecting to be warmly embraced by the community. Instead, he was met with a cool reception and was treated as an apostate because of his "weakness." He was devastated, and to prove he was not a deserter he left the security of Herrnhut once again and went back into Roman Catholic strongholds to preach. But he was not happy, and he gratefully welcomed a change in 1736 when he was sent to Holland to learn the Dutch language and then dispatched to South Africa in 1737 to work among the Hottentots. Zinzendorf had heard the reports of Ziegenbalg and Plütschau who, on their way to India, had become burdened for these oppressed Africans.

South Africa was a very harsh environment during the early eighteenth century. The Dutch colonists did not look favorably on missionary endeavors that might raise the social status of the Africans, and Schmidt's arrival among them was viewed with antagonism. Moreover, the Calvinistic Dutch Reformed ministers who were in the Cape Colony deplored the emotional and sentimental pietism of the Moravians. Schmidt himself did little to endear himself to them. According to one account, he was "a hypocrite and a sham, sometimes climbing on the low roof of the house. . . . There he knelt so that all . . . could see him, and pretended to pray."[16]

After residing at a military post for a time, Schmidt traveled inland to work among the Hottentots, who were regarded as "black cattle" by the colonists and were hunted down like animals in their effort to enslave them. They cautiously welcomed Schmidt, and, with the help of a Hottentot interpreter, he began preaching to them. In a very short time he had established a school with some fifty students.

All Moravians were expected to be evangelists, and there was little differentiation between those who ministered on the home field and those who went abroad.

As with other Moravian missionaries, Schmidt's ministry was not financed by supporters back home. All Moravians were expected to be evangelists, and there was little differentiation between those who ministered on the home field and those who went abroad. Schmidt worked among the people, and personal evangelism was simply conducted during his daily contacts with them. For a time he worked as a day-laborer, butchering, tanning hides, threshing wheat, pruning fruit trees, and doing other farm chores; and after a time he acquired livestock of his own as well as his own garden.

Life was not easy for Schmidt in South Africa. The winter of 1740 was particularly severe, and he and his neighbors survived a food shortage only by shooting a hippopotamus, an animal not normally used for sustenance. But to Schmidt, matters of day-to-day living were secondary. His sole purpose for being in Africa was evangelism. But in this area, too, he faced hard times and setbacks. His little flock of believers was unstable and given to backsliding. Even Africo, his interpreter and one of his most promising converts, fell back into his old ways. He went on drinking binges with his friends and nearly destroyed the fledgling church. Schmidt reacted harshly, and the men involved repented; but spiritual lethargy persisted. So discouraged was Schmidt that he wrote to Zinzendorf that he intended to return home.

Schmidt's problems in building a stable community of Christians were not only with the Africans but also with the Dutch residents and colonial authorities. Local farmers sought to ruin his reputation, some charging that he was living with a Hottentot woman, others claiming that he was a spy. And the colonial authorities, both religious and secular, deeply resented his continuing presence—the presence of an unordained laborer who had the audacity of assuming a position of spiritual leadership.

In an effort to stabilize the situation, Zinzendorf intervened. In a letter to Schmidt, he gave advice, outlined mission policy, and at the same time ordained him in absentia—hoping to quell the criticism:

> Why don't you baptize the children of the Hottentots who die in infancy? He who comes with water and blood, has died for them too. I ordain you for the case of a baptism or a communion . . . a minister of our church in the name of the Father, the Son and the Holy Ghost, Amen. . . . I am very pleased with you. But, my dear, you aim too much at the skin of the Hottentots and too little at the heart. . . . You must tell the Hottentots, especially their children, the story of the Son of God. If they feel something, pray with them, if not, pray for them. If feeling persists, baptize them where you shot your hippo.[17]

Receiving ordination was a great encouragement to Schmidt, and he immediately exercised his right to administer the sacraments by baptizing Wilhelm, who had been his first Hottentot convert. Soon others were baptized, and word spread to Dutch officials of what was happening. Rather than calming the situation, his ordination only intensified the animosity of the Dutch officials toward him. Reformed ministers at Cape Town insisted that the baptisms were invalid. They summoned two of the converts to come before them to undergo the standard catechism instruction and were surprised to find them as knowledgeable of doctrine as some of their own candidates for baptism. Nevertheless, Schmidt was ordered to leave South Africa and face officials back in Holland. Thus, in the spring of 1744 he sailed for Europe to argue the validity of his ministry before the Dutch authorities there.

Despite the efforts of Schmidt and other Moravian leaders, permission to return was never granted, and the little church among the Hottentots remained without pastoral leadership for nearly half a century until 1792. That year some Moravians returned to the valley. To their amazement, they found an old woman whom Schmidt had baptized more than fifty years before still cherishing the New Testament he had given her.

The second missionary endeavor in the Cape Colony by the Moravians was more successful than the first. Under the capable direction of Hans Hallbeck, the mission work thrived, and by the mid-twentieth century there were thirty-eight stations and nearly fifty thousand professing Christians under Moravian jurisdiction.

The success of Moravian mission work around the world was significant in its own right, but more than that, it served as a model for Protestant mission agencies that paved the way for the modern missionary movement. In 1800, as this movement was being launched, there was no other model that Protestants could easily envision as their own. Catholic religious orders were involved in mission enterprises throughout the world, but they were seen as extensions of a powerful religious bureaucracy headquartered in Rome. The Moravians, on the other hand, were more like an independent agency, and the missionaries sent out were sometimes married couples with families. The Moravians, with their mission posts scattered around the world, set an example through trial and error of how actual mission work could be carried out, and their writings were invaluable sources for new agencies that were emerging.

"The Moravian Church showed English Protestants the way forward," writes Mason. The founders of the Baptist Missionary Society, the London Missionary Society, and the Church Missionary Society found "the very necessary evidence with which to convince their followers that they too could maintain foreign missions, and be successful overseas."[18] William Carey regarded the Moravians as the best contemporary example of worldwide missions, strengthening his case against those who insisted that the time of world evangelism had either long since passed or had not yet come.

August Spangenberg was the premier Moravian missiologist whose writings became required reading for many early missionary candidates. His mission theology was taken primarily from the apostle Paul, whose tent-making vocation was particularly applicable to Moravian methodology. But it was Paul's defense of the gospel and his all-consuming passion for evangelism that Spangenberg emphasized as the foundation for any missionary venture. The early evangelists brought a simple gospel message that was easily transmitted across cultures, and that, he argued, was the model for all times.

Moravian missionary outreach would continue in the nineteenth and twentieth centuries, though it was often overshadowed by the burgeoning denominational and independent mission societies that were rapidly emerging. As time passed, too, the evangelical fervor of the early generations gradually receded.

SELECT BIBLIOGRAPHY

Bobé, Louis. *Hans Egede: Colonizer and Missionary of Greenland.* Copenhagen: Rosenkilde and Bagger, 1952.

Hamilton, J. Taylor, and Kenneth G. Hamilton. *History of the Moravian Church: The Renewed Unitas Fratrum, 1722–1957.* Winston-Salem, NC: Moravian Church in America, 1967.

Hutton, J. E. *A History of Moravian Missions.* London: Moravian Publication Office, 1923.

Kruger, Bernhard. *The Pear Tree Blossoms: A History of the Moravian Mission Stations in South Africa, 1737–1869.* South Africa: Genadendal Printing Works, 1967.

Langton, Edward. *History of the Moravian Church.* London: Allen & Unwin, 1956.

Mason, J. C. S. *The Moravian Church and the Missionary Awakening in England, 1760–1800.* United Kingdom: Boydell Press, 2001.

Weinlick, John R. *Count Zinzendorf.* Nashville: Abingdon, 1956.

PART 2

THE "GREAT CENTURY"

PART 2

The "Great Century"

The spread of Protestant Christianity in the three centuries following the Reformation, though notable, gave little indication of what was about to occur in the nineteenth century. In the year 1800, according to Stephen Neill, "It was still by no means certain that Christianity would be successful in turning itself into a universal religion."[1] Christianity appeared to be little more than a Caucasian religion that was being severely battered by a wave of rationalism that was sweeping across the Western world. Would the Evangelical Awakening in the eighteenth century make a difference? Would Christianity survive the modern era? The nineteenth century was crucial. Instead of falling before the onslaught of the Enlightenment, Christianity continued to be reinvigorated by an evangelical fervor that propelled missionaries throughout the world. It truly was the "Great Century" for Christian expansion.

There were a number of factors that made the nineteenth century conducive to worldwide Protestant missions. The Age of Enlightenment and the eighteenth-century rationalism had merged with a new Age of Romanticism. It was a time to question the excessive reliance on reason and to put more stock in the emotions and the imagination. Reform movements sprang up in the newly industrialized nations, and churches and Christian organizations were reaching out as never before through the participation of volunteer workers.

Changes in the world's religious environment no doubt contributed to the rapid spread of Christianity in the nineteenth century. It was a period of decline for the non-Christian religions. "Hinduism, Buddhism, and [Islam] were relatively quiescent in the nineteenth century," according to Martin Marty, and "Christians sensed that they could fill a vacuum."[2] Catholicism, too, was on the decline in many parts of the world. The French Rationalism of the seventeenth and eighteenth centuries had taken its toll on the church, and the French Revolution effectively cut the economic purse strings of Roman Catholic missions.

In Latin America especially, Roman Catholicism witnessed many reverses. National movements saw the church as "the last bulwark of an outmoded and oppressive regime."[3]

Protestantism, on the other hand, was thriving. The nineteenth century was a "Protestant era," and more specifically an era dominated by evangelical Protestantism. In the British Isles the evangelical Christians exercised powerful influence in the highest levels of government and commerce, and in America church membership increased from ten to forty percent during the course of the century. Denominations were developing rapidly, and the Sunday school movement in both Britain and America was growing at a fast pace.

Politically, the nineteenth century witnessed tremendous changes as well. Although there were revolutions and social upheavals in Europe and a bloody civil war in America, it was an era of relative world peace. Western nations, through scientific and technological advances, were quickly becoming world powers, and their wealth and prestige were viewed with envy and admiration by many nonindustrialized nations. Politically, it was also a period of secularization. "From the era of Constantine and the Christianization of the Roman Empire to the latter days of the eighteenth century," writes Marty, "western men assumed . . . that religion was to be established by law and sanctioned by the legal arm of the state."[4] But by the nineteenth century that was no longer true. Individuals were taking command of their own personal spiritual condition and their responsibility to reach out to others.

"Never before," writes Latourette, "had Christianity or any other religion had so many individuals giving full time to the propagation of their faith."

The eighteenth-century evangelical revivals that began in England with Whitefield and Wesley played an important role in awakening Christian leaders and laypeople to the responsibility for evangelism worldwide. "No longer," according to Harold Cook, "was the state held responsible in any sense for the propagation of the Christian faith."[5] Evangelism was the responsibility of the church and its leaders, and it was this once again rediscovered truth that launched the modern missionary movement with William Carey in England and Samuel Mills in the United States.

But belief was not enough. A vehicle was needed to turn the belief into action, and that vehicle emerged in the form of the mission society. The volunteer mission society, independent in some instances and denominationally oriented in others, transformed Christian missions, opening the way for ecumenical activity and lay involvement. "Never before," writes Latourette, "had Christianity or any other religion had so many individuals giving full time to the propagation of their faith. Never had so many hundreds of thousands contributed voluntarily of their means to assist the spread of Christianity or any other religion."[6] The first of these new societies was the Baptist Missionary Society (1792), soon to be followed by the

London Missionary Society (1795) and the Church Missionary Society (1799). From Continental Europe came the Netherlands Missionary Society (1797) and the Basel Mission (1815); and from the United States, the American Board of Commissioners for Foreign Missions (1810) and the American Baptist Missionary Board (1814). There would be dozens more as the century progressed, for it was, as Neill has pointed out, "the great age of societies."[7]

As important as the evangelical awakening and the new mission societies were to the spread of the gospel worldwide, without certain secular trends the foreign missionary cause would have been significantly curtailed. Both colonialism and industrialization had far-reaching effects on the expansion of Christianity. The Industrial Revolution had brought new power to Europe, and with that power came an urge to conquer. Colonialism and imperialism were on their way to becoming accepted government policies, and as such they had a significant impact on missions. "Commercial and colonizing schemes had brought the ends of the earth into new contact," writes R. H. Glover. "The Great East India Companies, Dutch and English, had—without intention or desire, it is true—paved the way for the missionary by making travel to, and residence in, Eastern countries more practicable and safe."[8]

The close tie between colonialism and missions has caused many historians to charge that the missionaries were merely "following the flag" as tools of imperialism. This is an issue that has been hotly debated by historians. In many cases the missionaries did "follow the flag" and aided colonial and imperialistic schemes. Others preceded the flag but even then, in many cases, bolstered colonialism. Livingstone, among others, pleaded for European commerce and settlements in Africa, and missionaries everywhere welcomed any privileges a favorable colonial power would grant them. Protestant missionaries strongly favored rule by Protestant countries and feared Catholic rule, and vice versa. However, by the year 1900 the majority of missionaries were not working in colonial territories ruled by their own home countries.

But despite this sometimes too cozy relationship between missionaries and the perpetrators of imperialism, the two groups were more often than not at considerable odds with each other. The commercial companies frequently stood in the way of the missionaries, and the missionaries, with few exceptions, decried the lifestyle of the traders and colonists. Rarely was the association harmonious. "The relation between missions and colonial expansion is complex," writes Andrew Walls. "But one thing is clear. If missions are associated with the rise of imperialism, they are equally associated with the factors which brought about its destruction."[9] Likewise, they are associated with social progress in underdeveloped nations. "Protestant missionary efforts in this period," according to Winter, "led the way in establishing all around the world the democratic apparatus of government, the schools, the hospitals, the universities and the political foundations for new nations."[10]

But valuable as such social progress was, it was not accomplished without the introduction of Western culture, accompanied in some cases by a rejection of native traditions and customs. As the missionaries spread out across Africa and Asia and into the island worlds, they brought their cultural baggage with them. "Only western man," writes Neill, "was man in the full sense of the word; he was wise and good, and members of other races, in so far as they became westernized, might share in this wisdom and goodness. But western man was the leader, and would remain so for a very long time, perhaps for ever."[11]

Imperfect as they were, it was the nineteenth-century missionaries—a tiny company in comparison to other forces impacting the nonwestern world—who, in a relatively short period of time, turned what some may have thought to be a declining Caucasian religion into the largest and most dynamic religious faith in the world. They were common people turned heroes, whose commitment and courage inspired succeeding generations to follow their example. This century was an age when little children dreamed of true greatness—of becoming a Carey, a Livingstone, a Judson, a Paton, a Slessor, or a Hudson Taylor.

5

South Central Asia: Confronting Ancient Creeds

The beginning of the Protestant missionary movement is conveniently dated as 1800. William Carey is the grand patriarch, and the setting is the subcontinent of India, where the world's oldest and most complex religions were born and where religious beliefs pervaded every facet of society. From a Western perspective—and in retrospect—this was an eventful moment in Christian missions. But in the eyes of the Indian people—the teeming millions who elbowed their way through the crowded marketplaces—nothing happened. If they had been aware of what was happening, they would have looked with scorn or indifference on those who would bring them a new religion. What could a "Western" religion offer them that Hinduism, Buddhism, Islam, Sikhism, or Jainism could not? And what appeal could there be in a religion whose proponents claimed that they alone possessed the truth? Hindus, with thousands of gods, prided themselves in their tolerance.

When Carey arrived in India, the vast country was going through a time of transition in its relation to the outside world. Nearly two hundred years earlier, Queen Elizabeth I had granted a charter to the East India Company. "No idea could be more erroneous," writes Mary Drewery, "than to suppose that Britain set out deliberately to conquer India with a view to territorial aggrandisement."[1] Trade was what the British were seeking. But other countries—particularly France—wanted that lucrative trade as well. Troops were needed to protect the trade, and with the India Act of 1784, the British government officially joined with the East India Company in its effort to wield control over the subcontinent.

The significance of Carey's ministry lies in its influence on Protestant missions more than on its influence on the Indian people, though he, unlike many missionaries before and since, was able to influence social and political reform. Christianity offered an alternative to the age-old caste system and release from the endless process of reincarnation—especially for the "untouchables." In spite of the tremendous barriers, Christianity was planted in India and elsewhere in South Central Asia. Through the influence of William Carey, who (in retrospect) symbolically ushered in the "Great Century" of foreign missions, the evangelism of the world began to be viewed as a primary obligation of the Christian church. South Central Asia, however, would never be a fertile field for Christianity, for still today only a tiny minority of the population professes the Christian faith.

William Carey

The year was 1800. The setting was in Bengal in the northeast of India along the banks of India's most sacred river, the Ganges. Into that polluted river went a native Indian and an Englishman—a man who had taken seriously the words of Jesus: "Go into all the world and preach the gospel, *baptizing* them...." After seven long years, William Carey was baptizing the first Hindu convert, Krishna Pal. What a momentous occasion it was—a moment to be remembered as a landmark in Christian missions—the "Father of Modern Missions" baptizing his first convert.

But this sublime scene is only part of the picture. Carey's wife, who had gone to India against her will, was now deemed "wholly deranged," and John Thomas, Carey's partner who had delayed the mission due to his credit problems, had also gone mad. A missionary observer to this momentous occasion filled in the details that we would rather not include in our stories of missionary heroes: "When Carey led Krishna and his own son Felix down into the water of baptism, the ravings of Thomas in the schoolhouse on the one side, and of Mrs. Carey on the other, mingled with the strains of the Bengali hymn of praise."[2]

William Carey, an impoverished English shoemaker, was an unlikely candidate to rise to the designation of "Father of Modern Missions." Indeed, some in recent years have strongly argued that such a title is not fitting. There were others who made significant contributions to the missions cause during this era and before, and whatever greatness Carey achieved was the result of teamwork. According to Christopher Smith, "layers of popular mythology still remain to be cut through before the actual contours of his career as a pre-Victorian mission leader will be uncovered."[3]

Yet whether based on popular mythology or not, Carey, more than any other missionary of this period, stirred the imagination of the Christian world and showed by his own humble example what could be done in a wide variety of ways to further the cause of world evangelism. Although he faced almost insurmountable trials during his forty-year missionary career, he demonstrated a dogged determination to succeed. His secret? "I can plod. I can persevere in any definite pursuit. To this I owe everything."[4]

Carey was born in 1761 near Northampton, England, the son of a weaver who worked on a loom in the family living quarters. Life was simple and uncomplicated. The Industrial Revolution had only begun to replace the cottage industries with grimy sweatshops and noisy textile mills. Carey's childhood was routine except for persistent problems with allergies that prevented him from pursuing his dream of becoming a gardener. Instead, he was apprenticed, at the age of sixteen, to a shoemaker and continued in that vocation until he was twenty-eight. He was converted through the influence of another apprentice, and from that time forward he became actively associated with Baptist Dissenters, devoting his leisure time to Bible study and lay ministries.

In 1781, before he reached his twentieth birthday, Carey married his master's sister-in-law. Dorothy was more than five years older than he, and like many eighteenth-century English women of her background, she was illiterate. From the beginning it was a mismatched union, and as time passed and Carey's horizons broadened, the chasm dividing them grew even wider. The earliest years of their marriage were filled with hardship and poverty. But despite the economic hard times, Carey did not turn aside from his study and lay preaching, serving as pastor of two very small Baptist churches while he continued making shoes. During these years in the pastorate, his philosophy of missions began to take shape, sparked first by his reading of *Captain Cook's Voyages.* But as he developed a biblical perspective on the subject, he became convinced that missionary work was the central responsibility of the church.

Drawing on certain Reformation teachings, many eighteenth-century churchmen believed that the Great Commission was given only to the apostles and therefore converting the "heathen" was no concern of theirs, especially if it were not tied to colonialism. When Carey presented his ideas to a group of ministers, one of them is said to have exclaimed: "Young man, sit down. When God pleases to convert the heathen, He will do it without your aid or mine."[5] But Carey would not be silenced. In the spring of 1792 he published an eighty-seven-page book that had far-reaching consequences in its influence on Christian missions.

In 1792 Carey published an eighty-seven-page book that had far-reaching consequences in its influence on Christian missions.

The booklet, *An Enquirey Into the Obligation of Christians to Use Means for the Conversion of the Heathens* (and that being a shortened title), very ably presented a case for worldwide missions and sought to deflate the arguments dramatizing the impracticality of sending missionaries to faraway lands. Soon after, Carey spoke to a group of ministers at a Baptist Association meeting in Nottingham, where he challenged his audience from Isaiah 54:2–3 and uttered the words that are most often associated with him: "Expect great things from God; attempt great things for God." The following day the ministers organized a mission agency, which became known as the Baptist Missionary Society. The decision was not made lightly. Most of the Baptist Association ministers were, like Carey, living on very meager incomes, and involvement in foreign missions meant tremendous financial sacrifices from both them and their congregations.

Andrew Fuller, the most prominent minister in support of the new society, became the first home secretary; and the first missionary appointee was John Thomas, a Baptist layman who had gone to India as a doctor for the royal navy and stayed on after his term of service to minister as a freelance missionary doctor and evangelist. Carey immediately offered himself to the new society as a "suitable companion" to Thomas and was accepted.

William Carey, the "Father of Modern Missions."

Although Carey had long been avidly interested in missions, the decision to offer himself for overseas missions was nothing less than rash. That his church was distressed at losing its pastor and his father judged him "mad" might be overlooked, but his wife was also strongly opposed. With three little ones and another on the way, it is no wonder Dorothy was adamantly opposed to leaving her homeland to embark on a hazardous five-month voyage (complicated by France's very recent declaration of war against England) to spend the rest of her life in the deadly tropical climate of India. Other women had willingly made such sacrifices, and thousands more would in the future, but not she. If there is a "Mother of Modern Missions," it was not Dorothy Carey. She refused to go.

However, if Dorothy thought her refusal to accompany her husband would change his mind, she was wrong. Carey was determined to go, even if it meant going without her. He went ahead with his plans, which included booking a passage for Felix, his eight-year-old son. In March of 1793, after months of deputation, Carey and Thomas were commissioned by the Society; and the following month they, along with Felix and Thomas's wife and daughter, boarded a ship on the Thames River that was to take them to India. But the trip to India ended abruptly at Portsmouth, England. Officials boarded the ship and refused to allow the party to leave the country until Thomas had satisfied his creditors.

The delay led to a dramatic change in plans. Dorothy, having delivered her baby three weeks before, grudgingly agreed to join the mission party with her little ones, provided that Kitty, her younger sister, could accompany her. Obtaining funds for the additional passengers was a difficult hurdle, but on June 13, 1793, they boarded a Danish vessel and set sail for India. The long and dangerous voyage around the Cape of Good Hope was at times terrifying, but on November 19 they arrived safely in India.

The time of their arrival was not favorable for establishing mission work. The East India Company was in virtual control of the country, and its hostility to mission work was soon made plain. The company feared anything that might interfere with its commercial ventures, and Carey was left with no doubts that he was very unwelcome. Fearing deportation, he moved with his family to the interior. Here, surrounded by malarial swamps, the Careys lived in dire circumstances. Dorothy and the two oldest boys became deathly ill, and family cares required his constant attention. She and Kitty were "continually exclaiming against"[6] him and were resentful of the Thomas family, who were living in relative affluence in Calcutta. After some months their plight was alleviated by the kindness and generosity of Mr. Short, an East India Company official who took pity on them and welcomed them into his home. Soon, however, the family moved on to Malda, nearly three hundred miles north, where Carey worked as an indigo factory foreman.

The years in Malda were difficult ones. Although Carey was content in his new position and found the indigo factory to be a choice language school and field for evangelism, family troubles persisted. Kitty had stayed back to marry Mr. Short, and Dorothy's health and mental stability steadily declined. Then the tragic death of their five-year-old son Peter in 1794 pushed her into serious mental illness.

Dorothy was apparently suffering from a delusional disorder that convinced her that her husband was unfaithful in their marriage. John Thomas wrote to Andrew Fuller about incidents that had occurred in 1795:

> Mrs. Carey has given us much trouble and vexation. . . . She has taken it into her head that C(arey) is a great whoremonger, and her jealously burns like fire unquenchable; and this horrible idea has night and day filled her heart for about 9 or 10 months past; so that if he goes out of his door by day or night, she follows him; and declares in the most solemn manner that she has catched him with his servants, with his friends, with Mrs. Thomas, and that he is guilty every day and every night. . . . She has even made some attempt on his life.[7]

Her mental delusions not only caused great personal turmoil for Carey but also created confusion and questions about his ministry and message. "He attempted to argue for the moral superiority of Christianity and how Christ could liberate Hindus and Moslems from the tragedies of paganism," writes James Beck. "But how could he evangelize with his wife following him through the streets accusing him in the vilest language of adultery?"[8] It was a distressing situation, and she was later described by coworkers as being "wholly deranged."

The circumstances, not surprisingly, took a toll on Carey, as is evident in his journal entries through 1795: "This is indeed the Valley of the Shadow of Death to me. . . . O what a load is a barren heart. . . . Oh that this day could be consigned to oblivion. . . . Much to complain of, such another dead soul I think scarcely exists in the world. . . . Mine is a lonely life indeed. . . . My soul is overwhelmed with depression."[9]

Despite his traumatic family situation and his continued factory work, Carey spent hours every day in Bible translation work and evangelism. By the end of 1795 a Baptist church had been established in Malda. It was a start, even though its entire membership equaled only four, and they were Englishmen. The services, however, drew curious onlookers among the Bengali people, and Carey asserted that "the name of Jesus Christ is no longer strange in this neighborhood." But there was no fruit. After nearly seven years of toil in Bengal, Carey could not claim even one Indian convert.[10]

In spite of his lack of outward success, Carey was satisfied with his missionary work in Malda and was keenly disappointed to leave in 1800. New missionaries had arrived from England, and in order to avoid continual harassment from the East India Company, they settled near Calcutta in the Danish territory of Serampore. Carey's help was urgently needed in setting up the new mission station to accommodate them, so he reluctantly set out for Serampore.

Serampore soon became the center of Baptist missionary activity in India, and it was there that Carey would spend the remaining thirty-four years of his life. Carey and his coworkers, Joshua Marshman and William Ward, referred to as the Serampore Trio, would become one of the most famous missionary teams in history. But "trio" is a misnomer. Hannah Marshman was as much a part of that team as were the men. The team is more correctly termed the Serampore quartet. "They were amazingly close-knit as a leadership team," writes Christopher Smith. "Indeed, very few people in Britain ever realized how dependent Carey was on his partners for insight and a wide range of initiatives."[11] The mission compound, which housed ten missionaries and their nine children, enjoyed a family atmosphere. The missionaries lived together and kept most things in common. On Saturday nights they met to pray and to air their grievances, "pledging themselves to love one another." Responsibilities were divided according to abilities, and the work progressed smoothly.

The success of the Serampore Mission during the early years can be credited, in part, to Carey's kindly disposition. His own willingness to sacrifice material wealth and to go beyond the call of duty was a continual example to the rest, and he easily overlooked the faults in others. Even in regard to Thomas, who mismanaged the mission funds—the man who had "set himself up in a fine house with 12 servants and a coach to carry him about the city"[12]—Carey could say, "I love him, and we live in the greatest harmony." Describing his coworkers, Carey wrote: "Brother Ward is the very man we wanted. . . . He enters into the work with his whole soul. I have much pleasure in him. . . . Brother Marshman is a prodigy of diligence and prudence, as is also his wife."[13]

The Serampore mission demonstrated effective teamwork, and there were results to show for it. Schools were organized, a large printing establishment was set up, and Carey's translation work continued. During his years at Serampore, he translated the whole Bible in Bengali, Sanskrit, and Marathi; helped in other whole Bible translations; and translated the New Testament and portions of Scripture into many more languages and dialects. His quality, however, did not match his quantity. Home Secretary Andrew Fuller scolded him for inconsistent spelling and other problems in the copy he sent back to England for printing: "I never knew a person of so much knowledge as you profess of other languages, to write English so bad. . . . You huddle half a dozen periods into one. . . . If your Bengal N.T. shd be thus pointed I shd tremble for its fate."[14] Fuller's fears were well-founded, and Carey, to his bitter disappointment, found that some of his work was incomprehensible. But he did not give up. He reworked his translations until he was satisfied that they could be understood.

Evangelism was also an important part of the work at Serampore, though it progressed slowly. By 1818, after twenty-five years of Baptist missions to India, there were some six hundred baptized converts and a few thousand more who attended classes and services.

Despite his busy schedule of translation and evangelistic work, Carey found time to do more. One of his greatest achievements was the founding of Serampore College in 1819 for the training of indigenous church planters and evangelists. The school opened with thirty-seven Indian students, more than half of whom were Christians. Another area of educational achievement involved his teaching at Fort William College in Calcutta, where he was invited to become the Professor of Oriental Languages. The position not only brought in much-needed income to the missionaries but also placed them in better standing with the East India Company and gave him an opportunity to improve his language skills while being challenged by his students.

As busy as he was, Carey neglected his children, failing to give them the parenting they so desperately needed. Even when he was with them, his easygoing nature stood in the way of firm discipline, a lack that was plainly exhibited in the boys' behavior. In speaking of this situation, Hannah Marshman wrote, "The good man saw and lamented the evil but was too mild to apply an effectual remedy."[15] Had it not been for her stern reprimands and William Ward's fatherly concern, the Carey boys would have gone entirely their own way.

In 1807, at the age of fifty-one, Dorothy Carey died. She had long since ceased to be a useful member of the mission family. In fact, she was a hindrance to the work. John Marshman wrote how Carey often worked on his translations "while an insane wife, frequently wrought up to a state of most distressing excitement, was in the next room."[16] Marshman himself suffered from mental illness—"terror and anguish"—which Carey described as "morbid depression."[17]

During his years at Serampore, Carey had developed a friendship with Lady Charlotte Rumohr, born into Danish royalty and living at Serampore, hoping the climate would improve her poor health. Though she came to Serampore as a skeptic, she attended services at the mission, was converted, and was baptized by Carey in 1803. After that she devoted her time and much of her money to the work of the mission. In 1808, only a few months after the death of Dorothy, Carey announced his engagement to Lady Charlotte, causing an upheaval in the usually tranquil mission family. So great was the opposition that a petition was circulated in an effort to prevent the marriage, but to no avail. The marriage, conducted by Marshman, took place in May, just six months after Dorothy had been laid to rest.

Carey's thirteen-year marriage to Charlotte was a happy one. Charlotte had a brilliant mind and a gift for linguistics, and she was a valuable assistant in his translation work. She also maintained close relationships with the boys and became the mother they had never had. When she died in 1821, Carey wrote, "We had as great a share of conjugal happiness as ever was enjoyed by mortals." Two years later, at the age of sixty-two, Carey married again, this time to Grace Hughes, a widow seventeen years younger than he. Though Grace was not as well-endowed intellectually as Charlotte had been, he praised her for her "constant and unremitting care and excellent nursing" during his frequent illnesses.[18]

One of the most devastating setbacks that Carey faced during his forty uninterrupted years in India was the loss of his priceless manuscripts in a warehouse fire in 1812. He was away at the time, but the news that his massive polyglot dictionary, two grammar books, and whole versions of the Bible had been destroyed devastated him. Had his temperament been different, he might never have recovered, but he accepted the tragedy as a judgment from the Lord and began all over again with even greater zeal.

Carey and his colleagues were conscious of communicating the gospel effectively in the Indian culture—though ever recognizing that their efforts were trifling in comparison to what native Indians themselves would be able to do. One of their means of cross-cultural communication was through music. "Hindu ballad singers were commonly seen on the streets and marketplaces of that day," writes Timothy George. "Carey, Marshman, and Ward assumed this role for themselves. Standing at a busy intersection of four roads, they began to sing a 'Christian ballad.' People looked out of their houses, stopped their business activities, and gathered around in astonishment at the sight." The ballad related the story of an Indian man who renounced various Hindu gods and put his faith in Christ. Printed copies were distributed to the curious bystanders.[19]

Carey's first fifteen years at Serampore were years of cooperation and teamwork. Except for occasional problems such as the one relating to his second marriage, the little Baptist community in India lived in harmony. But the peace did not last, and the fifteen years that followed were filled with turmoil. The spirit of unity was broken when new missionaries arrived who were unwilling to live in the communal fashion of the Serampore missionaries. One missionary demanded "a separate house, stable, and servants." There were other differences too. The new missionaries found their seniors—particularly Joshua Marshman—dictatorial, assigning them duties and locations not to their liking. The senior workers were settled into their system, and they were not open to change. Bitter accusations were made against the senior missionaries, and the result was a split between the two groups. The junior missionaries formed the Calcutta Missionary Union and began working only miles away from their Baptist colleagues. "Indelicate" was the word William Ward used to describe the situation.[20]

The ordeal became even more critical when the Home Committee received the news and became involved. The original committee headed by Andrew Fuller no longer existed. That little committee of three had grown, and most of the members knew Carey only through his letters. Fuller and one of the other original members had died, leaving the home committee clearly stacked in favor of the junior members whom it had personally commissioned as missionaries. While Fuller had been at the helm, he had insisted for two reasons that Serampore be self-governing: "One is, we think them better able to govern themselves than we are to govern them. Another is, they are at too great a distance to wait for our direction."[21] But the reconstructed home committee strongly disagreed. The members believed that all the important affairs of the Serampore Mission should be under their direct control. Finally, in 1826, after years of wearying conflict, the Serampore Mission severed its relationship with the Baptist Missionary Society.

The final split between Serampore and the Baptist Missionary Society was a financial blow to the Serampore missionaries. Although the Serampore team had been financially self-sufficient during most of its history, receiving only a small percentage of its funds from England, times were changing. There were missionaries at more than a dozen outstations who needed support, and medical care was needed for others. No longer could the Serampore team support them all. Carey and Marshman (Ward having since died) had no choice but to swallow their pride and submit themselves and the mission to the authority of the Society. Soon after that a substantial sum of money and kind letters arrived from the home committee. The healing process had begun.

Carey's goal was to build an indigenous church "by means of native preachers" and by providing the Scriptures in the native tongue.

Carey died in 1834, leaving a legacy for other missionaries to follow. In addition to evangelism, education, and translation, he had focused his attention on social issues—particularly in his long struggle against widow burning and infanticide. But otherwise, he sought to leave the culture intact. Carey was ahead of his time in missionary methodology. He had respect for the Indian culture, and he never tried to import Western substitutes as so many missionaries who came after him would seek to do. His goal was to build an indigenous church "by means of native preachers" and by providing the Scriptures in the native tongue, and to that end he dedicated his life.

But Carey's influence was felt well beyond India. His work was being closely followed not only in England but also on the Continent and in America, where the inspiration derived from his daring example outweighed in importance all his accomplishments in India.

Adoniram and Ann Judson

While Carey and his colleagues were conducting mission work in India, the Judsons were initiating mission outreach in Burma. Their destination had been India, but like so many missionaries before them, they discovered the East India Company to be an unyielding barrier to missionary work. After months of complications and delays, they were forced to leave India. They painfully separated from Carey and the other missionaries and sailed to Burma. There they would spend the rest of their lives under extreme hardship and privation in an effort to bring the gospel to the people of that closed and uninviting land.

Even as layers of popular mythology surrounded Carey, so also with Ann and Adoniram Judson, who became the heroes of America's first venture into overseas missions. As with many missionaries of this era, the biographical material is laudatory and limited by lack of original sources. According to his "official" biographer, Adoniram, due to "peculiar views of duty . . . had caused to be destroyed" all of his early family letters and personal papers. And later on, during his imprisonment, Ann destroyed his more current correspondence—no doubt fearing the letters would fall into the hands of Burmese authorities.[22]

Adoniram Judson was born in Massachusetts in 1788, the son of a Congregational minister. He was barely sixteen when he entered Brown University, and he graduated three years later as valedictorian of his class. During his student days, according to his biographers, he had grown close to a fellow student, Jacob Eames, who espoused deism, a denial of the personal God of the Bible. But Eames's views made a strong impact on young Judson, who had grown dissatisfied with the biblical faith of his father. After graduation Judson returned home to teach school, but he was restless. Disregarding his parents' pleas, he set out for New York City, hoping to become a playwright.

His stay in New York was short and unfulfilling. After a matter of weeks he was on his way back to New England, dejected and frustrated about his future. He stopped one night at an inn, during which time his sleep was interrupted by the groans of a sick man in the room next to his. In the morning, as the story goes, he inquired about the unfortunate traveler, only to be informed that the man—Jacob Eames—had died during the night. It was a terrible shock to the twenty-year-old Judson, a time for soul-searching as he slowly made his way home.

There was an air of excitement at the parsonage at Plymouth when Adoniram arrived home in September of 1808. His father was one of several ministers involved in establishing a new seminary at Andover that, unlike Harvard and the other New England divinity schools, would stand on the orthodox tenets of the faith. With the encouragement of his father and the other ministers, Adoniram agreed to enroll. He was admitted as a special student, making no profession of faith, but after only a few months he made a "solemn dedication" of himself to God.[23]

Soon after this commitment, Adoniram read a printed copy of a stirring missionary message given by a British minister. So moved was he that he vowed he would be the first American foreign missionary. Andover Seminary was hardly a beehive of missionary zeal, but there were other students who were very supportive, including Samuel Mills from Williams College, who had been the leader of the "Haystack Prayer Meeting" some years before. This outdoor prayer meeting, an unplanned event, was a landmark in American foreign missions. A group of missionary-minded Williams College students, known as the Society of the Brethren, often met outside for prayer. Caught in a thunderstorm one afternoon, they took shelter under a nearby haystack. It was there under that haystack that they pledged themselves to missionary service. The son of a minister, Mills listened to stories of the missionary pioneers from his mother. Though he never served as an overseas missionary, he was, according to Alan Neely, "a prime mover in the founding of the first foreign mission societies in North America."[24] He led in the formation of the American Board of Commissioners for Foreign

Adoniram Judson, pioneer missionary to Burma.

Missions, the American Bible Society, the United Foreign Mission Society, and other benevolent organizations.

Unable to secure the necessary funds for a missionary vocation from the newly formed American Board, Adoniram Judson sailed to England in hopes of obtaining funding for himself and six others through the London Missionary Society (LMS). The LMS, he discovered, was not averse to sponsoring an American missionary, but the directors were not willing to finance him under the American Board. He was prepared to offer himself and his colleagues to the LMS, but when word came of a sizable inheritance received by the American Board, he returned home.

Before he had gone to England, Adoniram had "commenced an acquaintanceship" with Ann ("Nancy") Hasseltine. Some years earlier Ann, like Adoniram, had undergone a life-changing religious conversion and had sensed a call to overseas missions—a call not prompted by "an attachment to an earthly object," meaning Adoniram, but because of an "obligation to God . . . with a full conviction of its being a call."[25] In February of 1812 she and Adoniram were married, and thirteen days later they set sail for India, arriving in Calcutta in mid-June.

Ann (Nancy) Hasseltine Judson, the first wife of Adoniram Judson.

For Adoniram and Ann the long sea voyage was more than an extended honeymoon. They spent many hours in Bible study—with a particular focus on the meaning and mode of baptism, a subject that had been weighing on Adoniram's mind. The more he studied the more convinced he became that the Congregational view of infant baptism by sprinkling was wrong. Ann was initially distressed, arguing that the issue was not crucial and stating that even if he became a Baptist she would not. After more study and much persuasion, however, she accepted his view, and after arriving in India they were both baptized by William Ward of Serampore.

When word reached home that the Judsons as well as Luther Rice (one of the other six missionaries commissioned to India by the American Board) had become Baptists, there was an uproar among the Congregationalists. How could their star missionary desert them after all they had invested in him? The Baptists, however, were pleased, and they quickly moved to form their own missionary society and underwrite the necessary support.

Unable to remain in India, the Judsons traveled from place to place until they settled in Burma, which had been Adoniram's first choice for mission work—until he heard frightening reports of brutal treatment of foreigners. Their arrival in Rangoon was a depressing and difficult time for them. Ann, who had undergone a stillbirth on the voyage, was bedridden. Unlike India, Burma had no European community. Poverty was everywhere. The narrow, filthy streets of Rangoon were lined with run-down huts. They were not the first Protestant missionaries in Burma. Others had come and gone, but only Felix Carey and his wife remained. They left soon after the Judsons arrived when Felix was offered a position by the Burmese government (to which his father had bitterly commented, "Felix is shriveled from a missionary into an ambassador"). Later Felix returned to India to join his father in the mission work there.

Two years after they had sailed from America, Adoniram and Ann were serving alone in Burma, spending up to twelve hours a day in language study. The large Baptist mission house in Rangoon had been left to them. Ann, through her daily contacts with Burmese women, caught on to the spoken tongue quickly, but Adoniram struggled laboriously with the written language, a continual sequence of letters with no punctuation or capitals and no divisions between words, sentences, or paragraphs.

Language was not the only barrier standing between the Judsons and the Burmese people. They could find no Burmese concept of an eternal God who personally cared for them. Their first attempts to share the gospel were discouraging: "You cannot imagine how very difficult it is to give them any idea of the true God and the way of salvation by Christ, since their present ideas of deity are

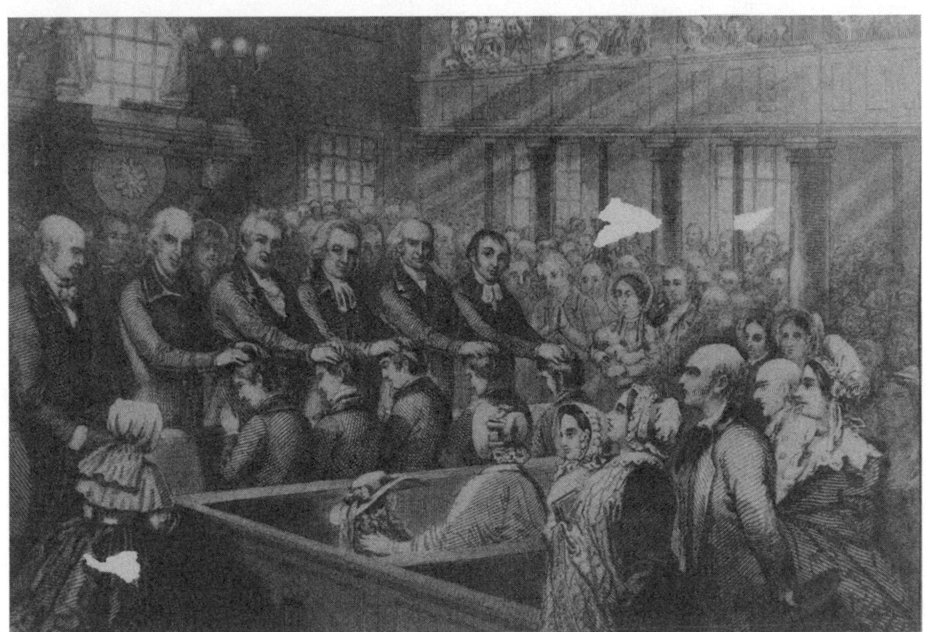

America's first foreign missionaries, commissioned February 5, 1812.

The Judsons aboard the Caravan *leaving Crowninshield's Wharf in Salem, Massachusetts, February 18, 1812.*

so very low." Buddhism was the religion of Burma, a religion of ritual and idol worship: "It is now two thousand years since Gaudama [Gautama], their last deity, entered on his state of perfection; and though he now ceases to exist, they still worship a hair of his head, which is enshrined in an enormous pagoda, to which the Burmans go every eighth day."[26]

The Judsons' status as the only Protestant missionaries in Burma was brief. Not long after they moved into the spacious mission house, their privacy ended as they made room for George and Phebe Hough and their children. Hough, a printer, came with his press and type and soon was printing portions of Scripture that Adoniram had slowly been translating. Within two years, two more families arrived; but death, disease, and early departures kept the mission force small.

Burma was a discouraging field of service. At times there were encouraging signs of interest, but then the inquiries would suddenly drop off as rumors of official crackdowns surfaced. Toleration of the missionaries fluctuated from one extreme to another with the continual turnover of viceroys in Rangoon. When the Judsons were in favor at the court, they were free to propagate the gospel and the Burmese responded to the relaxed controls; but when they were out of favor, they maintained a low profile, spending their time at the mission house in translation work.

From their early days in Rangoon, the Judsons were unhappy with the out-of-the-way location of the mission house. For a short while they moved out of the mission house and lived in a small dwelling among the teeming population of the city, but a fire ravaged their area and drove them back to the secluded mission house. However, their dream of attracting large numbers of people came to fruition through the concept of a *zayat*. A *zayat* was a shelter open to anyone who wanted to rest or to discuss the day's events or to listen to Buddhist lay teachers who often stopped by. It was a place to relax and forget the pressures of the day, and there were many such shelters in Rangoon. In 1819, five years after the Judsons arrived in Burma, they secured property not far from the mission house on the Pagoda Road, a well-traveled thoroughfare. Their *zayat* was a 20-by-20-foot hut with a wide veranda, all elevated on poles several feet off the ground. This was not to be an Asian version of a New England meeting-house. They attended a religious service at a nearby *zayat* to familiarize themselves with seating patterns and other cultural peculiarities.

The concept worked. Almost immediately visitors who would never have come to the mission house began stopping by, and the Judsons entered a new phase of their ministry. The following month Maung Nau made profession of faith at a Sunday service in the *zayat* packed with Burmese people. This was the beginning of the Burmese church in Rangoon, and by the summer of 1820 there were ten baptized members. From the beginning, the Burmese converts took an active role in evangelism: one woman opened a school in her house; a young man became an assistant pastor; and others distributed tracts. The work went forward even when the Judsons were away.

Both Adoniram and Ann suffered frequent bouts of tropical fevers, and baby Roger, born to them the year after they settled in Rangoon, died of fever at six months. In 1820 they returned to India for medical care for Ann, and two years later she took an extended sick leave back to the United States.

While Ann was away, Adoniram buried himself in his translation work, completing the New Testament in less than a year. In the meantime, his situation had drastically changed. Dr. Jonathan Price, a medical missionary working with Adoniram, was ordered to appear before the emperor at Ava, several weeks' journey upriver. Adoniram, fluent in the Burmese language, felt obligated to accompany him. For a time the two missionaries enjoyed the favor of the royal court, but by early 1824 the political situation in Burma began to look ominous. Ann had returned from the United States, and she joined Adoniram in Ava, but their reunion was brief. War broke out between Burma and England, and all foreigners were suspected of being spies. Both Adoniram and Price were arrested and confined in a death prison, where they awaited execution.

Life in prison was appalling. The missionaries were incarcerated with common criminals in a filthy, vermin-infested, dank prison house, with fetters binding their ankles. At night the Spotted Faces (prison guards whose face and chest

INDIA AND BURMA

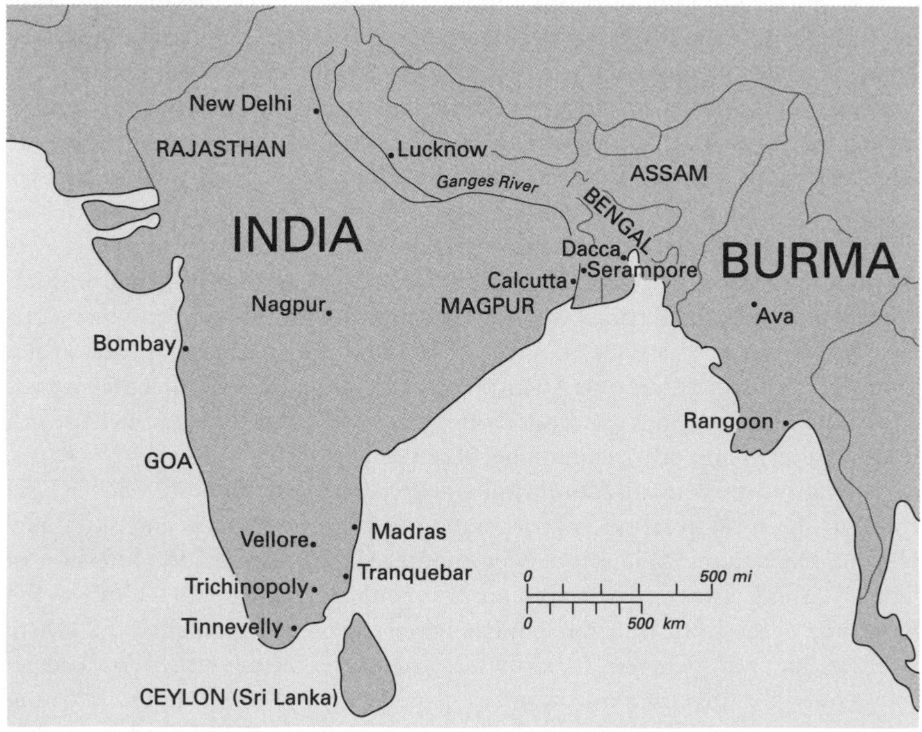

were branded for being one-time criminals themselves) hoisted the ankle fetters to a pole suspended from the ceiling, until only their heads and shoulders rested on the ground. By morning the weary prisoners were numb and stiff, but the daytime offered them little relief. Each day executions were carried out, and the prisoners never knew who would be next.

Adoniram's suffering was difficult for Ann. Daily she sought out officials, explaining that, as an American citizen, Adoniram had no connections with the British government. Sometimes her pleas and bribes allowed her a brief visit and gained Adoniram temporary relief; but all the while he continued to languish in prison. Her visits stopped for a time, but then in mid-February of 1825, eight months after Adoniram had been arrested, she returned carrying a small bundle—baby Maria, less than three weeks old.

The following May, with British troops marching toward Ava, the prisoners were suddenly removed from the prison house and forced on a death march to a location farther north. Having been bound in prison for most of a year without exercise, the prisoners were unprepared for the arduous pace under the scorching sun, and some died on the way. For Adoniram death would have been relief. His bare feet were raw and bleeding—each step was excruciating. As they marched, they crossed a bridge spanning a dry rocky riverbed, and for a moment he was tempted to hurl himself over the edge and end it all.

Within days, Ann arrived at the new location, once again pleading her husband's case. But her own life and baby Maria's was now in jeopardy. She was so ill that she could no longer nurse the baby. Sympathetic guards permitted Adoniram to go out of the prison twice daily to seek nourishment for his baby from other nursing mothers.

Finally, in November of 1825, after nearly a year and a half of prison confinement, Adoniram was released with the stipulation that he would help interpret peace negotiations with the British. He was also allowed a reunion with Ann and the baby. Of this time Ann wrote, "No persons on earth were ever happier than we were during the fortnight we passed at the English Camp."[27] After that, they returned to Rangoon for a short time and then went to Amherst, where Ann remained with Maria while Adoniram returned to help finalize the negotiations. The weeks dragged into months, and before he was able to return, Adoniram received a letter with a black seal. Ann had died of fever, followed a few months later by baby Maria.

Judson's immediate reaction to Ann's death was to drown his sorrows in work. But his heart was not in his labors.

Judson's immediate reaction to her death was to drown his sorrows in work. For more than a year he kept up a hectic pace of translation work and evangelism, but his heart was not in his labors. He attempted to suppress his guilt and grief, but he could not forgive himself for not being with Ann and the baby when he was needed most. As the depression increased, his output decreased, and he avoided contact with others—no longer eating with the other missionaries at the mission house. Finally, some two years after Ann's death, he went into the jungle, built a hut, and lived as a recluse. He dug a grave where he kept vigil for days on end, filling his mind with morbid thoughts of death. Spiritual desolation engulfed him: "God is to me the Great Unknown. I believe in him, but I find him not."[28]

Adoniram's mental problems raised great concern among both missionaries and native converts. They visited him and brought him food and prayed for him. Slowly, he recovered from the paralyzing depression—with a new depth of spirituality that intensified his ministry. He traveled in Burma, helping other missionaries at their outposts. As he did, he sensed a new spirit of interest "through the whole length and breadth of the land." It was a profound feeling: "I sometimes feel alarmed like a person who sees a mighty engine beginning to move, over which he knows he has no control."[29]

As exhilarating as Judson's itinerant ministry was, he knew that there was an even greater task to be accomplished—completing the Burmese Bible. That required setting aside two years and keeping up a pace of translating of more than twenty-five Old Testament verses each day from Hebrew into Burmese—

two enormously complex languages. He met his goal, but then followed more years of revision work. Not until 1840, fourteen years after Ann's death, was he able to send the last page of his Burmese Bible to the printer.

In the meantime, Judson had been concentrating on more than his revisions. In 1834, at the age of forty-six, he married Sarah Boardman, a thirty-year-old widow who had continued her mission work after the death of her husband. During the first ten years of their marriage, she gave birth to eight children (and buried two). The strain was too much. In 1845, the year after her last child was born, while they were en route to the United States, Sarah died.

Adoniram and three of their children who had accompanied Sarah arrived in America deeply sorrowful at a time that would have been a joyous reunion with family and friends. It had been thirty-three years since he had last seen his native land. Country towns and fishing wharves had turned into great cities and seaports. He hardly recognized the once-familiar New England countryside. Thirty-three years of progress had changed his homeland and had changed him. He suddenly found himself a celebrity. Everybody, it seemed, wanted to see and hear this man whose name had become a household word and whose missionary work had become a legend. Though he shunned publicity, he agreed to accommodate his enthusiastic supporters and began a tiring circuit of speaking engagements.

During his travels, Judson was introduced to Emily Chubbock, a young author of popular fiction written under the pseudonym Fanny Forrester. He was impressed with her lively writing style, but he was astounded that such brilliant talent of a professing Christian (and a Baptist at that) would be wasted on secular endeavors. His suggestion that Emily write a biography of Sarah was eagerly accepted, and their friendship quickly blossomed. He proposed marriage in January of 1846, less than a month after their first meeting. The decision to marry Emily was controversial. Judson was a venerated saint of Protestant America, and as such the prospects of his marrying a secular author still in her twenties, only half his age, was viewed with shock and displeasure. But the barrage of criticism did not dissuade them, and in June of 1846 they were married.

The following month they sailed for Burma, leaving Adoniram's three children in the care of two different families—never to see their father again. There were three more children who had been left behind in Burma. The Judson saga, as much as any missionary story, illustrates the trauma that missionary families endured—the trauma of crying, frightened little ones clinging to their parents, never comprehending why they were being torn from the only love and security they had ever known. Yet the children somehow weathered these ordeals. Of Judson's five children by Sarah who grew to adulthood, two became ministers, one a physician, another a headmistress of an academy, and another served in the Union Army until he was disabled in battle.

In November of 1846 Adoniram and his new bride arrived in Burma. Emily had faired the voyage well and was ready to fill Sarah's shoes to the best of her ability. She became a mother to Judson's little ones (only two of whom had survived), and she enthusiastically plunged into language study and missionary work, never forgetting her talent for writing. Through her pen came some graphic pictures of the stark reality of missionary life. She was bothered by the "thousands and thousands of bats," but most of the other little creatures she took in stride:

> We are blessed with our full share of cockroaches, beetles, lizards, rats, ants, mosquitoes, and bed-bugs. With the last the woodwork is all alive, and the ants troop over the house in great droves. . . . Perhaps twenty have crossed my paper since I have been writing. Only one cockroach has paid me a visit, but the neglect of these gentlemen has been fully made up by a company of black bugs about the size of the end of your finger—nameless adventurers.[30]

Adoniram and Emily served three years together in Burma. The birth of a baby girl brought happiness to them, but much of the time was marred by illness. In the spring of 1850, with Emily soon expecting another child, Adoniram, seriously ill, left on a sea voyage. Less than a week later he died and was buried at sea. Ten days later Emily underwent a stillbirth, and not until August did she hear of her husband's death. The following January she, along with her daughter and Adoniram's two young sons, sailed for Boston to make a home for the children in the United States. But her own health was broken. She died three years later at the age of thirty-six.

Adoniram Judson, unlike William Carey, left behind a legacy of evangelistic ministry that was carried on through succeeding generations. Maung Ing, his fourth convert, had shown his loyalty throughout Adoniram's prison term and worked with him after he was released. Ing's fourth daughter, Mei-Phaw, was also a Christian. Her life was threatened by her own son, Tha Doon Aung, who was a "king's man" and a "rigid Buddhist." In the very act of attacking his mother, Tha Doon Aung suddenly recognized the power of his mother's faith and was converted. His children and grandchildren carried on the faith, and his great-grandson, Tin Maung Tun, founded "Witnessing for Christ," an evangelistic movement that has continued to this day the work the Judsons started.[31]

George and Sarah Boardman

Sarah and George Boardman arrived in Burma from the United States at the close of the Anglo-Burmese War, soon after the death of Ann Judson. They knew well the perils of coming to such a land. In fact, their concern for Burmese missions and their subsequent marriage was stimulated by the untimely death of James Coleman, one of Judson's missionary colleagues. So deeply moved by this sacrifice was George Boardman, a graduate of Colby College, that he enrolled at Andover Seminary to prepare for missionary service. In much the same way Sarah Hall, a sober-minded teenager and the oldest of thirteen children, was touched by the tragedy. Her response was to write a poem about Coleman—lines that would change the course of her life. The poem, published in a religious journal, stirred the curiosity of Boardman. He was not satisfied until he located her, and within months after their initial meeting, they became engaged.

The Boardmans were known for their ministry among the Karens, a mountain tribe spurned by the more sophisticated Burmese. The Karens had a long tradition that white men would one day bring the "book of life" to them, and thus they were open to the teaching of the missionaries who had a *book*. Shortly after the Boardmans arrived in Burma, they left the comfortable mission confines of Moulmein to move to Tavoy for pioneer work among the Karens. With them they brought Ko Tha Byu, a converted criminal who by his own admission had committed some thirty murders. He was a native Karen who had a vibrant testimony and a contagious Christian faith—so much so that after revival broke out, his house was broken down as a result of people pressing in to see him. A letter requesting help was sent to Adoniram Judson: "We are in distress and send to you for relief. For the last several days, our house and the house of Ko Tha Byu, ten cubits square, have been thronged.... Karens are thronging in from many places."[32] The Boardmans worked with him in their evangelistic ministry, but George Boardman's health was seriously declining. He died in 1831 after less than five years in Burma. Unlike Judson, who served several years before he saw even one convert, Boardman had the privilege of seeing many make profession of faith. During the last two months of his life, fifty-seven Karens were baptized, and the Tavoy church alone had seventy members. In the years that followed, Ko Tha Byu continued on in work despite strong persecution from those who resented his effective evangelistic ministry.

Ko Tha Byu, a converted criminal, had a vibrant testimony—so much so that after revival broke out, his house was broken down as a result of people pressing in to see him.

After her husband's death, Sarah was tempted to return to the United States with little George, her two-year-old son, but through Judson's urging, she decided to continue in her ministry. She had established a girls' school and feared that it would falter were she to leave. For three years she remained with the Karens, spending her time teaching and continuing her husband's itinerant ministry into the mountain villages with her son, whom the Karens affectionately called "Little Chief."

In 1834, Adoniram Judson came to Tavoy to visit Sarah, and during his extended visit they were married. The following year the six-year-old "Little Chief" was sent to the United States to be properly educated. It was a traumatic experience for the boy, whom Sarah described as having "a clinging tenderness and sensitivity which peculiarly unfitted him for contact with strangers."[33] He never saw his mother again. The emptiness in Sarah's life was soon filled with more little ones, and she became encumbered with the duties of motherhood, but she never entirely set aside her ministry to the Burmese people. In addition to teaching a girls' school, she made effective use of her language skills. She wrote hymns and curriculum material in Burmese and translated other material, including part of *Pilgrim's Progress,* which she was working on at the time of her death.

Sarah's marriage to Judson did not mean an end to the missionary involvement with the Karens. Others came to work among them and to translate Scripture, and by the 1850s there were more than ten thousand church members.

Alexander Duff

One of the most innovative missionaries to serve in India was Alexander Duff, who arrived in Calcutta with his wife in 1830. Duff had not been impressed with the reports of missionary work in India, some of which claimed evangelism among the Indians was a complete failure. The critics charged that the few converts that had been made were largely among the outcastes, who then remained dependent on the mission with no influence on their fellow countrymen. While the reports may have been unduly pessimistic, it was true that no concerted effort had been made to reach high-caste Indians, and it was Duff's mission to remedy that situation.

Duff was born and raised in Scotland and educated at the University of St. Andrews. The evangelical awakening in Scotland during the 1820s transformed this young university student, and at the age of twenty-three he became the first overseas missionary of the Church of Scotland. But there were setbacks before he even began. On the voyage to India there were two shipwrecks, resulting in the loss of his entire personal library—a crushing blow to one as consumed as he was with scholarship and education.

On arriving in India, Duff put his plan into action—teaching arts and sciences in English to India's educated elite, who were very interested in Western ideas and education. The Bible would also be taught and studied, and through this method Duff was convinced that Christianity would be firmly planted in India. His critics were numerous—both missionaries and Indian educators—but he had two notable supporters: the aged and highly respected William Carey, and Ram Mohum Roy, an educated and liberal Brahman. Roy was a popular reformer with a wide following, and it was largely his influence that opened up opportunities. Roy prided himself in being open-minded and did not object to Duff's emphasis on the Bible. He had read the Bible without becoming a Christian, and he urged Duff's students to do the same and judge for themselves.

Within a few short months, Duff opened his school. He started out with five students under a banyan tree, but word spread quickly. By the end of the week there were more than three hundred students clamoring to enroll. The school was a success in its efforts to disseminate Western education and perhaps only slightly less so in its efforts to disseminate the gospel. Within three years he had baptized four converts, a small number for the size of his school. But even the news of those few conversions created such a disturbance that students left and his work for a time was jeopardized. Slowly students returned, however, and by the end of his first decade in India his school enrollment averaged eight hundred. Later he opened a school for high-caste girls that also attracted wide interest.

The major criticism of Duff's work was that the vast majority of his students came to his school only for the secular education, and of these thousands there were only thirty-three recorded converts during his lifetime. Most of those thirty-three, however, were young men from influential families who themselves became influential Christians. Some of them served as missionaries and ministers, and others became prominent Christian lay leaders.

Alexander Duff, missionary educator in India.

Duff was a staunch, sober, humorless Presbyterian whose monumental achievements were not fulfilled without sacrifice to his family life. In 1839 he and his wife returned to India after their first furlough, leaving their four little children (including their infant boy) behind with a "widow-lady," and they did not return until 1850, when that little boy was eleven years old—a time remembered with mixed emotions. Wasting no time to drill his son on his catechism, Duff, who was obviously not schooled in the principles of positive reinforcement, rebuked him: "The heathen boys in my Institution in Calcutta know more of the Bible than you do."[34]

Young Duff later described his father as having "no wit, no humour, and still less of rollicking fun." He resented his father's aloofness, and his own recollections of his parents' departure for India in 1855, when he was a teenager, certainly bear this out:

> I . . . well remember how my mother's and my own heart were well-nigh breaking, and how at the London Bridge my father possessed himself of the morning *Times,* and left us to cry our eyes out in mutual sorrow. . . . And so we parted . . . a sadder parting as between mother and son there never was.

> The father buried in his *Times* . . . parted from the son without any regret on the latter's part.[35]

If Duff failed as a father, he succeeded as a missionary statesman. During his second furlough he toured England, Ireland, Scotland, Wales, and the United States; and everywhere he went he was highly acclaimed. In the United States he preached to Congress and had a private meeting with the president. He has been described as "the most eloquent missionary orator"[36] of his century, and his impact on foreign missions was significant. Through his influence hundreds volunteered for foreign missionary service, and tens of thousands contributed financially to the cause. His concept of combining education and evangelism was copied the world over, despite the controversy the method frequently aroused.

While Duff was being hailed as an innovator in evangelizing the elite, others continued to work with the untouchables and the members of the degraded low castes. In 1865 John and Harriet Clough of the American Baptist Mission began their work at the Lone Star Mission at Ongole, India. Their ministry included famine relief, and in 1878 they witnessed a mass movement among the outcastes, baptizing some nine thousand converts during a six-week period. Clough strongly believed that converts should remain in their social setting as opposed to attaching themselves to a mission compound as was sometimes the case. "For this purpose his evangelistic work was centered on villages," writes Frederick Downs, "where he encouraged inquirers to wait until a family or group was ready to be baptized with them. Churches were organized in the villages in accordance with indigenous social structures." Clough also strongly promoted the ministry of native preachers, "encouraging them to adopt as their model the Hindu guru."[37]

There were other missionaries who strongly encouraged the ministry of Indian evangelists and whose ministry led to mass movements, among them the noted Methodist Bishop, James Thoburn. Sherwood Eddy, a leading figure in the Student Volunteer Movement, captured the spirit of Thoburn's ministry in his own recollections:

> My first contact with him was at the Northfield Students Conference in 1890. He made a powerful appeal, voicing the needs of India, and mentioning incidentally that very simple Indian workers could be supported for thirty dollars a year, though he made no request for money. Mr. Moody silenced the applause which greeted this address by saying it would be better to support some of Bishop Thoburn's workers than merely to applaud. He said that he and Mr. Sankey would each take one subscription, and that a leader on the platform would be ready to receive others. I was one of the hundred there who gave thirty dollars each, and Bishop Thoburn was left breathless as he received three thousand dollars contributed on the spot. At the end of the same year, when I was told that the Indian worker supported by my thirty dollars had brought over a hundred men to Christ, I took another subscription, and

> another, and finally sold the gold case of my watch to support yet one more evangelist.[38]

James and Isabella Thoburn

Born into an Irish immigrant family from Ohio, James Thoburn and his sister Isabella both served as missionaries to India, he as an evangelist, church planter, pastor, and later a bishop, and she as an educator. After completing studies at Allegheny College, James entered the Methodist ministry and sailed to India with his wife Sarah in 1859. Through his encouragement, Isabella joined them in 1866 in Luchnow, where "there was not one woman who could read or write, and there was bitter prejudice on the part of the Hindus against the education of women."[39] It was an inauspicious beginning with only six girls, but the enrollment quickly grew to more than twenty, and the mission purchased property for a boarding school. Bringing girls together to live and study was a monumental undertaking. Caste was the issue—an issue that would continue for generations to thwart mission work in India. In his biography of his sister, James Thoburn addressed this problem:

> Many differences, some of them petty and some of them painful, grew out of this question of race from time to time, and it is probable that Miss Thoburn at times suffered more acutely in her feelings on this account than from any other one cause during her whole life in India. She believed that in a country like India, where the very atmosphere seemed surcharged with caste and class feeling, it would be impossible to plant a pure and aggressive Christianity, unless the problem of raising up a people "of one mind and one heart" could be practically solved. She knew well that this problem could never be solved by artificial adaptations. The highest could not be brought down to the level of the lowest, nor the lowest all elevated to the plane of the highest. There could be no uniformity of salary, of occupation, of dress, of style, of taste, or of position. And yet there could be, and there must be, a blessed unity which would bind all hearts in a common family relationship.[40]

James Thoburn's ministry had also been impeded by caste. Initially he had conducted village evangelism and church planting, but the work was slow, and he was searching for new strategies. In 1870 he sought help from William Taylor, a controversial Methodist minister known for his successful evangelistic campaigns and for his emphasis on self-supporting missionaries and mission churches. Taylor conducted a revival ministry in India for most of five years, paving the way, he believed, for others to follow. In Calcutta, however, he was met with indifference. Not until after he left India and Thoburn moved his own ministry to Calcutta did the church there begin to grow. Indeed, according to Gerald Anderson, "Thoburn presided over an era of rapid growth of the Methodist

Church in India, with mass movements of converts into membership, and expansion into Southeast Asia."[41]

In the meantime, Isabella Thoburn's school was growing, and the young women who were graduating wanted further education. When she returned home for furlough in the 1880s, she spoke strongly for the cause and distributed a leaflet in which she had written: "There are over one hundred colleges in India for young men, but only one for young women, and that not Christian. Think what efforts we would make if there were only one college for women in America, and, in some measure, let us recognize the universal sisterhood and make like efforts for the women of India."[42]

In 1887 the Isabella Thoburn College opened its doors—the first Christian women's college in Asia. It was an impossible achievement—at least in the minds of many observers in India. The great missionary educator Alexander Duff had scoffed, "You might as well try to scale a wall fifty feet high as to educate the women of India."[43] But despite the obstacles, Isabella had fulfilled her dream—a dream that was shared with many of her supporters when she returned to America with Lilavati Singh, a brilliant student who later taught at the college. Singh impressed audiences with her academic excellence and her biblical insights. When she spoke at the Ecumenical Missionary Conference in New York in 1900, President Harrison, who was in the audience, reportedly said that if he had "given a million dollars to foreign missions," and Singh was all there was to show for it, he would have felt "amply repaid."[44]

Like her brother James, Isabella would leave a legacy of training Indian nationals for the gospel ministry. Speaking of her teacher, Lilavati Singh wrote:

> I shall never forget her Sunday afternoon prayer-meetings with us. How clearly she explained the laws of the spiritual kingdom.... Another thing that Miss Thoburn trained us in particularly was voluntary Christian work.... Sunday after Sunday, two by two, bands of Christian girls and teachers ... still go out to the native part of the city to teach the little girls in the zenana [harem] of the blessed Savior.[45]

The final decades of the nineteenth century were decades of optimism. James Thoburn expanded his horizons, initiating Methodist mission outreach in Burma in 1879, and six years later in Singapore, and on to the Philippines in 1899. But he never turned away from the work in India—the land where one day "the entire out-caste and the lowest caste ... may speedily be won to Christ in tens of millions."[46]

There was similar optimism regarding the whole region. In 1892 Henry Mabie, secretary of the American Baptist Missionary Union, enthusiastically reflected on the growth of the Baptist Church in Burma and elsewhere. With confidence he quoted Adoniram Judson, who some seventy years earlier had predicted that "The churches of Jesus will soon supplant these idolatrous monuments, and the chanting of the devotees of Buddha will die away before the Christian hymn of praise." Mabie was brimming with confidence as the centennial of Baptist mission work approached: "The Orient," he exulted, "is pulsating with the world-thrill of human and divine action."[47] In the generations that followed, as missionaries were no longer permitted entry into Burma and India, the air of triumphalism faded.

SELECT BIBLIOGRAPHY

Anderson, Courtney. *To the Golden Shore: The Life of Adoniram Judson.* Grand Rapids: Zondervan, 1972.

Beck, James R. *Dorothy Carey: The Tragic and Untold Story of Mrs. William Carey.* Grand Rapids: Baker, 1992.

Brumberg, Joan Jacobs. *Mission for Life: The Story of the Family of Adoniram Judson.* New York: Free Press, 1980.

Drewery, Mary. *William Carey: A Biography.* Grand Rapids: Zondervan, 1979.

George, Timothy. *Faithful Witness: The Life and Mission of William Carey.* Birmingham: New Hope, 1991.

Oldham, W. F. *Thoburn—Called of God.* New York: Methodist Book Concern, 1918.

Paton, William. *Alexander Duff: Pioneer of Missionary Education.* New York: Doran, 1922.

Richter, Julius. *A History of Missions in India.* New York: Fleming H. Revell, 1908.

Thoburn, James M. *Life of Isabella Thoburn.* New York: Eaton & Mains, 1903.

6

Black Africa: "The White Man's Graveyard"

African Christianity, according to Andrew Walls, should be seen as "potentially the *representative* Christianity of the twenty-first century." No longer is African Christianity a *missionary* religion. It carries distinctives all its own and exemplifies Christianity of the present and future. "The Christianity typical of the twenty-first century," continues Walls, "will be shaped by the events and processes that take place in the southern continents, and above all by those that take place in Africa.[1] This role for African Christianity—even if no more than symbolic—makes the study of the missionary movement to that region critical to our understanding of the church both present and future.

Black Africa, known for centuries as "the white man's graveyard," has claimed the lives of more Protestant missionaries than any other area of the world. Evangelism was a costly undertaking, but the investment paid rich dividends. Although Protestant missions got off to a late start in Subsaharan Africa (in comparison to Asia), it has been one of the most fruitful "mission fields" in the world—though not in the early generations of mission outreach. The rapid expansion of the church came primarily in the twentieth century. Indeed, church growth in the nineteenth century was often painfully slow, but it was the nineteenth-century missionary pioneers who risked all to open the way for Christianity in Africa.

Modern Protestant missions to Africa began during the eighteenth century in the Cape Colony with the Moravians. By the end of that century, the London Missionary Society had entered South Africa and, with Robert Moffat, began penetrating into the interior, though the majority of the missionaries remained in the healthier environment south of the Orange River and in the coastal regions. The thrust of Protestant missionary activity moved from south to north, and by the mid-nineteenth century the Baptists, Anglicans, and Presbyterians each had a solid foothold on the west coast. These were soon followed by permanent mission stations on the east coast, with almost all of Black Africa opened up to missionaries by the end of the century.

In spite of the tremendous sacrifice, African missions have been harshly criticized, particularly in regard to the missionaries' ties to colonialism and their exporting of European civilization. Moffat's philosophy of the "Bible and plough" was expanded by Livingstone's philosophy of "Commerce and Christianity," and even Mary Slessor insisted on the necessity of trade to raise the African standard of living and to make the people more suited to Christian ethical standards. In the eyes of the missionaries, the future of Christianity in Africa depended on European influence and trade, and few missionaries opposed the underlying concepts of imperialism that have come under fire in recent generations. But such harsh criticism may be unwarranted.

It is true that missionaries were often closely tied to colonialism, unashamedly identifying European civilization with the Christian message. But they, more than any other outside influence, fought against the evils that colonialism and imperialism brought. They waged long and bitter battles (sometimes physically) against the heinous traffic in human cargo. And after the demise of slave trade, they raised their voices against other crimes, including the bloody tactics used by King Leopold to extract rubber from the Congo. The majority of missionaries were pro-African, and their stand for racial justice often made them despised by their fellow Europeans. Indeed, it is no exaggeration to say that without the conscience of Christian missions, the crimes of colonialism might have been even more horrific.

The majority of missionaries were pro-African, and it is no exaggeration to say that without the conscience of Christian missions, the crimes of colonialism may have been even more horrific.

Missionaries have also been accused of being racists. They were. They were men and women of their time, and racist language and beliefs were commonplace. But perhaps more significant, they appear to have been significantly less racist than many of their contemporaries. It was the nineteenth-century intellectual of high society who viewed black Africans as inherently inferior—many rungs below Caucasians on the ethnologists' evolutionary ladder. Missionaries, on the other hand, were sometimes ridiculed in scholarly journals for their shallow thinking in regard to race, and most educated English citizens would have agreed with Mary Kingsley (whose Africa travelogue was widely circulated) when she criticized missionaries for their "difficulty in regarding the Africans as anything but a Man and a Brother" and their belief in "the spiritual equality of all colors of Christians."[2]

If missionaries frequently sounded like true nineteenth-century racists, it was because they viewed Africans (or any unchristianized peoples) to be degraded because of their lack of Christian moral teaching. Henry Drummond's views were characteristic. He described Africans as "half animal and half children, wholly savage and wholly heathen," but he qualified his blatant racism by concluding that "they are what we were once."[3]

Perhaps the greatest criticism of African missions has come from social scientists and anthropologists who have charged that Christian missions have wreaked havoc on African culture. It is true that missionaries of the nineteenth (and even the twentieth) century often failed to appreciate the distinctive qualities of unfamiliar cultures and failed to make Christianity compatible with the customs of other societies. But there were some customs, such as twin-murder and cannibalism and witchcraft, that did not contribute to a healthy environment. The missionaries' efforts to eradicate these practices helped preserve Africa's most valuable cultural asset—the people themselves.

The most significant missionary contribution that has profoundly affected African culture relates to Bible translation—an endeavor that influenced all aspects of life. This contribution "has few parallels, and should stand as a monument to the scaling down of cross-cultural barriers," writes Lamin Sanneh of Yale University. "We should give praise and honor to God that he raised in the Western church servants of his cause in Africa and elsewhere. The dry bones of many of these missionaries, rising from their unmarked graves, gave voices to our ancestors."[4]

The early Protestant missionaries to Africa, like Carey and his colleagues in India, were not ordained clergy. They were artisans and gardeners and factory workers who often spent much of their time as manual laborers and artisans in the mission work. Yet despite their mundane labors, they were missionary evangelists—and in some instances, notable Bible translators.

Robert and Mary Moffat

Robert Moffat is sometimes regarded as the patriarch of South African missions, a man who had a significant influence in that region for more than half a century. Yet even during his own lifetime, he was overshadowed by his famous son-in-law, often being referred to as "the father-in-law of David Livingstone." Moffat, nevertheless, was the far greater missionary of the two. He was an evangelist, a translator, an educator, a diplomat, and an explorer, and he effectively combined those roles to become one of the truly great missionaries to Africa.

Born in Scotland in 1795, Moffat was raised in humble circumstances that offered very limited education and no formal biblical training. His parents were Presbyterians with a strong missionary zeal, and on cold winter evenings his mother gathered the children around her and read aloud stories of missionary heroes. But young Moffat was not inclined toward spiritual things. He "ran off to sea" for a time, and at the age of fourteen he became apprenticed to a gardener, learning a skill that he would use the rest of his life.

At the age of seventeen, he moved to Cheshire, England, to begin his work as a gardener. There in 1814 he joined a small Methodist society that met in a nearby farmhouse—an association that offered him a harmonious blend of Scottish Calvinism and Methodist "enthusiasm." The following year, after making contact with William Roby, a director of the London Missionary Society (LMS), he applied to that board for missionary service. The society responded by saying that they could not "receive all who offered their services for missionary work" and were thus "obligated to select those who possess the most promising acquirements," which in their view did not include him. He was turned down.[5]

Undaunted by his rejection, Moffat secured a new gardening position near Roby's home and began studying theology with him on a private basis. After a year he again applied to the LMS, and this time he was accepted. Founded in 1795, the year of Moffat's birth, the LMS was an interdenominational evangelical mission board. In its twenty years it had seen steady growth and had missionaries stationed all over the globe. Moffat was sent to South Africa with four other new missionaries. After eighty-five days at sea they arrived in Cape Town to launch their missionary careers.

Moffat had hoped to begin his missionary career as a married man. During his last year as a gardener in England he had become interested in his employer's daughter, Mary Smith, whom he perceived as having a "warm missionary heart." Though her father was enthusiastic about Moffat's missionary plans, he was less excited about involving his only daughter into such work. So Moffat went to South Africa single, waiting more than three years before Mary's parents relented and agreed to let their twenty-four-year-old daughter join him.

In the meantime, Moffat was introduced to the realities of missionary work and African culture. He was distressed by the strong prejudice against missionaries by both the English and the Dutch colonists, and he was impatient when, for that very reason, government officials stood in the way of evangelism of the interior. But if he was disturbed by government policy, he was shocked by the open immorality and dissension among the missionaries themselves. Writing to the LMS secretary in London, Moffat lamented that "never was there a period when a body of missionaries were in such a confused and deplorable (and awful to add) degraded condition."[6]

Moffat was disturbed by government policy, but shocked by the open immorality and dissension among the missionaries themselves.

While the LMS had seen its share of problems (including moral lapses) with some of its Cape Colony missionaries, there were many who served honorably. The first missionary to South Africa was John T. Vanderkemp, a physician from Holland. Though the son of a Dutch Reformed pastor, the well-educated young Vanderkemp had become a religious skeptic and remained so until the tragic deaths of his wife and daughter in a boating accident, which he himself witnessed. With a renewed faith in Christ, he arrived in the Cape Colony in 1799 when he was past the age of fifty. He worked primarily among the Hottentots where, despite discouraging setbacks, he won hundreds of converts. Vanderkemp was greatly distressed by the slave trade he daily witnessed and spent thousands of dollars in freeing slaves, including a seventeen-year-old Malagasy slave girl whom he married when he was sixty—an act that created an uproar among the colonists and missionaries as well. Vanderkemp died in 1811 after only twelve years of missionary service, but he was recognized then and in the years that followed as one of the great pioneers of the LMS.

After several months of delays, Moffat and a married couple were granted permission to journey into the bleak arid regions of Namaqualand, hundreds of miles north of Cape Town. There he first met Afrikaner, a once-feared Hottentot chief, whose life had changed after coming in contact with a Dutch missionary. Moffat spent nearly two years at Afrikaner's camp and then invited him to travel to Cape Town so that the white colonists could see the change Christianity had made in this man, whose reputation for raiding colonists' farms was widely known. It worked, and Moffat's star as a missionary statesman began to rise.

Showing off Afrikaner was not Moffat's only reason for traveling back to Cape Town. In December of 1819, Mary Smith arrived from England, and three weeks later they were married. It was a happy union from the start and remained so for fifty-three years. Their honeymoon, a six-hundred-mile wagon trek northeast to Kuruman was a taste of their future together. There were parched deserts, dense forests, quagmire swamps, and raging rivers to be crossed, which no doubt made them grateful they were not alone. With them throughout their honeymoon was a single male missionary.

Kuruman was, in Moffat's eyes, a choice spot for a mission station. He had hoped Afrikaner and his people would move to the location, but Afrikaner died not long after their journey. The Moffats settled at the mouth of the Kuruman River, which was fed by a crystal-clear underground spring. "Here over the years," writes Adrian Hastings, "he built up the Mission of Kuruman with its canal, its irrigated gardens, its square stone houses standing in a straight line beside the canal, its fences, its fruit trees, its wheat, barley, grapes, and figs. By 1835, there were 500 acres under irrigation and a population of 700 souls."[7]

This model mission station consumed many years of arduous toil. Indeed, the Moffats' early years in Kuruman were filled with hardships. They lived in primitive conditions, their first home being a mud hut with the kitchen separate from the house. Although Mary was not used to doing heavy domestic work, she adapted to African life remarkably well. She washed clothes by hand in the river and cooked on an open fireplace. She soon overcame her aversion to cleaning the floors with cow dung and even recommended it: "It lays the dust better than anything, and kills the fleas which would otherwise breed abundantly."[8]

AFRICA

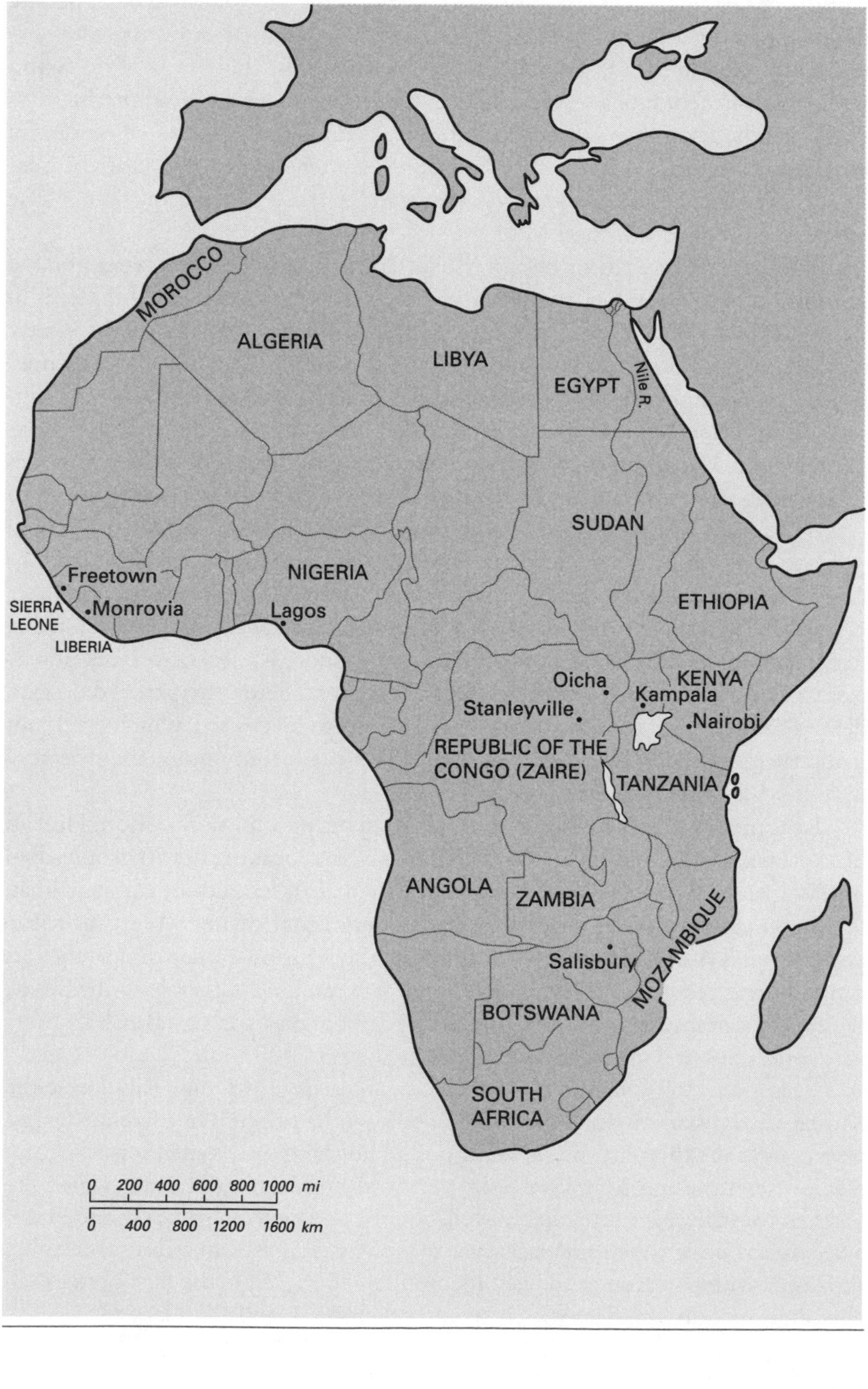

MOROCCO
ALGERIA
LIBYA
EGYPT
Nile R.
SUDAN
NIGERIA
Freetown
SIERRA LEONE
Monrovia
LIBERIA
Lagos
ETHIOPIA
KENYA
Oicha
Kampala
Stanleyville
Nairobi
REPUBLIC OF THE CONGO (ZAIRE)
TANZANIA
ANGOLA
ZAMBIA
MOZAMBIQUE
Salisbury
BOTSWANA
SOUTH AFRICA
0 200 400 600 800 1000 mi
0 400 800 1200 1600 km

The greater hardship at Kuruman related to their ministry. The Bechuanas, with whom the Moffats worked, were not receptive to the gospel message. Tribal superstitions prevailed, and when the official rainmaker could not prevent long periods of drought, Moffat was blamed. Theft also was common, and the Moffats' house was ransacked on many occasions. "Our labours," wrote Moffat, "might be compared to the attempts of . . . a husbandman labouring to transform the surface of a granite rock into arable land."[9]

As time passed, however, Moffat's prestige among the Bechuanas grew. In 1823, after only a few years at Kuruman, the situation in the area began to change. Waves of nomadic tribes began sweeping across the arid plains, and the very existence of the Bechuanas was in danger. Moffat exercised his diplomatic prowess, and through mediation and military arrangements with another tribe, he was able to avert the impending destruction of the Bechuanas. He became a civilian general of sorts, and on one occasion rode out to meet the enemy. Though his peace efforts failed and a fierce battle ensued, the invading Mantatee tribe was severely weakened and driven back.

From this point on, Moffat's leadership role at Kuruman was secure. As a diplomat and military leader, he commanded the highest respect, though there was little corresponding success in his evangelistic efforts. His converts were few. Polygamy was a nagging problem at Kuruman as it was elsewhere in Africa. How should the missionary counsel a convert who has many wives? Church membership was typically denied the individual, and consequently the church remained small. It was a discouraging situation, and Mary, particularly, was inclined to periods of despondency: "Could we but see the smallest fruit, we could rejoice midst the privations and toils which we bear; but as it is, our hands do often hang down."[10]

Perhaps the greatest reason for the slow progress of Christianity among the Bechuanas was simply a lack of understanding. Neither Moffat nor the Bechuanas fully comprehended the other's beliefs in spiritual matters. Moffat had little interest in the Bechuana religious traditions, and he sought to evangelize them with the mistaken impression that the tribe had no concept of or word for God. But an even greater handicap to his ministry was his failure to learn their language. For several years his sole means of communication was Cape Dutch, a trade language that some of the Bechuanas understood for rudimentary business transactions but that was hardly suitable for presenting a Christian message. Moffat wasted years of precious time trying to squeeze by on this shortcut, but he finally realized that learning the language, as difficult as it was, was the only solution to communicating the gospel. So convinced was he of this necessity that in 1827 he left Mary with their little ones, turned his back on his gardens, and went out into the bush to spend time with some of the men. For eleven weeks he immersed himself in language study.

On his return, he was ready to begin translating the Bible, a task that he began very slowly and that took him twenty-nine years to complete. Beginning with the gospel of Luke, he agonized over each sentence, and even then he was painfully aware that his translation was filled with errors. Only the patience of continual revising made the translation comprehensible. Printing the text also became a complicated ordeal. After traveling all the way to Cape Town in 1830, he found printers unwilling to print Scripture in a tribal tongue, fearing the equalizing tendencies it might have on the "inferior" race. His solution was to learn how to print himself and to secure a press for Kuruman.

Translating and printing the Bible often seemed like a fruitless, thankless task, but it also had its rewards. In 1836, while conducting a service in an outlying area, Moffat was astonished when a young man stood up and began quoting passages from the gospel of Luke. To Mary he wrote: "You would weep tears of joy to see what I had seen."[11]

But even before he was able to make his translation available to the people, Moffat was seeing positive results from his language study. His ability to speak the language of the people brought a new understanding of his teaching. He started a school with forty pupils, and soon his message began to take hold and a religious awakening followed. The first baptisms took place in 1829, nearly a decade after their arrival in Kuruman. In 1838 a stone church was built that still stands today.

The nucleus of believers at Kuruman never exceeded two hundred, but Moffat's influence was felt hundreds of miles around. Leaders from distant tribes came to Kuruman to hear his message.

Although Moffat's career is generally associated with Kuruman, his work extended far beyond that area. In fact, the nucleus of believers at Kuruman never exceeded two hundred, but his influence was felt hundreds of miles around. Chiefs or their representatives from distant tribes came to Kuruman to hear his message. The most notable instance of this occurred in 1829 when the great and fearsome Moselekatse, one of Africa's most infamous tribal chiefs, sent five representatives to visit Moffat and bring him with them on their return journey. The meeting of Moffat and Moselekatse was an unforgettable encounter. The naked Moselekatse was overwhelmed that the great white "chief" would come so far to visit him, and so began a thirty-year friendship built on a deep respect of one man for the other. Though Moselekatse himself was never converted to Christianity, in later years he did allow missionaries, including Moffat's son John and daughter-in-law Emily, to establish a mission station among his tribe.

As far away as Moffat often traveled, his thoughts were never far from Kuruman. Over the years, Kuruman had become a showpiece of African civilization, where his philosophy of "Bible and plough" was practiced. Their stone house had a large enclosed backyard where their five servants did domestic chores around a huge open brick oven. It was a homey atmosphere, with children always at play. (The Moffats had ten children, though only seven survived to adulthood; and of those seven, five became actively involved in African missions.) Though Kuruman was an out-of-the-way settlement, not on the main route to the interior, it attracted so many visitors that Moffat sometimes regretted the circus atmosphere that interfered with his Bible translation and revisions.

Robert Moffat, missionary patriarch of South Africa.

After fifty-three years in Africa with only one furlough (1839–43), the Moffats were ready to retire. They had suffered some severe tragedies, particularly the deaths of their two oldest children within the space of a few months in 1862, but the work was moving forward. There were several native pastors active in the work, and their son John, who had joined them at Kuruman, was prepared to take over the mission. It was a sad departure from Kuruman and perhaps an unfortunate mistake. Kuruman was the only home they had known for half a century, and readjustment back in England proved difficult, particularly for Mary, who died only months after their return. Moffat lived on for another thirteen years, during which time he became a noted missionary statesman, traveling throughout the British Isles challenging adults and youth alike with the tremendous needs of Africa.

David Livingstone

David Livingstone was the hero of Victorian England—and a hero for generations to follow. "After his death and his burial in Westminster Abbey," writes Geoffrey Moorhouse, his "reputation was secure from assault by anyone but the most reckless heretic. Even in the middle of the twentieth century, historians would still acknowledge him as the greatest missionary of them all. For almost a hundred years he would . . . be considered in the same breath as St. Francis of Assisi and St. Joan of Arc."[12]

Livingstone had unparalleled influence in the realm of African missions, but his own missionary work was slight. He was a frail, temperamental human being with serious personality flaws that hindered his ministry throughout his entire life. But despite his weaknesses, he, more than anyone else, focused the world's attention on the needs of Africa.

Like his father-in-law, Robert Moffat, David Livingstone was born in Scotland and raised in humble surroundings. But unlike his father-in-law, his brilliant mind and insatiable desire for learning impelled him to seek a higher station in life. His fourteen-hour days at a textile mill beginning at the age of ten did not prevent his education. He bought a Latin grammar book with his first week's pay, and he continued his schooling by enrolling in evening classes. He survived his difficult years of schooling by snatching glances at a book propped up on his spinning jenny and poring over homework assignments until midnight. His love for science caused a serious rift between him and his father and might have pulled him away from his Christian upbringing—but for the writings of Thomas Dick, who emphasized the compatibility of faith and science.

Livingstone grew up in a pious, church-going family who had left the established Anglican Church to attend an Independent chapel. After his conversion he dreamed of becoming a missionary doctor to China, but due to family hardships, further education was delayed. Finally, in 1840, at the age of twenty-seven, he was ready to begin his missionary career with a background in both theology and medicine.

Livingstone's application to the London Missionary Society was accepted in 1839, but his plans to sail for China were thwarted by international politics—friction between Britain and China, which eventually led to the Opium War. The LMS directors thought Livingstone should go to the West Indies instead, but in the meantime Livingstone had been introduced to the striking, six-foot-tall veteran missionary to Africa, Robert Moffat. Moffat had a profound influence on the eager missionary candidate and tantalized him with the thrilling opportunities for evangelism beyond Kuruman in "the vast plain to the north" where he had "sometimes seen, in the morning sun, the smoke of a thousand villages, where no missionary had ever been."[13]

It was with great anticipation that Livingstone sailed for Africa in December of 1840. After spending thirteen weeks in language study aboard ship, he arrived at the Cape in March of 1841 and remained there a month before beginning his journey to Kuruman, where he was to help with the work until the Moffats returned. He enjoyed his overland travel to Kuruman, describing it as a "prolonged system of picnicking." He was critical of the missionary work at Cape Town, however, where having large numbers of missionaries concentrated in a small area discouraged indigenous leadership. Further disappointment awaited him at Kuruman. With the mental image of "a thousand villages," he was surprised to find the region so sparsely populated, and he was shocked to discover the discord among the missionaries: "The missionaries in the interior are, I am grieved to say, a sorry set. . . . I shall be glad when I get away into the region beyond—away from their envy and backbiting." Livingstone's presence only complicated the situation, and most of the missionaries were only too anxious for him to "get away into the region beyond." He complained that there was "no more Christian affection between most if not all the 'brethren'" and himself than between his "riding ox and his grandmother."[14]

While waiting for the Moffats to return from their furlough, Livingstone made several exploration treks northward. Of his two-and-a-half-years at Kuruman, more than a year was spent away from his base, and this practice of "riding off" continued during the rest of his career. In 1843 Livingstone rode off to stay. He set out for the wooded and well-watered area of Mabosta, two hundred miles north, to establish a second Kuruman. With him was Roger Edwards, a middle-aged artisan-missionary, and his wife, both of whom had served for ten years at Kuruman. There were problems from the start. Edwards resented the imposed leadership of Livingstone, who was not only new on the African scene but was also eighteen years his junior.

Mabosta became Livingstone's first African home—a large house with glass windows brought up from Kuruman. There he first encountered the ever-present dangers of the African jungle. While taking part in a lion hunt he was attacked

WHEN in the act of ramming down the bullets I heard a shout. Starting, and looking half round, I saw the lion just in the act of springing upon me. . . . He caught my shoulder as he sprang, and we both came to the ground below together. Growling horribly close to my ear, he shook me as a terrier does a rat. The shock produced a stupor similar to that which seems to be felt by a mouse after the first shake of the cat. . . . The shake annihilated fear, and allowed no sense of horror in looking round at the beast. This peculiar state is probably produced in all animals killed by the carnivora; and if so, is a merciful provision by our benevolent Creator for lessening the pain of death. Turning round to relieve myself of the weight, as he had one paw on the back of my head, I saw his eyes directed to Mebalwe, who was trying to shoot him at a distance of ten or fifteen yards. . . . The lion immediately left me, and attacking Mebalwe, bit his thigh. . . . Another man . . . attempted to spear the lion while he was biting Mebalwe. He left Mebalwe and caught this man by the shoulder, but at that moment the bullets he had received took effect, and he fell down dead. . . . Besides crunching the bone into splinters, he left eleven teeth wounds on the upper part of my arm."

(David Livingstone, *Missionary Travels and Researches in South Africa*)

and badly mauled. Though he was grateful to have survived, thanks to his African companions, his left arm was severely injured and maimed for life.

By May of 1844, three months after the incident, he was feeling well enough to travel—on important business. He headed for Kuruman "to pay his addresses" to the Moffats' oldest daughter, Mary, who at twenty-three had just returned with her parents from England. His period of convalescence no doubt convinced him that there were drawbacks to being single, and so, during that summer, he "screwed up ... courage to put the question beneath one of the fruit trees." Later that year he wrote to a friend, "I am, it seems, after all to be hooked to Miss Moffat," whom he had described to another friend as being a "sturdy" and "matter-of-fact lady."[15]

The wedding took place at Kuruman in January of 1845, and in March the Livingstones left for Mabosta; but their stay there was short-lived. Further problems developed with the Edwards, and later that year, after delivering his first child, he moved his family to Chonwane, forty miles north. The time at Chonwane was a happy one for the Livingstones, but it only lasted eighteen months. Severe drought in that area necessitated a move with the tribe northwest to the Kolobeng River. In the summer of 1847, after their second child was born, they moved into their third home.

David Livingstone, the world-famous missionary-explorer.

For seven years, the family lived a seminomadic life in Africa. Sometimes Mary and the children stayed at home alone, and other times they joined the expedition. Neither situation was satisfactory. On one occasion, when Livingstone was away from Chonwane for an extended period of time, he wrote: "Mary feels her situation among the ruins a little dreary and no wonder, for she writes me that the lions are resuming possession and walk around our house at night."[16] But accompanying him was not suitable either. In 1850, after an exploratory trip with her husband, she gave birth to her fourth child, who died soon after, while Mary was suffering from temporary paralysis. All this became too much for the more sedentary Moffats of Kuruman to tolerate. In 1851, when they heard from their daughter (who was again pregnant) that Livingstone was planning to take her and the "dear children" on another long jungle trek, Mrs. Moffat wrote her son-in-law a stinging letter:

> Mary had told me all along that should she be pregnant you would not take her, but let her come out here after you were fairly off. . . . But to my dismay I now get a letter—in which she writes 'I must again wend my weary way to the far Interior, perhaps to be confined in the field.' O Livingstone what do you mean—was it not enough that you lost one lovely babe, and scarcely saved the other, while the mother came home threatened with Paralysis? And still you again expose her & them on an exploring expedition? All the world still condemn the cruelty of the thing, to say nothing of the indecorousness of it. A pregnant woman with three little children trailing about with a company of the other sex—through the wilds of Africa among savage men and beasts! Had you *found a place* to which you wished to go and commence missionary operations the case would be altered. Not one word would I say were it to the mountains of the moon—but to go with an exploring party, the thing is preposterous. I remain yours in great perturbation, M. Moffat.[17]

Whether the letter would have changed Livingstone's mind is impossible to say, but the fact is, he did not receive it until he and the family were well into their journey. On September 15, 1851, a month after departure, Mary delivered her fifth child on the Zouga River, an event to which Livingstone devoted only one line in his journal, leaving more space for his exciting discovery of crocodile eggs. Apparently ignoring his own culpability, Livingstone bemoaned his wife's "frequent pregnancies," comparing the results to the output of "the great Irish manufactory."[18] Yet, he seemed to have genuinely loved his children and in later years regretted that he had not spent more time with them.

LIVINGSTONE'S TRAVELS IN SOUTHERN AFRICA

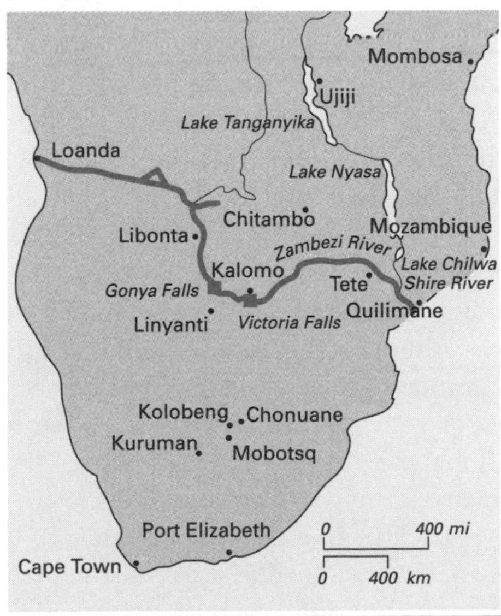

By 1852 Livingstone had come to realize that African expeditions were no place for a mother and little children. Earlier he had justified the risk: "It is a venture to take wife and children into a country where fever—African fever—prevails. But who that believes in Jesus would refuse to make a venture for such a Captain?" But no longer could he endure the criticism of his in-laws and others, so in March of 1852 he saw Mary and the children off from

Cape Town en route to England. How could he sacrifice his family for African exploration? "Nothing but a strong conviction that the step will tend to the Glory of Christ would make me orphanize my children."[19]

The next five years were depressing for Mary. A biographer wrote that she and the children were not only "homeless and friendless" but also "often living on the edge of poverty in cheap lodgings." It was rumored among the resident LMS missionaries that she had lapsed into spiritual darkness and was drowning her misery in alcohol.[20] But for Livingstone, now free to explore, it was an exhilarating time. He had little to show for his first eleven years—neither converts nor a mission station. Now he was free to move. The interior of Africa was beckoning.

Livingstone's first and greatest expedition took him across the continent of Africa along the Zambezi River. After seeing his family off at Cape Town, he leisurely headed back north, stopping at Kuruman and then going on to his favorite tribe, the Makololos, where he recruited a number of them to accompany him on the expedition. Beginning in central Africa, they followed the river northwest to the coast at Luanda. It was a hazardous journey with continual threats from hostile tribes and the dread of the deadly African fever, but Livingstone was never tempted to turn back. Although he was primarily an explorer, he never entirely abandoned evangelism. With him he carried a "magic lantern" (an early version of a slide projector) with pictures depicting biblical scenes. After six months of arduous travel, he and his men made history when they came out on the coast alive.

Despite offers from ship captains to return him to England, Livingstone, under a personal obligation to return the Makololo tribesmen to their homeland, turned back and started his trek down the Zambezi to the east coast. His journey east moved at a slower pace, hampered by dozens of bouts with African fever. In twelve months he reached Linyanti, his original starting point, and from there he continued on to the great falls that he named Victoria in honor of his queen. From this point, his single aim was to explore the Zambezi as a possible trade route from the East. The more he encountered the inhumane slave traffic of the Portuguese and the Arabs, the more convinced he became that only the combination of "Commerce and Christianity" could save Africa. He was convinced that slavery required the help of Africans (supplying slaves from enemy tribes), and his solution was to bring legitimate commerce to Africa by way of a navigable trade.

Although the expedition did not follow the Zambezi the entire route, Livingstone nevertheless arrived on the coast in May of 1856, confidently (though incorrectly) proclaiming the Zambezi to be navigable. It was a happy occasion, though he was disappointed again, as he had been on the West Coast, not to find a letter from Mary among all his mail.

Back in England in December of 1856 after fifteen years in Africa, Livingstone was heralded as a national hero. After only three days with his family, he went to London where he launched a year-long whirlwind speaking tour to adoring crowds and received some of the nation's highest awards. During this year in England, he also wrote his first book, *Missionary Travels and Researches in South Africa.* As a result of his high profile, new mission societies were formed—though he himself went in a different direction. Before returning to Africa in 1858, he severed his connection with the LMS and accepted a commission from the British government that allowed him more funds and equipment.

The remaining fifteen years of Livingstone's life could never recapture the glory of 1857. He returned to Africa with an official entourage for his second expedition, only to discover that the Zambezi River was not navigable. The section of the river he had bypassed on his previous journey contained rocky gorges and white rapids. Disappointed, he turned northward (nearer the east coast) to explore the Shire River and Lake Nyasa. Unfortunately, slavers followed in the wake of his discoveries, and thus for a time his exploration was doing more to open the area to slave traffic than to missions.

Missionaries also followed his paths to the Shire River region, but not without painful sacrifice. The Universities Mission to Central Africa (UMCA), founded as a result of Livingstone's rousing speech at Cambridge, entered the area with enthusiasm and false assurance of favorable living conditions. Livingstone was not an organizer, and soon the mission was in chaos. Bishop Charles Mackenzie, the leading cleric in the party, was a controversial figure. He was reported to have "arrived in East Africa with a crosier [bishop's staff] in one hand and a rifle in the other," and he did not hesitate to use his rifle and distribute others to friendly Africans for military action against the slave-trading Ajawa tribe.[21] His behavior created a scandal and seriously hurt the UMCA. In less than a year, however, Mackenzie was dead, and others in the mission party soon perished also, including Livingstone's wife, Mary, who had left the children in England to join her husband in 1861.

Livingstone returned to England in 1864, this time to much less acclaim. His second expedition had not been the success he had hoped it would be, and his reputation had been tarnished. Most of the members of his party, once enamored by their fearless leader, were complaining bitterly about his autocratic rule and difficult personality.

In 1865 Livingstone returned to Africa for the last time to begin his third and final expedition, this time for the purpose of discovering the source of the Nile. He took no Europeans with him, and in fact, did not see another European for nearly seven years. It was a difficult time for him. His body was racked by malnutrition, fever, and bleeding hemorrhoids, and often his supplies were stolen by Arab slave traders. Yet he was where he wanted to be. While he failed to discover the source of the Nile, he made other discoveries, and he was at peace with himself and his surroundings (except for the ever-present slave trade that tortured his conscience). As time passed, the Africans became used to the bearded, toothless, haggard old man who often spoke to them of his Savior.

During Livingstone's last years in Africa, rumors periodically surfaced that he had died. Though his reputation had been marred, people the world over still held him in awe and were strangely curious about this eccentric old man in the wilds of Africa. It was this curiosity that spurred the editor of the New York *Herald* to send an ambitious reporter, Henry Stanley, to find Livingstone, dead or alive. After several months of searching, Stanley caught up with Livingstone at Ujiji, near Lake Tanganyika, late in 1871. The initial meeting was awkward. After dismounting his horse, Stanley bowed and uttered the often-repeated phrase that soon became the butt of jokes: "Dr. Livingstone, I presume."

Stanley was a welcome sight to Livingstone. He brought medicine, food, and other supplies that Livingstone desperately needed. And perhaps more importantly, he brought companionship and news from the outside world. The two men developed a close and tender relationship; and in a moving tribute, Stanley described the months they shared together:

> For four months and four days I lived with him in the same hut, or the same boat, or the same tent, and I never found a fault in him. I went to Africa as prejudiced against religion as the worst infidel in London. To a reporter like myself, who had only to deal with wards, mass meetings, and political gatherings, sentimental matters were quite out of my province. But there came to me a long time for reflection. I was out there away from a worldly world. I saw this solitary old man there, and I asked myself, "Why does he stop here? What is it that inspires him?" For months after we met I found myself listening to him, wondering at the old man carrying out the words, "leave all and follow me." But little by little, seeing his piety, his gentleness, his zeal, his earnestness, and how he went quietly about his business, I was converted by him, although he had not tried to do it.[22]

Stanley would go on to follow in Livingstone's footsteps with his 999-day journey across Africa—an expedition that intrigued the world and sent missionary societies scrambling to stake their claims in the Dark Continent. Before that, he had written his bestseller, *How I Found Livingstone,* which served as another source to the unfolding legend of Livingstone.

Livingstone lived a little more than a year after Stanley departed. On May 1, 1873, an African servant found the "master" kneeling as if in prayer "by the side of his bed, his body stretched forward, his head buried in his hands upon the pillow."[23] It was a fitting way for this man of living legend to die. His faithful servants Susi and Chuma determined that there was no other way to pay their respects than to deliver his body and personal papers to his former associates at the coast. After burying his heart under a Mpundu tree, the body was dried in the hot African sun until it was mummified and then carried overland fifteen hundred miles to the coast.

In England, Livingstone was given a state funeral at Westminster Abbey, attended by dignitaries from all over the country. It was a day of mourning for his children, who came to say good-bye to the father they had never really known; but it was a particularly sad hour for the seventy-eight-year-old Robert Moffat, who slowly walked down the aisle in front of the casket bearing the man who decades before in that same city had caught a vision of "a thousand villages, where no missionary had ever been."

The death of David Livingstone had a tremendous psychological impact on the English-speaking world. Missionary fervor reached a high pitch as zealous young men and women volunteered for overseas duty, no matter what the cost.

George Grenfell

George Grenfell was one of the many British citizens inspired by the work of Livingstone and drawn to Africa in the wake of his death. He was born in Cornwall, England, in 1849. It was through reading Livingstone's first book that he committed himself to African missions. After working in a warehouse for a number of years while serving as a lay minister, he enrolled for a year at the Baptist College in Bristol to prepare for his missionary service.

In 1874, at the age of twenty-five, Grenfell was accepted by the Baptist Missionary Society (the same mission that commissioned William Carey some eighty years before), and the following month he left for the Cameroons. In 1876, he was back home in England for his marriage to a Miss Hawkes, who returned to Africa with him but died less than a year later, leaving him bereaved and regretful: "I have done a great wrong in taking my dear wife into this deadly climate of West Africa." He remarried two years later, this time to a "colored" woman from the West Indies who was also widowed.[24]

After a three-year apprenticeship in the Cameroons, Grenfell was assigned to do pioneer work on the Congo River, following on the discoveries of Stanley's 999-day journey. It was Grenfell's hope to pave the way for a network of mission stations across Africa. His mode of travel was a river steamer, the *Peace,* which he assembled himself after three engineers who were sent one at a time to carry out the task all died. The *Peace* became a home for Grenfell and his family, who accompanied him on his exploratory trips.

The Congo lived up to the reputation of a "white man's graveyard." Only one out of four missionaries survived their first term of service. Yet Grenfell pleaded for more missionaries: "If more men don't soon come, the Congo mission will collapse, and the work that has cost so much will be thrown away." His own family did not escape the clutches of death. Four of his children were buried in the Congo, including his oldest daughter, Pattie, who had come from England as a teenager to help in the work.[25]

But the disease-ridden jungle was not the only obstacle standing in the way of bringing Christianity to the Congo. Unfriendly tribesmen, known for their cannibalism, were a constant threat. Grenfell recalled as many as twenty harrowing experiences of "running away from cannibals." "The people are wild and treacherous, for several times after a period of apparently amicable intercourse, without any other cause than their own sheer 'cussedness,' as the Yankees would say, they let fly their poisoned arrows at us."[26]

Grenfell's own perspective on the situation was very different from that of others. Sam Lapsley, a young Presbyterian missionary, visiting in 1890, was disillusioned, according to Pagan Kennedy:

> But lingering day after day at this remote outpost with the famous Grenfell had unsettled the young missionary. Yes, the station appeared to be comfortable enough, with its machine shop, photography studio, and observatory, its tall palm trees and its steamship, Peace, docked in front. But Mr. Grenfell himself was a mess—"very anxious," Lapsley commented. Grenfell hated the natives, and they hated him. They had even threatened him with murder. . . . Was this what it meant to be a missionary? Hiding in your fancy house, terrified that the people you'd pledged to help might shoot you in the head?[27]

Lapsley's concerns were reinforced when he later encountered refugees from Grenfell's steamship *Peace* who were disoriented and starving. "According to the refugees, they had run off after being starved and then whipped," writes Kennedy. "Without enough rations, the *Peace* had become a floating torture chamber with hungry white men beating even hungrier black men."[28]

Grenfell, like many missionaries before and since, was in over his head. The dangers were real. That he had intentionally gone to Africa to torture the native people for his own benefit is an accusation that no serious historian would make. But it would be difficult to make the case that he was a true *friend* of Africa. He found himself caught between hostile Africans and the imperialistic power of Belgium's King Leopold, who viewed the Congo as his private domain. Grenfell's private maps and notes, and later his steamboat, were confiscated. His years in the Congo corresponded with the increasing atrocities against Africans—atrocities that were happening all around him. But "he was not willing to go public with what he knew, or even to protect the villages against encroaching State men," writes Kennedy. "It's no wonder some of the Africans wanted him dead."[29]

Grenfell found himself caught between hostile Africans and the imperialistic power of Belgium's King Leopold, who viewed the Congo as his private domain.

Despite these circumstances, Grenfell continued on in his missionary work, supervising the Baptist missions in the Congo for twenty years—with surprising success in later years. In 1902 he wrote: "You will be glad to know that here at Bolobo, shorthanded as we are, we are not without evidence of progress and blessing. People are more willing to hear, and give heed to the message they have so long slighted. In fact, many are professing to have given their hearts to the Lord Jesus, and there are signs of good times coming." Growth did continue, and soon there was a need for a larger chapel. He told of how twenty years before he had been driven off by spears, but now was greeted with the singing of "All Hail the Power of Jesus' Name."[30]

Though Grenfell was prevented by the Belgian government from completing a network of mission stations linking up with stations of the Church Missionary Society from the east, he continued to do pioneer work until his death from African fever in 1906.

After thirty years in Africa, Grenfell left behind a mixed legacy. Although he "had seen firsthand the full range of abuses, including Leopold's state employees buying chained slaves," he was mostly silent. In a letter home, he wrote that he was hesitant to "publicly question the action of the State."[31] There would be others, however, who would take a stand against this Mafia-like lawlessness. Among them was an African-American missionary whose writings drew the world's attention to this holocaust claiming an estimated ten million lives.

William Sheppard

A missionary overlooked in most mission histories has been William Sheppard, a black American who went to the Congo in 1890 as a missionary sponsored by the Southern Presbyterians. He was part of a broader plan of "recruiting missionaries from the African race," which coincided with the "back to Africa" movement engineered primarily by Southern whites. But whites were not the only ones attracted by the prospect of black missionaries in Africa. Returning to the land of their ancestors had long captured the imagination of many African Americans.

> *"The Bateke think there is nobody like 'Mundele Ndom,' the black white man, as they call Sheppard. . . . His temper is bright and even—really a man of unusual graces and strong points of character."*

Born in Virginia at the end of the Civil War, Sheppard had the rare fortune of acquiring a good education, first at Virginia's Hampton Institute and later in Tuscaloosa, Alabama, at the Colored Theological Seminary. He became a Presbyterian minister and served congregations in Montgomery and Atlanta, and then applied to the Southern Presbyterian Church for an appointment as a missionary in Africa. "For two years the Presbyterians put Sheppard on hold," writes Adam Hochschild. "Church authorities wouldn't let him go to Africa unless a white man was available to be his superior."[32] Samuel Lapsley, also a Presbyterian minister and a descendent of slave owners, agreed to serve in that position—the younger directing the older.

After surveying the prospects for mission work, the two made plans to establish a mission post far north on the Kasai River. They worked well together, and

Lapsley spoke highly of his partner: "The Bateke think there is nobody like 'Mundele Ndom,' the black white man, as they call Sheppard. . . . His temper is bright and even—really a man of unusual graces and strong points of character" and "a born trader."[33] The partnership was short-lived, however. In 1892 Lapsley, emaciated from African fever, journeyed downriver to the capital city. He never returned. When he learned of his partner's death two months later, Sheppard went into the forest "to pour out my soul's great grief."[34]

"Sheppard continued to thrive," according to Hochschild. "Unlike other missionaries, generally a pretty somber-looking lot, in photographs Sheppard seems to be enjoying himself." When pictured with native people, "He has the distinct look of a football coach showing off a winning team."[35]

Because of his contagious personality and sophisticated style—and his black skin—Sheppard suddenly found himself a dignitary among native Africans, welcomed as the returned spirit of a deceased king. He was the first outsider to obtain an audience with the intimidating Kuba king, Kot aMvweeky II, who received the stranger into his court. "Servants spread leopard skins for him to walk on whenever he approached the king, who sat on an ivory throne and wore a crown of beads and feathers." Of the Kuba tribe, Sheppard wrote: "They are the finest looking race I had seen in Africa, dignified, graceful, courageous, honest, with an open smiling countenance and really hospitable. Their knowledge of weaving, embroidery, wood carving and smelting was the highest in equatorial Africa."[36]

On furlough, Sheppard was also a celebrity. In London he lectured at Exeter Hall and was granted the honor of becoming a fellow of the Royal Geographical Society. Back in the United States, he visited with President Grover Cleveland and later Theodore Roosevelt and spoke at Princeton while Woodrow Wilson was president. During his first home leave he married Lucy Gantt, a teacher he had known during his student days. She gave birth to two children who survived, both of whom were raised by family back in the States.

As time passed, Sheppard encountered the increasingly terrible toll exacted by cruelties of colonialism, specifically, the rubber plunderers who had now moved into the Kasai River basin that was rich in rubber. Although he would later be acclaimed for publicizing the atrocities, he initially was reticent about challenging the white man's rule in the Congo. Pushed by his new mission director, however, he was assigned to go right into the heart of the rubber plundering. Here he pretended to be an official inspecting the work of the African agents. What he found was worse than he could have imagined. The dead and dying were everywhere, and further evidence of King Leopold's stranglehold on the country was offered by way of the grisly tradition of hand-collecting: "Malumba led Sheppard to a fire, outfitted with a grill. On top of it lay eighty-one right hands. Sheppard knew the exact number because he counted them."[37]

Sheppard's written reports and articles shattered the complacency of Americans and Europeans, and his role in exposing the atrocities was viewed as a threat by the powerful rubber racketeers. In a move to intimidate him and anyone else who would dare speak out, he was sued for libel. In the end he was vindicated, but more importantly, the court case helped bring the matter to the world's attention. Under the headlines AMERICAN NEGRO HERO OF CONGO AND FIRST TO INFORM WORLD OF CONGO ABUSES, the *Boston Herald* wrote, "Dr. Sheppard has not only stood before kings, but he has also stood against them. In pursuit of his mission of serving his race in its native land, this son of a slave . . . has dared to withstand all the power of Leopold."[38]

What Sheppard found was worse than he could have imagined. The dead and dying were everywhere, . . . and the grisly tradition of hand-collecting.

For all his fame and celebrity, Sheppard's life was not without controversy and scandal. Following the libel trial, he was forced to step down as a missionary and return to America because of adulterous affairs with African women, one resulting in the birth of a son. He confessed these affairs in a written statement, and after a time of probation, he returned to the ministry, initially as a traveling speaker and later settling in Louisville as the pastor of a small Presbyterian congregation, where his wife led the choir and conducted children's ministries.

Alexander Mackay

While Grenfell and the Baptists were penetrating Africa from the west, the Church Missionary Society (CMS, an arm of the Anglican Church) was moving from the east in an effort to fulfill Stanley's dream of spanning the continent with Christian mission stations. Johann Ludwig Krapf, a German Lutheran, was the first great CMS missionary to have this dream. He was one of many Lutherans from Germany who filled the ranks of the CMS when few Englishmen were willing to make the necessary sacrifices. Long before Stanley's expedition, Krapf pioneered Protestant missions on the east coast. In 1844, after being driven out of Ethiopia, he founded a station at Mombasa on the Kenya coast, a victory that was overshadowed by the death of his wife and baby. Krapf continued in pioneer missionary work for more than twenty years, making some notable discoveries but never realizing his dream of spanning Africa with the gospel.

The most noted missionary commissioned to the east coast by the CMS was Alexander Mackay, who arrived in Africa in 1876, a year and a half after the arrival of Grenfell on the west coast. Mackay was a well-educated Scot, an engineer by profession but a jack-of-all-trades with a keen mind for linguistics and theology. He was one of eight missionaries sent out by the CMS in 1876 in response to Stanley's rousing challenge to the Christian world that King Mtesa of Uganda had requested missionaries.

As the leader of this team of missionaries, Mackay felt an awesome responsibility, but his farewell message reflected the courageous determination such a venture required: "I want to remind the committee that within six months they will probably hear that some one of us is dead. Yes, is it at all likely that eight Englishmen should start for Central Africa and all be alive six months after? One of us at least—it may be I—will surely fall before that. When the news comes, do not be cast down, but send someone else immediately to take the vacant place."[39] Mackay's words were still ringing in the directors' ears when the news came that one of the eight had died. Five of them succumbed to the African graveyard in the first year, and by the end of the second year, Mackay was the only one left.

Though at times Mackay was at the point of death, he refused to give up. By 1878, two years after his arrival, he had constructed (with the help of African labor) a 230-mile road from the coast to Lake Victoria. But there was no joyous welcome. He arrived shortly after the murder of two fellow missionaries, and the rest of his colleagues had all left due to ill-health.

On reaching Lake Victoria, Mackay constructed a boat and then crossed the lake to Entebbe, where he met with King Mtesa. While Mtesa and his people welcomed him, there was opposition to his presence from other sectors—particularly Roman Catholics and Muslims. Mtesa himself was an unsavory character who almost daily executed his subjects for trivial offenses and allegedly had the largest store of wives of any man in history. With the protection of Mtesa, Mackay began preaching the gospel to the Baganda people, whom he found eager to learn. Soon he began translating the Scriptures. Long hours were spent at the printing press, but his labors were rewarded. Late in 1879, only a year after his arrival, he wrote: "Hosts of people come every day for instruction, chiefly in reading."[40] In 1882 the first baptisms took place, and two years later the local church had eighty-six African members.

With the protection of the unsavory Mtesa, Mackay began preaching the gospel to the Baganda people, whom he found eager to learn.

Church growth was not without hazards. There were numerous attempts on Mackay's life, and the situation became critical after Mtesa died in 1884 and was succeeded by his son, Mwanga. In 1885 more than thirty Christian boys were reportedly burned alive for refusing to succumb to Mwanga's homosexual exploits. Later that year James Hannington, an Anglican bishop attempting to enter Uganda from the east, was killed by orders of Mwanga. Tensions reached a climax when full-scale civil war broke out between Protestant and Catholic natives, ending with the bloody battle of Mengo. Through British military intervention the region was divided into Protestant and Catholic spheres of influence.

The Catholic presence in this area was largely a result of the intelligent, imaginative, and forceful leadership of Charles Lavagerie, who, according to Adrian Hastings, was "the most outstanding Catholic missionary strategist of the nineteenth century." Lavagerie was the founder of the White Fathers in 1868, and later the White Sisters. Unlike the Jesuits in previous centuries, the White Fathers conformed very closely to Rome on theological matters, but Lavagerie insisted that his missionaries otherwise conform to African customs. Developing an indigenous ministry was his prime concern. The growing conflict between Catholics and Protestants was not so much a matter of deep hostilities between the missionaries as it has been sometimes portrayed. Rather, it was the appeal of the Christian message from both sources that led to the tension. "Standard missiology," writes Hastings, "has portrayed the arrival of two competing societies ... as an evangelical disaster in a most promising field. The evidence suggests the contrary. It was the very tension between the two ... which created a genuinely intellectual challenge and made Christianity so intriguingly appealing."[41]

During these years Mackay was threatened repeatedly with expulsion, but his value as a skilled engineer served him well until 1887 when the Arabs finally convinced Mwanga to expel him. Mackay continued his ministry in Tanganyika on the southern end of Lake Victoria, where he continued translating and printing the Bible and serving Christian refugees from Uganda. In 1890, at the age of forty, this single and often solitary missionary died of malaria. After his death one of his grief-stricken colleagues lamented the irreplaceable loss in a simple but telling eulogy: "A score of us would never make a Mackay."

Mackay's death did not end the struggle to bring the gospel to Uganda. The CMS refused to be intimidated. In 1890, the year of Mackay's death, Alfred R. Tucker, a saintly Anglican bishop, arrived in Uganda and, through the invaluable assistance of African evangelists, built a church membership of sixty-five thousand. His unswerving commitment to racial equality stirred opposition among fellow missionaries, but his ideals triumphed, and the church in Uganda thrived.

One of the African evangelists to carry on the work of Mackay was Apolo Kivebulaya. He had first heard the gospel message from Mackay—a message that stayed with him during his military service and was later intensified through a vision. This was his call to preach to the pygmies. Christ "appeared to me in the form of a man and stood beside me.... He said to me, 'Go and preach in the forest because I am with you.'"[42] He followed that call and went into the forest to Mboga, where he encountered severe persecution. He was beaten repeatedly, on one occasion so badly that he was left for dead, "cast into the bush." The chief declared that "the wild beasts would soon make an end" of him.[43]

But miraculously, Kivebulaya survived. "Mboga was stirred to its depths; everyone flocked to see the dead man who had come to life again, foremost among them the startled chief.... He declared with weeping that God had spoken to him. After due teaching, he was baptized."[44] Kivebulaya continued on in the ministry for thirty years until he died in 1933. "It could be said that the entire Anglican province of today in eastern Zaire has grown out of Kivebulaya's work," writes Adrian Hastings, "a work wholly untouched by the pursuit of power, wealth, or any physical satisfaction whatsoever."[45]

Mary Slessor

The exploration and missionary work of Livingstone and Stanley inspired scores of others to embark on Africa—women as well as men. Most of the women, not surprisingly, envisioned their ministry sheltered within the confines of an established mission station, such as Kuruman where Mary Moffat spent most of her life. Exploration and pioneer work was not even an option for a single female missionary—until Mary Slessor arrived on the scene.

The story of Mary Slessor, as much as that of any missionary in modern history, has been romanticized almost beyond recognition. The image of her as a Victorian lady dressed in high-necked, ankle-length flowing dresses, escorted by tribal warriors through the African rain forests in a painted canoe, is far removed from the reality of the barefoot, scantily clad, red-haired, working-class woman who lived African-style in a mud hovel, her face at times covered with boils and often without her false teeth. Yet her success as a missionary pioneer was amazing, and the oneness she felt for the Africans has been equaled by few. She held the distinction of being the first woman vice-consul in the British Empire, but the greatest tribute she ever received was paid to her before her death by fellow missionaries who knew her well and, in spite of her faults and eccentricities, honored her as a great woman of God.

The image of Slessor as a Victorian lady dressed in high-necked, ankle-length dresses is far removed from the reality of the barefoot, scantily clad, working-class woman who lived African-style in a mud hovel.

Mary Mitchell Slessor, the second of seven children, was born in Scotland in 1848. Her childhood was marred by poverty and family strife due largely to the sporadic work habits of her alcoholic father, who had been known to throw her out into the streets alone at night after he had come home drunk. At age eleven she began working alongside her mother at the textile mills as a half-timer while she continued on in her schooling. By the time she was fourteen she was working ten-hour days, and for the next thirteen years she was the primary wage earner in the family.

Though she later referred to herself as a "wild lassie," there was little time or opportunity for leisure in the crowded, polluted working-class district where her family lived. Church activities, however, offered a fulfilling outlet from her miserable home life. She taught Sunday school, and when she was in her early twenties, she began working with the Queen Street Mission. Here she confronted street gangs that tried to break up her open-air meetings in the blighted neighborhoods of Dundee—neighborhoods that served as a training ground for her work in Africa.

Since early childhood, she had been deeply interested in overseas missions—particularly in the Calabar Mission (located in present-day Nigeria), established two years before her birth. Her missionary-minded mother hoped her only living son, John, would become a missionary, but his death shattered her dreams. However, the tragedy opened the way for Mary to escape the mills and to take her brother's place. The Calabar Mission had always made room for women, and she knew she would be a welcome addition to the staff. The death of David Livingstone clinched her decision.

In 1875 Slessor applied to and was accepted by the Calabar Mission, and in the summer of 1876, at the age of twenty-seven, she sailed for Calabar, long known for its slave trade and deadly environment. Her earliest years in Africa were spent at Duke Town, where she taught in a mission school and spent time in the nearby villages. But she was dissatisfied with her assignment, never feeling at ease with the social niceties and ample lifestyle of the missionary families comfortably stationed there. (And no doubt they also had reservations about her—a twenty-nine-year-old woman who admittedly had climbed every tree worth climbing between Duke Town and Old Town.) Life was too routine. Only a month after her arrival she had written, "One does need a special grace to enable one to sit still. It is so difficult to wait."[46] Her heart was set on doing pioneer work in the interior, but for that "privilege" she would have to wait.

CALABAR, WEST AFRICA

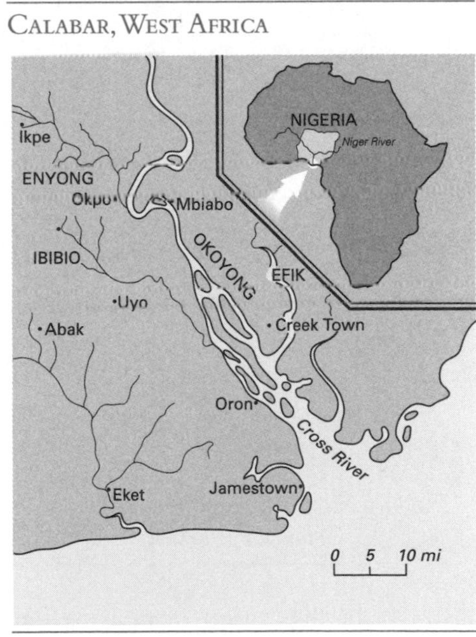

After less than three years in Africa and weakened by several attacks of malaria (and many more of homesickness), Slessor was allowed a furlough to regain her strength and reunite with her family. She returned to Africa, refreshed and excited about her new assignment at Old Town, three miles farther inland along the Calabar River. Here she was free to work by herself and to maintain her own lifestyle—living in a mud hut and eating local produce allowed her to send most of her mission salary to her family back home. No longer was her work routine. She supervised schools, dispensed medication, mediated disputes, and mothered unwanted children. On Sundays she became a circuit preacher, trudging miles through the jungle from village to village, sharing the gospel with those who would listen.

Evangelism in Calabar was a slow and tedious process. Witchcraft and spiritism abounded. Cruel tribal customs were embedded in tradition and almost impossible to eradicate. One of the most heartrending of these customs decreed that a twin birth was a curse. In many cases both babies were killed, and the mother was exiled to an area reserved for outcasts. Slessor not only rescued twins and ministered to their mothers but also fought the perpetrators, sometimes risking her own life. But after three years she was once again too ill to remain in Africa.

On her second visit home she was accompanied by Janie, a baby girl she had rescued from death. She and Janie were a sensation—so much so that the mission committee extended her furlough. She was also detained by her sickly mother and sister. In 1885, after nearly three years' leave, she returned to Africa, determined to penetrate farther into the interior.

Mary Slessor, pioneer missionary to Calabar, West Africa.

Soon after she returned, Slessor received word of her mother's death, and three months after that, of her sister's. Another sister had died during her furlough, and now she was left alone with no close ties to her homeland. She was despondent and almost overcome with loneliness: "There is no one to write and tell all my stories and troubles and nonsense to." But along with the loneliness and sorrow came a sense of freedom: "Heaven is now nearer to me than Britain, and no one will be anxious about me if I go up-country."[47]

"Up-country" to Slessor meant Okoyong, a remote area that had claimed the lives of other missionaries who had dared to penetrate its borders. Sending a single woman to that region was considered by many to be an exercise in insanity, but she was determined to go and would not be dissuaded. After visiting the area a number of times with other missionaries, she was convinced that such work was best accomplished by women, who, she believed, were less threatening to unreached tribes than men. So in August of 1888, with the assistance of her friend King Eyo of Old Town, she was on her way north.

Life was very difficult up-country—especially during the first months, as entries in her diary indicate:

> In the forenoon I was left alone with the mud and the rain . . . , with a gap round the window frame and more round the doorway. I looked helplessly on day after day at the rain pouring down on the boxes, bedding, and everything. . . . I am living in a single apartment with a mud floor and that not in the best condition. Moreover it is shared by three boys and two girls and we are crowded in on every side by men, women, children, goats, dogs, fowls, rats and cats all going and coming indiscriminately.[48]

For the next quarter of a century and more, Slessor would continue to pioneer missions in areas in which no white man had been able to survive. Her reputation as a peacemaker spread to outlying districts, and soon she was acting as a judge for the whole region. In 1892 she was appointed the first vice-consul to Okoyong, a government position she held for many years. In that capacity she acted as a judge and presided over court cases involving disputes over land, debts, family matters, and the like. Her methods were unconventional by British standards (often refusing to act solely on the evidence before her if she personally was aware of other factors), but they were well suited to African society.

Slessor was very isolated from outsiders during much of her missions career, but in 1893 she enjoyed a visit from Mary Kingsley, a British journalist who would later write *Travels in West Africa*. Though Kingsley confessed that she was not a believer, she greatly admired her missionary hostess. Of Slessor, she wrote:

> This very wonderful lady has been eighteen years in Calabar; for the last six or seven living entirely alone, as far as white folks go, in a clearing in the forest near one of the principal villages of the Okoyong district, and ruling as a veritable white chief over the entire district. Her great abilities, both physical and intellectual, have given her among the savage tribe a unique position, and won her, from white and black who know her, a profound esteem. Her knowledge of the native, his language, his ways of thought, his diseases, his difficulties, and all that is his, is extraordinary, and the amount of good she has done, no man can fully estimate. Okoyong, when she went there alone . . . was given, as most of the surrounding districts still are, to killing at funerals, ordeal by poison, and perpetual internecine wars. Many of these evil customs she has stamped out. . . . Miss Slessor stands alone.[49]

Slessor's life as a pioneer missionary was a lonely one, but she occasionally traveled back to England or to Duke Town. During one of her sick leaves to the coast, she met Charles Morrison, a missionary teacher who was much younger than she was. Their friendship grew, and Slessor accepted his marriage proposal, with the provision that he would work with her in Okoyong. The marriage, however, never took place. His health did not even permit him to remain in Duke Town, and for her, missionary service came before personal relationships.

She was probably not suited for marriage anyway. Her living habits and daily routine were so haphazard that she was no doubt better off remaining single. Women had tried to live with her but usually without success. She was careless about hygiene, and her mud huts were infested with roaches, rats, and ants. Meals, school hours, and church services were irregular—more suited to Africans than to time-oriented Europeans. Clothing, too, was a matter of little concern for her. She soon discovered that the modest, tightly fitted long dresses of Victorian England were not suited to life in an African rain forest. Instead, she wore simple cotton garments, often clinging to her skin in the dampness (causing one male missionary to insist on walking ahead of her on jungle treks so he would not have to look at her, even though she was the one who was familiar with the trails).

Though Slessor often failed to take the most basic health precautions and "lived native" (as other missionaries were prone to say), she outlived most of her fellow missionaries who were careful about health and hygiene. Nevertheless, she did suffer recurring attacks of malaria, and she often endured painful boils that appeared on her face and head, sometimes resulting in baldness. At times, however, she was surprisingly healthy and robust for a middle-aged woman. Her many adopted children kept her young and happy, and she could heartily say that she was "a witness to the perfect joy and satisfaction of a single life."[50]

Although she was highly respected as a judge and civic leader, she reported few conversions. She viewed her work as preparatory and was not unduly anxious about her lack of converts. She organized schools, taught practical skills, and established trade routes, all in preparation for others to follow. In 1903, near the end of her term at Okoyong, the first baptism service was held (with seven of the eleven children baptized being her own), and a church was organized with seven charter members.

In 1904, at the age of fifty-five, she moved on from Okoyong with her seven children to do pioneer work in Itu and other remote areas. Here she encountered great success with the Ibo people. Janie, her oldest adopted daughter, was now a valuable assistant in the work, and another woman missionary was able to take over the work at Okoyong. For the remaining decade of her life, she continued in this pioneer work while others followed behind her—their ministry made easier by her pioneering efforts. In 1915, nearly forty years after coming to Africa, she died at the age of sixty-six in her mud hut.

During the span of her ministry in Africa there had been a dramatic increase in missionary work. Independent faith missions were rapidly developing. The denominational missions supported by the Anglicans (who grew from a little over a hundred to more than a thousand during this period), Presbyterians, Methodists, and Baptists made dramatic increases in their overseas outreach. Likewise, such missions as the Christian and Missionary Alliance, the Evangelical Alliance Mission, the Sudan Interior Mission, and the Africa Inland Mission had all gained a solid foothold in the interior and were on their way to becoming a major missionary force in Africa.

SELECT BIBLIOGRAPHY

Buchan, James. *The Expendable Mary Slessor.* New York: Seabury Press, 1981.

Buxton, Meriel. *David Livingstone.* New York: St. Martin's Press, 2001.

Christian, Carol, and Gladys Plummer. *God and One Redhead: Mary Slessor of Calabar.* Grand Rapids: Zondervan, 1970.

Falk, Peter. *The Growth of the Church in Africa.* Grand Rapids: Zondervan, 1979.

Hastings, Adrian. *The Church in Africa, 1450–1950.* New York: Oxford University Press, 1994.

Jeal, Tim. *Livingstone.* New York: Dell, 1973.

Kennedy, Pagan. *Black Livingstone: A True Tale of Adventure in the Nineteenth-Century Congo.* New York: Viking, 2002.

Livingstone, W. P. *Mary Slessor of Calabar: Pioneer Missionary.* London: Hodder & Stoughton, 1915.

Morrison, J. H. *The Missionary Heroes of Africa.* New York: Doran, 1922.

Mueller, J. Theodore. *Great Missionaries to Africa.* Grand Rapids: Zondervan, 1941.

Northcott, Cecil. *David Livingstone: His Triumph, Decline, and Fall.* Philadelphia: Westminster, 1973.

———. *Robert Moffat: Pioneer in Africa, 1817–1870.* London: Lutterworth, 1961.

Ransford, Oliver. *David Livingstone: The Dark Interior.* New York: St. Martin's, 1978.

7

CHINA: "BARBARIANS NOT WELCOME"

The missionary enterprises established in India and Africa during the late eighteenth and early nineteenth centuries found no parallels in China, where isolationism prevailed and Christianity was unwelcome. Despite extreme opposition, Protestant missions began during the first decade of the nineteenth century. During that period only the small area of land known as Canton and the Portuguese colony of Macao were open to foreign residence, and thus missionary work was limited. But it was a start—enough to arouse Christian concern.

The underlying motivation for Chinese isolationism was national pride. The people were proud of their civilization and generally regarded outsiders as barbarians or, worse yet, as "foreign devils." China could boast an uninterrupted four-thousand-year national history and resented the implied superiority of the West. Both the culture and religion had a distinctly Oriental flavor that proved difficult for Western minds to grasp. Early Chinese religion developed around spirit and ancestor worship and consequently was diverse and disorganized. But with the introduction of the philosophies of Confucianism and Taoism in the sixth century B.C. and later the advance of Buddhism in the first century A.D. (and from there to Korea and Japan), the religious scene dramatically changed. Organized religious teachings and nationalistic pride blended together, and all efforts to introduce Christianity were rebuffed.

Christianity came to China in four stages. Nestorian Christians of the seventh century, who lived in Persia, were the first to come. Persecution was fierce, but the Nestorians maintained a foothold until the fourteenth century. The Roman Catholics entered China at the end of the thirteenth century. In 1293 Friar John, a Franciscan monk, arrived, and in less than a decade he had founded a church in Peking of some six thousand adherents. But soon persecution brought the work to a sudden end. In the sixteenth century the Roman Catholics, inspired by Francis Xavier, reentered China under the banner of the Jesuits. This time the Roman Catholic foothold remained, though the terrors of persecution were not over. The Catholic mission strategy here as elsewhere placed considerable focus on the baptism of infants. In fact, in 1843 the Society of the Holy Infancy was founded—an order that sought to baptize as many babies as possible, particularly those who were sickly and not expected to live. The practice increased the suspicion among Chinese that the infants were being poisoned.

The fourth and final stage of missionary enterprise to China was the Protestant thrust that began with Robert Morrison in the early nineteenth century. But for all practical purposes, China was still closed. Chinese authorities were fiercely resisting opium imports, and the only solution for a time seemed to be to ban all trade and close the coastal ports to foreign merchants—a defiance that Britain would not tolerate.

Opium smuggling was a lucrative business, and little concern was given to ethical matters. Marketing opium grown in India was the most profitable venture for the East India Company, and those profits helped pay for Britain's colonial administrative expenses. For that reason, British officials ignored the emperor's ban on opium in the early 1830s, and by 1836 opium production had tripled. The fact that debilitated opium addicts were dying in the streets and that the emperor's own three sons had died of addiction was conveniently ignored as many Britishers argued that opium was no worse than tobacco.

By 1839 the tense situation erupted into open warfare. At the same time, heated debates broke out in Parliament. The hawks prevailed, and Britain used its military might to subdue China. The Opium War ended with the treaty of Nanking that ceded Hong Kong to Britain and opened five coastal ports to foreign trade. It was an economic victory but hardly a moral one. "We have triumphed," wrote Lord Shaftesbury, "in one of the most lawless, unnecessary and unfair struggles in the records of history, this cruel and debasing war."[1]

There were other voices of protest—some from the missionary ranks—but many church and mission leaders believed that China should be opened to the gospel at all costs, even if it could only be accomplished by military force. Indeed, some missionaries were associated with opium smuggling itself. But smuggling ended in the 1850s when opium was officially legalized following a second Anglo-Chinese military outbreak. With this final humiliation of China, mission societies quickly moved in. Christianity, along with opium, could now be legally marketed in China, but not without paying a high price.

Many church and mission leaders believed that China should be opened to the gospel at all costs, even if it could only be accomplished by military force.

Robert Morrison

Robert Morrison was the first Protestant missionary to enter China, a noteworthy distinction, considering the formidable obstacles confronting foreigners in that hostile land during the first half of the nineteenth century. His prayer had been that "God would station him in that part of the field where the difficulties are the greatest, and to all human appearance the most insurmountable."[2] His prayer was answered. He persevered for twenty-five years in China, seeing fewer than a dozen converts.

Morrison was born in England in 1782, the youngest of eight children. His interest in missions developed as a youth—particularly as he read articles in missionary magazines. To become a missionary was his dream, but he faced one obstacle—his mother. There was a powerful bond of affection between them, and he promised not to go abroad so long as she lived. The delay was brief. She died in 1802 when he was twenty years old.

Soon after his mother's death, Morrison went to London for ministerial training. After two years he applied to the London Missionary Society and was accepted. The need for mission work in China weighed heavily on his mind, and he was soon studying with a Chinese scholar residing in London, while waiting to find a suitable colleague to accompany him. A partner was not to be found, so Morrison made plans to go alone. But obtaining passage to China was no simple task. The East India Company would have no part in a mission endeavor.

Finally, in January of 1807, nearly five years after the death of his mother, Morrison set sail on an American vessel to Canton via the United States. While in the United States, Morrison met with Secretary of State James Madison, who gave him a letter of introduction to the American consul in Canton. It was in America also that Morrison had his oft-quoted conversation with the ship's owner, who probed the young missionary: "And so, Mr. Morrison, you really expect to make an impression on the idolatry of the great Chinese Empire?" To which Morrison responded, "No, sir, but I expect God will."[3]

Morrison reached Canton in September of 1807, seven months after he had left England. Only then did his real problems begin. Further study of the Chinese language could be done only in the strictest secrecy, and his presence in Canton was under the scrutiny of the East India Company, whose officials prohibited evangelistic outreach of any kind. To make matters worse, he had little choice but to live in the high style of a company official, a waste that tried him sorely. Loneliness, too, was a grievous trial. Working without a partner was difficult enough, but his lack of communication from home (despite regular mails) only increased his depression. A year after his arrival he wrote to a friend: "I yesterday received your very welcome letter. It is but the second that I have received, after having written at least two hundred."

In spite of the restrictions placed on him, Morrison was able to secure language tutors and soon after began compiling a dictionary and secretly translating the Bible. So impressed were the East India Company officials with his dictionary that they offered him a position as a translator. He was convinced that such a move was the only way he could come to terms with the company. The generous salary was a further inducement.

At the very time that he was negotiating with the East India Company, Morrison was also negotiating another significant change in his life. After a brief courtship, he married Mary Morton, the daughter of an English doctor who was living in China at the time. Women were not allowed in Canton, so he arranged to live with her in Macao, a Portuguese colony, six months a year and spend the rest of the year in Canton working for the East India Company.

His early years of marriage were not happy ones. His separation from Mary, as well as her poor physical and emotional health, took a toll. To a friend he confided: "Yesterday I arrived in Canton. . . . I left my dear Mary unwell. Her feeble mind much harassed. . . . My poor afflicted Mary, the Lord bless her . . . she 'walks in darkness and has no light.'"[4] Mary's condition did improve for a time, but in 1815, six years after their marriage, she returned to England with their two small children. After a six-year separation, she and the children returned for a brief

FAR EAST ASIA

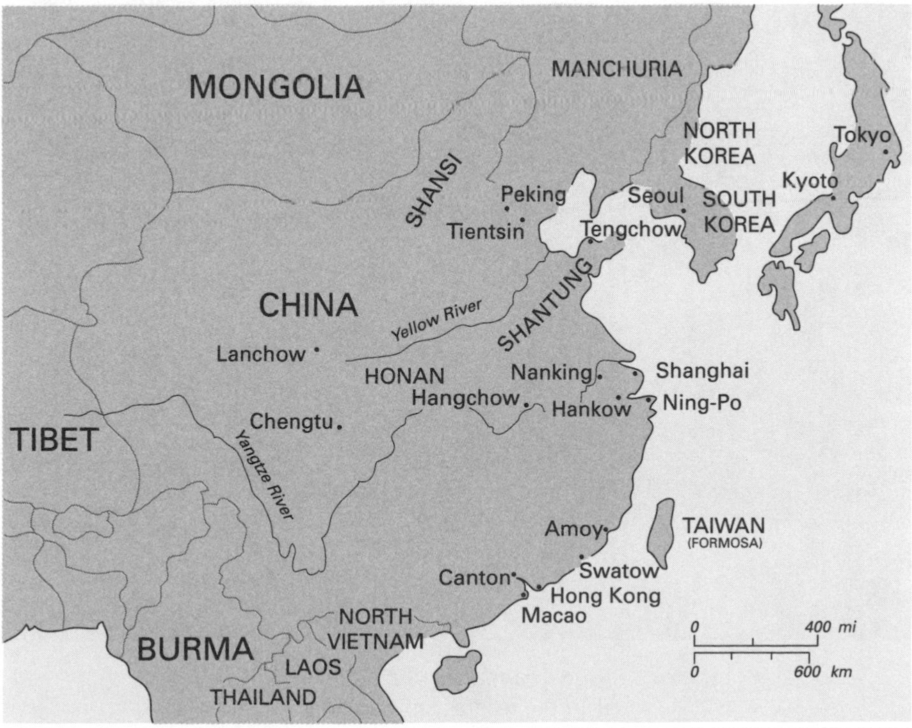

reunion before she died unexpectedly in the summer of 1821. The following year Morrison painfully parted with his nine-year-old Rebecca and seven-year-old John. He sent them back to England "to be brought up in a plain way; but above all things, to be taught the fear of the Lord."[5]

Morrison's long separations from his wife and children, as difficult as they were, had allowed him time for Bible translation, a task that he carried out with tireless energy. He begrudged the time he had to devote to the East India Company, always considering himself first and foremost a missionary, though never openly so. His Bible translation work was done in secret. In 1815 when his translation of the New Testament was made public, he was ordered dismissed by company officials—though it was never carried out.

That the East India Company would be irritated by Morrison's translation work was to be expected, but that other Christians would resent his labors caused him additional anxiety. In 1806, before he arrived in China, Joshua Marshman, Carey's colleague at Serampore, had begun to study Chinese with a view to translating the Bible. When Morrison heard of Marshman's plans in 1808, he wrote to Serampore, but there was no response. Marshman apparently wanted to be remembered as the first to have translated the Bible into Chinese. There was a sharp rivalry (though never expressed to each other personally), including an

Robert Morrison translating the Bible into Chinese with the help of his assistants.

unfair accusation of plagiarism against Marshman by some of Morrison's colleagues. In the end, Marshman won the race, but his translation, according to his own son, "was necessarily imperfect," to be valued "chiefly as a memorial to his missionary zeal and literary perseverance"[6]—and, to his stubborn pride. Morrison's translation, which was revised before printing (and thus delayed), was the better work. Morrison, rather than Marshman, is generally remembered for pioneering the translation of the Chinese Bible.

Such competition should not obscure the many instances of goodwill demonstrated among missionaries. Though Morrison, a Presbyterian, was overwhelmed with the immense challenge of reaching China with the gospel, he was not so consumed with his singular vision that he failed to give his attention to other mission endeavors. Indeed, he was so inspired by a sermon, "Asia Must Be Our Care," by Henry Martyn of the Anglican Church Missionary Society that he raised nearly three hundred dollars from Christians in Macao for Bible translation ministry in Calcutta.[7]

After completing his translation of the Bible, Morrison returned to England in 1824 for his first furlough in more than seventeen years. Although often overlooked while he was in Canton, he found himself a celebrity in England, continually besieged with invitations to speak. His primary emphasis was recruitment—not limiting his horizons to the male gender only. Morrison was ahead of his time in appealing to single women for mission service. In 1823, long before the advent of the Women's Missionary Movement, he had written that the ministry of missionary wives and mothers was often limited by domestic duties and

Old Canton, mission base for Robert Morrison.

poor health. His solution was single women: "Pious young women to acquire the pagan language & teach girls & grown women, would be very useful in the [missionary] Community."[8] So concerned was he for missions and for women's work that he organized a special class for women in his own home. Interestingly, one of the first to join this class was nineteen-year-old Mary Aldersey, who would later be remembered for her efforts to prevent the courtship and marriage of Hudson Taylor and Maria Dyer.

In 1826, after two years in England, Morrison returned to Canton, accompanied by his two children and his new wife, Elizabeth. He continued his translation of Christian literature and his clandestine evangelism; but his time was not his own, and there were increasing demands for him to serve as a negotiator between the conflicting commercial interests of England and China, which eventually culminated in war. In the midst of his busy schedule, he fathered five more children and was increasingly burdened by family responsibilities until 1832 when his wife and children returned to England. By this time his own health was failing, and he died in China in 1834. His death coincided with the forced departure of the East India Company from China and with the passing of another great missionary pioneer, William Carey, who had died less than two months earlier in India.

Amid his translation of Christian literature and clandestine evangelism, Morrison faced increasing demands to negotiate the conflicting interests of England and China, which eventually culminated in war.

During his twenty-seven years of ministry in China, Morrison could count no more than ten converts. His legacy is associated primarily with his translation work and his role in stirring interest in China missions. Like other China missionaries, his name was associated with the opium trade that led to the Opium War—and some mission enthusiasts would use that association to dismiss the seriousness of Western exploitation in China. For example, A. J. Broomhall writes: "The veteran and godly Robert Morrison remained a senior servant of the Honourable East India company, which controlled opium production in India and was the compelling force in producing it in such quantities. He had no scruples against traveling on Company ships"—or even in traveling with those who were smuggling opium into China.[9]

Liang Afa

Although Morrison's converts were very few in number, one of those went on to be an extraordinary evangelist and preacher—though his profession of faith actually came while he was working with William Milne, a missionary colleague of Morrison's. According to Broomhall, he "was to become one of the most notable Chinese Christians of all time and unknowingly the link in the chain of events which led to the devastating Taiping Rebellion against the Manchu dynasty."[10]

Born in 1789, Liang Afa was a printer and a devout Buddhist who was employed by Morrison to print his Scripture portions and tracts. But due to a crackdown by local authorities, he was sent away in 1815 for his own security and to assist Milne. As he continued to carve printing blocks for Bible passages, he began to absorb the message of Scripture. "After much internal struggle," writes Jonathan Spence, "Liang was won over, and on a November Sunday in 1817 he received baptism from Milne's hands."[11]

As a printer, Liang immediately began writing and printing his own literature, which would become his most lasting contribution:

> He called his first Chinese tract "An Annotated Reader for Saving the World." In thirty-seven pages he told of God's power as creator, and of His Ten Commandments, and used a variety of Paul's epistles to describe God's anger and His mercy. Carving the wooden blocks himself, Liang printed two hundred copies, and had just begun distributing them in and around Canton during the spring of 1819 when he was arrested by Chinese authorities, imprisoned, fined, and savagely beaten. The officials confiscated Liang's house and burned all the wooden printing blocks that he had made. Undeterred, over the ensuing months he converted his wife to Christianity and baptized her in person. Shortly thereafter, the couple prevailed on Robert Morrison to baptize their son.[12]

Throughout his ministry, Liang endured bitter persecution. He was repeatedly assaulted and robbed and imprisoned, but he was relentless in his determination to preach and to pass out literature. Morrison ordained him as an evangelist, and he later served as the pastor of his own congregation, all the while writing and printing tracts and translating Scripture. He traveled hundreds of miles from Canton, attempting to keep one step ahead of government officials—until he reversed his strategy. "He began to follow the itinerary of the Qing dynasty officials who went from town to town to administer the local Confucian examinations," writes Spence, "hoping thus that his tracts would reach the hands of the examination candidates, an influential audience—if not necessarily a sympathetic one." He further modified the strategy by distributing tracts near the hall in Canton where those who had passed local examinations came for their final tests. "In no other place in southeast China could one find a larger gathering of Chinese of proven education and of potential influence in their country's life."[13]

Liang's itinerant ministry did not go unnoticed by Chinese officials. He was "as intrepid as any of his foreign colleagues," writes Broomhall. But for him the stakes were higher. As a Chinese citizen, he was "publicly denounced as a traitor in a decree of 1833 which again prohibited the printing or sale of Christian books, those 'vile and trashy publications of the outside barbarians.'" But despite the decree there was a demand for the books—so much so that they "could not be printed fast enough."[14]

IT was every missionary's fantasy. In 1837 a Chinese national falls ill, slips into a coma, and has a vision in which he is taken up into heaven. Upon recovery he reads a gospel tract that seems to explain his dream. He converts to Christianity and becomes leader of a millennial movement that sweeps through six provinces of China.

It was every missionary's nightmare. Hon Xiuquan believes himself to be the younger son of Jesus Christ. He rewrites the Bible to fit his own beliefs, and his movement mutates into a regime combining the worst elements of Oliver Cromwell and Chairman Mao. Soldiers must recite the Ten Commandments each day, listen to daily sermons from their sergeants, and abstain from all contact with women.

(Philip Yancey, Untitled sidebar, *Christianity Today,* 28 April 1997)

Liang's literature was widely circulated in China, and many people found faith or were influenced by it—not the least of whom was Hong Xiuquan, the man who would become the leader of a vast movement, the Taiping Heavenly Kingdom, and the instigator of the failed Taiping Rebellion against the Manchu dynasty. Though influenced by Liang's writing and Western missionaries, Hong proclaimed himself the brother of Jesus, and his teachings veered significantly from Christian orthodoxy. Yet the movement gained a foothold, and Chinese Christians—including Liang's children—joined Hong's liberation army.

Karl F. A. Gutzlaff

The story of Christian missions in China would not be complete without a discussion of Karl Gutzlaff, who according to historian Stephen Neill "may be variously judged as a saint, a crank, a visionary, a true pioneer, and a deluded fanatic."[15] Gutzlaff was born in Germany in 1803, attended school at Basel and Berlin, and was in his early twenties when he was commissioned by the Netherlands Missionary Society to serve in Indonesia. There he reached out to Chinese refugees, though without board authorization. After two years he left the mission society to work independently.

From Indonesia he went to Bangkok, Thailand, where he adopted native dress and lifestyle, but his residence there was cut short due to ill health and the untimely death of his wife and infant daughter.

After leaving Thailand in 1831, Gutzlaff began making journeys along the China coast in any vessel from which he could obtain passage, be it a Chinese junk or an illicit opium clipper. On these voyages, which took him as far as Tientsin and Manchuria, with brief stops at Korea and Formosa, he attempted to verbally communicate the gospel but primarily distributed tracts and portions of Scripture, some of which were supplied to him by Robert Morrison in Canton. In 1833, after two years of traveling along the coast, he ventured inland to distribute literature and preach. His Chinese dress and his fluency in the language served him well until the outbreak of the Opium War in 1839.

During the Opium War, Gutzlaff, like Morrison, served as an interpreter for the British and helped to negotiate the Treaty of Nanking in 1842. After that he made his home in Hong Kong, and from that base he began to formulate his dream of reaching all of China with the gospel. His plan was to train Chinese nationals as evangelists and send them inland to preach and distribute literature. His goal was to evangelize China in one generation. Within half a dozen years he recruited more than three hundred Chinese workers, and the reports of their success were sensational. Thousands of New Testaments and countless more books and tracts were being distributed. People everywhere were flocking to hear the gospel messages, and the greatest news of all was that no fewer than 2,871 converts had been baptized "upon examination and satisfactory confession of their faith." It was a testimony for which every missionary dreams and a success story for which Christians back home were longing. Gutzlaff's detailed letters were met with an outpouring of enthusiasm. Financial support came from all over Europe.

> *Gutzlaff's plan was to train Chinese nationals as evangelists and send them inland to preach and distribute literature.*

In 1849, after recruiting two European associates, Gutzlaff arrived in Europe in person to share the wonderful news of what God was doing in China. He triumphantly traveled and preached throughout the British Isles and on the Continent. His story was thrilling, and it almost seemed too good to be true. It was. In 1850, while he was in Germany, his bubble burst. The whole endeavor turned out to be a grand hoax perpetrated by his Chinese workers, most of whom were thoroughly dishonest. The literature, instead of being distributed, was sold back to the printers, who then resold it to Gutzlaff. The tales of converts and baptisms were fabricated, and the money that had been so sacrificially donated had quickly found its way to the black-market opium trade.

As shocking as the news was to his supporters, Gutzlaff himself, as evidence indicates, was aware of the shady state of affairs before he left China for his European tour. Pride apparently compelled him to protect his own reputation and to turn his back on the mounting evidence. Following the exposure, Gutzlaff returned to China, vowing to reorganize the work, but he died in 1851, his reputation still tarnished. To some he remained a hero, and out of his missionary efforts was born the Chinese Evangelization Society (CES), the organization that commissioned Hudson Taylor to China in 1853. Gutzlaff, more than anyone else, influenced the missionary methods and goals of the enthusiastic young Taylor, and in later years Taylor referred to him as "the grandfather of the China Inland Mission."

J. Hudson Taylor

Few missionaries in the nineteen centuries since the apostle Paul have had a wider vision and have carried out a more systematic plan of evangelizing a broad geographical area than did James Hudson Taylor. His sights were set on reaching the whole of China, all 400 million people, and to that end he labored, though not single-handedly. He had a knack for organization, and he possessed a magnetic personality that drew men and women to him and to his point of view. The China Inland Mission was his creation and was a model for future faith missions. In his own lifetime the missionary force under him grew to more than eight hundred, and in the decades following his death it continued to expand.

But Hudson Taylor did not develop this vision alone. His first wife, Maria, was indispensable in setting the plan in motion, and his second wife, Jennie, was in the front lines carrying out the plan. Taylor's story is more than a story of a great missionary leader. It is a story of love, adventure, and unswerving faith in God, though not the story of the flawless saint that his early biographers created.

Taylor was born in Yorkshire, England, in 1832. His father was a pharmacist as well as a Methodist lay preacher who instilled in his son a passion for missions. Before he had reached his fifth birthday, the child was telling visitors that he wanted to some day be a missionary, and China (through the influence of his father) was the land that intrigued him the most.

Although family Bible reading and prayer were an integral part of his upbringing, Taylor had not made a profession of faith until he was seventeen years old. That was in the summer of 1849, when his mother was away for an extended visit with a friend. He was at home idly paging through papers in his father's library when he discovered some religious tracts. More interested in the stories than the spiritual applications, he began reading. He later wrote how he fell under a "joyful conviction . . . light was flashed into my soul by the Holy Spirit. . . . There was nothing in the world to be done but to fall down on one's knees and, accepting this Savior and His Salvation, to praise Him forevermore."[16] When his mother returned home two weeks later and he told her the news, she was not surprised. She told him that two weeks earlier while at her friend's home she suddenly felt the urge to pray for his salvation, so she excused herself to be alone and prayed until she was certain God had answered her.

From that point on, Taylor began planning for missionary work in China. Although evangelism was his sole motivation, he studied medicine in order to build relationships with the Chinese people. The zealous young Taylor also began a rigorous program of self-denial in preparation for missionary work. It was an effort to live entirely by faith. His diet was meager, a pound of apples and a loaf of bread each day, and his attic room was barren of the comforts he had been used to. He even refused to remind his employer of his long overdue wages. His rationale was clear—at least in his own mind—"When I get out to China I shall have no claim on anyone for anything; my only claim will be on God. How important, therefore, to learn before leaving England to move man, through God, by prayer alone."[17] Prayer alone did not sustain Taylor's physical strength. His already frail health declined with his meager diet, and his contact with an infected corpse during his anatomy training did not help the situation. He contracted a "malignant fever" that nearly ended his young life, forcing an interruption in his medical studies for several months.

J. Hudson Taylor, founder of the China Inland Mission.

Giving up physical comforts was easier for Taylor than setting aside romantic interests. "Miss V.," a music teacher, had become the object of his affections. Soon after their first meeting, he wrote to his sister: "I know I love her. To go without her would make the world a blank."[18] But Miss Vaughn had no vision for China. She perceived his passion for missions to be a passing fancy that he would forgo for her. Twice they were engaged, but China stood in the way. Taylor's commitment to missions was more powerful than his love for a woman.

The opening for Taylor to go to China came unexpectedly. His plans to complete his medical training were suddenly interrupted when word reached England that Hong Xiuquan, the leader of the quasi-Christian Taiping Rebellion, had become the emperor of China. With the prospect of China being freely opened to the gospel, the directors of the Chinese Evangelization Society, who had sponsored his medical training, decided to dispatch him immediately. So in September of 1853 the twenty-one-year-old Taylor sailed for China.

If Taylor had fantasized that he might be welcomed by emissaries of a new Christian emperor, he was mistaken. The Taiping Rebellion had failed. Nevertheless, Shanghai was a strange and exciting place for a young Englishman who had never ventured far from his Yorkshire home. It was a city of dragon-roofed

Buddhist temples, narrow shanty-lined streets, cheap coolie labor, subservient foot-bound women, pigtailed men, and a snobbish international settlement. There in the international settlement, Taylor found his first home; but loneliness soon engulfed him. The Chinese Evangelization Society was a small, disorganized mission board, and there was no one in China to initiate him into the work. There were many missionaries, but they looked down on the uneducated, unordained boy who had the audacity to call himself a missionary.

Soon after his arrival, Taylor found himself in financial straits. The visionary dream of evangelizing China quickly faded, and the memories of his boyhood days in Yorkshire filled his thoughts. Feelings of homesickness pervaded his letters to his family: "Oh I wish I could tell you how much I love you all. The love I have in my composition is nearly all pent up, and so it lets me feel its force. I never knew how much I loved you all before."[19]

Taylor's efforts to master the Chinese tongue only added to his frequent bouts of depression. His early months in Shanghai were filled with long hours of language study, and there were times when he feared he would never learn the language. Writing to the CES directors in England, he pleaded: "Pray for me, for I am almost pressed beyond measure, and were it not that I find the Word of God increasingly precious and feel His presence with me, I do not know what I should do."[20]

After some months of living at the London Missionary Society compound, Taylor moved out of the international settlement and bought his own shanty, which he described as having "twelve rooms, doors without end, passages innumerable, outhouses everywhere, and all covered with dust, filth, rubbish, and refuse."[21] It was hardly an ideal living situation. To make matters worse, civil war was raging close by, and the frigid temperatures of winter mercilessly invaded his walls. His initial experiment in independent living had failed, and he was grateful to be back in the international settlement.

Taylor, however, was never happy living among the other missionaries. In his eyes they lived in luxury. There was no place in the world, he said, where missionaries were more favored than in Shanghai. He viewed most of them as lazy and self-indulgent, and beyond that, he characterized the American missionaries as "very dirty and vulgar." He was only too anxious to get away from their "criticizing, backbiting and sarcastic remarks,"[22] so less than a year after he arrived in China he began making journeys into the interior. On one of these trips he traveled up the Yangtze River and stopped at nearly sixty settlements never before visited by a Protestant missionary.

Foreign missionaries had become commonplace in Shanghai, and the Chinese people took little notice of them, but the situation was very different in the interior. Early in his travels Taylor discovered that he was a novelty and that the people were far more interested in his dress and manners than in his message. To him there was only one logical solution: to become Chinese—to adopt Chinese dress and culture. Jesuit missionaries had long taken up Chinese ways, but most Protestant missionaries were more reluctant to closely identify with the people.

Adapting Chinese dress was a complicated ordeal for the blue-eyed, sandy-haired, Yorkshire-bred Taylor. The baggy pantaloons "two feet too wide around the waist," the "heavy silk gown," and the "flat-soled shoes" with turned-up toes would have been trial enough, but to blend in with the Chinese people, black hair and a pigtail were essential.[23] Taylor's first attempt at dying his hair was a fiasco. The top blew off the ammonia bottle and burned his skin, nearly blinding him. But despite the bad experience, he went ahead with his plans, "resigned" his "locks to the barber," and dyed his hair. But it was no fun. He found it to be "a very sore thing to get one's head shaved for the first time, when the skin is so irritable as the prickly heat makes it," and "the subsequent application of hair dye for five or six hours after does not do much to soothe the irritation." But the end result was worth the pain. With some "false hair plaited" in with his own to form a pigtail, and with some Chinese spectacles, Taylor blended in with the crowds: "You would not know me were you to meet me in the street with other Chinese. . . . I am not suspected of being a foreigner."[24]

To Taylor there was only one logical solution: to become Chinese—to adopt Chinese dress and culture.

As pleased as Taylor was with his new appearance, most of his fellow missionaries were unimpressed. He was an embarrassment to them and soon became the object of ridicule. Even his own family was shaken when they heard the news. But he persisted, and his adoption of Chinese dress and culture became his trademark. Not only could he move about more freely in the interior, but he found Chinese dress to be better suited to the climate.

Chinese dress by no means solved all of Taylor's problems of working in the interior, however. As he traveled and dispensed medical treatment, he was sometimes driven out of villages by local doctors. Traveling itself was risky. On one occasion Taylor's servant, who was hired to carry his belongings, absconded with his money and everything Taylor owned, forcing him to return to Shanghai, where he found refuge in the international settlement—until money came from England.

Taylor could not have survived his early years in China without private donations. Though his adopting Chinese culture and his residence in the interior had reduced his living expenses, his support from the CES was erratic and far less than he was able to live on, causing him to charge that the society had "acted disgracefully." In 1857, after three years of strained relations, Taylor resigned from the CES. From that point on he was entirely on his own, still unsettled and wandering through the interior of China, "not idle, but aimless," as one missionary characterized him.

The loneliness that Taylor had experienced during his early months in China still plagued him. He desperately longed for a wife. Although Miss Vaughn had refused to come to China with him, he could not forget her: "I am glad to hear of any news of Miss Vaughn you may have. She may get a richer and a handsomer husband but I question whether she will get one more devoted than I should have been.[25] Finally, with all hope for her fading, Taylor turned his attention to Elizabeth Sissons, another young woman whom he had known in England. He wrote to her, requesting a lock of her hair, and after he received it, he wasted no time in proposing marriage. Elizabeth accepted but quickly changed her mind. She did not answer his letters, and for a time he contemplated "giving up the missionary work" and returning to England to woo her.

During this time of depression and uncertainty Taylor arrived at Ningpo, and there he met Maria Dyer. Taylor was still pining over Elizabeth, and Maria was leery of the robed and pigtailed Englishman, but she was also intrigued: "I cannot say I loved him at once, but I felt interested in him and could not forget him. I saw him from time to time and still this interest continued. I had no good reason to think it was reciprocated; he was very unobtrusive and never made any advances." If Taylor seemed reticent to show any feelings for Maria, it was because he was still waiting for Elizabeth to write, and he no doubt feared a third rebuff were he to show interest in Miss Dyer. But in his diary he described her as "a dear sweet creature, has all the good points of Miss S. and many more too. She is a precious treasure, one of sterling worth and possessed with an untiring zeal for the good of this poor people. She is a *lady* too." As for the "very noticeable" and "decided cast in one of her eyes," the insecure Taylor was grateful: "I felt it gave me some chance of winning her."[26]

Maria Dyer Taylor, Hudson Taylor's first wife.

Maria Dyer had been born in China of missionary parents. Her father died when she was a small child, and her mother some years later. After that, she and her brother and sister were sent home to London for their education. But for Maria and her older sister, China was home. They returned when they were in their late teens to serve as teachers in Miss Mary Ann Aldersey's school for girls. Aldersey, the first single woman missionary to China, was a remarkable woman, but in the ensuing romance between Hudson Taylor and Maria Dyer, she played the role of the spoilsport, and it is that role for which she is remembered.

In March of 1857, several months after they had become acquainted, Taylor sent her a letter containing a marriage proposal. A mutual friend delivered the letter while she was teaching school. She waited until she was alone: "I then opened my own letter and read of his attachment to me, and how he believed God had given him that love for me which he felt. I could hardly understand that it was a reality. It seemed that my prayers were indeed answered . . . he asked me to consent to an engagement to him." Taylor went on to plead with Maria not to "send him a hasty refusal," intimating it would cause him "intense anguish." But she sent him just that—a "hasty refusal": "I must answer your letter as appears to me to be according to God's direction. And it certainly appears to be my duty to decline your proposals."[27] Miss Aldersey had stood over her timid teenage charge and dictated the response. With that accomplished, she wrote to Maria's uncle and legal guardian in England, strongly outlining her objections. He was uneducated, unordained, unconnected (with a mission society), and uncouth. And if that was not enough, he was short (Maria was tall), and he wore Chinese clothes.

Although Taylor was dejected when he received the response, he "strongly suspected that the hindrance lay with Miss Aldersey," and he refused to give up hope. In July of 1857, some months after his letter of proposal, Taylor secretly arranged an "interview" with Maria in the presence of another missionary. They shook hands, exchanged a few words, prayed, and then parted—a seemingly harmless meeting, but one that hurled the normally tranquil missionary community at Ningpo into the throes of dissension. Miss Aldersey threatened Taylor with a lawsuit; and Reverend W. A. Russell, her strongest ally, suggested Taylor "ought to be horsewhipped." Some were calmer in their reactions, suggesting that if Taylor were to return to England and finish his education, he would be worthy of her. Maria's response was eloquent: "I would wait if he went home in order to increase his usefulness. But is he to leave his work in order to gain a *name* for the sake of marrying me? If he loves me more than Jesus, he is not worthy of me—if he were to leave the *Lord's* work for world's honour, I would have nothing further to do with him."[28]

Reason, however, did not prevail. Maria was virtually placed under house arrest, and Reverend Russell would not allow her to take communion until she "should give evidence of repentance." In a letter home, Taylor wrote: "Dear Maria is charged with being a maniac, being fanatical, being indecent, weak-minded, too easily swayed; too obstinate and everything else bad."[29]

The months passed with only one brief meeting in October. Then in mid-November, with the help of a sympathetic friend, they met secretly and became secretly engaged. Wrote Taylor, "I was not long engaged without trying to make up for the number of kisses I ought to have had these last few months."[30] Back in England, William Tarn, Maria's uncle and guardian, was in a quandary. He had received not only Miss Aldersey's letter but also a letter from Maria and one from Taylor himself. Thousands of miles away, Tarn was outside the fray, and common sense directed him to calmly check out who the young man really was. So impressed was he with the reports, that he gave his unqualified approval of the match, and at the same time "condemned" Miss Aldersey's "want of judgement." His letters arrived in December, and the following month, on January 20, 1858, Hudson Taylor and Maria were married.[31]

Maria was the very woman Taylor needed to polish the rough edges of his personality and help focus his enthusiasm and ambitions, and from the start their marriage was a true partnership. They remained in Ningpo for three years, during which time Taylor was unexpectedly thrust into the supervision of the local hospital, a position that was clearly beyond his capability. Through that experience he became convinced that he needed to return to England for more medical training.

In 1860 the Taylors arrived in England for an extended furlough, one that would serve a number of purposes. Both were in ill health and needed a time of recuperation. It was also a time for further education. Taylor enrolled at the London Hospital, where he completed the Practical Chemistry course, the Midwifery course, and the Diploma for Membership of the Royal College of Surgeons. Another priority was translation work. Accompanying them to England was a Chinese assistant, and together with him and another missionary, Taylor made a revision of the Ningpo New Testament—an arduous task, sometimes consuming his energies for more than thirteen hours a day. But the most significant accomplishment during their extended furlough was organizational work. It was during this time that the China Inland Mission was born.

Taylor needed the backing of a mission organization, but there was none that suited his purposes—that is, none that would focus on reaching into the vast interior of China. As Taylor traveled through England, people were moved, not just by his enthusiasm, but also by his passion for lost souls: "A million a month dying without God" rang in the ears of his listeners, and many responded. They would form the support base for the new mission.

The China Inland Mission (CIM) was a unique missionary society molded around the experiences and personality of Hudson Taylor. It was an independent mission that appealed largely to the working classes. Taylor knew that China would never be evangelized if he had to rely on educated, ordained ministers to go, so he sought men and women among England's massive laboring classes. By appealing to this segment, he avoided competition with other mission boards, thus maximizing the missionary effort in China. His experience with the CES confirmed the need to establish the headquarters for the mission in China, where he would retain control. Indeed, as time went on he became a virtual dictator—though sensitive to the personal needs of those under him. As to finances and personal support, the CIM missionaries were offered no set salary but rather were to depend entirely on God for their needs. To avoid even the appearance of relying on human resources, offerings and other forms of direct appeals for money were strictly taboo.

Taylor knew that China would never be evangelized if he had to rely on educated, ordained ministers to go, so he sought men and women among England's massive laboring classes.

In 1865 the China Inland Mission was officially established, and the following year the Taylors returned to China with their four children and fifteen raw recruits, including seven single women. During his furlough Taylor had left his mark on England. In the words of the great Charles Haddon Spurgeon, "China, China, China is now ringing in our ears in that special, peculiar, musical, forcible, unique way in which Mr. Taylor utters it."[32]

The voyage to China was a remarkable one. Never before had such a large mission party set sail with the mission's founder and director on board, and the impact on the ship's crew was noticeable. By the time they had rounded the Cape, card playing and cursing had given way to Bible reading and hymn singing. But there were problems as well. The "germs of ill feeling and division" had crept in among them, and the once-harmonious band was sounding dissonant chords before it reached its destination. Lewis Nicol, a blacksmith by trade, was the ringleader of the dissenters. He and two other missionaries began comparing notes and came to the conclusion that they had received less substantial outfits than were usually received by Presbyterians and other missionaries. With that complaint came others: "The feeling among us appears to have been worse than I could have formed any conception of," wrote Taylor. "One was jealous because another had too many new dresses, another because someone else had more attention. Some were wounded because of unkind controversial discussions, and so on."[33] By talking to each missionary "privately and affectionately" Taylor was able to calm the dissention, but underlying feelings of hostility remained that would soon culminate in a near collapse of the infant CIM.

On arriving in Shanghai, Taylor ordered tailor-made Chinese clothes for each of the missionaries. They had been aware of his stand on the issue of Chinese dress and had agreed to it in principle, but this requirement, complicated by the ordinary pressures of culture shock, led to further turmoil. The initial discomfort of the clothing and the hair dyeing and head shaving were difficult enough, but the ridicule heaped on them by the resident missionary community in Shanghai was more than some could cope with, and the situation only seemed to worsen after the missionaries moved to the CIM compound at Hangchow. Taylor's leadership was challenged, and again the mission was caught up in strife. Even his most loyal supporters, Jennie Faulding and Emily Blatchley, had a falling out. Nicol and others flatly refused to wear native dress and began meeting

The Lammermuir Party that sailed from London on May 26, 1866 (from left to right, seated), 3rd and 4th, Mr. and Mrs. Lewis Nichol; 5th, Jennie Faulding; 6th and 7th, Hudson and Maria Taylor; (standing), 4th, Emily Blatchley.

separately for meals and devotions. The situation was tense, and the prospects for renewed fellowship seemed dim. Could anything save this visionary dream that had fallen into such shambles?

The price was high, but the mission was saved. During the heat of the summer of 1867, a year and a half after the missionaries had arrived in China, eight-year-old Gracie Taylor, whom her father idolized, became ill. For days Taylor sat beside her, giving her the best medical attention he was capable of giving, but her situation did not improve. The climate had also taken its toll on others; and during his vigil with Gracie, he was called away to treat Jane McLean, one of the missionaries who had strongly opposed him. Her illness was not as serious as supposed, and she soon recovered; but Taylor's delay in returning home to Gracie proved critical. He diagnosed water on the brain, but he was too late to be of any help. Her death was a heartrending tragedy, but it saved the CIM. The grievances were forgotten, and the outpouring of sympathy brought the missionaries back together, except for Nicol and his wife and the two single sisters, one of whom was Jane McLean. In the fall of 1867 Nicol was "put away" from the mission, and the McLean sisters resigned, allowing the mission family to move ahead in harmony.

The death of Gracie by no means ended the problems of the CIM. The greater crises were yet to come, and they revolved around the age-old hostility of Chinese for foreigners—a hostility that was magnified many times over in the interior. The first violent attack against the CIM missionaries occurred at Yangchow in 1868. The mission house was attacked and set on fire, and the missionaries, including Maria Taylor, barely escaped with their lives. As peaceable as the missionaries had been, it seems incredible that the incident could have brought on them the charge of their being warmongers, but such was the case. Although Taylor never sought for revenge or even requested British protection, certain hawkish politicians viewed the Yangchow incident as the perfect excuse to dispatch the gunboats of the Royal Navy to humiliate China, and the CIM suffered the consequences. Though shots were never fired, the *Times* of London despaired that England's "political prestige had been injured" and blamed it on "a company of missionaries assuming the title of the China Inland Mission."[34] The adverse publicity was devastating. Financial support plummeted, and prospective recruits suddenly lost interest.

While international controversy raged over the Yangchow incident, the CIM missionaries quietly returned to that city and continued their ministry. Their courage had been a testimony to the Chinese people, paving the way for more effective evangelism. A church was begun, and, wrote Emily Blatchley, "The converts here are different from any others we have known in China. There is such life, warmth, *earnestness* about them."[35]

In the aftermath of the Yangchow controversy, as critical newspaper editorials and private letters reached China, Taylor became deeply depressed—so much so that he lost his will to go on, even being tempted to end his own life. He was confronting the most serious spiritual battle of his life: "I hated myself; I hated my sin; and yet I gained no strength against it." The more he sought to attain spirituality, the less satisfaction he found: "Every day, almost every hour, the consciousness of failure and sin oppressed me." He was at the point of a mental collapse when he was, by his own account, rescued by a friend. Aware of Taylor's problem, the friend, in a letter, shared his own secret to spiritual living: "To *let* my loving Savior work in me *His will*. . . . Abiding, not striving or struggling. . . . Not a striving to have faith, or to increase our faith but a looking at the faithful one seems all we need." With that letter Taylor's life was changed: "God has made me a new man."[36]

His spiritual renewal came in time to sustain him through a period of severe personal testing. Soon after the Christmas season was over in January of 1870, the Taylors began making preparations to send their four older children back to England for their education. Emily Blatchley, who knew them well, offered to return with them and to care for them in England. But it was a painful time of trauma for the close-knit family—so much so that frail little five-year-old Sammy could not endure. He died in early February. Despite the tragedy, the decision to send the children away was firm. In March the Taylors sorrowfully parted with the other three children. They could not know that their kisses and hugs were the last they would ever give to their mother. During the hot summer that followed, Maria, who was late in another pregnancy, became seriously ill. In early July she delivered a baby boy, who lived less than two weeks. A few days after his death, Maria, at the age of thirty-three, died also.

Without Maria, Taylor was lonely. He had relied heavily on her support and good judgment and female companionship. In the months following her death, he renewed his friendship with Jennie Faulding, a twenty-seven-year-old single missionary who had been a close family friend. In England, Emily Blatchley, who had become a surrogate mother to the Taylor children, awaited his return—thinking that it would be natural for her to become Taylor's second wife. But when he arrived home, he was accompanied by Emily's former partner, Jennie, to whom he was now engaged.

Years earlier, when Emily and Jennie were living at the mission house in Hangchow with the Taylors, Lewis Nicol had spread rumors that Taylor was giving the young women good-night kisses and more. In his effort to discredit Taylor, he carried his charges to George Moule, an Anglican missionary who strongly opposed the ministry of single women. Moule called for an informal trial and questioned both Taylor and the young women. There was no evidence of wrongdoing—except bad judgment. The living arrangement that appeared inappropriate to some Western missionaries looked no different than polygamy to the Chinese.

Jennie Faulding, Hudson Taylor's second wife.

The news of Taylor's engagement to Jennie was devastating to Emily. "I feel sure from what I know of my own nature that I should, if I had had the chance, have been Mrs," she plaintively wrote in her diary. "And so it is in love and mercy my God cut off my flowing stream at which He perhaps saw I should drink too deeply. Such a sweet sweet stream, such a painful weaning! Therefore such a great blessing must await me for Jesus to bear to see me have so much pain."[37]

Returning to China in the fall of 1872 with Jennie, Taylor found himself increasingly involved in travel and administrative duties. He served as a troubleshooter and was continually called on to settle problems throughout China's many provinces as well as back in England. In 1874, after a two-year absence, he returned to England to bring together his children, who had been scattered due to Emily Blatchley's ill health. He returned to China in 1876, once again bringing with him more missionaries.

About all that Taylor could promise his new recruits was hardships and privations and negative publicity. Yet many volunteered to leave the drudgery of working-class Victorian England to answer God's call to missionary service. Financial support for the increasing numbers of missionaries—many of whom came from impoverished families—became an all-consuming endeavor. One of the interesting aspects of Hudson Taylor's ministry is his perspective on money. The impression given in CIM literature is that Taylor and Henry Frost, the American director, were relaxed about money, confident that the Lord would provide. In actuality, they were obsessed with money. In fact, four of the five "principles" of the CIM (requiring no debt, no guaranteed income, dependence on God alone, and no solicitation) related to money matters. Part of the obsession, according to Alvyn Austin, related to the very secretive nature of the organization.

> The old CIM was surrounded by an aura of secrecy which A. J. Broomhall . . . described as a "conspiracy of silence" and a "cocoon of silence" impossible for outsiders to penetrate. Within the mission, "family secrets" permeated every level: by the 1890s the rank and file in China were in open rebellion, London was not on speaking terms with Shanghai, Toronto would not reveal its finances to London, Australia was in debt, and Hudson Taylor was threatening to resign and take the work with him. The silence extended to the mission's archives, where Taylor decreed that "nothing detrimental to the mission be written and any documents which might prove an embarrassment in later years were to be destroyed." . . . The biggest secret was money.[38]

One such secret was the great sums of money that flooded into CIM coffers in later years, through donations as well as book publications. But the stories of privation were plenty, and the stories—like those of George Mueller's orphanages—had a similar theme, that of an extraordinary answer to prayer:

> More than once a dozen candidates and [Henry] Frost's six children sat down to the table without a scrap of food in the house; always, providentially, someone would appear at the door with a brace of partridges, a hamper of groceries, or a ton of coal, whatever was needed to survive the next day or week. These stories, repeated endlessly when the CIM became rich, reinforced the notion that it was always a poor faith organization.[39]

While hiding the millions in wealth, Taylor focused publicly on the millions of lost souls. The more Taylor worked and traveled in China, the greater his determination to reach the whole country became: "Souls on every land are perishing for lack of knowledge; more than 1,000 every hour are passing away into death and darkness."[40] It seemed like an impossible task, but he had a plan. If he could muster up one thousand evangelists, and if each of those evangelists could reach two hundred and fifty people a day with the gospel, the whole of China could be evangelized in a little more than three years. It was an impractical

THE "GREAT CENTURY"

1800 1810 1820 1830 1840 1850

INDIA AND CENTRAL ASIA

- (1793) William Carey arrives in India
- (1806) Henry Martyn arrives in India
- (1836) John Scudder begins
- (1834) Death of Carey
- (1812) First American missionaries set sail
- (1819) Founding of Serampore College
- (1830) Alexander Duff arrives in India
- (1824) Judson imprisoned
- (1845) Judson's
- (1850) Death

BLACK AFRICA

- (1799) Vanderkemp arrives at Cape
- (1816) Moffat begins missionary service
- (1825) Moffat settles at Kuruman
- (1841) Livingstone
- (1844) Krapf
- (1852)

THE FAR EAST

- (1807) Morrison arrives in Canton
- (1814) Morrison baptizes first convert
- (1840) Gutzlaff begins ministry on China coast
- (1842) Treaty of
- (1854)

THE PACIFIC ISLANDS

- (1796) *Duff* sails for South Pacific
- (1817) Williams arrives in South Seas
- (1819) Baptism of Pomare
- (1820) Hawaiian mission begins
- (1837) Coan begins revival
- (1838) Bible published
- (1839) Martyrdom
- (1848) Geddie

EUROPE AND NORTH AMERICA

- (1795) Founding of London Missionary Society
- (1799) Founding of Church Missionary Society
- (1810) Founding of the American Board of Commissioners for Foreign Missions
- (1835) Whitman leaves for
- (1837) Cherokee removal
- (1847)

1860 1870 1880 1890 1900

work in Madras

• (1870) Dr. Clara Swain arrives in India
furlough to U.S.
• (1878) John Clough's mass baptism
of Judson
• (1896) Amy Carmichael begins work in Tinnevelly

• (1864) Crowther consecrated bishop
• (1874) Stanley begins 999-day journey
• (1875) Grenfell arrives in Congo
arrives in Africa
• (1876) Mackay arrives in Uganda
arrives in Kenya
• (1890) Bishop Tucker arrives in Uganda
Livingstone begins
• (1892) Mary Slessor appointed British vice-consul
journey across Africa
• (1873) Death of Livingstone
• (1896) Death of Peter Cameron Scott

• (1865) First Protestant missionary arrives in Korea
• (1867) Death of Gracie Taylor
• (1868) Yangchow incident
• (1870) Death of Maria Taylor
• (1873) Lottie Moon arrives in China
Nanking
• (1877) Jennie Taylor returns to China alone
Taylor arrives in Shanghai
• (1885) "Cambridge Seven" sail for China
• (1859) Protestant missionaries arrive in Japan
• (1888) Goforths sail for China
• (1900) Boxer Rebellion

• (1855) Patteson sails for South Seas
• (1858) Paton arrives in Tanna
• (1866) Chalmers sails for South Seas
• (1871) Martyrdom of Patteson
in Hawaii
• (1873) Father Damien arrives on Molokai
in Tahitian
• (1882) Florence Young begins ministry at Fairymead
of Williams
• (1901) Martyrdom of Chalmers
arrives in Aneityum

• (1865) Founding of China Inland Mission
• (1886) Birth of Student Volunteer Movement
• (1887) Founding of Christian and Missionary Alliance
• (1890) Founding of Central American Mission
Oregon
• (1890) Founding of the Evangelical Alliance Mission
• (1892) Grenfell arrives in Labrador
Waiilatpu massacre
• (1893) Founding of Sudan Interior Mission
• (1895) Founding of Africa Inland Mission

numerical abstraction that allowed for no interaction and bonding. But while the plan itself had little merit, the CIM did leave an indelible mark on China. By 1882 the mission had entered every province, and in 1895, thirty years after its founding, it had more than six hundred and forty missionaries serving throughout China.

That Taylor sought to reach all of China with the gospel was certainly a lofty ambition, but that very goal may have been the decisive weakness of the CIM. In its effort to reach all of China, the policy of diffusion (as opposed to concentration) was implemented. According to the great missions historian Kenneth Scott Latourette, "The main purpose of the China Inland Mission was not to win converts or to build a Chinese church, but to spread a knowledge of the Christian Gospel throughout the empire as quickly as might be.... Nor, although Chinese assistants were employed, did it stress the recruiting and training of a Chinese ministry."[41] Such a policy led to problems. The hostility toward foreigners unleashed in the Boxer Rebellion and the Communist takeover some decades later illustrate the inherent weakness of a plan that did not make church planting an important goal.

The dark days were not long in coming for the CIM. The closing years of the nineteenth century were years of tension and unrest. The forces of modernization (and westernization) were clashing with the forces of tradition and nationalism. With imperial power moving to the side of the conservatives, the position of Westerners became more precarious. Then, in June 1900, an imperial decree from Peking ordered the death of all foreigners and the extermination of Christianity. The greatest disaster in the history of Protestant missions followed. One hundred and thirty-five missionaries and fifty-three missionary children were killed.

For Taylor, who was isolated in Switzerland, recuperating from severe mental and physical exhaustion, the news from China, though muted by those caring for him, was almost too much to bear, and he never fully recovered from the trauma. In 1902 he resigned his position as general director of the mission, and he and Jennie stayed on in Switzerland until 1904 when Jennie died. The following year Taylor returned to China, where he peacefully died the month after his arrival. In the years that followed, the CIM continued to grow. By 1914 it had become the largest foreign mission organization in the world, reaching its peak in 1934 with 1,368 missionaries. After the Communist takeover in 1950, the CIM, along with the other mission societies, was expelled from China. In 1964, after one hundred years of ministry, the CIM changed its name to the Overseas Missionary Fellowship, a name that was more indicative of its expanding missionary outreach in East Asia.

The contribution Hudson Taylor made to Christian missions was enormous. It is difficult to imagine where missions would be today without his vision and foresight. In the words of Ralph Winter, he was a "young upstart," whose impact on Christian missions rivaled or surpassed that of William Carey's—an impact that Winter goes on to perceptively summarize in light of later developments:

> With only trade school medicine, without any university experience much less missiological training, and a checkered past in regard to his own individualistic behavior while he was on the field, he was merely one more of the weak things that God uses to confound the wise. Even his early anti-church-planting missionary strategy was breathtakingly erroneous by today's church-planting standards. Yet God strangely honored him because his gaze was fixed upon the world's least-reached peoples. Hudson Taylor had a divine wind behind him. The Holy Spirit spared him from many pitfalls, and it was his organization, the China Inland Mission—the most cooperative servant organization yet to appear—that eventually served in one way or another over 6,000 missionaries, predominantly in the interior of China. It took 20 years for other missions to begin to join Taylor in his special emphasis—the unreached, inland frontiers.[42]

Taylor's greatest influence was with the thousands of like-minded missionaries of the CIM and later faith missions who sought to evangelize the "unreached inland frontiers." But there were others inspired by Taylor who went in entirely different directions. Timothy Richard (1845–1919) was one—a name revered today among many Chinese Christians as the greatest of all missionaries to China. His early years of missionary work convinced him that there were more effective ways of bringing Christianity to China. Itinerant evangelism, he argued, should be carried out by native evangelists, and the missionary should reach out to influential leaders. He also organized humanitarian endeavors and insisted that Western science and technology was an important means of bringing the faith to China.

Jonathan and Rosalind Goforth

Of all the missionaries who served in East Asia during the nineteenth and early twentieth centuries, perhaps no one witnessed greater immediate response than did Jonathan Goforth, who, according to J. Herbert Kane, was China's most outstanding evangelist. China was Goforth's base, but he also ministered in Korea and Manchuria, and wherever he went, revival followed.

Goforth, the seventh of eleven children, was born in western Ontario in 1859. He dedicated himself to ministry after reading the *Memoirs of Robert Murray M'Cheyne,* but his call to missions did not come until later when he heard a traveling missionary give a powerful appeal for workers in China: "As I listened to these words, I was overwhelmed with shame. . . . From that hour I became a foreign missionary."[43]

After graduating from Knox College, Goforth conducted city mission work in Toronto, where he met Rosalind Smith, a talented and sophisticated art student—an unlikely prospect for a missionary wife. But she looked beyond "the shabbiness of his clothes." For her, it was love at first sight: "It all happened within a few moments, but as I sat there, I said to myself, 'That is the man I would like to marry!'"[44] Later that year they became engaged, and at that time Rosalind got her first taste of the sacrifice she would encounter the rest of her life. Her dreams of an engagement ring were dashed when he told her that the money he would have spent for a ring must instead go for Christian literature.

Goforth initially applied to the China Inland Mission because his own church, the Presbyterian Church of Canada, had no missionary work in China. But before he received a response from the CIM, Presbyterian students from Knox College rallied to his cause and vowed to raise the money themselves to send him to China. Prior to his sailing, he traveled through Canada, speaking out for missions. His messages were powerful, as the report from a student illustrates:

> I was going up to the Alumni meeting in Knox College, Toronto, determined to do everything in my power to frustrate the crazy scheme which the students of the college were talking about, i.e., starting a mission field of their own in Central China. I also felt that I needed a new overcoat; my old one was looking rather shabby. So I thought I would go to Toronto to kill two birds with one stone. I would help sidetrack the scheme and buy an overcoat. But this fellow here upset my plans completely. He swept me off my feet with an enthusiasm for missions which I had never experienced before, and my precious overcoat money went into the fund![45]

Jonathan Goforth, missionary evangelist to China, Manchuria, and Korea.

In 1888 the Goforths sailed for China to serve in Honan province, where they began a life of hardships and lonely separations. They both suffered frequent illnesses, and five of their eleven children died. They endured fire and flood and barely escaped with their lives in a harrowing thousand-mile flight to safety during the Boxer Rebellion of 1900.

The Goforths' efforts to reach the Chinese were unconventional by most missionary standards, particularly their "open-house" evangelism. Their home, with its European interior design, and their furnishings (including a kitchen stove, a sewing machine, and an organ), were objects of curiosity to the Chinese, and they decided to relinquish their privacy in order to make contacts with the people of the province. Visitors came from miles around, once more than two thousand in one day, to tour the house. Before each tour began, Goforth gave a gospel message. He preached an average of eight hours a day, and during a five-month period some twenty-five thousand people came to visit. Rosalind ministered to the women, speaking to as many as fifty at a time who were gathered in their yard.

Rosalind Goforth, wife of Jonathan Goforth.

This type of evangelism paved the way for his future ministry of traveling from town to town conducting revivals, but not all of his colleagues approved: "Some may think that receiving visitors is not real mission work, but I think it is. I put myself out to make friends with the people and I reap the results when I go to their villages to preach. Often the people of a village will gather around me and say, 'We were at your place and you showed us through your house, treating us like friends.' Then they almost always bring me a chair to sit on, a table to lay my Bible on, and some tea."[46]

The Boxer Rebellion in 1900 interrupted their mission work, and after they returned to China their family life changed to accommodate his new plan for a broad itinerant ministry. Goforth had developed his idea before Rosalind returned, and soon after her arrival he confronted her with the scheme: "My plan is to have one of my helpers rent a suitable place in a large center for us to live in, and that we, as a family, stay a month in the center, during which time we will carry on intensive evangelism. I will go with my men to villages or on the street in the daytime, while you receive and preach to the women in the courtyard. The evenings will be given to a joint meeting with you at the organ and with plenty of gospel hymns. Then at the end of a month, we will leave an evangelist behind to teach the new believers while we go on to another place to open it in the same way. When a number of places are opened, we will return

Boxer poster showing Chinese attitude toward foreigners.

once or twice a year." As Rosalind listened, her "heart went like lead." It was not suited to a family. Exposing their little ones to the infectious diseases that were so prevalent out in the villages was too risky, and she could not forget the "four little graves" they had already left behind on Chinese soil.[47] Although she objected, he went ahead with his plan, convinced it was God's will.

Rosalind frequently had reservations about her husband's dedication to the family. As a wife she felt less than fully secure in her position. Before she and the children returned to Canada alone in 1908, she probed him concerning his commitment to her: "Suppose I were stricken with an incurable disease in the homeland and had but a few months to live. If we cabled you to come, would you come?" Goforth obviously did not want to answer the question. An outright "no" would have been too harsh, but Rosalind persisted until he gave his answer—in the form of a question to her: "Suppose our country were at war with another nation and I, a British officer in command of an important unit. Much depended upon me as commander as to whether it was to be victory or defeat. Would I, in that event, be permitted to forsake my post in response to a call from my family in the homeland, even if it were what you suggest?" What could she say? She had no choice but to sadly reply, "No."[48]

The itinerant ministry that Goforth began in the early years of the twentieth century was a stepping stone that led to the great revivals he conducted in the years that followed. This ministry began in 1907 when he and another missionary toured Korea and initiated a revival movement that swept through the churches there, resulting in an "amazing increase of converts." From there they ministered in Manchuria with similar results.

As he traveled through China and Manchuria in the years that followed, the revival ministry grew. Some within the mission were wary of what they deemed to be "fanaticism" and "Pentecostalism," but Goforth disregarded the criticism. In 1918 he conducted a two-week campaign with Chinese soldiers under the command of General Feng Yu-Hsiang, himself a Christian. At the end of the campaign nearly five thousand soldiers and officers took part in a communion service.

An issue that Goforth continually faced with his own mission board related to authority. He regarded the "Holy Spirit's leading" above the "hard-and-fast rules" of the presbytery under which he served. Thus, according to his wife, "with his convictions concerning Divine guidance *of himself,* he naturally came often into conflict with other members of the Honan Presbytery," making him "not easy to get along with." He insisted that each missionary should have "freedom to carry on his or her work as each one felt led." It was a difficult issue, and he often "found himself hampered and held back from following fully what he deemed was the Holy Spirit's leading."[49]

In the years that followed the problems did not diminish. Confrontations continued and friction increased, particularly in the 1920s when the Fundamentalist-Modernist controversy found its way to China. New missionaries, steeped in higher criticism, were arriving on the field, and Goforth "felt powerless to stem the tide." His only recourse was to "preach, as never before, salvation through the cross of Calvary and demonstrate its power."[50]

Goforth's ministry continued on into his seventies—even after the onset of blindness. At the age of seventy-four he returned to Canada, where he spent the last eighteen months of his life traveling and speaking at nearly five hundred meetings. He carried on to the very end, speaking four times on the Sunday before he died.

Mildred Cable

There are thousands of interesting missionary stories related to China—and to the China Inland Mission alone—but few exceed the enigma and intrigue of Mildred Cable and her two partners, Evangeline and Francesca French, known together as simply "the Trio." Born in England in 1877, Cable had served in China with the French sisters, teaching and conducting itinerant evangelism for some twenty years. Their work with the CIM could be considered routine—until they sensed the calling of God to China's great northwest, the "great cities where the name of Christ was not even known."[51]

They initially kept their calling to themselves. But word that these middle-aged women were requesting relocation leaked out. "Some wrote, saying in more or less parliamentary language, that there were no fools like old fools." It would be a drastic change for them, and many wondered aloud if they had misinterpreted what they perceived to be a call from God.

> To a good many people it had seemed just plain foolishness. Why leave this important and successful school work to go off on some harebrained scheme of roaming over vast deserts looking for a few isolated tent dwellers and remote villages, where there were literally tens of thousands of people near at hand all needing to hear the Gospel?[52]

With permission granted from the board, the trio began the long and arduous journey north, traveling for months by oxcart, which "rumbled and jolted over the uneven muddy mountain roads." On one occasion in particular, when they were waist deep in three feet of mud, "the call of the great Northwest was very faint." Their destination was the City of the Prodigals, the last border town before crossing into the vast Gobi desert—the town where criminals hid with a ready escape across the border. But it was also a city of traders and merchants.

> Little by little the Trio came to realize the tremendous importance of this network of trade routes, by means of which the cities of Central Asia are kept in vital contact with each other. The native news-distributing system whose speed, accuracy and simplicity baffles Western understanding might surely be made a means of spreading the knowledge of the Gospel, so that men in the marketplaces should hear, not only the political happenings of Europe or Afghanistan, but also that "Christ Jesus came into the world to save sinners."[53]

As time passed, the Trio developed a routine of spending their winters in the City of Prodigals, where they settled into teaching and preaching and church planting, and the remaining eight months of the year conducting itinerant evangelism in the vast desert beyond. Here there were scattered settlements in arable areas—their visits timed to correspond with fairs and festivals. Such gatherings gave them opportunities for street preaching and literature distribution. They kept records of their work, and one year they reported visiting nearly three thousand homes, conducting six hundred and fifty-six meetings, and selling some forty thousand portions of Scripture.

Long-term results were difficult to calculate, but when they visited the City of Sands after a five-year absence due to warfare in the region, they were pleasantly surprised by their welcome on a Sunday morning. "It was hoped that a few people would meet for public worship, but to everyone's amazement the inn room was crowded to the doors, and after the service was over, one and another stood and asked to have his name on a list of inquirers."[54]

Mildred Cable had begun her mission service in 1901, the year after the devastation of the Boxer uprising. Her work with the French sisters ended in 1936, when all foreigners were ordered out of the region. But tiny churches had been planted, and literature had found its way along the trade routes of the Gobi Desert and beyond. They had carried on the strategy of Hudson Taylor and the CIM well into the twentieth century.

There were others who went beyond the borders of China proper to carry the gospel to the ends of the earth. Among them was James O. Fraser (1886–1938), also serving with the CIM. He worked among the Lisu living in the mountains along the Tibetan-Burmese border. He encouraged indigenous family evangelism, and through that means some sixty thousand were baptized. Yet the work was difficult, and there were many disappointing setbacks. As he reflected on the work among the Lisu, he could have been speaking for the work throughout China in the nineteenth and early twentieth centuries:

> I am not painting a dark picture; I only wish to tell you the real position of things as candidly as possible. In some ways they are ahead of ordinary churchgoers at home.... But with the exception of a few, very few, bright earnest young people, there are not many who wish to make any progress or are really alive spiritually.[55]

SELECT BIBLIOGRAPHY

Barr, Pat. *To China with Love: The Lives and Times of Protestant Missionaries in China 1860–1900.* Garden City, NY: Doubleday, 1973.

Broomhall, A. J. *Hudson Taylor and China's Open Century.* Book One: *Barbarians at the Gates.* London: Hodder & Stoughton, 1981.

Broomhall, Marshall. *Robert Morrison: A Master-builder.* New York: Doran, 1924.

Cable, Mildred, and Francesca French. *Something Happened.* London: Hodder & Stoughton, 1934.

Crossman, Eileen. *Mountain Rain: A New Biography of James O. Fraser.* Southampton, UK: Overseas Missionary Fellowship, 1982.

Goforth, Rosalind. *Goforth of China.* Grand Rapids: Zondervan, 1937.

Latourette, Kenneth Scott. *A History of Christian Missions in China.* New York: Macmillan, 1929.

Pollock, J. C. *Hudson Taylor and Maria: Pioneers in China.* Grand Rapids: Zondervan, 1976.

Taylor, Dr. and Mrs. Howard. *J. Hudson Taylor: God's Man in China.* Chicago: Moody Press, 1978.

Thompson, Phyllis. *Desert Pilgrim.* Lincoln, NE: Back to the Bible, 1957.

8

The Pacific Islands: Preaching in "Paradise"

The islands of the Pacific have often been depicted as a paradise on earth. Explorers and traders came away with dazzling accounts of breathtaking beauty, and writers, including Herman Melville, Robert Louis Stevenson, and James Michener, masterfully adorned their novels with the enchantment of the island world. "Writers have vied with each other in their glowing descriptions of the wondrous picturesqueness of the scenery, the rugged mountains, deep valleys, and tranquil lagoons; the glistening fringe of sandy beach, the stately trees, feathery palms, and luxuriant creepers; the profusion of bright blossoms, delicious fruits, and gorgeous birds."[1] It was into this setting that missionaries came, first Roman Catholic monks who accompanied explorers, and later Protestants commissioned by mission societies.

Oceania, the term generally used to designate the Pacific islands, consists of some fifteen hundred islands divided into three major groupings: Polynesia, the largest group, extends from Hawaii in the north to New Zealand in the south; Micronesia, the group of small islands located between Hawaii and the Philippines, includes the Marianas and the Caroline, Marshall, and Gilbert Islands; and Melanesia, the islands south of Micronesia and north of Australia, includes Fiji, Santa Cruz, New Guinea, the New Hebrides, New Caledonia, and the Solomon Islands. The size of the islands ranges from New Guinea, the second largest island in the world, to tiny dots in the ocean such as the Marshall Islands, whose total land area is less than one hundred square miles. In fact, all of Micronesia is smaller in land area than the state of Rhode Island; and the population of Micronesia, and all of Oceania, was correspondingly small—excluding New Zealand, probably fewer than two million.

Nevertheless, this was a land of exotic tribal people—people who had never heard the gospel—and mission societies were eager to expend resources to reach them despite the geographical barriers. The first European mission endeavor consisted of Franciscan friars accompanying Magellan and his party of explorers in 1521. For Magellan, this historic expedition would be his last. He was killed, along with some of his crew, after trying to force natives to pay homage to the king of Spain. Later, during the sixteenth century, Roman Catholic missionaries returned to the islands, but their mission was short-lived.

It was Captain Cook's discoveries that captured the imagination of Protestants. The London Missionary Society was formed in 1795 by ministers and lay people for the purpose of sending missionaries to Tahiti "or some other of the islands of the South Sea." Soon other mission societies followed, including those founded by the Wesleyans, Congregationalists, Presbyterians, and Anglicans; and by the end of the nineteenth century, Oceania was considered a shining success story of Protestant missions.

Oceania was considered a shining success story of Protestant missions.

The first Protestant missionaries were from Great Britain and later from Australia, America, and Germany. When Catholics came to stay toward the middle of the nineteenth century, bitter rivalry ensued, with angry accusations from both sides: "Popery rises its hideous head," wrote Joseph Waterhouse (a Wesleyan missionary), "sanctioning the eating of human flesh, polygamy, adultery, and fornication!!"[2] Perhaps the greatest source of tension between Protestants and Catholics, however, was nationality. The Catholics were French, and there was a genuine fear among Protestants that French political and military power might prevail on the islands.

The geographical uniqueness of the Pacific islands had from the very beginning obvious implications on mission strategy. Transportation became an all-encompassing issue. It was simply not enough to send missionaries out to the South Seas, drop them on isolated islands, and expect them to be satisfied for a year or more until the next passing ship arrived. The small size and population of most of the islands fostered a sense of claustrophobia, and the missionaries who had ventured so far from their native land were suddenly isolated and hemmed in by the vast Pacific Ocean. Mission-owned ships soon became the logical solution to the problem. The *Morning Star* in Micronesia, the *John Williams* in Polynesia, and the *Southern Cross* in Melanesia—each name taken by a succession of mission ships that almost took on personalities of their own—played a key role in the evangelization of the island world.

With the use of mission ships, many of the European missionaries became traveling field directors who coordinated the work of native evangelists and teachers. "The native missionaries were to prove the main strength of Christian missions in the South Seas," according to Graeme Kent. "Lacking the prestige of the Europeans, they were ignored, bullied, and sometimes killed by islanders with

THE PACIFIC ISLANDS

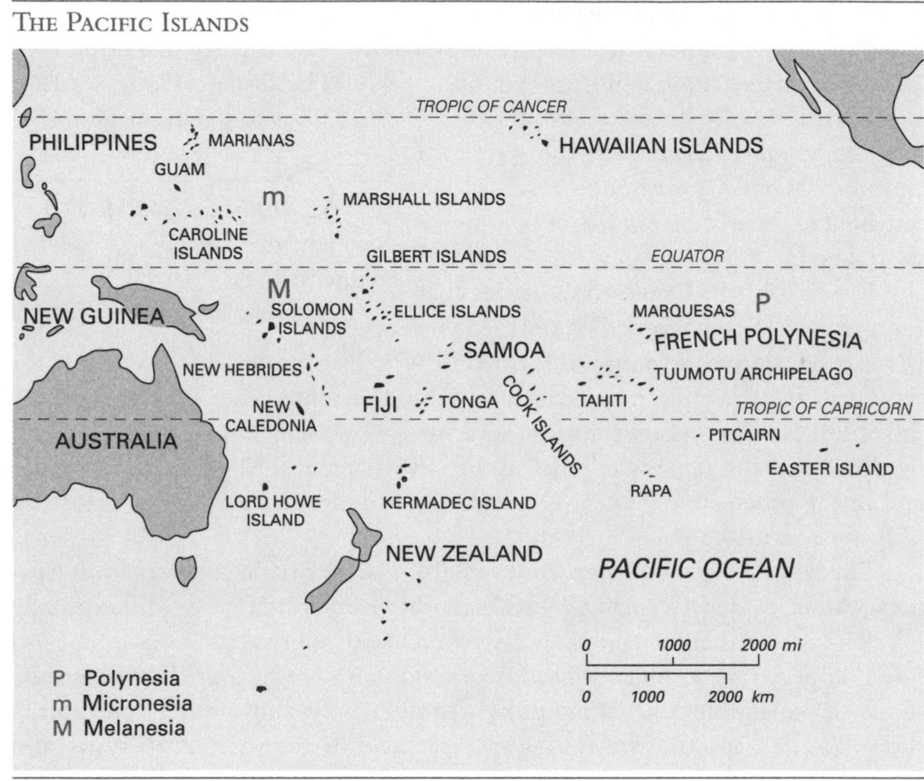

whom they cast their lot, but almost to a man [they] persevered, and between 1839 and 1860 most faiths owed more than they cared to admit to these island missionaries who went where few Europeans dared to venture."[3]

But life was also difficult for the Western missionary. Mission work was a life of hardship anywhere, but in the island world the hardships were exacerbated by the ever-present prospect of material gain and by the free lifestyle and sexual openness of the native people. The practice of "going native" was, according to Stephen Neill, "a much commoner happening than is generally reflected in the edifying accounts of these early missions."[4] Here in this island paradise missionaries faced temptations that had never confronted them in their sheltered backgrounds. Some overcame; others did not.

Despite the personal failures of the missionaries, the story of missions in this area of the world is a success story—at least compared to other areas. In many instances there were "people movements" that brought large families and sometimes whole tribes to Christianity. These mass movements have been meticulously documented by Alan R. Tippett in *People Movements in Southern Polynesia* and *Solomon Island Christianity*. He points out that in many instances there was no appreciable church growth until the missionaries realized the vital significance of the family and tribal unit. This realization helped bring about the unparalleled church growth that continued into the twentieth century.

Henry Nott and the *Duff* Missionaries

Unlike early Protestant missionary ventures elsewhere in the world, where missionaries trickled in one by one or in small groups, the entry into the Pacific islands began with a big splash. On a foggy London morning in August of 1796, thirty missionaries, along with six wives and three children, all sponsored by the London Missionary Society (LMS), boarded the mission ship *Duff* and began their seven-month ocean voyage to Tahiti. Such an extensive Protestant missionary endeavor had never before been launched, and it was a day to remember. There was an enthusiastic send-off as crowds of earnest supporters came down to the riverbank, "singing the praises of God," with high expectations of what their Christian ambassadors would accomplish in this most "uncivilized" area of the world.

After a less-than-tranquil voyage, the missionaries landed safely on Tahiti on Saturday, March 4, 1797, and on the following day they conducted a European-style church service, viewed with more than passing interest by the islanders. With the Sabbath behind them, the missionaries wasted no time getting settled, and within a matter of weeks Captain Wilson, himself a Christian, felt they were secure enough to be left on their own. He then proceeded to Tonga to establish ten missionaries on that island. The atmosphere at Tonga was less inviting than that of Tahiti, and Wilson left the missionaries with mixed emotions. But his job as a missionary chauffeur was still not finished; he had two remaining missionaries, William Crook and John Harris, to deposit on the Marquesas.

The missionaries confronted not spears and clubs, but a too friendly welcome—one their missionary orientation had not prepared them for.

It was on the islands of the Marquesas that the LMS encountered its first of many setbacks in the Pacific islands. The missionaries confronted, not the terrifying reception of spears and clubs, the dreaded and all-too-real vision of their nightmares, but a too friendly welcome—one their missionary orientation had not prepared them for. Hardly had the ship anchored when two beautiful unclad native women swam out into the surf and around the ship shouting "Waheine! Waheine!" (We are women). Although Wilson refused to let them board the ship and tried to discount their behavior, as a seasoned sailor he could not have been oblivious to what was ahead for his two rookie missionaries. Nevertheless, Crook and Harris had a job to do, and they dutifully loaded their belongings into a small boat and paddled ashore.

The following morning before lifting anchor, Wilson sent crewmen ashore to check on them. There on the beach they found Harris with his belongings, discouraged and very anxious to leave. After being separated from Crook, he was left to spend the night in the company of the chief's wife. Having encountered white men before, she no doubt believed such behavior would be well-received, but Harris rebuffed her. Leaving him alone, she went back to the village and, according to Graeme Kent, returned "accompanied by other women" and "swooped on the sleeping man and conducted a practical examination" to see if he was actually a man.[5] So distraught was Harris by the ordeal that he refused to remain on the island. Crook was left alone to establish the work on the Marquesas. But before the year had ended he left also, and the LMS was left with two outposts in the South Pacific, Tahiti and Tonga.

On Tonga, the missionaries faced entirely different problems. It did not take them long to discover that they were not the only Europeans on the island. Three sailors who had deserted their ships had made the islands their home. From the very beginning they were a "thorn in the flesh" to the missionaries. They viewed the missionaries as a threat to their easygoing lifestyle, and they sought to incite the natives against them. But physical danger was not their only ploy. They taunted the missionaries with their free and easy access to sexual pleasures and mocked their straitlaced celibate existence. The missionaries held firm in their convictions—except one, George Veeson, a bricklayer, who left his colleagues to join the beachcombers. The chief gave him land and servants, and he took for himself a harem of "wives."

The disgrace caused by Veeson was a deep humiliation for the LMS, but there were even greater problems facing the missionaries on Tonga. Civil war had erupted on the island. Three missionaries, caught in the middle of the warring factions, lost their lives, and the surviving six hid in caves until they were rescued by a passing ship. Only the renegade missionary Veeson remained, and even his days on the island were numbered. His conscience, though temporarily seared, prevented him from enjoying his promiscuous lifestyle, and he returned to England a repentant man and publicly confessed his sin, assuring his supporters that his experience was an isolated incident. "Considering all the obstacles," writes Kent, "it must be a great satisfaction to the promoters of the South Sea Mission . . . that no other of the missionaries . . . acted unbecoming their sacred character"[6] (an assumption that, unfortunately, was untrue). Though abandoned for a time, Tonga was again visited by missionaries in the 1820s—this time by Wesleyan Methodists. The most noted of their number was John Thomas, a blacksmith, who witnessed success during his twenty-five-year tenure on that island.

Meanwhile, the LMS work on Tahiti had been slowly moving ahead despite numerous setbacks. Three of the missionaries, like Veeson, had "gone native," and others had left, discouraged and ill. But for the perseverance of a stubborn, uneducated bricklayer, Henry Nott (who worked for sixteen years without any visible signs of success), the work there would no doubt have been abandoned. Nott was born in Broomsgrove, England, in 1774, and at the age of twenty-two sailed aboard the *Duff* as a single missionary. At first he was only one of many missionaries struggling to make even the slightest impact on the hearts and minds of the people. But as dangers and problems multiplied, other missionaries gave up (eleven departing at one time). Nott found himself left with only three others, and even they spoke of going home. Times were hard for the missionaries. In 1808 their house and printing press were destroyed and most of their belongings were stolen. To make matters worse, the *Duff* was captured by the French during the Napoleonic wars, and more than four years elapsed without news or supplies from home. With their food supply depleted, they were forced to forage in the mountains for wild berries and fruits. Nevertheless, Nott shunned any talk of retreat.

But for the perseverance of Henry Nott, the work on Tahiti would no doubt have been abandoned.

From the very beginning, the Tahitian missionaries had to contend with the hedonistic and authoritarian king, Pomare, who had a reputation for brutality, having offered some two thousand human sacrifices. Yet the missionaries needed him as an ally, and they sought to win his friendship. At times he responded favorably, but at other times he treated them as enemies. When he died in 1804, his son, Pomare II, came to power. He made peace with the missionaries, viewing them as a source for European goods, particularly muskets and ammunition. His profession of faith came while he was pleading for weapons to put down rebel forces. With increased rebel threats on their own lives, the missionaries agreed to supply Pomare and his professing Christian followers with guns and ammunition. It was a pragmatic move on which their very survival depended. According to a native observer, the rebels would have won "had not the native missionaries been taught to shoot as they have been taught to pray, and been given guns along with Bibles."[7]

During the rebellion the missionaries all fled Tahiti except for Nott, who bravely held his post, refusing to leave the island. He weakened only once, when he journeyed briefly to Australia to claim a special delivery from the LMS—one of four "godly young women" who had been sent out as wives for the lay missionaries. Nott, as did a number of other single missionaries, had taken a native wife, but bowing to the objections of his fellow missionaries, the union was "annulled by common consent, and no doubt conveniently forgotten when the four 'godly young women' arrived by special shipment."[8]

Nott may have been far happier and more compatible with his native wife than with the "godly woman" that was sent to him. Though described physically as having a "perfect curvature," she received less favorable reviews in regard to her temperament. A fellow missionary wrote: "Her Tong is daily employed in abusing her Husband in the most cruel manner and to slander others with the lest [*sic*] just cause. . . . Her Feet of late are never directed to the place where prayer is wont to be made but daily she joins with those who are studious in their design to perplex and thwart us."[9] She was generally regarded as a disgrace to the mission. Dr. Ross, an LMS missionary, lamented her drinking problem and claimed that "when intoxicated she is absolutely mad and cares not what she does or says." It was his opinion, when she died some months later, that she "drank herself to death."[10]

After the rebellion was over, Nott continued his forthright evangelism, ever pleading with Pomare to forsake his sinful ways. Pomare was not only a drunkard and a polygamist but also a promiscuous homosexual, and he seemingly had little intention of letting his professed Christianity interfere with such activities. Nevertheless, his final victory over the rebels in 1815 did signal a breakthrough for Christianity on the island. Pomare publicly renounced the pagan idols and altars. To demonstrate his sincerity, he gathered up his twelve personal idols and presented them to the missionaries (no doubt in response to their prompting) to be shipped to London and delivered to the LMS directors as evidence of what was taking place on Tahiti. The idols made a great sensation in England, where special prayer meetings had been conducted for the conversion of Pomare. They were just the curios the LMS needed to reestablish its reputation in the South Seas. Contributions poured in.

For Pomare, though, the renunciation of idols was not enough. He desired full status as a professing Christian, including baptism. But the missionaries were reluctant. Though hundreds, perhaps thousands, might as a result turn to Christianity, it would be a mockery in view of his continued lapses into immorality. After prolonged discussion and prayer, they agreed that he could be baptized—though they delayed it for seven years. When it finally occurred in 1819, it was a momentous occasion, with some five thousand people looking on, and it paved the way for many others to make their faith public. Soon after, a visiting Russian nobleman was amazed by the absence of infanticide, cannibalism, and war—which he credited to the European missionaries.

Elsewhere in the South Pacific the progress of missions during the early decades of the nineteenth century was laboriously slow. Other islands besides Tahiti were being evangelized, but for every apparent victory there seemed to be a comparable setback. Only in Hawaii, far to the north, was there marked evidence that Christianity was taking hold.

Hiram Bingham and Hawaiian Missions

The story of Christian missions in Hawaii (or the Sandwich Islands, as they were then called) is an unusual account of how a handful of American missionaries moved into an unfamiliar culture and within a few short decades dominated every facet of society. It is an intriguing tale of struggle and interpersonal conflict, so fascinating that in recent years it became the subject matter for James Michener's best-selling novel *Hawaii,* a novel that in many ways misrepresented

Christian missions in the islands. Michener's ranting, bigoted missionary, bent on destroying the native culture, is not typical of missionaries sent to Hawaii. True, they were tainted by the pervasive nineteenth-century sentiments of racial superiority, but they also shared concern for the well-being of the Hawaiians.

The Hawaiian Islands were inhabited around A.D. 900, but not until 1778 did Hawaii become known to the Western world, and then only by accident. Captain James Cook was sailing from Tahiti to the west coast of North America when he discovered this island paradise. During his first visit he was thought to be a god by the Hawaiians. But on his second visit in 1779, their reverence for him began to wane, and during a quarrel with one of the chiefs, Cook was killed. Despite this incident, contact with Hawaii continued, and the breach was soon mended. In the decades that followed, trade was established with the Western world, and the islands became a favorite stopover for ships trading in the Far East. During these layovers native boys were sometimes invited to sail with the crew, and some of the Hawaiian youths found their way to the United States.

It was this contact with the native people that sparked American interest in Hawaiian missions. The best known of these youths was Obookiah, who was found crying one morning on the steps of Yale College because of his unfulfilled desire for learning. Edwin Dwight, a student, began tutoring him, hoping that he would return to Hawaii and evangelize his people. Obookiah made a profession of faith, but he became ill and died during the winter of 1818. However, his story stirred enthusiasm for bringing the gospel to Hawaii.

Hiram Bingham, missionary to Hawaii.

The American Board of Commissioners for Foreign Missions (ABCFM) took the initiative, and within a year after Obookiah's death a contingent of missionaries were ready to sail to Hawaii. Perhaps fearing the enthusiasm might die down, the directors moved with a sense of urgency. Potential candidates were contacted and interviewed in record time and urged to secure wives and prepare to leave. The Board was conscious of the problems single missionaries faced in the South Seas. Of the seven couples who left for Hawaii in October of 1819, six of them were married within a matter of weeks before departure.

During the five-month voyage, Hiram Bingham, a graduate of Andover Seminary, assumed the leadership of the little band. He and Sybil had been married less than two weeks before sailing—and precisely two weeks after they first met. They were well suited for each other, and their leadership held the team together. On arriving in Hawaii wholly unprepared for what lay ahead, the New Englanders were shocked by what they found, as is evident from Bingham's telling description: "The appearance of destitution, degradation, and barbarism among the chattering and almost naked savages . . . was appalling. Some of our number, with gushing tears, turned away from the spectacle. Others with firmer nerve continued their gaze, but were ready to exclaim, 'Can these be human beings? . . . Can such things be civilized? Can they be Christianized? Can we throw ourselves upon these rude shores, and take up our abode for life among such people, for the purpose of training them for Heaven?'"[11]

Whether or not the Hawaiians made any adverse observations about their priggish New England visitors is unknown, but at least they had the courtesy to warmly welcome them—"far more courtesy," according to one historian, "than they deserved."[12] Fortunately for the missionaries, the timing of their visit was favorable. With a new king, a significant change had recently occurred. Idolatry and human sacrifice had been outlawed, and the long history of tribal warfare seemed to be over. The missionaries were given permission to go ashore and to begin their work.

The task that lay ahead was enormous, especially if they hoped to fulfill the assignment they had received from the Board: "You are to open your hearts wide and set your marks high. You are to aim at nothing short of covering these islands with fruitful fields, and pleasant dwellings and schools and churches, and of raising up the whole people to an elevated state of Christian civilization."[13] A "state of Christian civilization" meant a New England version, far removed from the easygoing lifestyle of the Hawaiians. Not surprisingly there was resistance, or if not that, at least a complete lack of understanding of the Puritan moral code.

The greatest resistance the missionaries confronted (as was the case in the South Pacific) came from their own people—sailors who were upset with interference in native lifestyle, which encouraged young women to go on board the trading vessels and sell themselves for a few cheap trinkets. As the missionary influence increased, the practice declined. More than once Bingham and his colleagues faced the wrath of the sailors. In one incident, sailors from the *Dolphin* came ashore and attacked Bingham with knives and clubs and would have no doubt killed him but for a rescue by faithful Hawaiians.

Despite the opposition, the progress of missions in Hawaii moved with amazing speed. Churches and schools were established, and soon they were overflowing with students hearing the gospel and learning to read. A school organized by Sybil Bingham enrolled several leading women, including the king's mother, who was baptized in 1823. The most noteworthy conversion was that of Kapiolani, a queen who had lived in dread fear of the goddess Pele who, according to tradition, resided in the fuming volcanic crater of Kilauea. After professing faith in front of hundreds of horrified onlookers, she flaunted Pele by climbing up the volcanic mountain and descending into the crater to demonstrate the impotence of this false god. She threw rocks and sacred berries into the lake of lava as she ridiculed the superstition of the people. Then, returning to the bystanders, she testified of her faith. It was a dramatic incident that did more to pave the way for Christianity in Hawaii than all the missionary diatribes against Pele put together.

Queen Kapiolani's dramatic flaunting of the goddess did more to pave the way for Christianity in Hawaii than all the missionary diatribes against Pele put together.

By 1830, after only a decade in Hawaii (and after a second group of missionaries had arrived), the missionaries had spread out to other islands. Bingham was held in high regard, and many chiefs looked to him as far more than just their spiritual leader. According to one observer, they even let "King Bingham" tell them what laws to make. "The blue laws of Connecticut are the laws of Hawaii," wrote another critic.[14]

But the blue laws did not fit Hawaii. It was a frustrating situation, according to Bradford Smith, particularly in dealing with sexual sins:

> Patiently the brethren tried to explain the seventh commandment. But in rendering it into Hawaiian they learned to their horror that there were about twenty ways of committing adultery Hawaiian-style. If they used any one of the twenty names, that left all the other avenues to pleasure wide open. They ended up with the vague phrase, "thou shalt not sleep mischievously," thus making the whole thing a state of mind.[15]

Even the most faithful Hawaiian Christians struggled with sexual immorality. In summing up the situation, missionary teacher Lorrin Andrews wrote that "adultery has been the crying sin of native teachers." Another missionary wrote, "Most teachers have lain with many or all of their scholars." The missionaries had believed they were aiding the cause of morality when they insisted converts wear clothes, "only to discover," according to Smith, "that the clothes the girls put on became a source of allurement to men who all their lives had taken nudity for granted!"[16]

The missionaries themselves stayed above the lax moral environment, but they did face other temptations, particularly in the area of materialism. Some of the missionaries were accused of marketing goods in competition with the foreign merchants and traders. Artemas Bishop, for example, was employing natives to manufacture cigars in exchange for educational materials, using the proceeds to build himself a home. Another missionary, Joseph Goodrich, acquired a sugarcane plantation and built his own sugar mill; still another was raising coffee beans.

Such commercial activity was not sanctioned by the American Board, and a hot debate over this issue and others raged between some of the missionaries and the directors. Writing home to his father, Lorrin Andrews castigated his superiors: "Are we to be made slaves of? . . . You are now paying your money to the A.B.C.F.M. to keep your son in bondage to the Prudential Committee."[17] Andrews and others wanted freedom from what they described as dictatorial control. Ironically, the economic situation in America gave them just that. Hard times caused by the Panic of 1837 forced the Board to cut back its support, and the missionaries had little choice but to diversify and to earn their own support.

Amid all of the problems of immorality and materialism and the controversy between the missionaries and the directors, evangelistic work continued with surprising success. By 1837 the missionary force numbered sixty, the majority of whom were hardworking and dedicated to the mission work. After twenty years of ministry, a spiritual awakening took place. Revival swept through the islands in the wake of Titus Coan's itinerant evangelistic ministry. Unlike some of his staunch New England brethren, he was not afraid of emotionalism and welcomed "the gushing tear, the quivering lip, the deep sigh, and the heavy groan."[18] Coan preached as many as thirty sermons a week as he traveled, and thousands professed faith in Christ. Churches grew rapidly, some reaching a membership of two or three thousand and more. More than twenty thousand Hawaiians were accepted into church membership during the revival, boosting the church roles almost twenty-fold.

By 1840 the New England missionaries could look back with a sense of accomplishment, but problems lay ahead. They were now faced with competition from Catholic priests, whose methods, according to Bradford Smith, had more appeal. "Instead of asking for contributions, Catholic priests were giving presents, especially to children who were brought to be baptized. They held short services with no sermons, had no objections to smoking or drinking, promised indulgence to the sinners and willingly received any to membership. Instead of building good Yankee houses they adopted the Hawaiian style of living."[19] Many of the Hawaiians who had flocked to hear Coan now turned to Catholicism. In less than a decade, evangelical Christianity was on the decline.

Sacrificial love often characterized the ministry of Roman Catholics more than it did the ministry of the Protestants. One striking example is that of Father Damien, a Belgian priest who, in 1873, volunteered to work on Molokai, a desolate, rocky, barren island inhabited only by the leprous "refuse" of the other islands. On his arrival, he immediately set up social programs and began an intensive evangelistic outreach. So successful was he that news of his work was carried all over the world, and financial assistance and supplies began pouring in. After more than a decade of tireless work, however, he realized that he himself had contracted leprosy. For four more years he continued his labor of love, now able to totally identify with those around him in the world of the "living dead." When he died in 1889 at the age of forty-nine, his work was world-famous.

Besides the influx of Roman Catholics, the departure of the Binghams (who returned permanently to the United States due to Sybil's ill health) contributed to the decline of Protestant missions. The most serious impediment to a vigorous missionary enterprise, however, was an ever-increasing drift toward materialism among the missionaries. Several missionaries were charged with land grabbing and were too involved in business ventures to give themselves wholly to the work. Many of the missionary children remained in Hawaii, holding political offices and becoming wealthy landowners. All this brought Hawaii into a close political relationship with the United States, but at the same time it adversely affected the church. By the turn of the century the once-vibrant Protestant church that had numbered well over twenty thousand had dropped to less than five thousand. The missionaries had succeeded in their commission to bring "civilization" to Hawaii but were less successful as missionaries.

John Williams

One of the most innovative and far-sighted missionaries to the Pacific islands was John Williams, sometimes referred to as the "Apostle of the South Seas" or the "Apostle of Polynesia" because of his widespread influence in missions in that part of the world. He was born in England in 1796, the year the *Duff* was dispatched to the South Pacific by the London Missionary Society. He grew up in a working-class district of Tottenham, and at fourteen was apprenticed to an ironmonger. During this time he joined a gang and turned his back on his spiritual upbringing. Then, on a January night in 1814 while he was loitering with friends on a street corner, his master's wife exhorted him to come to church. He reluctantly agreed, and that night in the Old Whitefield Tabernacle, his life was forever changed. From that time on, his leisure hours were spent teaching Sunday school, distributing tracts, and visiting the sick.

The pastor of the Tabernacle Church, Matthew Wilkes, took a special interest in Williams and encouraged him to enter the ministry and later to apply to the LMS. Although he was only twenty years old and had no formal Bible or missionary training, he was accepted. After a hastily planned marriage to Mary Chawner, they set sail for a small island near Tahiti.

In 1718 they moved farther west to another small island where they spent three months before finally settling on Raiatea, their base for the next thirteen years. Although Raiatea was a small island with a population of less than two thousand, it held great significance for the Polynesians because it was the home of the Polynesian god Oro, whose shrine was a center of human sacrifice. Williams and his family were warmly welcomed by the natives, but behind the cordial facade was a cultural heritage that placed little value on human life. Besides human sacrifice and the all-too-common practice of infanticide (usually burying the little one alive), the natives had a very lax moral code. According to

Williams, "men and women, boys and girls, completely naked, bathe together in one place, without shame and with much lasciviousness. . . . Promiscuous intercourse is as common, also, as it is abhorrent. When a husband is ill, the wife seeks his brother and when the wife is ill, the husband does the same. . . . When we tell them of the necessity of working they laugh at us."[20]

How to approach these people was Williams's first challenge. He was not trained in cross-cultural evangelism, so his first priority was to change the culture. He had come, not just to bring Christianity, but to bring civilization: "For the missionary does not go to barbarise himself, but to elevate the heathen; not to sink himself to their standard, but to raise them to his." To demonstrate the superiority of Western civilization, Williams erected a large seven-room house with a verandah overlooking the water and landscaped gardens on all sides. He encouraged the people to follow his example: "Many have built themselves very neat little houses and are now living in them with their wives and families. The king, through seeing ours and by our advice, has a house erected near to us. . . . Perhaps the advocates of *civilisation* would not be less pleased than the friends of *evangelisation,* could they look upon a portion of natives diligently employed in various useful arts."[21]

Williams had come to the South Seas, not just to bring Christianity, but to bring civilization.

Williams's emphasis on civilization did not diminish his zeal for evangelism. Despite all of his other activities, he conducted five services on Sunday and others during the week, and personal evangelism was a regular part of his daily routine. The bulk of missionary work, however, he assigned to native converts, who he believed could reach their own far more effectively than he could.

From his first months in the South Seas, Williams had felt confined by the small populations of the individual islands and the inability to travel freely from island to island. Commercial vessels visited the islands on occasion, but their irregularity made any hope of planned travel impossible. The obvious solution to the problem was for the mission to have a ship of its own. Other missionaries had tried to construct vessels, only to discover that the task was more complex than they had anticipated. One such abandoned project was just the enticement that Williams (an ironmonger by trade) needed to fulfill his dream of moving freely from island to island. He recruited the help of other missionaries, and soon the ship was ready for launching—a day that called for celebration.

But the joyous celebration of the missionaries was not shared by the mission directors back home. Viewing the situation from a distance, they failed to recognize the necessity of better transportation and communication for the island missionaries. They vetoed the plan and resolved that "the Society cannot allow itself to enter into any engagement with regard to ownership or employment of the vessel." The battle lines were drawn, and the years that followed were filled with conflict as Williams, in flagrant violation of the directors' mandate, continued his nautical activity. The first vessel that he had helped salvage was defective, but in 1821, on a visit to Sydney, he solicited funds to purchase the *Endeavour,* and quickly turned a profit of some eighteen hundred British pounds through his commercial ventures. The directors viewed the purchase as a "great evil" and accused Williams of "engaging in . . . commercial transactions" that were "calculated to divert . . . attention from the great object of their mission."[22]

By the time the directors' mandates reached Williams, the situation had usually changed, and their stinging rebukes no longer applied to the current situation. His commercial ventures had dwindled after heavy custom duties were imposed, so he dutifully promised to "avoid any and every future entanglement of every kind." But he did not back down on his determination to maintain a ship:

> A missionary was never designed by Jesus to get a congregation of a hundred or two natives and sit down at ease as contented as if every sinner was converted, while thousands around him are eating each other's flesh and drinking each other's blood with a savage delight. . . . For my own part I cannot content myself within the narrow limits of a single reef and if means is not afforded, a continent to me would be infinitely preferable, for there if you cannot ride, you can walk.[23]

Partly due to financial problems, Williams reluctantly agreed to give up the *Endeavour,* but not without the suggestion that the directors themselves may have been the Devil's tools in staying the progress of evangelism in the islands: "Satan knows full well that this ship was the most fatal weapon ever formed against his interests in the great South Sea; and therefore, as soon as he felt the effects of the first blow, he had wrested it out of our hands."[24]

Without ready access to a vessel, Williams's travel to other islands was curtailed, and he spent the next years building up the believers on the island of Raiatea and translating Scripture. Still he was frustrated by his confinement and the lack of additional reinforcements coming out from England. Evangelism of the South Seas was progressing too slowly. The LMS strategy simply was not getting the job done. Someone had to come to the rescue with forceful leadership, and Williams saw himself as that one. His on-site experience convinced him that he knew better than the directors how to conduct evangelism, which he maintained must involve extensive use of native missionaries. His plan was to commission and transport these missionaries to other islands and then periodically visit them and guide them in their ministry.

His plan required a ship, and once again he was at odds with the mission directors; nevertheless, he began the construction project. Soon the fifty-ton *Messenger of Peace* was ready to sail, and he began his itinerant ministry. By the time the directors learned about it, the plan was in operation and there was little they could do. Once again, Williams had flouted the will of the directors. He defended his action, convinced that he had sacrificed too much for the cause of missions to be stymied by short-sighted bureaucrats. Both he and his wife suffered from ill health, and seven of his ten children had died in infancy. There was too much at stake to relinquish his dream.

While many missionaries were grateful for the increased communication and freedom the *Messenger of Peace* brought, others resented the implied power and prominence Williams was gaining over the mission work. The directors too feared the consequences of his growing influence and prestige: "Take care that you give the glory to God—take care that you appropriate none of it to yourself—instead of yielding to the temptation . . . to become high-minded." That Williams was stung by the implied rebuke is indicated by his response: "The calculating suspicious spirit evident in your letter I am not aware of having merited at your hands. Letters written in such a strain produce in our minds feelings and sentiments toward the Directors of the Society that I never wish to cherish."[25]

Despite continuing conflict, Williams's plan moved forward with great success. Under his supervision, evangelism was conducted almost entirely by native teachers, most of whom had very limited training. Of them, Stephen Neill writes:

> But few marvels in Christian history can equal the faithfulness of these men and women, left behind among peoples of unknown speech and often in danger of their lives, to plant and build Churches out of their own limited stock of faith and knowledge, supported only by the invigorating power of the Holy Spirit and the prayers of their friends. Many watered the seed with their own blood; but the Churches grew, and far more widely than if reliance had been placed first and foremost on the European missionary.[26]

By 1834, after nearly eighteen years, Williams could say that "no group of islanders, nor single island of importance, within 2,000 miles of Tahiti had been left unvisited." It was a tremendous accomplishment, yet it was only a beginning. More funding and reinforcements were needed, and he was determined to return home and make an appeal in person.

Arriving with his family in England in the summer of 1834, the thirty-eight-year-old Williams found that his reputation had preceded him. The Archbishop of Canterbury had proclaimed that his ministry was adding a new chapter to the book of Acts, and others too had been lavish in their praise. In person, he was an overnight sensation. People flocked to hear the exotic tales of the Pacific islanders and the danger-filled life of a missionary. He met their expectations, sometimes donning a native costume—though not always with success, at least as he counted success. After one service he lamented, "I tried to work on their sympathies by giving them affecting accounts of heathen cruelties and wrung tears from their eyes, but only four pounds from their pockets. They are a cold-blooded lot."[27]

While Williams's meetings aroused lively interest and were well attended, it was his book, *A Narrative of Missionary Enterprises in the South Seas,* that brought in financial support. Copies were sent to wealthy and influential individuals, who responded with sufficient funds to purchase another ship. This time the directors did not object. They did not want to discourage the enthusiasm he had created in the LMS missionary work in the islands. The *Camden* (twice the size of the *Messenger of Peace*) was purchased in the spring of 1838, and after nearly four years of home leave, Williams was ready to sail with his family and new recruits—including his son and new daughter-in-law. It was a rousing send-off, and the speeches were laced with hyperbole. He was being hailed as the greatest missionary of his times.

Back in the South Pacific, Williams quickly resumed his work, visiting island stations and reinforcing the work of native missionaries, but disappointment met him on every hand. According to one historian, Williams "found that in spite of the glowing reports still being returned to Britain by LMS missionaries, matters had gone from bad to worse. . . . The islanders were turning away from Christianity, disillusioned and tired of the constant demands of the missionaries." There were problems, too, between the missionaries themselves, especially between the LMS missionaries and the Wesleyan Methodists. And even worse in Williams's eyes, the Roman Catholics were making "a most desperate effort to establish Popery in the islands."[28]

Williams's leadership and experience were desperately needed to help stabilize the situation and restore continuity to the islands he had opened to Christianity.

Williams's leadership and years of experience were desperately needed to help stabilize the situation and restore continuity to the scattered islands he had opened to Christianity. But he was more of a salesman than a repairman, and the unreached islands to the west were beckoning him. For years he had dreamed of expanding westward as far as the New Hebrides, and now, with the acquisition of the *Camden,* there was nothing standing in his way. The natives were dangerous, but he had risked his life before and was determined to do so again, despite his wife's objections.

In early November of 1839, he and several native missionaries boarded the *Camden* and set sail for the island of Erromango in the New Hebrides. Little was known of the people of these islands except that they had viciously attacked European traders who had exploited their sandalwood trees.

After a two-week voyage the *Camden* reached the island. Natives soon appeared on the shoreline and waded into the bay to receive gifts from their visitors who had come near shore in a small boat. After the initial encounter, Williams and two other European missionaries went ashore and began walking with the natives to their village. Suddenly, without provocation, the attack came. Williams had time to turn and make a dash for the beach, but he was clubbed to death as he tried to out-swim his assailants. One of the missionaries made it safely to the boat, and he and Captain Morgan rowed back to the *Camden*. Unable to go ashore to recover the bodies, Morgan sailed for Sydney to secure help. Two months later they returned, and after negotiating with the natives, were given the bones of Williams and his comrade, the flesh of which had been eaten by the natives.

The tragic death of Williams was in many ways a baffling enigma to his colleagues and friends. Knowing the treachery of the natives, especially in the wake of the sandalwood traders' fate, why did he not send native missionaries ashore first as was generally the practice? Their presence was far less threatening than that of Europeans who were presumed traders. Likewise, why did he not sense danger when he saw no women present? As a seasoned South Seas missionary, he certainly was aware that such a situation signaled impending peril. Why did he seem to blatantly ignore obvious precautions? Having just come down from a mountain peak of praise and adulation back home in England, he may have been dispirited by the dull routine of missionary work. As a courageous hero in the minds of his supporters, he had an illustrious reputation to uphold. Perhaps for a fleeting moment he lost himself in fanciful visions of his own invincibility.

John G. Paton

The international publicity surrounding the tragic news of the death of John Williams sent a shock wave through the Christian church, particularly in the British Isles, where dozens of young men vowed to take his place. The Presbyterians, represented by John Geddie, were the first Protestants with staying power to enter the New Hebrides in the years following the tragedy. Geddie, described as a "tough, humorless, single-minded and incredibly brave" missionary, had been intrigued by the accounts of missionary heroism in the South Seas since his early childhood in Nova Scotia. In 1848 he and his wife sailed for Aneityum, the most southerly of the islands of the New Hebrides, and there they spent their lives translating Scripture, conducting evangelism, and training native workers. So effective were they that virtually the entire population of the island turned to Christianity. An inscription commemorating Geddie in one of the churches he established underscored his powerful influence: "When he landed in 1848 there were no Christians here; when he left in 1872 there were no heathen."

Geddie's success stimulated more interest, and soon other Presbyterian missionaries began to arrive. One of these was John G. Paton, perhaps the best-known of the South Seas missionaries, who became immortalized largely because of his own play-by-play coverage of natives clubbing missionaries, published in his widely read, tension-filled autobiography. Paton, by his own account, tasted so many close calls at the hands of the natives that it was impossible to enumerate them all. Mere survival was a constant mental and physical strain, and staying alive was in itself an achievement worth noting.

John Paton was born in 1824 in Dunfries, Scotland, and grew up in a three-room thatched-roof cottage where his father earned a living by knitting stockings. The family was poor, and before he reached the age of twelve he was forced to quit school and spend his days working alongside his father to help support the family. The Patons were staunch Presbyterians whose lives were centered on church activities. Converted as a youth, he set his sights on missionary service that began in the Glasgow City Mission. He worked in the ghettos of Glasgow, where the impoverished industrial masses were spilling into the streets and where "sin and vice walked about openly and unashamed." It was a difficult assignment, but one that prepared him well for the trials he would face in the New Hebrides. There was violent opposition to his evangelistic street work, but Paton's philosophy did not allow for retreat: "Let them see that bullying makes you afraid, and they will brutally and cruelly misuse you, but defy them fearlessly, or take them by the nose, and they will crouch like whelps beneath your feet."[29]

After ten years of city mission work, Paton began contemplating the need for missionaries in the South Pacific. Friends sought to dissuade him. "You'll be eaten by cannibals," they warned. He needed no reminder of the cannibals. The fate of the great John Williams was never far from his thoughts.

In the spring of 1858, after a three-month speaking tour in Presbyterian congregations, he married Mary Ann Robson, and they set sail for the South Seas. They were assigned to the island of Tanna, where they suffered severe culture shock: "My first impressions drove me to the verge of utter dismay," wrote Paton. "On beholding these natives in their paint and nakedness and misery, my heart was as full of horror as of pity. . . . The women wore only a tiny apron of grass . . . the men an indescribable affair, like a pouch or bag, and the children absolutely nothing whatever!"[30]

It did not take him long to discover the harsh realities of the native lifestyle, and the problem of nakedness quickly paled by comparison. The natives were deeply involved in deadly warfare among themselves. Killings occurred almost daily and were accepted as a routine part of life, with occasional violent eruptions that threatened the whole population. It was a tension-filled time with hardly a moment for relaxation. Mary was continually plagued by illness, and childbirth only made her condition worse. On March 3, 1859, she died of fever, and less than three weeks later their infant boy died also. It was a time of despair for Paton. Only one short year had passed since they had solemnly repeated their wedding vows. "But for Jesus," he lamented, "I must have gone mad and died beside that lonely grave."[31]

During his first year Paton worked with native teachers who had come from Aneityum where John Geddie was serving. They not only effectively preached the gospel, but they also lived the Christian life—especially as it related to women. Women in the Tanna social structure were virtual slaves, often beaten by their husbands and occasionally killed. The example set by the native teachers and the protection they offered threatened the men, who attacked Paton and killed one of the native assistants. Disease also took a toll. When measles was brought to Tanna by European sailors, thirteen of the Aneityum teachers died. So severe was the outbreak, according to Paton, that one-third of the population of Tanna was wiped out.

By the summer of 1861, three years after Paton had arrived, the natives were on the verge of civil war, and Paton was in the middle of the conflict. At one point he and his one remaining Aneityum teacher locked themselves in a room for four days as natives waited outside to kill them. The coastal people despised him the most, and they were threatening all-out war against the inland tribes unless he left. Finally, in mid-January of 1862, the daily outbreaks of violence turned into a full-scale civil war. Using his gun for protection, Paton made his escape from Tanna to a trading vessel, leaving all of his belongings behind.

On leaving Tanna, Paton went to Aneityum and then to Australia, where he immediately began a tour of Presbyterian churches, telling the people of the terror he had endured in the New Hebrides. He was an effective speaker, and by the time his tour ended the offerings had netted him more than twenty-five thousand dollars to be used for the purchase of a mission ship, the *Dayspring*. In the spring of 1863 he sailed for the British Isles, where he continued his tour of Presbyterian churches, raising thousands more dollars for missions in the South Seas. While on tour he remarried, and in late 1864 he and his bride, Margaret, sailed for Australia, where they boarded the *Dayspring* and went on to the New Hebrides.

> *The example set by the native teachers and the protection they offered threatened the men, who attacked Paton and killed one of the native assistants.*

Soon after they arrived in the islands, Paton became embroiled in a controversy that nearly ruined his ministry. His own experience with the islanders and the experience of other Europeans had convinced a bellicose British commodore to sail his man-of-war through the islands and punish the natives of Tanna by destroying some of their villages—particularly the coastal natives who had so strongly opposed him. Paton later denied having "directed" the punishment, but he did accompany the expedition as an interpreter, thus making a direct link between missions and military action. Although the natives had been forewarned and there were few casualties, the incident nevertheless created an uproar. According to Paton, "The common witticism about 'Gospel and Gunpowder' headed hundreds of bitter and scoffing articles in the journals; and losing nothing in force, was cabled to Britain and America, where it was dished up day after day with every imaginable enhancement of horror for the readers of the secular and infidel press." Some of Paton's harshest critics, however, were not infidels but his own colleagues. A fellow Presbyterian missionary, John Geddie, who was on furlough at the time, was incensed when he heard the news, and he blamed Paton for this incident, which caused a negative fallout for missions. Paton himself complained that it made the "task of raising funds for our mission ship all the more difficult."[32]

John G. Paton, pioneer missionary to the New Hebrides.

Paton's second term in the New Hebrides was spent on the small island of Aniwa, since Tanna was still considered unsafe for Europeans. Once again he was accompanied by teachers from Aneityum, and he and his wife soon settled down to their new mission post. Although Aniwa was considered more peaceful than Tanna, the Patons and their native teachers still faced hostile threats. But now Paton had a psychological (if not physical) weapon to use against them. He warned them "not to murder or steal, for the man-of-war that punished Tanna would blow up their little island."[33]

In the decades that followed, the work progressed; and with the help of native Christians they built two orphanages, established a thriving church, and set up schools—one a girls' school taught by Margaret. Paton enacted strict laws, and crimes such as Sabbath breaking were punished. The people were expected to attend church. Of the first communion service on Aniwa, he wrote: "At the moment I put the bread and wine into those dark hands, once stained with the blood of cannibalism, now stretched out to receive and partake the emblems and seals of the Redeemer's love, I had a foretaste of the joy of Glory that well nigh broke my heart to pieces. I shall never taste a deeper bliss, till I gaze on the glorified face of Jesus himself."[34]

Paton spent the later years of his life as a missionary statesman, traveling in Australia, Great Britain, and North America, raising funds and speaking for the mission's needs in the New Hebrides. By the end of the century all but a few of the thirty inhabited islands had been reached with the gospel. A school had been established to train native evangelists, who numbered more than three hundred, and some two dozen missionaries and their wives were serving with them.

Paton spent his final years translating the Bible into the Aniwan language and preaching. At the age of seventy-three, while on a preaching tour, he wrote of his busy schedule: "I had three services yesterday, with driving twenty miles between; as I go along I am correcting proof sheets."[35] The Patons returned to the islands for a brief visit in 1904. Margaret died the following year and he two years later, leaving their work in the New Hebrides to be carried on by their son Frank.

John Coleridge Patteson

One of the most renowned missionaries to the South Pacific was John Coleridge Patteson, the first Anglican bishop of Melanesia, and a great-nephew of the English poet Samuel Taylor Coleridge. Patteson was born in 1827 into a well-to-do English family. His father, a distinguished judge, sent his son first to Eton and then Oxford, where Bishop George Selwyn, a family friend, encouraged him to enter the ministry. After graduation, Patteson sought ordination as an Anglican priest and then served briefly in a local parish before sailing to the South Seas in 1855—again influenced by Bishop Selwyn.

George Selwyn, the first Anglican bishop to New Zealand, was, like Patteson, affluent and well-educated. He had served in the South Pacific for more than a decade, and he needed the assistance of Patteson in overseeing his enormous diocese, the size of which was a controversial issue. A clerical error had mistakenly granted him authority over a vast area of the Pacific, including Melanesia, and he guarded the region as though it were his personal domain.

When Patteson arrived in New Zealand, he found a thriving mission enterprise with twenty-two mission stations and some fifty thousand adherents. The work had begun in 1814 with the arrival of Samuel Marsden, an Anglican chaplain from Australia. Most of the church growth had come since 1830 when, during a four-year period, more than thirty thousand people had been brought into the church for instruction, largely due to the completion of the New Testament translation into the Maori tongue. The Anglicans had joined with the Methodists in training the new converts and church planting. In 1851 the general secretary of the Methodist Mission had reported: "Scriptural Christianity has taken deep root in the native mind, and is generally received throughout the length and breadth of the land. Very few remain in heathenism. . . . Almost all the aboriginal families throughout New Zealand read the Scriptures, and pray together, both morning and evening."[36]

But this mission model for church growth was not to last. The mission work in New Zealand was closely tied to colonization, and smoldering barely under the surface was the burning issue of *land*. As was true with native Americans, the native people deeply resented the European colonists and their land-grabbing. As early as 1839 a missionary had warned of the impending danger of colonization: "An increase of settlers must affect the aborigines; and if colonization is carried forward in its various ramifications, we fear that . . . the people will soon be swept away."[37]

By 1870 there were seventeen Europeans to every three Maoris. Tensions were rising among the native people, and many of those who had professed faith turned away—particularly the second generation. Some joined cultic movements that revived native traditions and looked to a glorious future free from European colonists. They rose up in arms but were subdued. "This is a miserable end to a chapter," writes Alan Tippet, "that might have told of a glorious triumph."[38]

In 1856, soon after Patteson had arrived in New Zealand, he left with Bishop Selwyn for a tour of Melanesia. As they sailed from island to island on their mission ship, the *Southern Cross,* they recruited native boys to join them on the ship and be taken to New Zealand to be trained in a mission school. They were convinced that bringing the boys apart for a proper education and sending them back to their own people as evangelists and teachers was the only viable method of evangelizing the South Seas. Other missionaries had made good use of native teachers, but generally without giving them adequate education and training to effectively lead their native churches without depending on the Europeans.

> *Other missionaries had made good use of native teachers, but generally without giving them adequate education and training to effectively lead their native churches without depending on the European missionaries.*

Back in New Zealand, Patteson was given the enormous task of directing and bringing continuity to the training school that included students with different languages and social customs. But he had a brilliant mind for linguistics, and during the course of his missionary career he became fluent in some twenty different Melanesian languages and dialects. Unlike most of his predecessors, Patteson had no desire to "civilize" the natives. He often praised their culture and intelligence and insisted they not be discriminated against. Describing them as "friendly and delightful," he sarcastically queried, "I wonder what people ought to call sandalwood traders and slave masters if they call my Melanesians savages?"[39]

When their educational program was completed, Patteson accompanied the boys to their homes and then helped establish them in their ministry and recruited more to return with him for the school, which for a time had an enrollment of over fifty from twenty-four different islands.

As Patteson continued to minister in Melanesia, he noticed a change of attitudes among the people toward him and his ministry. The trust and confidence that they had once had seemed to be slipping. The outside commercial interests in the islands were rapidly expanding, and by the middle of the nineteenth century sugar and cotton plantations (particularly on the islands of Fiji and Queensland) were emerging as highly profitable ventures—ones that required an enormous labor force. This need created a new business in the South Pacific known as *blackbirding,* a system that made sandalwood traders appear benevolent by comparison. According to one historian, "The scum of the earth came to the Pacific in search of easy money in the blackbirding trade." Sometimes young men and boys were bribed or tricked into coming along willingly, but more often they were kidnapped. "Gangs of white seamen would go ashore and carry off men and youths at gunpoint." It is estimated that some seventy thousand young men were thus captured into slavery, rarely having the opportunity of returning home again.[40]

This terrible European blight on the islands of the South Seas, more than anything else, signaled the end to Patteson's ministry. Despite his condemnation of the blackbirders and his efforts to disassociate himself from them, his very methods created suspicion in the minds of many of the native people, and it became much more difficult for him to persuade young boys to come with him for schooling. But Patteson kept up his hectic pace, and in April of 1871 he again set out on another tour of Melanesia in the *Southern Cross.*

The journey was disappointing from the very start. Everywhere he went it seemed he was following in the wake of blackbirders. There were some joyful times, including a large baptismal service for more than two hundred people on the island of Moto, but no longer did he receive a warm welcome as he had in the past when the natives came down to the shore and greeted their "bishopi." They lived in terror, and if he wanted to see them, he had to seek them out.

During this tour on September 21, 1871, the brilliant young Anglican bishop made his final island stop. On board ship were the crew, another missionary, and several young Melanesians who were on their way to Norfolk Island for training. After the morning Bible lesson, which was on the martyrdom of Stephen, Patteson went ashore. It was a routine stop, but he sensed trouble almost as soon as he touched shore, and others who sought to follow him inland were driven back to the ship by a barrage of arrows. Back on ship, they anxiously waited for some sign of their missionary leader, but he did not return. Finally, some native boys decided to go in after him. As they made their way to the shore, they saw natives pushing what appeared to be an unmanned canoe out into the water toward them. When they reached the canoe, they found Patteson's body. It was marked by five separate wounds and covered by a palm with five knotted fronds, signifying that Patteson's life had been taken in revenge for five of their own men who had been seized by blackbirders. Despite the universal hatred for blackbirders, many of the islanders were appalled by the murder, and for that reason his body had been washed and returned to the ship. Patteson's body was buried at sea as were two native Christians who died of the wounds they had sustained.

Patteson's death drew world attention to the despicable business of blackbirding and helped eventually to bring about its demise. It also inspired many to dedicate their lives to South Seas missionary work.

Florence Young

The blackbirding business that had wrought such havoc in the islands of the South Pacific was ironically the very gateway that opened portions of the Solomon Islands to Christianity. While some missionaries such as John Coleridge Patteson bitterly fought this traffic in human cargo, others such as Florence Young seemed to accept it and work within the system. A native of Sydney, Australia, Young was the first to publicly express concern for the spiritual welfare of the South Seas plantation laborers. Her brothers were the owners of Fairymead, a large sugarcane plantation on Queensland, and her visit to that estate changed the course of her life. Whether her brothers were actually involved with the blackbirders is unclear, though even "legitimate" means of recruiting laborers involved inhumane practices.

A member of the Plymouth Brethren, Young had studied the Bible since early childhood and was well suited for her teaching ministry that began in 1882. Her first little class of ten men was an inauspicious beginning, but the numbers grew, and soon she had eighty in her Sunday class and half that many coming out each evening. The response was far greater than she had anticipated. Cutting cane in the scorching sun twelve or more hours a day was killing work—literally. Many workers died under the strain, including Jimmie, her first convert. Nevertheless, they sacrificed their hours of rest to come out and hear the gospel.

The success of Young's ministry at Fairymead encouraged her to branch out to other plantations on Queensland, where some ten thousand laborers lived in similar or even worse conditions. A monetary gift from George Mueller (also Plymouth Brethren) was the stimulant she needed to initiate the Queensland Kanaka Mission (*kanaka* being the term used for imported laborers). She secured the help of a male missionary teacher, wrote a circular letter to the planters in her district, and by the end of the century, through the work of nineteen missionaries, thousands had enrolled in classes, some carrying the message back to their own people.

Florence Young, Plymouth Brethren missionary to Queensland and later to the Solomon Islands, who also served a ten-year term in China under the China Inland Mission.

In 1890 Young had felt the call of missions to China and had left to serve under the China Inland Mission, but she returned to the South Seas in 1900 to direct the work of the mission as it moved into a different phase of the ministry. Laws forbidding blackbirding and the use of forced labor had been enacted, and by 1906 most of the native workers had been sent home. Follow-up was needed, and Young and other missionaries sailed to the Solomon Islands, where they worked with recently returned converts to establish churches.

In 1907 the mission changed its name to the South Sea Evangelical Mission, and Young's two nephews and niece, Northcote, Norman, and Katherine Deck, became very active in the work. As the years passed, ten more of her relatives found their way as missionaries to the Solomon Islands, where an evangelical church was planted that still thrives today.

In many respects the Pacific islands were the showpiece—the success story—of nineteenth-century evangelical missions. But the islands were also seen as the prime exhibit for the failure of the missionary enterprise. Whether from the news media or from novelists and anthropologists, missionaries were frequently portrayed as being the destroyers of culture. This was particularly true in the South Seas setting, commonly portrayed as an idyllic world until outsiders arrived, missionaries among them. "In Melville's view," writes William Hutchinson, "the missionaries, in Hawaii as throughout the South Seas, had participated all too willingly in the destruction of a once-happy people."[41] Although Herman Melville's novels and other widely read pieces of fiction often exaggerated the carefree life in the islands, these writings had a profound impact on the missionary enterprise—causing some to turn their back on missions altogether and others to seriously reexamine their strategies of cross-cultural evangelism.

SELECT BIBLIOGRAPHY

Bell, Ralph. *John G. Paton: Apostle to the New Hebrides*. Butler, IN: Higley, 1957.

Griffiths, Allison. *Fire in the Islands: The Acts of the Holy Spirit in the Solomons*. Wheaton, IL: Shaw, 1977.

Gunson, Neil. *Messengers of Grace: Evangelical Missionaries in the South Seas, 1797–1860*. New York: Oxford University Press, 1978.

Gutch, John. *Beyond the Reefs: The Life of John Williams, Missionary*. London: McDonald, 1974.

Kent, Graeme. *Company of Heaven: Early Missionaries in the South Seas*. New York: Nelson, 1972.

Lennox, Cuthbert. *James Chalmers of New Guinea*. London: Melrose, 1902.

Paton, John G. *The Story of Dr. John G. Paton's Thirty Years with South Sea Cannibals*. New York: Doran, 1923.

Pierson, Delavan L. *The Pacific Islanders: From Savages to Saints*. New York: Funk & Wagnalls, 1906.

Smith, Bradford. *Yankees in Paradise: The New England Impact on Hawaii*. New York: Lippincott, 1956.

Tippett, Alan R. *People Movements in Southern Polynesia: Studies in the Dynamics of Church-planting and Growth in Tahiti, New Zealand, Tonga, and Samoa*. Chicago: Moody Press, 1971.

9

The Muslim World: Mission Field in the Desert

The first significant Christian mission to the Muslims was conducted in the thirteenth century by Raymond Lull, who was almost alone among Christians in his concern to evangelize Muslims rather than fight them. And in the centuries following, according to Stephen Neill, the "Muslim lands" were "neglected by Christian missions in comparison with more productive fields." That changed in the late nineteenth century, a period "marked by the beginning of a real encounter between the faith of Jesus Christ and the faith of Mohammed."[1] Henry Martyn's short tenure among Muslims was followed decades later by fellow Anglicans. Other denominations hesitantly became involved, but it was Samuel Zwemer, a student volunteer initially without denominational support, who more than any other individual coordinated Muslim missionary efforts and sought to draw the attention of other evangelicals to the Muslim population and its need for Christ.

Several models have been used in the difficult challenge of evangelizing Muslims, as outlined by John Mark Terry in a historical study of this topic. Henry Martyn's ministry, according to Terry, represents the *confrontational approach* used by Raymond Lull and many of the early Protestant missionaries to Muslims. They arranged public debates and published polemical literature. "This approach is not widely used today," says Terry. "First, most Muslim countries do not allow it. Those earlier missionaries often worked under the protection of colonial governments. Second, today's missionaries prefer to emphasize the positive nature of the gospel, rather than expose objectionable elements in Islam. Finally, this method is not usually successful. Occasionally, a Muslim intellectual is convinced, but the debates do not move the masses."[2]

The second model Terry cites is the *traditional evangelical model,* of which Zwemer is a representative—though initially he was more polemical and confrontational. In *The Disintegration of Islam* (1915) and *Mohammed or Christ* (1916), he argued that Muslim converts must completely reject Islam—that there must be a "radical displacement" of the religion. With time, however, he developed a softer approach. "Zwemer in later years advocated witnessing to individuals and small groups. He advised his students to engage in friendship evangelism. He believed the human personality was the best bridge for conveying the gospel."[3] The same could certainly be said for Martyn, but Zwemer's writing is more indicative of this second model.

The three remaining models suggested by Terry are institutional, dialogical, and contextual; as is true with the first two, many missionaries used more than one model. By the early twentieth century, many mission societies believed that the only way to make inroads into the world of Islam was through medical or educational centers, the *institutional model*. The *dialogical model*—that of emphasizing respectful interaction between the missionary and the Muslim—has always been used, but it was particularly representative of the ministry of Temple Gairdner, and even more so by Kenneth Cragg. And finally, the *contextualization model,* whereby missionaries seek to enter the culture of Islam in the least offensive way possible, "calls for changes in missionary lifestyle, worship forms, theological terms, and strategy."[4]

While the contextualization model would appear on the surface to be the least offensive, it is considered by many to be a less-than-honest means of making Christianity more acceptable to unwary Muslims. In the final analysis, none of these models offered the solution to penetrating the very difficult field of Islam. Among the reasons for this, according to J. Dudley Woodberry, are sociological factors of close family and community ties, theological issues (that include an outright Islamic rejection of trinitarian claims), political issues (the inseparability of religion and politics in Islam), and finally, the association of Christianity with Western culture.[5]

Despite the obstacles, the mission outreach grew steadily from the mid-nineteenth century until the late decades of the twentieth century, by which time it had become the last frontier, so to speak, in evangelical missions. With the terrorist events of September 11, 2001, however, the future for Muslim outreach in many areas of the world appeared more grim than ever before.

The mission outreach grew steadily from the mid-nineteenth century until the late twentieth century, by which time it had become the last frontier in evangelical missions.

It is sometimes easy to imagine that the interest in Islam and the philosophical debates that encompass that religion are of recent origin, passed down to our own generation. But Islam was a much-debated topic in nineteenth-century Victorian times—and not only in missionary circles. In England there were two main schools of thought, both claiming Christian foundations. Charles Foster (1787–1871), an Anglican minister, represents the position that was considerably more favorable toward Islam than the other side, which saw little if anything that was positive about the religion. Foster's book, *Mahometanism Unveiled,* was considered by many to be an authority on the topic, though many Christians strongly questioned his biblical and theological underpinnings. His interpretation was rooted in the story of Abraham and his two sons, Ishmael and Isaac. Foster emphasized that the covenant with Ishmael's lineage, though often ignored, carried material as well as spiritual blessings. Thus, Islam should be viewed as opening the way for the gospel. He criticized Christians who held Mohammed to the standard of Christ—a standard he did not know. Rather, insisted Foster, he should be viewed alongside Moses and seen as one who also sought to have a positive impact on morality. Foster "believed that Islam was gradually converging toward Christianity . . . so that eventually Isaac and Ishmael would be reunited."[6]

Foster's "infidel theory" was harshly criticized by most supporters of Christian missions. One critic fumed that if Muslims were "truly entitled to the pedigree and praise bestowed it by Mr. Foster . . . our societies ought to . . . [print] cheap Korans [and send] missionary Moulahs to the heathen."[7] These critics rejected this "conciliatory" school of thought in favor of the "confrontational" position—though both offered reputable scholarship on Islam.

Sir William Muir (1819–1905), principal at Edinburgh and author of *Life of Mahomet* (1861), was representative of the confrontational school. One observer notes:

> In his 1845 review of Foster's book, Muir not only rejected the view that Islam contained any spiritual value but also the idea that it prepared the way for the reception of Christian faith. Instead, it presented an "impenetrable barrier . . . which effectively excludes every glimmering of the true light." Muhammad, too, should be judged not against Moses, but against Christ and so judged stands condemned: his cruelty, craft, artifice, and licentiousness outweigh his urbanity, loyalty, moderation, and magnanimity. . . . Muir wrote, "The Islam of today is substantially the Islam we have seen throughout history. Swathed in the bands of the Koran, the Moslem faith, unlike the Christian, is powerless to adapt to varying time and place, to keep pace with the march of humanity, direct and purify the social life and elevate mankind. . . . Among missionaries, Muir's work was thought definitive.[8]

During the Victorian era, Muir represented the school of thought that viewed Christianity in opposition to the very threatening faith of Islam. The battle was being waged both between Christians of opposing views and between two powerful religions. Muir identified with Henry Martyn, whom he called "champion of England's honour" in first entering the "sacred contest."[9]

Henry Martyn

Henry Martyn is sometimes described as the pioneer Protestant missionary to Muslims—though as a chaplain with the East India Company assigned to India, he was not technically a missionary. Yet it was his intention, when he arrived in India in 1806, not only to serve as a spiritual counselor to employees of the company but also to minister to Indian nationals—though he assumed those native people would be Hindus. But his focus quickly turned to Muslims and their lack of Scripture translations. He recognized his own lack of understanding and confessed that he was reading "everything I can pick up about the Mohammedans." Indeed, he had gone to India "without having first read a single word of the Koran."[10] In many ways his company ties served him well. Missionaries were forced out of the country and harassed in other ways, but he was permitted far greater freedom.

Martyn was born in Cornwall, England, in 1781. His father was a merchant who provided well for his gifted child. After Martyn completed his formal training, he went on to Cambridge, where he graduated with top honors in mathematics. Though he had turned away from God during his youth, the death of his father and the influence of friends and family, as well as the writings of David Brainerd, led to a spiritual transformation and a vision for missions.

Like Brainerd, Martyn spent many hours each day in prayer and devotion to God: "I thought of David Brainerd and ardently desired his devotedness to God. I feel my heart knit to this dear man. I long to be like him. Let me forget the world and be swallowed up in a desire to glorify God." In his effort to glorify God, Martyn began practicing self-denial, which included eating his breakfast and reading while "standing at a distance from the fire though the thermometer was at freezing point."[11]

Celibacy was another aspect of his self-denial. He was thankful he was "delivered from all desires for the comforts of married life," preferring a "single life in which are much greater opportunities for heavenly mindedness." But that was before he fell helplessly in love with Lydia Grenfell, his cousin's sister-in-law, who was six years older than he. It was this "idolatrous affection" that more than anything else distracted him from his single-minded goal of following in the footsteps of Brainerd: "I felt too plainly that I loved her passionately. The direct opposition of this to my devotedness to God in the missionary way excited no small tumult in my mind." Lydia had captured his heart. He could not stop thinking about her, waking in the night with his "mind full of her."[12]

Martyn would not have been the first (nor the last) to have been deterred from foreign missions by romance, but though Lydia consumed his thoughts, he refused to be turned aside from his spiritual commitment. He was convinced that he could more effectively serve God unencumbered by marriage, and it was highly doubtful whether Lydia would have accompanied him to a foreign land anyway. He spent most of a year making plans to sail to India, all the while pining over Lydia but claiming to be "cheerfully resigned to do the will of God and to forego the earthly joy" of marriage.[13]

In 1803 Martyn was ordained as a curate, and two years later as an Anglican priest, and then was appointed a chaplain to the East India Company. He was well aware of the scorn this commercial company had for missionaries. The minutes of a directors' meeting are anything but subtle: "The sending of missionaries into our eastern possessions is the maddest, most extravagant and most unwarrantable project . . . ever proposed by an enthusiastic lunatic."[14]

In the summer of 1805 he bade farewell to Lydia and sailed for India. On his arrival he met William Carey and the other Serampore missionaries, who immediately recognized his brilliance and encouraged him to do Bible translation work. As a chaplain, his main responsibilities were to the employees and families of the East India Company; but his heart was in missions, and he was eager to begin translation work. For four years he served at military posts, preaching to both Europeans and Indians, establishing schools, and at the same time working on translations of the New Testament into Urdu and later into Persian and Arabic. His closest assistant was Nathaniel Sabat, a Muslim convert.

Martyn had a profound confidence in Scripture that was expressed with passion—as few missionaries and Bible translators before or since have had. "Henry Martyn's implicit faith was that once readers had the Christian page before their eyes, the reading mind would understand," writes Kenneth Cragg. "For him, the translator's work—given the right diligence in seeking out the 'conveyance' of the Word—would turn the key of comprehension. . . . He was sure that . . . the text would be its own perfect advocate." His devotion to this task is perhaps best summed up in his prayer before the open Greek New Testament: "Tell me where . . . I may find India." He was so assured of the power of the translated text that, with its publication, he believed "rival Scriptures" would be set aside—that "the Qur'an would pale into insignificance."[15]

Martyn was so assured of the power of the translated text that he believed "rival Scriptures" would be set aside—that "the Qur'an would pale into insignificance."

His vision, however, was not realized. Even while he worked with his translation helpers, he encountered hostility. Their being paid out of his private funds did not lessen their disdain for the work. Of one of them, he wrote: "He said with dreadful bitterness and contempt that after the present generation . . . a set of fools would perhaps be born such as the Gospel required . . . who would believe that God is a man and man is God. . . . He sometimes cuts me to the very soul." He conceded at times that doctrinal debates were often of little use—that the gospel must be transmitted through proclamation and through demonstration of Christ's

Henry Martyn, Bible translator in India and Persia.

love: "I wish a spirit of enquiry may be excited," he wrote, "but I lay not much stress upon clear arguments. The work of God is seldom wrought this way."[16]

Martyn's translation work progressed, but the scorching temperatures of Central India took a toll on his already frail health. In 1810, with his Urdu New Testament ready for the printer, he left on a sea voyage to Persia, hoping to restore his health and at the same time revise his Persian and Arabic translations. Here he wrote tracts that set the stage for debates with Muslim scholars. And, with improved health, he continued translation work alongside some of the most recognized scholars in Persia. But soon his condition again deteriorated along with his optimism. "What surprises me," he wrote, "is the change of views I have here from what I had in England. There my heart expanded with hope and joy at the prospect of the speedy conversion of the heathen. But here the sight of the apparent impossibility requires a strong faith to support the spirits."[17]

Martyn's Bible translation work was widely known and even praised by some unlikely sources. When the British ambassador presented a copy of the New Testament to the Shah, he praised the work as one "in a style most befitting sacred books" and "a source of pleasure."[18]

By 1812 he determined that an overland trip to England was his only hope of regaining his health, and it would also be an opportunity for him to renew his relationship with Lydia. Although she had rejected his invitations to come to India and marry him, he longed to see her again and to tell her in person what he had been saying in letters for the past six years. But the opportunity never came. He died in Asia Minor in the fall of 1812, at thirty-one years of age. When he had first arrived in India, he had written in his diary, "Now, let me burn out for God." That he did.

Samuel Zwemer

The name most associated with Protestant missions to Muslims is that of Samuel Zwemer. Sometimes referred to as the "Apostle to Islam," Zwemer more than anyone else put the Muslim world on the map. He was born near Holland, Michigan, in 1867, the thirteenth of fifteen children. His father was a Reformed

Church pastor, and it seemed natural for Samuel as he was growing up that he should enter Christian service. Four of his five surviving brothers entered the ministry, and his sister, Nellie Zwemer, spent forty years as a missionary to China. During his senior year at Hope College, while listening to the persuasive preaching of Robert Wilder (who was on tour recruiting student volunteers), he and five of his seven classmates volunteered for foreign missionary service.

After seminary studies and medical training, Zwemer and a fellow seminarian, James Cantine, offered themselves to the Reformed Board to serve in the Arab world. They were turned down, however, because of the prevalent belief that such a mission would be "impractical." Undaunted, the enthusiastic pair formed their own mission, the American Arabian Mission, and began raising support, Zwemer traveling some four thousand miles visiting churches in the West, while Cantine traveled in the East. Their method of deputation was unique. Rather than appealing for funds for themselves, Zwemer requested support for Cantine, and Cantine for Zwemer. The biggest obstacle was the "lethargy of the pastors," wrote Zwemer.[19]

By 1889 Cantine's tour was over and he sailed for Arabia, with Zwemer following in 1890. Their determination and dedication did not go unnoticed by their church leaders. In 1894 the mission was invited to become incorporated into the Reformed Church in America. The slow progress and opposition Zwemer faced during the early years of his ministry in the Persian Gulf region did not discourage him but only verified what he had anticipated. Initially, he and Cantine lived with an Anglican missionary couple, but when the Anglican couple was relocated, they were on their own, except for a young Syrian convert who had come to work with them. His untimely death less than six months after he arrived was a painful setback to the work.

In 1895, after five lonely years as a single missionary, Zwemer began courting Amy Wiles, a missionary nurse from England sponsored by the Church Missionary Society of the Anglican Church. Their plans for marriage, however, were impeded by the Church Missionary Society's "very strict rules about their young lady missionaries having gentlemen friends." According to Zwemer's biographer, the mission "did not surrender their prize without something of a struggle. As is the custom with most Societies, a portion of transportation cost must be refunded if a new person does not remain a certain time on the field. It was necessary to meet this rule, so . . . Samuel Zwemer purchased his wife in true oriental fashion."[20]

After sailing to the United States for furlough in 1897, the Zwemers returned to the Persian Gulf to work among the Muslims on the island of Bahrein. They distributed literature and conducted evangelism in public thoroughfares and in private homes, but rarely did they witness a positive response. Living conditions further complicated efforts for a successful ministry. In an age before air conditioning, the heat was almost unbearable—"107 in the coolest part of the veranda." Personal tragedy also interrupted the work. In July of 1904, the Zwemers' two little daughters, ages four and seven, died within eight days of each other. Despite the pain and hardship, Zwemer was content in his ministry, and he could look back on this period some fifty years later and say, "The sheer joy of it all comes back. Gladly would I do it all over again."[21]

By 1905 Zwemer had established four stations, and though they were few in number, the converts showed unusual courage in professing their faith. In that year the Zwemers returned to the United States, and, though they did not know it at the time, it would mark the end of their pioneer missionary work. Back in the United States, Zwemer traveled and spoke in behalf of missions to the Muslims and aggressively raised funds. Then in 1906 he served as chairman of the first general missionary conference on Islam that was convened in Cairo.

While in the United States, he accepted a call to become the traveling secretary for the Student Volunteer Movement, a position that suited him well. At the same time, he served as field secretary for the Reformed Board of Foreign Missions, so that his time was taken up in traveling and speaking. Unlike his work with the Muslims, this work elicited an enthusiastic response, and many students responded to his appeals for missionaries. Nevertheless, he was eager to go back to his position in Arabia. In 1910, following the Edinburgh Missionary Conference and a return trip to America, he sailed for Bahrein to continue his work.

Zwemer's wife and two youngest children accompanied him back to the Gulf region, but not to remain long. Living arrangements for the two older children back home had not been satisfactory, nor had the education of the two younger children on the field. Thus, Amy returned to the United States to oversee the family matters, a situation that placed the family, as Zwemer described, on "three horns of a dilemma"—a problem with no real solution. "If the wife went home with the children, some would remark that the missionary did not love his wife to let her go like that. If the children were left in the homeland, they were thought to be neglected by their parents. If husband and wife both spent more than usual furlough time at home, they would be accused of neglecting the work on the field."[22]

Back on the field, Zwemer found it difficult to reestablish himself in the work. His leadership abilities were in great demand, and conference planning and speaking engagements frequently called him away from his post. Then in 1912 he received a call from the United Presbyterian Mission in Egypt, requesting that he relocate in Cairo and coordinate the missionary work to the entire Islamic world. The Nile Mission Press, known for its literature distribution to Muslims, also joined in the call, and so did the Young Men's Christian Association (YMCA) and the American University of Cairo. The decision was clear: Zwemer accepted the call.

In Cairo he encountered a much more open society, where educated young adults were eager to listen to this impressive missionary intellectual from the West. He spent hours each week on university campuses and, according to Sherwood Eddy, even "gained access to the leaders of the proud and influential Muslim University El Azhar." On some occasions he conducted meetings with as many as two thousand Muslims present, but actual conversions were rare, and opposition remained intense. Once he was forced to leave Cairo on the grounds that he had illegally distributed tracts among university students, but the incident contributed to the conversion of one of those students. An infuriated professor tore to bits one of his tracts in front of his class, and a student, curious as to why a small leaflet should create such an outrage, later picked up the fragments and pieced them together. Subsequently, he was converted to Christianity.

During his first year in Cairo, Zwemer was joined by William Borden, a young student volunteer from Yale who had signed the "Princeton Pledge" as a result of his preaching. Borden's humility and eagerness to pass out tracts as he rode through the teeming Cairo streets on his bicycle belied the fact that he had been born into wealth and was an heir to the vast Borden fortune. Before venturing to the mission field he had given hundreds of thousands of dollars to various Christian organizations, while at the same time denying himself a car—"an unjustifiable luxury." His single-minded goal was to serve out his life as a missionary. That he did, though his term was short. After four months in Cairo he died following an attack of spinal meningitis.

Although his converts were few, Zwemer's greatest contribution to missions was that of stirring Christians to the need for evangelism among Muslims.

For seventeen years Zwemer made Cairo his headquarters, and from there he traveled all over the world, participating in conferences, raising funds, and establishing work among Muslims in India, China, Southeast Asia, and South Africa. His evangelistic methods were a combination of traditional confrontational interaction and the more contemporary concept of presenting the love of Christ that was characteristic of the student volunteers. Although his converts were few—probably less than a dozen during his nearly forty years of service—his greatest contribution to missions was that of stirring Christians to the need for evangelism among Muslims.

In 1918 he was asked to join the faculty at Princeton Theological Seminary, but he believed the urgency of his work in Cairo was too great. In 1929 his work was well established, and when a call again came from Princeton, he was able to leave with good conscience and to begin a new career as Professor of History of Religion and Christian Missions, where he continued until 1937. He spent his "retirement" years teaching at the Biblical Seminary of New York and Nyack Missionary Training Institute.

During his teaching career he continued speaking and writing. For forty years he edited the *Moslem World,* and he wrote hundreds of tracts and dozens of books. To the very end he was filled with "nervous energy." A traveling companion once glumly recounted his overnight stay with him: "He could not stay in bed for more than half an hour at a time . . . for then, on would go the light, Zwemer would get out of bed, get some paper and a pencil, write a few sentences and then again to bed. When my eye-lids would get heavy again, up would come Zwemer, on again the light, and another few notes. . . . Then off to bed again."[23]

Throughout his life, Zwemer faced tragedy and hardship. He mourned the deaths of his little daughters, of close associates, and of two wives (his first in 1937, and his second in 1950). Yet he remained remarkably content and optimistic, and in many ways his personality was uniquely suited to his years of toil in the barren ground of the Islamic world. "A lifelong student of Islam," writes Alan Neely, "he never ceased to contend for the finality of Christ."[24]

Temple Gairdner

William Henry Temple Gairdner, a contemporary of Samuel Zwemer and probably the most noted British missionary to the Muslim world in the early twentieth century, was born and raised in Scotland. His father was a professor of medicine at Glasgow University; his mother, "Lady Gairdner," an "elegant" and "distinguished" woman. The religious environment in his home was not what could be described as evangelical, but after he enrolled at Oxford University, his life began to change. There he encountered the Oxford Inter-Collegiate Christian Union, a group considered fanatical by most students. He had hoped he could participate as a "silent" witness, but there was no such option. Writing to his family he confessed his struggles:

> I know that in Oxford one is thought a mild type of imbecile if one displays any *personal* enthusiasm for the cause that is one day to conquer the world. . . . I do feel that at the risk of being thought a prig or a fanatic one must hang out one's colours. . . . It is hard, I find it awfully so here; but it will be always hard whatever our sphere of life, and yet it will be always our business. . . . I am asked, "Are you better than those here, that you speak to them?" Nay, but Christ is better—I do not speak of myself but of Him.[25]

Gairdner did not fit the evangelical mold in many respects and was accused by some of the evangelical students of not being fully one with them. He was open-minded on matters of biblical criticism, and he "took a strong line" on the destination of the lost and refused to believe in any "physical flames of everlasting fire." His passion for overseas missions was further inspired by two Americans, John R. Mott and Robert Speer, who were touring England as representatives of the Student Volunteer Movement. Of one of the meetings, he wrote in his diary: "Holy Communion . . . deep impression of new era. . . . Evening, Speer simply God-inspired. 'Evangelization of the World in this Generation.' Never heard anything like it."[26]

His decision to serve as a missionary in Cairo—not just as a missionary, but worse than that as a missionary to Muslims—was troubling to both friends and family as a waste of a brilliant mind. Speaking for others, one friend lamented that they "deplored his devoting his life to a mission to educated Mohammedans—spending years of labour, we hear, in making one proselyte." In Cairo, Gairdner was met by friends who were already involved in ministry, and he learned the language well enough to become involved in teaching in less than a year. And despite his friends' dire predictions, he made more than one "proselyte" during that very early time of ministry. But, as he would discover later on many occasions, the joy of winning converts could quickly turn to heartbreak: "It was a story only too familiar to those who know the Near East. . . . Two members of the Church gave way. . . . Both made public recantations of Christianity for Islam, as usual accompanied with slanders concerning the leaders of the Church they left. It darkened all the sky for Gairdner. He could not rest for thinking of the failure of these souls, of the failure of the Church to hold them."[27]

Reflecting on the situation, Gairdner wrote: "I *now* begin for the first time to see that the character of Judas Iscariot is possible and human." This was his first such experience, though certainly not his last. It had a deep and personal impact on him, as he confessed to the young woman to whom he was engaged to be married:

> I seem to have left the uncloudiness, the boyhood of life behind me forever, and have entered into what I feel to be a sadder life. . . . For I look ahead, darling, and I see the same thing in front—this apparently hopeless effort to cope with Islam, the weariness of the climate and the sense of duties left untouched, and above all, these terrible disappointments. That's the life I've chosen; that's the life—God help me—I've asked you to come and share.[28]

Gairdner and Margaret Mitchell were married in Nazareth in the fall of 1902. She had been assigned to conduct mission work in India, but after their engagement was reassigned to a location where she could easily study Arabic. After their marriage, they made their home in Cairo—a home that would include their four children and become a center for mission activity. Both Temple and Margaret were musicians; he specialized on the keyboard, and she on the violin. They hosted concerts for Christians and Muslims alike. Although Gairdner was a classical musician, he "hoped for the day when the Church would discover and use the beauty of her own Eastern airs." Among missionaries, he was ahead of his time. "The reward that he saw in his lifetime," writes Constance Padwick, "was to have some member of his congregation (once a Moslem) ring him up begging that a best beloved Eastern tune of his collection might be sung in Church next Sunday, or to hear the utterly pure beauty of a few girls' voices as they sang on Good Friday one of his haunting Eastern airs."[29]

Gairdner's mission activities as a teacher and evangelist and writer were diverse—activities that came together in his role as a Christian apologist to Islam. Through the course of his ministry, his "approach to Muslims shifted from polemics to apologetics," writes James Tebbe, "which meant, if not a more positive view of things Islamic, at least an approach that was less confrontational." In his survey of Christian literature written for Muslims, Gairdner had found it to be very argumentative—an insight that prompted him "to move away from an attack on Islam to a focus on explaining to Muslims problems they faced with various Christian beliefs." But he continued to believe that Christian missions would always have a "decisive 'quarrel' with Islam, which irenic sensitivity must refine but could in no way loyally evade." For him, there was one motive for evangelism: "All 'debate' or 'dialogue' was with intent to save, not crudely to score, nor idly to compare, nor cosily to converse."[30]

Gairdner was prompted "to move away from an attack on Islam to a focus on explaining to Muslims problems they faced with various Christian beliefs."

"We need the *song* note in our message to Moslems," he insisted, "not the dry cracked note of disputation, but the song note of joyous witness [and] tender invitation." The song note was evident in his evangelism and apologetics through his artistic endeavors. He was more than a musician. He wrote and directed dramas, most of which were performed in schools and hospitals. His greatest production was "Joseph and his Brothers, an Old Testament Passion Play," which was performed five times in a Cairo church and viewed by some seventeen hundred people. "But suddenly at the height of this creative joy," writes Padwick, "came a short, sharp arrest." Word came from his mission board, concerned that "the idea of plays in church should prove too shocking to supporters of the Society and money gifts should be lost."[31]

One of the most difficult problems Gairdner faced during his nearly three decades of ministry was lack of help. He was convinced that the progress being made in Cairo would spur excitement and would result in the assignment of more workers to the area. With the death of his longtime partner Douglas Thornton, he lost not only a dear friend but also half of his publishing and ministry team. There were many inquirers, but no time to follow up. He was trained to be a missionary, but much of his time was consumed with routine office work. The Church Missionary Society had given him a year to study Islam with some of the best scholars in the world, but when he returned to Cairo he was so inundated with work that he had no time to publish his insights or pursue his studies any further. "With all my heart," he lamented, "I could have gone in for the research work, and I feel that I might have done some decent work in it." But, writes Padwick, "the dream was dead."[32]

Throughout his tenure as a missionary in Cairo, Gairdner sought to bring unity in the church and diffuse the opposition among Muslims. He was distressed by the lack of goodwill among Christians—"sect upon sect, each more intolerant than its neighbour, each practically excommunicating the others in the name of the One Lord—and that in the face of an Islam which loathes all alike." Unlike most missionaries to Egypt, he had good relations with Coptic Christians, but he found precious few among them who had a heart for evangelism. He longed for the day "when there shall emerge a reformed Orthodox Coptic Church, showing at last those two lost 'notes' of a Church—evangelical militancy and Catholicity."[33]

The most difficult conflict for Gairdner, however, was that which arose within his small group of converts. In 1914 "an extraordinary outburst of Moslem opposition" erupted, "quite unlike any we have before experienced." The outburst was well organized and financed, and it was difficult to counteract. "At that very hour of danger, I became aware of some serious weakness in our own ranks," he later wrote. "For a fortnight I suffered more than I can tell you—days sick with anxiety and evil news and rumours and restless, dreaming nights." This was the Easter season, and he referred to the time as "Black Holy Week." He gathered the group together and went to the desert where there was a cave. There he admonished them with the words of Paul that they should "deliver such an one unto Satan for the destruction of the flesh, that the spirit may be saved in the day of Jesus Christ":

> We invoked the divine power. There was a rallying, and only one or two fell away. We breathed again and are now praying for and believing for the manifestation of divine power. . . . We're not the first to cope with this. The men who *really* had a hard time were the people in the first centuries when there was no Church history. We have only to look up the Early Fathers to see that our troubles have been survived before. Blessed be God for History![34]

Gairdner died in 1928 at age fifty-five after suffering for several months from a lung disease. Surviving were his wife and four children and the ministry in Cairo that continued on without its extraordinary leader. He left behind a legacy of printed materials that were used and improved upon in the decades that followed. But more than that, he left behind a zeal for Muslim outreach that fueled mission enthusiasm in his own Anglican Church and beyond.

Constance Padwick

Constance Padwick began working with Temple Gairdner in Cairo in 1916, and after his death, having previously written a biography of Henry Martyn, she wrote a biography of him. Padwick was a missiologist—a mission strategist—and she was convinced that biography was the most effective means of presenting not only inspiring and sacrificial lives but also mission methods and theories that would challenge others to become involved in Muslim missions. She had a broad understanding and involvement with Islam from her experience in Egypt and later in Palestine, Sudan, and Turkey.

Born and raised in Sussex, England, in 1886, Padwick was active in the Student Volunteer Movement as a youth. But in her mid-twenties she visited Palestine, and out of that experience came her lifelong concern for the Muslim world. Her desire to serve abroad was initially denied due to health problems. For five years she worked in the home office of the Church Missionary Society, and finally, after she had proven herself on a short-term assignment, the CMS agreed to sponsor her as a missionary—a career that extended over most of four decades.

Padwick's primary ministry involved writing. In addition to editing *Orient and Occident* (thus relieving Temple Gairdner of that enormous task), she wrote a wide variety of materials for Muslims. But she was far more than a writer: she was also an effective organizer. She "inspired and became the energetic mainspring of the Central Literature Committee for Muslims," which sought to coordinate the scattered mission efforts to provide literature for Muslims.[35] The director of the CMS in Africa praised the "remarkable ventures in the field of literature which owe so much to the genius of Temple Gairdner and Constance Padwick." Like Gairdner, she was critical of much of the existing literature—literature that was often "filled with the spirit of disputation rather than of worship and love, and apt to hammer rather than to woo and win."[36]

In addition to writing biographies and literature for Muslims, Padwick wrote for Christians in the West. She lamented that the church had too long ignored the Islamic world. The all-pervasive theme that runs through her writing is that it is an *obligation* of the church to reach out to Muslims. There were many, however, who believed that the Islamic world was essentially a lost cause. She did not sidestep the issue: "Can it be right, when in mass movement areas souls are pressing into the Kingdom, for when we cannot find shepherds," she asked, "can it be right in these circumstances to send men and women to an Islam that consistently rejects their message?" Her response was unequivocal and without apology:

> The church through long centuries showed not only the negative of neglect but the positive of hostility and retaliation. Therefore are we bounden (as members of that Church of Christ whose communion and solidarity is not limited to those contemporary with us on earth) to go, not in superiority but in penitent love to the Muslim, to make what loving reparation is allowed us to the heart of our forgiving Lord and to the unforgiving Muslim world. And this duty lies upon us, inescapable, whatever are the opportunities of joyful service elsewhere.[37]

Padwick's vision was to develop a mission strategy that would effectively resonate with Muslims. Others before her had held high that same vision, but primarily with an apologetical approach. She emphasized a relational approach, though other missionaries had emphasized that as well. One proponent of this principle was Agnes De Selincourt, who gave an impassioned address at the second mission conference on Islam in 1911 in Lucknow. De Selincourt particularly challenged women missionaries to reach out to upper-class Muslim women:

> We need to give a larger place in our missionary plans to what has been well termed the Ministry of Friendship. It means infinite expenditure of time and sympathy and love to place ourselves alongside of these women, to enter into their lives, to share their aspirations in so far as these are rightful; it means willingness also to lay ourselves open to not a few snubs and repulses. In many ways it is harder than contact with the poorer classes, who often quickly and gratefully respond, and do not so speedily pull us up by their hot resentment the instant we show the cloven hoof of our fancied superiority and behave as if we had come to India to "work among them," rather to love them and seek their friendship.[38]

As she studied Islam and mission outreach to Muslims, Padwick became convinced that one of the most effective means of building bridges between Christianity and Islam was through a common spirituality. Her work that best offers insights into this realm is *Muslim Devotions*. It is a compilation of Islamic devotional writings, the understanding of which she believed was essential in the task of communicating the gospel with Muslims.

Much of Padwick's mission strategy was conveyed through her biographical works. In addition to her full-length biographies of Henry Martyn and Temple Gairdner, she wrote a lengthy biography of Lyman MacCallum, entitled *Call to Istanbul*. Here she emphasized what she believed to be the very foundation of effective ministry. In the introduction, she wrote: "The significance of Lyman MacCallum's life, and the reason why it should be recorded, lies in his behaviour. . . . He differed radically from most of the missionaries . . . in that he did not feel, and indeed was essentially *not,* a foreigner among the Turks." She quoted a testimonial to him from a Muslim Turk—a testimony that she hoped would stand as a model for all missionaries: "I came to know one Christian who did away with the chasm which separated us from all Christians. He filled it in completely and made the path absolutely level. I have tested him for years. I came to believe that if there could be one such real Christian, there must be many more. I love him and in his person loved all Christians."[39]

The title of one of Padwick's many articles was "Lilias Trotter of Algiers." Lilias Trotter (1853–1928) was a contemporary of Padwick's—one she admired greatly. Like Padwick, Trotter had been a mission society reject due to her ill health, but she refused to be hindered in her calling to reach Muslims with the gospel, despite the temptation to pursue her lifelong love of art. Raised in an affluent home in London, she traveled to Venice where she studied under the noted artist John Ruskin. But she was convinced that her talent was one she must sacrifice for her call to missions—though she would continue to paint throughout her years in North Africa. Padwick opens her biographical sketch of Trotter with the words: "There is a peculiar loveliness about the artist-saints." But was it worth the sacrifice? Padwick asks, and then answers that question:

> Her gift to Algeria was twofold: the creation, with her much-loved comrades, of an evangelistic band of some thirty members scattered in fifteen stations and outstations, and the creation of an evangelistic literature, chiefly in leaflet form but none the less noteworthy for its story-parables with their human freshness and the note of oriental beauty in colour and line.
>
> These things were the outward and visible achievement of her life, and the inevitable question arises, were they worth while? Had they, when all was said and done, made the slightest dint on the Moslem life of North Africa? . . . Her journals drive home the . . . impression of soul after soul led Christward just in time to die. Again and again did Lilias Trotter hear from dying lips in a Moslem household some phrase like "Jesus has all my heart."[40]

Most of the missionaries to Muslims were not artists and writers and scholars as Martyn, Zwemer, Gairdner, Padwick, and Trotter were. They were, except for Zwemer, Anglicans who held scholarship in high regard. But there were also many missionaries in the Muslim world who served as simple evangelists or were involved in humanitarian endeavors and gave little thought to the religious tenets of Islam. Lillian Trasher, whose connections were with the Assemblies of God, is an example. She broke a marriage engagement to serve as a missionary in Egypt, and during her half-century of tireless labor, beginning in 1910, she established an orphanage and through the decades reached out to more than eight thousand homeless children. Her work was highly regarded among the people, as was evident at the time of her death: "As the gilded horse-drawn hearse carried Lillian Trasher's earthly remains through Assiout to the cemetery, people everywhere wept. In every window, every balcony the procession passed, people stood remembering this great woman who had loved so deeply and given so much."[41]

Equally intrepid was Maude Cary—though at her death she would be honored by no such procession.

Maude Cary

By the early twentieth century women were equaling or outnumbering men in most mission societies, and in some countries the mission work would have virtually collapsed had it not been for the single women. Such was the case for a time in Morocco with the Gospel Missionary Union. One of five Protestant missions in that country, the GMU had struggled since 1894 to reach the Muslims with the gospel. Despite these efforts, there was little visible progress against the seemingly impenetrable wall of Islam, and discouragement as well as disease took its toll on the missionary force. For some, the logical solution would have been to close the mission stations and concentrate on other fields; but the single women, among them Maude Cary, remained and served with unusual distinction during a difficult time. Her story is relevant as it intersects with missions to Muslims, and perhaps even more so as it relates to her personal life.

Maude Cary, missionary to Morocco.

Cary was born on a Kansas farm in 1878 and was introduced to missions by the traveling evangelists and missionaries who frequently conducted meetings in the Cary home. Her mother, an independent woman, was a talented musician who had trained at the Boston Conservatory of Music, and an outstanding Bible teacher as well. Maude inherited this independent spirit, and at age of eighteen she enrolled at the GMU Bible Institute in Kansas City, Missouri, to be trained for a ministry in overseas missions.

In 1901 she sailed to Morocco with four other GMU missionaries to begin her fifty years of service there. The first months were devoted to language school, and from the beginning there was evidence of personality friction between her and the other students. A bright and competitive student, she was not about to be outscored by the others, including F. C. Enyart, the only male in the small class. Although Enyart was as competitive as she was, he felt that since he was a male, it was his prerogative to maintain the highest grades in class (and, in fact, he outscored her by a fraction of a percentage point). But it was she who was accused of pride and aggressiveness. Women needed to be independent and courageous enough to forsake all for a missions career, but they were expected to accept their secondary status alongside men. Cary, however, recognizing the error of her ways, "prayed daily," according to her biographer, "for cleansing from the sin of pride."[42]

Cary's first summer in Morocco was filled with new experiences. It was the mission policy to spend the summer months doing itinerant evangelistic work

MOROCCO

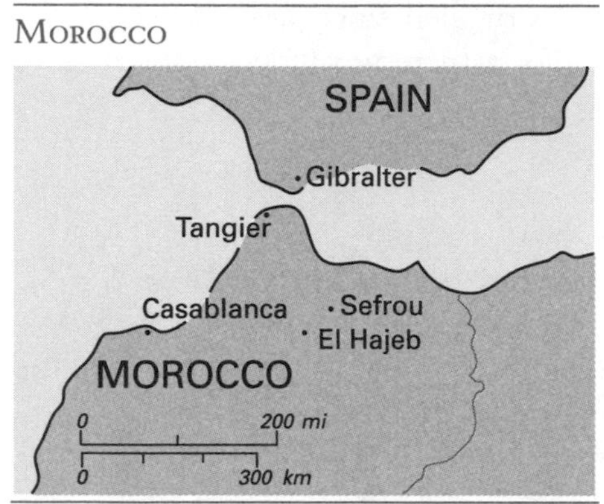

in the villages, and it was an exciting time as the missionary caravan started out into the rural areas. The excitement soon faded, however, as the harsh realities of the primitive camp life became apparent. And the difficulty in presenting the gospel proved even more frustrating. Every family kept a "pack of fierce dogs whose bite was worse than their bark," but "even when they were held back from attacking the foreign visitors, they would bark noisily in the background," drowning out what the missionaries were trying to say. Despite the obstacles, there were encouraging times, especially for the women missionaries, who, once outside the village, were able to talk with the women at a river or spring where they carried water or washed their clothes. Many listened with interest, "but if a man appeared in the distance, the women melted away, apparently fearful of being caught listening to the heretics."[43]

More threatening than the dogs and the men who occasionally caught their wives conversing with the missionaries was the general political situation in Morocco that soon turned against the missionaries, forcing them to relocate near the coast. Work continued, but not without heartache for Cary. At the field mission conference following her second year in Morocco, one of the meetings was opened to group discussion on the topic of grievances and complaints the missionaries had toward each other. According to her biographer, she soon found herself to be the brunt of much of the criticism: "From all that was said, her first two years on the field had been a total failure. The mission would have been better off without her. She was selfish and forgetful. She had written at least one unspiritual letter. She didn't always pray with the Muslims to whom she witnessed. Gaiety, friendliness, laughter—these had all been misconstrued. Added to her tendency to idle talk and her pride of dress, they became a mountain over which her coworkers had stumbled."[44]

Within weeks after that devastating meeting, the president of the GMU, who was visiting Morocco at the time, advised her to prepare to return home. Her health problems, along with her personality quirks, combined to make her a greater liability than an asset to the mission. She was crushed. How could she ever face her family and friends back home?

Ironically, the ordeal she endured relating to her pride (both during her language school days and again at the annual field meeting) was not an unusual or isolated occurrence for women in missions. Many other single women encountered similar circumstances. The very qualities that made them supremely capable for missionary service were viewed with suspicion by their weaker sisters and were threatening to their male colleagues. Isobel Kuhn, in her book *By Searching,* tells of a similar experience when she was applying for mission candidacy to the China Inland Mission. On the basis of a personal reference, she was charged with being "proud, disobedient, and likely to be a troublemaker." Though she was "conditionally" accepted, her departure for China was delayed, allowing the council time to keep an eye on her. She was promised that if she "conquered her problems," she would be "fully accepted." Dr. Helen Roseveare, similarly, was nearly denied candidacy because of the council's judgment that she was "proud, always knowing better than others, unable to be told things or warned or criticized, difficult to live with, and so on."[45]

The very qualities that made women capable for missionary service were viewed with suspicion by their weaker sisters and were threatening to their male colleagues.

In Cary's case, she was already on the field, and sending her home would have been devastating; in the end she was allowed to stay. There would, however, be more humiliating experiences ahead of her. In addition to her language study in Arabic, she was studying the language of the Berbers, an ancient tribe that inhabited the area long before the Arabs moved across North Africa. She had worked with this tribe before her relocation near the coast. But as she struggled with the language, she searched her motives, wondering if she would be so interested in going back to those people if it were not for a single male missionary, George Reed, who was working among them. She and Reed had corresponded with each other, and she secretly hoped her study of the Berber language would further stimulate his interest in her. It apparently did, and soon after the 1907 field conference, they became engaged. But whether because of her ill health or a combination of reasons, Reed soon had second thoughts. He encouraged her to return to the United States, and when she refused, he returned to work with the Berbers without her, though not officially breaking off their engagement.

Still single on her thirtieth birthday, she, according to her biographer, "chose a new motto for her life. It was 'Seek Meekness,' chosen, in part at least, because George Reed said he wanted a humble wife."[46] But humility or not, the marriage never took place, though she was to be strung along for six more years before she would know for sure. In 1914 George decided to leave Morocco and open a new work in the Sudan (a decision that may have been precipitated by his seeming inability to call off the engagement), and his departure signaled the end of their relationship. Only then did she reluctantly accept her fate—spending the rest of her life, as she put it, as an "old maid missionary."[47]

After twenty-three years Cary returned home for her first furlough, still wearing the same style dress and hat she had worn when she left the United States in 1901. America was reveling in Roaring Twenties, and she seemed entirely out of place. Yet it was a time to care for her aged parents, both of whom died during her furlough, and it was also a time for reflection. What had she accomplished in those twenty-three years? Had churches been founded? Were mission schools filled with eager students? Were converts evangelizing their own people? No. In terms of outward success, very little had been accomplished against the power of Islam. And of the handful of "converts," the most promising one had turned away from the faith in the face of persecution. Was it truly worth the sacrifice? She was convinced that it was; and besides, at forty-seven, she was now alone, and the only home she really knew was Morocco.

Back in Morocco, the very slow progress of the previous decades seemed to be starting to reverse itself, and Cary began to see signs of success. More women were openly defying their cultural mores and coming out for Bible teaching. Likewise, there were two young male converts whose courageous stand inspired the whole Moroccan missionary community. But despite her optimism, the GMU missionary force continued to dwindle, and new recruits were few in number. By 1938 she found herself alone with one other single missionary to man the GMU stations in that most discouraging field of service. Two more single women arrived just before the outbreak of World War II, but then the doors were closed. It was a troubling time. The four single women might have isolated themselves in an out-of-the-way station and waited out the war. Instead, they split up in order to keep the three stations in operation—Cary and the other more experienced missionary each to a station by themselves, and the two new missionaries working together. Finally, in 1945, the war was over, and surprisingly, according to Cary's biographer, "The work had suffered very little, thanks to the faithful, sacrificial labors of our single women who chose to remain on the job."[48]

Following the war, new GMU missionary recruits began entering Morocco, eleven by 1948, and most impressive of all, "Three of them were men!" Cary, now the mission's elder statesman, conducted language school and helped new recruits become situated, but her pioneering days were not over. Still plagued by a shortage of workers, the GMU assigned her, at the age of seventy-one, accompanied only by a young woman still in language study, to "open the city of El Hajeb to resident missionary work." Elsewhere the work also went forward, and in 1951 a Bible institute was organized to train young Moroccan men. Three students were enrolled, two of whom were from her new station at El Hajeb.

Although the Bible institute had long been a dream of Cary's, she was not present at its dedication in January of 1952. Some months before she had been flown back to the United States for medical treatment. No one expected her to return, but late that year, at the age of seventy-four, she was back and once again involved in the work. For three years she continued her ministry, but due to recurring health problems the mission began arranging for her retirement. Her departure in 1955 coincided with the end of the French occupation of Morocco and an exciting new era of relaxed restrictions against the missionaries. For twelve years the missionaries worked openly and freely among the Muslims, and many responded. Some thirty thousand of them enrolled in correspondence courses, and Bible studies flourished.

But the good times were not to last. In 1967 the Moroccan government closed the door to all foreign missionaries. Seventy-five years of service ended for the GMU. Radio broadcasts continued to beam the gospel to those who would listen, but for all practical purposes the tiny Moroccan church was on its own. In that same year, back in the United States, an obituary appeared in the local newspaper, and "a small handful of people, seven of whom were ministers, attended the funeral. There were only two sprays of flowers and hardly any tears."[49] Maude Cary had gone to be with her Lord.

SELECT BIBLIOGRAPHY

Bentley-Taylor, David. *My Love Must Wait: The Story of Henry Martyn*. Downers Grove, IL: InterVarsity Press, 1975.

Padwick, Constance E. *Call to Istanbul*. London: Longmans, Green, 1958.

_______. *Henry Martyn: Confessor of the Faith*. New York: Doran, 1922.

_______. *Temple Gairdner of Cairo*. London: Society for Promoting Christian Knowledge, 1930.

Stenbock, Evelyn. *"Miss Terri": The Story of Maude Cary, Pioneer GMU Missionary in Morocco*. Lincoln, NE: Good News Broadcasting, 1970.

Wilson, J. Christy. *The Apostle to Islam: A Biography of Samuel M. Zwemer*. Grand Rapids: Baker, 1952.

______. *Flaming Prophet: The Story of Samuel Zwemer*. New York: Friendship, 1970.

10

KOREA AND JAPAN: A CONTRAST IN RECEPTIVITY

One of the great puzzles of mission history relates to the contrast between Korea and Japan (or Korea and other Asian countries) in the growth of the Christian faith. Church growth in Korea has been the subject of many studies—not so with church growth in Japan. The world's largest church is located in Korea, as is a rapidly expanding overseas missions movement. Why has one Asian culture been receptive to the Christian faith and another been so closed to what is considered a Western religion?

Korea was known as the "Hermit Kingdom" for good reason. "In part this related to the simple fact that few Americans knew anything about Korea prior to 1880," writes Everett Hunt. "Even after that date it is unlikely that many Americans could accurately pinpoint Korea's place on the map, to say nothing of describing any of Korea's cultural distinctives." The *New York Times* described Korea as "the only country on the globe which is now closed to the rest of the world."[1] But that all began to change after 1880—especially after American missionaries began to take residence in that once-closed country. Indeed, Korea is one of the few areas of the world where virtually all of the pioneer nineteenth-century missionaries were Americans.

Protestant mission boards didn't enter Japan until the late 1850s, and even then the progress was painfully slow. Korea remained without resident Protestant missionaries even longer, with the first missionary, R. J. Thomas, not arriving until 1865, and then not to put down roots. He visited again the following year on board an American vessel, but his life and the lives of the crew were taken when the ship was burned by Koreans who felt threatened by American power and presence.

When resident missionaries did arrive in Korea in 1884, the political situation, though still unstable, served them well. King Kojong welcomed medical and educational work, and the early missionaries were moderately compliant with his ban on preaching and evangelizing. But the king was by no means tenaciously protecting Korea's religion. "The Koreans offer the spectacle," wrote Elliot Griffis in 1888, "of a nation without a religion waiting for one." He was overstating the case, but there was some truth in what he said. "Confucianism had become more a rigid code for the legal and ceremonial conduct of government," according to Hunt, and Buddhism had been "out of favor" for centuries. Shamanism was widely practiced but was not a unifying force in society. "Thus," continues Hunt, "while the encounter between Christianity and other religions has often been a central issue in the introduction of Christianity in other nations, in the Korea of 1885 it was almost no issue at all."[2]

"The Koreans offer the spectacle," wrote Elliot Griffis in 1888, "of a nation without a religion waiting for one." There was some truth in this statement.

Protestant missionary work to Korea began in earnest in the 1880s, and within a relatively short time there was a receptive response—unlike the hostility the Roman Catholics had faced barely two decades earlier. One of the reasons for this may have been the Protestants' use of the Korean term *Hananim* for God, avoiding the imported Chinese term that the Catholics used. "The choice of *Hananim,*" according to Don Richardson, "could not have been more providential for Protestant missions in Korea! Preaching like houses afire in cities, towns, villages or in the countryside, Protestant missionaries began by affirming Korean belief in *Hananim*. Building upon this residual witness, Protestants masterfully disarmed the Korean people's natural antipathy toward bowing before some foreign deity."[3]

Besides encouraging the Koreans to retain their own term for God, the missionaries quickly established a pattern of encouraging them to develop their own churches. In 1890 the arrival in Seoul of John L. Nevius, a veteran Presbyterian missionary from China, paved the way for mission strategy that soon characterized Korean missions in general. The Nevius method called for "self-governing, self-supporting, and self-propagating" churches, promoting indigenous Christianity virtually free from outside influences.

Roman Catholic missionaries, who were in Korea much earlier, had encountered fierce opposition, but they courageously carried on the work. The period between 1784 and 1884, sometimes referred to as "the century of Roman Catholic missions," was a time of growth despite persecution. In 1866 thousands of Korean Christians were martyred, along with three French priests. An edict against "foreign learning" was issued in that same year, making the teaching of this outside religion punishable by death. The French military retaliated—an act of aggression that only increased negative feelings among Koreans about the outside world. The individual who more than anyone else had been behind the great persecution was Tai Won Kun. Of him and his family connections, Samuel Moffett writes:

> It was at the orders of this man of blood that the church had been almost annihilated in 1866. But when he died some thirty years later, the faith, so far from being dead, had moved into his own home. His wife had become a Christian, baptized secretly at night by Bishop Mutel, who twice crept into the persecutor's palace, once to baptize her and once to give her Holy Communion. The year they buried Tai Won Kun, in 1898, there were forty thousand Roman Catholics in Korea.[4]

The first Korean Protestant community was born out of the ministry of John Ross, a Scotch Presbyterian. While serving in Manchuria, he extended his evangelistic outreach to the border of Korea in 1873. Here he met with Sang Yoon Suh, who agreed to help Ross and his partner in Bible translation. That involvement led to his conversion and to his returning to the village of Sorai in the Northwest of Korea, where he introduced his relatives and neighbors to his newfound faith. "In the winter of 1884 Ross and his colleagues visited the Korean immigrants in the northeastern valleys of Manchuria," writes Roy Shearer, "where they baptized seventy-five men. . . . These men served as the link for the first Protestant work in Korea proper, and some of them became the foundation for the young Church in Korea."[5]

Horace Allen

It is not uncommon in the history of missions for missionaries to become involved in political or economic or cultural dealings in the country of their residence. William Carey was involved in Indian reform movements; Robert Morrison and his son were connected with the East India Company and involved in treaty negotiations during the Opium War; David Livingstone resigned his mission post to become an employee of the British government; and missionaries and their children in Hawaii were deeply involved in political and economic endeavors. But Dr. Horace Allen (1858–1932), the first Protestant resident missionary to Korea, went a step further than these mission predecessors when he left his vocation as a missionary medical doctor to become a diplomat representing the interests of Korea. This was no loss to the missionary community. He was a man with diplomatic skills in international affairs but utterly lacking in such skills in personal affairs.

Allen was born and raised in Ohio and, after completing his medical training, was appointed by the Presbyterian Church to serve, with his wife Frances, as a missionary in China. However, he was dissatisfied with his situation there—getting calls from opium addicts through the night so that, by his own testimony, "sleep was quite out of the question" and his "life was made miserable." In 1884, after less than a year in China, he was permitted to transfer to Korea. But he was unhappy with his assignment in Korea as well—especially as it related to other missionaries. "Mission work is a farce," he protested. "Heron [Dr. John] has every other week wholly to himself and all but 2–3 hours of other weeks. Yet he does not study. Underwood has as much leisure. So have the Methodists. I think it is a pretty soft thing."[6]

In reality, these colleagues were conscientious and hard-working, and Allen said as much on various occasions. But wherever Allen went, conflict followed. "Most, if not all these difficulties," writes Everett Hunt, "centered around Horace Allen and his strange personality."[7] Yet it was Allen more than anyone else who paved the way for the long-term presence of Protestant missionaries in Korea.

It was Allen more than anyone else who paved the way for the long-term presence of Protestant missionaries in Korea.

Allen was able to maneuver amid the political strife that was simmering beneath the surface when he arrived. The king supported the "progressives" who were open to Western, particularly American, ideas. They were opposed to those who were clinging to the old ways and fearful of modernization. In the fall of 1884, when the conflict erupted into open hostilities, the queen's nephew was wounded. Allen came to the rescue, and the young man's life was saved. "This whole affair has been trying," wrote Allen. "But it has admitted me to the palace and given me a prominence I could not have gotten otherwise. Already the people know me, and our work will not suffer from this event."[8] The progressives had lost ground during the skirmishes, and any hope for mission opportunities could have ended at that time, but for the medical service of Allen.

Early in 1885, after only months of residence in Korea, Allen was invited to help serve the medical needs of the king and queen and was granted his request to establish a hospital in Seoul. He was modest about his achievement. "My professional efforts have been crowned with far greater success than my experience deserves," he conceded. "I have had some most astonishing recoveries and all I believe in answer to prayer." Allen's medical work continued during the precarious political situation, though he feared it would be jeopardized by other missionaries (with no medical skills) who were trickling in. But it continued to grow. In his first annual report for 1886, Allen's calculations indicated that his hospital had served more than ten thousand patients. This achievement was due in part to his sensitivity to the Koreans. He asked Korean officials to serve as directors of the hospital—except for making medical decisions—and he also invited them to give the hospital a name of their own choosing.[9]

Despite the apparent success he was experiencing, Allen's stormy friction with other missionaries persisted. Then, in 1887, the opportunity came for him to leave what had become a very unsatisfactory situation. The Korean king asked him to head up a diplomatic delegation to America. He was to escort and introduce the delegates to government officials in Washington. But before his official duties had even begun, he was grumbling again. On board ship the delegates were "smoking in their rooms which smell horribly," and his meetings with them were curtailed because he could not "stop long in their rooms as I have had to point out lice to them on their clothes."[10] Nevertheless, Allen effectively represented Korea in Washington, and through his encouragement of American business investments, he helped to stimulate the Korean economy. He strongly defended Korean independence and, unlike many of his mission colleagues, strongly opposed Japanese incursions.

In 1889 Allen returned to his mission vocation, first to Pusan and then to Seoul, where he practiced medicine; but again he found the circumstances unsatisfactory. By 1890 his second mission term was behind him, and he was back in diplomatic service, this time working for the U.S. government in Seoul, which eventually led to his being appointed U.S. Minister and Consul General to Seoul in 1897. But he was a mere diplomat, and his strong views did not prevail in Washington. In 1903 he returned to his nation's capital to plead Korea's cause with President Theodore Roosevelt, but to no avail. As Wi Jo Kang points out, "In his discussion with the president . . . Allen's pro-Korean and pro-Russian views clashed sharply with Roosevelt's pro-Japanese attitude. Allen attacked Japan's aggressive behavior, but he was unable to sway the president."[11]

Allen's strong views led to his recall in 1905. "There was little question," writes Kang, "that Allen was dismissed because he strove for Korean sovereignty in opposition to Japanese imperialism."[12] Back in Ohio, Allen practiced medicine and continued to be a great promoter of Korea through writings and speeches. He translated some of the best-loved Korean folk legends into a condensed version that he published as *Korean Tales*. In his book *Korean Things,* he sought to win American support for Korea's struggle against Japan, and his book *A Chronological Index* was a historical overview of Korea's foreign diplomacy from 97 B.C. to 1901.

In many respects Horace Allen, the failed missionary, became the greatest missionary to Korea. When he died in 1932, according to Kang, he left behind "a rich legacy of Christian witness to political justice as the first Protestant missionary to Korea."[13]

Henry Appenzeller

On Easter morning, April 5, 1885, Reverend Horace G. Underwood and Reverend Henry G. Appenzeller, the first ordained missionaries, arrived in Inchon, Korea. The story is that they held each other's hands and jumped ashore together so that no one might later say that either the Methodists or the Presbyterians had arrived first. That Horace Allen had already been serving as a Presbyterian missionary in Korea was apparently dismissed because of his lack of ordination—though ordination credentials had hardly been a prerequisite for most pioneer missionaries. The desire for unity across denominational lines was commendable—though from the beginning there was considerably more denominational conflict among the Korean missionaries than such hand-holding symbolism would imply.

That the beginning of Methodist work should be dated that Easter morning was very important to Appenzeller, who was forced to return to Japan less than a week later, and he wanted to make certain of that for the history books and for his own denomination, as he penned in a letter: "The Methodist Church may rightfully be said to have entered Korea at this time as we left part of our goods behind." He repeatedly wrote of his plans for "the success of Methodism" and his hopes that "Methodism will flourish."[14] If the Presbyterians had less denominational loyalty, they were not without apprehension about their competition. Allen wrote to the home board that he wished the Methodists would "blow their trumpet a little more mildly and not scare an exclusive nation." And Underwood reiterated those concerns: "I am afraid the Methodists may come into Korea and jeopardize matters. They are welcome if they will only be judicious." The issue of who arrived on the scene first was also important to the mission directors back home. Of the Methodists, the Presbyterian mission secretary responded with some apparent haughtiness: "If they have been outrun in the occupation of the field, they should submit to it pleasantly."[15]

Henry Appenzeller (1858–1902) grew up in a German Reformed church in Pennsylvania and was reared "with a strong devotion to the Bible and the Heidelberg Catechism."[16] But at twenty-one he joined the Methodist Church, "probably because of its evangelistic outreach and lively fellowship." He served for a short time as a Methodist minister before going to Drew University to study theology. Only weeks before receiving his assignment to serve in Korea as a missionary, he married Ella Dodge, a Baptist. Despite his diverse denominational connections, Allen referred to him as "a most ardent Methodist of the John Wesley type."[17]

Like many American missionaries of his era, Appenzeller was an American patriot, and he was eager to bring to Korea all that was good in American culture. Although he "ventured beyond Seoul in search of places to plant Christian churches," writes Edward Poitras, "he seems never to have considered adapting to Korean cultural ways."[18] This may have been due in part to his strong bias against the Catholic missionaries who wore Korean dress and adapted Korean culture to a large extent. He believed (now decades after Hudson Taylor had made native dress an accepted part of Protestant mission work) that such practices compromised true Christianity. He was convinced, according to Daniel Davies, "that God commissioned the Anglo-Saxon race (led by the United States) to spread Protestantism throughout the world as the vehicle to remove all forms of corruption from human life."[19]

Yet he was a strong supporter of Korean independence long before such a notion was internationally endorsed—though "he believed that Koreans could master their own destiny only through Western-style knowledge and political institutions." Unlike Allen, who was very conscientious about submitting to Korean authority and laws, Appenzeller was more autonomous and unrestrained by the authorities, be they Korean or American. He "pursued direct evangelistic activities when they were expressly forbidden by Korean law and the orders of missionary supervisors and colleagues." He was convinced that he was bringing not only God's message but also God's methods. He had come to Korea to remove "the rubbish of idolatry, superstition and custom" in order to pave the way for "a bright, positive life free of the dark, enervating work of Satan."[20]

Despite the unsettled political situation in Korea and his own deficiencies in contextualizing the gospel, Appenzeller encountered surprising success during his early—and later—years of ministry. He opened a boys' school less than a year after his arrival, and within six months he had more than thirty students receiving a standard liberal arts education. The purpose of the school from his perspective was evangelism, but at that time any type of proselytizing was officially prohibited. Preaching—not teaching—was Appenzeller's calling, and the school was a cover for his real reason for being in the country. But as time passed, the school consumed more and more of his time and served his purposes as an evangelistic ministry—"the foundation stone on which he would build the Methodist Church in Korea." In September of 1887 the new school building was officially dedicated, and Korean officials were invited. But it was not merely a dedication service. Appenzeller was careful to turn it into one more momentous *first*: "This is the first public service of a religious kind ever held by anyone in Korea."[21] In 1890 required chapel services were part of the curriculum, and three years later a theological program was initiated.

Appenzeller was convinced that he was bringing not only God's message but also God's methods.

As much as Appenzeller felt compelled to preach, his time was consumed primarily with other activities and a schedule that would quickly dispel any accusations of laziness. He served at different times as both treasurer and superintendent of the mission; he purchased tracts of land and acted as general contractor of various building projects; he translated portions of Scripture; he edited and wrote various publications for both Korean and American audiences; he was actively involved in several ecumenical projects, including the Bible Society, the Literature Society, and the Seoul Union Club; *and* he was the pastor of the first Methodist church in Korea.

During the early years of mission work, the missionaries met for a "union" service—Methodists and Presbyterians together. In fact, for all the competition between the two groups, they accomplished a remarkable amount of ministry together, including Bible translation work. The first baptism of a Korean—on

Easter Sunday of 1886, one year after they arrived—was officiated by Methodist Appenzeller, with Presbyterian Underwood assisting. In 1888 the new year brought both denominations together for a week of prayer, but denominational loyalties and significant theological differences kept them apart. Just a month after that special week, they came together for a conference the purpose of which was to divide up Korea between the two denominations.

The work of both the Methodists and the Presbyterians progressed on through the 1880s, but as it did, opposition increased. Appenzeller was often quick to place the blame on the Catholics, as he did in 1888, after the government had placed a ban against Christianity: "The Catholics here are putting up a building in a part of the city objectionable to the King who very generously offered them another plot and damages on the present lot if they would move. This they refused to accept. The King then ordered Christian work to cease and of course we 'innocent ones' suffer with the guilty."[22] Appenzeller himself had ignored the king's decrees against evangelizing and was believed to have contributed to the backlash as much as had the Catholics. The situation worsened by the summer of 1888, when rumors began to circulate that missionaries were in the business of kidnapping and killing Korean children and eating them—in the basement of Appenzeller's Christian school no less. The king came to the rescue, issuing "a proclamation calling for the arrest of all persons circulating false rumors."[23]

Despite his shortcomings, Appenzeller's mission work was characterized by sacrifice and self-denial.

More than anyone else, Appenzeller laid the foundation for Methodism in Korea. "His emphases on evangelism and individual conversion, conservative biblical hermeneutics, strict morals, and social implications of the Christian faith have all been carried forward." But "to the extent that he remained insensitive to the implications of Western cultural domination," writes Poitras, he has been viewed less favorably.[24] Yet during Appenzeller's seventeen years heading up the Methodist ministry in Korea, forty-seven Methodist churches had been established. In summing up all the statistics, he concluded, "What hath God wrought!"

Despite his shortcomings, Appenzeller's mission work was characterized by sacrifice and self-denial. His wife would "create a home that would make a visitor feel like they had dropped in on a family in Pennsylvania," yet Asia would never be home to them. Early in his ministry he had written to his brother-in-law, who was considering coming to Japan for a business venture, that he should stay in America: "As a missionary I am glad I came and expect to stay, but I would not remain, much less come for any other purpose. I would much rather have a salary of $1,000 at home than $10,000 out here."[25]

Appenzeller gave his life for the work. In the summer of 1902, while traveling by steamship to the southern tip of Korea for a meeting of the Bible translation committee, there was a collision in the fog with a Japanese steamer. According to accounts passed along, he died in circumstances fitting a true missionary hero: he "lost his life in an attempt to save his Korean assistant in the translation work and a Korean child entrusted to his care." He was forty-four years old. "Thus ended the life of a man in his prime, and the blow to the Methodist Episcopal mission in Korea proved staggering, if not crippling."[26]

Horace and Lillias Horton Underwood

If Appenzeller was overly concerned about establishing the Methodist church in Korea—with the proper date corresponding to that of the Presbyterians, Horace Underwood was overly concerned about how he should properly impress the Korean people themselves. The mission secretary back home had received word that he was wearing "an Oxford coat and a ministerial dress generally," and counseled him that "the true course for a Protestant American in a country where everything is yet so unsettled would be to throw off all ministerial dress and ministerial manner."[27]

The competition between the Presbyterians and Methodists touched Underwood's life in a very personal way. The Presbyterians, with the first medical doctor in Korea, had a decided advantage in the court of the king—a fact that was not overlooked by the Methodists. But both sides were very conscious that a male physician had severe limitations in matters that pertained to the queen and any other female royalty. So the race was on. Which side would be first to offer the court the services of a woman doctor? Appenzeller had written to the home board about the urgency of this matter because the Methodists were "at great disadvantage" to "our sister society." Presbyterian Dr. Allen, however, had an ace in the deck in the person of his bachelor colleague: "If one [woman doctor] could come out soon and marry Mr. Underwood, our prospects here would be grand indeed." With a touch of humor, he added, "If you are quick we may convert the Wicked Queen of Korea. Otherwise the Methodists may have that pleasure."[28]

The Presbyterians won the prize when one of their own arrived to become the first woman "doctor" in Seoul. Allen was pleased to announce that "Dr." Ellers would become the queen's physician. There was only one problem—if indeed it was a problem. Annie Ellers was a nurse. But this fact apparently went unnoticed by the queen, and Ellers served her with distinction and married a missionary—though not Horace Underwood. But as Allen had hoped, Underwood would marry the first woman physician, Dr. Lillias Horton, who arrived in Korea in 1888 and served the queen as Ellers' successor.

Horace Underwood (1859–1916) was born in London and emigrated with his family to America when he was a youth. After graduating from New York University, he continued his education at New Brunswick Theological Seminary and was ordained to the ministry in the Reformed Church in America. Unlike virtually every other denomination, however, the Reformed Church did not send missionaries overseas to perpetuate one more denomination. Rather, it supported missionaries to work with churches that were already established in other countries. Thus, it was natural for Underwood to be appointed to serve with the Presbyterian Church in Korea and to work with the Presbyterian mission board.

Learning the language was the greatest obstacle Underwood faced when he first arrived in Korea, but once he was able to communicate, the people showed unusual interest:

> As soon as we had secured a little knowledge of the language, we regularly went out in the lanes and byways, sitting down under some tree near a frequented road, or beside some medicinal spring to which the people were in the habit of flocking. We would take out a book and start reading and when several gathered around us to ask questions, we would attempt to explain to them the book, its truth and what it meant.[29]

Like Appenzeller, Underwood would have a cover for his preaching ministry so that he would have a legitimate vocation. He established an orphanage and was encountering success equal to that of the Methodists with their schools—though the Presbyterians funded only about half as much as did the Methodists from their mission board. Underwood also spent time in Bible translation and was eager to spend more of his time in preaching. Like the Methodists, the Presbyterians were amazed at the progress they were able to make in such a short time: "Now we have been here but a little over two years and the work has opened up so wonderfully that there is really more to be done than we can undertake."[30]

For Underwood there would be the additional good fortune of inheriting church growth that had been initiated by others.

The circumstances for missionaries were truly unusual in Korea, and Underwood and his colleagues often expressed their amazement. He confessed that he arrived "with the expectation that we would have to wait many years before we would be able to do any work, looking forward to a steady work in the line of learning the language and translating the Scriptures for several years to come."[31] This had been the normal way things progressed in other mission settings, so there was genuine surprise when the faith took hold so quickly.

For Underwood there would be the additional good fortune of inheriting church growth that had been initiated by others—John Ross, Sang Yoon Suh, and others who had evangelized in the remote village of Sorai far to the northwest. Without warning he was visited by four men who had walked more than two hundred miles, requesting baptism from him. They asked him to visit their area where several more were awaiting baptism. When he visited them, he baptized seven more. Sorai has since been called "the cradle of Protestant Christianity in Korea."[32]

These baptisms and the organization of a church in Sorai were not without controversy. Dr. Horace Allen, Underwood's close colleague, was upset that the law prohibiting evangelism was being ignored and would potentially risk the entire mission endeavor. Underwood argued that he had merely baptized—that the evangelism had been done by others. How could he have done other than grant their request, he argued, building his support from Scripture and church history: "I can find no warrant for such action denying them baptism either in the history of mission, in the story of the Acts of the Apostles or in the teaching of Christ."[33]

After Allen left the mission to serve in diplomatic service for the government of Korea, Underwood's close connection to the Korean royalty came through a doctor with whom he would have a more stable relationship—Dr. Lillias Horton, whom he married in 1889, the year after she arrived. In the years that followed, she "became such a familiar figure at court" that "she was able to dispense with the formality of an interpreter when she was talking with the queen," and "she often forgot that she was not chatting with an intimate friend." Yet she recognized her place as an outsider, and for that reason was reluctant to make a forthright presentation of the gospel.

All the missionaries were praying for the conversion of the queen, but their hopes were dashed in 1895, when the Japanese began a period of oppressive rule. The Japanese perceived the queen as their enemy, and on October 8, 1895, "Japanese cutthroats, under the eyes of the Japanese army officers, rushed the palace guard and murdered her." It was a terrible loss to the mission community, and to Lillias Underwood in particular, but she would continue her medical work in Korea despite the setback.[34]

John L. Nevius

The name most associated with the first decade of mission work in Korea is that of John L. Nevius (1829–93), a missionary to China who spent only two weeks in Korea. But those two weeks, some would say, transformed the Protestant mission endeavor and the future of the church in Korea. The "Nevius method" is often credited with the rapid growth of the church in Korea—making the difference between the church in Korea and that in Japan.

The "Nevius method" is often credited with the rapid growth of the church in Korea—making the difference between the church in Korea and that in Japan.

Nevius was born in western New York into a family of Dutch Reformed heritage. His father died when he was young, and he was brought up in the faith by his mother, who had lamented his moving south "to seek his fortune" as a young man. "John," she implored, "if you were going away to be a missionary to the heathen, and I should never see you again in this world, *that* I could bear; but *this* I cannot."[35] He later wrote to her that he was determined to serve God rather than seek a fortune. Soon after that he enrolled at Princeton Theological Seminary, where he not only immersed himself in studies but set up for himself a strict program of spiritual disciplines, the last one which read: "16. Every Saturday night to eat sparingly or nothing at all, and spend a part of the evening in looking over these rules, seeing how far I have transgressed them, how much I can improve them, and myself by them; and in preparation for the Sabbath."[36]

In 1853 Nevius and his wife, Helen, sailed from Boston to China, where they would continue to serve for the next four decades. His approach was to do itinerant ministry and train converts to conduct basic evangelism. The Nevius home became a center for short-term training, with as many as forty men coming from outlying areas to study the Bible and learn how to more effectively reach out with the gospel. He was a critic of much of the mission work in China, believing that the progress was slow in part because too many missionaries settled into "mission station" life and because they hired Chinese Christians to do the work of itinerant evangelism. But he was not just a critic; he had laid out a method of evangelism that he was convinced would be far more effective, and he was invited to present his ideas at the Second General Missionary Conference of China, convened in Shanghai. There were over four hundred missionaries in attendance, and Nevius was one of the prominent speakers.

In China, however, after more than a half century of mission outreach, missionaries tended to be set in their ways. But word of his ministry and of his presentation at this conference reached Korea, and there was immediate excitement. The year was 1890, barely six years after the work in Korea had begun, and the missionaries were not yet set in their ways. They were open to new ideas, and they invited Nevius to present his ideas to them. Thus, on their way home for a furlough, he and his wife spent two very important weeks in Korea.

During this time, Nevius clearly pointed out the differences between the "old system" and the "new system": "The Old uses . . . the more advanced and intelligent of the native church members in the capacity of paid colporteurs, Bible agents, and evangelists, or heads of stations; while the New proceeds on the assumption that the persons employed in these various capacities would be more useful in the end by being left in their original homes and employments."[37] He accused missionaries of employing nationals to produce quick growth so that they could send favorable reports back home, but he insisted that such methods only resulted in an uncommitted church leadership, with converts who are doing evangelism only for the money they received.

What the missionaries heard from Nevius was not a new strategy of mission. Many others had said essentially the same thing, but he came as an experienced practitioner having a clear plan of action. Charles A. Clark later summed up his method in nine points:

1. Missionary personal evangelism through wide itineration,
2. Self-propagation: every believer a teacher of someone, and a learner from someone else better fitted, . . .
3. Self-government: every group under its chosen unpaid leaders; circuits under their own paid helpers, will later yield to pastors, . . .
4. Self-support: with all chapels provided by the believers, . . .
5. Systematic Bible study for every believer under his group leader and circuit helper,
6. Strict discipline enforced by Bible penalties,
7. Co-operation and union with other bodies, . . .
8. Non-interference in lawsuits or any such matters,
9. General helpfulness where possible in the economic life problems of the people.[38]

Following their two-week stay in Korea, the Neviuses continued their voyage home for furlough and then returned to China in 1892. The following year, as he was ready to leave on an extended tour of visiting the churches he supervised, he suddenly died of a heart attack at age sixty-four. His most enduring work for missions had been his forty years of service in China, but his name would become known for his influence on Korean missions during its early, most impressionable stage.

How much Nevius influenced the rapid church growth in Korea is debatable. Most would agree that there were many other factors as well. But whatever the various factors were, the church in Korea grew rapidly in comparison to the church in other Asian settings—and in comparison to almost anywhere else in the world. One of the young missionaries who had arrived only six months before the definitive visit of Nevius was Samuel Moffett. According to Alan Neely, "Moffett stressed two facets of the plan especially: intensive Bible study for all believers and evangelism by all believers. . . . Three years later he moved to Pyongyang, where the response to the gospel and the growth of the church became legendary."[39]

Beginning in 1895, there was what some described as an "explosion" of church growth, and there was evidence that the Nevius method was being employed. In Pyongyang, according to one report, the church was "beginning to develop, to expand and to make itself felt as a factor in the life of the city and surrounding country." The main reason for this was further explained: "A cause for rejoicing is the earnest evangelistic work carried on by the members and catechumens. The men have been doing the work and we [missionaries] have been receiving calls to follow up their work."[40]

The church in Korea continued to grow in the years and decades that followed, despite the fact that Korea was in the midst of very hard times during most of this era. Indeed, some observers have suggested that the hard times actually fostered growth in the church. Elsewhere in Asia, persecution of Christians had typically come primarily from fellow citizens. But in Korea much of the persecution came from the hated Japanese, who had formally annexed Korea in 1910. Prior to this annexation, the Korean church had experienced the "great revival" of 1907, which did not necessarily increase membership but rather marked the "spiritual rebirth" of the church. Then in 1910–11, the "Million Souls for Christ" campaign was inaugurated, though again with no significant church growth.

Perhaps more significant than these spiritual revivals were political movements—particularly the Independence Movement that developed in the churches apart from any missionary influence. "The Church became a rallying point for the oppressed Korean people," writes Shearer. "Missionaries had no part in planning this 'Independence Movement,' and the official mission board reports denied that it had any religious character" even though many of the signers of the Declaration of Independence in 1919 were prominent Christians, as were many of the participants in the street demonstrations.[41]

What followed was a very bleak time for Christians in Korea. Many were imprisoned for their political involvement, and churches were burned. According to one local report, "almost all the men of these two churches took part in the demonstrations and fight," and most were either arrested or fled the area.

> It seemed a black day for the Church. Many churches stood almost empty.... Christian schools had to be closed, and the country itineration of missionaries stopped temporarily. Colporteurs could not sell literature anymore, and it looked as if the year 1919 was a black year for the Church in Korea. Yet within the space of a year it was evident that 1919 was ... instead the bright mark of a new era for the kingdom of God in Korea.... The fact that Korean people came to Christ under the prison conditions gives us a hint of the nation's great receptivity to the Gospel and a clue to the rapid growth of the Church for the next seven years.[42]

During the 1930s the church in Korea continued to grow under continued persecution. This was an era when Koreans were required to give obeisance at Shinto shrines—though the Japanese rulers insisted that such acts were not religious in nature but rather reverence for ancestors. For not complying, Christian schools lost government recognition, and many people lost their employment. In Pyongyang, Samuel Moffett made the decision, along with other missionaries, that they would close the seminary and college rather than submitting to the ultimatum that they take part in ceremonies at the local Buddhist shrine. For his part in what was considered to be obstructing authority, he was forced to leave the country. It was a time of testing for the church in many ways, and it was also a time when independent movements and what some described as "fanatical" groups of Christians became more prominent. As the 1940s and World War II approached, missionaries were evacuated from Korea, and the church would continue to be even more free of outside influence.

Protestant Mission Initiatives in Japan

Protestant mission work began in Japan in 1859 and grew in the decades that followed, with many mission agencies involved in the work. But unlike the situation in Korea, no conspicuous leaders or personalities stood out in those early years, and there was no comparable church growth to report to mission societies in the homeland. Some of the early missionaries transferred from China and maintained close contacts with their colleagues there. Most, however, were sent from their headquarters to transplant their respective denominations in Japan. One of the common descriptions of Japanese Christianity is that it is Western and not truly Japanese. Whether due to a different political situation or a different set of "pioneer" missionaries or the lack of the widespread use of the "Nevius Method," Japanese church growth remained very slow, with professed Christians probably never exceeding more than one percent of the population.

One particular mission endeavor that did experience rather significant growth in the late nineteenth and early twentieth centuries was the Russian Orthodox outreach headed by Ivan Kasatkin, who took the name Nikolai after he was ordained a priest. His initial assignment in 1861 was to serve Russian diplomats, but his vision was to do missionary work, and with that in mind, he spent the next years in language study of both Chinese and Japanese. In 1868 he baptized his first three converts, and within a year he had a fellowship of twelve baptized believers and twenty-five catechumens.

Unlike many of the Protestant missionaries who had very close ties with their denominations and mission organizations back home, Nikolai was determined from the start that this was to be an Orthodox mission to the Japanese people, "entirely independent of the Russian state and its traditions." To accomplish this, he laid out a strategy to train catechists, "the best among whom might later be ordained," writes Stephen Neill. "Japan was to be evangelized by the Japanese. Laypeople were to be drawn into the administration of the Church in a way that was almost unknown in other Orthodox churches."[43] By 1882 there were upwards of eight thousand baptized members, that number growing to some twenty-six thousand by the turn of the century.

Nikolai's loyalty remained with the Japanese Orthodox churches during a time of great testing for him personally. War broke out between Russia and Japan in 1904. In light of the predicament, he wrote a pastoral letter to the churches under his care:

> Brothers and sisters, carry out all the duties that are demanded of you as loyal subjects in this situation. Pray to God that he may give victory to your imperial army; thank God for the victories that have been given; make sacrifices to meet the needs of the war.... But in addition to our earthly fatherland, we have another, a heavenly fatherland. To this all men belong without distinction of nationality, since all men are equally children of the heavenly Father.... It is for that reason, brothers and sisters, that I do not separate myself from you, but remain in your family as though it was my own.[44]

One of the unique aspects of Protestant mission work in the early years was the emergence of evangelistic bands of youthful converts. Beginning in the 1870s, these young men were developing into Japan's church leaders of the future. Guido Verbeck, a Dutch Reformed missionary, had organized one of these bands in Nagasaki soon after he arrived in Japan. His primary evangelistic method was to teach English by using the Bible as his text. When he opened a school for Japanese interpreters, he added the U.S. Constitution as a source. He was involved in a number of educational ventures and served for a time as Japan's official translator of government documents, but his vision was to train students for ministry and government service. Another American who organized an evangelistic band and had a profound influence in Japan was William Smith Clark, a man who today would be described as a short-term, tent-making missionary.

William Smith Clark and Kanzo Uchimura

William Smith Clark (1826–86) was the president of Massachusetts Agricultural College when his contributions to the field of agriculture came to the attention of visiting dignitaries from Japan. They invited him to come to Japan to set up a similar institution in their own country. His tenure was short, but his accomplishments were enormous, as David Mitchell summarizes:

> In July 1876 the dynamic Clark reached Sapporo, capital of Japan's newly colonized northern island, and within eight months set up a college, preparatory school, and experimental farm, introduced crops and trees, agricultural buildings and methods, and converted all sixteen students to Christianity. The young believers, exemplifying his parting words, "Boys, be ambitious," won all the second class who also signed Clark's "Covenant of Believers in Jesus." The zealous group became known as the Sapporo Band, whose most notable member was Kanzo Uchimura.[45]

Kanzo Uchimura (1861–1930), writes Andrew Walls, was "one of the outstanding Christian figures of his day in Japan."[46] He was born in Tokyo, the son of a prominent samurai official who was also a Confucian scholar. His early schooling was a traditional Confucian education, but his father was concerned that his son be prepared to confront the modern world and urged him to enroll in Sapporo Agricultural College, where he was awarded a full scholarship. Here Uchimura was suddenly confronted with the Christian faith. Clark had returned to America, but his students remained—and they formed the tenacious Sapporo Band. Uchimura's conversion in 1878 was prompted in part by his disillusionment with Shinto. "As a child, he had been taught that there were more than 8,000 Shinto gods and goddesses. . . . Sometimes the demands of these gods were contradictory. . . . This troubled the serious young Uchimura, and he now found a solution in Christianity and its one God."[47]

Uchimura was baptized by a Methodist missionary, but he felt no particular loyalty to that denomination. He soon gathered a group of friends to help him plant a church in Sapporo—friends who, likewise, felt no special loyalty to the Western denominational church through which they had been baptized. Their evangelism and building project was suddenly halted, however, when one of the Methodist missionaries, who had granted them $698 for the new Sapporo church building and who had assumed the church would be a Methodist one, realized that Uchimura did not intend to affiliate the church with the Methodist mission. He became angry and demanded immediate repayment. The young men repaid the money from their own earnings—a considerable amount, but well worth the sacrifice. "S. Church is Independent," wrote Uchimura. "Joy inexpressible and indescribable! The result of two years economy and industry was our freedom." Not surprisingly, "the sectarianism Uchimura encountered regarding the building of the church," writes Chung Jun Ki, "enhanced his negative feelings toward the Western missionaries in Japan."[48]

This was the beginning of what would become known as the *Mukyokai,* or "Non-Church Movement," which Uchimura emphasized should not be viewed negatively, "as one sees in anarchism or nihilism; it does not attempt to overthrow anything. 'Non-church' is the church for those who have no church." Recognizing that it could become another sectarian denomination, he emphasized the need for a continual spiritual "revolution"—always moving away from the "old" *mukyokai* while recreating *mukyokai.* There was no hierarchy or any kind of organized religious system; rather, the movement was to be simply "a gathering of Christians in a communal atmosphere, where Christ is the center and love and faith draw them together."[49]

Discipleship was the movement's philosophy of missions. As followers matured in the faith, they invited friends and neighbors to their homes and began to teach them. The movement would spread as the members moved from place to place. He was convinced that this concept was the key to bringing Christianity to Japan—"that the Japanese could easily be taught Christianity if they were properly instructed, that is, if they were directed to the teachings in the Bible and not instructed in the rites and formalities of church institutions."[50]

Some missionaries viewed the movement as cultic because of its separation from Western denominations, and Uchimura was harshly criticized for using the term "Japanese Christians" for his followers. He was a man of strong national pride, and he regarded Japan as "a peaceful, prosperous nation, a model for other nations." In defending his national pride, he was quick to point out the same national spirit among the missionaries:

> I am blamed by missionaries for upholding Japanese Christianity. They say that Christianity is a universal religion, and to uphold Japanese Christianity is to make a universal religion a national religion.... Why blame me for upholding Japanese Christianity while every one of them upholds his or her own Christianity?... Is not Episcopalianism essentially an English Christianity?... Why, for instance, call a universal religion "Cumberland Presbyterianism"? If it is not wrong to apply the name of a district in the state of Kentucky to Christianity, why is it wrong for me to apply the name of my country to the same. I think I have as much right to call my Christianity Japanese as thousands of Christians in the Cumberland Valley they live in.
>
> When a Japanese truly and independently believes in Christ, he is a Japanese Christian, and his Christianity is Japanese Christianity.[51]

Uchimura's most enduring legacy to Japanese Christianity was found in his writings. He published hundreds of issues of his monthly journal, *The Biblical Study,* and along with that a 22-volume Bible commentary. His writings were widely used by Christians outside his movement, many of whom were not connected with the more established denominations as had been the case in Korea. His writings, some of which have a contemporary tone that rings as true today as when they were written, are still used and quoted. He was a profound social critic, as is demonstrated by a piece that was published in 1926 in the *Japan Christian Intelligencer:*

> Americans themselves know all too well that their genius in not in religion.... Americans are great people; there is no doubt about that. They are great in building cities and railroads.... Americans have a wonderful genius for improving the breeds of horses, cattle, sheep and swine; they raise them in multitudes, butcher them, eat them, and send their meat-products to all parts of the world. Americans too are great inventors. They invented or perfected telegraphs, telephones, talking and hearing machines, automobiles ... poison gasses.... They are great in democracy.... Needless to say, they are great in money.... They first make money before they undertake any serious work.... To start and carry on any work without money is in the eyes of the Americans madness.... Americans are great in all these things and much else; but *not in Religion,* as they themselves very well know.... Americans must *count religion* in order to see or show its value.... To them big churches are successful churches.... To win the greatest number of converts with the least expense is their constant endeavour. Statistics is their way of showing success or failure in their religion as in their commerce and politics. Numbers, numbers, oh, how they value numbers!... Mankind goes down to America to learn how to live the earthly

> life; but to live the heavenly life, they go to some other people. It is no special fault of Americans to be this-worldly; it is their national characteristic; and they in their self-knowledge ought to serve mankind in other fields than in religion.[52]

Uchimura had lived and studied in America, but most of his perspectives on Americans came from his association with them in Japan, primarily with American missionaries. Many of the early missionaries were independent or sponsored by independent faith missions, and they sometimes seemed to mirror the description that Uchimura had drawn—Americans bringing to Japan a religion of numbers and money and strategies. Charles and Lettie Cowman, with their ties to the Holiness movement, could have been the very Americans he was describing.

Charles and Lettie Cowman

Charles and Lettie Cowman came to Japan as independent missionaries in 1901 and later founded the Oriental Missionary Society and worked closely with the Holiness Church in Japan. Their commitment to missions had come several years after they had married and settled into an affluent lifestyle—Charles, in management at Western Union Telegraph Company, and Lettie the daughter of a banker. They had only recently been converted and were attending a mission conference at Moody Church in Chicago where A. B. Simpson (founder of the Christian and Missionary Alliance) was the speaker. Following the emotionally charged message, an offering was taken. So moved was Charles that he contributed "a roll of bills that represented a month's salary." But the offering had just begun. "Then, as the enthusiasm mounted higher, people wanted to give their jewelry and even watches. At the announcement of this second offering, Charles disentangled his solid gold watch and chain, and looked down at the large diamond in Lettie's engagement ring, as if to say: 'Surely you are going to come along with me in this, aren't you?'"[53]

The connections with Moody Memorial Church, A. B. Simpson, the Holiness Movement, and their student days at Moody Bible Institute put the Cowmans squarely in the camp of turn-of-the-century Fundamentalism—as did their concerns about separation from the world. After her conversion, Lettie had stood by her piano and "yielded" her stacks of dance music, operas, popular songs, and secular books to God, never to again be involved in such worldly amusements.[54] At about the same time, her husband received a very specific message from God that he wrote in his Bible: "Called to Japan. August 11, 1900, at 10:30 A.M."[55] But their obvious piety did not make them immune from what Uchimura would have called "this-worldliness," that "national characteristic" of Americans.

Numbers and money and statistics and strategies were the threads that held the Cowman's ministry together from the very beginning. In her leather-bound birthday book, Lettie had written what her biographer describes as "her financial hymn of praise, her monetary missionary psalm"—not to be mistaken for "an audit-account of finance."

Received to date	$ .25	
November 1, 1900	300.00	
	70.00	Japan
	464.00	Nakada
	50.00	China
	25.00	India
	909.00	
December, 1901	$1,000.00	from a stranger
	500.00	from a stranger
	1,000.00	from a stranger for missions
February 28, 1903, to date	$7,000.00	
January, 1909, to date	$104,000.00	praise God!
February 1, 1919, to date	$510,000.00	praise God!
May 1, 1939, to date	$5,000,000.00	praise God![56]

Despite the significant growth in income in less than forty years, there was never enough. There was always a shortage of funds, as Lettie's biographer writes on page after page:

> Days and nights are given to prayer for funds. . . . How thrilling (with an empty treasury!) to have young Bud Kilbourne come rushing in from town, waving a cabled order from America for $2,000.00. . . . Funds begin to flow more freely. She [Lettie] is learning to be a campaigner on the deputational field. . . . Soon the funds are gone once more. New friends must be raised up to maintain the advance of the work. . . . As they return to Japan, she sees the crusade vision burn like a fever in Charles' heart. *Faster-farther!* Are his watchwords. He knows that time is short. . . . Things look dark. Funds are falling off at a fearful rate. She goes at once to the bankbook of heaven. . . . Millions of dollars will be needed, but millions of dollars are nothing to God.[57]

"Numbers, numbers, oh, how they value numbers!" wrote Uchimura. For the Cowmans, numbers did not just relate to money, though specific amounts of money were very significant. For instance, a bill for $878.05 arrived at the office (for the purchase of 100,000 Gospels). When all the receipts for money that had arrived over the following weekend were calculated, the adding machine tape totaled exactly $878.05.[58] Money was a critical element. Under the title "What would I do if I fell heir to a million dollars," Charles penned a wish list for his mission dreams.[59]

Equally important figures were those used for calculating numbers of people and households and souls saved. Like many other missions, the Cowman's worked with evangelistic bands during their ministry in Japan. "One band has increased to seven bands, with a total of seventy-eight crusaders. . . . It is thrilling—two hundred saved yonder, a hundred here. Day by day the tally grows. Thousands are numbered among the redeemed."[60] The mission strategies hinged on numbers:

> Charles E. Cowman's vision for Japan is carried out through crusade bands, pledged to visit every house in the Empire. They have the benefit of military maps which the government has released. (God provided them for this hour; not before, nor since, have these been available.) They are large maps representing five-mile squares of territory. Marked on every road and path is each house, Buddhist monastery, Shinto temple, wayside shrine, or tenant shack.
>
> Charles makes definite assignments, receives personal reports, believes in achieving day-by-day goals. His room takes on the activity of a combined business, missionary, and military headquarters. . . . Mission stations are multiplying. Nightly meetings and nightly converts swell the totals.[61]

In 1918 the plan that the Cowmans had initiated after they had arrived in Japan was declared finished: "The initial work of the mission has been completed. . . . The pioneer 'Every Creature Crusade' has been completed. Ten million three hundred thousand homes of Japan have received a first gospel message—all in seventeen years!"[62] Then, in 1924, after suffering from a serious heart condition for several years, Charles died.

During her husband's long illness, Lettie had written and published a devotional book, *Streams in the Desert*—a book that would become an evangelical bestseller and classic. Following his death, she was nearly paralyzed with grief, but eventually she began to write books again, including a biography of her late husband. Then in 1928, after the death of Ernest Kilbourne, who had succeeded her husband as president of the Oriental Missionary Society, Lettie herself assumed the presidency, a position she held until 1949. Seven years later, "at 6:00 A.M. on Sunday morning, August 10, 1936, the Lord speaks: 'I sanctified thee and I ordained thee a prophet unto the nations' (Jer. 1:5). She sees that before she was born, God planned her life." God, she was convinced, had given her a "new thing" to do, and that was nothing less than "the evangelization of the world." She believed God was calling her to finish the work Charles had started—he was "God's pioneer in putting the gospel into every home in one nation." She would put the gospel in every home in the world.[63]

From that point on, her story reads almost like an atlas. She started her campaign in Finland, then went on to Lapland and the other Baltic States, and to Russia and other European countries. Egypt, Israel, Ethiopia, India, Cuba, Haiti, Mexico, Korea, Columbia—one country followed on another—though when her world tour was over, most of the world was still untouched by her ministry.

In many places she was hosted by government dignitaries, and in every country she visited—and some she did not—she sought to carry out her evangelization of the world by having evangelistic bands distribute Gospels in every home. In Mexico alone, the number of Gospels distributed was 1,455,000.[64]

Still counting to the very end, this banker's daughter died April 17, 1960, one century old, minus a decade.

Mabel Francis

Mabel Francis was a contemporary of the Cowmans and, like them, influenced by turn-of-the-century Fundamentalism, but her life and ministry was very different. Indeed, most of her life was spent in obscurity. Her missionary work in Japan would have appeared utterly insignificant, with no "Every Creature Crusades" and millions of dollars to account for. Yet at the end of her fifty-six-year mission tenure in Japan, she was the country's most celebrated foreign "citizen."

Mabel was born in 1880 and grew up in New Hampshire. After the untimely death of the young man she hoped to marry, she became an itinerant evangelist and store-front preacher. Then, at age nineteen, she felt God calling her to be a missionary in Japan, where she began her ministry with the Christian and Missionary Alliance ten years later in 1909. In 1913 her brother joined her in the work, and together they planted twenty churches. In 1922 her widowed sister, Anne, also joined her, and she and Mabel spent much of the next forty years together, with Mabel doing evangelism and Anne teaching.

Mabel Francis, Japan's most celebrated foreign "citizen."

In the 1930s, during the Great Depression, the Alliance, strapped for funds, recalled their missionaries from Japan. But unlike their colleagues, the sisters refused to come home. The needs in Japan were too great to abandon the work. Money trickled in from supporters back home, but life was very difficult. Mabel conducted her evangelistic outreach by bicycle, though she often thought "how nice it would be to have money to ride the bus." And how nice it would be to have men come and do the work: "O Lord, where are the men who ought to be riding these bicycles up and down these trails?" She was a single woman who had longed for a husband, as she later confessed:

> You see, when I was so discouraged and the job seemed so terribly big, I thought, "Well now, if I was married, I could follow on with my husband, and there would be something doing, but what can a little person like myself do?" I just felt so hopeless!
>
> And then the Lord said, "You are on the wrong track. I have a plan for your life and it is not for you to be married.... Well, you know the whole thing passed out of my life like a cloud passing away, and that was many years ago. The thought of marriage has meant nothing to me since that time—nothing![65]

The difficult times during the 1930s were only exacerbated after the bombing of Pearl Harbor. Initially the sisters were permitted to remain in their home—officially under house arrest. But later they were taken to an internment camp set up in a Catholic monastery. After the war Francis was heavily involved in humanitarian efforts, but she was distressed by the lack of supplies and fellow workers. "That's where America failed in Japan," she lamented. "Our churches didn't grasp the opportunity—they didn't send a thousand missionaries. During the first ten years after the war, the Japanese people were really very open and seeking.... Now ... it is much harder to reach them."[66]

Though never trained in cross-cultural communication, Francis won the hearts of the Japanese people that she came to know. One of the Japanese converts as a young girl had been intrigued by a foreign woman, and she inquired of a friend who this bicycling woman was—this woman who was always smiling. When she was later invited to attend a service, "much to her surprise," wrote Francis, "she found out I was the preacher when she got into the church."[67] Francis was open and honest about her own struggles—particularly in her desire to organize and plan the ministry in a culture that was not her own. She writes of one such incident that reveals her seriousness as well as her sense of humor:

> For instance, we had an elderly Japanese man in one of our groups who had been wonderfully saved. It was indeed a miracle, and he would faithfully get up and give long testimonies, magnifying the Lord.
>
> But he had lost his teeth, and he could not talk plainly. No one could really understand him very well.
>
> I used to sit there and pray, "O Lord, stop him. He is spoiling the meeting. Everything will go to pieces here."
>
> So one night the Lord spoke to me and said, "I can bless right over that old man. He is standing there trying to glorify me."
>
> "But you do bother Me," the Lord said to me, "by sitting here and fretting over it."
>
> Oh, wasn't I ashamed of the spirit I had! I saw it. And that's the way He took that fretting spirit out of my life. I just committed it to Him.[68]

More than a decade after the end of World War II, Japanese officials honored Mabel and Anne for their long years of service in Japan, and they were invited to speak at official functions. In 1962 the emperor honored Mabel Francis with Japan's highest civilian honor, membership in the exclusive Fifth Order of the Sacred Treasure. This was one of many ways she was singled out for her sacrifice for "the welfare of the Japanese people in their distress and confusion at the time of their defeat."[69] The award had come after a furlough in America. She had returned to Japan to continue her ministry. She was eighty-three.

SELECT BIBLIOGRAPHY

Chung, Jun Ki. *Social Criticism of Uchimura Kanzo and Kim Kyo-Shin.* Seoul: UBF Press, 1988.

Cowman, Lettie B. *Charles E. Cowman: Missionary—Warrior.* Los Angeles: Oriental Missionary Society, 1939.

Davies, Daniel M. *The Life and Thought of Henry Gerhard Appenzeller (1858–1902).* Lewiston, NY: Edwin Mellen, 1988.

Francis, Mabel. *One Shall Chase a Thousand.* Harrisburg, PA: Christian Publications, 1968.

Hunt, Everett N., Jr. *Protestant Pioneers in Korea.* Maryknoll, NY: Orbis Books, 1980.

Pearson, B. H. *The Vision Lives: A Profile of Mrs. Charles E. Cowman.* Grand Rapids: Zondervan, 1961.

Shearer, Roy E. *Wildfire: Church Growth in Korea.* Grand Rapids: Eerdmans, 1966.

PART 3

The Expanding Involvement

PART 3

THE EXPANDING INVOLVEMENT

Profound changes were occurring in the world as the nineteenth century came to a close. The "European century throughout world history"[1] was over. The colonialism and imperialism unleashed by Western powers were being resisted and challenged, and the era of relative world peace was coming to an abrupt end. As the twentieth century opened, there were rumblings of war in Asia, and by 1904 Russia and Japan were battling each other in armed conflict. The outcome was a victory for Japan, and on a larger scale for Asia. No longer could the Western nations assume they were the only military powers in a rapidly expanding world.

The real break in international stability did not come until a decade later when, in the words of Stephen Neill, "The European nations, with their loud-voiced claims to a monopoly on Christianity and civilization . . . rushed blindly and confusedly into a civil war which was to leave them economically impoverished and without a shred of virtue." And, "the second world war," he continues, "only finished off what the first had already accomplished. The moral pretensions of the West were shown to be a sham."[2]

If Christianity was not the answer to the world's problems, then what was? To many people in Europe it was Marxism. The revolutionary ferment that had erupted periodically during the nineteenth century had not been purged, and the disillusionment resulting from World War I only added to the dissatisfaction with capitalism and its class-oriented structure of society. The Bolshevik Revolution of 1917 was just one manifestation of this discontent, but it was a significant one. With a solid foothold in Russia, Marxism was on its way to becoming a grave threat to Western capitalism. This turn of events brought an added incentive to twentieth-century missionaries, many of whom viewed their mission as one of disseminating a combined philosophy of Christianity and capitalism to combat atheistic Marxism.

Along with the threat of Marxism came an anti-Western sentiment that was seen in much of the third world. Nationalism was on the rise and there was a growing movement toward independence. Westerners, though armed with advanced technology and social programs, were associated with economic exploitation. The white man was seen as both a "deliverer and destroyer," according to Neill, and "the missionary, too, would come to be regarded as both friend and foe."[3]

Western society itself was undergoing major social changes. In the United States, the late nineteenth century had seen growing discontent among farmers and laborers. The Populist movement championed a wide variety of rural causes, and William Jennings Bryan became a symbol of rural radicalism. In the cities, labor unions were on the upswing and strikes were numerous and violent. The Progressive Movement was the middle class expression of social concern, out of which came a variety of legislative reforms, including antitrust laws, child labor prohibition, and laws to protect industrial workers. In the churches, the social gospel was gaining momentum with less emphasis on an individual's inner relationship with God and more of a focus on broad human social needs in the here and now.

The white man was seen as both a "deliverer and destroyer," and "the missionary, too, would come to be regarded as both friend and foe."

One of the most far-reaching social concerns of the late nineteenth and early twentieth centuries related to women's rights. The suffrage movement that had begun decades earlier climaxed in 1920 with the passage of the nineteenth amendment. But the women's movement involved much more than suffrage. World War I had created a vacuum in the labor force, and women more than ever before were entering the workplace in large numbers. With the close of the war, young women began dreaming of professional careers, and more and more were enrolling in the nation's colleges and universities.

This new liberation had a direct impact on overseas missions. As in other professions, women began entering the field in vast numbers. When the nineteenth century opened, missionaries were men. Many of these men had wives, and the wives served faithfully alongside their husbands, but they were not generally viewed as missionaries in their own right. By the close of the century, however, the situation was vastly different. Single women in large numbers began volunteering for missionary service, and married women were beginning to assume a more active role.

The social changes taking place in society were accompanied by intellectual changes, most noticeably in the fields of philosophy and religion. By the twentieth century the theological liberalism so prominent in Germany had begun to draw a wide following in America. Higher criticism—based on rationalism and the scientific method—was in vogue, and much of traditional Christianity was being stripped of its essential beliefs. "In essence, it stripped Christianity of its supernatural elements," writes Robert Linder, "especially its miracles and the deity of Christ. It taught instead what it considered to be the essential Christian virtues of the fatherhood of God, the brotherhood of man and the necessity of living in love. The Bible, historically the authority for faith and practice in the Protestant churches, was no longer considered trustworthy, but embracing errors and contradictions."[4]

All this had a profound effect on missions. Virtually all Protestant missionaries during most of the nineteenth century were evangelicals who held the authority of Scripture and staunchly defended the cardinal doctrines of the faith. But by the end of the century, carrying the title of missionary was no guarantee that an individual was orthodox in his Christian beliefs. The fallout from higher criticism, the Darwinian theory of evolution, and the social gospel was beginning to be felt on the mission field.

This trend toward theological liberalism at home and abroad, however, did not go unchallenged. In Europe, Neoorthodoxy was the answer for many. The teachings and writings of Germany's Karl Barth and his American counterpart, Reinhold Neibuhr, were widely respected by Protestant intellectuals as a compromise between the old orthodoxy and the new liberalism. In America, the reaction was much more conservative. Neoorthodoxy gained a wide following, but the more prominent opposing force was Fundamentalism. "For nearly a generation," writes Linder, "Christians fought an exhausting war for the minds and souls of American church members. When the smoke of battle cleared, every major denomination had been affected and a number of them split by the quarrel."[5]

The new breed had no qualms about evangelizing "nominal" Christians, and areas regarded as already evangelized were not off limits.

In part as a reaction to this trend, another new breed of missionaries emerged, not necessarily so different from their forebears, but intensely determined to keep the faith pure and to trust God only for their needs. They were largely Bible institute and Christian college graduates, and they founded and filled the ranks of the new faith mission societies that arose in the late nineteenth and early twentieth centuries. Unlike a certain few of their predecessors, they had no qualms about evangelizing "nominal" Christians; and areas of the world traditionally regarded as already evangelized were not off limits, Latin America and Europe being prime examples.

One of the most significant changes in Protestant missions during the first half of the twentieth century related to the nationality of the missionaries themselves. After the turn of the century, the home base of missions shifted from England to North America. Although thousands of missionaries continued to pour out of England, Europe, Australia and New Zealand, and Scandinavian countries (Norway and Finland sent out an amazing number in proportion to their Christian population), North America took the lead. This was due in part to the active role the United States began playing in international affairs. "American imperial expansion," writes Winthrop Hudson, "was accompanied by a mounting enthusiasm among the churches for overseas missions."[6] Foreign policy was in some cases justified in the name of world evangelism. In regard to the acquisition of the Philippines, President McKinley explained, "There was nothing left for us to do but to take them all and to educate the Filipinos and uplift and civilize and Christianize them, and by God's grace do the very best we could by them, as our fellowmen for whom Christ also died."[7]

By the third decade of the twentieth century mainline mission outreach was on the wane. The number of students volunteering for foreign missions, according to the Foreign Missionary Conference report, also fell drastically—from 2,700 in 1920 to only around 250 in 1928. Even the very philosophical basis for missions came under fire as William E. Hocking and his colleagues, who compiled the *Laymen's Inquirey,* warned against "conscious and direct evangelism."

But what seemed apparent in statistics and publicized reports failed to tell the whole story. In fundamentalist-evangelical circles the missionary spirit had never died, and during the 1930s, despite the woes of the Depression, there was a conscious and growing movement to speed the pace of world evangelism with whatever means were available. It was during that decade that Clarence Jones and others initiated missionary radio broadcasts, that William Cameron Townsend began training missionary linguists, and that many medical ventures were launched, while still others were testing the practicality of aviation services for missionaries. World War II, however, frustrated the plans of many of these missionary activists, and it was not until the end of the war that the real thrust of missionary specialization got underway.

The emphasis on specialization in missions, coming largely as a response to technological, political, social, and religious changes during the twentieth century, included not only medicine, translation work, radio, but also dozens of other areas such as education, literature, and agriculture. One of the factors influencing the growth of such specialized ministries has been the increase in the number of Christian liberal arts colleges, many growing out of one-time Bible institutes and Bible colleges. Graduates from these schools, often through the aid of INTERCRISTO (a computerized Christian placement service) have discovered countless opportunities to utilize their education and skills on the foreign field.

The ministry of Christian literature alone expanded many times over during the course of the twentieth century. In 1921, a survey of contemporary missionary trends concluded that "one hundred and sixty presses are conducted by the Protestant missions boards in various parts of the world, and they issue annually about four hundred million pages of Christian literature."[8] After World War

II, that number vastly increased as specialized ministries were launched, such as the Christian Literature Crusade, the World Literature Crusade, Operation Mobilization, the Evangelical Literature League, the Pocket Testament League, and Evangelical Literature Overseas. One of the largest literature organizations was the Moody Literature Mission, which distributed literature in nearly two hundred languages.

By the middle of the twentieth century the United States had become the missionary "sender" of the world. Who were these Americans, and why were they so willing to leave the luxuries of the freest and most prosperous nation on earth? Their profile had changed in some significant respects. They were different in many ways from their missionary forebears. They were women in increasing numbers, and they were better educated with stronger theological views—university-educated student volunteers, avowed Fundamentalists, and everything in between. Like their predecessors, they were hardy individualists, tempered by waves of revivals and spurred on by a pioneering spirit, but along with that pioneering spirit, they often brought a specialty—and the latest technology—to advance the gospel.

11

SINGLE WOMEN MISSIONARIES: "SECOND-CLASS CITIZENS"

From the earliest times, women have been actively involved in evangelism. Beginning in the New Testament and throughout the period of the early church and the Middle Ages and on into the era of modern missions, women have served effectively. Among Protestants, there were few opportunities for single women to serve in ministry until the mid-nineteenth century. Before that time the wives of missionaries—though not missionaries in their own right—stand out in many instances for their dedicated service. But there were other wives thrust into missions who did not want to be there. Dorothy Carey is a notable example. Edith Buxton, in her book *Reluctant Missionary*, tells of her struggles and of the unhappiness she felt for many years; and Pearl Buck writes of the years of discontentment her mother endured in China.

Yet if some married missionary women secretly resented their station in life, there were countless more single women who longed to be missionaries. Married women missionaries, with household duties and little children to care for, simply could not carry the load of work that needed to be done. "They glimpsed the promise of what might be achieved in women's work for women and children," writes R. Pierce Beaver, "but they longed for colleagues who would have more freedom and who could devote themselves solely to such activity."[1] Some men also saw the need for single women, but public opinion throughout much of the nineteenth century was opposed to the idea. Nevertheless, beginning in the 1820s, women were venturing overseas in a steady trickle.

> *Despite public opinion, beginning in the 1820s, women were venturing overseas in a steady trickle.*

Even before this, however, there were Roman Catholic women who were conducting effective ministry in mission settings. One of the most remarkable of these women was Ann Marie Javouhey (1779–1851). She grew up in the French countryside during the time of the French Revolution and entered a convent as a young woman. Soon thereafter, she had a visionary call to serve as a missionary. She founded the Sisters of St. Joseph, and in 1822 began working in Africa. Within decades her blue-robed sisters were stationed all over the world. She was a strong woman, claiming God was her only authority—not her bishop. Stung by the insubordination, her bishop forbade her to participate in the Eucharist. She appealed to the archbishop, again demonstrating her strength of character: "I am not only the Superior General of the Congregation of St. Joseph of Cluny; I did not merely cooperate in the foundation of that Order; I am its sole and solitary foundress. I am its Mother General as God is its Father."[2] The archbishop ruled in her favor. When she died, there were some nine hundred nuns serving under her banner throughout the world.

In Protestant circles women were not involved in founding mission organizations until the last half of the nineteenth century, and none of those mission societies had a worldwide influence comparable to that of the Sisters of St. Joseph. Betsy Stockton was the first unmarried Protestant woman from America to serve as an overseas missionary. She was a black woman and former slave who went to Hawaii in 1823. Believing that God had called her to serve as a missionary, she applied to the American Board, and the directors agreed to send her abroad—but only as a domestic servant for another missionary couple. Despite her lowly position, Stockton was considered "qualified to teach" and was allowed to conduct a school. Later on in the 1820s, in response to a need for a single woman teacher, Cynthia Farrar, a native of New Hampshire, sailed for Bombay, where she served faithfully for thirty-four years under the Marathi Mission.

Not until the 1860s, with the beginning of the Women's Missionary Movement, did single women in large numbers begin serving overseas. The idea for separate organizations for women first surfaced in England, but it quickly spread to America. By 1900 there were more than forty women's mission societies in the United States alone. Largely because of the "female agencies," the number of single women in missions rapidly increased; and during the first decade of the twentieth century, women, for the first time in history, outnumbered men in Protestant missions—in some areas by large proportions. In the Chinese province of Shantung in 1910, for example, among the Baptists and Presbyterians there were seventy-nine women and only forty-six men. In the decades that followed, the number of single women missionaries continued to climb until women outnumbered men in some areas by a ratio of 2:1 (with single women, married women, and married men each comprising approximately one-third).

In her classic book on missions, *Western Women in Eastern Lands,* published in 1910, Helen Barnett Montgomery wrote of the amazing strides taken by women in world evangelism:

> It is indeed a wonderful story.... We began in weakness, we stand in power. In 1861 there was a single missionary in the field, Miss Marston, in Burma; in 1909, there were 4,710 unmarried women in the field, 1,948 of them from the United States. In 1861 there was one organized woman's society in our country; in 1910 there were forty-four. Then the supporters numbered a few hundreds; today there are at least two millions. Then the amount contributed was $2000; last year four million dollars was raised. The development on the field has been as remarkable as that at home. Beginning with a single teacher, there are at the opening of the Jubilee year 800 teachers, 140 physicians, 380 evangelists, 79 trained nurses, 5,783 Bible women and native helpers. Among the 2,100 schools there are 260 boarding and high schools. There are 75 hospitals and 78 dispensaries.... It is an achievement of which women may well be proud. But it is only a feeble beginning of what they can do and will do, when the movement is on its feet.[3]

Overseas missions attracted women for a variety of reasons, but one of the most obvious was that there were few opportunities for women to serve in vocational ministry in the homeland. Ministry was considered a male profession. Some nineteenth-century women, such as Catherine Booth, broke into this male-dominated realm, but not without opposition. Wrote Booth, herself a Bible scholar, "Oh, that the ministers of religion would search the original records of God's Word in order to discover whether ... God really intended woman to bury her gifts and talents, as she now does." Other women simply entered secular work. Florence Nightingale felt called to the ministry, but there were no opportunities: "I would have given her [the church] my head, my hand, my heart. She would not have them."[4] So the "foreign field," far away from the inner sanctums of the church hierarchy, became an outlet for women who desired to serve God.

Besides the opportunities for Christian service, missionary work was an outlet for adventure and excitement. While men could fulfill their heroic fantasies as soldiers, seamen, and explorers, women had no such available options. Likewise, women such as Mary Slessor from poor, working-class backgrounds were able to raise their station in life through missionary careers. But the common thread among virtually all of the single women missionaries who sacrificially served abroad was a sense of calling from God—and equally important, a sense that they could make a difference. Their most universal concern beyond that of saving souls was to help their sisters living under oppression in "heathen" lands. They desired to offer women a taste of "civilization" that they enjoyed.

Missionary women were part of the larger missionary manifest destiny movement and came with a "can do" spirit of Western superiority. Although they "seldom wielded political power," writes Dana Robert, "they worked in a context where American citizenship meant to have special privileges." She continues:

> Yet in its practice, "Woman's Work for Woman" bore an ambiguous relationship to the realities of cultural imperialism. What appeared as a "holistic

> mission" from the missionary perspective was often perceived by the missionized as cultural imperialism designed to tear down their own customs and societies. The emphasis on social change toward western norms, couched in the language of helping to bring about God's kingdom on earth, made "Woman's Work for Woman" a partner with the myths of western superiority so prominent during the late nineteenth century. At the same time, its focus on global sisterhood and the essential unity of humankind was a valuable corrective to patriarchal notions that valued men over women and boys over girls in many parts of the world.[5]

One of the most effective nineteenth-century missionaries whose term of service was devoted to "Woman's Work for Woman" was Adele Fielde, an individual who in many respects was an unlikely candidate for missionary greatness.

Adele Marion Fielde

The life and public service of Adele Fielde (1839–1916) intersected with many facets of life besides overseas missions. Following her years of ministry in Thailand and China, she returned to the United States where she became a strong voice in the women's movement and involved herself in scientific research. She was a confident, determined, and resourceful woman, whose missionary career powerfully illustrates the second-class status that confronted women who often sacrificed so much just to be permitted to give their lives in service to God.

Fielde grew up in East Rodman, New York, in a working-class family who were Baptists "of the tolerant New England kind." But young Adele, "with her parents' blessings, chose to be a Universalist, a more tolerant sect which believed in universal redemption, the salvation of all human beings." She studied at the State Normal College in Albany and then became a school teacher. Still single at age twenty-five, she was regarded by some as a "confirmed old maid." Then in 1864, she was introduced to her best friend's brother, Cyrus Chilcott, a Baptist missionary candidate to Thailand. They became engaged, and she agreed to become a Baptist and to follow him to Thailand once he was settled there.[6]

What was expected to be a hundred-day sea voyage for Fielde turned into a much longer and more perilous and harrowing journey that ended in heartbreak. Fielde was an excellent writer, and lines from her journal tell the story best:

> Great flakes of snow fell slowly on the deck as we stood watching the receding shore of native land.... During the ensuing night the waves rose high and for many consecutive days we were unable to leave our bunks.... In the Indian Ocean we encountered a typhoon that mauled and drove our ship for days.... As our ship passed slowly through the straits between Java and Sumatra ... jungle fever seized all on board save the captain.... A chill like that of ice in the veins was followed by scorching fever.... While in a state of coma, I was

> thought to have died.... On a clear morning in May we entered the harbor of Hong Kong. Ten of the crew were carried ashore for burial.... I was barely able to stand, and Miss Sands, who had partially recovered, arrayed me in white.[7]

Dressed and ready, Fielde expected the groom to appear, and there on the ship they were to be married by the captain. But there was no groom. She soon learned that he had died of typhoid fever in Bangkok ten days after she had sailed from New York. The captain tried to convince her to sail back to New York with him, but she insisted that she must go on to Thailand. If she did not, she would live with an emptiness and incompleteness for the rest of her life. Her letter, published in the *Baptist Missionary Magazine,* tells of that time of anguish:

> I have journeyed seven weary months over tempestuous seas and in strange lands to meet my beloved and I found his grave with the grass upon it seven months old. I have come to my house; it is left unto me desolate. While I stood holding out my hand for a cup of happiness, one of fearful bitterness was pressed violently to my lips. I looked joyful to Providence and it turned upon me a face of inexpressible darkness. And because I believe in God I have been able to endure it.[8]

The Baptist mission work in Bangkok had been opened by William Dean in the 1830s, and the ministry was primarily aimed at Chinese people living there. Bangkok was only one of many locations where, due to prohibitions against mission work in China, "missions run by sixty Protestant missionaries had been established among Chinese immigrants." Once China opened up after the Opium War, the Bangkok mission was relegated to secondary importance. That is how Fielde found it when she arrived in 1865. She was determined to continue Chilcott's ministry, but that is not what the mission director had in mind: "Though Dean was sympathetic to Adele's plight, he did not consider her to be a suitable addition to the Bangkok mission. He treated her not as a single woman but as a widow, and he hoped that she might attract a young male missionary." Yet, due to her special predicament, the American Baptist Missionary Union permitted her to remain, "though it was against policy." The more proficient in the language she became, however, and the more effective her ministry was, "the more Dean tried to restrict her."[9]

The Baptist mission work in Thailand could not be considered a success story. In 1868 Fielde reported that since Dean had begun the work more than thirty-five years earlier, the fifteen missionaries who had served in the mission, on an average, could account for the conversion of "fewer than three native Christians," and even some of those conversions were considered dubious at best. But she was optimistic: "I don't believe our Lord sends His servants on useless errands."[10]

Fielde's commitment to the ministry was often tested by what she viewed as unfair mission policies. As a teacher she had a salary three times what her mission salary was, and she soon discovered that a single male missionary received nearly double her four-hundred-dollar annual allotment. She was straightforward in her appeal to the mission board back home: "I cannot see why an unmarried woman giving all her time to missionary work, paying all her own expenses, having precisely the same or equal expenses—does not require and should not receive the same salary as an unmarried man."[11] After two years of debate over the matter, the mission increased her salary, with retroactive pay for one year.

Fielde was optimistic about her mission work: "I don't believe our Lord sends His servants on useless errands."

Fielde's relationship with William Dean continued to deteriorate, particularly after she began appealing for more single women to come to Thailand—single women, without family, who were more cost effective than married men with their families. Dean accused Fielde of being "dangerous to the interests of the cause." She was also accused of not being "a true Baptist, but a Universalist who chose to consort with the European community, bankers, diplomats, and other 'unbelievers.'" Likewise, "she indulged in card-playing and attended dancing parties, forbidden by Baptists." When she was called up short on her behavior, Dean was shocked when she responded: "I desire to be *good*. But I do not wish to be *Pious*." When the mission board secretary wrote to her saying that the "incredible charges" that had been made against her put her ministry in "extreme peril," she sought to defend herself, agreeing that card-playing was a mindless diversion but insisting that dancing was a wholesome exercise.[12]

The controversy over Fielde raged for months, and in the end she was ordered to return home, after most of six years of ministry in Thailand. To calm her nerves during her final months, she made herself a pipe and "smoked six thimblefuls of the *kang cha* [hashish]"—though she did not confess that indiscretion until years later. On her return trip to America, Fielde had a stopover at the Chinese port of Swatow on the South China Sea. There she was befriended by William and Eliza Ashmore, who invited her to return and work with them. They were impressed with her "high motives," her good-natured personality, and her proficiency in the Chinese language.[13]

When she returned home, she discovered that she had become somewhat of a celebrity—largely because of her writings. She took speaking engagements, and with the mission board's approval returned to work in China. With the Ashmores, Fielde reveled in the late-nineteenth-century triumphalism that characterized evangelical missions. Missionaries were "winning splendid victories," Ashmore had written. They were "entering no battle but to conquer. . . . Hinduism, Buddhism, Confucianism, are but the shadows of their former strength, and seem on the point of extinction."[14]

Soon after she returned to China, Fielde became involved in the training of Bible women. "It was said that the conversion of one woman was worth the conversion of twenty men, and if the women could not be reached, there was no hope for the evangelical movement in China." Training Bible women was not an idea introduced by Fielde; others had effectively conducted such work. But Fielde "institutionalized the program, explicitly defining its structure, mode of operation, and aims, and she implemented the plan with vigor, fully employing her organizational skills, and her capacity for hard work." She had students ranging from their early twenties to their mid-seventies. "Overall, about five hundred passed through her school in a twenty-year period."[15]

Her mission strategy was simple and served as a model for training Bible women throughout China:

> It was Miss Fielde's practice to gather Christian women for instruction and to teach them thoroughly one lesson from the Gospel. When they had learned it, she sent them out, two by two, into the country about to tell the lesson to villagers. After a time they were gathered at Swatow and received another portion of the truth and having obtained a thorough grasp of it, went forth to carry the good news of salvation.[16]

Fielde's writing skills made her a priceless asset to the mission, as she wrote stories to be published and consumed by mission supporters. "She had each Bible woman tell her story, which she translated and published in magazines," writes Leonard Warren. "Their heart-rending sagas proved enormously appealing to American women, who could sympathize with their suffering Chinese sisters."[17] She later compiled the stories into a book, *Pagoda Shadows*. In addition to her teaching and writing, she compiled a *Dictionary of the Swatow Dialect,* which went through many publications.

In 1883 she returned to America for home leave, spending part of her time on a speaking tour and nearly two years studying at the Academy of Natural Sciences in Philadelphia—the "happiest" years of her life. At the end of her furlough, she was asked to serve as president of Vassar College, but she turned down the offer, determined instead to return to her ministry in China with her faithful Bible women.

Fielde had trained her best students to train others, so when health problems developed, she was relieved that she could return home with good conscience. In 1889 she resigned the mission and spent the next two years traveling home through India, the Middle East, and Europe. Her last years were devoted to the suffragist movement, public lecturing, organizational work, humanitarian endeavors—and most notably, science. She conducted biological research on ants and published her findings in scholarly scientific journals. She was fascinated by the theories of the century's most noted scientist, Charles Darwin, and found no discrepancy between science and religion.

In many respects, Fielde was an enigma regarding religious matters. A freethinker from childhood, she broke from her family's Baptist roots to become a

Universalist, only to be baptized as a Baptist prior to her anticipated marriage. She faithfully served as a Baptist missionary for two decades and then turned to science. "After breaking with the Baptist Missionary Union, and shedding the certainties of sectarian Christianity," writes Warren, "she never again joined any religious organizations. . . . Yet Fielde had not the slightest hesitation in proclaiming that Christianity was the best of all possible religions."[18] When she died in 1916, she left behind not only scientific research and writings on racial reconciliation but also Bible women who were training other Bible women and literature in Chinese that would be used for decades to follow.

At the time of her death, her Baptist mission society did not even publish her obituary in its official magazine. Ten years later, however, she was eulogized as the "mother of our Bible women and also the mother of our Bible schools."[19]

On the surface, Adele Fielde had much in common with another unmarried Baptist woman from America who arrived in China in 1873, the very same year that she did (though she had been serving in Thailand previously). In a letter to this other woman, H. A. Tupper, secretary for the Southern Baptist Foreign Mission Board, had written: "I estimate a single woman in China is worth two married men."[20] On the average that may have been true, but few could have argued—then or now—that Adele Fielde and Lottie Moon combined were "worth" more than four married men.

Charlotte (Lottie) Diggs Moon

Lottie Moon was one of the most prominent missionary activists of the nineteenth century. Her impact on missions—particularly Southern Baptist missions—was enormous. Indeed, she is sometimes referred to as the "patron saint" of Baptist missions. And that remains true today. "No one—missionary, pastor, or denominational leader," writes Alan Neely, "is as powerful a symbol in Southern Baptist circles as Lottie Moon. Her name is a mission shibboleth. Her life epitomizes foreign missions."[21]

Charlotte ("Lottie") Moon was born in 1840 into an old Virginia family of Albemarle County and grew up on Viewmont, a tobacco plantation near three famous presidential homes—Monticello, Montpelier, and Ashlawn. She was one of seven children and was deeply influenced by the staunch faith, ambitious drive, and independence of their mother, who was widowed in 1852. Her oldest brother became a respected physician, and her sister Orianna, also a physician (and reputedly the first female doctor south of the Mason-Dixon line), served as a missionary in Palestine until the outbreak of the Civil War and then returned home to serve as a medical doctor in the Confederate Army.

Like her brothers and sisters, Moon was well educated and cultured. During her college years she rebelled against her strict Baptist upbringing, but a campus revival changed her life: "I went to the service to scoff, and returned to my room to pray all night." After college she went home to help run Viewmont while other family members, both male and female, "marched out to fight for the Stars and Bars," performing "splendid service" as spies and elite guerrilla soldiers. Moon was left out of the excitement, and it was this vacuum, according to Irwin Hyatt, "that would eventually send her to China."[22]

Following the war, Moon pursued a teaching career, but she desired ministry and adventure beyond what her little school in Cartersville, Georgia, offered. Unlike so many women, she did not feel deterred by her sex. The strong women in her family who had performed as "doctors, executives, and spies," according to Hyatt, "further demonstrated what determined females could do." In 1872 Lottie's sister Edmonia sailed for China, and in 1873, she followed.[23]

Edmonia Moon's tenure in China was short. She was only in her late teens when she sailed for China and was unable to cope with the pressures of missionary life. Besides physical ailments, she suffered from seizures and, according to coworkers, did "queer and unreasonable things" and was "very burdensome" to the missionary community. Even her sister was exasperated by her "good for nothing" behavior, and finally, in 1877, after four years in China, she returned home to Virginia. Although her departure freed Moon from the drudgery of being her sister's nursemaid and allowed her to actively participate in missionary work, it also plunged her into a period of depression. To her home committee she wrote: "I especially am bored to death living alone. I don't find my own society either agreeable or edifying. . . . I really think a few more winters like the one just past would put an end to me. This is no joke, but dead earnest."[24]

Loneliness, however, was not the only factor frustrating her ministry in China. Crawford Toy, a Confederate Army chaplain who had first "come a-wooing" while she was living at Viewmont following the war, had entered her life again. Now teaching at a Southern Baptist seminary in South Carolina, he talked of marriage and suggested they work as a missionary team in Japan. It was a tempting offer but one that Lottie reluctantly refused. While the prospect of going to Japan appealed to her, there were other factors to consider. Toy, "influenced by the new ideas of the German scholars," also held to the Darwinian theory of evolution, a view that had already created controversy for him within the Southern Baptist Convention. Moon was aware of his position, and after studying the subject she concluded that evolution was an "untenable position." She broke off their relationship. Years later, when asked if she had ever had a love affair, she responded, "Yes, but God had first claim on my life, and since the two conflicted, there could be no question about the result." Toy later became a professor of Hebrew and Semitic languages at Harvard University, and Moon, in her own words, was left to "plod along in the same old way."[25]

If Moon had hoped that coming to China would allow her to have a ministry comparable to that of a man, she was mistaken. The Southern Baptists had distinct roles for women, according to Catherine Allen:

> Moon's assignment in China was "women's work." This title denoted two philosophies that shaped her ministry and her world. First was the missionary strategy known as "woman's mission to woman." Second was the staunchly defended prohibition against women seeming to teach, preach, or exercise authority over men.[26]

Moon's work in China continued to be drudgery, and the romantic ideal of missionary work had long since faded. As a cultured "Southern belle," she found it difficult to identify with the Chinese people, and as a teacher she found it almost impossible to penetrate their "dull" minds. Had she really given up her thriving school in Cartersville, Georgia, for this? She had come to China to "go out among the millions" as an evangelist, only to find herself chained to a school of forty "unstudious" children. Relegating women to such roles, she charged, was "the greatest folly of modern missions." "Can we wonder," she fumed, "at the mortal weariness and disgust, the sense of wasted powers and the conviction that her life is a failure, that comes over a woman when, instead of the ever-broadening activities she had planned, she finds herself tied down to the petty work of teaching a few girls." "What women want who come to China," she insisted, "is free opportunity to do the largest possible work. . . . What women have a right to demand is perfect equality."[27]

> *"What women want who come to China," she insisted, "is free opportunity to do the largest possible work. . . . What women have a right to demand is perfect equality."*

Such a view was a radical position for a female missionary—especially when published in missionary magazines. There was immediate reaction, particularly by those who found such signs of female liberation "repulsive." One such response came from one of her colleagues, a Mrs. Arthur Smith, wife of a Congregational missionary to China, who suggested Moon was mentally unbalanced for craving such "lawless prancing all over the mission lot." Mrs. Smith argued that the proper role of a female missionary was to attend "with a quivering lip" her own children.[28]

With no children of her own, Moon was determined to expand her ministry to fit her own concept of fulfillment. She began traveling out into the country villages, and by 1885 she concluded that her ministry would be more effective if she were to move to Pingtu and begin a new work there on her own. Besides her desire to be involved full-time in evangelistic work, she wanted to get out from under the high-handed authority of her field director, T. P. Crawford. His philosophy of missions did not allow for mission schools, so Lottie's teaching ministry was in jeopardy anyway, and his dictatorial methods of dealing with other missionaries had even alienated his own wife. Moreover, she feared that under his authority single women missionaries might be relegated to the place of Presbyterian women missionaries, who had no vote in their mission, and she threatened to resign over this very issue. "Simple justice," she insisted, "demands that women should have equal rights with men in mission meetings and in the conduct of their work." She wrote to the home board, criticizing Crawford and his new plan of operation (including the closing of schools and the "regulation of mission salaries") and concluded with the terse comment, "If that be freedom, give me slavery!"[29]

Moon's critical remarks were not those of a heady adolescent. She was forty-four years old and a twelve-year veteran of China missions, and she justifiably resented the lack of choices women were allowed. But her move to Pingtu did not solve all her problems. Pioneer evangelism was extremely difficult work. The cries of "woman devil" followed her as she walked down the narrow village streets. Only slowly and after weary persistence did she win friends among the women, and even then it was difficult to make an impact on women until she had won the confidence of the men.

Her first opportunity to reach Chinese men came in 1887, when three strangers from a nearby village appeared at her door in Pingtu. They had heard the "new doctrine" being whispered about by the women and were eager for her to tell them more. She visited their village, where she found "something I had never seen before in China. Such eagerness to learn! Such spiritual desires!" So excited was she that she canceled plans for a long-overdue furlough and summoned Martha Crawford, the wife of her field director, to come and help her. Their efforts were rewarded. She wrote home, "Surely there can be no deeper joy than that of saving souls." Despite local opposition, she established a church, and in 1889 the first baptisms were conducted by an ordained Baptist missionary. The church grew, and within two decades, under her policy of keeping "the movement as free from foreign interference as possible," Li Shou Ting, the Chinese pastor, baptized more than a thousand converts, and Pingtu had become the "greatest" Southern Baptist "evangelistic center . . . in all China."[30]

Between 1890 and her death in 1912, Moon lived two separate lives in China. Part of the year was spent in villages doing evangelistic work, and the other part was spent in Tengchow, where she trained new missionaries, counseled Chinese women, and enjoyed her Western books and magazines. She continued to write articles that paved the way for her extraordinary influence among the Southern Baptists. Although she returned home on furloughs and occasionally spoke before large audiences, it was chiefly her pen that stirred the hearts of Baptist women in the South.

Most of her writing appealed for greater support of foreign missions and for more recruits, sometimes taunting the men. "It is odd," she wrote, "that a million Baptists of the South can furnish only three men for all China. Odd that with five hundred preachers in the state of Virginia, we must rely on a Presbyterian to fill a Baptist pulpit [here]. I wonder how these things look in heaven. They certainly look very queer in China." But if the men would not come to the rescue of foreign missionary work, women would have to. The

China missionary work of the Southern Methodists had almost collapsed before it was rescued by "enlisting of the women." And if Methodist women could save their foreign missionary program, so also could Baptist women.[31]

She called for a week of prayer and a special Christmas offering to be handled solely by women and to be directed exclusively toward missions. She also appealed for "vigorous healthy women" to come to China. The first Christmas offering in 1888, according to Hyatt, "exceeded its goal by a thousand dollars, enough to pay for three new ladies instead of two." Moon responded with enthusiasm: "What I hope to see is a band of ardent, enthusiastic, and experienced Christian women occupying a line of stations extending from Pingtu on the north and from Chinkiang on the south, making a succession of stations uniting the two . . . a mighty wave of enthusiasm for Woman's Work for Woman must be stirred."[32]

In the years that followed, the Christmas offering increased and there were more single women to serve in China, but the early years of the twentieth century following the Boxer uprising were devastating times in China. Outbreaks of the plague and smallpox, followed by famine, and then a local uprising in 1911 brought mass starvation to the region. She organized a relief service and pleaded for funds from the United States, but the board, unable to meet other financial obligations, declined assistance. She contributed from her personal funds, but her efforts seemed trifling in the face of such tragedy.

With the last of her savings drawn from her small bank account, she lapsed into depression—no doubt due in part to the fact that her sister Edmonia had, while lying in bed, "put a gun to her head" and ended her life.[33] She quit eating, and her health declined. A doctor was sent for, and only then was it discovered that she was starving to death. Arrangements were made for her to return home in the company of a nurse, but it was too late. She died aboard ship while at port in Kobe, Japan, on Christmas Eve 1912, one week after her seventy-second birthday.

What she could not do in life, she accomplished in death. In the years that followed, the "Lottie Moon Christmas Offering" increased, and the Lottie Moon story was repeated over and over again. By 1925 the offerings had surpassed three hundred thousand dollars, and by the last decades of the twentieth century, more than twenty million dollars was collected annually. For Southern Baptist women, she had become a symbol of true womanhood and of what women could accomplish for missions. The highest compliment the *Foreign Missions Journal* could pay her at the time of her death was to say she was "the best man among our missionaries."[34]

Amy Carmichael

Probably the only woman missionary whose fame exceeded that of Lottie Moon in the early twentieth century was Amy Carmichael. She served in India for fifty-five years, from 1895 to her death in 1951. During that time she founded Dohnavur Fellowship and wrote some thirty-five books, a number of which were translated into more than a dozen languages. One of them, *Gold Cord,* has had sales of more than a half-million. She founded a religious order, the Sisters of the Common Life, made up primarily of Indian women, who along with Carmichael pledged themselves to celibacy and sacrificial ministry. To many people she was a living saint. Sherwood Eddy, a missionary statesman and author, was impressed by the "beauty of her character"; and character, according to Eddy, was the key to successful world evangelism. "Here is the point where many a missionary breaks down. Every normal missionary sails with high purpose but as a very imperfect Christian. . . . His character is his weakest point. . . . [But] Amy Wilson Carmichael was the most Christlike character I ever met, and . . . her life was the most fragrant, the most joyfully sacrificial, that I ever knew."[35]

Amy Carmichael was born in 1867 into a well-to-do North Ireland family whose little village of Millisle was dominated by the prosperous Carmichael flour mills. She lived a carefree life until her father died when she was eighteen and, as the oldest of seven children, heavy responsibility fell on her shoulders. Her father had left the family in severe financial straits, and soon afterward they moved to Belfast. Here Carmichael was introduced to city mission work and the "deeper life theology" of "victorious living." Then came her call to missions.

In 1892 Carmichael heard the words "Go ye" as her missionary call, and one year later, at the age of twenty-four, she was in Japan. But the Japanese language seemed impossible to her, and the missionary community was not the picture of harmony she had envisioned. To her mother she wrote, "We are here just what we are at home—not one bit better—and the devil is awfully busy. . . . There are missionary shipwrecks of once fair vessels." Her health was also a problem. To Sherwood Eddy she later confided that she had "broken down from nervous prostration during the very first year of . . . service, suffering, as some foreigners do, from what was called Japanese head." "The climate," she had written her mother, "is dreadful upon the brain."[36]

Amy Carmichael, founder of Dohnavur Fellowship in India.

After fifteen months in Japan she departed. Without even notifying the Keswick Convention, the mainstay of her support, she sailed for Ceylon.

Her explanation was simple: "I simply say that I left Japan for rest and change, that when at Shanghai I believed the Lord told me to follow Him down to Ceylon, and so I came."[37] After a short time she left Ceylon and returned home. But after less than a year in the British Isles, she was back in Asia—this time in India, where she would remain for more than fifty-five years without a furlough.

Carmichael's ministry was primarily one that reached out to children—child widows, temple prostitutes, and orphans. Her compound, Dohnavur Fellowship, became a center for humanitarian services. By 1913, twelve years after she began her ministry, she had 130 children under her care, and in the decades that followed, hundreds more found a home at Dohnavur.

Carmichael's ministry was primarily one that reached out to children—child widows, temple prostitutes, and orphans.

Dohnavur Fellowship was a unique Christian ministry. The members wore Indian dress and lived communally. To critics who accused her of focusing too much on humanitarian activities, she responded, "One cannot save and then pitchfork souls into heaven. . . . Souls are more or less securely fastened to bodies."[38]

Years before, while in Japan, she had dealt with the matter of singleness. It was a difficult struggle and one that she was unable to write about for more than forty years—and even then she only shared it privately with one of her "children," whom she was admonishing to follow the same course:

> On this day many years ago I went away alone to a cave in the mountain called Arima. I had feelings of fear about the future. That was why I went there—to be alone with God. The devil kept on whispering, "It's all right now, but what about afterwards? You are going to be very lonely."
>
> And he painted pictures of loneliness—I can see them still. And I turned to my God in a kind of desperation and said, "Lord, what can I do? How can I go on to the end?" And he said, "None of them that trust in Me shall be desolate." That word has been with me ever since. It has been fulfilled to me. It will be fulfilled to you.[39]

That others should follow her in forsaking marriage and a family was to Carmichael both a practical and spiritual commitment. The ministry needed staff who would serve as mothers and spiritual counselors to the children. That led her to form the Sisters of the Common Life for single women.

Carmichael insisted—at least outwardly—that reports of the work not be embellished. She was criticized for her book *Things as They Are* because it gave a negative perspective of missions: "It is more important that you should know about the reverses than about the successes of the war. We shall have all eternity to celebrate the victories, but we have only the few hours before sunset in which to win them. . . . So we have tried to tell you the truth—the uninteresting, unromantic truth."[40]

But as forthright as Carmichael was about the difficulties and downside of mission outreach, she was very careful to shield from public view any negative aspects of her private life or of life inside Dohnavur Fellowship. She was also concerned that Dohnavur might become contaminated with the outside world. "O to be delivered from half-hearted missionaries!" she wrote. "Don't come if you mean to turn aside for anything—for the 'claims of society.' . . . Don't come if you haven't made up your mind to live for *one thing*—the winning of souls." She insisted that those who worked with her not associate with other missionaries. Even when taking a rest at a retreat house in the hills, "you had to be insulated there from other missionary ideas and certainly from the rest of the European community."[41]

Her individualism and eccentricity are seen in her autobiographical writing. In one story, she tells about riding her horse wildly. "Oh, that you could see us as we tear along," she wrote. "We are called the mad riders of Kotagiri." While riding along a road, they came upon a group of people, including the retiring Anglican bishop, the new bishop, his wife, and "various old ladies." The people "parted with alacrity as we shot through, and we caught a fleeting glance at the gaze of astonishment and horror." There is a tone of contempt as she concludes her story: "Once I ran over a man. I did not mean to—he wouldn't get out of the way and one can't stop short in mid-gallop."[42]

Another aspect of her separation from the world was her "Victorian sensitivities"—though the Victorian era was ending as she was beginning her mission work in India. The most extreme form of modesty reigned over Dohnavur. So offended by the English word *leg* was she, writes Elisabeth Elliot, that "even the doctors found themselves inserting [the Tamil word] *kaal* into an English sentence when it was necessary to refer to that unspeakable limb." And despite the medical work conducted at Dohnavur, "a missionary who worked with her many years later insisted that Amy not only did not then know the truth about sex, but never learned."[43]

Carmichael was a hard taskmaster. When those who worked with her "raised the question of furlough or even just a weekend off," they were denied the request. Even the nature of the ministry was rigidly guarded. When an elderly Indian coworker, Saral, asked if she could teach Hindu women how to knit with some pink wool yarn she had been given, Carmichael explained that "the Gospel needed no such frills." The woman "protested that there was nothing in the Bible which bore upon pink wool and knitting needles." But Carmichael insisted there was. She quoted Zechariah 4:6 (KJV), "Not by might, nor by power, but by my spirit, saith the Lord of hosts."[44]

She had utter contempt for non-Christian religious practices. Once while walking in the hills with Saral, they came upon three stones under a tree, which

Saral identified as "heathen idols." Carmichael was incensed: "To see those stupid stones standing there to the honor of the false gods, in the midst of the true God's beauty, was too much for us. We knocked them over and down they crashed." She also took a militant stance against Hinduism when it related to evangelism. Speaking of a high-caste woman who she hoped would openly express interest in the gospel, Carmichael responded: "If so, we shall be in the very thick of the fight again—Hallelujah!" Regarding another such woman, she wrote, "Will God move in [her] heart so that she will dare her husband's fury and the knife he flashed before her eyes? If so, our bungalow will be in the very teeth of the storm, angry men all around it, and we inside, kept by the power of God."[45]

Not surprisingly, other missionaries strongly disapproved of her approach. "There arose during the early years of the Dohnavur work," writes Elliot, "a fairly strong 'Get-Amy-Carmichael-out-of-India' movement among missionaries and Indian Christians." As the years passed, she was more often ignored than opposed by other missionaries. But the criticism continued. "Someone suggested that her efforts to save temple children were nothing more than a stunt, meant to draw attention to herself. . . . She was a dictator, she opposed marriage, her Indian girls worshipped her."[46]

Carmichael believed she was divinely directed in her work and her decision making. "Our Master . . . demands obedience," she wrote, and it was her duty to obey the instructions. "Sometimes the Spirit of Jesus gave a direct command. . . . Sometimes an angel was sent, sometimes a vision. . . . In the end our God justifies His commands."[47]

Carmichael was accused by some of being a dictator—particularly some of those who came to Dohnavur to work with her, including the Neill family, who arrived in 1924—the parents, both physicians; their daughter; and their son Stephen, a recent graduate of Cambridge. Within six months after their arrival, the elder Neills had severed their ties with Dohnavur, but Stephen continued on for more than a year. Carmichael was impressed with his brilliance—particularly his quick grasp of the language, but she resented his efforts to change things God had already ordained. He introduced interscholastic athletics, bringing Dohnavur boys in contact with "the outside." This she viewed as perilous. In other ways he sought to bring Dohnavur closer to the missionary community, but she feared contamination.[48]

The stormy relationship continued until November 28, 1925, when, according to Elliot, Stephen Neill was dismissed from Dohnavur. For Carmichael it was "one of the saddest nights of my life." There had previously been an altercation that caused "a dreadful time of distress." She wrote in her diary: "Never such known before. I am beginning to sink. Lord, save me." A year after Neill left Dohnavur, she wrote to a friend: "I long over him still, miss him and want him and long to be one in affection. The scab is not even beginning to skin over. It's just red raw."[49]

From Neill's perspective, this period of time was equally distressing, as he confessed in his autobiography: "During that first year, fellow Christians had brought into my life such darkness and suffering that it took me many years to recover from the injuries, and the scars are still there."[50] Neill recalled his initial meeting with her as "an impression of power"—that not even the "smallest disagreement" was permitted. Those who came to Dohnavur found it to be a "myth." The compound was thoroughly separated from the surrounding area and "flooded with Europeans." He later confessed, "I gave my whole soul to Dohnavur," but his time spent there only brought him lifelong wounds.[51] "Some of the experiences of my first year in India," he writes, "were so excessively painful that by January 1926 the darkness was complete. A year in England helped, but this time of trouble did not really clear itself up until 1933."[52]

Neill went on to write dozens of books, most notably *A History of Christian Missions,* and he served for many years as the Anglican Bishop of Tinnevelly—the district that included Dohnavur, though by that time Carmichael had severed her ties with the Anglican Church.

Though her final twenty years (following a serious fall) were spent as an invalid, Carmichael continued to write books and to plead for the cause of her "dear children." She died at Dohnavur in 1951 at the age of eighty-three.

Johanna Veenstra

Perhaps the most striking aspect of single women in missions was the status the profession conferred to otherwise very ordinary individuals. This was also true in certain cases with men, but not to such a great extent. A man had to excel. He had to attain some kind of distinction in his missionary service to be rated a "missionary hero," but a woman could became a heroine just by having the courage to strike out on her own and go to a distant land. This was true of Johanna Veenstra, in many ways representative of the vast army of single women who went abroad after the turn of the twentieth century, who was repeatedly referred to as a "heroine" by her admiring biographer (Henry Beets, Director of Missions of the Christian Reformed Church). An obscure stenographer turned celebrity in Christian Reformed circles, she was in many ways very ordinary. Her life, however, sheds light on the sacrifice as well as the expectations placed on her and her fellow "heroines" of the faith.

Veenstra was born in Paterson, New Jersey, in 1894, two years before her father left his carpentry trade to train for ministry. But only months after completing his ministerial training and beginning his pastoral ministry, he contracted typhoid fever and died. His death brought hardship and poverty to the widow and her six small children. She returned to Paterson where she opened a general store. Johanna attended Christian schools until she was twelve and then trained to become a secretary. At the age of fourteen she became a stenographer in New York City, commuting every day from Paterson.

Johanna was active in her Christian Reformed church, but it was while attending a Baptist church that she underwent a religious experience that sparked her interest in missions. At the age of nineteen she enrolled at the Union Missionary Training Institute in New York City and then applied to the Sudan United Mission (SUM) for missionary service in Africa. Mission policy, however, required candidates to be twenty-five, so in the interim she took further schooling at Calvin College, where she became the first woman member of the Student Volunteer Board. Before sailing to Africa, she returned to New York for medical training and graduated from the midwifery course.

Veenstra's assignment under the SUM involved pioneer work at Lupwe, not far from Calabar (where Mary Slessor had served some years earlier). The station at Lupwe was new and consisted only of a few unfinished and unfurnished huts with dirt floors, but she adjusted to the very primitive conditions quickly—or at least gave that impression when writing home: "When having my evening meal, here were those creatures, in swarms, sticking fast in hand, dropping in the food—and I concluded a plague was upon us. There was no 'shutting' them out because in these native huts we have no ceiling." The rats, too, were bothersome, but she did not complain. God had called her. "There has never been a single regret that I left the 'bright lights and gay life' of New York City, and came to this dark corner of his vineyard. There has been no sacrifice, because the Lord Jesus Himself is my constant companion," she wrote.[53]

Johanna Veenstra, Christian Reformed missionary to Africa.

One of her first projects was to set up a boarding school to train young men as evangelists. It was an all-consuming project, but she found time for medical and evangelistic work. Sometimes her treks into neighboring villages lasted for several weeks at a time. There were rarely outward professions of faith. Just obtaining an attentive audience was a major sign of success. But if on "rare occasions" she witnessed "people weep as they were hearing the story of the death of our Lord" and "gasp with wonder and clap their hands in gratitude to God for His gifts," there were "very discouraging" times too:

> I took one trek through the hills, walking from place to place for nine days. . . . We planned to stay over Sunday at a certain village but it proved that we were not welcome. They did not want to provide food for the carriers and the others who were with me. So they suffered a good deal of hunger. Rain hindered the people coming to meetings. I sat at a hut door, with an umbrella to keep me dry, while the people were huddled together inside the hut about a fire. On Sunday afternoon a heavy thunderstorm arose. The rain came down in torrents. The hut where I camped was a grass-walled one, and the rain came rushing in until the whole place was flooded. . . . Early the next morning we started off for a long walk to another hill. . . . The chief was at home, but he was sick. We stopped here one night, and decided to go home. How glad we were to see our Lupwe compound.[54]

Veenstra's usual means for traveling from village to village was a bicycle, but it was slow and very tiring pedaling uphill in rough terrain, especially considering her tendency toward portliness. She secretly envied some of the male missionaries who were moving about in relative ease on their motorcycles, so after her second furlough in 1927 she returned to Africa with a new motorcycle. Her matronly appearance no doubt made for a curious sight as she began her motorized journey inland over the bumpy trails, but no one could question her pluck. Despite her initial enthusiasm and determination, she soon discovered that "dirt-biking" was not her niche. Less than forty miles out, she unexpectedly hit sand and was thrown from the bike. Badly bruised in body and spirit, she sent for help and resigned herself to go back to pedaling.

Although she willingly lived in a native hut and accepted the Africans for who they were, she entered their world with a spirit of domination. "It is necessary," she wrote, "that the missionary continually hold an attitude of superiority. Not in the sense of 'we are better than you.' God forbid! But rather in the sense of claiming and using authority. The missionary must prove himself or herself to be 'boss' (not bossy), commanding and demanding obedience."[55] This kind of paternalism (or maternalism in this case) was the norm, and she as much as any missionary was a product of her generation. But such attitudes nevertheless contributed to the bitter animosities that led to violent revolution in that part of the world only a few decades later.

But during the 1920s and 30s, while she was pouring her life into Africa, there seemed to be little evidence of resentment. Her medical work was particularly appreciated, and it was considered a privilege to attend her boarding school. It was thus a great sorrow to the people of Lupwe and neighboring villages when they received word of their missionary's untimely death in 1933. She had entered a mission hospital for what was thought to be routine surgery, but she never recovered.

Back home the news was received by her family and friends with disbelief and sorrow. But they were God-fearing Christian Reformed people who never questioned God's sovereignty in such matters. Their "heroine" had merely been promoted to a higher position and was now enjoying far greater riches than she so willingly relinquished on earth. Ironically, a letter that arrived from her after her death, though written about an African Christian who had died, was titled appropriately for Veenstra herself: "From a Mudhut to a Mansion on High."[56]

Gladys Aylward

If sex discrimination had been a factor in the past for women who had been denied missionary appointments, this was not the case with Gladys Aylward. She applied to the China Inland Mission (a mission with a longstanding reputation for its acceptance of women) in 1930 only to be turned down after a probationary term at the mission's training center. She simply was not missionary material. At twenty-eight, her age was not in her favor, but the primary reason for rejecting her was her poor academic showing—which may have been caused by a profound learning disability. Although she was bright conversationally, book learning seemed impossible for her. She studied as hard as the other students, but according to one biographer, "when it came to imbibing knowledge by normally accepted methods, Gladys's powers of mental digestion seemed automatically to go into neutral, and occasionally reverse."[57] But despite this handicap, she became one of the most noted single woman missionaries in modern history.

She was born in London in 1902 into a working-class family, and it was among that segment of society that she seemed doomed to carry out her existence. She entered the workforce at the age of fourteen and settled into a life of domestic service. She was a parlor maid, a genteel term for a house servant—a position that included heavy chores, long hours, and low pay—and a job that trapped some single women for the whole of their lives. The days were routine and dull, and the occasional nights off were cut short by an early curfew. Only in her fantasies did she break out of her drab existence. Here she moved in fast circles—drinking, smoking, dancing, gambling, and attending theaters.

This combination of fantasy and reality dominated Aylward in her twenties and perhaps would have continued on into her thirties and beyond but for a significant change in her life. Although she had attended church occasionally, it was not until she was confronted by a stranger that she made profession of faith. With her conversion, her life changed, and she began dreaming about being a missionary. This dream brought her to the CIM headquarters in 1929, and the dream did not die when she was denied candidacy after her probationary term was over. She was convinced that God was calling her, and if she could not obtain a mission's sponsorship she would go on her own.

So alone in her little bedroom, once again employed as a parlor maid, she began planning for mission work in China. She began depositing all her scant savings with the ticket agent at the railway station. (Rail passage through Europe,

Russia, and Siberia was the cheapest transportation available.) She also began reading and inquiring about China, which brought her in contact with Jeannie Lawson, an elderly widowed China missionary who was eager to have assistance. For Aylward that was a direct sign from God, and on October 15, 1932, tickets in hand, she departed from the Liverpool Street Station en route to China.

Bundled up in an orange frock worn over a coat, she was a curious looking traveler, resembling a gypsy more than a missionary. Besides her bedroll, she carried suitcases (one stocked with food) and a bag clanking with a small stove and pots and pans. Despite the language barriers, her trip through Europe was relatively uneventful. Russia, however, was in the midst of an undeclared border war with China, and after passing through Moscow the train was packed with Russian troops. At every stop the validity of her tickets and passport was questioned.

Alone with hundreds of soldiers, crossing the stark Siberian landscape, she had second thoughts about her decision, but it was too late to turn back. Finally, the monotony of the train clanging along the frozen tracks ended. Without warning, she was told that she had gone as far as she would be allowed to travel. Only soldiers were allowed to stay on the train. She refused to get off, thinking that every mile was bringing her closer to China. The train continued several miles down the track, and then it stopped again. The sound of gunfire could be heard

GLADYS AYLWARD'S TRAVELS THROUGH EUROPE AND ASIA

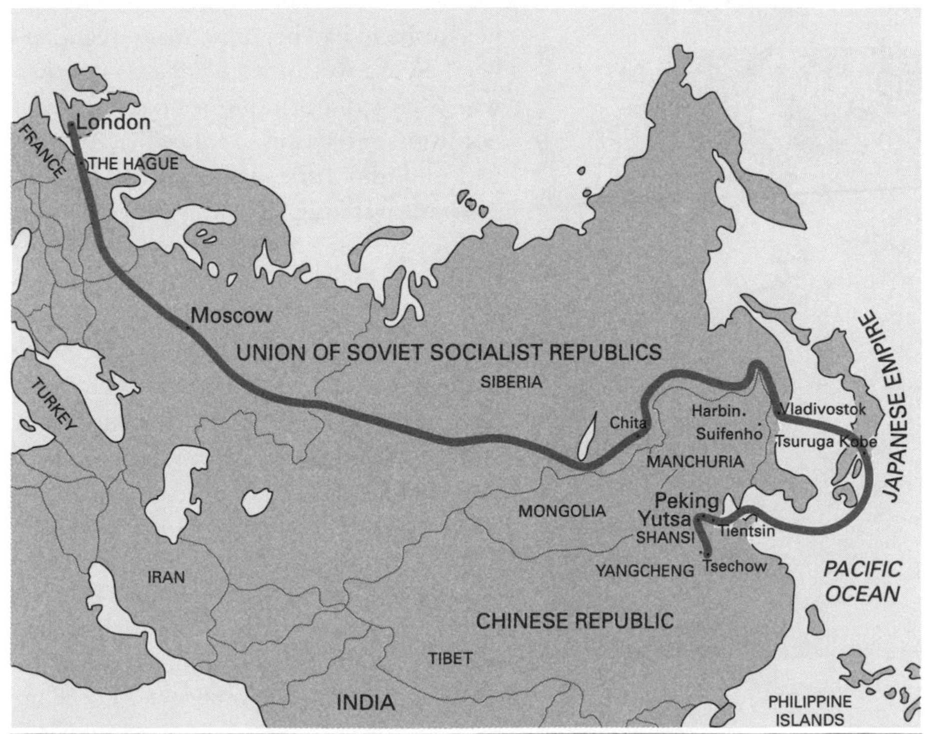

in the distance as the soldiers and supplies were unloaded. She found herself all alone in a deserted train only hundreds of yards away from the war zone. She had no choice but to trudge back on the snow-covered tracks to Chita. Her biographer, Alan Burgess, vividly recounts the ordeal:

> The Siberian wind blew the powdered snow around her heels, and she carried a suitcase in each hand, one still decorated ludicrously with kettle and saucepan. Around her shoulders she wore the fur rug. And so she trudged off into the night, a slight, lonely figure, dwarfed by the tall, somber trees, the towering mountains, and the black sky, diamond bright with stars. There were wolves near by, but this she did not know. Occasionally in the forest a handful of snow would slither to the ground with a sudden noise, or a branch would crack under the weight of snow, and she would pause and peer uncertainly in that direction. But nothing moved. There was no light, no warmth, nothing but endless loneliness.[58]

By dawn, after having taken a two-hour rest next to her little alcohol stove, she could see the lights of Chita in the distance. The worst ordeal of her journey was over. From Chita she was able to get rail passage into Manchuria, but even then she was able to get into China only by making an unscheduled trip to Japan, where she received help from the British consul.

Once in China, she began the arduous trek across the mountains to Yangcheng, where Jeannie Lawson was faithfully continuing the work she and her husband had begun so many years earlier. Lawson welcomed her, but in her own way. She was a brusque woman who was not impressed by any sacrifice that Aylward had endured. After being shown around, Aylward was assigned the work of being a missionary—operating an inn for muleteers who passed through Yangcheng on their route west. For Lawson it was an opportunity to share the gospel with the muleteers each evening, but for Aylward it was hard work—making her domestic work back in London seem like a genteel profession.

Gladys Aylward, shortly after her arrival in China.

Despite the hard work and few rewards, this was an opportunity for her to become immersed in the culture. What she never could have learned in formal language training, she was readily picking up as she dealt with the muleteers. The Chinese tongue was not just a language of complex written characters, but a language of emotion and feeling, and it was through this facet of the language that she learned to communicate. But if she was making progress in communicating with the Chinese, she was regressing in her ability to communicate with Lawson—if, in fact, they ever had truly communicated. Lawson's set ways and Aylward's independent spirit clashed, and finally, after a heated argument (less than a year after her arrival), Aylward was ordered to leave. With nowhere else to go, she moved in with some CIM missionaries in another town; but when word came some time later that Lawson was ill, she rushed back to be at her side and cared for her until she died several weeks later.

With the death of Lawson, she no longer had the financial support needed to operate the inn, but a new opportunity opened up—one that gave her a far wider influence. She was asked by the Chinese magistrate of Yangcheng to become the local foot inspector. It became her job to go from house to house, making sure the new laws against female foot-binding were being upheld. It was an exciting opportunity for her to improve her language skills, to get to know the people, and to share the gospel.

As she traveled around, her ministry blossomed. Wherever she went, people came out to see her and to listen to her Bible stories. As she visited and revisited villages, her prestige grew, and the people began to view her as an authority figure—so much so that on one occasion she was called on to use her prowess to put down a prison riot. She made friends and converts, and the future for her ministry seemed bright. But outside her little world around Yangcheng in the Shansi Province, massive plots and military maneuvers were taking place. The yet-obscure guerrilla leader Mao Zedong (Mao Tse-tung) was building his revolutionary force, and Japan was amassing thousands of troops on the Manchurian border.

Aylward made friends and converts, and the future for her ministry seemed bright. But outside her little world, massive plots and military maneuvers were taking place.

But life went on in Yangcheng as usual until the summer of 1937 when the once-peaceful mountain villages of Shansi suddenly became targets of Japanese bombing raids. Aylward, who had recently become a Chinese citizen, stayed on; and in the spring of 1938, when Yangcheng itself was bombed, she refused to leave until the last casualties were accounted for.

The war had a profound effect on her. On the one hand, it brought courage and physical endurance that she herself did not recognize. She moved behind enemy lines, bringing supplies and assistance to villagers, and served so effectively as a spy for the Chinese military that there was a price on her head. But on the other hand, the ravages of war made her realize how very alone and vulnerable she really was. To those around her she was strong, but deep down inside she longed for a husband.

Marriage was something that she had never ruled out. Even before the war she had prayed for a husband and dreamed that one day her Prince Charming might come walking into Yangcheng. He never came—at least the one of her fantasies. But the war did bring another man into her life. His name was Linnen, a Chinese military officer—the man who convinced her to become a spy against the Japanese. At first it was mutual patriotism that brought them together, but as time passed a romantic relationship developed, and as the suffering and hardships of war increased, her desire for marriage and security grew more intense. She wrote home to her family in England that she was planning to marry him. But the marriage never took place. In the devastated, war-torn countryside nothing short of death seemed certain, and plans were made to be broken.

There were others who needed her love and attention more than Linnen. She had children to care for. Ninepence was her first child—a tiny abandoned girl she had purchased for that amount. As the years passed she "adopted" more, and in addition to her own, there were dozens of war orphans that depended on her for sustenance. This overwhelming responsibility loomed above all else, impelling her to leave Shansi with her brood of nearly one hundred children in the spring of 1940 and to cross the mountains and the Yellow River (the Huang) into safety beyond the border.

The journey was a harrowing one. Enemy troops were never far away, and moving unnoticed with nearly one hundred noisy children was a constant emotional strain. When at last they reached their destination, she collapsed from mental and physical exhaustion, and the children were scattered in refugee housing. After months of care by a missionary couple, Aylward slowly regained her strength, but mentally she remained impaired—suffering hallucinations and wandering around the village unable to find her way home. But as the months passed, the period of mental confusion decreased, and she was able once again to reestablish contact with her scattered children and minister to others.

By 1943, with the Japanese retreating, she was back again in China, living with CIM missionaries. But she was restless and moved on, finally settling in Chengtu, where she eventually became employed by a local church as a Bible woman—a role heretofore reserved for native Chinese women. Yet that lowly position was one she accepted with honor, serving the church in evangelism and charity work.

In 1949, after nearly twenty years in China, she was persuaded to make a visit home, and during that furlough the "small woman" of China won her way into the hearts of the British people. Ill at ease in Western culture, she would have preferred to remain in the background, but her mother, serving as her daughter's agent, had different ideas for her. For many years her mother had eagerly accepted speaking invitations to deliver her one and only address, "Our Gladys in China." And now that her daughter had returned home, she proudly introduced her to her audiences.

In the years that followed, through a popular biography (*The Small Woman* by Alan Burgess), a film (*The Inn of the Sixth Happiness,* starring Ingrid Bergman), and a *This is Your Life* feature on BBC, Aylward became an international celebrity. Though she returned to minister and make her home in Taiwan in 1957, she continued her world travel and was never out of the limelight, speaking in such places as the Hollywood First Presbyterian Church and dining with such dignitaries as Queen Elizabeth.

Yet through all the service she had rendered and the fame she had acquired, she was never fully secure in her calling—particularly that God really wanted to entrust a woman with the responsibilities he had given her. In an interview during her later years, she confided her doubts to a friend: "I wasn't God's first choice for what I've done for China. There was somebody else. . . . I don't know who it was—God's first choice. It must have been a man—a wonderful man. A well-educated man. I don't know what happened. Perhaps he died. Perhaps he wasn't willing. . . . And God looked down . . . and saw Gladys Aylward."[59]

SELECT BIBLIOGRAPHY

Allen, Catherine. *The New Lottie Moon Story*. Nashville: Broadman, 1980.

Beaver, R. Pierce. *American Protestant Women in World Mission*. Grand Rapids: Eerdmans, 1969.

Beets, Henry. *Johanna of Nigeria: Life and Labors of Johanna Veenstra*. Grand Rapids: Grand Rapids Printing Company, 1937.

Burgess, Alan. *The Small Woman*. New York: Dutton, 1957.

Elliot, Elisabeth. *A Chance to Die: The Life and Legacy of Amy Carmichael*. Old Tappan, NJ: Fleming H. Revell, 1987.

Houghton, Frank. *Amy Carmichael of Dohnavur*. London: Society for the Propagation of Christian Knowledge, 1954.

Hyatt, Irwin. "Charlotte Diggs Moon." In *Our Ordered Lives Confess: Three Nineteenth-Century American Missionaries in East Shantung*. Cambridge, MA: Harvard University Press, 1976.

Robert, Dana. *American Women in Mission: A Social History of Their Thought and Practice*. Macon, GA: Mercer University Press, 1996.

Stevens, Helen N. *Memorial Biography of Adele M. Fielde: Humanitarian*. New York: Fielde Memorial Committee, 1918.

Thompson, Phyllis, *A Transparent Woman: The Compelling Story of Gladys Aylward*. Grand Rapids: Zondervan, 1971.

Tucker, Ruth A. *Guardians of the Great Commission: The Story of Women in Modern Missions*. Grand Rapids: Zondervan, 1988.

Veenstra, Johanna. *Pioneering for Christ in the Sudan*. Grand Rapids: Smitter Book, 1926.

Warren, Leonard. *Adele Marion Fielde: Feminist, Social Activist, Scientist*. New York: Routledge, 2002.

12

Student Volunteers: Forsaking Wealth and Prestige

Unlike the single women who typically raised their status in life by entering overseas missions, the student volunteers were primarily young men who in the eyes of the world lowered their status; and unlike the women, they generally entered the mission married or married soon after they arrived. In the minds of many people it was commendable that the Gladys Aylwards and the Johanna Veenstras went to the distant shores to evangelize the "heathen," for all they would have amounted to was to be parlor maids or stenographers anyway; but to send brilliant young university graduates to "waste" their lives among the pagans was a crying shame.

The Student Volunteer Movement (SVM) was born in Mount Hermon, Massachusetts, in 1886, though the impetus for its development occurred even earlier when seven Cambridge University students turned their backs on their career ambitions and committed their lives to foreign missions. The movement prospered for some fifty years, during which time, according to J. Herbert Kane, "it had been instrumental in sending 20,500 students to the foreign mission field, most of them from North America."[1] During the early twentieth century it is estimated that student volunteers constituted half of the total Protestant overseas missionary force. Most of them worked among the people of the older developed civilizations of Asia—particularly China, where approximately a third of them served. The next largest concentration was in India. Mission leaders passionately pleaded for "men and women of literary tastes" to go to China, and the call was answered.

By 1920, at the Des Moines Convention, the movement had passed its peak, and from then on it declined. "It was inevitable," writes Harold R. Cook, "that the same liberal trend affecting the major denominations should touch the Student Volunteer Movement. By the late 1920s it was already losing ground. Then came the Great Depression and the critical 'Laymen's Report' on foreign missions with disastrous effects on the whole missionary enterprise."[2]

Despite their failures, the student volunteers were among the most dedicated missionaries ever to enter missionary service. In an era when some (or "most," in the evaluation of Hudson Taylor) missionaries had become "self-indulgent and idle," the student volunteers were a striking contrast. They were driven by an intensity of purpose that has rarely been equaled, and they were committed to evangelizing the world by whatever means was necessary.

Student volunteers were driven by an intensity of purpose that has rarely been equaled, and were committed to evangelizing the world by whatever means was necessary.

Such intensity, combined with their liberal university training, often lead the student volunteers to be far more accommodating to other religions and religious practices in order to show respect and bring greater numbers under the umbrella of Christianity. They were different from their missionary forebears, whose chief education had been centered in the Bible. Many of the student volunteers had also spent their formal education grappling with Kant's *Critique of Pure Reason* and Darwin's *Origin of Species* and had not been ordained to the ministry.

Because of the regularly scheduled Quadrennial Conventions sponsored by the Student Volunteer Movement, there was an interdenominational bond among the student volunteers that had never before occurred in a broad-based missionary movement. The outcome of this association was a beneficial cooperative effort among missionaries that had rarely been seen before, and it also paved the way for the ecumenical movement. This concern for unity, along with a modern critical approach to Scripture, had long-term effects on world evangelism. "Protestant liberalism, de-emphasizing and demythologizing miracles and biblical authority, introduced the powerful but crippling secularism into Chinese Christianity." According to Kenneth S. Latourette, this "secularizing movement" was the most important factor influencing Christianity's losses in China in the face of communism.[3]

For many student volunteers, the whole world rather than one country was their mission field. While many did settle in one location and dedicate their lives to one small area, others traveled throughout the world in an effort to reach the elite—the educated classes who could wield the most influence on their fellow citizens. With them the student volunteers brought the YMCA and other organizations that provided a network for Christian students throughout the world.

During the first half of the twentieth century, the student volunteers made an indelible impact on foreign missions. Their names—C. T. Studd, J. E. K. Studd, Robert Wilder, John R. Mott, Joseph H. Oldham, Robert E. Speer, W. Temple Gairdner, William Paton, Fletcher Brockman, E. Stanley Jones, and others—will forever be remembered in the annals of missionary literature as ones who willingly forsook professional careers, wealth, and comfort to serve in a cause to which they were wholeheartedly committed.

Sherwood Eddy spoke for many student volunteers when he wrote of his own experience and of the movement as a whole:

> In retrospect, I find I have spent half a century along the far-flung battle line of missions. I was one of the first of sixteen thousand student volunteers who were swept into what seemed to us nothing less than a missionary crusade. We were considered fanatical by some, and we made numerous mistakes which we ourselves came to realize later in bitter experience. Many sacrificed early plans and ambitions for wealth, power, prestige or pleasure, to go to some distant country about which they knew little save its abysmal need. Not wholly unlike the unity of Christendom achieved during the Middle Ages was the feeling of these student volunteer missionaries that they were one team, working for one world, under one Captain. We felt much as Wordsworth did about the French Revolution—which he doubtless idealized as we did our crusade:
>
> Bliss was it in that dawn to be alive,
> But to be young was very Heaven![4]

C. T. Studd

One of the most famous of the student volunteers was C.T. Studd, an illustrious college athlete and son of a wealthy Englishman. Charlie Studd strikingly exemplifies the willingness of the student volunteers to sacrifice wealth and prestige and to boldly confront the task of world evangelism with intense dedication. He possessed almost fanatic zeal—particularly in later life—zeal that caused him to disregard his own well-being and the well-being of his family in his self-imposed effort to further the kingdom of God. This unrelenting discipline, combined with personality flaws, made him one of the most controversial missionary figures the evangelical church has known in modern history. His management style as the founder and director of the Worldwide Evangelization Crusade illustrates the critical importance of leadership in cross-cultural mission endeavors.

Wealth and luxury surrounded the young C.T. Studd as he grew up in the 1870s on Tedworth, the family estate in Wiltshire. Edward Studd, his father, had made a fortune as a planter in India and then returned to England to live a life of leisure. Horse racing was his passion, and it was a day of celebration when his own horse won the Grand National. With such a reputation, it came as a surprise to many when word spread that Edward Studd had been converted at one of D. L. Moody's evangelistic campaigns. The effect was immediate. He sold his horses and gave up racing, began holding gospel meetings at Tedworth, and invested his energy in seeking to convert his friends and relatives. His three sons were special targets of his persistent witness, and according to C.T., "Everyone in the house had a dog's life of it until they were converted."[5]

All three sons were converted before their father's untimely death two years later, but it was not until some six years later, following a near-fatal illness of his younger brother, that C. T. went to a Moody campaign on his own and there committed his life to missionary service. His decision created a sensation. He was the captain and best all-around player of the famed Cambridge Eleven, considered by many to be "England's greatest cricketer." Added to the sensation of his decision was word that six other brilliant and talented Cambridge students had made the same commitment. The "Cambridge Seven," as they were dubbed, were determined to sail to China together to serve with the China Inland Mission. "Never before in the history of missions," wrote a newspaper reporter, "has so unique a band set out to labor in the foreign field."[6] To many people, including members of Studd's own family, the decision of the seven university students was a rash move and a tremendous waste of intellect and ability.

The "Cambridge Seven" after they arrived in China (with C. T. Studd standing on the left).

Studd's tenure in China lasted less than a decade, but it was filled with activity. Soon after he arrived, he met and married Priscilla Steward, who was serving in China with the Salvation Army. Four daughters were born to them on Chinese soil, but their time in North China was filled with difficulties. "For five years," lamented Studd, "we never went outside our doors without a volley of curses from our neighbors."[7] But as they established themselves their ministry expanded—Priscilla in her evangelistic work with women, and C.T. in his work with opium addicts. Although he had received a substantial inheritance (equivalent to more than a half-million dollars by today's standards) from his father's estate, he gave it away in order live entirely by faith as other CIM missionaries did, many times facing severe financial hardship.

Ill health forced the Studds to return to England in 1894, and the next six years were spent speaking in behalf of the Student Volunteer Movement in the United States and England. According to Kane, "students by the thousands flocked to his meetings, sometimes six a day, . . . and hundreds, caught up in the revival movement, volunteered for missionary service."[8] In 1900 Studd moved with his family to India for six years to minister to planters and English-speaking people there, but again plagued by ill health, he returned to England and continued his itinerant speaking ministry.

A sign on a door inscribed with the words "Cannibals Want Missionaries" changed the course of Studd's life. On further inquiry, he heard of hundreds of thousands of tribal people in Central Africa who had never heard the gospel because "no Christian had ever gone to tell of Jesus." The shame sank deep into his soul: "I said, 'Why have no Christians gone?' God replied, 'Why don't you go?' 'The doctors won't permit it,' I said. The answer came, 'Am I not the good physician? Can I not take you through? Can I not keep you there?' There were no excuses, it had to be done."[9]

C. T. Studd, missionary to China, India, and Africa.

His decision to go to Africa was devastating to Priscilla, who was suffering from a debilitating heart condition. How could he just leave her and pursue such a wild scheme? He was fifty years old, sickly, and without financial backing. She strongly objected, but convinced of his calling, he left for an exploratory trip in 1910, returning the following year to make plans for his new mission to Africa, HAM—the Heart of Africa Mission. In 1913, with one assistant, Alfred Buxton, who would later become his son-in-law, Studd began his eighteen-year venture to the Belgian Congo in "the heart of Africa." Though he received word on his journey that Priscilla had suffered further heart complications, he refused to turn back. The work of the Lord, he firmly believed, came before family concerns. When he returned home in 1916 (his only furlough) to secure new recruits for Africa, he found Priscilla no longer an invalid and more active than she had been in years, effectively carrying out the work of the home office.

In the years that followed, more recruits arrived in Africa, including his daughter Edith, who married Alfred Buxton, and his daughter Pauline, who arrived with her husband, Norman Grubb. But as more missionaries came, doctrinal and personal differences surfaced that continually plagued the infant mission. Even his daughters and sons-in-law found him to be a most difficult individual to work with. He had sacrificed everything for Africa, and he expected his missionaries to do the same. He worked eighteen-hour days, and, according to Norman Grubb, "There was no let-up . . . no diversions, no days off, no recreation." The missionaries were expected to live African style, avoiding any appearance whatever of affluent European lifestyles.[10]

Doctrinal controversies also arose between Studd and many of the missionaries—particularly between him and new recruits arriving in Africa. Studd had written home about the incredible breakthroughs he was making. In fact, in 1918, after only five years on the field, he wrote: "The progress is simply wonderful; people are coming to us from every quarter and from very long distances. We are having pretty nearly weekly baptisms. The converts are evangelizing far and near." But when the missionaries arrived, according to Grubb, they found a very different situation:

> But what shocked us most was his attitude toward professing African Christians, five hundred of whom would gather on a Sunday morning. Where we had been told to expect a concourse of shining saints, C. T. was saying that sin was rampant, and nobody who continued in sin entered heaven, no matter how much he was supposed to have been born again; and that he doubted, holding up the fingers of his two hands, whether ten of these five hundred would really get there. We thought this awful. Our theology was . . . that once a person was born again . . . he could not be unborn. C. T. took no count of that. His stand was "without holiness no man shall see the Lord."[11]

Living in sin, to C.T., did not just mean gross immorality. It included a wide range of "sins," including ones related to a man's work ethic. "One of the worst sins of these people," wrote Studd, "is a terrible laziness. To sit about on a chair and talk is the desire of everybody. To work is folly." For Studd, the regular work day began at 6:00 A.M., and he expected Africans and missionaries alike to follow suit. Personal devotions were to be over with by then, so that the day's activities could begin. When Grubb suggested on one occasion that the Africans and missionaries hold special prayer meetings for revival, C.T. responded, "I don't believe in praying in work hours. Let's have a meeting at 4 A.M." When Grubb rose at 4 A.M. for his own devotional time, he could hear from across the compound "the old man's banjo going. He had gathered a 4 A.M. prayer meeting of some of the Africans."[12]

Priscilla Stewart Studd, wife of C. T. Studd.

Living such a rigorous Christian life was too much for many of the Africans and missionaries as well, but Studd had no time for anyone who, in his mind, was less than totally committed, even if it meant dismissing his own daughter and son-in-law, Edith and Alfred Buxton. It was a demoralizing time for them, especially for Alfred, who had sacrificed so much to begin the work in Africa with Studd. Other close relationships of past years were also deteriorating, and by the late 1920s, despite his hard work and dedication, Studd was rapidly losing the support of the home committee—particularly after Priscilla's death in 1929. His rigorous demands on missionaries and his negative view of African Christians were well known to the home committee, but now other issues were creating controversy—one surrounding a booklet he had written, entitled "D.C.D." In response to the lethargy he had found among Christians, he wrote, "I want to be one of those who doesn't care a damn except to give my life for Jesus and souls." D.C.D. stood for "Don't Care a Damn," which offended many of his staunchest supporters.[13]

If the pamphlet was not enough to prompt committee action against him, reports that he had become a morphine addict were. His ill health and eighteen-hour days were taking a toll on him physically and emotionally, and after discovering the relief that a shot of morphine gave him, he began taking tablets dispensed by a medical doctor from Uganda and brought in by missionaries "without declaration because of difficulties which might have been raised." "With this news reaching home . . . the Committee," according to Grubb, "decided that the only thing to do was to remove him from the mission." What followed, in the words of Grubb, "was the darkest chapter in the mission's history."[14] With the home committee prepared to reorganize and start a new mission without Studd, Grubb (who, with Studd, had also been dismissed from the mission) and David Munro, also Studd's son-in-law, took the "drastic action" of going into the mission headquarters early one morning and removing the records to their own safekeeping.

But even with the records in hand, the mission was in shambles, and there seemed to be little hope of recouping the losses. Was there anything that could give the fledgling WEC (the Heart of Africa Mission was now the Worldwide Evangelization Crusade) a fresh start? There was. Within weeks came the news of Studd's death. A tumultuous era was over, and with the leadership of Norman Grubb the mission got a fresh start—though never to forget the tireless dedication of the mission's founder, C. T. Studd.

What went wrong? How could one of Britain's most prestigious young missionaries come to such an end? Certainly the intensity of his dedication contributed to his downfall—an intensity that was characteristic of the student volunteers. "We do need to be intense," wrote Studd, "and our intensity must ever increase."[15] But it was that intensity, viewed by many as "fanaticism" or "extremism," that brought him down. C. T. often referred to himself as a "Gambler for God." But it could be said that he gambled and lost.

Following C.T. Studd's death in 1931, Norman Grubb became the director of the Worldwide Evangelization Crusade. Four years later he went through his dark night of the soul.

I HAD begun to have a thirst for enlarged understanding and deeper reading, the kind of student mentality I should have had fifteen years before. I could only be a dabbler in my busy life, but one book I picked up was William James' *Varieties of Religious Experience.* It hit me like a boxer's knock-out blow. That itself is an evidence of my immaturity in thinking things through; for as I read the psychological explanation of Paul's conversion on the road at Damascus, it suddenly struck me that perhaps this was only some inner change in Paul's psychological make-up, and that there is no reason to postulate a divine revelation; and that perhaps there really is no God—just the human race. I don't think James himself meant this if I had gone on to finish the book; but here was I, a missionary of fifteen years' standing, and a secretary of a missionary society, and I was questioning the existence of God. . . . Life blanked out on me. . . . I did try once to speak at a meeting for which I was booked, and it was simply hell—to speak of one whose existence I was doubting. . . . By the end of a year the mist had cleared. I can't exactly say how except that it was while I was reading John of the Cross's *Assent of Mount Carmel,* and the result has been worth all the agony of that year."

(Norman Grubb, *Once Caught, No Escape: My Life Story*)

In the years after Studd's death, the World Evangelization Crusade grew steadily, and by the 1970s it was reaching all over the globe with more than five hundred missionaries—among them the noted doctor Helen Roseveare, who began her service in Ibambi where Studd himself served. In analyzing the phenomenal comeback of the WEC, it would be difficult to overestimate the leadership of Norman Grubb, a man possessed of a rare honesty in admitting his own shortcomings and who, though a relentless defender of his father-in-law, was wise enough to recognize his flaws and to learn from them.

John R. Mott

While C.T. Studd and his fellow classmates of the "Cambridge Seven" captured world attention as student missionary volunteers, John R. Mott, perhaps more than any other individual, influenced the surge of students into overseas missions in the decades that followed. Though a layman and never an actual missionary in the strictest sense of the word, his influence was enormous. His role model was David Livingstone, "whose heroic, Christlike achievements," in the words of Mott, "furnished the governing missionary motive of my life."[16] Like so many of the student volunteers, Mott passed over opportunities of wealth and prestige in his commitment to world evangelism. He declined diplomatic posts and opportunities for financial gain, but he could not elude fame. He was a friend and counselor of presidents, a winner of the Nobel Peace Prize, and one of the most influential world religious leaders of the twentieth century.

Mott was born and raised in Iowa, the son of a prosperous lumber merchant. He was converted as a youth and became active in the local Methodist church. In 1881, at the age of sixteen, he left home to attend Upper Iowa University, where he became a charter member of the YMCA, an international organization then committed to Christian evangelism. He then transferred to Cornell, where he studied political science and history. There, under the preaching of J. E. K. Studd, he underwent a life-changing experience, committing himself to evangelism. J. E. K. Studd, the brother of C. T., had come to the United States to tour university campuses at the invitation of D. L. Moody and YMCA leaders. According to Mott's biographer, it was hoped that Studd "would attract students to hear his missionary message and description of the 'Cambridge Seven' who had rejected status and wealth to volunteer for foreign missions."[17]

Although Studd emphasized missions, Mott did not personally commit himself to the cause until the following summer, when he attended the first Christian Student Conference at Mount Hermon, Massachusetts (sponsored by D. L. Moody and later held at the nearby Northfield conference grounds). As a delegate from Cornell, along with some two hundred and fifty other students from nearly one hundred colleges and universities, he spent a month under the tutelage of Moody and other Bible teachers. On the last day of the conference, Robert Wilder, a missions enthusiast from Princeton, presented a missionary challenge that turned into an aggressive appeal for personal commitment. As a result, one hundred students, later dubbed the "Mount Hermon Hundred," signed the "Princeton Pledge" ("I purpose, God willing, to become a foreign missionary") that would soon become the initiation oath into the Student Volunteer Movement. Mott was among the one hundred who signed, and that meeting was the beginning of the Student Volunteer Movement for Foreign Missions (officially organized in 1888), an organization that he would lead for more than thirty years.

Following this meeting, Wilder, at the encouragement of Moody and others, began a tour of college campuses to make his challenge nationwide. With his emotional appeal, his urgent slogan ("The Evangelization of the World in This Generation"), and his "Princeton Pledge," he provided the impetus for the movement. Wilder had grown up in India with his missionary parents. His concern to motivate students was inspired in part by his father, who had been a member of the "Society of the Brethren" at Andover, a missions-oriented club that had originated in 1806 with Samuel Mills and the Haystack Group (an informal mission fraternity formed while waiting out a thunderstorm). Following his tour, Wilder returned to India to work with students, while Mott and others took over the leadership on the home front.

As a leader and organizer of the SVM, Mott confronted an enormous task, especially if the movement's slogan was to be taken seriously. He was determined to mobilize thousands of students to carry the gospel to the ends of the earth. He was convinced that the SVM was uniquely suited to carry out this task because the movement encompassed young adults from a wide spectrum of religious backgrounds.

Closely associated with Mott's activities with the SVM were his activities with the YMCA, an organization he served for more than forty years, sixteen of them as general secretary. In these capacities travel became a way of life, and as soon as one world tour was over, he was already planning for another. As he traveled, he worked with resident missionaries as well as international students and sought to develop a worldwide network of unified missionary activity. In realizing this goal, he helped to organize the World Student Christian Federation, a loose international organization of Christian students that under his leadership grew to include societies in some three thousand schools.

One of the most receptive areas for Mott's appeal to students was China, among the literati, "the scholars of that great land of scholars." During his first tour of that country in 1896, the prospects for reaching that class seemed dim, but according to Mott, the atmosphere soon changed:

> Five years later the walls of Jericho were beginning to crumble.... The ancient literati were beginning to give way to the modern literati.... When I reached Canton, I found to my surprise that they had hired the largest theater in China, a building that holds thirty-five hundred people. On the night of the first meeting as we neared the theater, I saw crowds in the streets and asked, "Why do they not open the doors?" Someone came to tell us that the doors had been opened for an hour and that every seat was taken.... On the platform were about fifty of the leading educated Chinese of Canton, many of them young men who had studied in Tokyo and in American universities.[18]

By the time the series of meetings was over, more than eight hundred had become "inquirers," and within a month nearly one hundred and fifty of those "had been baptized or were preparing for baptism." In two other Chinese cities where Mott conducted meetings, he received a similar response.[19]

The highlight of Mott's career as a missionary statesman was the Edinburgh Missionary Conference of 1910, which he organized and chaired. This ten-day conference, composed of 1,355 delegates, was the first interdenominational

THE TWENTIETH CENTURY

1900 1910 1920 1930

BLACK AFRICA

- (1910) C. T. Studd arrives in Africa
- (1915) Death of Mary Slessor
- (1913) Schweitzer arrives in Africa
- (1928) Carl Becker sails for the Congo
- (1931) Death of C. T. Studd

THE FAR EAST AND PACIFIC ISLANDS

- (1905) Martyrdom of Eleanor Chestnut
- (1907) Goforth begins revival ministry in Korea and Manchuria
- (1930) Gladys Aylward
- (1932) Martyrdom
- (1934) Martyrdom of the Stams

LATIN AMERICA

- (1917) W. C. Townsend arrives in Guatemala
- (1929) Townsend completed Cakchiquel NT
- (1931) HCJB begins broadcast from Quitc
- (1936)

THE NEAR EAST, NORTH AFRICA, AND CENTRAL ASIA

- (1900) Ida Scudder begins medical work in India
- (1901) Maude Cary sails to Morocco
- (1907) E. Stanley Jones arrives in India
- (1912) Zwemer begins work in Cairo
- (1918) Ida Scudder founds Vellore Medical College
- (1928) Jerusalem World
- (1933) Death
- (1938)

EUROPE AND NORTH AMERICA

- (1908) Grenfell rescued from drifting ice
- (1910) Edinburgh Missionary Conference
- (1920) SVM Des Moines Convention
- (1932) *Rethinking*
- (1934)
- (1939)

1940 1950 1960 1970 1980

- (1953) Helen Roseveare arrives in the Congo
- (1960) Congo independence
- (1964) Simba rebellion
- (1964) Death of Paul Carlson
- (1964) Attack on Kilometer Eight
- (1977) Festo Kivengere escapes Uganda

- (1948) FEBC begins broadcasting in Manilla
- (1954) Myron Bromley enters Balim Valley

goes to China
- (1958) Cho begins tent ministry in Korea

of eleven TEAM missionaries
- (1962) Don Richardson arrives in Irian Jaya
- (1962) Capture of Mitchell, Gerber, and Vietti
- (1940) Gladys Aylward leads children to safety
- (1968) Death of Betty Olsen
- (1945) Death of R. A. Jaffray in Japanese prison camp
- (1945) Death of Eric Liddell

- (1948) Nate Saint arrives in Ecuador
- (1956) Auca massacre
- (1956) Marianna Slocum completes Tzeltal NT
- (1957) Rachel Saint and Dayuma tour U.S.
- (1941) Walter Herron begins aviation ministry
- (1943) Martyrdom of five New Tribes missionaries in Bolivia

Ken Pike begins work in Mexico
- (1964) TWR broadcasts from Bonaire
- (1981) Martyrdom of Chet Bitterman

- (1951) Death of Amy Carmichael
- (1962) Viggo Olsen arrives in East Pakistan
- (1967) Morocco closed to missionaries
- (1972) JAARS crash in New Guinca
- (1973) Death of E. Stanley Jones

Missionary Conference
of Johanna Veenstra
Madras World Missionary Conference

- (1942) Founding of New Tribes Mission
- (1945) Founding of MAF
- (1946) First triennial "Urbana" Missionary Convention held by IVCF in Toronto

Missions published
- (1950) Founding of World Vision

Founding of Summer Institute of Linguistics
Joy Ridderhof founds Gospel Recordings

- (1954) Founding of Trans World Radio
- (1955) Death of Mott
- (1974) Lausanne Conference on World Evangelization
- (1976) Founding of the U.S. Center for World Mission

missionary conference of its kind and became the impetus for the ecumenical movement that took shape in the decades that followed. The conference was a high point of missionary enthusiasm; and the call to evangelize the world "in this generation" was still in the air. With some forty-five thousand missionaries on the field and the prediction that the number might be tripled in the next thirty years, delegates were optimistic about the prospects for world evangelization.

But in the years following Edinburgh, interest in missions waned in most mainline denominations. The 1920 annual meeting of the SVM in Des Moines was tension-filled. Here, according to C. Howard Hopkins, it began the process of "correcting that fateful fascination with ... the Orient that had hypnotized their forebears and sent them off to China" far away from "the slums of Chicago or the injustices of sweated labor." The focus for the future would be "the visible pressing social maladjustments at hand rather than 'traditional questions of missionary work.'"[20]

Mott had all along stressed the social dimensions of world evangelism, but never to the extent of making it a primary focus. Yet he was forced to come to terms with the "social gospel shift" that was emerging in missions. Social service, he insisted, is "one of the most distinctive calls of our generation," and one intrinsically tied to personal evangelism: "There are not two gospels, one social and one individual. There is but one Christ who lived, died, and rose again, and relates himself to the lives of men. He is the Savior of the individual and the one sufficient Power to transform his environment and relationships."[21]

Social service, Mott insisted, is "one of the most distinctive calls of our generation," and one intrinsically tied to personal evangelism.

It was Mott's more traditional stance that led to his declining influence during the last years of the SVM. The younger generation was more concerned with social problems on the home front. There were others who criticized Mott as well. His name was associated with the Laymen's Foreign Missions Inquiry and its report, *Rethinking Missions,* and for that reason he was viewed by some as having become too open and progressive in his mission outlook. That report sought to redefine the aim of missions: "To see the best in other religions, to help the adherents of those religions to discover, or to rediscover, all the best in their own traditions, to cooperate with the most active and vigorous elements in the other traditions in social reform and in the purification of religious expression. The aim should not be conversion."[22] Although Mott acknowledged the value of the inquiry and subsequent report, it clearly did not reflect his own position. Throughout his life he viewed conversion of non-Christians to be the most important aim of missions.

The last years of Mott's life were filled with activities at home and abroad. He took part in the formation of the World Council of Churches, an organization he believed could strengthen the influence of Christianity in the world.

Though he sought to remain above the bitter fundamentalist-modernist debate, he, along with Robert Speer, became a target for criticism among fundamentalists.

John R. Mott at the Whitby World Conference meeting in 1947.

Throughout his life, despite all his travels, Mott remained a strong family man. Leila, his wife of sixty-two years, traveled and worked with him, often speaking to groups of college women and ministering to women missionaries all over the world. Her death in 1952, at the age of eighty-six, came as a heavy blow to Mott, but he continued his travel in behalf of world evangelism without her. In 1953, at the age of eighty-eight, he remarried, and in 1954 he made his final public appearance at the World Council of Churches assembly in Evanston, Illinois. But his traveling days were not over. "Death," he told a reporter, "is a place where I change trains." He made that transfer on January 31, 1955.

Robert E. Speer

A close associate and lifelong friend of Mott and a man described as "the incarnation of the spirit of the Student Volunteer Movement" was Robert E. Speer, who, like Mott, served the foreign missionary cause as a layman. Unlike Mott, his ministry was dedicated largely to a single denomination—the Presbyterian Church—serving for forty-six years as the Secretary of the Board of Foreign Missions. The Presbyterian Church was one of the most fervent of the mainline denominations in its missionary zeal, and Speer's own enthusiasm for foreign missions only enhanced the church's stand. Though Speer was a highly respected and popular figure within his own denomination and in ecumenical circles, his ministry spanned a stormy period of his denomination's history; and despite his efforts to play the role of peacemaker, he was often the brunt of criticism. Nevertheless, during his tenure the denomination greatly expanded its role in overseas evangelism.

Born in Pennsylvania in 1867, Speer was the son of an attorney and two-term Democratic congressman who brought up his children in a strict Puritan-Presbyterian atmosphere. Educated at Andover and Princeton, he twice held the office of class president and gained a reputation as a hard-hitting defensive tackle on the varsity football team. During his second year at Princeton, Speer, under the persuasive preaching of Robert Wilder, became a "pledge-signing" student volunteer, along with several of his classmates. He left behind his ambition to follow his father into the legal profession and began setting his sights on overseas missions. "There are many who regard us as possessed of a strange delusion," he confessed, "many who count us carried away by some fanatical madness."[23]

After graduation from Princeton, Speer became the traveling secretary for the Student Volunteer Movement; and though he served for only one year in that capacity, he signed up more than a thousand volunteers for foreign missions. With the intention of serving abroad himself, he returned to Princeton for seminary training. But after less than two years his studies were interrupted when he unexpectedly received a call from the Presbyterian Board of Foreign Missions to fill its highest administrative post. The call, according to Sherwood Eddy, "upset Speer's equilibrium, and he fought hard against it. He certainly did not want to stay at home when he had asked a thousand volunteers who had signed the declaration to undergo the hardships of the foreign field."[24] But he reluctantly accepted the offer, challenged by the potential influence he could exert for missions through such a key position.

Though an activist, he is best remembered for his philosophical influence on missions. During a time when many voices from the younger generation were calling for social activism in missions, he insisted that the "Supreme and Determining Aim" of missions be religious:

> We cannot state too strongly in an age when the ... body has crept up on the throne of the soul, that our work is not ... a philanthropic work, a political work, a secular work of any sort whatsoever; it is a spiritual and a religious work.... Religion is spiritual life. I had rather plant one seed of the life of Christ under the crust of heathen life than cover that whole crust over with the veneer of our social habits ... of Western civilization.[25]

Speer took a strong stand against the Laymen's Foreign Missions Inquiry Report of 1932, separating himself from many of his more liberal colleagues. But the real clashes that he confronted as a missionary statesman were not with the so-called modernists but with the fundamentalists, though he himself had helped write the last volume of *The Fundamentals.* The modernist-fundamentalist controversy that was being waged in the Presbyterian Church at home was also being waged abroad, and Speer was caught in the middle, distressed by the unfortunate effect the infighting was having on the work of evangelism. "I wish we could get up such a glow and fervor and onrush of evangelical and evangelistic conviction and action," he wrote to a missionary in China, "that we would be swept clear past issues like the present ones so that men who want to dispute over these things could stay behind and do so, while the rest of us could march ahead, more than making up by new conquests for all the defections and losses of those who stay behind."[26]

During this time Speer himself was attacked for alleged unorthodoxy and was accused by J. Gresham Machen and others of "malfeasance in appointing allegedly unorthodox missionaries." It was a trying time for one who had served so long and so faithfully for his church (filling its highest position as moderator in 1927), but he weathered the storm and was vindicated by the General Assembly, which gave him an overwhelming vote of confidence.

The modernist-fundamentalist controversy being waged at home was also being waged abroad, and Speer was caught in the middle, distressed by the unfortunate effect the infighting was having on the work of evangelism.

Unlike many other denominational leaders of his day, Speer strongly supported women in ministry. "It would be strange and anomalous to deny to women equality in the church," he argued, "which is the very fountain of the principle of equality. It is Christ who has made women free and equal. Is she to be allowed this freedom and equality elsewhere and denied it in the Church, where freedom and equality had their origin?" Likewise, he praised "the Christian Churches on the foreign mission field" that were "apprehending the measure of the Gospel in this better than we.... God shuts no doors to His daughters which He opens to His sons."[27]

At the age of seventy, after forty-six years of service, he retired from his leadership position in Presbyterian missions. For the next decade he traveled, lecturing at campuses and conferences, never relinquishing his all-consuming commitment to world evangelism. The intensity that had so characterized him in his earlier years continued to the very end. "When he boarded a train," according to his biographer, "his bag of papers and books were with him. Out of the battered brown bag came papers and reports from the office, or a book. He plunged at once into their perusal."[28] Although terminally ill, suffering from leukemia, he insisted on keeping a previously arranged speaking commitment only three weeks before he died in 1947. To the end he was self-deprecatory—particularly in comparison to those who were serving on the front lines. When a friend requested to write his biography, he responded: "Nix on the biography ... merely say the cuss lived; he worked; he died; there are others coming along."[29]

Fletcher Brockman

The thrill of seeing the brilliant young men of the Student Volunteer Movement dedicate their lives to foreign missions was tempered when the methods and ideology of some of their numbers became known. Conservative evangelical missionaries were often distressed by the new concepts introduced by the young intellectuals. This conflict was particularly evident in China, and one of the young missionaries who vocally expressed his progressive views was Fletcher Brockman.

Brockman was reared on a cotton plantation in Georgia and educated at Vanderbilt University, graduating in 1891. On graduation he served as the national secretary for the YMCA, working with college students in the South and promoting overseas missions. As a Methodist, Brockman first offered his services to his own denominational mission board, but his bishop suggested that interdenominational sponsorship of the YMCA might be more appropriate for the broad-based ministry he hoped to have with students in China. The YMCA accepted his services, eager to respond to the invitation of many China missionaries who had called on the organization to enter that field.

In 1898, along with his wife and small son, Brockman sailed for China, arriving at a critical time just prior to the Boxer uprising. Although he survived the terrors of that violent period, other student volunteers did not. Horace Pitkin, the leader of the Yale volunteer band, had been in China only four years when he was executed in Paoting by Boxer insurgents in the summer of 1900. But his death was not in vain. Fourteen years later, Sherwood Eddy, another Yale volunteer, visited that same city in China at the invitation of Brockman, and he reminded his audience (which included some three thousand students) of Pitkin's sacrifice:

> When I came to the story of the cross and of Pitkin's death the interpreter broke down under deep emotion and stood silent, unable to speak. It is considered a shameful disgrace for a Chinese to weep in public. The audience bowed their heads in sympathy and shame. Many were in tears. When, after a pause, we quietly gave the invitation, some decided for Christ and many became honest inquirers. More than ten thousand Christian books were sold in a single day in the city where Pitkin had been martyred.[30]

With the Boxer uprising over, Brockman settled into missionary work, but he soon discovered that his personal philosophy of missions was rapidly changing. "In America," according to Sherwood Eddy, "Brockman had been preparing to go out and work for the conversion of what he then called the 'heathen' in the Orient. It was only after he had reached China and had humbly sat at the feet of Confucius, in his language study, that he learned that 'all within the four seas are brothers.'"[31] In his book *I Discover the Orient,* Brockman wrote of his search for the meaning of Chinese philosophy and religion: "The next ten years were largely taken up with discovering and untangling the true from the false without destroying my sense of mission."[32]

Though he always remained a Christian missionary and evangelist, Brockman shocked many of his friends by his open view toward other world religions and their leaders.

Brockman, like many other student volunteers in China, was well received by the Chinese literati because he was tolerant and sympathetic toward Confucianism, Buddhism, and other Oriental religions—an attitude that was a bold departure from traditional evangelical missionary perspectives. Though he always remained a Christian missionary and evangelist, he shocked many of his fellow missionaries and supporters back home by his open view toward other world religions and their leaders. "I am rich," he wrote in *I Discover the Orient*. "I have come into a great inheritance. My wealth has been gathered for thousands of years. Confucius, Mencius, Mo Ti, Buddha, Abraham, Moses, Isaiah, Paul, Jesus—I have entered into their inheritance. I am heir of the ages. I am sent not to dig up roots but to gather in the harvest."[33]

As Brockman studied the Chinese writings and learned from Chinese scholars, he won their hearts. But learning was not enough. He believed that he should reciprocate and teach them of his way of life, which included sharing his Christian faith; but more importantly from the Chinese standpoint, it also included teaching them of modern science and technology—a subject students craved to learn more about. Realizing his own deficiency in this area, he wrote to Mott and, in the words of Eddy, "implored him to secure the best man in America with scientific training to meet China's need." C. H. Robertson, professor of mechanical engineering at Purdue University, who had been in the Christian Association during his student days, was sent, and "within a few years Brockman's dream was realized in a remarkable way. The popular young educational genius Brockman had secured from America was addressing the largest audiences of officials, gentry, ancient scholars, and modern students that had ever listened to any man, Chinese or foreign, in all the history of China."[34]

Fletcher Brockman (left) and John R. Mott with a Chinese Christian leader.

One of Brockman's main tasks in China was to establish the YMCA in cities across the land. This required financial backing, and Brockman relied heavily on the Chinese—particularly the more tolerant Confucianists—for this help. Although the control of the YMCA was to be in the hands of the Christians, some of the organizations later fell into the control of other segments of the population, and today the YMBA (Young Men's Buddhist Association) has become a part of Asian society.

So respected was Brockman in China that after less than fifteen years there he was offered the post of presidency of Peking University. At the advice of Mott, he declined the offer. Mott believed that Brockman's organizational ministry with Chinese students was too great a calling to forsake for a secular pursuit. Then, only three years later, Mott called upon Brockman to leave China in order to help shore up the YMCA in America. Brockman left China with deep regrets.

"Mott," according to Latourette, "almost forced him to do so," and the years that followed were not happy ones. Brockman's tenure under Mott's direct authority was "self-denying," "difficult," and "exhausting."[35] Before he retired in 1927, Brockman was able to make return trips to China and to again work among the people he so loved and respected.

E. Stanley Jones

The enthusiasm that Brockman had for introducing Western science and technology to China found no parallel in E. Stanley Jones's effort to reach the intelligentsia of India. In fact, Jones shunned any effort to align Christianity with Western civilization, believing rather that Christ should be interpreted by the Indian people according to their own customs and culture. Even using science lectures as an opening for the gospel, he believed, was making an association that was misleading. One of the greatest detriments to the growth of Christianity in India, he believed, was the presumed relationship between Christianity and Western civilization, and missionaries were the culprits in perpetuating this ill-advised union.

Jones, born in Maryland in 1884, was only two years old when Wilder inspired the hearts of the "Mount Hermon Hundred." His commitment as a student volunteer came many years later while attending Asbury College, and his first inclination was to serve as a missionary in Africa (a calling that Jones humorously related was fulfilled only in the mind of a student who wrote on an exam that it was "Stanley Jones" who was sent to find Livingstone after his long disappearance). But the Methodist Missionary Society requested that he serve in India.

Before going to India, Jones endured a humiliating experience that changed the course of his ministry. The occasion was his "very first sermon":

> The little church was filled with my relatives and friends, all anxious that the young man should do well. I had prepared for three weeks, for I was to be God's lawyer and argue His case well. I started on rather a high key and after a half dozen sentences used a word I had never used before and I have never used since: indifferentism. Whereupon a college girl smiled and put down her head.... Her smiling so upset me that when I came back to the thread of my discourse it was gone. My mind was an absolute blank. I stood there clutching for something to say. Finally I blurted out: "I am very sorry, but I have forgotten my sermon," and I started for my seat in shame and confusion.... As I was about to sit down, the Inner Voice said: "Haven't I done anything for you? If so, couldn't you tell that?" I responded to this suggestion and stepped down in front of the pulpit—I felt I didn't belong behind it—and said, "Friends, I see I can't preach, but you know what Christ has done for my life, how He has changed me, and though I cannot preach I shall be his witness the rest of my days." At the close a youth came up to me and said he wanted what I had found. It was a mystery to me then, and it is a mystery to me now that, amid my failure that night, he still saw something he wanted. As he and I knelt

> together, he found it. It marked a profound change in his life, and today he is a pastor, and a daughter is a missionary in Africa. As God's lawyer I was a dead failure; as God's witness I was a success. That night marked a change in my conception of the work of the Christian minister—he is to be, not God's lawyer to argue well for God; but he is to be God's witness, to tell what Grace has done for an unworthy life.[36]

Jones began his missionary career in 1907 as an ordained Methodist minister of an English-speaking church in Lucknow. He preached on Sundays and immersed himself in language study the rest of the week. After three years he transferred to Sitapur, where he ministered to outcasts, which was where most mission work was concentrated because there was less resistance to the gospel. But as Jones lived among the people, he realized that India was far more than a land of impoverished outcasts. He turned his attention to high caste intellectuals.

Working among educated caste Indians was challenging but also debilitating. Jones often found himself on the defensive, being challenged by some of the keenest intellects he had ever encountered. The strain was too much. After eight and a half years and more than one mental breakdown, he returned to the United States to recuperate and rest. But back in India after his furlough, his mental problems continued. "I saw that unless I got help from somewhere I would have to give up my missionary career. . . . It was one of my darkest hours." Soon after, Jones underwent a deep spiritual experience: "A great peace settled into my heart and pervaded me. I knew it was done! Life—abundant life—had taken possession of me." Never again was he afflicted with the agony of mental illness.[37]

With his life changed, Jones became one of the world's most renowned evangelists, and as his reputation spread he traveled beyond the borders of India—always with the message of Christ. Christ was the focal point of Jones's evangelism, not Christianity. And he was quick to emphasize the difference. Christianity as the world knew it was a Western institutional church; and it was Christianity, brought to India by the Western missionaries, not Christ, that had been rejected by the Indian intellectuals. Jones was convinced that if the educated Indians had the opportunity to see Christ without all his Western garb, they would gladly receive him.

But Jones went further than merely disassociating Christ from Western civilization; he also disassociated him from the Old Testament: "Christianity must be defined as Christ, not the Old Testament, not Western civilization, not even the system built around him in the West, but Christ himself." Jones viewed his own mission as to "refuse to know anything save Jesus Christ and Him crucified." Sidestepping difficult passages in the Old Testament was a matter of pragmatism:

> I still believed in the Old Testament as being the highest revelation of God given to the world before Jesus' coming; I would inwardly feed upon it as Jesus did. But the issue was further on. A Jain lawyer, a brilliant writer against Christianity, arose in one of my meetings and asked me a long list of questions regarding

> things in the Old Testament. I replied, "My brother, I think I can answer your questions, but I do not feel called on to do so. I defined Christianity as Christ. If you had any objections to make against Him, I am ready to hear them and answer them if I can." He replied, "Who gave you this authority to make this distinction? What church council gave you this authority?" I replied that my own Master gave it to me.... Revelation was progressive, culminating in him. Why should I, then, pitch my battle at an imperfect stage when the perfect was here in him? My lawyer friend saw with dismay that a great many of his books written against Christianity had gone into ashes by my definition.[38]

Neither the Bible nor Christian doctrine, according to Jones, made Christianity unique among the world's religions; it was Christ. Therefore he believed that Christ alone should be exalted. On one occasion, when he was complimented by a Hindu for being a "broadminded Christian," he responded: "My brother, I am the narrowest man you have come across. I am broad on almost anything else, but on the one supreme necessity for human nature I am absolutely narrowed by the facts to one—Jesus." Jones went on to explain, "It is precisely because we believe in the absoluteness of Jesus that we can afford to take the more generous view of the non-Christian systems and situations."[39]

Jones's "generous view of the non-Christian systems" made him a target for criticism, especially among fundamentalists, who believed he was compromising Christianity in order to make it more appealing to other religious groups. "Jones accommodates himself to sinful pride, heathen thought and the growing nationalism," wrote Chester Tulga, a Conservative Baptist. "His Christ looks much like an Indian nationalist. His Biblical universality shrinks to Indian nationality.... The Christ of the modernist missionary ... becomes a false Christ, with no saving power and no historical authenticity."[40]

In presenting Christ to the non-Christians of India, Jones sought to use methods that were a natural part of Indian society. His Round Table Conferences and his Christian ashrams were examples of this. The Round Table Conferences began after he had been invited to a Hindu home to join other intellectuals in philosophical discussions as they all sat in a circle on the floor. With that example, Jones began doing the same thing, inviting Christians as well as adherents of Hinduism, Jainism, and Islam. These discussions, though intellectually oriented, became an avenue for evangelism: "There was not a single situation that I can remember where before the close of the Round Table Conference Christ was not in moral and spiritual command of the situation."[41]

The Christian Ashram movement that Jones founded was also an accommodation to Indian social life—an alternative to the Western church:

> The Church is for the most part a worshipping institution used once or twice a week. This makes the fellowship a momentary thing of an hour or two in seven days. After those few hours, each goes back into his compartmentalized life. The

> Indian mind—in fact, the human mind—wants something that will gather the whole of life into a central control and make it into a fellowship which will not be for an hour or two, but something continuous and all-embracing.[42]

The setup of the Christian ashram was very similar to its Hindu counterpart. The "family" was required to rise at 5:30 A.M. and spend its day in a combination of activities, including private devotions, manual labor, and group discussions, the latter being eliminated on the one day a week that was specified as a day of "complete silence." While the main purpose of the ashram was for personal spiritual growth, its greatest effect in India was to break down caste and political barriers that otherwise separated Christians in their daily workaday life. By 1940 there were some two dozen Christian ashrams located throughout India.

Jones's reputation as an evangelist and Christian statesman made him a highly respected individual in India and all over the world. He counted Mahatma Gandhi and Jawaharlal Nehru among his friends, and both men paid him great respect, though neither converted to Christianity. But Jones was more than just a missionary to India. In the words of Sherwood Eddy, "No one can more appropriately be called a world evangelist, no one has more consistently maintained his evangelistic work—for over forty years—in the spirit of a crusader, than E. Stanley Jones." Japan was just one of the countries he visited on his evangelistic tours, and according to J. Herbert Kane, the meetings there "attracted vast audiences in all parts of the country and tens of thousands registered their decision for Christ."[43]

As a renowned world evangelist and Christian leader, Jones was an influential voice in the twentieth-century ecumenical conferences, but he was frequently at odds with his colleagues—particularly on the issue that Jesus, rather than institutional Christianity, must be paramount. At the Madras Conference in 1938 he took issue with Hendrick Kraemer and others who supported the proposition, "The Church is, under God, the hope of the world." Only God, as seen through Jesus Christ, Jones argued, was absolute. "The Church is a relativism. . . . The Conference was thus betrayed."[44] Because of his weak view of the institutional church, Jones did not entirely fit in with other ecumenically minded missionary statesmen, and he was often criticized by both liberals and conservatives.

Although Jones had long since turned away from denominational exclusiveness in his ministry and had embraced a broad concept of Christian unity, he was nevertheless regarded highly among peers in the Methodist Church and was elected bishop at the General Conference. Before the consecration ceremony, however, he resigned. "I am an evangelist," he wrote, "not a bishop."

First and foremost, Jones was always an evangelist. Though he "revered all that was good and true in Oriental religions and did his best to meet them halfway," according to Kane, "he spoke on the finality of Jesus Christ and the uniqueness of the Christian Gospel" and "always ended up with 'Jesus and the Resurrection.'" His task as an evangelist was not to expand the institutional church but to introduce people to Jesus and then let them come to know Him in their own way, as his writing so powerfully conveyed:

> There is a beautiful Indian marriage custom that dimly illustrates our task in India, and where it ends. At the wedding ceremony the women friends of the bride accompany her with music to the home of the bridegroom. They usher her into the presence of the bridegroom—that is as far as they can go—then they retire and leave her with her husband. That is our joyous task in India: to know Him, to introduce Him, to retire—not necessarily geographically, but to trust India with the Christ and trust Christ with India. We can only go so far—He and India must go the rest of the way.[45]

That philosophy of world evangelism was the theme of Jones's widely circulated book, *The Christ of the Indian Road,* a book that had a significant impact on twentieth-century missions. When he died in 1973, he was mourned by Christians around the world.

SELECT BIBLIOGRAPHY

Brockman, Fletcher S. *I Discover the Orient.* New York: Harper & Row, 1935.

Eddy, Sherwood. *Pathfinders of the World Missionary Crusade.* Nashville: Abingdon-Cokesbury, 1945.

Fairbank, John K., ed. *The Missionary Enterprise in China and America.* Cambridge, MA: Harvard University Press, 1974.

Grubb, Norman P. *C. T. Studd: Cricketer & Pioneer.* Fort Washington, PA: Christian Literature Crusade, 1972.

______. *Once Caught, No Escape: My Life Story.* Fort Washington, PA: Christian Literature Crusade, 1969.

______. *With C. T. Studd in Congo Forests.* Grand Rapids: Zondervan, 1946.

Hogg, William Richey. *Ecumenical Foundations: A History of the International Missionary Council and Its Nineteenth-Century Background.* New York: Harper & Row, 1952.

Hopkins, C. Howard. *John R. Mott, 1865–1955: A Biography.* Grand Rapids: Eerdmans, 1979.

Johnston, Arthur P. *The Battle for World Evangelism.* Wheaton, IL: Tyndale, 1978.

Jones, E. Stanley. *Along the Indian Road.* New York: Abingdon, 1939.

______. *The Christ of the Indian Road.* New York: Abingdon, 1925.

Mackie, Robert. *Layman Extraordinary: John R. Mott, 1865–1955.* New York: Association, 1965.

Mott, John R. *The Larger Evangelism.* Nashville: Abingdon-Cokesbury, 1944.

Tulga, Chester E. *The Case Against Modernism in Foreign Missions.* Chicago: Conservative Baptist, 1950.

Wheeler, W. Reginald. *A Man Sent from God: A Biography of Robert E. Speer.* London: Fleming H. Revell, 1956.

13

"Faith" Missionaries: Depending on God Alone

During the years that the Student Volunteer Movement was recruiting young intellectuals from the universities and colleges, the "faith" missionary movement was building momentum. Like the SVM and the Women's Missionary Movement, the missionaries it represented came from many mission societies and denominations (or independent churches). It had its origins in 1865 with the founding of the China Inland Mission by Hudson Taylor, who directly or indirectly influenced the founding of over forty new mission boards. With the founding of such missions as the Christian and Missionary Alliance (1887), the Evangelical Alliance Mission (1890), the Central American Mission (1890), the Sudan Interior Mission (1893), and the Africa Inland Mission (1895), independent "faith" missions became a significant feature of world evangelism, whose "glorious achievements," according to J. Herbert Kane, are "stranger than fiction and more marvelous than miracles." While most of the infant faith missions struggled for survival, others, such as TEAM, founded by Fredrik Franson as the Scandinavian Alliance Mission, grew with amazing speed. Within eighteen months it had commissioned some one hundred missionaries to China, Japan, India, and Africa.

From the very beginning, faith missions have been associated with conservative evangelicalism, and the majority of the recruits have been either without higher education or graduates of Bible institutes or Christian colleges such as Nyack Missionary College, Moody Bible Institute, and Wheaton College. Moody Bible Institute particularly stands out as a training ground for faith missionaries, having graduated thousands of young adults who have served with hundreds of mission agencies around the world.

The term *faith mission* has often been associated with those missions whose financial policy guarantees no set income for its missionaries, and some such missions carry the policy to the point of refusing to solicit funds or even make known the needs of the missionaries, thus professing to rely entirely on God for financial needs. But the concept of living entirely by faith went far beyond the matter of finances. The missions were born out of faith, often at great risk and resulting in a high mortality rate among the early faith missionary pioneers.

For faith missionaries, the purpose of missions was to save lost souls from the eternal torment of hellfire and brimstone.

Risking their lives to bring the gospel to those who had never heard was not taken lightly. The faith missionaries were motivated by a vivid picture of hell. For them, the purpose of missions was to save lost souls from the eternal torment of hellfire and brimstone. "May we who know Christ," implored Jim Elliot, "hear the cry of the damned as they hurtle headlong into the Christless night without ever a chance.... May we shed tears of repentance for those we have failed to bring out of darkness."[1]

While faith missionaries were not oblivious to the physical and social needs of the people to whom they ministered, evangelism was paramount, always with a focus on cutting-edge concepts and technology. "Most of the innovations in twentieth-century missions have been introduced by the faith missions," according to Kane, "including radio, aviation, Bible correspondence courses, gospel recordings, tapes, cassettes, saturation evangelism, and theological education by extension."[2] A prime example of this was Harry Strachan's founding of the Latin America Mission (LAM) in 1921 for the unique purpose of mass campaign evangelism. Using the latest techniques in advertising and communications, he, along with his wife, Susan, and other missionary personnel conducted entertaining programs in theaters and public halls throughout South and Central America, attracting huge crowds. The gospel was presented, and converts were left in the care of local mission societies and churches. "There is hardly a mission of any size in Latin America," writes Kane, "which does not count among its members converts won in the campaigns conducted through the years by the LAM."[3]

This emphasis on evangelism sharply increased the spread of Christianity, and the faith missions grew to meet the challenge. By the late twentieth century, faith missions were among the largest mission societies in the world. Though diverse in their geographical locations and their evangelistic methods, they developed loose organizational ties through the Interdenominational Foreign Mission Association, founded in 1917 to promote the growth of faith missions.

A. B. Simpson and the Christian and Missionary Alliance

Though not a missionary himself, A. B. Simpson had an enormous influence on missions, particularly in his impact on the founding of faith mission societies in America. The founders of both the Sudan Interior Mission and the Africa Inland Mission were deeply influenced by him and studied at his missionary training school; and evangelical denominations, especially those within the holiness movement, were launched into missionary activity largely through his missionary zeal. Beginning in 1883, he orchestrated interdenominational conventions held in cities throughout the United States and Canada, featuring missionaries from various denominations and mission societies. These conventions led to the formation of Simpson's own international mission society, the Christian and Missionary Alliance.

Albert Benjamin Simpson's interest in missions began early in life. He was born on Prince Edward Island in 1843 and was baptized by John Geddie, the first Canadian missionary to the South Seas. The "missionary atmosphere" in his home had a lasting impact on him, and as a youth he was deeply affected by a biography of John Williams, martyred on the island of Erromango. At Knox College in Toronto missions continued to interest him, but after his graduation his reputation for preaching elicited a call to serve as pastor of the large and fashionable Knox Church in Hamilton, Ontario.

After eight years of ministry in Canada, Simpson accepted a call to Chestnut Street Church in Louisville, Kentucky, which offered him an impressive yearly salary of five thousand dollars. Yet he was not comfortable with the dignified respectability that pervaded the congregation, nor with his own tendency to cater to the wealthy and ignore the poor. Then a spiritual crisis caused him to realize how "barren and withered" his ministry had become and that his "true ministry had scarcely begun." After a "lonely and sorrowful night . . . not knowing but it would be death," his "heart's first full consecration was made." After that the Chestnut Street Church became a center for evangelism in Louisville.[4]

During his Louisville pastorate, Simpson traveled to Chicago to visit friends, and during this time he had a powerful visionary experience:

> I was awakened one night from sleep, trembling with a strange and solemn sense of God's overshadowing power, and on my soul was burning the remembrance of a strange dream through which I had that moment come. It seemed to me that I was sitting in a vast auditorium, and millions of people were there sitting around me. All the Christians in the world seemed to be there, and on the platform was a great multitude of faces and forms. They seemed to be mostly Chinese. They were not speaking, but in mute anguish were wringing their hands, and their faces wore an expression that I can never forget. I had not been thinking or speaking of the Chinese or the heathen world, but as I awoke with that vision on my mind, I did tremble with the Holy Spirit, and I threw myself on my knees, and every fibre of my being answered, "Yes, Lord, I will go."[5]

Following that vision, he "tried for months to find an open door, but the way was closed." The greatest obstacle confronting him was his wife Margaret. She agreed to leave her beloved Canada to go to Louisville, but not to China! With six children, she had no interest in forsaking the comfortable lifestyle the

Chestnut Street Church afforded them: "I was not then ready for such a sacrifice. I wrote him that it was all right—he might go to China himself—I would remain home and support and care for the children. I knew that would settle him for a while."[6]

Simpson was not a Livingstone, and he simply could not abandon his wife and six children, but he soon became convinced that God was calling him "to labor for the world and the perishing heathen just the same as if [he] were permitted to go among them."[7]

But Louisville was not the place to launch his enterprise for world evangelism, so in 1879 he accepted a call from Thirteenth Street Presbyterian Church in New York City. After two years, however, he resigned, realizing that the church did not champion his vision for evangelism. Without any steady income, he launched his new ministry. It was an impulsive decision that stunned not only the church and his associates, but also his wife, Margaret. A. W. Tozer poignantly described her feelings:

> The wife of a prophet has no easy road to travel. She cannot always see her husband's vision, yet as his wife she must go along with him wherever his vision takes him. She is compelled therefore to walk by faith a good deal of the time—and her husband's faith at that. Mrs. Simpson tried hard to understand, but if she sometimes lost patience with her devoted but impractical husband she is not for that cause to be too much censured. From affluence and high social position she is called suddenly to poverty and near-ostracism. She must feed her large family somehow—and not one cent coming in. The salary has stopped, and the parsonage must be vacated. . . . Mr. Simpson had heard the Voice ordering him out, and he went without fear. His wife had heard nothing, but she was compelled to go anyway. That she was a bit unsympathetic at times has been held against her by many. That she managed to keep within far sight of her absent-minded high soaring husband should be set down to her everlasting honor. It is no easy job being wife to such a man as A. B. Simpson was.[8]

With an advertisement in the newspaper, Simpson launched his new movement. His first meeting was held on a Sunday afternoon and was open to the public, except for his former parishioners, whom he had specifically instructed not to attend. He did not want to be accused of splitting the church. That meeting was well attended, but only seven remained after the service to dedicate themselves wholly to his new ministry. These seven, however, along with Simpson, formed a nucleus, and through their zealous evangelism the crowds soon overflowed the rented hall in which the services were being held. For the next eight years the group moved from place to place until a permanent building, the Gospel Tabernacle, was erected.

Simpson's ultimate aim was to organize a body of believers committed to world evangelism, but he was not satisfied with confining the movement to his

New York City followers. To broaden the appeal, he launched a missionary magazine, *The Gospel in All Lands,* and organized conventions in North American cities. In 1887 he founded two organizations that would merge in 1897 to form the Christian and Missionary Alliance. In the meantime, he established a missionary training school that would later become Nyack Missionary College.

Simpson pleaded for missionaries with a sense of urgency—not just to save souls from hell but to hasten the return of Christ. His key text was Matthew 24:14: "And this gospel of the kingdom will be preached in all the world as a testimony to all nations, and then the end will come." The Christian and Missionary Alliance quickly spread out all over the world, and within five years it had nearly one hundred and fifty missionaries in fifteen countries.

A. B. Simpson, founder of the Christian and Missionary Alliance.

Yet there was severe testing during the earliest years. The first to go abroad as missionaries were five young men who sailed to the Congo in 1884, three years before the mission was officially organized. Within a few months after their arrival, the leader of the party had died. In both the Congo and the Sudan, the early attempts at evangelism were costly in lives. "Those deadly climates," writes A. E. Thompson, "exacted such an awful toll of lives that for years the missionary graves in both fields outnumbered the living missionaries."[9] In China the Boxer uprising of 1900 claimed the lives of thirty-five Alliance missionaries and children.

But the work went forward, and by the time of Simpson's death in 1919, the mission was securely grounded on every continent. By 1919 his missionary training school was also well established at its permanent location in Nyack, New York, and his legacy in the area of Christian education extended far beyond the corridors of one institution. His missionary training concept launched the Bible institute movement that spread out across North America and became the primary recruiting grounds for independent faith mission societies in the decades that followed.

When Simpson contemplated the world, he envisioned millions of people dying without hope of eternal life—a burden that was summed up in one of his plaintive hymns:

A hundred thousand souls a day
Are passing one by one away,
In Christless guilt and gloom.
Without one ray of hope or light,
With future dark as endless night,
They're passing to their doom.

He often felt as though he alone was carrying this burden, and there were times when he buckled under the weight. Soon after he moved to New York, he plunged "into a Slough of Despond so deep that . . . work was impossible." "I wandered about," he later recalled, "deeply depressed. All things in life looked dark and withered." He recovered, but he was always susceptible to periods of despair. For a time prior to his death, "he went under a spiritual cloud," according to A. W. Tozer, and "felt that the face of the Lord was hidden from him."[10]

To many friends and associates his bouts of despair were puzzling. How could a spiritual giant like Simpson experience such profound depression? Tozer's analysis is insightful: "It is characteristic of the God-intoxicated, the dreamers and mystics of the Kingdom, that their flight-range is greater than that of other men. Their ability to sweep upward to unbelievable heights of spiritual transport is equaled only by their sad power to descend, to sit in dazed dejection by the River Chebar or to startle the night watches with their lonely grief."[11] Such highs and lows were a part of Simpson's earthly pilgrimage, and if he seemingly lost his sense of direction on his descents into the valleys, it was while he was flying high that he caught and carried out his global vision of evangelism.

Fredrik Franson and TEAM

Fredrik Franson's mission outreach in many ways paralleled that of A. B. Simpson, a man with whom he was closely associated. Born in Sweden in 1852, he is remembered primarily for his role in founding The Evangelical Alliance Mission (TEAM). As a youth, he emigrated with his family to Nebraska, and as a young man, like many of the mission leaders of the late nineteenth century, he was deeply influenced by D. L. Moody and Hudson Taylor. His concern for world missions did not develop until he was in his thirties, when he traveled through Eastern Europe and the Middle East. He had one goal: "To be able to do something on a larger scale to help the masses of people who are rushing into perdition."[12]

In 1890 Franson initiated his "11-day evangelist course" in Chicago for the purpose of training itinerant missionaries to serve in China with the China Inland Mission. But the following year he formed his own mission committee, which was the beginning of TEAM. The mission grew rapidly. In the spring of 1892 he reported: "The Alliance Mission [not to be confused with Simpson's

International Missionary Alliance] now has 59 missionaries in China proper, 14 in Japan, 10 on the way to Tibet, and 8 on the way to Africa, a total of 91."[13]

Perhaps more than any other mission strategist of his day, Franson was consumed with numbers. He calculated that one million Christians could evangelize the whole world of 1.4 billion people if each one reached fourteen hundred people. His hopes for the evangelization of the world intersected with those of Hudson Taylor, who called for one thousand missionaries for China who could evangelize the whole of China if each of these missionaries reached fifty families a day for one thousand days.

On a more practical level, Franson, like Taylor and Simpson, called for women missionaries to be very actively involved in worldwide mission outreach. In an era when many were insisting that there were severe biblical restrictions on the ministry of women, he insisted otherwise:

> There is no prohibition in the Bible against women's public work, and we face the circumstance that the devil, fortunately for him, has been able to exclude nearly two-thirds of the number of Christians from participation in the Lord's service through evangelization. The loss for God's cause is so great that it can hardly be described.... There are, so to speak, many people in the water about to drown. A few men are trying to save them, and that is considered well and good. But look, over there a few women have untied a boat also to be of help in the rescue, and immediately a few men cry out; standing there idly looking on and therefore having plenty of time to cry out: "No, no, women must not help, rather let the people drown." What stupidity![14]

During Franson's lifetime and following his death in 1908, TEAM continued to expand both in numbers of missionaries and in numbers of countries being served. But Franson's call for a primary role for women in all aspects of mission outreach was being heeded less and less as the twentieth century progressed.

Rowland Bingham and the Sudan Interior Mission

The visions of Simpson and Franson were to send missionaries all over the world. Other mission leaders of the era, following the example of Hudson Taylor, concentrated their efforts on more specific geographical areas. Like the Student Volunteers, many of the forerunners were deemed religious extremists and exhibitionists who needlessly risked their own lives and those of others. It was what they perceived to be the *call* of God that propelled them onward.

This evangelistic zeal of a few inexperienced men was what led to the opening of a vast region of the interior of Africa. What was then known as the Sudan appeared to be nothing short of a hopeless cause. Failure, death, and despair marked the beginnings of the Sudan Interior Mission (SIM). The Sudan was a vast, forbidding region south of the Sahara that has since been divided into a number of separate nations. Yet through the persistence of Rowland Bingham, SIM International became a dynamic mission venture in Africa, and today it is one of the largest faith mission societies, now reaching far beyond that continent.

The story of SIM began with Walter Gowans, a young Canadian of Scottish descent. He became convinced that the Sudan, with its more than sixty million people without any missionaries, was where God wanted him. But from the beginning, he confronted enormous obstacles, especially in obtaining sponsorship and support. With no mission societies in North America willing to risk sending personnel into the disease-infested Sudan, he sailed to England, hoping to find support there.

In the meantime, his mother and staunchest supporter sought additional recruits to join in the venture with her son. That she had already sent a daughter to China did not dampen her enthusiasm. She was an ardent missions supporter, as Bingham readily observed. She had invited him to her home after hearing him speak. Convinced that he would make an ideal partner for her son, she passionately presented to him the needs of the Sudan. She was a persuasive woman, and "the next morning," wrote Bingham, "when I went to call on Mrs. Gowans, it was to announce that I expected to sail in two weeks to join her son in a common enterprise. Was she glad? She was the whole board and I was accepted on the spot."[15]

Rowland Bingham was born in 1872 in Sussex, England, where he had a carefree childhood until financial devastation hit the family after the death of his father. At the age of thirteen he quit school to work, and three years later he emigrated to Canada. He had been converted in England through the ministry of the Salvation Army, and soon after arriving in Canada, "God made it clear," he wrote, "that He wanted me to preach the Gospel, and following His leading I joined the Salvation Army as an officer." It was through this ministry that he first met Mrs. Gowans.

After committing himself to the new missionary venture, Bingham traveled to New York, where he contacted Thomas Kent, a friend of Walter Gowans, and persuaded him to join the venture. They sailed together in the spring of 1893 to join Gowans and to begin their trek into Africa from the West Coast. On arriving in Lagos, the trio quickly learned why other missions had been so wary about sending missionaries into the Sudan. The head of the Methodist Mission in West Africa gave them an ominous warning: "Young men, you will never see the Soudan; your children will never see the Soudan; your grandchildren may."[16] Missionaries from other societies also

The head of the Methodist Mission in West Africa gave them an ominous warning: "Young men, you will never see the Soudan; your children will never see the Soudan; your grandchildren may."

offered gloomy predictions, but the fact that no other missionaries were preaching the gospel in the Sudan was the very reason for which they had come, and they refused to turn back. However, their hope of setting off together as a team was dashed when Bingham contracted malaria and remained on the coast to set up a supply base.

In less than a year after they left on their eight-hundred-mile overland journey, both Gowans and Kent, true to the pessimistic predictions, had succumbed to malaria. When word of their deaths, only three weeks apart, reached Bingham, he was devastated. He returned to England, uncertain about his future and his faith:

> My faith was being shaken to the very foundation.... Why should those most anxious to carry out the Lord's commands and to give His gospel to millions in darkness be cut off right at the beginning of their career? Many questions faced me.... Was the Bible merely an evolution of human thought, even biased thought, or was it a divine revelation? For months the struggle over this great issue went on before I was finally brought back to the solid rock.[17]

His faith renewed, Bingham returned to Canada, determined to go forward with the mission. Realizing his own inadequacies for mission work, he took a basic medical course at a Cleveland hospital and then, in the fall of 1895, he enrolled in Simpson's Bible school in New York City, the same school Gowans and Kent had attended. Before returning to Africa in May of 1898, he established the Sudan Interior Mission. In that same month he married Helen Blair, the daughter of a man to whom Bingham owed a debt of gratitude: "Just five years before, when her father had emptied his bank account to help send me to Africa, he little thought that I might some day return and ask his daughter to share in that work. In view of the fact that our first effort had nothing to show but two lonely graves, he found the first gift easier than the second."[18]

By 1900, seven years after his first attempt, Bingham and two young volunteers were ready to try again to reach the Sudan. This time he found the missionaries in Lagos "more than ever out of sympathy" with his plans, and they strongly expressed their views to his partners. More discouragement followed, and within weeks Bingham, seriously ill with malaria, returned home. Though his young recruits had promised to go on without him, they lost heart after hearing more dismal predictions, and they returned home on the next ship.[19]

The news plunged him once again into the depths of depression: "It would have been easier for me, perhaps, had I died in Africa, for on the homeward journey I died another death. Everything seemed to have failed, and while I was gradually regaining strength in Britain, a fateful cable reached me with word that my two companions were arriving shortly, I went through the darkest period of my whole life."[20] Still he refused to give up. He returned to Canada, met with the council, and found four more recruits to join him for the third attempt to reach the Sudan.

This third attempt, made in 1901, was successful, resulting in the first SIM station in Africa, located at Patigi, some five hundred miles up the Niger River. But with each step forward there were two steps backward, and within two years only one of the original party of four remained. One had died and two were sent home physically debilitated, never to return. Though barely hanging on, with only a few converts made during the first ten years at Patigi, the SIM gradually spread out to new stations and became firmly grounded in that desolate region of Africa.

One factor influencing the staying power of SIM in Africa after the turn of the century was the perfected use of quinine as a cure for malaria. With the proper use of that drug, missionaries no longer had to fear the dreaded disease. Another factor, according to Bingham, was Mrs. Gowans. She was "one of the greatest prayer helpers that ever blessed and strengthened" the SIM. "With her prayer and faith she carried us from the first seven barren years into the years of harvest."[21]

Besides malaria, the missionaries faced other obstructions that were in some ways equally frightening. "There is the constant invisible warfare," wrote Bingham, in reference to the demonic world he had encountered in Africa:

> It is fashionable in the Western world to relegate belief in demons and devils to the realm of mythology, and when mentioned at all it is a matter of jest. But it is no jest in West Africa or any other mission field for that matter. One has not to go far in the jungles of Nigeria, the Sudan or Ethiopia and visit a few of the African villages to believe in devils and demons. They are all around you, and soon, very soon, one begins to share the beliefs of the pagans as to the reality of these malign agencies without, of course, as a Christian sharing their fears or their vain oblations to propitiate them. Fetish men, devil men, ju-ju, lycanthropy, witches, wizards, ordeal by poison all flourished unchecked in the early days of the Mission.[22]

As the missionaries battled the "powers of darkness" and preached the gospel, they realized they could not ignore the physical needs of the people around them. Leprosy in particular was a dreaded African disease, and SIM soon became actively involved in eradicating its awful scourge among the people. The work began among the lepers in the 1920s, and by the 1960s the mission was treating more than thirty thousand leprosy patients in Nigeria alone. Many of the Africans who sought treatment were Muslims, and "many made their choice for Christ in spite of their early Muslim teaching and their parents' threats."[23]

As SIM grew and spread out across Africa, the needs of Ethiopia became apparent, and the church that was established there by SIM missionaries was a fitting climax to Bingham's sacrificial life of service for Africa. In 1928 Dr. Thomas Lambie had opened up the southern provinces of Ethiopia to mission work and settled in the province of Wallamo, where he practiced medicine and conducted evangelistic work. Other SIM missionaries joined the effort, and for several years they poured themselves into the work with few results. Then, in 1935, when the Italian military forces moved against Ethiopia, the situation became grim. The American and British embassies advised all their citizens to leave immediately, but the SIM missionaries stayed on—with the blessing of their general director, Rowland Bingham. "You are under higher orders than those of the King of England or the President of the United States. Get your instructions from Him and we are one with you."[24]

At this time there were only seventeen baptized believers in Wallamo, and the missionaries realized that their days were numbered. "Because we knew our time was short," wrote one missionary, "we did everything we could to teach the Christians and get the gospel message out. . . . It was unsafe to leave the mission compound, but the urgency and importance of using the little time which remained to further train the young Christians warranted the danger."[25]

The last nineteen missionaries and seven children remaining in Ethiopia were forcibly evacuated in 1937—giving them nearly two years of "borrowed time" to build the little Wallamo church. But even with the added time the number of believers remained small—only forty-eight—and the missionaries left with a deep sense of sadness and doubt:

> As we turned the last corner around the mountain and saw in the distance the wave of their hands in farewell, we wondered what would happen to the little flickering flame of gospel light that had been lit in the midst of so much darkness. Would these young Christians, with no more of the Word of God in their own language than the Gospel of Mark and a few small booklets of selected Scripture portions to guide and teach them, be able to stand under the persecution that would inevitably come?[26]

And persecution did come—severe persecution that tested even the most faithful as it had in the early church. But despite the oppression the church rapidly grew. "The warm love displayed by the Christians toward one another in the times of severest persecution made a great impression on the unbelievers. . . . Word of such love, hitherto unknown and unheard of, spread far and wide."[27]

By 1941 the war in Ethiopia was over, and the following year the first missionaries were allowed to return—though only by working under the British government. What they found amazed them. The forty-eight Christians they had left five years before had grown to some ten thousand, and instead of one fledgling church there were nearly one hundred congregations spread out across the province. It was one of the greatest stories of Christian evangelism in African history—one that overwhelmed the sixty-nine-year-old Rowland Bingham.

The painful losses of his early years in Africa had turned around, and he had just completed a book on the fifty years of SIM, *Seven Sevens.* Amid the celebration, he made plans to go to Ethiopia, but before he left Canada in December of 1942, he died suddenly of an apparent heart attack.

In the years after his death, SIM witnessed both victories and setbacks in Africa. When Sudanese[28] independence was declared in 1955, the missionaries found themselves in the midst of political turmoil, and when civil war broke out between the southern tribal people and the northern Muslim Arabs, they were accused of aiding the southern rebels. The new government nationalized mission schools, and in 1964 the Muslim-controlled government expelled all missionaries in the south. With the missionaries gone, life for the Sudanese Christians only seemed to get worse. The northern government armed some southern tribes to fight other southern tribes, exploiting tribal animosities to weaken southern resistance. Some of the tribes in the south were ruthlessly crushed, and over a half million died. Christians were tortured and churches were burned.

By the early 1970s, however, the political climate in Sudan turned around. The Soviet advisors were dismissed, and the missionaries were allowed to return. A small Bible school was established, and many health care programs were initiated. In Ethiopia political turmoil increased as the Soviet Union became involved and a Marxist government was established. By the late 1970s the SIM missionary force there was only a fraction of what it had been, though there remained some twenty-five hundred churches and dozens of Bible schools connected to the mission.

Peter Cameron Scott and the Africa Inland Mission

The AIM, like the Sudan Interior Mission, barely survived its turbulent infancy. The torture of the African environment took its toll on the Western missionaries, and for a time the dream of fulfilling Johann Krapf's vision of establishing a line of mission stations across Africa from the east coast turned into a grueling nightmare. The venture that had begun with promise in 1895 was within a few years barely alive. Yet by 1901 the situation had begun to reverse itself, and AIM was on its way to becoming the largest mission in East Africa.

The Africa Inland Mission was founded by Peter Cameron Scott, a young missionary who had served for a short time in Africa under the International Missionary Alliance (later the Christian and Missionary Alliance) but was forced to return home due to repeated attacks of malaria. He was born in Glasgow in 1867, emigrated to America when he was thirteen, and settled in Philadelphia, where, as a gifted vocalist, he trained with an Italian maestro. Although his parents objected to his pursuing a career in opera and insisted he learn the trade of printing, the lure of the stage was strong. But on the steps of an opera house, as he was on his way for an audition, he made the crucial decision to serve God in missions rather than to pursue a career in music.

With that decision behind him, he enrolled at the New York Missionary Training College founded by Simpson to prepare for missionary service in Africa. In 1890, at the age of twenty-three, he was ordained by Simpson, and the following day he sailed for the west coast of Africa to begin mission work. Within months after he arrived, he was joined by his brother John, but the reunion was short lived; John joined the multitude of other missionaries in "the white man's graveyard." Peter constructed a crude coffin and dug the grave himself. There were no church bells or flowers or eulogies, but alone at the grave, he recommitted himself to preaching the gospel in Africa.

Peter Scott would return to Africa and lay down his life, if need be, for the cause for which Livingstone had lived and died.

Back in England some months later, broken in health, he found inspiration again at the tomb of David Livingstone in Westminster Abbey as he knelt and read the inscription, "Other sheep I have which are not of this fold; them also I must bring." He would return to Africa and lay down his life, if need be, for the cause for which this great man had lived and died.

From England, Scott returned to America and there met with others to lay out a strategy for penetrating Africa from the east, moving beyond the coastal regions where the Anglicans were serving and on into the "unreached tribes of the interior." Among those involved in the first planning sessions were A. T. Pierson and C. E. Hurlburt, men who would play significant roles in AIM in the years to come. The Bible Institute of Pennsylvania became the headquarters for the new mission and the scene of the farewell service in August of 1895 when Scott and seven others, including his sister Margaret, were officially commissioned to service in Africa.

Peter Cameron Scott, founder of the Africa Inland Mission.

The missionary party arrived in Zanzibar, and from there they traveled inland to establish the first of several mission stations that would be located in Kenya. Within months after founding the first station, Scott was scouting out new mission sites. More recruits, including his parents and younger sister, Ina, were on the way, and he was optimistic about the future. In 1896, when he submitted his first annual report of AIM, he recounted the significant accomplishments that had occurred in only one year. Four stations had been opened, houses had been built, educational and medical programs had been set up, and there was steady progress in language acquisition.

But hardly had Scott's first annual report been issued when word came that he had become ill. The harsh African environment had once again brought him down, and his hectic travel schedule on foot—covering some 2,600 miles in a year—only aggravated the situation. His mother patiently nursed him, but to no avail. He died in December of 1896, just fourteen months after the work had begun.

Scott had been the lifeblood of AIM, and with his death, according to Kenneth Richardson, "The young mission passed through deep waters. . . . One after another, several of its valuable workers passed away. Others had to give up for health reasons. Still others—including the remaining members of the Scott family—left to serve Africa in other ways." By the summer of 1899 the only missionary remaining on the field was William Gangert, a solitary symbol that AIM was in Africa to stay. He was soon joined by two new recruits, and the rebuilding process began. Then in 1901, C. E. Hurlburt, who had been appointed general director of the mission, uprooted his wife and five children (all of whom later became AIM missionaries themselves) and relocated in Africa, where he could have a closer scrutiny of the work and become involved himself.

By 1909, AIM had expanded its work into Tanzania and later into the northeastern part of the Congo—but not without powerful political influence. In 1908, while on furlough in the United States, Hurlburt had been summoned to the White House to meet President Theodore Roosevelt and to advise him concerning a safari he was planning in East Africa. When he visited Africa the following year, Roosevelt renewed his acquaintance with Hurlburt and laid the cornerstone for Rift Valley Academy, offering to use his influence should the mission ever need it. Hurlburt remembered that pledge in 1910 when he confronted Belgian authorities blocking AIM's entrance into the Congo, and he called upon the ex-president for help. True to his word, Roosevelt contacted the Belgian government and permission to enter was granted. A communications mix-up caused the local chiefs to believe Roosevelt himself was on his way in, so the first contingent of missionaries received an unexpected royal welcome.

Hurlburt had surprised many people by bringing his five children to Africa, but he was convinced of the importance of a stable family life and did not think children should be sent back to the homeland for their education. He became one of the pioneers of the missionary children's school—a boarding school located on the field. Rift Valley Academy was established soon after he arrived in Africa; and in the years since, it has expanded to serve hundreds of missionaries in East Africa with a schedule of three months at school and one at home, allowing children to return to their families three times each year.

Hurlburt was a leader in the 1913 conference in Kenya that sought to encourage missionary cooperation based on the authority of Scripture and the Apostles' and Nicene Creeds. "It seemed tragic," writes Richardson, "that the denominational differences which divided Christians in the homelands should be imported into Kenya."[29] Although there was adverse reaction to the proposals of unity (especially from some Anglicans), a loose alliance was formed that fostered cooperation among mission societies.

There were other difficult issues confronting Hurlburt—particularly ones relating to the African tribal customs. During the 1920s the practice of female circumcision created a crisis that nearly destroyed the young Africa Inland Church. This custom, accompanied by tribal rites, involved circumcising girls at the age of puberty. The young girls were taken to a secluded forest camp where they were mutilated without anesthesia by older women using unsterilized, crude instruments that frequently resulted in serious infections as well as complications at the time of childbirth.

Within the African churches feelings ran high on both sides of the issue, but the mission insisted that the African church leaders condemn the practice or lose their positions. Only twelve refused to comply, but the crisis was not over. For taking a stand against this time-honored tribal practice, some African Christians were persecuted, and self-appointed circumcisers went out into villages in search of uncircumcised girls.

Then came the ultimate act of degradation. "It was bound to happen," write James and Marti Hefley. "An elderly, deaf AIM missionary, Hilda Stumpf, was found choked to death. First reports said she had been killed by a thief. Then the real facts came out. She had been brutally mutilated in a fashion that pointed to the work of circumcision fanatics." This "shocking murder caused some of the tribal zealots to back off. But the deeper conflict between Africans and Europeans dragged on and culminated in the bloody Mau Mau rebellion of the 1950s."[30]

Following this uprising, AIM leaders realized the urgent necessity of releasing more control of the mission activities to the Africans themselves. In 1971 AIM turned over its properties to the Africa Inland Church. The mission continued its work in Africa as set forth by Peter Cameron Scott in 1895, but at the invitation of the African church.

C. I. Scofield and the Central American Mission

During the same decade that A. B. Simpson was commissioning missionaries all over the globe and Bingham and Scott were penetrating central Africa, another American, who would later become famous for his popular edited Bible, was laying the groundwork for a gospel witness in Central America. C. I. Scofield was not the first to catch a vision for Central America, but when that area of the world came to his attention in the late 1880s, "there was only one Spanish-speaking Gospel witness" in that region.[31]

Scofield was born in Michigan in 1843 and raised in Tennessee. During the Civil War he joined the Confederate forces and served in Lee's army. Following the war he studied law, served in the Kansas State Legislature, and then became a U.S. Attorney under President Grant. Later, in 1879, while practicing law in St. Louis, he was converted through the witness of a client. For Scofield, "a slave to drink," the conversion was dramatic. He began an intense study of the Bible, and in 1883 he was ordained as a Congregationalist minister. For the next thirteen years he served as a pastor in Dallas. Later he became a conference speaker and the founder and first president of Philadelphia College of the Bible. In Dallas his concern for missions developed.

For several summers Scofield had attended the Niagara Bible Conference, and there he formed a lasting friendship with Hudson Taylor. Then, in the summer of 1888, he learned of the needs of the people in Costa Rica. When he returned to Dallas, he formed a prayer fellowship with its focus on that small country. In the fall of 1890, with the help of others, he organized the Central American Mission (CAM), and within four months its first candidate, William McConnell, was serving in Costa Rica, soon to be joined by his wife Minnie and their three sons.

C. I. Scofield, Bible editor and founder of the Central American Mission.

When McConnell arrived in Costa Rica, he met two women, Mrs. Ross and Mrs. Lang, both married to coffee plantation owners living in San José. They were active in a church founded by the Scotch Presbyterians and had been meeting together to pray for missionaries. Years later, McConnell described the women as "the first to heartily welcome us to the country and encourage us in the work," adding that they had been "loyal friends and helpers ever since."

By 1894 there were seven CAM missionaries in Costa Rica, and the following year the mission began work in Honduras and El Salvador. In 1899 missionaries arrived in Guatemala, and the following year in Nicaragua. In its first decade the mission had twenty-five missionaries working in five Central American countries, and despite setbacks, the work continued to grow, with some three hundred missionaries serving in six Central American countries and Mexico by the late twentieth century.

South and Central America

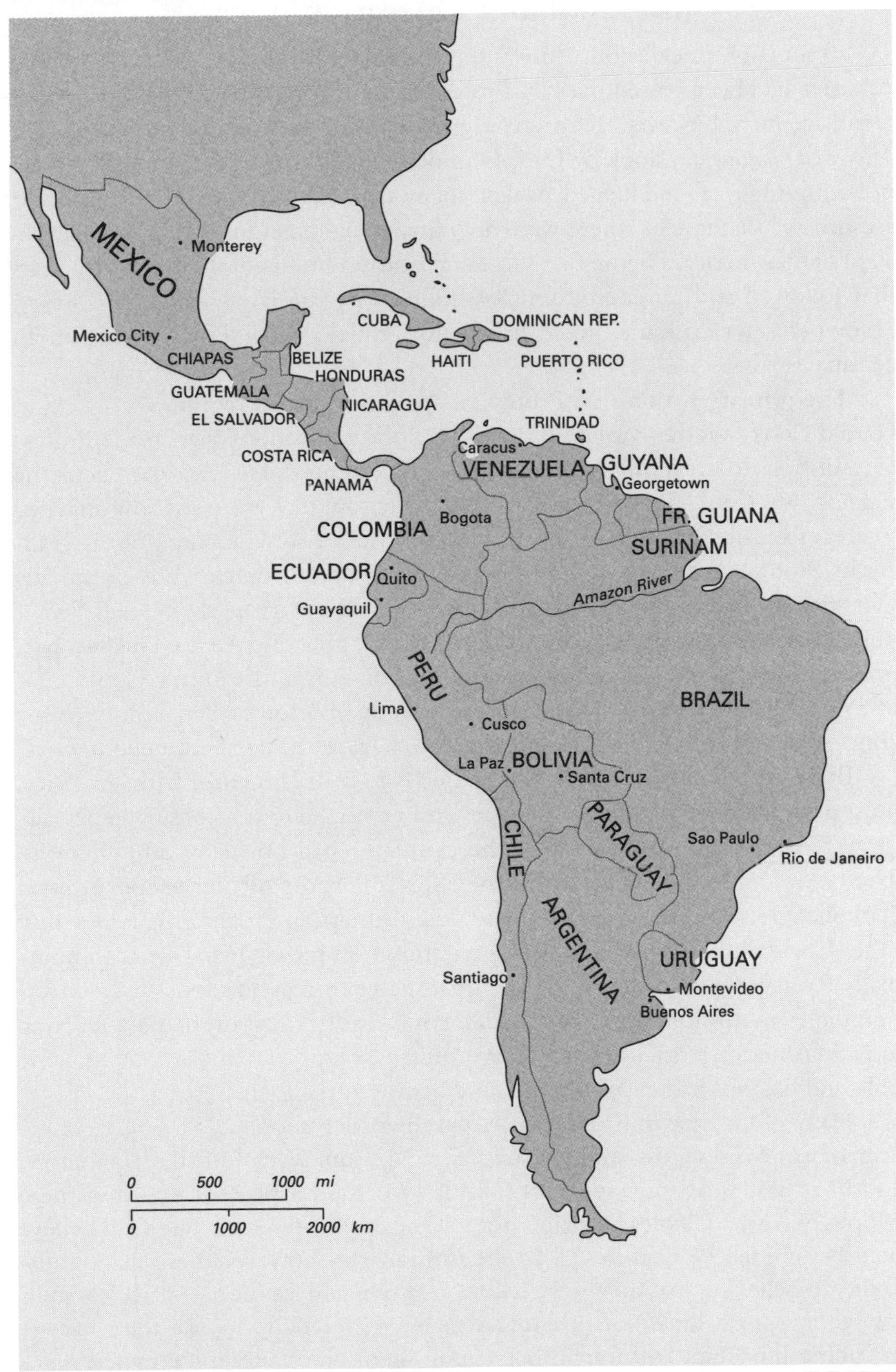

Jim Elliot and Operation Auca

Although Scofield's concern was specifically for Central America, all of Latin America had been passed over by Protestant missions. By the end of the nineteenth century, however, there was a growing awareness of this oversight. *The Neglected Continent,* a book by Lucy Guinness, underscored the "spiritual neglect of South America" and helped awaken many Christians to their responsibility. It is estimated that in 1900 there were only fifty thousand evangelical Christians in all of Latin America, a figure that increased nearly a hundredfold in the fifty years that followed and numbered tens of millions by the late twentieth century. "Nowhere," writes Kane, "has Christianity grown so rapidly in the twentieth century."[32]

The primary reason that Protestants passed over this region, according to Harold Cook, was the "violent Roman Catholic opposition" that "made Protestant missions to Latin America unattractive if not impossible." Another factor, he suggests, was that Latin America "lacked the glamour that was somehow attached to areas like the Orient, Africa or the South Seas." Likewise, some of the leaders of Protestant mission societies argued that Latin America was nominally Christian, so Protestant activity in that area could not properly be classified as missions in the same sense as the work in India, China, and Africa. This was particularly true of some of the delegates at the Edinburgh Missionary Conference of 1910.[33] It was also true of some of the "faith" mission leaders whose prime concern was to reach inland frontiers where Christ had not even been named.

But if certain individual mission societies hesitated to enter Latin America, most mainline denominational societies and newer "faith missions"—especially those founded around the turn of the century—had no such compunctions. They moved into the region "with the express purpose of 'converting' Roman Catholics." Historically, writes Stephen Neill, "American Protestants, unlike most other Christians, have never had any hesitation over proselytizing work in nominally Roman Catholic countries, and treat such efforts as 'missions' without distinction from missions in non-Christian countries."[34] Most of the people living in Latin America, particularly the native Indians, were Roman Catholic in name only and had not had even minimal instruction in the faith.

Many of the new missions focused on the native peoples. The South American Indian Mission, the Andes Evangelical Mission, Wycliffe Bible Translators, and New Tribes Mission were all founded for the purpose of reaching these people, of whom Charles Darwin wrote, "One can hardly make one's self believe that they are fellow creatures."[35] To the missionaries, however, there was no difficulty in believing that they were fellow creatures and far more—priceless souls for whom Christ died. For this, missionaries were willing to risk their lives—including Jim Elliot and four other young men who were killed by the Auca

Indians of Ecuador in 1956. The tragedy became the missionary headlines of the century, with magazine covers, books, and a film all reporting the details.

The most stunning aspect of this incredible story is that it was a virtual repeat of a tragedy that had occurred a decade earlier in Bolivia when Cecil Dye, his brother Bob Dye, and their three companions, all with New Tribes Mission, entered the jungle in an effort to open the way for mission work among the *bárbaro.* This was a tribe, they were told, that "uses short arrows with such deadly effect that even the neighboring tribes . . . are terrified of them." Others who heard of the missionaries' plans also warned of danger: "They . . . attack any civilized person who comes near them"; "impossible to tame"; "you won't come back alive"; "they'll club their victims in their hammocks at night." But the determined party refused to be dissuaded. "God had called them to reach this so-called 'hardest tribe' first." "Of course it is risky going to them," wrote George Hosback, the youngest member of the team, "but didn't God stop the mouths of lions by His angels . . . and is He not 'the same yesterday, today and forever'?"[36]

After the men entered the jungle by foot, they were never heard from again, although early in 1944, months after they departed, items belonging to them were found by a second search party. During the years that followed, rumors surfaced periodically about the men—one in 1946 reporting that they had emerged from the jungle in a remote area of Brazil. "We wondered," wrote Jean Dye, "how much more we could bear of these waves of hope—raised only to be dashed." In the meantime, the wives of the missing men remained in Bolivia "more determined than ever to win these souls to Christ"[37]

In August of 1947 the first real breakthrough with the Ayorés occurred. The painstaking work of Joe Moreno, a self-described "flunky" missionary not chosen for the team, had paid off. He had inquired about Ayoré customs and began leaving gifts in their abandoned camps near the perimeter of their territory. Eventually, native men followed the gifts to the settlement where the missionaries were stationed; and as more time passed, the missionaries learned the language and presented the gospel to them. It was not until 1949 that the wives learned conclusively that their husbands had been killed.

That such a tragedy as this could recur in such similar circumstances a decade later illustrates how truly independent many twentieth-century faith missionaries had become, and it also shows the degree of cooperation that existed among missionaries from different evangelical mission societies. Operation Auca, which claimed the lives of five young men, was not a project designed by a mission society. Rather, it was a hastily drawn-up plan devised by members of three different missions with

Operation Auca was not a project designed by a mission society. Rather, it was a hastily drawn-up plan devised by members of three different missions with virtually no consultation with experienced individuals.

virtually no consultation with their leaders or with senior missionaries on the field. They were "faith" missionaries operating "by faith," depending on God for direction.

That is not to suggest, however, that they ignored pertinent data relating to the Indians and the experience of other missionaries. Indeed, as they planned the contact with the Aucas, they pored over the details of the New Tribes tragedy in Bolivia the previous decade, noting with grave interest their mistakes and vowing not to fall into any of the same traps themselves.

The five missionaries involved in Operation Auca were all what might be termed junior missionaries. Nate Saint, a pilot working under Mission Aviation Fellowship (MAF), was the most experienced, having served in Ecuador for seven years. The others had only two or three years of experience each. Roger Youderian was serving with the Gospel Missionary Union; and Jim Elliot, Pete Fleming, and Ed McCully were with Christian Missions in Many Lands, an organization with ties to the Plymouth Brethren. This organization channeled money to some thirteen hundred missionaries, though it claimed it was "not a mission board, nor . . . in any way a mission society." It encouraged its missionaries to "depend directly on the Lord for guidance in their work," reminding them that they were not "answerable to any mission board—only to God"—an approach that opened the way for such a project as Operation Auca.

Operation Auca was born in the Ecuadorian jungle in the fall of 1955 in an effort to reach one of the most hostile Indian tribes in all of South America with the gospel. For centuries the Aucas, like the Ayorés in Bolivia, had been the subject of hair-raising stories. "Spanish conquistadors, Catholic priests, rubber hunters, oil drillers—all had been targets of Auca spears. Dozens, perhaps hundreds, had been killed. No outsider had ever been able to live in Auca territory"—so said Dave Cooper, a veteran missionary to Ecuador. The most recent publicized killings by the Aucas had occurred in 1943, when eight Shell Oil employees lost their lives at the hands of this most unfriendly tribe. These very accounts held a certain fascination for the five young missionaries. What a glorious victory it would be if such a tribe could be converted to Christianity!

Jim Elliot had graduated from Wheaton College in 1949 and was preparing for missionary service in Ecuador. His single-minded enthusiasm to reach South American Indians deeply influenced Pete Fleming, a graduate of the University of Washington. In 1952 they left together for Ecuador, both still single, though that would soon change.

Also arriving in Ecuador that year was Ed McCully, with his wife Marilou. He, like Elliot, was a graduate of Wheaton College, where he had been a star football player. Also a Wheaton alumnus was Nate Saint, who, with his wife Marj, had served in Ecuador since 1948. Roger Youderian, a World War II paratrooper and graduate of Northwestern College in Minneapolis, was the most recent arrival, coming in 1953 with his wife Barbara and infant daughter.

Although Youderian was an enthusiastic participant in Operation Auca, his brief tenure as a missionary working among the headhunting Jivaros had not been a satisfying time, and he had been on the verge of giving up and going home. "There is no ministry for me among the Jivaros or the Spanish," he had written in his dairy, "and I'm not going to try to fool myself. I wouldn't support a missionary such as I know myself to be, and I'm not going to ask anyone else to. Three years is long enough to learn a lesson and learn it well . . . the failure is mine. . . . This is my personal 'Waterloo' as a missionary."[38]

But Operation Auca changed all that. The excitement of being involved in what was hoped to be one of the great missionary breakthroughs in modern history brought new life into his missionary work. For the others too, Operation Auca provided, in the words of Nate Saint, "high adventure, as unreal as any successful novel,"[39] a welcome change in the midst of routine missionary work. Though Jim, Pete, and Ed had been invited by Chief Atanasio to come and teach his tribe of Quichuas, it was the fearsome Aucas that captured their imaginations.

The dream of reaching the Aucas had been in the minds of the missionaries for years. Ever since Nate had arrived in Ecuador and heard stories of them, he had dreamed of one day sharing the gospel with them. Pete and Jim had also been deeply burdened for them. In December of 1953 Pete wrote of this burden in his diary:

> Last night with Nate and Cliff [a visitor from the States] we talked a long time about the Auca problem. It is a grave and solemn one; an unreachable people who murder and kill with a hatred which causes them to mutilate the bodies of their victims. It came to me strongly then that God is leading me to do something about it . . . I know that this may be the most important decision of my life but I have a quiet peace about it. Strangely enough I do not feel my coming marriage as prohibiting myself from being eligible for this service.[40]

The first breakthrough came nearly two years later, on September 19, 1955. As Nate Saint flew over Auca territory in his single-engine Piper Cruiser, he spotted for the first time an Auca village. In the weeks that followed, regular visits to the "neighbors" began. As he was at the controls, one of the other missionaries would drop gifts (including machetes, knives, clothing, and life-sized pictures of themselves) and shout friendly Auca greetings learned from Dayuma, an Auca woman living outside the tribe. On one occasion while circling above, Nate used a rope to lower a bucket containing gifts, and he was excited to pull it back up filled with gifts from the Aucas—a live parrot, peanuts, and a smoked monkey tail. This response was taken as a genuine sign of friendship.

The speed with which the missionaries moved forward in this dangerous undertaking, and the secrecy that surrounded it, have in the years since been the most controversial aspects of the effort. "The whole project," wrote Ed McCully

ECUADOR

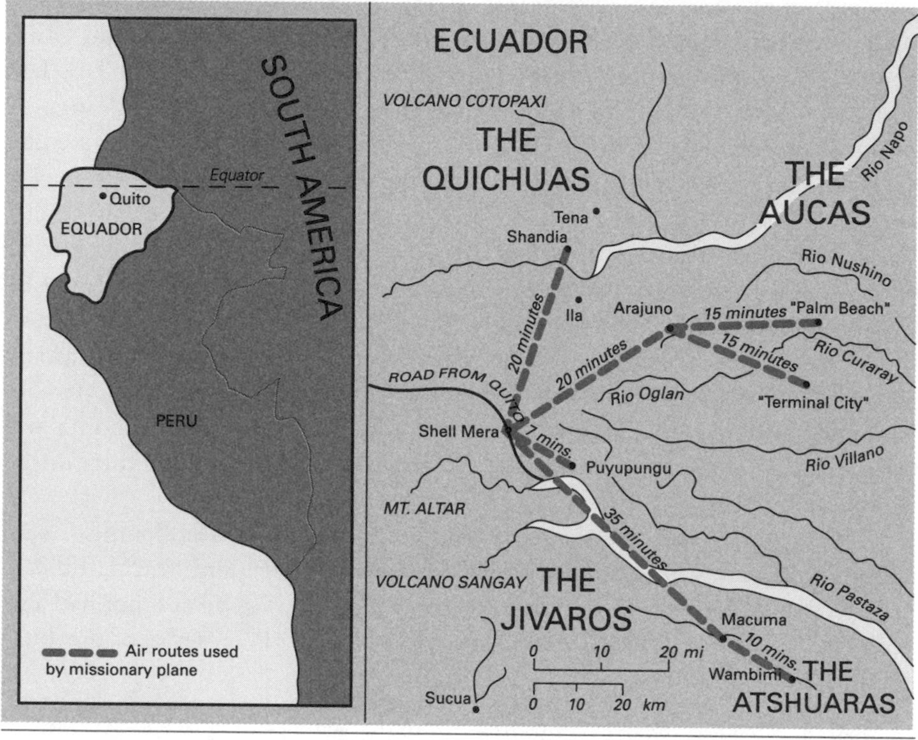

to Jim Elliot, "is moving faster than we had originally dared to hope." But why such haste? "The reason for the urgency," wrote Nate Saint, "is the Brethren boys feel that it is time now to move." Presumably he was referring only to Jim and Ed, as Pete Fleming had warned against moving ahead quickly—especially before they had a better command of the language. Jim, who was "always quick to make decisions," was described as "chewing the bit," while Nate was cautioning that nothing be done suddenly, allowing each advance to "soak in" before another step was taken. Yet less than three months after the first gift drop, the men had landed in the midst of Auca territory.[41]

But if speed was a top priority, secrecy was even more so. A code system was developed so that the missionaries could communicate over short-wave radio without their plan being discovered. They themselves were sworn to secrecy. No one other than their wives and Johnny Keenan, an MAF pilot who would provide backup support should they need it, was to know. Nate Saint wrote to his family back home requesting special prayer, hinting at what was underway, but couching even the vaguest clues in such phrases as "do not mention," "CONFIDENTIAL," "guard your talk," and "tell no one."[42]

The reason for the strict secrecy, according to James Hefley, was that "they feared that if word got out, a horde of journalists, adventurers, and curiosity seekers would make contact impossible." But the veil of secrecy extended to others who could be trusted and who could have given invaluable assistance. Frank Drown, with twelve years experience among the Indians, was not told of the venture until the plans had been finalized.

Another key individual left out of the planning was Rachel Saint, Nate's sister, who had spent months studying the Auca language with Dayuma, who had fled from her people. Rachel hoped to reach them with the gospel herself, but she knew the necessity of extreme caution. From Dayuma she had been warned: "Never trust them....They may appear friendly and then they will turn around and kill."[43] Such warnings were probably not what Jim Elliot wanted to hear, nor did he want to risk her reporting their planned venture to her supervisors at Wycliffe.

Certainly the five missionaries were aware of the danger, but they were convinced that no risk was too great to take for God. "He is no fool who gives what he cannot keep to gain what he cannot lose," was Jim Elliot's motto; and he solemnly vowed that he was "ready to die for the salvation of the Aucas."[44] They were all looking to God for guidance, and they saw signs of what they viewed to be God's direct intervention. The Curaray River, for example, seemed to shrink from its banks, providing a beach airstrip at a time when the beach normally would have been flooded.

Nevertheless, there was great trepidation as the time approached for the landing in Auca territory. Aside from the fierce nature of the Aucas, there were other serious safety factors to consider, particularly concerning the landing and takeoff from the short sandy beach along the river. Nate Saint was a skilled pilot, but he knew all too well that a sandy beach was not the same as a packed dirt airstrip. This awesome responsibility kept him awake most of the night on January 2, 1956.

The alarm clocks rang before 6:00 A.M. on Tuesday, January 3, and the adrenaline was flowing as the men began dressing. For Olive Fleming, married to Pete for only a year and a half, it had been a "rough night." Her apprehension could not be disguised. Jim Elliot had initially advised against Pete's going since it would mean risking the lives of three of the four male missionaries who knew the Quichua language, but by late December the consensus of opinion seemed to have changed. On December 27, Pete wrote in his diary: "It was decided that perhaps I ought to prepare to go on the expedition in order to gain by numbers more relative security for all."[45] The decision was made that Pete should fly out with Nate each night. Reports of previous Auca attacks indicated they invariably struck during the predawn hours.

The plan called for Nate Saint to make several trips to Palm Beach (the name designating a sandy shoreline along the Curaray River), ferrying the missionaries and equipment in. The first landing and takeoff were crucial: "As we came in . . . we slipped down between the trees in a steep side slip. . . . As the weight settled on the wheels I felt it was soft sand—too late to back out now. I hugged the stick back and waited. One softer spot and we'd have been on our nose—maybe our back. It never came." On takeoff, after leaving Ed alone on the beach, "the sand really grabbed the wheels," but within seconds Nate was airborne and on his way back to the base to begin his second trip.[46]

January 3 was a busy day on Palm Beach as Nate ferried in the missionaries and equipment. By nightfall the men had constructed a tree house, and three of them slept there while Nate and Pete flew back to the base at Arajuno to spend the night. They returned the following morning and spent a relaxing uneventful day with the other three on the beach before flying out again in the late afternoon. Thursday was much the same. Then on Friday, things began to happen. At 11:15 A.M., three naked Aucas (two women and a man) suddenly appeared out of the jungle from across the river. Jim waded out to meet them, and a friendly exchange took place. They accepted gifts and appeared to be at ease with their hosts. That night the Auca visitors departed, and Saturday was another uneventful day.

By Sunday the missionaries were restless and anxious for something to happen, wondering if their visitors had forgotten them. Nate decided to fly over the Auca village, which appeared deserted. On the way back he spotted a band of Aucas "en route" to Palm Beach. "That's it, guys! They're on the way," he shouted as he touched down on the beach. The missionaries waited. At 12:30 P.M. Nate made his scheduled radio contact with Marj at Shell Mera, promising to contact her again at 4:30.

The 4:30 contact never came. Nate's watch (later found smashed against a stone) had stopped ticking at 3:12 P.M. But Marj refused to believe the worst. Perhaps the radio transmitters had broken down. It was a sleepless night as she prayed and thought of the unthinkable. Early the next morning Johnny Keenan was in the air flying over Palm Beach. His report back to Marj was grim—a report that Marj relayed on to Elisabeth Elliot: "Johnny had found the plane on the beach. All the fabric is stripped off. There is no sign of the fellows."[47]

"Suddenly, the secrecy barrier was down," writes Russell Hitt. Word spread rapidly. Missionaries and government officials organized a search party. A *Time* magazine correspondent and a *Life* magazine photographer were dispatched to the scene. The story was on news wires, and people around the world waited for news. On Wednesday afternoon two bodies were sighted from the air, and on Friday the ground search team reached the site. "The missionaries in the ground party," according to Hefley, "pulled four badly deteriorated bodies from the river. Some still had palm wood spears sticking through their clothing. From personal belongings, they identified Jim, Pete, Rog, and Nate. Ed McCully's body apparently had been washed away." It was a somber scene. "The darkening sky indicated a jungle storm would soon be upon them. Hurriedly, the missionaries dug a shallow grave. As the rain came down in sheets, Frank Drown offered a quick committal prayer."[48]

At Shell Mera the five widows congregated to hear the grim details. Ahead of them was the task of putting their lives back together. For the stoical Elisabeth Elliot, there were "no regrets." It was God's will. "This was not a tragedy. . . . God has a plan and purpose in all things."[49] For Olive, who was left alone with no children, the trauma might have been unbearable. During her brief marriage she had endured the strain of two miscarriages and now the tragic death of her husband. But the very Bible passages she and Pete had been reading together before his death became her strength during this time of desperation, especially 2 Corinthians 5:5: "He who has prepared us for this very thing is God."

As with the slaying of the five missionaries in Bolivia in the previous decade, the public response was mixed. From everywhere came an outpouring of sympathy for the families; and many Christians, on seeing the commitment of these five, dedicated themselves to God and to missionary service. But to others the incident was "a tragic waste" of young lives.

> *What happened was God's will. "This was not a tragedy. . . . God has a plan and purpose in all things."*

Despite the trauma that ended Operation Auca, the Aucas themselves were not forgotten. MAF pilots resumed the gift drops, and Rachel Saint continued her study of the Auca language. But no more dramatic entries into Auca territory were planned. The effort proceeded with caution, and after nearly two years, some of the Aucas slowly began to make overtures to others outside their tribe. Then, in September of 1958, Dayuma returned to her tribe with two Auca women, and three weeks later they reappeared and invited Rachel Saint and Elisabeth Elliot to visit them. So began mission work with the Aucas. There were no newsmen or photographers to record the breakthrough, for there was nothing to record except that two women were once again venturing into the jungle to preach the gospel—routine missionary work.

In the aftermath of the tragedy there were many theories put forth as to why the Aucas killed the five missionaries—for example, that internal issues among the Aucas were contributing factors. Perhaps so. But the overriding factor was that the Aucas were territorial people. Outsiders entering their territory were considered enemies. To protect their families, by the dictates of their worldview, they had no choice but to eliminate their adversaries. The missionaries failed to appreciate and recognize that worldview.

"For those who saw it as a great Christian martyr story," Elisabeth Elliot later reflected, "the outcome was beautifully predictable. All puzzles would be solved. God would vindicate Himself. Aucas would be converted and we could all 'feel good' about our faith." But that is not what happened. "The truth is that not by any means did all subsequent events work out as hoped. There were negative effects of the missionaries' entrance into Auca territory. There were arguments and misunderstandings and a few really terrible things, along with the answers to prayer."[50]

Eliza Davis George and the Elizabeth Native Interior Mission

While many faith missions such as the Sudan Interior Mission, the Africa Inland Mission, the Christian and Missionary Alliance, New Tribes Mission, and Christian Missions in Many Lands grew rapidly during the course of the twentieth century, each sponsoring hundreds of missionaries, others remained small and obscure, though not without making an impact among the people they encountered. One such mission is the Elizabeth Native Interior Mission founded by Eliza Davis George for the purpose of training young Liberian nationals to evangelize their own people.

It was not easy for a woman to establish her own mission society, especially if that society was not specifically a Catholic religious order or a Protestant "female agency." But complicating matters for Eliza Davis was the fact that she was a black woman. Merely obtaining a missionary appointment was a major hurdle for such a person. Others before her had struggled against racism in their efforts to answer God's call to missionary work. Most had given up, but she refused to be intimidated and founded a mission despite the great odds.

Mary McLeod Bethune offers an example of the difficulties faced by black women who desired a missionary vocation. She was one of seventeen children born to an impoverished South Carolina farm family. Her secondary education was funded through scholarships, and with the financial aid of a kindly Quaker woman she enrolled at Moody Bible Institute. There she prepared for missionary work in Africa with a Presbyterian mission board, but after graduating in the 1890s she was told that "there were no openings for black missionaries in Africa." Despite this rejection, she "accomplished remarkable things in her eighty years," writes Elliott Wright. "She built a college and hospital for blacks in Daytona Beach, Florida. She mothered the influential National Council of Negro Women." She "advised presidents, had a hand in shaping the Charter of the United Nations, and worked for voting rights for all American women." Only missionary work to Africa was denied her.[51]

Eliza Davis (1879–1980) faced similar obstacles. She grew up in Texas in the late nineteenth century. Soon after she completed her studies at Central Texas College, during the heyday of the Student Volunteer Movement, she dedicated her life to foreign missions at a prayer meeting at her alma mater, where she had been asked to stay on as a teacher and matron. During a long prayer, while the leader went "all the way around the world and halfway back again," praying

> for India, China, Japan, and Africa, Eliza's heart was suddenly filled with an overwhelming desire to see her brothers and sisters in Africa. . . . As clearly as if she were there, she saw black people from Africa passing before the judgment seat of Christ, weeping and moaning, "But no one ever told us You died for us."[52]

The immediate response to Davis's disclosure that she had been called to be a missionary was, "You don't have to go over there to be a missionary—we have enough Africa over here." That was only the beginning of the opposition she faced. When she sought denominational support from her church, the Southern Baptist Convention, she was rebuffed. Never before had a black woman from Texas become an overseas missionary, and church leaders "did not believe she was able to take on such pioneering work." Finally, however, she was permitted to present her case at a special meeting. Her words gripped the hearts of those obstinate men.

> Eliza sat down, realizing that she had never once even looked at the notes clenched in her hand. Then, startled, she heard the board members applauding. Dr. Strong stood up, cleared his throat to bring the members to attention, looked at Eliza, and said:
>
> "Miss Davis, your eloquence and sincerity have moved us deeply. I for one can no longer stand in the way of your fulfilling your life's ambition."[53]

Davis arrived in Liberia in 1914 and began working with another single woman in the interior, where they established a Christian trade school, the Bible Industrial Academy. Within two years the school had an enrollment of fifty boys, who were housed in a bamboo building with a thatched roof. "Even more thrilling to Eliza was the response to the gospel among the tribal people. Within the year more than a thousand converts had accepted Christ in the villages."[54] But news from home was not so positive. The Texas Baptist Convention had separated from the National Baptists, who were in charge of the work in Liberia. Since Davis was from Texas, her appointment and support were now in jeopardy.

With an uncertain future, Eliza Davis felt vulnerable and alone. It was in that frame of mind that she made a critical decision that would haunt her for years to come. Her acquaintance with C. Thompson George, a native of British Guyana who was working in Liberia with a Portuguese company, led to a marriage proposal from him, which she initially turned down. "I didn't come here to marry," she responded in a short note. "I came here to work for the salvation of the souls of these natives, and nothing will deter me from my course." But that was before she received the letter from the Convention telling her that a Reverend and Mrs. Daniel Horton would be replacing her at the Bible Industrial Academy, the school she had worked so hard to establish.[55]

With that devastating revelation still ringing in her ears, George's promise that he would leave his job and help her start a new mission suddenly became more appealing. "Though she didn't love this little man with his English accent and his vast experience, she did respect and admire him. . . . And he was offering her the only hope she had to remain in Africa." Initially they worked together as a team, George keeping his promise to forsake his worldly ventures for her ministry. Very quickly, however, problems developed. She "had not found the physical intimacies of marriage easy, but she attributed this to the fact that she had been an 'old maid' when she married. But to have her husband smell of liquor repulsed her."[56]

Despite their marital conflicts, Eliza and Thompson continued to work together in the years that followed, often in the face of heavy financial difficulties. Yet they continued to make progress in their work. They traveled around holding revivals in churches as well as in areas where there were no churches. They trained more than fifty boarding students at the thatched-roofed mud school they operated. And many of the students became future leaders in Liberia.

In 1939, after more than twenty years of marriage, Thompson died. A friend who knew them both later assessed the marriage:

> She was very sad about that situation. I don't think it could have worked; in the light of her character, her gifts, and her calling, it would have been difficult to have found a suitable husband. She was too absorbed in working for people to give sufficient affection, attention, and time to her husband. He would have to have been exactly like her. But husbands want to take the lead and want the wife to give them a certain amount of time. It would have been hard for her unless he had changed.[57]

In the years after Thompson's death, Eliza witnessed the greatest growth and progress ever in her work. By 1943 her mission work included four substations besides her mission center at Kelton, and the local churches were cooperating in the work. But once again she faced opposition from church leaders in America. She was sixty-five, and the National Baptist Convention (from which she had received some support) was determined to retire her and replace her with one of her Liberian former students who had gone to America for a college education. The letter bearing this pronouncement indicated concern for her health, but she knew that once again her work had been undermined. Determined to stay on and continue without any denominational support, she sought to put the incident behind her. In her recorded memoirs she simply states the hard facts: "In 1945 the Foreign Mission Board of the National Baptist Convention of America saw fit to discontinue my services as a missionary."[58]

From that point on, Eliza worked "by faith," supported largely by "Eliza Davis George Clubs" in the United States. She continued her independent mission work in Liberia, which became known as the Elizabeth Native Interior Mission. The mission acquired thousands of acres of land in the years that followed, and by 1960 there were twenty-seven churches in the Eliza George Baptist Association, which was closely related to the mission. She continued to be actively involved in the work until she was past the age of ninety, and she lived to reach one hundred. When she died, the work was carried on by capable nationals who had worked beside her over the years.

SELECT BIBLIOGRAPHY

David, Raymond. *Fire on the Mountains: The Story of a Miracle—The Church in Ethiopia.* Grand Rapids: Zondervan, 1975.

Elliot, Elisabeth. *Through Gates of Splendor.* New York: Harper & Row, 1958.

Hitt, Russell T. *Jungle Pilot: The Life and Witness of Nate Saint.* Grand Rapids: Zondervan, 1973.

Hunter, J. H. *A Flame of Fire: The Life and Work of R. V. Bingham.* Scarborough, ON: Sudan Interior Mission, 1961.

Johnson, Jean Dye. *God Planted Five Seeds.* Woodworth, WI: New Tribes Mission, 1966.

Kane, J. Herbert. *Faith Mighty Faith: A Handbook of the Interdenominational Foreign Mission Association.* New York: Interdenominational Foreign Mission Association, 1956.

Richardson, Kenneth. *Garden of Miracles: The Story of the Africa Inland Mission.* London: Africa Inland Mission, 1976.

Spain, Mildred W. *"And in Samaria": A Story of More than Sixty Years' Missionary Witness in Central America, 1890–1954.* Dallas: Central American Mission, 1954.

______. *Witness in Central America, 1890–1954.* Dallas: Central American Mission, 1954.

Thompson, A. E. *The Life of A. B. Simpson.* New York: Christian Alliance Publishing, 1920.

Torjesen, Edvard P. *Fredrik Franson: A Model for Worldwide Evangelism.* Pasadena, CA: William Carey Library, 1883.

Tozer, A. W. *Wingspread: A. B. Simpson: A Study in Spiritual Altitude.* Harrisburg, PA: Christian Publications, 1943.

14

INNOVATION AND INGENUITY: THE CALL FOR SPECIALIZATION

The typical nineteenth-century missionary, if there was one, was an evangelist. His time was largely consumed with saving souls and planting churches. Even if he practiced medicine or translated Scripture, he was first and foremost a preacher of the gospel. By the twentieth century that concept of a missionary was changing. Missionary work was becoming far more diversified. By mid-century many mission societies had been founded for the express purpose of promoting certain mission specialties, and in the decades that followed, it was assumed that a missionary would specialize in a particular aspect of ministry.

The base for this new trend in mission specialization was primarily the United States. It had actually begun in the nineteenth century as missionary doctors and educators went abroad, sponsored by denominational mission societies. In the following decades the trend continued, and by the middle of the twentieth century there were entire mission agencies that concentrated on one particular specialty.

During the years following World War I, there was a decline in religious fervor, and this was reflected in an ambivalence toward foreign missions. "The mood of the Protestant churches in the 1920s," according to Winthrop Hudson, "was remarkably complacent." There was "a growing missionary apathy," and "missionary giving steadily declined during this period of booming prosperity."[1] The number of students volunteering for foreign missions fell significantly—from 2,700 in 1920 to only around 250 in 1928. The very motivation for missions was challenged by William E. Hocking and

By the middle of the twentieth century there were entire mission agencies that concentrated on one particular specialty.

his colleagues in the *Laymen's Inquirey,* warning against "conscious and direct evangelism."

In fundamentalist-evangelical circles, however, the missionary spirit had never died. Even during the 1930s, despite the Great Depression, there was a growing movement to speed up the pace of world evangelism through innovative means. During that decade Clarence Jones and some of his visionary colleagues made the earliest attempts to establish missionary radio. At that time also, William Cameron Townsend began training missionary linguists and Joy Ridderhof was implementing her ideas for gospel recordings, while others were testing the practicality of aviation on the mission field. World War II, however, frustrated the plans of many of these missionary activists, and it was not until the end of the war that the real thrust of missionary specialization got underway.

The close of World War II brought a revival of religious fervor in America. Though nearly all religious groups played a role in this new religious spirit, it was the evangelicals, according to Hudson, "that gave the revival its most vigorous leadership."[2] Such newly formed organizations as Youth for Christ and the National Association of Evangelicals gave the evangelical movement a broader base. The close of the war also saw the emergence of a new missions association, the Evangelical Foreign Missions Association, that was openly opposed to the religious liberalism of the twentieth century.

Spurred on by this wave of evangelical fervor, the embryonic specialty missions conceived in the 1930s began to blossom. With servicemen coming home from abroad, there was a new awareness and sense of urgency for world evangelism. Organizations such as Mission Aviation Fellowship, Far East Broadcasting Company, Far East Gospel Crusade, and Greater Europe Mission were all formed through the efforts of World War II veterans.

By the 1950s the "Iron Curtain" had barred mission work from much of Eastern Europe and the Soviet Union, and vast portions of Asia were effectively closed to the gospel as well. Radio and literature were seen as the only viable means of reaching such people, and as a result, missions such as the Slavic Gospel Association, Trans-World Radio, and those promoting Bible smuggling found a solid base of support.

After World War II, Christian literature as a missionary tool expanded rapidly. Several organizations were founded that were geared almost exclusively to an overseas ministry, including the Christian Literature Crusade, the World Literature Crusade, Operation Mobilization, the Evangelical Literature League, the Pocket Testament League, Moody Literature Mission, and Evangelical Literature Overseas.

The mission specialties that became most associated with the new missionary "heroes" of the mid-twentieth century were those centered around medicine, translation and linguistics work, radio, and aviation. These specialties were often closely tied to one another, all dedicated to the goal of world evangelization.

Medical Missions: "Angels of Mercy"

From the beginning of the modern missionary period, medical work was a significant aspect of world evangelism, but not until the late nineteenth and early twentieth centuries did medical missions became a distinct specialty in its own right. By 1925 more than two thousand doctors and nurses from America and Europe were serving throughout the world, and mission-run hospitals and clinics were increasing rapidly.

The ministry of missionary medicine has been a monumental humanitarian effort the world over. But despite their goodwill, medical missionaries have often found themselves in direct competition with traditional doctors and types of medicine. Sometimes the opposition manifested itself in threats and attacks, and other times in deep suspicion. A missionary doctor in Africa waited eight years before he treated his first native patient. In China medical missionaries faced open hostility; yet in 1935 over half of the hospitals in that country were mission-operated facilities.

Medical doctors have generally received the most acclaim for their service in medical missions, but dentists, nurses, and other medical personnel have also made noteworthy contributions to the cause. Likewise, some missionaries with virtually no training in medicine learned by trial and error how to treat diseases, thereby alleviating suffering and death while paving the way for an evangelistic ministry.

The first noted medical missionary in the modern period was Dr. John Thomas, who preceded William Carey to India and later worked alongside him. Though Thomas was emotionally unstable, Carey praised his work, claiming that the "cures wrought by him would have gained any physician or surgeon in Europe the most extensive reputation." Dr. John Scudder was the first noted American missionary to specialize in medicine and was the patriarch of a long line of medical missionaries to serve in India and elsewhere in the world.

Some missionaries with virtually no training in medicine learned by trial and error how to treat diseases, thereby alleviating suffering and death while paving the way for an evangelistic ministry.

Perhaps the most famous medical missionary of all time was the famed Albert Schweitzer, a medical doctor, musician, and biblical scholar, whose controversial theological views were widely disseminated in his book *The Quest of the Historical Jesus.* His career as a medical missionary began in West Africa in 1913, where he established a hospital at Lambarene. There, except for a period of imprisonment by the French during World War I, he devoted his life to medical work in Africa. Although he was a sought-after author, lecturer, and concert organist and

Wilfred Grenfell, missionary doctor to Labrador.

could have enjoyed a very comfortable life at home, he chose instead to serve "the brother for whom Christ died."[3]

Though the field of missionary medicine was dominated in the early years by men, women began entering the field in the late nineteenth century, and soon their achievements were being heralded all over the world. Clara Swain, a Methodist and the first woman missionary doctor from America, arrived in India in 1870, and within four years had opened her first hospital. The first missionary nurse was Miss E. M. McKechnie, who arrived in Shanghai in 1884 and later founded a hospital there.

There were few regions of the world that medical missionaries did not enter. While most medical missionaries in modern history have spent their lives in tropical climates fighting against the ravages of fever, leprosy, and other tropical scourges, Wilfred Grenfell conducted an effective medical ministry along the frozen coastline of Labrador. In 1885, while completing his medical training in London, he attended a revival campaign where he was inspired by the words of D. L. Moody and C. T. Studd. Grenfell, also a cricket player, was deeply moved, and that night he was converted. Soon afterward he volunteered to serve as a missionary doctor for the Royal National Mission to Deep Sea Fishermen, and then, in the 1890s, he began ministering to people in the scattered villages where families were entirely without medical services.

To reach these villages, the adventurous doctor navigated his own steam-powered launch along the dangerous coastline, "taking risks," according to a biographer, "that would have made a professional sailor die of fright." He "threaded the launch between islands and a fearful collection of submerged rocks ... through fog and ... against the strong winds and heavy seas."[4] In addition to his medical work, he was involved in economic endeavors that helped the impoverished villagers.

Grenfell traveled and spoke in churches, telling exciting stories of his work and his exploits. His fame spread, and money poured in as "Grenfell Societies" sprang up across the United States and Canada. He died in 1940, but his memory lives on today along the rugged coasts of Labrador.

Ida Scudder

The most renowned medical missionary family was the Scudders, who served for generations in India and elsewhere. In 1819 John Scudder left his growing practice in New York City and sailed for Ceylon with his wife and child. They served for thirty-six years in Ceylon and India, and during that time thirteen more children were born. Of the nine who survived to adulthood, seven became missionaries, most of them specializing in medicine like their father. In four generations, forty-two members of the Scudder family became missionaries, contributing well over one thousand combined years of missionary service. Among those forty-two was Ida, the daughter of John Scudder's youngest son, also named John and also a medical missionary to India.

Ida Scudder was born in India in 1870 and grew up well-acquainted with the trials of missionary life, particularly the pain of separation from loved ones. When she was a youth, her family returned to America for furlough, after which her father sailed to India alone. Two years later her mother joined him, leaving her daughter with relatives in Chicago. It was a traumatic time, according to her biographer:

> The memory of that night could still bring a stabbing pain. The rain outside had been as wild as her own fourteen-year-old helpless grief. She had not even been allowed to go to the station to see her mother off for India. When her clinging arms had been finally, regretfully, unloosed, she had rushed upstairs and sobbed all night into her mother's empty pillow. . . . With the passing weeks and months the aching loneliness had never ceased, merely subsided.[5]

After high school she remained in the United States to attend a "young ladies' seminary" in Northfield, Massachusetts, founded by D. L. Moody. She had no intention of joining the family tradition and becoming a missionary, but shortly after her graduation in 1890, she received an urgent cablegram informing her that her mother was seriously ill. Within weeks she was on her way to India, that "horrible country, with its heat, dust, noise, and smells." Her purpose was to care for her mother, and when that obligation was met, she would return to America to pursue her own dreams.

Scudder's stay in India was longer than she had planned. In addition to caring for her mother, there was other urgent work to be done. She soon found herself in sole charge of a school of sixty-eight girls. Although she was happy to be reunited with her family, she felt pressured from her parents and extended family to not shirk the Scudder duty of becoming a missionary. But she wanted more than the toil of missionary life. Then came the "three knocks in the night," her "call" to medical missions—a parable that was pulling her back to India. Three different men—a Brahmin, another high-caste Hindu, and a Muslim—came to the door during the course of one night, pleading for her to assist in difficult childbirths, refusing the assistance of her physician-father because custom prohibited such contact.

> I could not sleep that night—it was too terrible. Within the very touch of my hand were three young girls dying because there was no woman to help them. I spent much of the night in anguish and prayer. I did not want to spend my life in India. My friends were begging me to return to the joyous opportunities of a young girl in America. I went to bed in the early morning after praying much for guidance. I think that was the first time I ever met God face-to-face, and all that time it seemed that He was calling me into this work. Early in the morning I heard the "tom-tom" beating in the village and it struck terror in my heart, for it was a death message. I sent our servant, and he came back saying that all of them had died during the night. Again I shut myself in my room and thought very seriously about the condition of the Indian women and after much thought and prayer, I went to my father and mother and told them that I must go home and study medicine, and come back to India to help such women.[6]

The following year she returned to America, and in the fall of 1895 she enrolled at Women's Medical College in Philadelphia. In 1898, when Cornell Medical College opened its doors to women, she transferred there to take advantage of its higher ranking accreditation, and she received her M.D. degree from Cornell. When she returned to India, accompanied by Annie Hancock, a good friend who had come to work with her and to conduct evangelism, she brought with her a ten-thousand-dollar check for a new hospital given by a wealthy woman supporter.

Her dream of serving her internship under the brilliant tutelage of her father was shattered when he unexpectedly died of cancer. To make matters worse, the people, though desperate for medical attention, did not trust her. As the months passed, her practice slowly grew, yet she continued to encounter superstitious practices that counteracted her best efforts. Medicine was prohibited on certain feast days, and critically ill patients were sometimes moved from place to place to escape evil spirits. On one occasion, after cleaning a serious wound she stepped aside to prepare the dressing, and when she turned back she was distressed to see the girl dabbing "holy ashes" in the wound.

Building a nursing school for women became Scudder's all-consuming goal, and fund-raising became an important part of her ministry.

Soon after she arrived in India, construction began on the hospital at Vellore that she had pleaded for before leaving America. But she quickly realized that an educational facility was also necessary. Indian women needed to be properly trained to go out among their own people in the villages. Building a nursing school for women became her all-consuming goal. From then on, fund-raising became an important part of her ministry. While home on furlough, she captivated her largely female audiences by her stories of the hopeless plight of the Indian women, and every meeting brought more money for the project. When the nursing school opened, she was deluged with applicants, and her first graduating class ranked high in the government exams.

In addition to her medical courses, Scudder taught a four-year Bible course on the apostle Paul and the Pauline epistles. But medical work consumed the vast majority of her sixteen-hour work day. In addition to running a hospital, a medical college, and village dispensaries, with her mother's help she operated a small orphanage. More than twenty homeless children were taken into the Scudder home, and frequently she brought one or more of them along on her rounds. Her mother's death at the age of eighty-six was a profound loss to her. Sixty-three years earlier, this tenacious woman had been denied mission-board support because of frailty. Her husband agreed to accept responsibility for her, and for a quarter of a century after he died, she continued on in the work.

As Scudder's medical work grew, vast sums of money were needed to defray expenses and to update equipment. Women's groups from four denominations were supporting the work, but still the funds were inadequate. Then, in the early 1920s, she received word that her work, along with other Christian schools in India, would be eligible for a one-million-dollar Rockefeller grant if two million dollars could be raised elsewhere. She returned to America for the grueling fund-raising campaign that netted three million dollars, a large portion of which went to build a new medical complex at Vellore.

Ida Scudder, missionary doctor in India.

In spite of the new facilities, Vellore Medical College could not keep pace with the new government requirements during the years following independence. A 1937 ruling required all medical schools to be affiliated with the University of Madras. For Scudder, "it sounded the death knell for her beloved medical school."[7] In the midst of the Great Depression, raising the necessary funds seemed impossible. The men's Christian medical schools were being consolidated, but there were no other women's medical schools. For many, including John R. Mott, a coeducational school was the logical solution, and some suggested that Vellore would be the ideal location.

Scudder enthusiastically shared the proposal with her supporters back home, only to be thrown into the most bitter controversy she had ever endured. Thousands of women had been mobilized to raise money to support medical missions for women in India, and the thought of sharing all they had worked so hard for with the men was unthinkable. Hilda Olson, a governing board member of the Vellore Medical compound, responded tersely to the proposal: "Vellore is as you say, God's work, but I would like to add God's work *for women*. Every dollar would have to be given back to the givers."[8]

The governing board was bitterly divided on the issue, and Lucy Peabody, who had been one of Scudder's staunchest supporters through the years, became her most caustic critic, accusing her of disloyalty to everything the board stood for. It was a depressing time for Scudder, but in the end, after years of sharp debate, the board voted to join the men, and Vellore became the site of the new coeducational school.

During these years and following, Scudder became widely recognized for her accomplishments. She was interviewed by reporters, and many stories were written about her work. The *Reader's Digest*, among other magazines, gave her flattering coverage:

> This extraordinary white-haired woman has, at 72, a spring in her step, a sparkle in her eye and the skilled, strong hands of a surgeon of 45. For 18 years she had been head of the medical association in a district with a population of 2,000,000. Doctors all over India send her their most difficult gynecological cases. Women and children come just to touch her, so exalted is her reputation for healing.[9]

She retired in 1946 at the age of seventy-five and was succeeded by one of her most distinguished pupils, Dr. Hilda Lazarus. It was a graceful retirement, according to her biographer. "She who had been all her life a leader—some had called it dictator—now found it possible to be a follower."[10] But she remained active for more than another decade. She taught her weekly Bible class (to both men and women), advised doctors on difficult cases, entertained friends and dignitaries at Hill Top, her beautiful Indian residence, and played a fast game of tennis. Although she was not what she had been at the age of sixty-five (when during a tournament she had beaten her teenage opponent in two sets, winning every game—after the girl scornfully objected to having to play a "grannie"), she continued to play regularly, and even at the age of eighty-three, according to her biographer, "she was still serving a wicked tennis ball."[11]

So famous had she become that when a letter addressed simply "Dr. Ida, India" arrived on the subcontinent populated by some three hundred million people, it was sent immediately to her at Vellore.

Another well-known missionary doctor who served in south-central Asia was Viggo Olsen, who is most remembered for his widely read autobiography,

Daktar: Diplomat in Bangladesh. Becoming a missionary was not something he had contemplated when he began his medical training. "I viewed Christianity and the Bible through agnostic eyes," he writes, "feeling that modern science had outmoded much of this religious sentiment."[12] Following his conversion, however, he felt "God's call" to overseas medical missions. Then, "three days later came the acid test." In the mail was a letter: "We are happy to inform you that you have been accepted for a fellowship in the department of Internal Medicine of Mayo Clinic." But he turned down the opportunity for a higher calling. He and his family began their ministry in East Pakistan with the Association of Baptists for World Evangelism (ABWE) in 1962, and four years later, amid political turmoil, opened Memorial Christian Hospital.

During the 1970s, when the Muslim majority fought for independence from West Pakistan, he remained at the hospital while his wife and children were evacuated. In the midst of the ravages of war, he was able to save the hospital, and after a time of home leave, he returned to his hospital to serve the people in the new country of Bangladesh.

Carl Becker

Carl Becker was one of Africa's most beloved doctors of the twentieth century. He began his medical studies in 1916 after working at a foundry for several years to help support his widowed mother and sister. But with the outbreak of World War I, he enlisted in the United States Medical Corps, which provided him training and a small salary. With his training over, he warned his fiancée that he had promised to give God his life if God would give him an education. "I don't know if it means I'll go to China or Africa as a missionary or what," he told her, "but he has first claim on my life."[13]

As he became settled into his practice in Pennsylvania, however, his promise to God was ignored until he received a letter from Charles Hurlburt of the Africa Inland Mission, a man he had met some years earlier. Hurlburt's daughter-in-law, a medical doctor who was serving in the Congo, had died suddenly, and he was urgently seeking a doctor to take her place. Becker rejected Hurlburt's request, but Hurlburt persisted, and in the summer of 1928, the Beckers sailed for Africa, leaving "a $10,000-plus income to earn $60 a month . . . to go to a primitive outpost he knew nothing about."[14]

The Beckers' first home in the Congo was a mud hut that Marie creatively turned into a "mud mansion." In 1934 he moved with his wife and two children to the tiny mission station of Oicha in the dense Ituri forest to work among the Pygmies and other forest tribes. There his ministry bloomed. Walled in by the giant mahogany trees, he built a medical compound out of nothing—primitive in comparison to the facilities he had been used to back home, but that met the needs of the African jungle. He was not an organizer or a long-range planner, nor was he public-relations minded. Otherwise, writes his biographer, "he might have raised a large sum of money by promoting it as a memorial hospital in honor of some dear-departed saint." As it was, he added room additions and buildings as they were needed, with "no overall general plan."[15] There was no budget for hospital construction, so much of the expense came out of his $60-a-month salary.

Evangelism was the primary purpose for Becker's work in Africa, and weekends were devoted to itinerant work in the villages. Though without formal Bible training, he communicated the gospel effectively to the Africans. Bible stories were told with the use of his own crude drawings that became so popular that he began mimeographing them for distribution. On one occasion when he entered an outlying village, he noticed a crowd gathered in the road, and to his surprise he discovered an illiterate Congolese soldier sharing the gospel, using a set of his picture stories.

Despite his effective evangelistic work, Becker, as were countless other medical missionaries before and after him, was consumed with meeting the physical needs of the people. "What is the spiritual value of all this?" he frequently asked himself. The question could only be answered through seeing the results of his work:

> In fact, far from imagining that medical work was only the soil-breaker for the seed—only the John the Baptist for the Messiah—he came to see it was a complete missionary ministry. It was an opportunity for mass evangelism, for where else could he find several hundred needy Africans each day, coming from distant places to one site where the gospel could be preached? It was also an opportunity for Christian nurture. With the inpatients he had a chance to help young Christians grow in their Christian life, to provide a sort of hothouse climate for young plants. And Dr. Becker felt, too, that it was an unparalleled opportunity to build a responsible African church.[16]

In many instances medical missions paved the way for evangelizing tribes that were otherwise very difficult to reach. Such was the case with the Pygmies of the Ituri forest. Long the brunt of discrimination by other Africans, the Pygmies withdrew into the jungle and shied away from all outsiders, but their need for medical services eventually overcame their extreme isolationism. They slowly developed a trust in the missionaries, and many were converted to Christianity. Likewise, medical missions played a crucial role in reaching lepers with the gospel. They too had been the brunt of discrimination, but the love and care they received from Becker and his staff gave them a renewed sense of worth.

The Pygmies' need for medical services eventually overcame their extreme isolationism. They slowly developed a trust in the missionaries.

Although he treated every disease and injury imaginable, the problem of leprosy concerned Becker the most, and he desperately sought to find a cure that would relieve the terrible suffering. Word of his compassion spread, and lepers by the thousands came to him for treatment. By the early 1950s he was treating some four thousand resident patients at his eleven-hundred-acre leprosy village, and the results were impressive—so much so that leprosy specialists from all over the world were visiting him and borrowing the notes on his research. Even Dr. Robert Cochrane from Cambridge, the world's leading authority on leprosy, was impressed with his findings.

During this time Becker, with the help of nurses, was performing upwards of four thousand major and minor operations and delivering some five hundred babies each year. He nevertheless found time to branch out into other areas, including psychiatry, and he eagerly experimented with the most up-to-date treatments. Among his patients were some severely disturbed individuals who were viewed by their families as demon possessed. He established a mental ward and a psychiatric clinic, and he was the first doctor in equatorial Africa to use electric shock treatment—though he "remained convinced that simple Christianity was the soundest general therapy for the mentally upset, that 'the Gospel of love and hope alone can banish superstition and fear.'"[17]

BANGLADESH

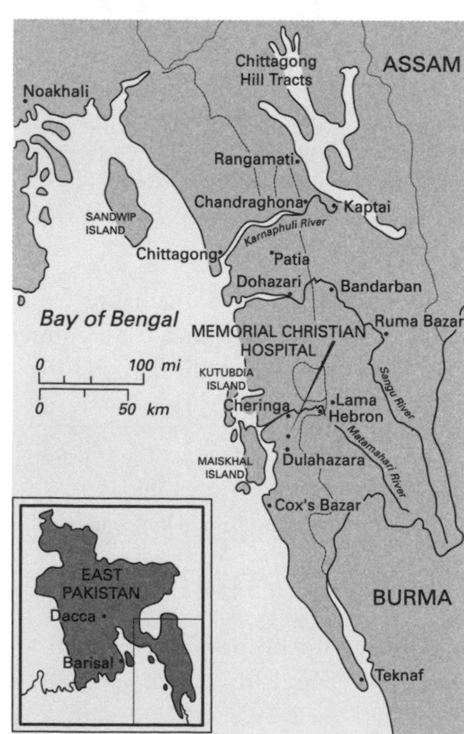

In spite of his selfless service in behalf of the people of the Congo, Becker did not remain immune to the violence that broke out in the 1960s. While most missionaries fled to East Africa for safety, he stayed on at Oicha until the summer of 1964, when it was learned that he had been targeted by the Simbas to face a firing squad. At the age of seventy, he bade farewell to his beloved African associates and, with his wife, three nurses, and a young associate, barely escaped the Simba guerrillas.

Considering his age, the evacuation in 1964 would have been an opportune time to begin retirement. But for the Beckers, Africa was home. In the words of his biographer, he was "allergic to furloughs," and he had no desire to return to the United States. Although he recognized that he was slowing down, he wanted to remain in Africa as long as he could be of useful service. So after a year in the relative security of East Africa, the Beckers were back in Oicha to rebuild what the guerrillas had destroyed.

Becker was eighty-three before he agreed to return to the United States and retire. Art Buchwald, the well-known American newspaper columnist, wrote of him: "In all of Congo, the man who made the greatest impression on us was an American missionary doctor named Carl K. Becker. . . . We couldn't help thinking as we left Oicha that America had its own Dr. Schweitzer in Congo."[18] But the greatest tribute ever paid Becker may have been made by an African medical trainee: "Many missionaries had preached Jesus Christ to me, but in the *munganga* [doctor] I have seen Jesus Christ."[19]

William Cameron Townsend and Bible Translation

Bible translation, like medicine, can be viewed properly as a twentieth-century missions specialty, but virtually all pioneer Protestant missionaries were Bible translators—even as they were amateur medical specialists. William Carey is remembered as one of the first and most prolific of these missionary translators, but more than a century earlier the dedicated and energetic John Eliot translated the Scriptures for the Algonquin Indians of Massachusetts. It was Carey who made Bible translation an accepted, integral part of missionary work. Other well-known Bible translators included Robert Morrison, Adoniram Judson, Ann Judson, Robert Moffat, and Henry Martyn.

Not until the twentieth century, however, did Bible translation take on a new image. This came about with the introduction of the science of linguistics—and the tireless efforts of W. Cameron Townsend and his twin organizations, Summer Institute of Linguistics and Wycliffe Bible Translators, which became the largest independent mission agency in the world. Summer Institute of Linguistics (SIL) was founded in an Ozark farmhouse in 1934 as Camp Wycliffe by Townsend and L. L. Legters, both of whom were concerned about linguistics training for prospective Bible translators. But as important as SIL was to the work of Bible translation, it soon became evident that with its secular nature, it was not suitable as a mission support organization. Thus, in 1942 Wycliffe Bible Translators (WBT) was officially established for the purpose of receiving funds for the support of missionary translators and to publicize the ongoing field work. The twin organizations, though separate, had interlocking directorates and the same goals and philosophy, but different duties to perform.

Cam Townsend was born in California in 1896 during the difficult economic period following the Panic of 1893, and much of his early life was plagued by poverty. After high school he enrolled in Occidental College, a Presbyterian school in Los Angeles. During his second year there he joined the Student Volunteer Movement and was further challenged by missions when John R. Mott came to the campus to speak. Then, during his junior year, the Bible House of Los Angeles appealed for Bible salesmen for Latin America. Townsend volunteered and was assigned to Guatemala.

Accompanied by a college friend, he left for Guatemala in 1917. Selling Bibles in Central America seemed like a worthwhile ministry, but he soon discovered that most of the Cakchiquel Indians could not read Spanish and that their own language was yet unwritten. Some people seemed offended by his preoccupation with selling Spanish Bibles. "Why, if your God is so smart," asked an Indian one day, "hasn't he learned our language?"[20]

> *"Why, if your God is so smart," asked an Indian one day, "hasn't he learned our language?" The question changed Townsend's life.*

Townsend was taken aback by the blunt question—a question that changed his life. He dedicated the next thirteen years to learning their language, reducing it to writing, and translating the Scriptures. Without prior linguistic training, he faced tremendous obstacles. The language, for example, had four different "k" sounds that to him were barely distinguishable, and the verb forms were mind-boggling. One verb could be conjugated into thousands of forms, indicating time, location, and many other ideas besides simple action. It all seemed like an impossible task until he met an American archaeologist who advised him to quit trying to force the Cakchiquel language "into a Latin mold," and instead seek to find the logical pattern on which the language is based. That advice changed the course of his language study, and it led eventually to his forming a linguistics training program.

From the very beginning of his ministry, Townsend's strong will and independence often clashed with the more conservative views of those around him. When his work as a Bible salesman ended, he joined the Central American Mission, only to realize that evangelism, not translation work, was what the mission expected of him—a factor that created strained relations. During this time, he married Elvira Malmstrom, who was also serving as a missionary in Guatemala, and her physical and emotional difficulties added to the strain with the mission—and to the marriage. Though she had at one point insisted that there was no problem "with my mind"—that rather "my problem pure and simple has been selfishness," Townsend blamed her problem on "extreme nervousness," during which time "she loses control of herself and says and does things painful to me and hurtful to our work."

Whatever the cause, the mission board had censured her because her "condition is still causing considerable embarrassment to the work," adding that "there is a difference of opinion as to the extent to which you are responsible for your actions."[21] Despite the problems, Elvira continued on in the work until her untimely death in 1944.

After ten years of translation work, the Cakchiquel New Testament was finished, and Townsend was eager to translate the Scripture for other tribes. But the mission wanted him to remain with the Cakchiquels. Because of these and other philosophical differences, he eventually resigned. Working under the authority of others was difficult for him, and he had insisted that administrators from the home office should not be making decisions of strategy for missionaries on the field. In 1934, with L. L. Legters, he founded Camp Wycliffe in Arkansas—a disorganized and unimposing venture that grew into the world's largest independent Protestant mission organization.

Over the years, Townsend was embroiled in numerous controversies. The most often-repeated criticism was that he was attempting to gain an entrance in foreign countries under a false pretense, while at the same time being less than honest with supporters at home. To government officials, critics charged, the linguists claimed to be merely language specialists and literacy teachers, when in fact they were missionary Bible translators. To their mission supporters, their identity was reversed. So heated was the controversy that one veteran missionary returned from Central America to warn churches about the "dishonesty" and "fakery" of Townsend.[22]

Good relations with foreign governments was a top priority, but again critics cried foul—particularly when Townsend was perceived as serving the agenda of socialist regimes. He was also perceived as being too friendly with Roman Catholics. In Latin America the hostilities ran deep between Catholics and Protestants. The vast majority of evangelical missionaries believed that there should be no cooperation with Catholics, but Townsend was more tolerant. "It's possible to know Christ as Lord and Savior," he wrote, "and to continue in the Roman Church."[23] The test came when Paul Witte, a Catholic scholar, applied to become a translator under Wycliffe. Townsend sent a letter of support to the entire Wycliffe membership: "We must not depart from our nonsectarian policy one iota if we are to keep entering countries closed to traditional missionary organizations."[24] But despite his plea, Witte was denied membership by a two-thirds majority of the WBT voting delegates.

Roman Catholics were not the only unacceptable candidates for Wycliffe membership. In 1949, with the application of Jim and Anita Price, the issue of accepting Pentecostals flared into a heated floor debate. Most of the members, while not denying the sincere Christian faith of Pentecostal believers, felt that they would be incompatible with the non-charismatic evangelicals that filled the ranks of the organization. Again Townsend upheld the nonsectarian policy of Wycliffe, asserting that the theological issues involved were "nonessentials" and threatening to resign his position as general director if the Prices were rejected. This time he won the battle.

His tolerance also extended to race. During a time when many evangelicals were still defending segregationist policies, he appealed to blacks and other ethnic minorities to become involved in Bible translation work. He deplored race prejudice, and in a letter to the board in 1952 he wrote, "Our constitution has nothing that savors of discrimination. You won't find it in the New Testament either. Please send along all the non-Caucasian workers you can, if they make out good in courses."[25]

His call for equal opportunities for women was another issue that aroused controversy among members and supporters. Allowing single women to work with married couples was an accepted fact in mission circles, but permitting them to go in pairs into remote tribal areas was quite another issue. He himself expressed doubts when single women first requested tribal work, but he quickly agreed that there would be no restrictions on their service. Despite loud objections from protectors of the "weaker sex," by the 1950s there were several pairs of single women translators in Peru alone, among them Loretta Anderson and Doris Cox, who served as his prime example in defense of women translators.

They initiated their work in 1950 among the Shapras, one of the most feared headhunting tribes of the Peruvian jungle, led by the infamous Chief Tariri, who had won his position by killing his predecessor. Though "scared most of the time during the first five months," they were committed to "the agonizingly slow job of learning the language."[26] Soon Chief Tariri began helping them as a language informant, and a few years later he turned away from witchcraft and murder and became a Christian as did many in his tribe. Years later he confessed to Townsend, "If you had sent men, we would have killed them on sight. Or if a couple, I'd have killed the man and taken the woman for myself. But what could a great chief do with two harmless girls who insisted on calling him brother?"[27]

William Cameron ("Uncle Cam") Townsend, founder of Wycliffe Bible Translators and the Summer Institute of Linguistics.

Unlike some mission founders and leaders, Townsend avoided authoritarian leadership. When SIL was first organized, he proposed that he be under the executive committee and ultimately under the vote of the membership. This, according to James and Marti Hefley, "was something new in the history of missions—a founder-director telling a crew of young green members, some unhappy with past decisions, to take charge. But he believed it was dangerous for one individual to have control. It meant he would have to use persuasion and charisma in attempting to put across his policies."[28] Because of this self-imposed policy, he was frequently stymied in carrying out his innovative plans. After one heated debate between him and his executive committee, one of the committee members commented, "Uncle Cam is probably right. He may be ten years ahead of the rest of us as usual."[29]

Following the death of his first wife, he married Elaine Mielke, a former supervisor of special education in Chicago. The Townsends served for seventeen years in Peru, during which time their four children were born. They then moved on to conduct translation work in Colombia. Though he would become recognized the world over as a great missionary statesman, Townsend always thought of himself first and foremost as a Bible translator—with one more language to go.

After fifty years of ministry, rather than contemplating retirement, he was preparing to go to the Soviet Union with Elaine. Having learned that there were some one hundred languages spoken in the Caucasus, many of which had no Bible translation, he was determined to become involved at the grassroots level once again. So at the age of seventy-two, with Elaine at his side, he found himself in a hotel overlooking Red Square in Moscow, studying Russian several hours a day. After their initial period of study was completed, they traveled into the Caucasus to confer with linguists and educators.

Throughout his life one single philosophy motivated him more than any other: his high view of the Bible. "The greatest missionary is the Bible in the mother tongue," he was fond of repeating. "It never needs a furlough, is never considered a foreigner."[30] But among the greatest missionaries of the twentieth century was Cam Townsend—a missionary who ranks alongside William Carey and Hudson Taylor in the nineteenth century. When he died in April of 1982, Bernie May emotionally spoke for the entire organization:

> When the word came that Uncle Cam was gone, I had the feeling I've had on several occasions when flying a twin-engine airplane and one engine suddenly goes dead. All at once your goal becomes very important. You instantly turn to your guidance system. You keep on flying, but with a new intensity of reaching your destination as quickly as possible.... There are still 3,000 languages without the Bible.... This is our challenge. This is our call.[31]

During his lifetime and following his death, many of Townsend's protégés effectively carried on the work. One of those was Kenneth Pike, who served for many years as director and president of SIL. Recognized the world over for his contributions to linguistics, he was the author of numerous scholarly works and was a professor at the University of Michigan. But he was also a missionary Bible translator in Mexico and other underdeveloped areas of the world where the Bible was unavailable in the native tongue. He felt as comfortable talking with an illiterate Mixtec Indian as he did with a distinguished French university professor; and with all his contributions to linguistic science, he remained first and foremost a missionary, eager to share the gospel with those who had never heard.

After graduating from Gordon College, Pike applied to the China Inland Mission but was rejected for missionary service due to his nervous disposition and his language difficulty. He then applied to other missions, but the only one to accept him was Wycliffe Bible Translators. When he arrived for training in 1935, Legters reportedly lamented, "Lord, couldn't you have sent us something better than this?"[32]

In addition to translating the New Testament into the San Miguel Mixtec language, Pike helped other translators solve difficult linguistic problems, and every summer he taught at SIL. Making courses practical was always a top priority, and sometimes his lectures were as entertaining as they were scholarly. Even more entertaining than his lectures, however, were his language demonstrations that were often given to large public audiences—demonstrations showing how quickly an unknown language could be learned without an interpreter. On stage with Pike, along with several blackboards and a few props (sticks, leaves, and simple objects of various sizes), would be a stranger whom Pike had never met and whose language he did not know. Before the session was over, however, the two would be communicating amazingly well with each other.[33]

Kenneth and Evelyn Pike

Few linguists in history have received more honors and awards than did Dr. Kenneth Pike. With his first book, *Phonetics*, he "revolutionized the thinking of the field," according to Professor Eric Hamp of the University of Chicago. And that was only the beginning, continues Hamp:

> It is fair to say that something like one-half of all the raw data from exotic languages that has been placed at the disposal of theoretical linguists in the past quarter century can be attributed to the teaching, influence, and efforts of Kenneth Pike.... The boyish enthusiasm of Pike in all his studies and his modesty in attacking every fresh problem would scarcely suggest to the unprepared onlooker that he is in the presence of one of the few really great linguists of the 20th century.[34]

Clarence W. Jones and HCJB

At the beginning, missionary radio was not seen as a tool to be used independently of traditional missionary outreach. But though some missionaries were skeptical at first, they soon realized the value of having radio pave the way for them. "It has given traditional missionary effort a tremendous weapon and means to spread the gospel," according to Abe Van Der Puy of World Radio Missionary Fellowship. "Until recently, in many parts of Latin America, missionaries had a very difficult time getting people to talk with them about the gospel. These people, however, have been willing to listen in the privacy of their own homes. . . . Many times when personal workers are dealing with individuals about the gospel, the person being dealt with will say, 'Oh, that means you are like those of HCJB.'" In recent decades, with the increasing size of transmitters and the greater affordability of transistor radios, Christian broadcasts are reaching more people than ever. According to Barry Siedell, "There is virtually no square foot on earth that isn't reached sometime during the day by a gospel radio broadcast."[35]

Like other specialized areas of missions, missionary radio had to fight its way into acceptance with the Christian public. Clarence W. Jones was a pioneer in this field who was not afraid to use the "tool of the devil." People from his home church termed it "Jones's folly." Only a fool would go off to a foreign land to set up a radio station when there were only six receiving sets in the whole country. But Jones was convinced that missions had to be in the forefront of the field of communications if the world was to be evangelized.

Born in 1900 in Illinois, the son of Salvation Army officers, Jones played the trombone in the Salvation Army band from the age of twelve. In 1921 he graduated from Moody Bible Institute as class president and valedictorian, even though he had only completed two years of high school. During the years following his graduation, he worked with Paul Rader in his tent-meeting evangelism and later in his evangelistic ministry at the Chicago Gospel Tabernacle. Among other things, Jones played his trombone in a brass quartet and became program director for the Tabernacle's radio broadcasting that began with the start of Chicago's first commercial radio station.

In 1928, despite the skepticism of his friends and associates, Jones made an exploratory trip to South America, hoping to find an opening in Venezuela for radio ministry. As he traveled through the villages and towns, he was overwhelmed with the need for evangelism, as his diary indicates:

> How endless the task of missions seems here in Venezuela at our present slow rate of response! This country is only a small portion of a whole great continent, with many places having no witness for missions. Missionary work could be supplemented and speeded up by the perfectly possible procedure of regular

> Spanish radio broadcasts. I am more and more impressed with the opportunity for evangelism in all Venezuela, and am spending much time in prayer these days, asking the Lord to do *the great and mighty things*.[36]

But instead of "great and mighty things," the Venezuelan government officials refused his request. Before returning home, he visited Columbia, Panama, and Cuba with similar requests, but the answer was the same. Back home, he was frustrated and embarrassed. All the time and money that had been invested in his exploratory trip had come to nothing. Even his wife was discouraged: "Her initial reckless zeal had worn off, and with two little ones to care for, she just did not want to go to 'the foreign field.' Not at all."[37] For Jones it was a depressing period in his life:

> Then there was the day of such discouragement that Clarence, desperately needing some money for his family, unable to shake off the feelings of total inadequacy and failure, and chagrined that this obsession with South America had made him look like a fool, decided to chuck it all—his work at the Tabernacle, his call to the mission field, his family—and went down to enlist in the Navy. He was rejected for lack of 20/20 vision.[38]

Jones's dream of missionary radio might have faded away had it not been for a devoted couple that entered his life in the months that followed. Reuben and Grace Larson had been serving in Ecuador under the Christian and Missionary Alliance since 1924, and during their furlough in 1930 they visited the Chicago Gospel Tabernacle to present their work. To the Larsons, Jones's trip to South America was not a fiasco; he had simply gone to the wrong countries. He had bypassed the beautiful land of Ecuador, not even seeking entrance until after he had met the Larsons, two individuals who would provide the key to missionary radio in South America.

Although Ecuadorian officials were at first skeptical about a Protestant radio station, Larson was persistent; and on August 15, 1930, he sent a cable to Jones, urging him to come as soon as possible, informing him that a twenty-five-year contract had been granted. "Clearly we saw the hand of God moving on the whole Congress of Ecuador," he wrote, "causing them to allow, in this closed Catholic country, a ministry of gospel radio."[39] Jones, however, had not waited for Larson's cable. So anxious was he to begin his work that he was already on his way to South America when the cable arrived.

The weeks following Jones's arrival in Ecuador were discouraging ones. Hardly had the ink on their permit dried when the missionaries were told by engineers as well as by American State Department officials that Ecuador—particularly Quito—would never be suitable for radio transmission. The mountains and the close proximity to the equator would be insurmountable obstacles. But "unreasonable, illogical though it seemed," in the words of Lois Neely, "Clarence was absolutely certain that Quito was God's place for his voice to South America."[40] So he went ahead with plans, and in the year that followed, despite more disappointments, Radio Station HCJB (Heralding Christ Jesus' Blessings) became a reality.

It was a historic day. The world's first missionary radio program was broadcast live on Christmas Day 1931, coming from a 250-watt transmitter located in a sheep shed in Quito, Ecuador. With organ music in the background, Jones played his trombone and Larson preached in Spanish. All thirteen receiving sets in the country were tuned in, and the Voice of the Andes was on the air.

In the months that followed, the World Radio Missionary Fellowship was officially incorporated, and the daily broadcasts continued, though not without periods of crisis. As the Depression deepened back in the United States, contributions fell off. During the entire year of 1932 less than one thousand dollars was donated to the new mission. In 1933 the bank through which Jones and his associates had been receiving their monthly checks folded, and later the Chicago Gospel Tabernacle, the mainstay of the mission's support, went bankrupt. The future of the fledgling radio station was in serious doubt. On his knees in a little tool shed, Jones pleaded with God for one whole day for direction: "Are we to carry on with HCJB, or pack it in and go home?"[41]

That day was a "low spot" in Jones's life, but he left the tool shed with the assurance that God would see him through the crisis, and that night there was a buoyant enthusiasm in his voice as he went on the air with the evening broadcast. Within days, through a financial loan from a friend and a mortgage on the transmitter, the immediate crisis was averted, and HCJB slowly climbed out of its economic peril.

One of the reasons for HCJB's survival was the growing recognition it received from the government and the people of Ecuador. From the very beginning, Larson and Jones had cooperated fully with government officials, agreeing to make their programming not only religious but educational and cultural as well. When gospel programs were aired, they were always presented in a positive vein to avoid antagonizing the Roman Catholic Church. Patriotism was a key element of their philosophy; the president of Ecuador had an open invitation to use the broadcasting facilities and often did so, especially on holidays.

One of the reasons for HCJB's survival was the growing recognition it received from the government and the people of Ecuador.

As word of the radio station spread, the number of receivers in Ecuador grew rapidly, and HCJB, according to Neely, "was cutting across every level of society, breaking down barriers to the gospel. Missionaries (many whom had in fact strongly opposed the idea of Christian radio) were finding that where previously they were persecuted and stoned on the streets, now they could minister openly. And even when they encountered a 'Protestants Not Welcome' sign on a door, inside they could hear *La Voz de los Andes,* HCJB. Everyone seemed to be listening."[42]

The decade of the thirties was one of tremendous growth for HCJB. The first major power addition was a thousand-watt transmitter that reached far beyond the borders of Ecuador; and before the decade closed, a ten-thousand-watt transmitter was installed. On Easter Sunday 1940, President Andres Cordova of Ecuador threw the switch to begin broadcasting over the new transmitter that would carry the gospel farther than ever before. How far was anybody's guess, but even the most optimistic observers were surprised when letters began pouring in from New Zealand, Japan, India, Germany, and Russia. That a mere ten thousand watts would broadcast over such great distances was due to the location. Though Jones had been advised against locating near the equator, it was later determined to be the finest location for north-south broadcasting because the equal distance from magnetic poles makes it "the one place in the world freest from atmospheric disturbance."[43] The high elevation in the mountains near Quito was an added benefit. The hundred-foot tower perched on a 9,600-foot mountain was almost equivalent to a ten-thousand-foot antenna.

As the size of HCJB grew, so did its reputation for quality programming. Jones was a perfectionist who demanded excellence in every area of broadcasting, and some considered him "tyrannical." Even his children feared his authoritarian control and were occasionally pulled from the program when their playing did not meet expectations.

Throughout the 1950s and 1960s HCJB continued to grow, increasing its power to more than a half million watts. But the good times were accompanied by personal traumas for Jones and his family. In 1953 a head-on collision left Katherine in a coma and Clarence with such severe facial injuries that it was doubted whether he would every play his trombone again. Their recovery was slow, but by the end of the year both had returned to the ministry. Then in 1966, in another automobile accident, their only son, Dick, who with his wife and children was serving as a missionary in Panama, was killed. In both instances, Jones went back to the work with even greater zeal for radio evangelism.

In 1981, with Jones living in retirement in Florida, HCJB celebrated its fiftieth anniversary. But in the half-century since its founding, the World Radio Missionary Fellowship had become far more than a mere radio station. Its ministry included two hospitals, mobile clinics, a printing press, and television programs—all in addition to its 24-hours-a-day radio station in Quito (broadcasting in fifteen languages) and two sister stations in Panama and Texas.

In the decades following the founding of HCJB, there were other ventures in missionary radio, including the Far East Broadcasting Company, founded by John Broger, a young military officer who fought in the Pacific in World War II. He returned from the war with a desire to reach Asia with the gospel, and missionary radio was his vision. With two friends, Robert Bowman and William

Roberts, and a combined total of one thousand dollars, they formed a nonprofit corporation and filed the necessary papers. All that remained was to raise one hundred thousand dollars. During the first three months of publicizing their venture, some ten thousand dollars was donated, and with that encouraging beginning, it was decided that Broger should return to the Far East to lay the groundwork for their proposed ministry. Despite setbacks, construction for FEBC in Manila began in the late fall of 1946. Programming began with the hymn "All Hail the Power of Jesus' Name" as "the first of the Far East Broadcasting Company's transmitters hummed with power . . . at 6:00 P.M., June 4, 1948, releasing the words of this majestic hymn to the waiting airways of the Orient."[44]

After fourteen years of service, John Broger returned to military service and Robert Bowman became the president. By 1970 FEBC had twenty-one stations ranging from a thousand to 250,000 watts, broadcasting nearly fourteen hundred program hours each week in more than forty languages. After 1979, when China relaxed its barriers with the West, more than ten thousand letters came in during one twelve-month period from China alone—primarily from people interested in learning more about the gospel message.

TRANSMITTING TOWERS OF TRANS WORLD RADIO

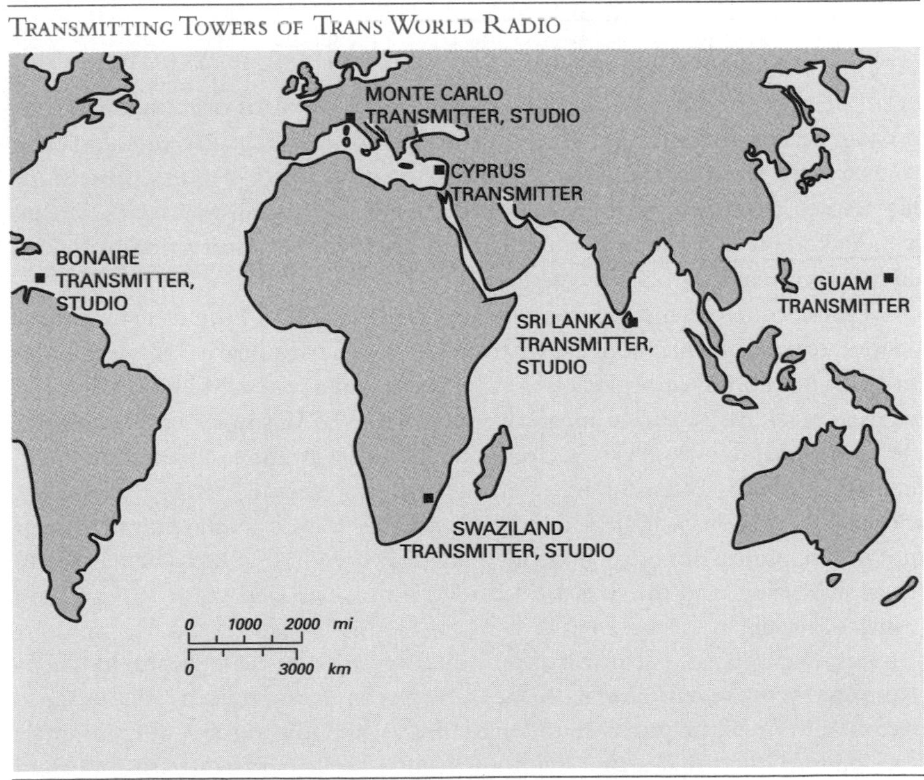

Of all the missionary broadcasting organizations, the largest and most geographically diverse is Trans World Radio. Founded in 1954, TWR grew to more than five million watts of power capable of reaching eighty percent of the world's population. From towers in Monte Carlo, Bonaire, Swaziland, Cyprus, Sri Lanka, and Guam, its giant transmitters beamed out Christian programs in more than eighty different languages and dialects.

As was true with HCJB and FEBC, Trans World Radio would never have been born, but for the vision of one man, Paul Freed—and his father. Having grown up in the Middle East, the son of missionaries, Freed sold his home and car to launch TWR. With that matter settled, he needed to secure a station director—"the best possible man." Who else but his own father, a veteran missionary teaching at Western Canadian Bible Institute? But when he phoned, he learned that just three days earlier his father had accepted the presidency of the school. Paul was devastated. "I did not know what to say. I could not offer him anything that remotely resembled the financial security or prestige of this fine school."[45] Nevertheless, a few days later his father called back accepting the challenge. In the years that followed, despite massive financial and governmental obstacles, Paul Freed's vision became a worldwide ministry—a ministry that stands as a monument to personal sacrifice and strong faith.

Elizabeth "Betty" Greene and Mission Aviation

Seventeen days in a dugout canoe, besieged by swarms of mosquitoes, traversing steamy jungle-lined rivers infested by poisonous snakes and alligators. Such was the travel of the jungle missionary—a twentieth-century professionally trained evangelist, severely impeded by outmoded transportation. It is no wonder that the introduction of aircraft to supplement missionary work was considered a godsend to those whose lives it changed.

This need led to the founding in California in 1945 of the first missionary aviation service organization, the Christian Airmen's Missionary Fellowship, later renamed Mission Aviation Fellowship. As important a role as MAF has played in overseas missions, it became apparent early on that MAF simply could not meet the high demand for its services. Consequently, other aviation organizations were formed, the largest and most geographically dispersed being JAARS (Jungle Aviation and Radio Service), an arm of Wycliffe Bible Translators and Summer Institute of Linguistics. But other missions, including New Tribes Mission, the Sudan Interior Mission, and the Africa Inland Mission, developed their own aviation services as well.

It is no exaggeration to say that missionary aviation has revolutionized Christian missions in the past several decades. The weeks and months of arduous travel became a thing of the past, and no longer do isolated missionaries in remote villages endure months at a time without needed health services, fresh food, and mail deliveries. Today a single MAF pilot covers as much territory in a matter of weeks as David Livingstone covered in a lifetime of African exploration and with much less strain on health and family relationships.

It is ironic that the founding of one of the most male-oriented and male-dominated mission agencies was strongly influenced by a woman. Though Betty Greene denies that she was the founder of Mission Aviation Fellowship, she was the first full-time staff worker and the first pilot to fly for the newly formed organization. She had served in the U.S. Air Force during the early months of World War II, flying radar missions, and later was assigned to developmental projects that included flying B-17 bombers in high-altitude equipment tests. But military service was not Greene's career objective. Her vision was mission aviation, and before the war was over, she began laying the groundwork for her life ministry as a missionary pilot.

Though Betty Greene denies that she was the founder of Mission Aviation Fellowship, she was the first full-time staff worker and the first pilot to fly for the newly formed organization.

Her interest in flying began as a young girl, and at the age of sixteen she began taking flight lessons. During her college years at the University of Washington, she enrolled in a government civil pilot training program in preparation for her dream of one day flying as a missionary. But when World War II intervened, she enlisted in the WASP (Women's Air Force Service Pilots) in a spirit of patriotism and also to acquire the training and experience she would later need in mission service. During the war years she published an article in *HIS* magazine about the need for missionary aviation. The article was spotted by Jim Truxton, a navy pilot. He contacted her, asking her to join him and two fellow pilots in forming an organization for missionary aviation.

With her term of service with WASP over, Greene moved to Los Angeles, where she set up headquarters for the newly formed Christian Airmen's Missionary Fellowship (later MAF). Soon after, in 1945, an urgent request came for assistance, and Greene was the only one available to go: "We were asked by Wycliffe Bible Translators to help them in Mexico with their jungle camp program," she later recalled. "I went down in 1945 to see what the situation looked like. We bought an airplane in early 1946, paid in part by the savings of one of the MAF men in the military. It was a Waco cabin plane with a 229-horsepower engine. I flew the plane down to Mexico in February of 1946—the men were still tied up with Uncle Sam."[46]

After several months of service in Mexico, Cam Townsend, founder of Wycliffe, asked Greene to help out in Peru. She agreed to go, and George Wiggins, a navy pilot, was sent to replace her. Then came the first real blow to the fledgling MAF. When Greene was "checking out" Wiggins for his new assignment, they crash-landed after clipping a small building near the runway. Neither one was hurt, but the plane was so damaged that Nate Saint, a skilled mechanic, was called down from the States to fix it. Greene went ahead with her plans to serve in Peru, where she flew a war surplus Grumman Duck amphibian biplane that Wycliffe had acquired. Her assignment involved flying missionaries and supplies into the interior, each time crossing the towering peaks of the Andes, winning the distinction of being the first woman pilot to do so.

After a year in Peru, she returned to the United States, where she again worked in the MAF home office. Her next overseas assignment was in Nigeria, where she flew support missions over varied terrain from the dense Nigerian jungle to the vast Sahara Desert. Then it was back home for another stint in Los Angeles, where she involved herself in much-needed public relations work in an effort to shore up the home base. After three years, she went to East Africa to serve as a pilot for the Sudan Interior Mission.

In 1960, after another stint in the home office, she went to Irian Jaya. To receive flight service, each mission outpost had to build its own airstrip, and before landings could be made, a qualified pilot had to make the overland trip to check it out. Most of her previous work had been in the air, and she soon realized that she was no match for her robust female companion, Leona St. John, or the carriers who were used to the daily tropical rainstorms, the frayed vine bridges, and the slippery mud embankments. "I didn't know how hard it would be," she recalls. "I suppose the carriers were perfectly aware of the trail, but for most of the way I wasn't even sure there was one. The place we were going was supposed to be thirty miles away, but I think the map meant horizontal miles, and most of ours were straight up and down."[47] The physical discomfort was quickly forgotten when the party realized that it had inadvertently come upon a tribal war—a terrifying scene of death and carnage that the two missionaries and their carriers watched in horror.

All the misery she had endured on the arduous trek was worth it when they were greeted by the villagers and the resident missionary couple with a tumultuous celebration. The airstrip was deemed suitable for landings and takeoffs. The next day a coworker flew in with much-needed supplies, and Greene flew out with him for her next assignment.

Following her nearly two years in Irian Jaya, she retired from active flying duty and returned to headquarters to represent the mission and recruit more pilots—male pilots in particular. Despite her own success as a pilot, she never sought to interest other women in the field. In fact, she argued against female missionary pilots. When asked during an interview in 1967 if she would encourage girls to go into this sort of work, she answered: "MAF definitely frowns upon it, and so do I. . . . We have three reasons why we do not accept women for this work: (1) Most women are not trained in mechanics. (2) Much of the work connected with missionary aviation is heavy work. There is bulky cargo to load, in some cases impossible for a woman to handle. (3) The other is flexibility. For instance, if there is a place where it is necessary to base a pilot alone for a few days or weeks, you can't do this with a woman."[48]

Despite MAF's past policy, women nevertheless continued to enter the field of missionary aviation and to serve with distinction. Even Greene, with her indisputable qualifications and experience, was written off as a "woman driver" in the mind of Nate Saint before he discovered firsthand that she was "a pilot of such caliber that local airline and military pilots regarded her with great respect."[49] Her acceptance by her male counterparts in those early years no doubt had a lot to do with the fact that she willingly accepted their view that missionary aviation was a man's world and that she was an isolated exception to the rule.

Perhaps the best known missionary pilot has been Nate Saint, whose role in the Auca tragedy made him a household name in evangelical circles. Unlike Greene, he was a pilot-*mechanic*, and as such, he was well suited for mission aviation. But Saint was also a risk-taker—a "dare-devil" in the minds of some. Not long after he became involved with MAF, he had a serious crash in Ecuador that left him in a full-body cast. The accident was "not a matter of inadequate equipment but the pilot's inexperience." He offered his resignation, but MAF was determined rather to focus on better training of pilots.[50]

Nate Saint, missionary pilot to Ecuador, martyred by the Aucas in 1956.

Although Saint had initially scorned the idea of becoming a "grease monkey for the Lord," he became a very innovative pilot-mechanic. He developed, for cxample, a technique of dropping large quantities of canned goods and other supplies by a parachute device. "Immodest of me to say so," he wrote, "but I get a big bang out of these 'bombing runs.' I enjoy my work to the full."[51] A far more difficult item to transport by plane was aluminum sheeting for roofs. But he was not deterred by the size or bulkiness of an item, so he improvised a harness sling and began transporting seven-foot lengths of aluminum to the grateful missionaries. When word of his rash experiments reached the "slide-ruling brethren," there was anxious concern and an immediate rebuke. He responded by assuring the directors, conceding his poor judgment and adding: "I must admit I am completely defenseless."[52]

It was a combination of Saint's impulsiveness and his evangelistic zeal that so suddenly ended the life of this brilliant and dedicated young pilot in January of 1956, when he and his colleagues were slain by the Aucas. It was through his own ingenious bucket drop that the Aucas were thought to be friendly, and through his exceptional skill as a pilot that the men were landed safely in Auca territory. But skill and technique were not enough, and missionary aviation lost one of its finest pilot-mechanic-inventors on that fateful day. His contribution to missionary aviation did not end with his death, however, for his testimony lived on and others dedicated their lives as missionary pilots as a result of hearing his story.

Saint's contribution to missionary aviation did not end with his death, because others dedicated their lives as missionary pilots as a result of hearing his story.

If the airplane was a godsend to missionaries in jungle regions, it was perhaps even more so in Arctic regions, where nomadic bands roamed the vast ice-covered wasteland and where weather conditions prevented extensive travel by other means. The sparse population and the scattered missionaries in the Arctic regions did not generally make missionary aviation support services practicable, so missionaries in that area of the world frequently became their own pilots. One such pilot-evangelist was Gleason Ledyard, the chairman-director of the Eskimo Gospel Crusade, who began his ministry in the Hudson Bay region in 1946.

Missionary aviation work in the Arctic was in many ways more strenuous than in the jungle. The long flying distances with few landmarks, combined with unpredictable, rough weather made every flight a calculated risk. Emergency landings due to ice on the plane were common occurrences that meant building an igloo miles from nowhere and waiting out the storm. With temperatures reaching forty and fifty degrees below zero, the engine had to be kept warm with blow pots, and sometimes there was a two- or three-day wait before the journey could be resumed. Because of the sub-zero temperatures, high-altitude flying was rare, and sometimes, to avoid sudden wind gusts and icing, the planes were flown as low as ten feet off the ground.

Despite harrowing ordeals, the rewards of reaching remote bands of Eskimos were worth the risks involved, as Gleason later related concerning one such experience:

> After the spring break-up season was over, and the lakes were free of ice, God gave me a most joyful experience—the joy of teaching a band of Eskimos, for the first time, the words of life.... Never before had I experienced such an eagerness to learn.... Every word uttered would be repeated after me. If something was not clear a pause would result. I would restate my thought. As soon as they got the meaning, they would repeat it in unison.[53]

He insisted that he was not "interested in taking anything of the Christian Church" to these remote people but only Christ, and it was this message and a man with an airplane that opened the door to the gospel among the remote peoples of the Arctic.[54]

Mission pilots, as did all missionaries, made many personal sacrifices for their profession. The Christmas story of Bernie May, a pilot for Wycliffe Bible Translators before he became the U.S. director, illustrates this. Three days before Christmas he had delivered emergency medical supplies to a remote village in the Amazon jungle. He had landed his pontoon plane safely on the river, and with the cargo unloaded, he set up a make-shift shelter for the night. But during the night it began raining, and the rain continued, leaving him in the jungle, wallowing in self-pity, as he later recalled:

> It was Christmas Eve and night was descending on the jungle. There was no way I could get back home. Back in Pennsylvania, my folks would have returned from church and Mother would be getting the turkey ready. Outside the snow would be falling. . . . In Yarinachcha, six hours away, Nancy and the boys would be sitting at home alone. They knew by now, because I had been able to radio back that I was stuck in the jungle. I would not be with them for Christmas.
>
> "Oh God," I moaned, "I'm in the wrong place." . . . That night, under my mosquito net I had a visitation from God—something like those shepherds must have had on the hills of Bethlehem. There were no angels, and no bright light. But as I lay there in my hammock, desperately homesick, I felt I heard God say: "My son, this is what Christmas is all about. Jesus left heaven and on Christmas morning He woke up in the 'wrong place'—a stable in Bethlehem. Christmas means leaving home, not going home. My only begotten Son did not come home for Christmas—He left his home to be with you."

SELECT BIBLIOGRAPHY

Buckingham, Jamie. *Into the Glory: The Miracle-Filled Story of the Jungle Aviation and Radio Service*. Plainfield, NJ: Logos, 1974.

Buss, Dietrich G., and Arthur F. Glasser. *Giving Wings to the Gospel: The Remarkable Story of Mission Aviation Fellowship*. Grand Rapids: Baker, 1995.

Cook, Frank S. *Seeds in the Wind: The Story of the Voice of the Andes, Radio Station HCJB, Quito, Ecuador*. Opa Locka, FL: World Radio Missionary Fellowship, 1976.

Cowan, George M. *The Word That Kindles: People and Principles That Fueled a Worldwide Bible Translation Movement*. Chappaqua, NY: Christian Herald, 1979.

Freed, Paul E. *Towers to Eternity*. Nashville: Sceptre, 1979.

Hefley, James C. *The Cross and the Scalpel*. Waco, TX: Word, 1971.

Hefley, James, and Marti Hefley. *Uncle Cam: The Story of William Cameron Townsend, Founder of the Wycliffe Bible Translators and the Summer Institute of Linguistics*. Waco, TX: Word, 1974.

Hitt, Russell T. *Jungle Pilot: The Life and Witness of Nate Saint*. Grand Rapids: Zondervan, 1973.

Kerr, J. Lennox. *Wilfred Grenfell: His Life and Work*. New York: Dodd, 1959.

Ledyard, Gleason H. *And to the Eskimos*. Chicago: Moody Press, 1958.

______. *Sky Waves: The Incredible Far East Broadcasting Company Story*. Chicago: Moody Press, 1968.

Neely, Lois. *Come Up to This Mountain: The Miracle of Clarence W. Jones and HCJB*. Wheaton, IL: Tyndale, 1980.

Olsen, Viggo, with Jeanette Lockerbie. *Daktar: Diplomat in Bangladesh*. Chicago: Moody Press, 1973.

Peterson, William J. *Another Hand on Mine: The Story of Dr. Carl K. Becker of Africa Inland Mission*. New York: McGraw-Hill, 1967.

Pike, Eunice V. *Ken Pike: Scholar and Christian*. Dallas: Summer Institute of Linguistics, 1981.

Roddy, Lee. *On Wings of Love: Stories from Mission Aviation Fellowship*. Nashville: Thomas Nelson, 1981.

Steven, Hugh. *Wycliffe in the Making: The Memoirs of W. Cameron Townsend, 1920–1933*. Wheaton, IL: Harold Shaw, 1995.

Wallis, Ethel E., and Mary A. Bennett. *Two Thousand Tongues to Go: The Story of the Wycliffe Bible Translators*. New York: Harper & Brothers, 1959.

Wilson, Dorothy Clarke. *Dr. Ida: The Story of Dr. Ida Scudder of Vellore*. New York: McGraw-Hill, 1959.

PART 4

The Era of the New Millennium

PART 4

THE ERA OF THE NEW MILLENNIUM

During the last decades of the twentieth century, there were tremendous changes occurring throughout the world. "The most obvious outward trait" of the period, writes Ralph Winter, "was the unprecedented 'Retreat of the West'"—a "collapse of four hundred years of European empire building in the non-Western world."[1] As the superpowers and their allies aligned against each other, the once politically insignificant countries of Africa, Asia, and South America became the much sought after "powers" of the Third World. Underdeveloped nations long ruled by colonial powers suddenly captured world attention—often through revolutionary movements or by blatant acts of aggression by petty dictators. Oil became the world's most coveted raw material as the demand for energy expanded, and the proliferation of nuclear weapons increased. By the 1990s, America alone held the designation *superpower* and was held in awe in many parts of the world—while at the same time deep hostilities and resentment boiled to the surface.

The turbulent changes that occurred in the Third World had a decisive impact on the foreign missionary movement—an impact that had been felt through the course of the twentieth century. By the 1960s, however, attacks against missionaries increased, particularly in the face of revolutionary movements. There were deaths among the members of almost every mission society active in troubled areas of the world, and there were calls for missionaries to go home. Many mainline denominations withdrew missionaries as their own numbers declined in their homeland. But with a new focus on unreached people groups and social outreach programs, interest increased among evangelicals and Catholics.

With increasing opposition to mission work in many areas of the world, there was a heightened sense of urgency and an expanding interest in mission strategy—particularly in relation to cultural anthropology, church growth case studies and statistics, mission partnership, and Muslim evangelism. The field of missiology that was in its infant stages at the beginning of the century had become a widely recognized discipline by the new millennium.

Perhaps the greatest change in mission outreach that occurred during the course of the twentieth century was the increasing involvement of non-western Christians. From the dawn of modern missions, nationals had played a significant role in evangelizing their own people, but as the twentieth century progressed they increasingly reached out cross-culturally. And, at the same time that missionaries were being threatened by acts of violence by their so-called enemies, they were confronting tense situations with their friends. Third World Christians were no longer willing—if, in fact, they had ever been—to submissively bow to the will of the Western missionaries. They demanded leadership positions and control of their own affairs that in some cases had long been denied them.

One of the factors that has aided national leadership and participation in church ministries has been expanded Christian education. The training of national pastors and evangelists was revolutionized during the last half of the twentieth century through the introduction of TEE (Theological Education by Extension). This program served many national Christians in remote areas—especially men with families who were unable to enroll in Bible schools or seminaries because of factors of cost and distance. By the middle of the 1970s, some fifty thousand men and women in more than seventy countries were receiving advanced Bible training through TEE.

Another important influence during this era was the Lausanne movement that began with the Lausanne Congress on World Evangelization in 1974, where one-third of the nearly twenty-five hundred delegates came from Third World churches, with one hundred and fifty countries represented. The movement sent a strong message that completing the Great Commission was not just the white man's burden. In a secondary sense, the movement provided an opportunity for delegates from the Third World to air their grievances. Among them was Dr. Rene Padilla, who charged "that the gospel some European and North American missionaries have exported was a 'culture-Christianity,' a Christian message . . . distorted by the materialistic, consumer culture of the West."[2]

The Lausanne Committee on World Evangelization, which grew out of the 1974 Congress, sponsored many regional congresses in the following years, all reflecting the large number of outstanding national leaders in all parts of the world. A second world level meeting in Pattaya, Thailand, in 1980 again involved a large number of church leaders from the non-Western world, but "the lack of women in positions of prominence," writes A. Scott Moreau, "was evident and a point of contention for some in attendance."[3]

The Lausanne movement sent a strong message that completing the Great Commission was not just the white man's burden.

The Lausanne movement also reflected a charismatic influence in the worldwide church. The fastest growing segment of the Christian church during the twentieth century was the Pentecostal and charismatic wing. During the decade of the 1960s the Assemblies of God and a number of other Pentecostal denominations and missions increased their missionary personnel by more than 50 percent. This mission expansion spurred growth worldwide. "The explosive growth of indigenous Pentecostal churches in Chile, Brazil and South Africa," writes Robert Clouse, "has caused some to predict that the future center of Christianity will be in the Southern Hemisphere among non-Caucasian Pentecostals."[4]

Other evangelical groups also witnessed significant growth. During the 1970s the conservative evangelical missionary force increased by almost 40 percent, encompassing a total of more than thirty-two thousand missionaries. "It is well known," writes Robert T. Coote, "that the North American conservative agencies, taken as a whole, have experienced dramatic growth since the late 1960s. By 1980 they accounted for ten out of eleven North American Protestant career missionaries working overseas."[5] In fact, by 1983 Wycliffe Bible Translators alone was sending out twice as many missionaries as the combined total of the member denominations in the National Council of Churches.

There is indeed reason for optimism in viewing the overall picture of worldwide missions. The Protestant missionary "movement still vibrates with life and action," wrote Herbert Kane in 1979. "Today there are more missionaries in more countries of the world than ever before in the history of the Christian church." But, as he pointed out, there were other reasons for optimism. "Never before have the non-Christian people of the world been so open.... Some countries are now difficult to enter because of visas, resident permits, and red tape, but once in, missionaries find the people more receptive than ever before."[6]

In 1982 there were more volunteers for missionary work among the Muslims than ever before, and during that same year some ten thousand students (many influenced by Inter-Varsity's triennial Urbana Conference) spent their summer vacation in short-term mission work. Some organizations such as Operation Mobilization, founded in 1958 and headed by George Verwer, and Youth with a Mission, specialize in sending young adults on short-term assignments involving literature distribution and evangelistic work.

As the number of short-term missionaries increased, so has the number of nonprofessional missionaries, or "tentmakers," as they have been termed. Tentmaking "is the wave of the future," writes Herbert Kane. "Today there are millions of Americans traveling and residing overseas. If all the dedicated Christians among them could be trained and persuaded to be effective witnesses for Jesus Christ, they would add a whole new dimension to the missionary movement. The spiritual potential here is enormous."[7] Nonprofessional tentmaker missionaries were being trained by such organizations as Campus Crusade for Christ and the Navigators, both of which have extensive overseas ministries. In the era of the new millennium the North American base for mission outreach was shifting to the non-Western world—though North America still retained a powerful financial advantage which was demonstrated by its continuing dominant role.

So, what is the future of Christian missions? Is the age of the traditional life-term missionary over? Will Third World missionaries, short-term evangelists, and nonprofessionals carry the burden of future missionary outreach? The last decades of the twentieth century were a time when large numbers of career North American missionaries were retiring, many of which were not replaced. The fastest growing mission agencies were based in the Two-Thirds world. But despite the new trends, the age of the pioneer missionary who spends a lifetime in cross-cultural evangelism and church planting is not over.

In its two-thousand-year history, mission work has changed dramatically. But in many ways it still remains the same. Christians whose lives have been transformed reach out to their neighbors and across the world. Like many in the earliest centuries, there are ones who give their lives for the cause, whether dying at the hands of enemy bullets, or at the end of a long life spent in reaching out to the poorest of the poor in Calcutta and around the world.

15

Twentieth-Century Martyrs: "Yankee, Go Home"

The twentieth century opened with the Boxer uprising in China that took the lives of more Protestant missionaries than any other such crisis in history—a crisis that in some ways was a preview of the rest of the century. As independence movements emerged in developing nations, foreigners were viewed as oppressors, with little differentiation made between diplomats or merchants or missionaries. All whites were suspected of being part of an imperialist conspiracy to exploit the weaker nations of the world.

Political turbulence, then, confronted missionaries more and more as the twentieth century progressed. No longer did the idea of martyrdom conjure up images of missionaries being eaten by cannibals, but rather images of missionaries facing hostile mobs, guerrilla warfare, and terrorist attacks. Asia, Africa, and Latin America were torn by militarist movements during the second half of the twentieth century, and missionaries and national Christians were sometimes slain in the process.

But that is not to say that much of the persecution and martyrdom of Christians in the twentieth century was not religiously oriented. Indeed, the century ended with the appalling murder and martyrdom of Graham Staines and his two sons, ten-year-old Phillip and six-year-old Timothy. Staines, a native of Australia, had gone to India in 1965, and was the director of the Leprosy Mission in Baripada, Orissa. Thirty-four years later, on the night of January 23, 1999, while ministering at a jungle outpost, he and his sons were burned alive while they slept in their jeep. Those responsible for the crime were seeking to eradicate Christianity from India.

As horrendous as such incidents have been, national Christians have paid an even higher price in their commitment to the gospel. During the Boxer Rebellion, hundreds of dedicated Chinese evangelists were martyred for their faith—

none more heroically than Chang Sen. Though blind, Chang had been one of the most effective itinerant evangelists Manchuria had ever known, but his success made him the brunt of severe persecution. At the height of the Boxer uprising, he was singled out for retribution. Fearing the worst, he hid in a cave, but when word reached him that fifty Christians would be killed if his whereabouts were not disclosed, he willingly came out of hiding, knowing full well the consequences. Even in death, however, he had a vibrant testimony—one that made his executioners so fearful that they insisted his body be cremated, fearing that he, like Christ, would rise from the dead.

World War II sparked many violent attacks against missionaries, including what became known as the Hopevale massacre of 1943 that cost the lives of a dozen American missionaries. Hopevale was the name given to the makeshift mountain camp in a deeply wooded area on the island of Panay in the Philippines where the missionaries had fled to safety. Among them were Dr. Frederick Meyer, a graduate of Yale Medical School, and Dr. Francis Howard Rose, a graduate of the University of Chicago—both beloved and respected doctors among the Filipinos. For more than a year they hid themselves at the camp, continuing all the while to minister physically and spiritually to the people in the nearby villages. Then, in December of 1943, they were discovered and executed by Japanese soldiers.

Following the war, except for the Soviet Union and Eastern Europe, there was a relative lull in religious persecution worldwide. But beginning in the 1960s with the outbreak of violent independence movements in several areas of the world, the persecution and martyrdom of Christians once again hit the front-page headlines.

Despite such threats, the church in these regions sometimes grows faster than in areas of the world that are free from persecution and violence. Centuries ago St. Augustine of Hippo singled out Christian martyrs for special praise—words that have provided comfort through the ages:

> Martyrs are holy men of God who fought or stood for truth, even unto death, so that the Word of God may be made known and falsehood and fictions be overcome. Such a sacrifice is offered to God alone, thus the martyr is received in heavenly honor. This means that God has rewarded the faith of the martyr with so much grace that death, which seems to be the enemy of life, becomes in reality an ally that helps man enter into life.[1]

It is misguided, however, to presume that persecution and martyrdom have a positive effect on the Christian community. "Many contemporary authors and church leaders continue to assume," writes Vernon Sterk, "that where there is persecution, the growth of the church will inevitably follow, reflecting Tertullian's well-known statement 'The blood of the martyrs is the seed of the church.'" Such an inference is unfounded. "The conclusion of my study and experience,"

Sterk says (referring to his many years of ministry in Chiapas, Mexico), is that "persecution negatively affects the growth of the church.... Probably the most common and widely recognized negative result of persecution is that of the reversion of Christians."[2]

Sometimes Christian missionaries are attacked because they are seen to be part of an opposing political regime, are caught in the crossfire, or are seen as a threat to the lives of the native people.

Persecution and martyrdom are closely connected—though the definition of martyrdom is not always precise. Sometimes Christian missionaries are attacked because they are perceived to be part of an opposing political regime or because they are caught in the crossfire or because they are seen as a threat to the lives of the native people—as in the case of those slain by the Aucas of Ecuador. So the verdict is still out as to whether the term applies only to those who are killed specifically for their professed Christian faith—as was often the case in the early church—or whether the term is applied more broadly to those who died while serving amid danger and disease.

Martyrdom in the early church was often considered a death so holy that it was something to be sought after or longed for, and that perspective was expressed in more recent times when missionaries served in places where an untimely death was almost inevitable. Ann Martin Hinderer is an example. By going to Africa in the early 1850s, she proclaimed her willingness to lay down her life. "I longed to be a martyr.... When I see what is the need, I feel that if I had twenty lives, I would gladly give them."[3]

That willingness—or eagerness—to lay down one's life, however, was not the missionary mentality, especially among Protestants, as the twentieth century progressed. In fact, the focus was on safety and evacuation of mission personnel when life was in danger—sometimes leaving national Christians at a greater risk. But mission agencies drew the line at paying ransoms to free missionaries, reasoning that if by kidnapping, terrorists could reap financial rewards, they would be more likely to repeat their actions. This matter of paying a ransom was broached when Betty and John Stam were taken hostage in 1934 and would arise again and again in the decades that followed.

In 2003, after Martin and Gracia Burnham, of New Tribes Mission, were taken hostage in the Philippines, the matter came to a head with a *Christianity Today* cover-story entitled, "Did Martin Die Needlessly?" "Gracia Burnham is unapologetic in her support of ransom payments to free hostages," writes Ted Olsen. To those who would argue that ransom risks the lives of other missionaries, her response was that they would feel the same way she did if they experienced what she had. Nor did she express concern about the fear that "blood money" would be used for evil purposes. She quoted her husband's rationale: "If we can trust the Lord for a million dollar [ransom], which is something totally beyond our reach, we can trust the Lord that the million dollars never buys a weapon or blows anybody up."[4]

The case of the Burnhams that drew wide media coverage might imply that religious persecution and martyrdom is so rare that it makes headlines. However, Paul Marshall strongly argues otherwise. His book *Their Blood Cries Out* focuses primarily on the unnamed believers who live in regions where religious freedom is unknown:

> This book is about a spiritual plague. It tells of massacre, rape, torture, slavery, beatings, mutilations, and imprisonment. It also tells of the pervasive patterns of extortion, harassment, family division, and crippling discrimination in employment and education. This plague affects over two hundred million people, with an additional four hundred million suffering from discrimination and legal impediments.[5]

Betty and John Stam and China Martyrs

During the years following the Boxer uprising, China was anything but free from hostility toward foreigners. Missionaries were viewed with the deepest suspicion, even though their work was largely humanitarian in nature. They were blamed for spreading a cholera epidemic that swept across the northern provinces in 1902, and as a result, two CIM missionaries were killed by a mob. Another brutal attack against missionaries occurred near Hong Kong in 1905 and resulted in five deaths, including that of the greatly loved Dr. Eleanor Chestnut.

After coming to China in 1893 under the American Presbyterian Board, Chestnut built a hospital, using her own money to buy the bricks. Even before the hospital was completed, she was performing surgery—in her own bathroom for want of a better place. One such operation involved the amputation of a coolie's leg. Complications arose and skin grafts were needed. Later, the doctor was questioned about a leg problem from which she herself was suffering. "Oh, it's nothing," she answered, brushing off the inquiry. But a nurse revealed that the skin graft for the "good-for-nothing coolie" had come from Dr. Chestnut's own leg while using only a local anesthetic.[6]

During the Boxer Rebellion, Dr. Chestnut remained on her post longer than most missionaries, and she returned the following year. Then in 1905, while she was busy working at the hospital with four other missionaries, a mob stormed the building. Although she escaped in time to alert authorities, she returned to the scene to help rescue her colleagues. It was too late. Her colleagues had been slain. But there were others who needed her help. Her final act of service to the Chinese people whom she so loved was to rip a piece of material from her own dress to bandage the forehead of a child who had been wounded.

Despite such incidents, the early years of the twentieth century in China were relatively peaceful ones during which the Christian community greatly expanded. By the 1920s, though, the Chinese political scene was in chaos. Sun Yat-sen's authority was being challenged on every side. There were more than a dozen "governments" centered in various cities, and military factions ruled the countryside. In 1925 Sun Yat-sen died, and the fate of foreigners in China became more tenuous than ever. The Communists, under the leadership of Mao Zedong, were gaining influence, and several missionaries were killed as a result of apparent Communist instigation. The situation only seemed to worsen when Chiang Kai-shek arose as an opposition leader. By 1927 his southern armies were sweeping across China, leaving thousands dead in the wake. Missionaries were ordered out, and during 1927 alone some fifty percent of all foreign missionaries in China left, never to return again.

It would seem that such chaotic political turmoil would have resulted in a curtailment of missionary work for the CIM, but to the contrary, "just when the general situation was at its worst in 1929, Hoste [the general director] telegraphed to the home countries an appeal for 200 workers (the majority to be men) in the next two years." The goal was met numerically and on schedule, but "disappointingly, only eighty-four were men."[7] Despite the dangers they knew lay ahead, young women eagerly volunteered. Among them was Betty Scott, a graduate of Moody Bible Institute and the daughter of Presbyterian missionaries to China.

While at Moody, Scott had attended the CIM weekly prayer meetings, and there she became acquainted with John Stam, who also was prepared to volunteer to be one of the two hundred called for. But although Betty and John were attracted to each other and their future ambitions were pointing in the same direction, a personal desire for marriage was seen as secondary. To his father John wrote:

> Betty knows that, in all fairness and love to her, I cannot ask her to enter into an engagement with years to wait.... The China Inland Mission has appealed for men, single men, to itinerate in sections where it would be almost impossible to take a woman, until more settled work has been commenced.... Some time ago I promised the Lord that, if fitted for this forward movement, I would gladly go into it, so now I cannot back down without sufficient reason, merely upon personal considerations.[8]

In the fall of 1931 Betty sailed for China, while John remained at Moody to complete his senior year. As the class speaker for his graduation ceremony, he was well aware of the depressed American economy and the political crises abroad. Yet he challenged his fellow students to go forward with the task of world evangelism:

> Shall we beat a retreat, and turn back from our high calling in Christ Jesus; or dare we advance at God's command, in the face of the impossible?... Let us remind ourselves that the Great Commission was never qualified by clauses calling for advance only if funds were plentiful and [there is] no hardship or

self-denial involved. On the contrary, we are told to expect tribulation and even persecution, but with it victory in Christ.[9]

There was reason to expect persecution. The situation in China remained grim. There were many acts of violence against missionaries in 1932, though none more shocking than the killing of eleven missionaries in Sian serving under the Scandinavian Alliance Mission (now TEAM).

Following his graduation in the fall of 1932, John Stam sailed for China, not expecting to see Betty. Just before he arrived in China, however, she had returned to Shanghai for medical reasons, and their reunion resulted in their engagement. A year later they were married at the home of Betty's parents in Tsi-nan, and during the year that followed, they continued their language study while serving at the CIM mission compound in Süancheng.

In September of 1934, Betty gave birth to a baby girl, Helen Priscilla, and that fall they were assigned to a station in the province of Anhwei where missionaries had been evacuated two years earlier. Communist activity, they were told, had diminished, and the local magistrate personally guaranteed their safety, assuring them that there was "no danger of Communists" in the area.[10] CIM officials, anxious to reopen the station, were also convinced that the area was reasonably safe. But both the Chinese and the CIM officials had seriously misjudged the situation. The Stams arrived at the end of November, and before the first week of December had passed, they had been attacked in their home by Communist soldiers. Though placed under heavy guard, John was permitted to send a letter to his superiors:

Tsingteh, An.
Dec. 6, 1934

China Inland Mission,
Shanghai.

Dear Brethren,

My wife, baby and myself are today in the hands of the Communists, in the city of Tsingteh. Their demand is twenty thousand dollars for our release.

All our possessions and stores are in their hands, but we praise God for peace in our hearts and a meal tonight. God grant you wisdom in what you do, and us fortitude, courage and peace of heart. He is able—and a wonderful Friend in such a time.

Things happened so quickly this a.m. They were in the city just a few hours after the ever-persistent rumors really became alarming, so that we could not prepare to leave in time. We were just too late.

The Lord bless and guide you, and as for us, may God be glorified whether by life or by death.

In Him,
John C. Stam[11]

The day after the letter was written, the Stams were forced to make a grueling march to another town. Not only were their own lives at stake, but they could overhear their guards discussing plans to kill their baby girl to avoid the bother of bringing her along. Little Helen's life was spared, but no such fortune awaited them. After they arrived at their destination, they were stripped of their outer clothes, paraded through the streets, and publicly ridiculed while the communist guerrilla leaders urged the townspeople to come out in full force to view the execution.

A week after the execution, baby Helen was delivered in a rice basket to the home of another missionary family a hundred miles across the dangerous mountain terrain. A Chinese evangelist had found her abandoned in a house some thirty hours after the execution and took the responsibility of bringing her to safety.

The execution of the Stams was a distressing blow to the CIM, but many young people, inspired by their sacrifice, dedicated their lives to missions, and the year 1935 saw the greatest amount of money come into the mission since the stock market crash in 1929.

There were other missionary martyrs in China in the years that followed. Among them was John Birch, a man whose tireless work as a missionary has long been lost to the political society that was named after him. Birch began his missionary career in Hangchow under a Baptist mission organization in 1940 when China was at war on all fronts with the Japanese invaders. Almost immediately he was recognized for his courage as he traveled about the war-torn countryside, "slipping through Japanese occupation lines and preaching in villages where missionaries had not dared to go since the war began."[12] Later he became involved in evacuating missionaries and Chinese evangelists from the war zone, conducting a one-man rescue operation that defied all risks, bringing out as many as sixty at a time. Following the war, he remained in China despite the growing threat of communist guerillas. He continued his widespread evangelistic activity, knowing full well the risks, and it was on one such trip north that he was ambushed and killed by communist forces.

John and Betty Stam, martyred in China in 1934.

Another well-known name inscribed on the missionary death registry for China was Eric Liddell, the great Olympic athlete of 1924 whose story was portrayed in the award-winning film *Chariots of Fire.* Liddell grew up in China, the son of missionaries, and in 1925, only a year after his momentous Olympic victory, he returned to serve as a missionary in his own right. His ministry there spanned the period of the Sino-Japanese War, and he and his family knew firsthand the hardships and danger of missionary life. With the outbreak of World War II the political situation in China worsened, and in 1941 Liddell decided to send his wife and two children to his wife's home in Canada until the worst of the dangers was over. Later that year, along with six other members of the London Missionary Society, he was placed under house arrest by the Japanese, and there he remained until his death early in 1945.

Though Liddell's death was not a direct result of his imprisonment, the malnutrition and lack of adequate medical care may have contributed to it. After an extended illness and what was thought to be a nervous breakdown, later complicated by a stroke, he died. The autopsy report, however, revealed that he had suffered from a massive hemorrhage on the brain caused by a tumor. His sudden death came as a shock to his family and friends and to his fans the world over, but it was also a testimony of the sacrifice of a man who had so consistently put his faith in God above personal ambition and fame.

Paul Carlson and the Congo Martyrs

Not since the Boxer Rebellion of 1900 had so many missionaries been killed in a single year as in the Simba Rebellion in 1964 and 1965. The terror unleashed on innocent Congolese Christians and Western missionaries left thousands dead and even more to suffer from physical and emotional scars that would stay with them the rest of their lives. Dr. Helen Roseveare, beaten and raped and held captive for months, and Dr. Carl Becker later returned to serve in the Congo, but many others had their lives cut short by the very people they had come to serve. Among them was another doctor, Paul Carlson, who had served in the Congo less than two years. Most of the thirty other Protestant missionaries and nearly two hundred Catholic missionaries who were slain had served considerably longer than he and in some instances with greater distinction, but it was his story that became the most published of the Congo martyrs.

Born in California in 1928, Carlson dedicated his life for missionary service as a teenager. Following a semester at UCLA and a short stint in the navy, he enrolled in North Park College in Chicago for premed studies. While there he met Lois Lindblom, a nurse from Menominee, Michigan, and after their engagement in 1949 he returned to California to continue his medical course at Stanford University. Eight years later, with a wife, two babies, and an M.D. degree, he was ready to begin his residency. It was a hectic time, and according to Lois, "the subject of medical missions was mentioned less and less" until "eventually it disappeared completely from our discussions." Spiritually, he was going through a difficult period in his life, questioning "the very existence of a Triune God."[13]

But his repressed commitment to missions was suddenly reawakened in 1961 when he received a letter from the Christian Medical Society presenting an urgent need for medical doctors in the Congo. What caught his attention was that it was not a request for lifetime service. In fact, a follow-up letter indicated that a four-month term would be welcomed. Perhaps subconsciously hoping to fulfill his teenage commitment in four months, he accepted the call, and in June of 1961 he left Lois and the two children in Michigan and flew to the Congo.

Just one year earlier—with little warning—the Congo had been granted independence from Belgium, and the political situation was highly volatile. The new premier, Patrice Lumumba, ordered Belgians to leave, and many other foreigners followed. The government was in chaos, stripped of its leaders and civil servants. Bands of soldiers and teenage gangs roamed the cities and countryside. Professional and technical personnel were in short supply. This was the atmosphere Paul encountered when he stepped off the plane in Leopoldville in 1961.

But despite the unsettled political environment, Carlson's five-month term in the Ubangi Province convinced him of the critical need for medical missionaries. The need was greater than he could have imagined, and the opportunities of presenting the gospel were endless. His call to missions was coming into focus. "The Paul Carlson who had returned from Congo was a new person," Lois discovered. "His attitudes had changed, his ideals shone forth again, his purposes in life were well defined, his outlook on the future was confident. I knew that Paul had come back to himself and back to his God."[14]

The need was greater than Carlson could have imagined, and the opportunities of presenting the gospel were endless.

Despite his renewed commitment to medical missions, leaving the United States and returning to the Congo with his family was not an easy move. During the year following his five-month term in Africa, he joined a practice with doctors with whom he had worked during his residency. The security of a comfortable income was something he and Lois had never before enjoyed, as she recalled:

> It was so easy to look to the undemanding side of life, to look forward to a comfortable existence, to expect the things that all women and families would like to have. It was easy to look forward with our medical colleagues to a better standard of living, as we Americans term it, in that we have all the comforts money can buy. We were on the verge of attaining that kind of life, and now we were faced with the decision that had to be made, that we had known would have to be made—and it had to be made by both of us.[15]

In the summer of 1963 the Carlsons arrived in the Congo as full-fledged medical missionaries—this time serving under their own denomination, the

Evangelical Covenant Church of America. They were assigned to Wasolo, a mission station in a remote section of the Ubangi Province where Paul had worked before and where there were only three other medical doctors in the entire province. Almost immediately he was consumed with routine hospital work, attending to an average of two hundred patients a day, while Lois was adjusting to running a household with no modern conveniences.

The first year went by quickly and relatively uneventfully, but by the beginning of their second year at Wasolo the scene began to change. Though Wasolo was often referred to as the "forgotten corner" of the Congo, it was not immune to rebel infiltration, and by August of 1964 the Simbas were threatening the government defenses in that area. Not wanting to take unnecessary risks, Paul escorted Lois and the children across the border to the Central African Republic and then returned to the hospital to make final preparations before he himself would evacuate.

During the days that followed, he was busy handling routine cases as well as combat casualties. He crossed the river on Sunday to visit his family, promising to return the following Wednesday. But the visit never took place. The Simbas moved in, and before he could escape, he was taken into captivity. He would endure three months of mental and physical torture before his life would be taken.

The publicity surrounding Carlson's death in some ways overshadowed the heroic sacrifices made by other missionaries in the Congo—particularly American missionaries, who were identified as tools of American imperialism. Some, though, were killed indiscriminately by Simba guerrillas. Irene Ferred and Ruth Hege, single Baptist missionaries, were attacked in their house out in the Kwilu bush by drunken teenage rebels, and only Ruth survived to tell the story.

Hector McMillan, a Canadian, was another missionary to die at the hands of the Simbas. He, his wife Ione, and his six sons, along with several other UFM (Unevangelized Fields Mission) missionaries, were trapped at Kilometer Eight, their mission station just outside Stanleyville. Escape routes were closed, and there was no place to go. For Ione the trauma of those harrowing days was ironic. Her own call to missions had been influenced by the deaths of John and Betty Stam. She felt God wanted her to go to China to help fill the void they had left behind. But China closed its doors, and Ione went to serve in the Congo instead, where she met and married Hector McMillan. Now in 1964 and six sons later, she found herself and her family in the midst of violent conflict no less terrifying than what the Stams had faced.

The attack on Kilometer Eight came suddenly. Hector was gunned down point-blank by a Simba rebel, and two of the McMillan boys were wounded. It was a day of infamy, but for Ione and the other missionaries there was no time to grieve. They had to get out as soon as possible. Al Larson, the senior UFM missionary in the area, arrived with government mercenaries soon after the attack to help evacuate the survivors. Space on the trucks was limited. There was no room for baggage, the mercenaries insisted—only room for "living" people. Hector's body would have to remain behind.

What might have been the ultimate devastation for Ione turned into a testimony of God's grace—a testimony she had been strangely prepared for by reading a biography of Adoniram Judson. Judson's mental breakdown following the death of Ann had been exacerbated by morbid thoughts of her decaying body, and that account made a deep impression on her. The day before the tragedy, she had vowed that she would never allow the same to happen to her: "If a member of my family is ever taken in death, by God's help I am not going to waste time and the energies He gave me worrying over a body of clay." "Why this decision just yesterday?" writes Homer Dowdy. "Why had she read so recently about Adoniram Judson's bitter experience? Why had someone once bought this book, perhaps put it aside, only for her to pick it up years later? Why had the great missionary struggled through this grievous vale? It was part of God's plan—God's perfect will—for her at this precise moment."[16]

Another North American missionary brutally murdered by the Simbas was Jay Tucker, who grew up in Arkansas. Like the McMillans, Jay and his wife were married after coming to the Congo, and for twenty-five years they carried out a fruitful ministry under the auspices of the Assemblies of God. In early November of 1964, Jay was arrested by the Simbas; and some three weeks later, when the rebels realized the government troops were closing in on them, they retaliated and turned their vengeance on their captives. An Italian priest was the first to be singled out for execution. Jay Tucker was next.

> In the near darkness someone swung a bottle across the missionary's face. With a dull thump the bottle broke; blood covered the face that in agony turned to grovel in the dirt. In the glassy-eyed glee that their hemp afforded, the Simbas began to whoop as they searched for sticks to finish the job. Those finding sticks made use of them, others their rifle butts. They took turns at hitting the missionary. Starting at the neck, they worked slowly down his back, striking again each time their victim squirmed.[17]

The nearly three months of captivity had been ones of mental and physical torture for Paul Carlson. Even before his captivity, articles had surfaced in American newspapers telling of his courageous and sacrificial medical work, and after his capture more articles appeared, giving him publicity that may very well have complicated his situation in the Congo. The Simbas did not want the world to think they were persecuting a saintly hero, so they twisted the facts; and by late October, Radio Stanleyville was broadcasting reports of the upcoming trial of "Major Carlson," an American mercenary who was charged with being a spy. For more than two weeks there was no further news, but then in mid-November, the news flashed over the wires that he had been tried and was facing execution.

Realizing his value as a hostage, the rebels postponed his execution when negotiations seemed imminent.

On November 24, 1964, only hours before Hector McMillan was slain at Kilometer Eight and Jay Tucker was murdered at Paulis, Paul Carlson was shot down in the streets of Stanleyville. After two days of relative peace, the hostages had awakened that morning to the sound of planes overhead and tense confusion all around them. The rescue operation had begun. Belgian paratroopers were filling the streets, and the sound of machine guns was coming closer. The prisoners were herded outside, where they fell flat on the street, hoping to avoid the crossfire. After a time the shooting stopped. It was an eerie silence—no comfort to the exposed prisoners lying in the street. They were sitting ducks. They had to run for cover—or so they thought. In an act of desperation, Paul and several others raced to the closest building. It was a fatal mistake. The other prisoners made it, but Paul, who was behind and had difficulty scaling the wall after helping another missionary get over it, was riddled with bullets. In a matter of minutes, the rescue operation was over, but for Paul it was too late.

Only hours before Hector McMillan was slain at Kilometer Eight and Jay Tucker was murdered at Paulis, Paul Carlson was shot down in the streets of Stanleyville.

The funeral, conducted by Congolese pastors, was a moving scene. Hundreds of Congolese Christians, carrying flowers and palm branches, poured into the village of Karawa where the service was held. It was their way of showing appreciation to a man who had sacrificed all for them—a man whose life's creed was summed up in the verse on his grave marker, written in the Lingala tongue: "Greater love has no one than this, that he lay down his life for his friends."[18]

Betty Olsen and the Vietnam Martyrs

While missionaries were flooding into China during the nineteenth century, little attention was being paid to what was then referred to as Indo-China—the three small Buddhist countries to the south: Vietnam, Laos, and Cambodia. Not until the twentieth century did Protestant missionaries enter that region, and even then the work was conducted primarily by one mission, the Christian and Missionary Alliance—until the missionaries were expelled in the 1970s. From the outset, the region had been a very difficult area for Christian missions. In many instances the nationals themselves were receptive to the gospel, but there was opposition from the ruling powers. During the French colonial regime, evangelistic work was severely curtailed, and when the Japanese moved in during World War II, the missionaries who refused to leave were confined to internment camps.

The defeat of the Japanese in 1945 that brought an end to the war in Asia brought no lasting peace to Indo-China. For eight years, beginning in 1946, Ho Chi Minh and his communist guerrillas fought the French colonial regime in Vietnam until the French withdrew and left the country divided along the seventeenth parallel. But still there was no peace, and when Vietnamese civilians began fleeing from the communist-controlled North to the South, pressures from the North increased. Communist guerrillas began terrorizing villagers, and the government in Saigon retaliated. Then, with the introduction of the American soldiers, the conflict developed into a full-scale war, and American missionaries were in danger as never before.

Even before full-scale American military involvement, missionaries had been the brunt of guerrilla hostility. The very fact that the United States was assisting South Vietnam militarily outraged the Viet Cong and Hanoi officials, and missionaries were viewed as part of a capitalist-imperialist conspiracy to control the region. Some missionaries were evacuated, especially from areas known to be heavily infiltrated with Viet Cong. Nevertheless, it came as a shock when three American missionaries were taken captive in 1962. That they were serving at a leprosy hospital had given them a false sense of security. Dr. Ardel Vietti, a medical doctor; Archie Mitchell, the hospital director; and Dan Gerber, a Mennonite staff worker, were taken at gun-point into the dense jungle, never to be heard from again. Rumors of their whereabouts surfaced periodically, but no word as to their fate at the hands of their captors.

The fact that the United States was assisting South Vietnam militarily outraged the Viet Cong and Hanoi officials, and missionaries were seen as part of a conspiracy to control the region.

Left unscathed from the attack at the leprosy compound were Betty Mitchell and her children, and a nurse, Ruth Wilting, who on the day of the attack was sewing her wedding dress for her upcoming marriage to Dan Gerber. They escaped the following morning to the nearby provincial capital of Banmethuot and continued in their mission duties, hoping every day for news of their loved ones.

It was in Banmethuot, six years later, that the greatest loss of missionary lives occurred. On January 30, 1968, the day of Tet (the Vietnamese year of the monkey), the Viet Cong moved into the mission compound, killing five American missionaries (including Ruth Wilting) and a four-year-old child. Less fortunate than the dead were Betty Olsen and Hank Blood, who were taken captive, along with Mike Benge, an American AID officer. For several months they suffered indescribable torture and humiliation before Olsen and Blood also died.

Betty Olsen did not fit the profile for a missionary hero. Many of those who had known her in earlier years doubted her usefulness in missionary service altogether. Yet in the early hours of Tet, she risked her life as she nursed the critical wounds of little Carolyn Griswold (who later died), and in the grueling months of suffering that followed, she served faithfully.

Olsen, a "self-possessed, trim redhead," was thirty-four years old at the time of the Banmethuot killings.[19] She was a registered nurse who had served for less than three years with the Alliance in Vietnam. Missionary work, however, was not new to her. She had been raised in Africa, the daughter of missionaries, and some of her happiest memories were of her time spent there. But her childhood days were also filled with turmoil. Her earliest recollections were of her parents consumed in the work of the mission, often away for days at a time visiting African churches. When she was eight years old, she was sent away to school for eight months each year, where she spent many homesick nights crying herself to sleep. For her, boarding school was not a pleasant experience. She rebelled against the rules and resisted close relationships with others, fearing the hurt that would inevitably come when separations occurred. Her insecurities as a teenager were only exacerbated when, just before her seventeenth birthday, she lost her mother to cancer.

She completed high school in the United States and then returned to Africa, still struggling with emotional insecurities and craving love and attention from her father, whose attention was focused on his hectic schedule and plans for remarriage. After he remarried, she returned to the United States and took nurses training at a hospital in Brooklyn before enrolling at Nyack Missionary College to prepare for a missionary career.

Yet there was no real happiness. She desperately wanted marriage and a family of her own, but the relationship she hoped for never developed. After graduating in 1962, she was convinced that the Alliance would not accept her as a candidate on her own merits, so she went to Africa on her own to work with her father and stepmother. It was difficult, however, for her to suppress her anger, and after a time she became so difficult to work with that she was asked to leave.

At the age of twenty-nine she found herself in Chicago working as a nurse and thoroughly defeated in her Christian life. So depressed was she that she contemplated suicide. But after sessions with her church youth counselor, she was prepared to move ahead. The counselor was Bill Gothard, who went on to develop a seminar known as Institute in Basic Youth Conflicts, "based largely on the questions Betty Olsen asked."[20]

For weeks Olsen, along with Hank Blood and Mike Benge, was forced to march twelve to fourteen hours a day, sustained only by meager rice rations.

If ever principles of Christian living were desperately needed, it was during the months that Olsen endured mental and physical torment at the hands of her Viet Cong captors in the steamy insect-infested jungle. For days and weeks at a time she, along with Hank Blood and Mike Benge, was forced to march twelve to fourteen hours a day, sustained only by meager rice rations. All three suffered from dengue fever that caused high fever and chills. Parasitic skin diseases brought on extreme discomfort; and for Olsen, who remained clothed in the dress she was captured in, bloodsucking leeches by the dozens clung to her legs as she was prodded on without stopping to rest.

Awful as her ordeal was, she was the healthiest of the three during most of those agonizing months of the jungle death march. Benge contracted a severe case of malaria and for more than a month was delirious. Blood, however, suffered the most during the early months of captivity. A middle-aged man and father of three whose eight years in Vietnam as a Wycliffe Bible translator had involved sedentary work, he simply could not withstand the rigors and deprivations of the debilitating marches. Kidney stones, painful boils, and finally pneumonia that was left untreated during days of drenching rain led to his death in mid-July after more than five months of agony.

By September, after nearly eight months on the jungle trails, the end seemed near for Olsen and Benge as well. "Their hair turned gray. They lost their body hair, their nails stopped growing. Their teeth were loose with bleeding gums"—all signs of malnutrition.[21] Olsen's legs began swelling, making it extremely difficult for her to walk, especially at the pace the guards insisted on. When she fell down, she was beaten. She pleaded with her captors to go on and let her die on the jungle path, but her cries were ignored. Her final days defy description. Suffering from dysentery that caused severe diarrhea, she "became so weak she couldn't get out of her hammock" and "she had to lie in her own defecation."[22] Benge nursed her the best he could, but her condition only deteriorated. Her thirty-fifth birthday found her moaning in pain in her filthy hammock, and two days later she was dead.

Shortly after she died, Benge was taken to a POW camp, where he was imprisoned with other Americans. There he endured beatings and nearly a year in solitary confinement before he was transferred to the "Hanoi Hilton," where again he was kept in solitary for much of the time. In January of 1973, after nearly five years of captivity, he, along with most of the other POWs, was released as a condition of the American military pullout.

The exhilaration of being released was tempered by the grueling ordeal of recounting to the families of Hank Blood and Betty Olsen the grim details of their agonizing captivity. His story included more than the nightmare of the Vietnam jungle though. He told how he himself put his trust in God through their selfless witness to him, and how they hid their own meager rations to share with captured native Christians whose rations were even less. In Olsen, the once angry young woman, Mike found "the most unselfish person he had ever known." Her love was more than he could comprehend: "She never showed any bitterness or resentment. To the end she loved the ones who mistreated her."[23]

Chet Bitterman and Latin America Martyrs

In the 1970s and 1980s, terrorism periodically sent shock waves through the missionary community—often accused of plotting to overthrow revolutionary governments or of being informants for the CIA (charges that were apparently true in some instances). But missionaries were not the targets of leftist guerrillas only. In Latin America and elsewhere, missionaries (particularly Roman Catholic) were sometimes associated with leftist movements, and in several instances terrorist attacks on them were instigated and carried out by right-wing government factions. Such was apparently the case in the 1980 deaths of three American Maryknoll nuns and a lay worker in El Salvador. Though their work involved caring for homeless children displaced by the war, they were perceived as aiding the rebel cause and were brutally murdered as a result.

In December of 1981, on the anniversary of the nuns' deaths, the Catholic Church, at the prompting of its missionaries to Latin America, began a year of commemoration called the "Year of the Martyrs." Those commemorated were not only the "El Salvador Four" but also scores of other missionaries and lay workers whose lives had been lost in Latin American civil strife. Among them was Stanley Rother, a red-bearded Catholic priest from Okarche, Oklahoma, who only months earlier was found shot in the head in his house at a Guatemala village where he had worked among the Cakchiquel Indians for thirteen years. Though he was considered "a real low-key type," and was the "most conservative" of the Catholic priests in the area,[24] his name was nevertheless placed on a right-wing hit list, and as such he became the ninth priest in less than nine months to die as a result of Guatemala's political turmoil.

The most publicized Protestant to be shot by Latin American terrorists during these years was Chet Bitterman, but he was not alone in being victimized by such a senseless outrage. In September of 1981, John Troyer was shot and killed in Guatemala. The twenty-eight-year-old Mennonite missionary from Michigan was gunned down in front of his wife and five children by a band of terrorists shouting anti-American slogans. His partner, Gary Miller, though shot in the chest, survived the ordeal. The gunmen were later identified as a leftist group calling themselves the Guerrilla Army of the Poor.

Acts of terrorism did not take mission leaders by surprise. They were well aware of this newest threat to their work, and some made policy decisions regarding their response in the event of such action. In 1975 Wycliffe members voted that the mission should not yield to terrorists' demands, recognizing that while concessions might free an individual hostage, such action would only serve to jeopardize other missionaries the world over.

That statement of policy, combined with the excessive demands, prevented Wycliffe Bible Translators and the Summer Institute of Linguistics from even considering submitting to Colombian terrorist demands early in 1981 when Chet Bitterman was kidnapped and held for forty-eight days. While government and mission officials worked feverishly to secure his release, capitulating to the terrorist demands that Wycliffe leave the country was never an option.

Years earlier, Wycliffe members had voted that the mission should not yield to terrorists' demands, recognizing that such action would only serve to jeopardize other missionaries the world over.

Bitterman was new on the scene in Colombia, having arrived in the summer of 1979 with his wife Brenda, who was pregnant with their second child. He was the oldest of eight children, all born and raised in Lancaster, Pennsylvania. After high school he enrolled at Columbia Bible College, and in 1976 he married Brenda Gardner, the daughter of Wycliffe missionaries to Colombia. Although he was determined to become a missionary linguist even before he met her, linguistics did not come easy for him. He attended the Summer Institute of Linguistics for two summers but became discouraged by the slow progress he was making.

The Bittermans had initially hoped to serve as missionary linguists in Malaysia, but Wycliffe officials requested that they go to Colombia instead. Once in Colombia they encountered obstacles as they sought to become involved in the work. They had unsuccessfully attempted to begin work with three different language groups and had finally made arrangements to go to the Caryona-speaking Indians when Chet became ill and was sent to Bogota for gall bladder surgery.

The kidnapping occurred while Chet was staying at the SIL residence in Bogota awaiting surgery. Terrorists knocked at the door at 6:30 A.M. and then burst in with revolvers and machine guns. Sylvia Riggs, a Wycliffe member, later described what happened after she was awakened by one of the hooded terrorists: "They took us all to the living room and made us lie facedown on the floor while they tied our hands and feet and gagged us. There were 12 of us adults and five children. . . . During the course of the hour that we lay there, my hands began to hurt from the rope tied around my wrists and I began to tremble from the cold of the cement floor."[25] The paralyzing fear that gripped those seventeen helpless victims as they lay on the floor that morning of January 19, would never be forgotten, but for sixteen of them the physical trauma was over by 8:00 A.M.

For Bitterman the nightmare had only begun. Soon after the terrorists had attacked, it became apparent that the individual they really wanted was Al Wheeler, the director of the Bogota SIL office. When they discovered he was not among the group, they chose Bitterman instead, forcing him at gun-point into a car. Then they drove away, giving no clue as to their motives. The first real indication of why he was kidnapped came four days later when the terrorists, identifying themselves as the "M–19," expressed their demands in writing: "Chet

Bitterman will be executed unless the Summer Institute of Linguistics (SIL) and all its members leave Colombia by 6:00 P.M. February 19."[26]

Once the demands were made known, attempts were made to negotiate, and pleas came from everywhere begging the terrorists to spare his life. Garcia Herraros, a Catholic priest, wrote an open letter that was printed on the front page of a Bogota newspaper: "We want to ask the kidnappers to free this man who has dedicated his life to the extremely noble task of translating the Bible into an Indian language. We can't become insensitive or indifferent to the pain of our Protestant brothers. We esteem and respect them. We appreciate their efforts of sharing the love of Christ. We are with them in this moment of pain."[27]

When the February 19 deadline passed, there was a sense of relief. Perhaps the terrorists would realize that their goals were futile. But every glimmer of hope was quickly dashed by the reality of the situation. New and conflicting deadlines were set, and rumors surfaced almost daily that the execution had already been carried out. It was a nightmare for Brenda and her fellow WBT/SIL colleagues. For Bitterman the ordeal may have been less traumatic than it was for his loved ones.

During the forty-eight days of his captivity, he was treated reasonably well. He shared the gospel with them, argued with them, and played chess with them. "We've even become friends," he wrote, "and we respect each other, though we view the world from opposite poles."[28] What "friendship" was established between him and his captors, though, did not stay his execution on March 7. He was shot once through the heart, and his body was left in a bus along a street in Bogota.

> In Columbia, South Carolina, Chet's brother learned of the news as a result of a chance look at a teletype machine. In Huntington Beach, California, Wycliffe's U.S. director Bernie May was awakened by a long-distance telephone call.... In Lancaster, Pennsylvania, Chet's parents got the word from a local newspaper reporter. And in Bogota, Colombia, the early-morning stillness was jarred for Chet's wife when a nearby shopkeeper banged on the gate yelling a message that couldn't wait: "They've found Chet's body in a bus."[29]

The publicity surrounding Chet Bitterman's kidnapping and death brought an outpouring of sympathy and support for the Bitterman family and for WBT/SIL. Cam Townsend reported that more than two hundred individuals had volunteered to take his place. Townsend, in Colombia for the memorial service, was overwhelmed with the response. "The whole country was expressing sympathy to us. Everyone from the president to the policeman who had tears in his eyes when he called on us, was wonderful."[30]

For Bitterman's family, the news of his death was accepted with an amazing serenity. Yet there were the inevitable questions. Why had God allowed the ordeal to end the way it did? The problem with his death, Chet's father confessed, "is that we so completely misread God's intent."

> We fully expected Chet to lead his captors to the Lord.... We expected God to release Chet, perhaps in some miraculous way, so the capture of missionaries would become less attractive to revolutionary-type people.... God is still God. We know that, but how can we make the media people recognize it? We anticipated telling the news reporters when Chet was released, "See what God has done?" But how is He going to do something now in a way that'll make sense to the world?... We've almost concluded there's very little, if anything, we can do to explain Chet's death to our unsaved friends and the media people, because the answer is to be found at the spiritual level.[31]

William Donald McClure

For some missionaries who were killed in the line of duty, it was the untimely and unjust death that most defined the sacrificial service. But for others it was the life of ministry that far overshadowed the grievous death. This was true of William Donald "Don" McClure (1906–77), who, with his wife Lydda, served for nearly fifty years in Africa with the American Presbyterian Mission. In 1977 he was gunned down by guerrilla terrorists at a mission outpost on the border of Ethiopia and Somalia. His life was "a pilgrimage of service," according to his biographer: "He started in the desert region around Khartoum along the Nile, traveled across the lush forests of the Upper Nile plain from Doleib Hill in the Sudan on the Sobat River among the Shulla people, to Akobo on the Pibor River among the Anuaks, to Pokwo on the Baro River, to the Gilo River, to Addis Ababa, and finally across Ethiopia to Gode among the Somali people along the Webi Shebelle at the southern edge of the vast Ogaden desert."[32]

Like many missionaries, McClure was a jack-of-all-trades—a teacher, evangelist, mission strategist, agriculturist, diplomat, veterinarian, and handyman. But Africans knew him as "Dr." McClure. He was an untrained and unlicensed physician whose clinics attracted people from miles around and surrounding districts. On one occasion, when he "had to operate on what I think was cancer of the mouth," he lamented his frustration about his role: "Who am I to attempt such things and why does the Lord allow me to work alone out here? I am the only 'medical officer' for 25,000 Anuaks."[33] Most of his medical work involved treating malaria and eye infections and other more routine procedures, and through it all he tried to preserve his sense of humor, as is illustrated in one of his letters:

> Then after dark I started for the house to clean up a bit for supper, but I was called to the river bank. Another canoe had come in through the rain and this time a young girl was lying in bloody water.... Then I saw her trouble was caused by an umbilical cord which had not been removed and trailed behind her as they dragged her out of the boat and laid her on the ground naked.... I was told that she had given birth to a still born baby yesterday and the placenta would not detach itself.... I stooped over to pick her up in my arms and

> bring her into the house where I could treat her. As I lifted her and straightened up, she suddenly clutched my neck and screamed in pain, and I heard one of the women cry, "It is out." . . . I dare say this is the only case on record where a placenta was removed in this manner. . . . She is now sleeping quietly in my study and already feels much better.[34]

Amidst all his medical work, McClure did not neglect evangelism, nor was he subtle in his strong views on the subject. Indeed, he was very critical of fellow missionaries with the American Presbyterian Mission: "Our missionaries have been working here in Khartoum for thirty years, and we do not have even one *outstanding* convert who can attract others to the Christian faith. . . . I am convinced the fault lies with us. . . . The apostle Paul preached, converted, and then taught. We on the other hand, teach a lot of classes, then preach some, but no one is converted."[35]

His emphasis on evangelism, however, did not detract him from community development. "Our primary task among these people is to lead them to a saving knowledge of Jesus Christ," he wrote, "but hand in hand with that program we must teach them to improve their social and economic standard of living."[36] He introduced irrigation and new crops that provided far more nutritional value than the *durra* they were then growing. He also helped market crops so that the people might rise above their subsistence living standard. Yet the Shulla church brought him the most satisfaction: "We pushed the cattle out of the cattle barn, which was the largest building in the village, but the group kept getting larger and larger. One Sunday morning we had more than a hundred people packed into stalls. . . . Already we have ten other Sunday schools started in different centers. . . . This church . . . was only the beginning of a great movement among our surrounding villages that is still growing."[37]

His success was due partly to his insistence that converts not be "required to memorize the catechism, the Apostles' Creed, the Lord's Prayer, and certain passages of Scripture"—as had been the approach of other missionaries. "We will never have a villager who is able to perform such mental gymnastics," he argued. "I want to set a new precedent. I believe that for the Shulla people, we should perform baptisms as soon as they show a desire to live a Christian life and can assure us of their sincerity in giving up their pagan worship."[38]

Long before McClure was killed by guerrillas, his life was threatened on many occasions by practitioners of traditional religions. His response, however, was not to retreat.

Throughout his ministry, McClure trained others to conduct evangelistic ministry, and the churches he planted grew significantly, though not without strong opposition from the powerful tribal witchdoctors. Indeed, long before he was killed by guerrillas, his life was threatened on many occasions by practitioners of traditional religions. His response, however, was not to retreat. On one occasion, when a witchdoctor's treatment nearly killed one of his patients, he was "determined to find the man and whip him publicly," but he changed his mind, he confessed, after "my savage anger had cooled." He recognized the urgency of reaching these feared individuals with the gospel because, he said, "There are hundreds of Shullas who want to become Christians, but they are too afraid of the curses of the witchdoctors, whose powers over these people is unbelievable to a foreigner." It was a great day then, when a new Christian, La Amoleker, brought the witchdoctor to church: "Today hundreds and hundreds of people came in from the villages round about. The church was crowded to overflowing, and many had to stand outside. . . . Suddenly there was a stir of excitement. A lane opened up from the back for La Amoleker and Kaimybek, who was the most renowned and feared witchdoctor in all this country. He has been an enemy of this mission for forty years. . . . Gradually La [Amoleker] led Kaimybek to a knowledge of the Lord Jesus Christ."[39]

McClure's diplomatic and evangelistic encounters included not only witchdoctors but also an emperor—Emperor Haile Selassie of Ethiopia, who paved the way for new ministry opportunities for him. But his friendship at court ended when Haile Selassie was deposed by a military junta after six decades of ruling Ethiopia. That power vacuum led to McClure's being shot to death by guerrillas just before he had arranged to be airlifted out of the region. His son Don, on hearing the news, left his own mission post some distance away and risked his life to go and bury his father—in Africa, the land he loved.

SELECT BIBLIOGRAPHY

Carlson, Lois. *Monganga Paul: The Congo Ministry and Martyrdom of Paul Carlson, M.D.* New York: Harper & Row, 1966.

Dowdy, Homer E. *Out of the Jaws of the Lion: Christian Martyrdom in the Congo.* New York: Harper & Row, 1965.

Hefley, James, and Marti Hefley. *By Their Blood: Christian Martyrs of the 20th Century.* Milford, MI: Mott, 1979.

______. *No Time for Tombstones: Life and Death in the Vietnamese Jungle.* Wheaton, IL: Tyndale, 1976.

Lyall, Leslie. *A Passion for the Impossible: The China Inland Mission, 1865–1965.* Chicago: Moody Press, 1965.

Marshall, Paul. *Their Blood Cries Out: The Untold Story of Persecution against Christians in the Modern World.* Dallas: Word, 1997.

Partee, Charles. *Adventure in Africa: The Story of Don McClure.* Grand Rapids: Zondervan, 1990.

Taylor, Mrs. Howard. *The Triumph of John and Betty Stam.* Philadelphia: China Inland Mission, 1960.

16

Third World Missions: Younger Churches Reach Out

Korean Christians evangelizing their own people and reaching out to others across the ocean. This is a scenario that has continued for many decades and is being repeated the world over. The era of the Western missionary is not over, but the burden of world evangelism is now being carried to a large extent by Christians from outside the Western world. Historically, Western missionaries depended heavily on native converts to serve as assistants in carrying on the ministry, but during the twentieth century the "younger churches" came of age and the situation was reversed, with Western missionaries serving as assistants at the invitation of the national church leaders.

This turnaround in missions has been underscored by mission leaders in various places on the world scene. From an Asian perspective, Theodore Williams, the head of the Indian Evangelical Mission, observed in 1978 that the rise of indigenous missionary movements in Asia, Africa, and Latin America was a "significant development" indicating that "we are in an exciting period of mission history." He went on to acknowledge that "Third World missions have just made a beginning."[1]

In the decades since Williams spoke of "Third World" missions, the terminology has changed. A major news magazine used the term in 1975 within an economic framework to describe "have not" nations, still undeveloped, "whose interests don't jibe with those of developed nations in the other two worlds—that is, the communist and the non-communist world."[2] In more recent times, the term "Two-Thirds World" has been used in the mission context to designate areas outside the so-called Western world.

Although much of the non-Western world is not underdeveloped or economically depressed, the churches in this region, on the average, have far fewer financial resources than do churches in the West. Indeed, according to Williams,

"Missions in the Two-Thirds World are missions within a context of poverty."[3] Yet, Williams and others argue, despite poverty, missions is a responsibility of this region of the world. Observing the mission scene in 1990, Luis Bush wrote:

> Missionaries from the Two Thirds World? Just a few years ago the idea would have seemed unthinkable. But not now! Today the rapidly growing Two Thirds World mission force is one of the most remarkable factors in world evangelism. . . . This vital resource has the potential to reach the whole world with the Gospel. The consequences could be incalculable.
>
> *However, unless this enterprise is adequately financed, the whole opportunity could be lost.*[4]

Luis Bush himself has been a key figure in the expansion role of the non-Western church in cross-cultural missions. Born in Argentina, the son of an English businessman, he later moved with his family to Brazil. Like his father, he was headed for a career in business until his life took a sharp turn. He went to seminary in Texas, where he studied theology. After graduating, Bush and his wife moved to San Salvador, where he served as the pastor of Iglesia Nazaret, a mission-oriented church that in seven years grew to more than a thousand, supporting some three dozen missionaries and planting seven daughter churches. Then in 1986 he accepted a call to serve as the head of Partners International, a ministry that has brought Western churches and individuals into partnership with some seventy indigenous missions in fifty countries. During this time he also worked closely with COMIBAM, a consultation for thousands of leaders from Latin America.

It was Bush who, at the Lausanne II Conference in Manila in 1989, coined the phrase "10/40 Window" to designate a rectangular area of Africa and Asia, from ten degrees latitude north of the equator to forty degrees latitude north of the equator, where most of the world's "unreached peoples" lived. In more recent years, Bush took up the leadership of the AD2000 & Beyond Movement, with its goal, "A church for every people and the gospel for every person by AD 2000."

Through all of his tireless activity, Bush has strong ties in both the Western and non-Western worlds, seeking to bring partnership in mission outreach. Speaking of his native land, he lamented that "for all the ambitions to send out missionaries, the economic realities facing Argentina are overwhelmingly difficult." Its economic vitality has been depleted by a massive national debt and rampant inflation among other factors. Neighboring Brazil faces similar problems, as do most Two-Thirds World nations. Thus, *partnership*, he argues, is a necessity for the contemporary and coming generations of missions.

Most of the funds raised in the West for mission work are designated for the support of Western missionaries. This fact prompted a Seattle chiropractor, Dr. N. A. Jepson, in 1943 to found CNEC (Christian Nationals Evangelism

Commission, since renamed Partners International), an organization committed to the support of Christian nationals. The support was limited to Chinese nationals in the early years, but by 1982 the organization was assisting more than a thousand nationals in thirty-six countries.

One such national Christian leader was Anand Chaudhari, the son of a high-caste Brahman priest. Following his conversion, he left his home in Goa to serve in Rajasthan, an area with virtually no Christian witness. Through decades of tireless work, thousands of Indians turned to Christianity. He founded the Rajasthan Bible Institute and began weekly radio broadcasts that are heard all over India. In 1978 he organized a team of more than thirty evangelists to spread out over India with Christian literature, and from that effort more than sixty thousand people requested correspondence courses on the Bible.

Because of his own background, Chaudhari has been able to effectively communicate with high-caste Hindus. Among those who became Christians was a high-caste political science professor and author—a man who initially kept his conversion a secret. Chaudhari understood this man's fear, and he remembered well the painful ordeal of visiting his own family and telling them of his conversion. They would rather he had died. Soon after that visit he received word that his family, along with hundreds of others, had been killed by an elephant stampede during a Hindu festival. It was only his Christian faith that brought him through the crisis—a gripping testimony that reached the hearts of other Hindus.

In the Philippines, Partners International contributed to the support of the Philippines Missionary Fellowship, a locally controlled organization that has sponsored hundreds of missionaries, many of whom have been trained at the Philippines Missionary Institute, founded in 1961. By assisting in the support of such missions, Partners International was serving the cause of world missions by the most efficient means possible. Nationals living in their own country are far more cost-effective than foreign missionaries. They likewise are free of language and cultural barriers and are not barred from "closed" countries. The charge that Partners International is "spoiling" nationals and denying their own people the privilege of supporting them is not convincing, considering the fact that most of the organization's financial aid supplements ministries that are already effective and that are being supported by nationals, as in the case of the Philippines Missionary Fellowship, which has been largely supported by Filipinos.

Bush insists that there still is a need for Western missionaries, though he concedes that the presence of North American missionaries in some areas is offensive and that "missionaries from other countries are often better able to fill" the need. "The role of the American Christian," he emphasized in an interview in 2003, "continues to change to an increasingly partnership and servant role in support of nationals."[5]

Partnership and servanthood have been complex issues in cross-cultural missions in recent decades. While Bush argues that "money should not be the central concern in missions," money continues to command power, and that power belonged to North America during the twentieth century and on into the twenty-first—while at the same time the rapid growth of the church and the spiritual leadership was moving to the Two-Thirds World. The influential Christian leaders of that part of the globe who have played significant roles in mission and evangelistic outreach are far too numerous to designate, but their names are recognized worldwide. Luis Palau, born in Argentina in 1934, is widely regarded as one of the world's premier evangelists. Known primarily for mass campaigns in large cities, his ministry has also focused on radio and print ministries, as well as church-planting.

Partnership and servanthood have been complex issues in cross-cultural missions in recent decades.

From South Africa, the name Desmond Tutu is recognized worldwide—a Christian leader whose pivotal role in bringing an end to apartheid stands as a monument to effective Christian leadership. From Uganda, Festo Kivengere is remembered as a great Anglican bishop who helped bring peace to a war-torn country through a time of great religious revivals. David Cho (formerly Paul Yonggi), as the pastor of the world's largest church, has an extensive ministry that reaches far beyond his homeland of Korea. And from China, mission leaders such as Jonathan Chao are having as great an impact in the West as in their homeland. These individuals and many more rise out of the heritage of great missionaries and mission leaders of past generations from the Two-Thirds World.

Pandita Ramabai

As the Christian faith took root in Asia and elsewhere around the globe, it was embodied by individuals who had very different perspectives on life than the perspectives brought by Western missionaries. This often led to conflict between East and West, while at the same time paving the way for a more authentic and culturally sensitive form of the gospel. Sometimes the differences were denied, as native converts attempted to become westernized, but in other instances the differences surfaced in painful personal disputes, as was the case with Pandita Ramabai and Sister Geraldine.

Ramabai was born in 1858, the daughter of a high caste Brahman scholar who believed that his wife and daughter should have the same opportunities for education that he had had. She began studying Sanskrit at age seven, and by the time she was twelve she had memorized thousands of the classical sayings. When she was still a young child, her father lost his wealth and began a religious pilgrimage—an intense search for God. After her parents died, she, accompanied by her brother, took up the search, ever grateful for her father's influence and legacy: "I am a child of a man who had to suffer a great deal on account of advocating Female

Education," she wrote. "I consider it my duty, to the very end of my life, to maintain this cause, and to advocate the proper position of women in this land."[6]

As she continued the pilgrimage her parents had begun, Ramabai discovered many things about her religious heritage that troubled her. Hindu belief was varied and inconsistent, but on one issue, she insisted, there was uniformity—"that women of high and low caste, as a class, were bad, very bad, worse than demons, as unholy as untruth" and that their only hope of being liberated from karma "was the worship of their husband"—the "woman's god."[7]

Determined to reform Hinduism, Ramabai began at age sixteen to lecture on women's education. Her fame quickly spread. Within a few years she "was the news of the hour, and papers all over the country trumpeted her accomplishments," writes John Seamands. "She was a woman of purest Brahman birth, twenty years old and unmarried, beautiful, and scholarly." She spoke six languages and easily conversed with the country's noted scholars.[8]

Following the death of her brother, Ramabai married a lawyer, but he was of the Shudra caste, and in the eyes of many people she had disgraced herself—a disgrace that was intensified when she was widowed soon after. Yet she continued her lectures and founded the Aryan Women's Society for the purpose of banning child marriage and promoting women's education.

During this time, Ramabai encountered Christians, and through their influence and her desire to further her education, she traveled to England. Before going, she made a vow to friends that she would never convert to Christianity, but while there she became acquainted with some Anglican nuns who encouraged her to read the Bible. Then, through the encouragement of Sister Geraldine, she made a profession of faith and was baptized into the Church of England—a denominational name that she recognized as offensive to her as an Indian. Indeed, she feared that she was betraying her heritage, as she expressed in a letter to Sister Geraldine:

> I am, it is true, a member of the Church of Christ, but I am not bound to accept every word that falls down from the lips of priests or bishops. . . . I have just with great efforts freed myself from the yoke of the Indian priestly tribe, so I am not at present willing to place myself under another similar yoke by accepting everything which comes from the priests as authorized command of the Most High.[9]

Sister Geraldine was distressed by Ramabai's independent spirit and her questioning Anglican doctrine. "I regret that I have been the cause of making you feel yourself wrong for the part you acted in my baptism," she confessed to Sister Geraldine. "I wish I knew that your Church required a person to be quite perfect in faith, doubting nothing in the Athanasian Creed, so that he had left nothing to be learnt and inquired into the Bible after his baptism." Sister Geraldine urged her to make a complete break from her Hindu heritage, insisting that her refusal to eat puddings made from eggs indicated that she was "clinging to caste prejudice which ought to have been thrown to the winds" when she became a Christian. Ramabai fired back:

> You may, if you like, trace my pride in pies and puddings.... I confess I am not free from all my caste prejudices, as you are pleased to call them.... How would an Englishwoman like being called proud and prejudiced if she were to go and live among the Hindus for a time but did not think it necessary to alter her customs when they were not hurtful or necessary to her neighbors?[10]

For many missionaries and Western Christians, Ramabai's refusal to completely separate from her Hindu heritage was a concern—particularly her insistence on referring to herself as a Hindu Christian. She maintained close friendships with Hindus and lectured at Hindu functions—and she continued to read from the Hindu scriptures. She was also very independent in her perspectives on matters relating to the education of girls, thus finding herself the target of criticism from all sides. But she was undaunted: "I am having a right good time in the story of public indignation that is raging over my head."[11]

One of the specific reasons she was criticized was her open policy of permitting girls at her school to maintain caste rules and to read the Hindu scriptures, which were available along with the Bible. But the opposition was not limited to the Christian community. Hindus were upset that some students were requesting Christian baptism. So angry was the protest that twenty girls were removed from the school, but she continued on in her educational ministry—primarily with orphans and child widows.

During this time she also became involved in mission outreach. Her inspiration came from reading the biographies, as she later testified:

> About twelve years ago, I read the inspiring books, "The Story of the China Inland Mission," "The Lord's Dealings with George Muller," and the "Life of John G. Paton," founder of the New Hebrides Mission. I was greatly impressed with the experiences of these three great men, Mr. Hudson Taylor, Mr. Muller and Mr. Paton, all of whom have gone to be with the Lord within a few years of each other. I wondered after reading their lives, if it were not possible to trust the Lord in India as in other countries. I wished very much that there were some missions founded in this country that would be a testimony to the Lord's faithfulness to His people, and the truthfulness of what the Bible says, in a practical way.
>
> I questioned in my mind over and over again, why some missionaries did not come forward to found faith missions in this country. Then the Lord said to me, "Why don't you begin to do this yourself, instead of wishing for others to do it?"[12]

As time passed, she expanded her school and opened an orphanage and Rescue Home for "fallen girls," at one point housing nearly two thousand girls at various locations, including a one-hundred-acre farm. There were many times of famine and privation, but the Mukti Mission, as it was known, carried on with the ministry. In 1900, during a severe drought, she wrote of God's sustaining care:

> Two of our large wells were quite dried up, and very little water left in our other two wells. Many of our friends were praying that God would give us water—and so He did. Although there was none for cultivating the vegetable garden, God gave water for all our people. More than 1,900 people, besides over one hundred cattle . . . required a great deal of water. Each of the two wells had all its contents used up every day; every evening one could see the bottom. . . . But there came a fresh supply in the morning to each well, and it lasted all day.[13]

Ramabai became known worldwide after a revival broke out at the Mukti Mission in 1905 that sparked another well-known revival, as Colin Melbourne writes:

> Pandita is typically low key here about this remarkable revival at Mukti and beyond. She was encouraged by news of the 1904 Welsh revival to start the prayer circle she mentions. She requested supporting prayer of the annual Keswick convention, in England, and in 1905, the praying girls and women sparked a genuine Spirit-filled revival with signs, wonders, tongues, miracles, visions, deep repentance, and thousands of conversions between 1905–07. . . .
>
> The accounts of the Holy Spirit outpourings in the Welsh 1904 and Mukti 1905 revivals encouraged the believers at Azusa Street, Los Angeles, USA, to seek the Baptism, and they too received the Pentecostal experience in 1906. One of its leaders, Frank Bartleman, declared that the "revival was rocked in the cradle of little Wales" . . . "brought up" in India, and then became "full grown" at Azusa Street.[14]

Ramabai may have been one of the first mission leaders from the non-Western world to reverse roles and invite a Western missionary to serve as her assistant. Minnie Abrams, a Methodist who had grown up in Minnesota, had served in India for more than a decade before she became an administrative assistant at the Mukti Mission. Their ministries complemented each other, and the results were remarkable. "Shortly after the 'fire fell' [during the 1905 revival] at Mukti," writes Gary McGee, "Abrams and her 'praying bands' of young women from the Mission carried the revival to various places of ministry. On a broader scale, 48 bands with 15 members each went out twice weekly to the surrounding countryside to preach in the villages. Mukti would do its part in preparing a contingent of the 100,000 female evangelists."[15]

Amid all her other responsibilities, Ramabai took on the challenge of translating the Bible in Marathi, her own native tongue. The only translation available was stiff and formal, and she was determined to provide a translation that captured the energy and the personal dynamics of the book she so dearly loved.

"Her aim was to produce a translation in pure but simple Marathi that even the common villager could understand." After studying Greek and Hebrew, she devoted time every day for most of fifteen years before the enormous task was completed—only months before her death in 1922.[16]

There were many other Indian Christians who gave their lives to mission outreach. V. S. Azariah (1874–1945) was ordained in 1909 as the first Indian bishop in the Anglican church, but he is perhaps better remembered for his passion for indigenous mission work in India and beyond. He "was the most successful leader of grassroots movements of conversion to Christianity in South Asia," writes Susan Billington Harper. "During the early twentieth century ... he actively recruited Indians to serve as Christian missionaries in India," challenging "his countrymen ever more insistently to evangelize their own land."[17]

Another Indian mission leader's story began in 1908 when Watkin Roberts from Wales came to preach the gospel among the Hmar tribe in the Indian state of Manipur. Government authorities forced him to leave only five days after he arrived, but during that time he had made five converts, including Chawnga, who followed him out of the region and became his disciple. Chawnga memorized the gospel of John and returned to his people and many became Christians. But the tribe had no Scriptures in its own language, and Chawnga was determined that his son, then ten years old, would one day accomplish the task of translating God's word into the Hmar language.

In the decades that followed, his son, Rochunga Pudaite, not only translated the New Testament into Hmar, but he became the president of an evangelical denomination that has some three hundred churches with more than forty thousand members, a hospital, dozens of village schools, and four high schools. But his influence had reached far beyond the Hmar tribe. In 1971 his vision expanded to the whole of India—and to the whole world. He founded Bibles for the World, a ministry whose goal is that of reaching all the people listed in the phone books in India and beyond. Since that time more than 14 million copies of the New Testament have been mailed to people in more than one hundred countries, and supporting the mailings are short radio programs that offer gospel messages in drama and storytelling, and personal interviews. Pudaite's journey from the jungle in northeast India to a missionary statesman to the world is told in a musical sung by India Children's Choir, "Headhunters to Heart Hunters."

K. P. Yohannan, founder and president of Gospel for Asia, has also made an imprint on missions in India and beyond. Born into a poor family in a remote village in South India, he credits his spiritual development and call to missions to the prayers of his mother. As a child he was so shy and timid that he "trembled when asked to recite in class." But after listening to a powerful missions challenge from George Verwer of Operation Mobilization, he was convinced that God wanted him to devote his life to bringing the gospel to his people.

In 1978, after completing biblical studies and serving in a pastorate, Yohannan founded the mission organization that became Gospel for Asia, which in the next quarter-century planted more than twenty thousand churches and mission stations and trained thousands of evangelists in its dozens of Bible schools. But Yohannan was convinced that the task of evangelizing the Two-Thirds World was one that belonged to the whole world—the West included. In his book *The Coming Revolution in World Missions*, he strongly challenged Christians in the West to join in the privilege of financially supporting the Christian workers in developing countries.

William Wade Harris

He "flashed like a meteor through parts of West Africa." Known as a prophet, William Wade Harris was described by a Western missionary as "Africa's most successful evangelist [who] gathered in a few months a host of converts exceeding in number the total church membership of all the mission in Nyasaland now after fifty years of work." In less than two years, more than one hundred thousand Africans were baptized as a result of his ministry that challenged his followers to prepare to be discipled by the "white man with the Book." His influence in Africa has been compared to that of Albert Schweitzer.[18]

The son of a Methodist mother and "heathen" father, Harris was born in Liberia around 1860 and professed faith as a young adult. According to his testimony, "The Holy Ghost came upon me. The very year of my conversion I started preaching."[19] He served first as a Methodist lay minister and later as a teacher and evangelist supported for some fifteen years by the Episcopal mission, which was actively working among his own Glebo people. "Tragically, this period was marked by intensive conflict between indigenous and immigrant Americanized blacks," writes David Shank. "If at the beginning Harris was committed to the 'civilizing' pressures of the Episcopal Church and the foreign patterns of the Liberian republic, it is also quite clear that halfway through the period a major shift in his loyalties was starting to take place."[20]

Harris was eclectic in his preaching and prophecy, drawing primarily from Scripture and his Methodist and Episcopal background, but he was thoroughly African in his outlook.

Harris joined with others in political involvement, seeking to turn Liberia into a British protectorate. For a time, in fact, he threatened local chiefs with violence and occult curses in an effort to procure their support. In 1909, after a failed coup, he was tried, convicted of treason, fined, imprisoned, and paroled, only to be imprisoned again after breaking the terms of his parole by preaching against the ruling regime.

While he was in prison, he testified to a visionary experience—a visitation from the angel Gabriel who told him that he would be the prophetic voice of the end times. He was instructed to forsake his fetishes and his Western fashions and shoes and become a wandering barefoot prophet wearing a white robe and preaching Christian baptism. Harris was eclectic in his preaching and prophecy, drawing primarily from Scripture and his Methodist and Episcopal background—especially in his emphasis on the Lord's Prayer, the Ten Commandments, and the Apostles' Creed. But he was thoroughly African in his outlook, and communing with the spirits of those who had gone before—whether Moses, Elijah, or Jesus—was a natural aspect of his spirituality. Nor did he limit his sources of knowledge to mainstream teachings. His eschatology was influenced by Charles Taze Russell, founder of the Jehovah's Witnesses, and he viewed World War I as a pivotal time in history to be followed by a seven-year period of tribulation.

He initiated his ministry in 1910, beginning along the Liberian coast and later extending his travels to the Ivory Coast and Gold Coast. He "dressed in a white cassock and turban with a cross-topped staff in one hand and a Bible and baptismal bowl in the other," according to Shank. He was a "striking and original figure" in his ministry of assailing demonic powers. "In response, all the village people would bring their religious artifacts to be burned; then they would kneel for baptism while grasping the cross, and receive a tap of confirmation with the prophet's Bible." He was sometimes criticized for baptizing people who had not been instructed properly and did not understand even the basics of Christian belief, but that very factor has also been suggested as one of the primary reasons for his effectiveness in making converts and keeping "people from returning to the old powers." For him, baptism was "a preventative measure."[21]

His reputation for performing signs and wonders quickly spread, and people often sought him out—fearing God's wrath if they did not. Although certain government officials testified to his leaving behind a higher moral and ethical climate than when he had entered the area, he was nevertheless perceived by many as he traveled the Gold Coast to be a troublemaker. In 1915 he and three women singers (who some said were his wives) were arrested and beaten and then sent back to Liberia. His repeated attempts to return to the Ivory Coast were thwarted by authorities; nevertheless, he continued his preaching in Liberia and Sierra Leone. Despite the revival that followed in the wake of his preaching, most missionaries distanced themselves from him because of his refusal to condemn polygamy. Yet he continued to have a tenuous relationship with the Methodists to the end of his life, and when he died in 1928, an Episcopalian minister officiated at his funeral.

The legacy of William Wade Harris on the West Coast of Africa was enormous. He left behind an indigenous Christian church largely free of ritual sacrifice and fetishism, with converts affiliating with not only the Methodist and Episcopal churches but also Baptists, the Christian and Missionary Alliance, and the Catholic Church. Indeed, here in Africa was one of the remarkable instances of mission history when a religious figure was "prophet" to both Protestants and Catholics. He was regarded by Catholics as the instrument used for the "salvation of the Ivory Coast." This was true also in Ghana, where revival among Catholics was described as "divine fire lit by the grace of the divine Master." Likewise, in Liberia, Father Ogè reported in 1920 that the Catholic mission was growing "by leaps and bounds" because "the pagans, deprived of their old gods, stream to our churches and ask for religious instruction." All this he credited to the teachings of the "famous prophet Harris."[22]

Harris also left behind in the Ivory Coast the Ѐglise Harriste. This church was formed when there were no mission churches close by. After he had baptized converts and given basic instruction in Christian beliefs, he appointed twelve apostles to lead the new church, and many of these churches thrived in the years that followed. This African movement reported some 200,000 members by the late twentieth century; and since his death, other "prophets"—both male and female—have come to the fore, claiming comparable authority. Summing up this "Pentecost in Africa," Frederick Price wrote: "Many of these people may be members of the invisible church of Christ even though we cannot admit them into full membership in the local assembly."[23]

Harris's message was simple and was given to all who would listen without the expectation of reward or recognition. "He was not teaching a gospel other than that he had learnt from the missionaries," writes Adrian Hastings. "It was rather that his visions had provided the biblical message with a greater immediacy. He believed himself, indeed, to be an Elijah, a John the Baptist, but he expected his converts to become Methodists or Roman Catholics, and many of them did."[24] He died a poor man, and no denomination or indigenous movement could claim him as distinctly their own.

Semisi Nau

Most missionaries from the non-Western world, like the vast majority of those from the Western world, lived and died in relative obscurity, with no great revivals during their lifetime and with no legacies of achievement that commanded later biographies. This was true of Semisi Nau (c. 1866–1927), who served faithfully as one among more than a thousand Pacific Island missionaries. "The difficulties involved in recovering Semisi Nau's story underscores the problems of missionary invisibility," writes Allan Davidson. "Yet our understanding of mission history is incomplete while we are unable to take into account the contribution of all those involved. It highlights the danger of writing only 'from above,' from the perspective of the missionary society, its board, administration, supporters, and European staff."[25] What is most remarkable about Semisi is that he left behind an autobiography that was not published until some seventy years after he died.

Semisi was born in Fiji, the son of a Methodist minister and missionary. He prepared for his missionary training at Tupou College in Tonga and then volunteered to do mission work in New Guinea, but he was not deemed suitable as a single man. Following his marriage, he again pleaded for an opportunity to serve in missions no matter how lowly the position—"If it is only to chop wood or carry water in the service of God, I want to go." He had come through "a time of great difficulty and darkness," having mourned the deaths of three of his four children. This time the Methodist mission agreed to commission him, and in 1905 he sailed to the Solomon Islands to serve under John Goldie, who had begun work there three years earlier.

It was an extremely difficult assignment from the very beginning. The native people on the remote coral ridge of Ontong Java refused to allow him and his Samoan partner to come ashore, so for more than three months the two men waited in a boat. "The endurance of the missionaries raises questions," writes Davidson, "about the propriety of Goldie's leaving the two men in such a precarious position and the wisdom of the missionaries remaining in a situation where they were clearly unwanted."[26]

The vast majority of native missionaries were not independent leaders in their own right, as were Kanzo Uchimura, Pandita Ramabai, William Wade Harris, John Sung, and others. And in many respects, Semisi's story illustrates the unfortunate circumstances of these evangelists and church planters under the authority of Western missionaries. After being stranded offshore, Semisi and his companion moved on to a rival village, where they were allowed to come ashore. Later he returned to the village where he was rebuffed, and after two more weeks of waiting, he was permitted to come ashore. His message was one the chief could understand. He offered a Spirit more powerful than the spirits they worshipped. There was no concept of individual salvation. The question was: "Do you want the Lotu to come to this place?—*Lotu* meaning the Christian way of worship, replacing traditional spirit worship." Through "power encounter" and Semisi's persuasion, "a people movement followed with a ready acceptance of the Christian Lotu or way of worship."[27]

In many respects, Semisi's story illustrates the unfortunate circumstances of native evangelists and church planters under the authority of Western missionaries.

But the mass movement became entwined with local and international religion and politics. The local chief whose conversion was influenced by the expectation of power became convinced that there was more to gain with a European missionary and threatened to switch his allegiance to the Catholics unless Semisi was replaced. Thus, he was exchanged for an inexperienced Australian missionary, who "quickly alienated the chief and the traditional priests with his heavy-handed, confrontational approach."[28] The anticipated mass movement to Christianity never came to fruition.

In the meantime, Semisi was sent to another area in the Solomon Islands, only to be replaced once more—this time by native missionaries. Though he remained devoted to Goldie, it is perhaps not surprising that in his autobiography he expressed some resentment for how his own calling and concerns had often been disregarded by the mission from the very beginning. Yet there were times of great satisfaction in his ministry, particularly when he returned to Tonga; and through his enthusiastic preaching for missions, more than one hundred people volunteered for missionary service—though only two of those were actually received into service.

Semisi later returned to Ontong Java to try to reconstitute the people movement left in ruins by the Australian missionary, but he was never able to return to the days when hundreds of people were attending church. In 1918, after little more than a dozen years of missionary service, he returned to Tonga, where he settled into pastoral ministry until his death less than a decade later.

John Sung

Like many other church and mission leaders in the non-Western world, John Sung (1901–44) often found himself in conflict with Western missionaries, whose influence dominated Chinese Christianity during his lifetime. He was the sixth child of a Methodist minister from the Hinghwa district of Southeast China. His mother had been an ardent Buddhist until she nearly died giving birth to her fifth child—a frightening experience that led to her conversion. His own conversion occurred when he was nine years old during a revival known as the "Hinghwa Pentecost," when thousands in this Buddhist stronghold made profession of faith. Soon after that he began traveling with his father, sometimes preaching himself and often referred to as the "little pastor" of Hinghwa.

After completing secondary school, Sung received an offer from an American woman to fund his education at Ohio Wesleyan University. In 1923, after three years of undergraduate studies in physics and chemistry, he graduated with highest honors and was elected to Phi Beta Kappa. Although he was awarded scholarships at Harvard and other universities, he continued his studies at Ohio State University, earning his Ph.D. in chemistry in 1926. So remarkable were his achievements that his story appeared in newspapers around the country, and there were invitations to teach at prestigious universities. But despite the opportunities and accolades, he felt unfulfilled, remembering the call to ministry he had sensed as a child. He was determined to continue his education—turning from science to seminary. At the advice of a friend, he enrolled at Union Theological Seminary in New York, where he studied under Henry Sloan Coffin, Harry Emerson Fosdick, and other notable liberal scholars.

Instead of preparing him for ministry, the courses he took caused him to question the very foundations of the Christian faith. The Bible, he was taught, was one of many sacred texts of the world's great religions—not God's special revelation. As such, it made no sense to seek to convert people to Christianity. He questioned his own conversion, and in desperation, he began studying the religion of his ancestors and chanting Buddhist scriptures. "My soul wandered in a wilderness," he later confessed. "I could neither sleep nor eat. My faith was like a leaking, storm-driven ship without captain or compass. My heart was filled with the deepest unhappiness."[29]

During this time of depression and doubt, Sung was invited to attend Calvary Baptist Church to hear a visiting scholar—with the hope that the scholar might have answers to counteract the scholars at Union Seminary. But the night he attended, the scholar was unable to speak, and in his place was a fifteen-year-old evangelist, Uldine Utley. Like he had been, she was a "little preacher," and he was captivated by her message. He returned for the following four nights to hear her, vowing that he would pray until God gave him the same power to preach that this girl had. His life was transformed, and in the weeks and months that followed, he spent his time reading the Bible and Christian biographies and testifying of his newly reclaimed faith. When he was given a gift of a globe by a stranger, he took it as a sign from God that he would one day preach the gospel around the world. Instead of chanting Buddhist scriptures, he began singing hymns as he walked the halls of the seminary—behavior that was viewed by some of the seminary officials as a sign of mental instability.

Sung's life was transformed, and in the months that followed, he spent his time reading the Bible and Christian biographies and testifying of his newly reclaimed faith.

Sung was ordered to submit to psychological exams and then was confined, against his will, to the psychiatric ward of Bloomingdale Hospital. During this time he testified of his faith to other patients and read through the Bible forty times, later referring to the hospital and this time of confinement as his real theological seminary. With the help of the Chinese consul, he was released in the summer of 1927 and returned to China to preach the gospel—turning away opportunities to teach science at Chinese universities.

In the years that followed, Sung worked with the Bethel Mission as an itinerant evangelist, sometimes speaking more than five times a day. During a six-month period some fourteen thousand people made professions of faith, and nearly three thousand of them volunteered to serve in evangelistic teams—forming some seven hundred, which were named Bethel Bands.

In 1930 Sung became an evangelist for the Hinghwa Conference of the Methodist Church. By this time his reputation was preceding him, and people were coming from great distances to hear him preach. He held evangelistic campaigns in most of the major cities of China, including Shanghai, Nanking, Tenghsien, and Amoy. In Amoy, when the crowds overflowed the largest church, "a special mat-shed was erected to accommodate twenty-five hundred people." On another occasion, five thousand people came to a campaign that was held at a football field.[30]

Sung was an animated preacher, often pacing back and forth across the platform, and is sometimes compared with Billy Sunday. Those who were moved by his preaching often wept openly and confessed their sins. It was through his ministry that the "Holy Ghost revivals of 1933–36" broke out. But along with success came criticism—particularly from missionaries and Chinese leaders, who blamed him for speaking ill of the Western missionaries. In his book *I Remember John Sung*, William Schubert writes of this animosity:

> Then I went to the missionary, who was a friend of mine, and I asked, "Why do you oppose Dr. Sung?" He replied: "Because he criticizes us missionaries; he stands up there and says, 'You hypocrites of missionaries on the back seat.'" I told him, "Now Frank, I'll tell you what to do: You sit in front of me, and whatever you can't take, you throw it over your shoulder to me; I need it."[31]

Sung did not limit his ministry to China. In the years that followed his great revivals in China, he traveled to Taiwan, the Philippines, Singapore, Malaysia, Indonesia, and Thailand—in some cases returning several times. Everywhere he went there were conversions and churches were planted. His demands and expectations were high. When he visited Java on his third missionary journey to Indonesia in 1939, he announced to the congregation at Surabaja that he had twenty-two messages to give during his one-week visit, insisting that people attend three meetings a day. Shops were closed, and children were taken out of schools to attend the meetings. But attendance was only one aspect of the week-long training. Adults and youth were expected to go out in teams and evangelize neighboring villages.

Sung was an evangelist and missionary, but perhaps even more than this outward ministry, he was known as a man of prayer. David Smithers writes of this aspect of his life:

> When John Sung was not actively preaching or organizing a new evangelistic team, he usually could be found writing in his diary or adding to his ever growing prayer list. He carefully prayed over an extensive list of people's needs, which was accompanied by dozens of small photographs. . . . Everywhere he went, he urged the people to give themselves to prayer. . . . John Sung made it his regular habit to be up every morning at 5 A.M. to pray for two or three hours. "Prayer for John Sung was like a battle. He prayed until the sweat

> poured down his face." At times he would literally collapse upon his bed and uncontrollably weep and sob under the burden of travailing prayer. John Sung believed that prayer was the most important work of the believer. He defined faith as watching God work while on your knees.[32]

In the midst of his hectic schedule, Sung sought to fulfill his duties as a husband and father. His marriage had been arranged before he returned to China, but according to Seamands, the marriage proved quite successful, and Mrs. Sung became John's faithful companion through all their eighteen years of life together. They had three daughters and two sons who, in addition to their Chinese names, were given "biblical" names: Genesis, Exodus, Leviticus, Numbers, and Joshua.

Sung died of cancer and related causes before he reached his forty-third birthday, but his legacy lives on as one of China's greatest missionary evangelists.

Elka of the Wai Wai

Certain celebrities are known by only one name. So it was with Elka, one of the most celebrated witchdoctors and chiefs of the Wai Wai people of British Guiana and far beyond in the Amazon jungle. A witchdoctor might seem like an unlikely candidate for conversion to Christianity. But Elka had been drawn to spiritual things from the time he was a child—receiving dreams from the spirit of a pig telling him that Kworokyam, the god of the Wai Wai, wanted him to sing his songs and be his servant.

"While Elka dreamed of pigs controlled by evil spirits," writes Homer Dowdy, "hundreds of miles away three brothers with another vision were planning a move that would bring them face to face with the Wai Wai." Neill Hawkins, the oldest brother at thirty-three, and his two younger brothers, Rader and Bob, had grown up in the "old-time religion" of a Christian home in Texas, and their mother was determined to one day send her three sons off as missionaries. They all joined the Unevangelized Fields Mission to serve in South America—in Brazil and British Guiana.[33]

When Neill and Bob Hawkins began their work among the Wai Wai in 1949, they were the first white men that many of the people had ever seen, and they were initially thought to be enemies who had come to kill the people. But they slowly settled into the tribe, hired men to build a runway, and brought in their wives and children on what the native people referred to as the canoe from the sky. Elka, the chief and witchdoctor, quickly became fascinated with "God's paper," the Bible that had written words about God, and he eagerly agreed to serve as a language informant for Bible translation into his yet unwritten language. He had often felt insecure about the messages he was getting from the spirits and the Wai Wai god, but here the words were on paper, and he was learning to decipher that message himself.

> Elka did more than try to make the strange scratches on paper talk back to him. He was not content until he knew what the scratches said—not just what they said out loud, but what they spoke to his mind. In the Sunday lessons, in the reading classes, and in the long language-informant periods with Bahm [Bob Hawkins] he learned about God and his Son, Jesus Christ.
>
> Most of his people were slow to learn. But Elka had a yearning to know that made him awake each morning eager for another session.... Bahm had once thought he was presenting God to Elka in a spiritual vacuum. He was wrong. Elka believed in the spirit world with more conviction than he did in the physical.... It was not hard for him to believe that God was a spirit.[34]

But Elka was not ready to forsake his role as witchdoctor for the Wai Wai people. He wanted to believe what the missionaries were teaching without having to give up Kworokyam, the god of his people. Initially, the tension between the two belief systems stimulated his thinking and brought excitement into his life, but as time passed, the tension was "fought in the pit of his stomach," "brought despondency," and "worried Elka constantly." When he was told that "God's paper said he could not serve both God and Kworokyam," he knew he would have to make a choice. Finally, after a long struggle, he recognized what God wanted him to do—how God wanted him to serve his people. He made his decision—to be "Christ's witchdoctor."[35]

Being Christ's witchdoctor, however, meant that Elka would no longer use his charms to heal the sick and drive away evil spirits. This caused great distress among the tribal elders, who insisted that he could "walk with Jesus" and use his charms at the same time. In the midst of this tribal conflict, most of the people continued coming to the Sunday services, and Bahm taught Bible classes to some of the men in small groups.

Within a matter of years, the Sunday preaching was turned over to Wai Wai Christians, a practice that began when one of the Hawkins brothers lost his voice and Elka volunteered to fill in.

As Elka studied the Bible every day, he spent more time with the missionaries and visited their homes. And "seeing the tools of the white man's culture, he developed an appetite for the things they had." He wanted a high chair to keep his baby off the floor, even as they had for their baby. He wanted an outboard motor for his canoe as they had, and he wanted a light in his house at night. "He wanted to exchange his loincloth for shorts." These were difficult issues that had no easy answers, and the missionaries "tried to explain that they did not want to make the Wai Wai dependent on the white man's world." There was often strain between the two sides. "But this mood did not dominate his life," writes Dowdy. "He lost no occasion ... to be a witness for Christ."[36]

The patient and persistent work of the missionaries, with the tribal leadership of Elka, resulted in a continual stream of conversions. Within a matter of years, the Sunday preaching was turned over to Wai Wai Christians, a practice that began when one of the Hawkins brothers lost his voice and Elka volunteered to fill in. His sermon on Daniel was a "revelation" of "Elka's ability to speak with . . . a ring of conviction in his voice."[37]

With the growing community of believers came a desire to reach out beyond their own clan. "Elka was concerned about the Wai Wai who still lived across the high mountains. . . . He wanted them to learn the way of Christ." So as chief, he commissioned his brother to go to them and invite them to come back and learn God's way. That was the beginning of mission outreach, and it continued as Elka commissioned others to go even farther with the message of God's paper.

> They made a start by inviting the Shedeu and the Mawayana, people very like themselves, to come and hear the Gospel. But there were strange tribes farther away, people they did not know or people they had always feared, who still lived without hope in fear and suspicion, hatred and killing. . . .
>
> For the Wai Wai it was a hard choice. They would have to leave their familiar land, travel . . . through strange towns of the white man's civilization. . . . Who knew whether they would ever return?[38]

Among those who went to the *regions beyond* as a *foreign* missionary was Elka, who sent prayer letters back home telling of his experiences and encouraging the Wai Wai to remain faithful to God. While he and the other missionaries were away, others planted their fields and took care of their domestic needs. When he returned, Elka had colorful stories to tell about the natives' customs—other tribes that were so different from their own, including tribes of white people who took their bath in a "shower." He found the little community of believers among the Wai Wai to have grown, as outsiders came and joined the original group. The clan of 200 had grown to 350. But there were always the temptations of people going back to their old ways.

For Elka, there were new ways that he was obliged to adopt. His missionary work required contextualization: "The Waica men wanted us to cut off our pigtails and look like them," he told his people. "At first we didn't want to. It would take many rain seasons to grow long again. But then we felt it was no sacrifice at all, if by cutting off our hair we could make the Waica know that because of Jesus we loved them."[39]

As the Wai Wai took over the leadership of their own church and reached out in mission, the two Hawkins families moved on in their ministry, Neill and his family to conduct mission work with the Trio Tribe in nearby Surinam, and Bob and his family to finish up the translation of the Wai Wai Scriptures. "By 1962 the Wai Wai had gone on as many missionary trips in as many directions as a man had fingers and toes," writes Homer Dowdy. "A few of the trips were with the white missionaries. Most of them were on their own and by themselves. . . . Some Wai Wai travelers ran out of food. Others got sick on the trail."[40]

These were the trials and tribulations of missionaries from the time of Jesus, and the Wai Wai were part of that tradition.

SELECT BIBLIOGRAPHY

Adhav, Shamsundar Manohar. *Pandita Ramabai*. Madras: Christian Literature Society, 1979.

Bush, Luis, and Lorry Lutz. *Partnering in Ministry: The Direction of World Evangelism*. Downers Grove, IL: InterVarsity Press, 1990.

Davidson, Allan K., ed. *Semisi Nau: The Story of My Life: The Autobiography of a Tongan Methodist Missionary Who Worked at Ontong Java in the Solomon Islands*. Suva, Fiji: Institute of Pacific Studies, 1996.

Dowdy, Homer. *Christ's Witchdoctor*. Grand Rapids: Zondervan, 1973.

Dyler, Helen S. *Pandita Ramabai: Her Vision, Her Mission and Her Triumph of Faith*. London: Pickering & Inglis, n.d.

Harper, Susan Billington. *In the Shadow of the Mahatma: Bishop V. S. Azariah and the Travails of Christianity in British India*. Grand Rapids: Eerdmans, 2000.

Hefley, James, and Marti Hefley. *God's Tribesman: The Rochunga Pudaite Story*. New York: Holman, 1974.

Keyes, Lawrence E. *The Last Age of Missions: A Study of Third World Missionary Societies*. Pasadena, CA: William Carey Library, 1983.

Lyall, Leslie T. *Flame for God: John Sung and Revival in the Far East*. London: Overseas Missionary Fellowship, 1976.

Seamands, John T. *Pioneers of the Younger Churches*. Nashville: Abingdon, 1967.

Schubert, William E. *I Remember John Sung*. Singapore: Far Eastern Bible College Press, 1976.

Yohannan, K. P. *The Coming Revolution in World Missions*. Altamonte Springs, FL: Creation House, 1986.

17

New Methods and Strategy: Reaching Tomorrow's World

From the time of the apostle Paul, mission strategy has been a key element in the advance of the gospel. Yet there have always been misgivings and a degree of apprehension between the one who, propelled by a sense of duty and calling and passion, simply obeys God's command and resolutely preaches the gospel, and the one who contemplates and plans and questions methods and strategies before launching into an evangelistic endeavor that may be ill-advised.

In the generations that followed the New Testament era, ordinary Christians were the missionaries who spread the faith in private homes and the marketplace, while at the same time apologists contemplated how best to make the faith comprehensible in the wider Greco-Roman world. This continued through the centuries as the gap between the lay Christian with a passion for evangelism and the missions administrator or missions professor in the ivory tower continued to grow. But the most influential and capable of the long line of mission strategists were those who were thinkers and practitioners at the same time. In recent generations, being a strategist-practitioner has become an aspiration of virtually all missionaries—though few actually attain that status.

The most influential and capable of the long line of mission strategists were those who were thinkers and practitioners at the same time.

"The New Missionary" was the title of a *Time* magazine cover story in 1982 about men and women devoting their lives to bringing Christianity to some of the most remote and impoverished areas of the world. Who is this "new missionary"? From the perspective of *Time*, the "new missionary" is not really very different from the missionary of generations past. Both are characterized by a sacrificial devotion to carrying the gospel to the ends of the earth. However, there are some significant differences between the new and the old missionary style. The "new missionary" is, in many ways, much better trained and more professional in outlook than was the "old missionary." These men and women tend to be more concerned with methodology and principles of mission strategy, more aware of population growth and other relevant statistics, more eager to make use of the latest technology, and, as *Time* pointed out, more careful than ever to avoid any tactics that would associate them with Western imperialism. They are also more likely than ever to seek to preserve colorful cultural traditions that were once viewed as unchristian.

Paralleling the development of the "new missionary" has been a significant advance in the field of missiology in recent decades, as evidenced by scholarly journals, recognized schools of mission, and an impressive task force of forward-thinking missiologists. Once a description given only to a handful of scholarly mission board directors, today the term *missiologist* is associated with hundreds of professional specialists involved in developing more effective mission strategies. In 1970 the American Society of Missiology did not exist, but a decade later, eight years after its founding, it had several hundred members. By the 1990s more seminaries and schools of religion were offering studies in missiology—a specialty coming of age in the broad field of theology and world religions.

The greatest area of interest and controversy in missiology in the 1990s was religious pluralism. Christianity's place among other religions was an issue as old as the faith itself. Pluralism "was known as a theological *problem* to the earliest Church," writes Geoffrey Wainwright, "but Western Christendom was not obliged to confront it—except in the shape of Islam at its circumference" and Jews "in its midst." However, that changed in modern times with "a widespread awareness of the rest of the world," and the development of Enlightenment rationalism supplied "a normative intellectual framework for a relativistic account of the various religions that systematically undermined the certainty of the Christian faith concerning the absoluteness of Christ."[1]

In the late twentieth century John Hick became a leading figure in espousing *religious pluralism*. It was his own Copernican Revolution, with Christianity no longer at the center of the universe, so to speak. Christianity was simply one of many religions—one of many paths to God. While such positions had long been held, Hick, more than anyone else, brought the matter to the forefront of missiological discussions. Karl Rahner, a Jesuit theologian, added his own unique concept to the mix by introducing a version of *inclusivism* by his term "anonymous Christian." Such are people in other religions who are saved through Christ even as Christians are—though they do not know it. Amid the new publications and ensuing controversies, evangelicals and conservative Christians of all stripes upheld the traditional position, referred to as *exclusivism*—insisting that salvation comes exclusively through Christ.

As important as the issue of religious pluralism has become, however, it is only one cultural aspect of the contemporary scene in world evangelism. The most striking characteristic of cross missions is the diversity of methodology and philosophy. Some mission strategists have conducted their work almost as though the debates were not taking place. Their concerns were church growth and how to effectively reach the most people with limited time and resources. Among the leading proponents who focused on "people groups" or "hidden peoples" were Donald McGavran, Ralph Winter, and Don Richardson, whose concepts were being supported by many mission agencies.

By the time of the annual meetings of the IFMA (Independent Foreign Missions Association) and EFMA (Evangelical Foreign Missions Association) in the fall of 1982, there were few among the nearly two hundred mission agencies of these two largest associations that were not by then already using these terms and making plans for expansion into new frontiers in order to reach these "hidden peoples." The concept was widely adopted by the younger generation of evangelical mission leaders and became a dominant theme in the last decades of the twentieth century.

Many issues that came to the fore during the last decades of the twentieth century had been topics of mission concern much earlier in the century. Although the modern missions era is generally dated with William Carey's early work in India around the turn of the nineteenth century, it was not until a century later that *missiology*—the science of mission studies—was born. That is not to say that there were not major mission thinkers before that time, but the beginning of systematic *scientific* study of missions is usually associated with Gustav Warneck, who was a professor of missions at Halle in Germany from 1897 to 1908. Another early-twentieth-century missiologist who has had a significant influence on mission theory and strategy was Roland Allen (1868–1947).

Allen was an Anglican minister who served as a missionary in China for several years before returning to England due to health problems. After serving for a time in a local parish, he resigned from the priesthood and directed his energy to lecturing and writing. "The crises of his early experience," writes Charles Henry Long, "led him to a radical reassessment of his own vocation and the theology and missionary methods of Western churches."[2]

He was a harsh critic of the mission station formula set in motion by Carey (and others before him), arguing that the missionary task was to plant self-supporting, self-governing, and self-propagating churches. His widely disseminated mission concepts were enunciated in one book—the book for which he is primarily known—*Missionary Methods: St. Paul's or Ours?* Published in 1912, this classic has influenced generations of missionaries. He wrote with passion about a Pauline style of evangelism that can all too easily become a mundane aspect of another mission *program* or *strategy*:

> St. Paul expected his hearers to be moved. He so believed in his preaching that he knew that it was "the power of God unto salvation." This expectation is a very real part of the presentation of the gospel. It is a form of faith. A mere preaching which is not accompanied by the expectation of faith, is not a true preaching of the Gospel, because faith is part of the gospel. Simply to scatter the seed, with a sort of vague hope that some of it may come up somewhere, is not preaching the gospel.... St. Paul expected to make converts, but ... others expected it also. This accounts for the opposition which his preaching created. People were afraid of his preaching, and fear is a form of expectation: it is a form of faith.... St. Paul did not scatter seeds, he planted. He so dealt with his hearers that he brought them speedily and directly to a point of decision, and then he demanded ... they make a choice and act on their choice.[3]

Dutch scholars also made significant contributions to the field of missiology in the early twentieth century, among them Hendrick Kraemer (1888–1965) and J. H. Bavinck (1895–1964), who both served as missionaries in Indonesia. Kraemer is remembered for taking a stand against liberalizing tendencies in missiology—particularly his defense of the uniqueness of Christ and the biblical message in relation to world religions. Bavinck also focused attention on world religions. "The central problem in Bavinck's thinking," writes J. van den Berg, "was that of the relationship between religious experience and God's revelation in Jesus Christ."[4] He was particularly interested in eastern mysticism, confessing that he himself "was born with an Eastern soul." The two works for which he is most remembered are *An Introduction to the Science of Missions* and *The Church Between Temple and Mosque*.

As a missionary and as a professor, Bavinck was deeply committed to evangelism and ecumenical endeavors. "He was ecumenical," writes Johannes Verkuyl, "not because he felt forced to be showy or stylish, but simply because with childlike simplicity he thankfully and joyously recognized the Spirit of Jesus Christ in whichever human beings and church communions He was revealing Himself."[5] Yet, despite his "radical devotion to Jesus," he struggled with "powers of darkness" in his own life. In his book *Faith and Its Difficulties*, he confessed his own struggles in believing:

> In all the voices that reach my ear, in all the books I open, I recognize and see Him, the mighty Unknown, the Regent of life, the Ruler of all nations. And with every step I take, I have difficulty understanding that the Unknown God is the same as the God who spoke to me in Jesus Christ. And sometimes I am oppressed with fear and anguish that I can see no confluence of these two, that I cannot see them proceeding in one direction, and that everything will be demolished and destroyed. That is our tension and our strain. And we shudder![6]

This tension that Bavinck experienced reflected the tension of many Christians in modern and postmodern times and set the stage for missiologists like Lesslie Newbigin, who would, like Bavinck, bring East and West together in one heart and mind. With the same spirit, though in a very different way, Ken Strachan sought to bring North and South together in his ministry in Latin America.

R. Kenneth Strachan

A widely hailed—and sometimes controversial—mission strategy of the mid-twentieth century known as "saturation evangelism" was advanced by Ken Strachan. His development of Evangelism-in-Depth was extolled as a "Revolution in Evangelism," as the title of a book on the subject suggests. His concepts still stimulate debate and claim loyal disciples, though he died in 1965. Yet his basic premise, "that the growth of any movement is in direct proportion to its ability to mobilize its entire membership for continuous evangelism," was not new.[7] Others had operated under the same theory, but none had developed it into a well-defined missionary thrust. It was left to Strachan to do that, in part as a reaction to the weaknesses he saw in his own father's evangelistic ministry.

Ken Strachan (1910–65) was born and raised in Latin America, the son of Susan and Harry Strachan, cofounders of the Latin America Mission (originally called the Latin American Evangelization Campaign). Most of his early years were spent in Costa Rica, his mother being responsible for the oversight of LAM headquarters while his father conducted evangelistic tours. Roberts writes that Harry Strachan, "as ubiquitous as the fabled Don Quixote, had moved up and down the continent in unceasing evangelistic activity, setting up, coordinating, and carrying on evangelistic campaigns in all the principal cities of Latin America. He was advance man, follow-up man, coordinator, master of ceremonies, song leader, and sometimes the evangelist himself."[8] But impressive as his individual pursuits were, he was unable to inspire others to join the ministry with equal enthusiasm. And as his health declined, so did the evangelistic efforts of the mission.

That the son could ever fill his father's shoes seemed out of the question. "Squirt" was his nickname at Wheaton College, and there was little else about him that would have pointed to a future missionary statesman. He "lacked his father's commanding pulpit presence, his singing voice, his natural authority, and his ability as a preacher and evangelist. Little wonder that he should be plagued all his life by an inferiority complex in this area of his ministry."[9]

Moreover, throughout his young adult life, Ken Strachan was plagued by spiritual battles. During his college years he frankly admitted such in a letter to his mother:

> Things have not been going very well, Mother, and I hate to tell you about it, but I know you'd rather hear it from me than elsewhere.... I tried hard to get right with God.... I had a fight for several days ..., and in the end I lost out.... It would not have been so bad if it were only that I had backslidden religiously, but I have lost any traces of manhood. I have no willpower or self-control, I have not made myself do the things I know I should have done, and

> as a result, I am failing not only in Christian life but even more so than the most worldly man. . . . I feel so heartily ashamed of myself when I think of what I should have done and didn't, and yet I haven't the strength or haven't gone far enough to turn back.[10]

In 1945 his father died, and he was suddenly thrust into a position of leadership that he did not relish. Immediately, there were decisions to make, and the differences between father and son became readily apparent. While Ken saw the need for publicity and promotional work, he had an instinctive aversion for it. He tried to continue his father's evangelistic emphasis, but big-time evangelism was simply not his niche. He saw "inconsistencies, contradictions, and even phoniness" in things "others seemed to accept with ease." Another area that troubled him was the tightrope he was forced to walk "between the Fundamentalists and the Inclusivists, whose controversies were highly distasteful to a man of such vision for cooperation."[11]

Strachan's position in the mission became that of codirector with his mother, and he served in that capacity until she died in 1950. Then, as the director of the Latin America Mission, his leadership qualities blossomed. The mission expanded its radio, literature, educational, and medical services; and by 1960 the missionary force had increased to 144, an 82 percent increase since the death of his mother a decade earlier.

More important than the increased membership from North America, however, was the Latin-Americanization of the ministry. For years Strachan had been concerned about the "race question" (not black versus white per se, though he may have been alone as a white evangelical mission leader to maintain membership in the NAACP). He had taken issue with his mother when she had been insensitive to employing Latins in the mission; and later, when he stepped into the directorship, he took steps to bring Latins in on an equal par with North Americans.

"Latinizing" the mission did not simply mean bringing in more Latin members and allowing them opportunities for leadership. It also meant bringing the mission policy itself in line with Latin culture and thinking. The issue of mixed marriages, for example, was a sore point. Most of the North American missionaries had opposed such marriages—a position perceived by the Latins as one of implied superiority. Strachan faced the issue squarely and insisted that such "obstacles to full fellowship be eradicated."[12] To further incorporate Latins into the mission, Spanish became the language in which all business was conducted.

Cooperating effectively with the Latin Americans came much more easily than did cooperation with fellow North American missionaries outside the LAM. He wanted to work with others in cooperative ventures even if they were not within the fundamentalist camp. He quickly realized, however, that such an approach threatened to dry up contributions from zealous supporters back home.

After walking the tightrope for several years, he became convinced that the Scriptures did not teach separation as fundamentalists perceived it, and LAM began to take a more cooperative approach to evangelism. By broadening the appeal in an effort to expand the evangelistic outreach, the mission lost support and was accused of "flirting with apostasy both in the Ecumenical Movement and the Roman Catholic Church."[13]

Earlier in his ministry, Strachan had renounced any association with groups tied to the World Council of Churches, but by the 1960s his position toward both the WCC and the Roman Catholic Church had softened. The greatest threat to Latin America, he had come to believe, was communism; and to combat the evils of that system, Christians had to work together. This radical departure from traditional evangelical thinking surfaced publicly at the 1961 convention of the National Association of Evangelicals, where he made the statement that "Rome is changing," and "we may have to stand beside Rome against Communism."[14] Though he later qualified his optimism about the changes occurring in Catholicism, he nevertheless created a stir that would widen the gap between him and other conservative evangelical missions and supporting churches.

Many evangelicals did not acknowledge the positive changes that were occurring in Latin America through the influence of Pope John XXIII and Vatican II. Although Strachan did not live to steer his mission through this new era of relaxed religious tension, the LAM, under the leadership of others, continued to maintain an openness toward Catholics, thereby isolating itself more and more from many of the evangelical missions. As controversial as his softening toward Catholicism was, however, in the minds of some it was no worse than his friendship and cooperation with Pentecostals. To him a "ministry of reconciliation" was far more conducive to missions and to an evangelistic program than was a strict separatist position, and that attitude pervaded the Evangelism-in-Depth campaigns and the total ministry of LAM.

The evangelistic crusade ministry of LAM that he had continued after the death of his father came to a climax in 1958 following the Billy Graham Caribbean crusade. It was an exhilarating time, but despite the outward signs of immediate success, he had become convinced that such an approach was not effective evangelism. He believed that "the church, rather than the visiting evangelistic team, was ... central in God's program of evangelistic outreach."[15] Total mobilization of the church became his theme—a theme that he developed after observing and reading abut the success of three rapidly expanding groups: Communists, Jehovah's Witnesses, and Pentecostals.

His first experiment with Evangelism-in-Depth was a seven-month endeavor in Nicaragua, which he launched with a retreat for interested Christian workers. Following this four-day conference of seminars and Bible studies, those present fanned out across the country and began developing visitation programs and witnessing teams in local churches. This was followed by area-wide evangelistic campaigns and climaxed by a nationwide crusade in Managua. Follow-up was a key element; new believers were established in local churches and discipled by more mature Christians. Judged on the basis of the traditional crusade, this program was "fabulously successful."[16] It was truly a national effort, and as a result some twenty-five hundred reportedly were converted.

What happened in Nicaragua was seen by many as an encouraging new trend in missionary outreach that was ideal for anywhere in the world. "Here is a well-organized effort to meet the demands of this hour," wrote Arthur Glasser. "We are being shown what can be accomplished when the total Christian strength of a country is mobilized for a united effort."

"We are being shown what can be accomplished when the total Christian strength of a country is mobilized for a united effort," wrote Glasser.

Despite the praise, Strachan was not satisfied with the Nicaraguan effort. Although nationals had undertaken the major responsibility for the extended campaign, the initiative had come from the outside, and "it could not truthfully be said that a revolution had been effected in the work and attitudes of the churches."[17]

The next Evangelism-in-Depth experiment was in Costa Rica. Here, as in Nicaragua, there were many decisions for Christ, but again the lasting tangible effect on the local churches was less than had been anticipated, and the local committee was left strapped with a large debt after the five-month effort was completed.

The mental and physical strain of the Costa Rican campaign and the lackluster results left Strachan spiritually and psychologically depressed. Serious doubts arose as to whether LAM should move ahead with a planned Evangelism-in-Depth program for Guatemala. The mission was in deep financial straits, and the future looked dismal. Then, during a meeting in September of 1961 at Keswick Grove, New Jersey, the picture suddenly changed. As he later recalled, "in that moment . . . a promissory note was written on a piece of scratch paper and laid before the Lord. Suddenly we were brought out of the distress of mind to the perfect haven of assurance that God would provide."[18]

The Guatemalan effort went forward, and the end result was "not only the biggest and the toughest but also the 'deepest' of the Evangelism-in-Depth movements to date." When the year of concentrated outreach ended, the "harvest had only begun." "The conclusion was inescapable," according to Dayton Roberts. "Guatemala had been shaken spiritually during 1962 as never before."[19]

The Guatemalan campaign marked the end of Ken's very active involvement with Evangelism-in-Depth. His health was declining, and in 1963 his doctors diagnosed his condition to be Hodgkin's disease—a deteriorating condition that took his life in 1965. The principles that he had developed through Evangelism-in-Depth, however, would not die. His colleagues in Latin America continued the efforts he had begun, and in nine years eight countries were reached, resulting in more than one hundred thousand conversions. As word of such successes spread, missionaries and church leaders from all over the world took notice. Invitations to conduct Evangelism-in-Depth campaigns came from as far away as Hong Kong and Japan, and LAM officials had the unique opportunity of teaching their principles to others who would carry out the actual ministry.

Evangelism-in-Depth changed over the years, but the basic principle of mobilizing laypeople and Christian workers remains. And in the years since Strachan's death, the work of LAM, known for its progressive views in regard to the relationship between the mission and the national church, continued to move forward. Instead of opting for "the most common solution . . . of two parallel but independent organizations on the same field—the association of local churches and a continuing mission structure with a coordinating committee as go-between," the mission "took a bold step in organizing each entity in Latin America under Latin leadership."[20] Some North Americans found the policy difficult to adjust to, but it represented the far-sighted mission philosophy that Ken Strachan so ably promoted.

Orlando Costas

Mission leadership and independence in Latin America was coming of age, with or without the encouragement of Ken Strachan, and among the voices raised from that part of the world was Orlando Costas (1942–87). He had participated in Evangelism-in-Depth, and that experience opened his eyes to the divisiveness of Christians in Latin America—among old-line Protestants, evangelicals, charismatics, and Catholics. A major aspect of his ministry was to build bridges and nurture dialogue among these groups. He also sought to build a bridge between Latin America and North America.

Costas was born in Puerto Rico and at age twelve immigrated to the United States with his family—exchanging the "island of enchantment" for "Hispanic ghettoes of large U.S. cities." He might have taken a turn toward gangs and crime, but with his Methodist heritage, he turned toward Madison Square Garden and a Billy Graham Crusade, which he speaks of as his first conversion—to saving faith in Christ. His second conversion was his rediscovery of his Hispanic roots, and his third was his conversion to social activism. As a student at Bob Jones University through the influence of a Puerto Rican friend, his concern for communicating the gospel took root. But another concern also took root that year: "I came face to face with Anglo-Saxon culture in its worst form . . . the puritanical value system . . . the shameless defense and justification of racism . . . and the triumphalistic belief in the divine (manifest) destiny of the United States."[21]

Costas left the university and returned to the North. In the years that followed, he served in pastoral positions, studied at Nyack Missionary College, and then returned to Puerto Rico with his wife Rose to continue in pastoral ministry and university studies. "These studies led me to rediscover my Puerto Rican identity, to affirm my Latin American cultural heritage, to begin to question the political hegemony of the United States in Latin America and to consciously break with its culture," he said. Referring to an incident in 1965 when Marines landed in the Dominican Republic to support a military coup, he lamented, "I had a chance to see for myself how a powerful nation quenched the hopes and aspirations of a people."[22]

> *"I came face to face with Anglo-Saxon culture in its worst form . . . the puritanical value system . . . the shameless defense and justification of racism."*

After returning to the States for seminary studies, Costas and his wife served in Costa Rica as missionaries with the Latin America Mission, where he taught at the Biblical Seminary in San José and worked with Evangelism-in-Depth. During the decade of the 1970s he was deeply involved in the turmoil and excitement that was occurring within the context of Latin American missiology—particularly as it related to liberation theology. Biblical seminary itself "became the focus of a bitter controversy at the center of which was liberation theology." The issue became so polarized that he left the school and the vision behind. "The dream we had," he writes, "of making the Seminary an Evangelical institution committed to the Latin American context and independent from American missionary power centers had been frustrated (at least for me)."[23]

During those turbulent 1970s Costas took his doctoral studies at Free University in Amsterdam with the noted missiologist Johannes Verkuyl and then relocated in Birmingham, England, where he taught at the missionary training center at Selly Oak Colleges, where Lesslie Newbigin also taught. By the time he returned to Latin America for his second term of missionary work, his name was becoming well known in the field of missiology—far beyond that region of the world. In 1980 he relocated again—this time to Pennsylvania, where he would teach at Eastern Baptist Theological Seminary and later at Andover Newton Theological Seminary in Massachusetts.

In his widely heralded book *Christ outside the Gate*, Costas addressed several key issues related to the church and mission, including what he viewed to be a continuing alliance between mission endeavors and Western imperialism. "It was not by accident that mission work took an entrepreneurial shape," he argued. "It occurred because the modern missionary movement is the child of the world of free enterprise." His seeing the United States as "a New Macedonia" was a reversal of how the Central American Mission and other mission societies viewed Latin America as "Samaria"—the next door neighbor that should be evangelized. Instead, he saw the United States as "a mission field for Third-World Christians." He sensed a visionary call to Latin American Christians and other minorities in

North America to bring the simple gospel of Jesus Christ to Americans for whom the gospel has been distorted.

Costas was at the height of his missions vocation when he was diagnosed with terminal cancer. "On November 5, 1987, at the age of forty-five, the man who had crossed so many borders as a missionary crossed the final border to meet his Lord."[24]

Donald McGavran

One of the most recognized missiologists of the late twentieth century was Donald McGavran, whose specialty was church growth. Not content with the age-old mission station approach, for more than a half century he was a missionary activist vitally involved in cross-cultural evangelism. "His thesis," writes Arthur Glasser, "is that the social sciences can be harnessed to the missionary task. Research and analysis can result in the removal of hindrances to the growth of the church. Indeed, he is the Apostle of Church Growth."[25] McGavran brought a new twist to the subject of church growth that thrust him into the very center of the fiery debate. In fact, much of the debate on mission strategy in the 1970s and 1980s were focused on his ideas. "He has been lauded, and he has been blasted," writes David Allen Hubbard, "but he has not been ignored."[26]

McGavran was born in India in 1897, the son and grandson of missionaries. He initially rebelled against the thought of a lifetime of "missionary barrel" life style: "My father has done enough for the Lord," he reasoned. "It is time for me to strike out for myself and earn some money."[27] His student days at Butler University foreshadowed his later missions career. As president of his senior class and a debater, he looked forward to a career in law. But through the influence of the Student Volunteer Movement his aspirations changed. After graduating from Yale Divinity School, he and his wife went to India to begin their life as missionaries—a life filled with adventure that harks back to the missionary pioneers of an earlier generation—adventure that included fending off a wounded tiger on one occasion and a wild boar on another, checking "almost single-handed a cholera epidemic," climbing in the Himalayas, and trekking through the jungles of remote islands in the Philippines.

But his adventures also included conducting seminars across Africa, producing a motion picture, and writing more than a dozen books. Retirement, however, was not among his accomplishments. In 1973, during his seventy-sixth year, he wrote three books, taught classes, and conducted research projects. In 1983 he conducted seminars in India and Japan, and his active ministry continued in the years that followed.

McGavran's missionary career began in Harda, India, as the superintendent of a mission school, serving under the United Christian Missionary Society. He later served in other capacities relating to education and medical services and was active in translation and evangelistic work. In the mid-1930s his missionary work was briefly interrupted by further graduate studies that culminated in a Ph.D. at Columbia University.

For two more decades he ministered in India, during which time he was deeply involved in studying the phenomenon of mass movements, but by the mid-1950s his mission board began to use him in broader activities. He was interested in missiological issues—particularly the mission strategy of church growth. He had long realized that much of the work that was being conducted by missionaries was accomplishing very little toward the goal of world evangelization, and he wanted to study new concepts of evangelism. At that time he began teaching in the field of missions at various Christian institutions, and in 1961 he founded the Institute of Church Growth, with which his name has been associated for more than two decades.

Like Ken Strachan, McGavran studied evangelistic activities of others to discover principles and methodology that resulted in church growth. No method was sacred or beyond the scrutiny of scientific investigation. Even Strachan's Evangelism-in-Depth was eventually put to the test. "Careful research on several Latin American republics," according to C. Peter Wagner, "could not come up with any cause and effect relationships between year-long Evangelism-in-Depth efforts and increased rates of growth in the churches."[28] For McGavran and his disciples, the actual incorporation of converts into the church—not necessarily the numbers of "decisions"—was the key factor in evaluating missionary methodology. If crusade evangelism resulted in church growth, McGavran sought to discover why, and then he applied the principles he had discovered elsewhere.

For McGavran and his disciples, the actual incorporation of converts into the church was the key factor in evaluating missionary methodology.

Through his Institute of Church Growth this field of missiological research developed more fully than it had anywhere previously. Beginning in 1961 at Northwest Christian College in Eugene, Oregon, with one student, it moved to Fuller Theological Seminary in Pasadena in 1965. McGavran "was goal-oriented to the core," writes Wagner. "He dealt with principles, not methods. Methods were accepted or rejected . . . on the basis of what he called 'fierce pragmatism.' Research became his chief tool."[29]

From his research, McGavran concluded that not only had traditional methods of mass evangelism contributed little to real church growth, but that the main missionary thrust of the whole nineteenth and much of the twentieth century had been misdirected. The mission station approach that dominated missions for nearly two centuries had not fostered the kind of spontaneous expansion that characterized the early church. Although missionaries had worked diligently to establish indigenous churches, Christianity continued to be focused around the mission station.

"These mission station churches," writes McGavran, "are lacking in the qualities needed for growth and multiplication." The basic reason is that converts are often segregated from their former social relationships and find their only fellowship with other mission station Christians. They generally feel "immeasurably superior to their own unconverted relatives," and thus they have limited influence on them for evangelism. What results is the unintentional and misguided creation of a new tribe, a new caste, a separate society that is dependent on the mission station for employment and social services. Such Christians may "draw the easy conclusion that if more people become Christians, the resources of the mission will be spread thinner," resulting in instances where "they have actually discouraged possible converts from becoming Christian."[30]

The solution, according to McGavran, is people movements—movements of whole tribes or "homogeneous units" toward Christianity. Such "multi-individual" conversions, rather than individual conversions, were, in his mind, far more lasting and stable for real church growth. Such movements had occurred in the past but had "seldom been sought or desired." In India most such movements were in fact "resisted by leaders of the church and mission where they started," in part because of the "Western preference for individual decision" over "corporate decision."[31]

The most controversial aspect of McGavran's people-movement concept, called the Homogeneous Unit Principle, became widely disseminated after he addressed a plenary session at the Lausanne Congress in 1974. He argued that a consciousness of race should be seen, not as a negative factor, but rather as a positive one in the process of world evangelization. "It does no good," he insisted, "to say that tribal peoples ought not to have race prejudice. They do have it and are proud of it. It can be understood and should be made an aid to Christianization." He was not defending race prejudice. Rather, he insisted that becoming free from race prejudice could not be made a prerequisite to becoming a Christian. He defined two stages of Christianization: "discipling" and "perfecting." It was only in the second stage, he believed, that real progress toward eradicating race prejudice might be accomplished.[32]

One of his most pointed critics was John H. Yoder, an Anabaptist theologian, who questioned the honesty of McGavran's approach. "I would think the missionary was cheating," he charged, "if he told me after I was baptized that I had to love blacks when he had not wanted to tell me before." "If we have not said the Christian church is an integrated community initially," he asked, "what authority will we have to call for a movement toward integration later?"[33]

Another critic of McGavran's Homogeneous Unit Principle was Rene Padilla, a missiologist from Latin America. In his view, the homogeneous unit is "sub-Christian" and sinful:

> The idea is that people *like* to be with those of their own race and class and we must therefore plant segregated churches, which will undoubtedly grow faster. We are told that race prejudice "can be understood and should be made an aid to Christianization." No amount of exegetical maneuvering can ever bring this approach in line with the explicit teaching of the New Testament regarding the unity of men in the body of Christ.[34]

McGavran's critics have accused him of "stressing quantity at the expense of quality; of being so concerned with the saving of souls that he neglects the serving of human needs; of pushing for church extension and being blind to the needs of social justice; and of relying on human effort instead of the Holy Spirit."[35] But his writings brought new energy into the field of missiology. According to Arthur Glasser (writing in 1973), he is "more widely quoted" and "more hotly debated than anyone else in the field of missions today." He "has completely upset the old, traditional and largely nonproductive missionary methodology that dominated all missions . . . prior to 1955."[36]

When McGavran died in 1990 at the age of ninety-two, he left behind a long legacy of mission research and continuing debate surrounding his church growth concepts. In many respects, his significance lies not so much in the correctness of his answers as in the questions he raised. He helped to elevate the study of missions from introductory courses in a few Christian schools into a widespread professional discipline. He had himself been influenced by other scholars, but the one who had the most profound influence on him as a missiologist was an Indian woman whose words changed his life.

One day while walking through the mission compound after church, he encountered an Indian woman who, with her family, had lived and worked on the headquarters compound for many years. He struck up a friendly conversation, in the course of which he asked, "How is it that you have been with Christians for all these years, yet none of you has ever become a Christian?" She told him they probably would have long ago if anyone had cared. No one had ever urged her, or anyone in her caste, to make such a decision.

"That went through me like a knife," McGavran remembers. He was shaken that a family living on the mission compound had never been asked to take Jesus as Lord. He was working twelve hours a day as an administrator, but he began to spend one night out of every week evangelizing her family and her caste.[37]

Ralph and Roberta Winter

Ralph Winter has arguably been the twentieth century's premier missionary statesman—a practitioner, strategist, scholar, organizer, innovator, motivator, and enthusiast. Indeed, it would be difficult to single out anyone else who has been more involved in as many facets of missions as he.

Winter was born in Los Angeles in 1924 and, except for his years spent in school or overseas, had lived in the same house since the age of two. Following high school, he entered California Institute of Technology to pursue an engineering career as his father had done. After graduating from Cal Tech and serving in the navy, he went on for further education, eventually culminating in a Ph.D. from Cornell University and a degree in theology from Princeton Theological Seminary in preparation for missionary service.

After ten years of mission work in Guatemala with his wife Roberta, Donald McGavran invited him to join the faculty of the Fuller School of World Mission, where he taught for a decade. Then, in 1976, he and Roberta gave up the security and salary of teaching and set out with no financial backing to found the U.S. Center for World Mission (USCWM) and purchase a college campus in Pasadena. "They believed this would be the ideal base of operation to bring together men and women with the purpose of reaching the unreached. The cost: $15 million. They had $100 between them."[38]

In the years since its founding, the USCWM has "faced imminent foreclosure" and "seemed destined to die at the loan desk," until "last-minute funds rolled in."[39] But the focus of the battle has never been centered on mortgage payments. The focus, rather, has been on the estimated seventeen thousand distinct people groups—over two billion people—where the Christian church was not in existence.

The USCWM is a "beehive of energy"—a cooperative "think-tank" to which mission agencies assign people to work together in the research and mobilization necessary to reach these "hidden peoples." "There's more to it than just the creative genius of its director," writes David Bryant. "From what I sense in many quarters, the Center's great appeal lies in the models of pioneering faith it has rallied to itself (Winter being one of them), whose zeal of the glory of God renews the faith of many (including myself) in what God *can* and *will* do *through* His people for Christ's global cause." Bryant has compared the center with the town Rivendale, in Tolkien's *Lord of the Rings*: "the place where visions can be born, where fragile dreams can become reality, where battle plans can be laid for great battles ahead, and faith renewed in ultimate, inevitable success."[40]

The USCWM, however, is not the only brainchild of Winter's "fertile mind." He was active in the founding of the William Carey Library (a publishing house specializing in books on Christian missions), the American Society of Missiology, Theological Education by Extension, Frontier Fellowship, and the William Carey International University, an international undergraduate and graduate extension program.

For Winter, mission work is not just a vocation. It encompasses his whole life. He and his family have maintained what he calls a "wartime lifestyle," not to be confused with a "simple" lifestyle. "A wartime lifestyle," according to him, "may be more expensive or less expensive than simple. If a man is out in a trench and he's eating K rations, he's not using up much money, but a guy who's flying a fighter plane may be using up $40,000 a month of technology. In other words, during wartime one doesn't judge according to the same model of lifestyle. What's important is getting the job done."[41]

The model is evident in their everyday life. While using the latest computerized equipment in their offices and taking advantage of express mail services to facilitate projects, he was often seen driving his 1965 Dodge station wagon that was into its third hundred-thousand-mile cycle and wearing a blue sport coat that he picked out of the "missionary barrel."

Through his various organizations and personal contacts, Winter has been primarily involved in the North American scene in mobilizing others for the cause of cross-cultural missions. "Roberta and I would be back on the field," he wrote to supporters, "if we were not convinced that the biggest task is that of extending mission vision to the American Church. Right now only two percent of the people in our congregations have that vision." The very reason for the U.S. Center for World Mission and the cause for which he has given most of his life is summed up on the center's website:

Could "staying home" do more to accomplish that than going to the field?

> Missionaries do all kinds of good things, but the truly unique task of missions is not "winning more souls." (We will always have the job of evangelism.) Neither is it social involvement. (Life and culture will always be under attack.) The unique task of missions is to establish a viable growing church movement among every tribe, tongue, people and nation on the earth.
>
> Until we are sure there is a strong church movement within every one of the people groups, our task is not finished.
>
> Yes, until a people group has a rugged, believing fellowship within its culture, it is unfair to expect very many individuals to make a truly meaningful decision about Christ and His claims. Until individuals in every group can see how their "new life" relates to their culture, as it has in thousands of others throughout history, they will not feel comfortable or have the fellowship necessary to be reproductive followers of Christ.[42]

Lesslie Newbigin

The premier missiologist of the late twentieth century was Lesslie Newbigin, whose scholarly writings and lectures were profoundly informed by his lifelong service in the church and its evangelistic and missionary outreach. His life intersected with the religious cross-currents of East and West in a way that allowed him to speak perceptively in either setting with recognition and credibility accorded to few individuals in the history of Christianity.

Newbigin was born in England in 1909, the son of devout Christian parents. After completing his secondary schooling, he "abandoned the Christian assumptions of home and childhood." But during his college years, through the Student Christian Movement and its connections with missions leaders "whose sheer intellectual and spiritual power was unmistakable," he "began to explore the faith again." That exploration had also been triggered by a visionary experience while working for a social service center at a mining camp in Wales—"a vision of the Cross, but it was the Cross spanning the space between heaven and earth"—a vision that changed his life:

> I saw it as something which reached down to the most hopeless and sordid of human misery and yet promised life and victory. I was sure that night, in a way I had never been before, that this was the clue I must follow if I were to know how to take bearings when I was lost. I would know where to begin again when I had come to the end of all my own resources of understanding or courage.[43]

Evangelism became a foundation for Newbigin's energized faith—evangelism that included old-fashioned, open-air, soapbox preaching that demanded the fortitude "to stand up to heckling" and answer "the serious questions of working men and women." He used this same method of evangelism when he was serving as a missionary in India: "I fitted a wooden box to the back of my bike and stocked it with cheap paperback copies of the Gospels which could be sold for one anna. Every now and then I would stop, prop up the bike, open the box and take out a Gospel to read. At once a small crowd would collect."[44]

In India, Newbigin's concept of mission outreach developed slowly as he was influenced by "a lonely prophet"—Roland Allen—whose writings from a generation earlier were still fresh. "I fought against his ideas, but it was a losing battle," he confessed, and he gradually came to realize that the advance of the gospel would come through the "spontaneous expansion of the church" as one native convert reached out to another.[45] He sought to put these ideas into practice and transmit them to others as he continued his ministry as the first bishop of the newly formed United Church of South India.

Newbigin challenged many of the assumptions of McGavran, his noted American counterpart, whose ties were also with India. He agreed with both Roland Allen and McGavran that the missionary should not settle into a mission station. "But against McGavran and with Allen," writes Wainwright, "Newbigin distinguishes between rapid *spread* and rapid *growth*," citing Paul as one who was focused more on the faithfulness of the new communities and converts than on the numbers. Regarding the Homogeneous Unit Principle, McGavran argued that new converts be organized in separate groups according to their caste origins, whereas "Newbigin joins with the majority of [Indian] Christians in judging that such a policy would run counter to the essential witness of an evangelical ethic concerning the unity of all in Christ."[46]

Newbigin was a practicing missiologist during his thirty-five years in India, but his greatest contributions to the field came after he officially retired. Back at home in Birmingham at age sixty-five, he had imagined that he would spend his remaining years teaching and writing. Instead, he discovered that England had become a "foreign mission field" in his absence. He found England much more closed to the gospel than India had been: It was "much harder than anything I met in India. There is a cold contempt for the Gospel which is harder to face than opposition." He quickly became convinced that "the development of a truly missionary encounter with this very tough form of paganism is the greatest intellectual and practical task facing the Church."[47]

Newbigin discovered that England had become a "foreign mission field" in his absence.

Five years after he retired, Newbigin was involved in a church council charged with closing a dying church in Birmingham across from the Winson Green prison. He insisted that the church must continue—that "if the Church abandoned such areas in order to settle in the relatively easy circumstances of the suburbs it would forfeit the claim to be a missionary Church."[48] His side prevailed in the debate, but only after he agreed to become the pastor of the church—without salary. Concerned for the large population of Asians in the neighborhood, Newbigin requested the help of a young man who was a native of India. "As I visited the Asian homes in the district, most of them Sikhs or Hindus," he later recalled, "I found a welcome which was often denied on the doorsteps of the natives"—referring to his own countrymen.[49]

In seeking to identify with contemporary Western culture, Newbigin discounted many of the concepts of contextualization and cross-cultural communication that have been touted in recent decades. The gospel, in his mind, should be countercultural—should challenge the self-absorbed mind-set that is so prevalent. "This missionary mindset is quite distinct from evangelistic enthusiasm," writes Tim Stafford. "Evangelism can be (and usually is) carried on within the constraints of a culture. For example, Jesus can be preached as satisfying modern desires for self-fulfillment. The missionary, however, sees the gospel as an invasive force, challenging culture, compelling a higher allegiance."[50]

As a missionary, Newbigin also saw the gospel challenging his own faith and theological presuppositions—particularly his Reformed perspective on election, the teaching that God chooses or predestines certain people. George Hunsberger captures the essence of Newbigin's understanding of what has often been perceived to be a harsh doctrine:

> Newbigin stands among those who search for the purpose of election. It is to him a betrayal of trust for believers when their minds "are concerned more to probe backwards from their election into the reasons for it in the secret coun-

> sel of God than to press forward from their election to the purpose for it, which is that they should be Christ's ambassadors and witnesses to the ends of the earth."...
>
> Fundamental to Newbigin's perspective, then, is his conviction that election is about the purpose God intends by the choice, not the reason God has for making the choice.... It is so that we are reminded that election is "not special privilege but special responsibility."[51]

During the last years of his life, Newbigin became the most respected and revered missiologist in the world, and the missionaries and mission scholars worldwide influenced by this work probably number in the thousands. In his last addresses before a conference sponsored by the World Council of Churches, he challenged the notion that "the sins of the old missionaries" are only redressed by giving of ourselves and making no exclusive claims for Jesus. "I am an old missionary, and I have committed most of those sins," he confessed, "but it would be wrong to respond, 'I will refrain from talking about Jesus and will instead offer my own life as a witness that will enable people to believe.'"[52]

He died in 1998 at the age of eighty-eight—an old missionary with a message as old as the cross.

SELECT BIBLIOGRAPHY

Allen, Roland. *Missionary Methods: St. Paul's or Ours?* 1912.

Bavinck, J. H. *Faith and Its Difficulties.*

Elliot, Elisabeth. *Who Shall Ascend: The Life of R. Kenneth Strachan of Costa Rica.* New York: Harper & Row, 1968.

Hunsberger, George R. *Bearing the Witness of the Spirit: Lesslie Newbigin's Theology of Cultural Plurality.* Grand Rapids: Eerdmans, 1998.

Roberts, W. Dayton. *Revolution in Evangelism: The Story of Evangelism-in-Depth in Latin America.* Chicago: Moody Press, 1976.

______. *Strachan of Costa Rica: Missionary Insights and Strategies.* Grand Rapids: Eerdmans, 1971.

Wainwright, Geoffrey. *Lesslie Newbigin: A Theological Life.* New York: Oxford University Press, 2000.

Winter, Roberta H. *Once More Around Jericho: The Story of the U.S. Center for World Mission.* Pasadena, CA: William Carey Library, 1978.

18

SAINTS AND CELEBRITIES: APPEALING TO THE MASSES

It has been the destiny of some missionaries to become celebrities. That was certainly true of David Livingstone, the greatest missionary celebrity of modern times, second only perhaps to Mother Teresa. But Adoniram Judson was also a celebrity. When Judson was speaking to a Baptist audience during a furlough in 1845, a Brown University professor wrote of the adulation expressed by the crowd:

> Hundreds were gazing for the first time upon one, the story of whose labors and sorrows and sufferings had been familiar to them from childhood, and whose name they had been accustomed to utter with reverence and affection as that of the pioneer and father of American missions to the heathen. They recalled the scenes of toil and privation through which he had passed, they remembered the loved ones with whom he had been connected, and their bosoms swelled with irrepressible emotions of gratitude and delight.[1]

Ann Judson was also revered. "If she had lived in legendary instead of historical times," wrote one of her biographers, "she would have ranked with Saint Agnes and Saint Cecilia."[2]

C. T. Studd, England's most outstanding cricket player, and six other Cambridge athletes and scholars became instant celebrities when they volunteered to serve as missionaries with the China Inland Mission. It did not hurt their image that they were all from wealthy (or at least affluent), well-bred English families. The back cover of Studd's biography by Norman Grubb presents the contrast between youth and wealth, on the one hand, and sacrifice and self-denial, on the other:

> Nurtured in the lap of comfort, educated at Eton and Cambridge, the hero of the British sport-loving public, C. T. Studd, whose Cambridge career has been

> described as "one long blaze of cricketing glory," created a stir in the secular world of his youth by renouncing wealth and position to follow Christ. He was captain of the Eton XI in 1879, and of Cambridge University in 1883, being accorded in the latter year . . . "the premier position as an all around cricketer for the second year in succession."[3]

Amy Carmichael was a celebrity—through her writings—though she never returned home to be surrounded by admiring crowds. Lottie Moon's celebrity status only flowered after she died (conveniently on Christmas Eve). As the twentieth century progressed, there were other mission leaders and missionaries who gained celebrity status, among them John R. Mott, who won the Nobel Peace Prize, and Gladys Aylward, who was the subject of a Hollywood film. Celebrities in missions, like celebrities in the movies or in music or in sports, were often in the right place at the right time. Their ministries in many cases did not necessarily rise high above that of their nameless colleagues, but a particular event or a compelling personality or an admirer in a key position was the catalyst that launched them into a public role.

This has been true of Mother Teresa. She was not alone in devoting her life to sacrificial ministry. Indeed, "there may be hundreds of Mother Teresas doing similarly valuable work the world over," writes Anne Sebba, but "the importance of the [Malcolm] Muggeridge film can hardly be overestimated." It was not just the film but how she was portrayed: "She comes over very well on the screen because she does exude humility, there is nothing bogus about her. She was a symbol and so was Muggeridge, in his case a symbol of someone searching for goodness in the twentieth century." People who met her often spoke of it as a spiritual encounter—sometimes transmitted through a third party. "Through meeting Muggeridge," writes David Porter, one of her biographers, "I sensed that I was meeting her and, at a sort of third hand, meeting the Lord Himself."[4]

Mother Teresa sprang from a centuries-old lineage of celebrated saintly lives in the Catholic tradition. Like her, they were known for self-denial and sacrificial service, and like her, they performed miracles. The stories of these saints is often categorized as *hagiography*—biographies that minimize or ignore the flaws of the subjects while accentuating the virtues. Hagiography is not limited to Catholic stories of the saints, however. In *A Chance to Die*, Elisabeth Elliot writes of Amy Carmichael that those who worked with her "found it nearly impossible, after her death, to think of any faults" they could attribute to her.[5] In reference to Una Roberts Lawrence's biography of Lottie Moon, published in 1927, Alan Neely writes:

> It ranks with the "best" of twentieth-century missionary hagiographies, such as Rosalind Goforth's account of her husband [Jonathan], *Goforth of China* (1973); Russell T. Hitt's *Jungle Pilot: The Life and Witness of Nate Saint* (1973); James and Marti Hefley's *Unstilled Voices* (1991); and Steve Estes' *Called to Die* (1986), the story of Chet Bitterman, a Wycliffe translator.[6]

The old hagiography so prominent for centuries in Catholic and later in Protestant writings—particularly in accounts of missionaries—is no longer as treasured as it once was. Readers demand more honesty. Yet new missionary celebrities and heroes arise with every generation—sometimes, as in the case of Dr. Helen Roseveare, commended because of confessions of flaws and failures.

Bob Pierce

The danger of the celebrity status is the possibility of being pushed off the pedestal—as was the case with Bob Pierce, the founder of World Vision. The motto inscribed in his Bible succinctly summed up his outlook on life: "Let my heart be broken with the things that break the heart of God." Yet with a heart that reached out to the whole world, he was unable to sustain the most intimate bonds of love with his own family. The love that he gave so freely to homeless orphans and ravished flood victims was given so sparingly to the ones who needed it most—particularly his wife Lorraine and his three daughters. Even before he had grown to celebrity status, he had left his family and threatened divorce, and the new worldwide ministry only seemed to exacerbate the problems.

For nearly a decade "Dr. Bob" held the distinction of being one of the "ten most traveled men in the world," and everywhere he went he was hailed as a godsend.

"Dr. Bob," as he was affectionately called, had become a saintly legend throughout the Far East. But his ministry was not confined to that area of the world. For nearly a decade he held the distinction of being one of the "ten most traveled men in the world," and everywhere he went he was hailed as a godsend. Back in the United States he traveled from coast to coast, awakening American Christians to the needs of the underprivileged world, raising hundreds of thousands of dollars for orphanages, hospitals, and evangelistic ministries. When he returned home from his ten months of travel a year, family conflict inevitably ensued. There were also increasing difficulties with his board of directors. The friction continued for many years until 1967, when matters reached a boiling point and he resigned in a rage. "The next day World Vision presented him with legal documents of agreement, and Bob Pierce signed his life's work away."[7]

In 1968 Pierce traveled to the Far East with Lorraine on a "Good-bye Tour" sponsored as a final parting gesture by World Vision—no doubt in part to maintain their contacts in that part of the world. Near the end of that trip a call came from their depressed oldest daughter, Sharon, pleading with her father to come home. But he refused to interrupt his schedule. Lorraine flew home immediately, only to "discover her daughter had slashed her wrists in an attempt to end a life she found too painful to endure." Later that year Sharon did take her life, at age twenty-seven.[8] Suffering from physical and mental exhaustion, Pierce separated himself even more from his family, and never again would they enjoy a sustained happy relationship.

In later years he began traveling again, and with World Vision support he founded Samaritan's Purse, an organization that provided assistance to missionaries in Asia. He died in September 1978, remembered by many people around the world as "Dr. Bob," the man with the big heart. He was a deeply flawed man who, despite his failures, gained worldwide recognition for his good works—no small legacy to leave behind.

Bruce Olson

While Bob Pierce was flying around the world funding humanitarian ministries, Bruce Olson was essentially lost to the outside world, deep in the jungles of Colombia—though he would emerge often enough to win celebrity status that in some ways would rank with that of "Dr. Bob." He wrote a best-selling book that tells of his mission work that won him the personal friendship of five presidents of Colombia, appearances before the United Nations and the Organization of American States, and many other honors. His fascinating autobiographical account entitled *Bruchko* (the name given to him by the natives) is summarized on the back cover:

> What happens when a 19-year-old boy leaves home against his parents' wishes and heads into the jungles to evangelize a murderous tribe of South American Indians? . . . What Bruce Olson discovered by trial and error brings a revolutionary message to traditional missionary activity. Olson has lived with the Motilones since 1961. He has reduced their language into writing. He has translated several New Testament books into the Motilone language. He has taught the Motilones health measures, agricultural techniques and the value of preserving their cultural heritage. . . . This epic account marks an exciting milestone in the history of missions.[9]

In 1988, a decade after he published his autobiography, Olson was taken hostage by ELN, a guerrilla group, which accused him of doing work that was detrimental to the native Colombian people. The group announced that he had been sentenced to death, but he was released after a nine-month captivity through the combined efforts of the Red Cross, the U.S. Embassy in Bogota, and the State Department.

Mother Teresa

The greatest celebrity saint of the twentieth century in the minds of many people was Mother Teresa. In common with Bob Pierce, she gained worldwide recognition for good works, but without the glaring personal flaws. Like him, she struggled with administrative failures, though unlike him, she had an adoring throng of followers who did not try to interfere with her uncontested leadership of the mission. Her detractors focused primarily on matters of administration or philosophy such as her adamant stance against birth control and family planning—rarely attacking her personally except as related to authoritarian leadership. But no amount of criticism has been able to dim the shining star of Mother Teresa of Calcutta. "As you fly into Calcutta today, city of twelve million and growing, you are welcomed" by a giant billboard, writes Anne Sebba, "which announces this as the city of Tagore the poet, Ray the film maker and Teresa the nun. Extraordinary as it may seem, she has become a tourist attraction. Of the three, it is Teresa who is the best known internationally and it is she who has made Calcutta famous anew in the West."[10]

Born Agnes Bojaxhiu in Albania in 1910, the youngest of three children, she lived a life of modest comfort until her father died in 1919, leaving his business ventures to his partners. Despite poverty, her mother was known in the community for helping others, and her example did not go unnoticed by her youngest daughter. Her mother's devout faith and devotion to Mary also had a profound influence on young Agnes, who was assured of her mother's blessing when she announced that she was going to be a missionary in India. At age nineteen, she did just that. "She was caught in a wave of enthusiasm," writes Edward Le Joly, for "spreading the gospel in the missions, an enthusiasm generated by the writings of Pope Pius XI."[11]

In the winter of 1929 Teresa was sailing up the Hooghly River to Bengal, as William Carey had done 135 years earlier. For two years she trained as a novice, and in 1931 she took her vows to become a Loreto sister, serving as a teacher specializing in geography—a position she held several years until she was named headmistress.

Teresa's call to minister to the poorest of the poor did not come from a sense of pity for the sick and homeless in Calcutta—a point that is repeatedly emphasized by those who have been closest to her:

> "This is how it happened," she told her spiritual director, Father Julien Henry. "I was travelling to Darjeeling by train [for my annual retreat], when I heard the voice of God." Father Henry then asked her how she had heard his voice above the noise of a rattling train and she had replied with a smile: "I was sure it was God's voice. I was certain that He was calling me. The message was clear: I must leave the convent to help the poor by living among them. This was a command, something to be done, something definite. I knew where I had to be. But I did not know how to get there."[12]

Apart from the "voice of God," however, Mother Teresa may have heard voices from the past. She had never imagined herself spending her life cloistered behind the walls of a girls' school for India's elite. The stories she had read in *Catholic Missions* as a girl were stories of self-denial and danger—stories about "sisters so poor that they lived in thatched huts with wild animals rampaging through the encampments and hardly enough money for food and clothes . . . and one issue told how a Mother Superior was saved by her orphans from a snake poised to bite her, another of a lucky escape from a tiger."[13]

It took two years before Mother Teresa was granted permission to leave the convent, and soon she had three followers join her—all students from the Loreto school. That same year she obtained Indian citizenship and applied to Rome to form a new congregation, Missionaries of Charity. From the beginning, it was different from other religious orders—most significantly, it had no "walls" of security. "Our Sisters must go out on the street," she insisted. "They must take the tram like our people, or walk to where they are going. That is why we must not start institutions and stay inside. We must not stay behind walls and have our people come to us."[14]

Mother Teresa, missionary to India who was awarded the Nobel Peace Prize.

During the 1950s the Missionaries of Charity grew steadily, and in 1960, when Mother Teresa left India for the first time in more than three decades, there were more than one hundred sisters in the movement. Her travels took her to America and Europe, and as she spread the message, funds poured in. Like Hudson Taylor a century earlier, she emphasized that she would not ask for money because she had no need to. "She was entirely dependent on the providence of God," writes Sebba. "But she did remind her audience that she was giving them, too, a chance to do something beautiful for God. This, rather than directly appealing for donations, was a far more powerful method of raising money."[15] In the years that followed, the number of sisters grew to the thousands. Houses were established in cities all over the world, and the aura of saintliness accorded Mother Teresa was bestowed on them as well—at least in the words of Malcolm Muggeridge, a one-time agnostic who became their greatest champion:

> Their life is tough and austere by worldly standards, certainly: yet I never met such delightful, happy women, or such an atmosphere of joy as they create. Mother Teresa, as she is fond of explaining, attaches the utmost importance to this joyousness. The poor, she says, deserve not just service and dedication, but also the joy that belongs to human love.... The Missionaries of Charity ... are multiplying at a fantastic rate. Their Calcutta house is bursting at the seams, and as each new house is opened, there are volunteers clamoring to go there. As the whole story of Christendom shows, if everything is asked for, everything—and more—will be accorded; if little, then nothing.[16]

In December of 1979 Mother Teresa accepted the Nobel Peace Prize, bringing the spotlight of the world on her selfless missionary service. When asked how she identified herself, she responded: "By blood and origin, I am all Albanian. My citizenship is Indian. I am a Catholic nun. As to my calling, I belong to the whole world. As to my heart, I belong entirely to Jesus."[17] Wherever she went, she was esteemed—whether speaking at a Harvard University graduation or at a Capitol Hill luncheon, as Dee Jepson, whose husband was a U.S. Senator, related: "In came this tiny woman, even smaller than I had expected, wearing that familiar blue and white habit, over it a gray sweater that had seen many better days.... As that little woman walked into the room, her bare feet in worn sandals, I saw some of the most powerful leaders in this country stand to their feet with tears in their eyes. Just to be in her presence."[18]

Mother Teresa died in 1997, her death overshadowed by the tragic auto accident that took the life of Princess Diana of the United Kingdom the same weekend—an old nun and a young princess who considered each other friends.

Brother Andrew and Open Doors

While Mother Teresa and Bob Pierce were seeking to evangelize the world through humanitarian acts of charity, others, like Brother Andrew, were taking a more combative approach. *God's Smuggler*, the title of a popular book about him, is the title most frequently associated with this unordained Dutchman whose controversial ministry has frequently been the focus of international attention. He has been described as "the James Bond of the cloth," though he insists that his 1967 bestseller is a "curse" because it portrays him as a hero—an unusual claim, since he is the author of that book. The book brought him celebrity status, reportedly selling over ten million copies in twenty-seven languages.

His mission outreach, known as Open Doors, was initially focused on Eastern Europe and the Soviet Union, but since that region of the world opened up to mission ventures, his attention has been largely on China and the Muslim world. Defying government laws and authorities, Open Doors is guided by the philosophy that it is far better to "obey God rather than men."

In many ways the daring risks involved in smuggling Bibles across the borders of enemy countries was well suited to the young Dutch army commando whose childhood days in the 1930s had been filled with war games with neighborhood friends. Brother Andrew (a pseudonym) was born into a proud Protestant family who, like most Hollanders, suffered immensely during the Nazi occupation of their land. After that devastating war he joined the army and soon found himself fighting to maintain Dutch rule in the tropical jungles of Indonesia. This was not a setting where heroes were easily made, but by his own testimony he quickly established a reputation for himself: "I became famous throughout the Dutch troops in Indonesia for my crazy bravado on the battlefield. I bought a bright yellow straw hat and wore it into combat with me. It was a dare and an invitation. 'Here I am!' it said. 'Shoot me!' Gradually I gathered around me a group of boys who were reacting as I did. . . . When we fought, we fought as madmen."[19]

It was inevitable that someone from the enemy camp would challenge his dare, and Andrew was soon on a hospital ship headed for home, nursing a badly wounded right ankle. During his hospitalization he spent many hours reading the Bible, a book that he had never had time for before. Back in Holland in 1950, he was converted, and almost immediately he was challenged to become a missionary. But to serve under the Dutch Reformed Church would have required twelve years of further schooling, so he looked elsewhere for sponsorship. Through the help of friends, he went to London to learn English and then on to Glasgow, Scotland, to study at the WEC (Worldwide Evangelization Crusade) training school, from which he graduated in 1955.

Although it had been his intention to serve as a missionary with WEC, that organization had no ministry behind the Iron Curtain—an area of the world that captured his attention. Just before his graduation, he had come across an advertisement for a youth festival in Warsaw. It was a colorful piece of propaganda intended to lure Western youth to that beautiful city to see firsthand what socialism could offer them, but for him it was an opportunity for ministry in a country that had been forgotten by Christians in the West.

> *"That night I promised God that as often as I could lay my hands on a Bible, I would bring it to these children of His behind the wall that men had built."*

His initial trip to Warsaw paved the way for speaking invitations back home in Holland and stirred his interest in visiting other Eastern European countries. His second trip took him to Czechoslovakia, where the rigid crackdown on religion became evident immediately. What impressed him most was the scarcity of Bibles, unavailable even at the largest religious bookstore in the country. In Belgrade, Yugoslavia, he discovered the same problem. While speaking at a religious meeting, he learned that out of the entire group, only seven people, including the pastor, owned a Bible. "That night," he later wrote, "I promised God that as often as I could lay my hands on a Bible, I would bring it to these children of His behind the wall that men had built. How I would buy the Bibles, how I would get them in, I didn't know. I only knew that I would bring them—here to Yugoslavia, and to Czechoslovakia, and to every other country where God opened the door long enough for me to slip through."[20]

For fifteen years Brother Andrew and his recruits smuggled Bibles behind the Iron Curtain with few arrests. The work remained relatively obscure until after his widely circulated book *God's Smuggler* was published. People from all over the world wanted to become involved, and contributions to the work dramatically increased. At the same time that the book was informing the Christian world of his work, it was also informing communist authorities—a development that brought a virtual halt to his trips into Eastern Europe.

But he continued to seek out risky ventures. On the day that the Russians moved into Czechoslovakia in 1968, he tells how he packed his station wagon with Bibles and headed for the border. "I didn't need a prayer meeting to tell me what to do. I figured if the Russians were coming to meet me halfway, I'd better get moving!" According to him, there was so much confusion at the border that the patrol officers waved him through without asking to see a visa or checking his vehicle. On his way to Prague, he encountered two divisions of the Soviet army, but he managed to get through without being detained. There he was invited to preach in a church, and afterwards the people tearfully thanked him for coming. Then, with a group of Czech Christians, he went out into the streets and distributed tracts and Bibles. "The Czech citizens took them like starving men taking bread. Czech authorities were too busy coping with the Russians to worry about arresting us, and we gave away tens of thousands of tracts before we finally depleted our supply and I headed back for Holland."[21]

In 1965 he made his first trip to mainland China, where he found Christians requesting Bibles, and once again he began smuggling operations. Following the fall of Saigon in 1976 and the Communist takeover of Laos and Cambodia, he turned his attention to those countries. The most publicized and controversial Bible smuggling operation he conducted occurred in the fall of 1981. "Operation Pearl," as it was dubbed, was, according to *Time* magazine, the "largest operation of its kind in the history of China." Led by an ex-Marine, it was "executed with military precision." More than two hundred tons of Bibles, packed in waterproof containers, were shipped from the United States to Hong Kong and from there were transported on a barge to the southeast China port city of Swatow, all at the cost of some six million dollars. There were harrowing moments when the crew feared they had been discovered, but the Bibles were unloaded without incident, and not until four hours after the barge had departed did authorities storm the beach. Hundreds of the estimated twenty thousand Chinese believers who had come to help were arrested, but those in charge claimed that well over half of the Bibles ended up in the hands of Chinese Christians for whom they were intended.[22]

As a result of this illegal operation, Chinese officials tightened restrictions on religious activities, causing an outcry against his organization, Open Doors, by some Western and Chinese churchmen who feared that such efforts only served to further alienate Chinese Christians from their leaders. Others criticized Brother Andrew on ethical grounds. In response, he wrote a small book entitled *The Ethics of Smuggling*, defending his work:

> We do it because we know what we are doing. This world is enemy-occupied territory, filled with souls to whom Christ holds the rightful claim. Under his explicit command, we go in by every possible means—partial truth, concealment of truth, interpretation, change and opposition, or any other form of strategy that will help us get in there with the gospel....
>
> It's time we stop this silly bickering and instead use Holy Spirit boldness to see the nations as God sees them....
>
> We are not facing an ethical issue but a loyalty issue. If we are true followers of the Lord Jesus Christ, we simply go into all the world because he sends us. We need no welcome, we need no invitation, we need no permission from the government, we need no red-carpet treatment, we need no VIP reception—unless it means Very Important Prisoner for Christ's sake.[23]

But with the criticism came praise. "Operation Pearl ... inspired calls from potential donors willing to finance massive new Bible-smuggling ventures to China or behind the Iron Curtain."[24] By the turn of the twenty-first century most of the criticism of Bible smuggling related to the high cost of such operations—particularly into China—where inexpensive Bibles printed there were readily available.

In an interview in 1995 with Michael Maudlin of *Christianity Today*, Brother Andrew, in what some might regard an exaggerated claim, stated that Muslim radicals had disclosed their political plans with him:

> *Hamas* has outlined to me their plan to take over that area [Lebanon]. They've told me their timetable and what they're going to do. And yet there's no group in the Middle East more open to the presentation of Christ than *Hamas*. *Hezbollah* has even begged me for very open publicized dialogue with evangelical Christian leaders. But I cannot find any Christians who are willing.[25]

In the face of widespread criticism, Brother Andrew emphasized that "smuggling" is "only a small part" of the total ministry of Open Doors. Yet he conceded that it is the "smuggling" aspect that had an adventurous appeal to many people. The label has served him well. As "God's Smuggler," he entered the third millennium in his seventies, still drawing crowds.

Helen Roseveare

One of the most sought-after speakers of the late twentieth century on the international missions circuit was Dr. Helen Roseveare, whose harrowing adventures as a missionary doctor in the Congo captured the attention of her listeners. Such attention and adulation would have been incomprehensible during her early years in Africa when she clashed with her colleagues and mission board on matters of medical education and community health.

Roseveare was born in Cornwall, England, in 1925. Her father, who had been knighted for his patriotic service during the war, was a renowned mathematician, keenly interested in the education of his children. At twelve Helen was sent away to an exclusive girls' school, and after that to Cambridge, where she received her medical degree. During her freshman year at Cambridge, she turned away from her Anglo-Catholic background and joined the ranks of the Evangelicals. Her commitment for missionary service was natural. Her father's brothers and her mother's sister had served as missionaries, and from childhood she had contemplated being a missionary herself. That day came in 1953, when she sailed for the Congo to serve with the Worldwide Evangelization Crusade.

WEC's focus was evangelism, and medicine was only a secondary sideline, which suited Roseveare, who envisioned her own ministry as primarily evangelism. Once in the Congo, however, she found the medical needs overwhelming. Her solution was to establish a training center where nurses would be taught the Bible and basic medicine and then sent back to their villages to handle routine cases, teach preventive medicine, and serve as lay evangelists. It was a far-reaching plan, but from the start she was blocked at every turn by her colleagues, who believed that a mission should not become involved in training the nationals in such fields as medicine.

Through sheer determination Roseveare prevailed, however. Two years after arriving in the Congo, after spending months in the building process, she had set up a medical center in Ibambi, and her first four students had passed their government medical exams. But with hardly a chance to catch her breath, she was relocated at Nebobongo in an old leprosy camp that had become overgrown by the jungle. She had forcefully argued against the move, but to no avail. There she built another medical center and continued training African nurses. She had worked hard against insurmountable odds, and she had succeeded. It was hers, and she was proud of what she had accomplished.

Roseveare's strong will and determination might easily have been overlooked in a male medical doctor, but she was perceived as a threat to many of her male colleagues. So, apparently in an effort to keep her in her place, a decision was made at the annual field conference in 1957 to relocate John Harris, a young British doctor, and his wife to Nebobongo to head the medical work. Roseveare was devastated:

> In her terms, he's just taken over Nebobongo—*her* place, which she'd built up out of nothing, out of her dreams, out of her heart, out of the money she'd raised. This was the place where she'd dug the water holes, cleared the ditches, fired the bricks. She had acknowledged the facts that you could not have two people in charge, that he was a man, and that in Africa a man was the superior being, so she handed over the keys. Then she found she couldn't take it. Perhaps she had been her own boss too long. But now she had lost everything. She had always taken morning prayers: he took them now. She had always taken Bible class; Dr. Harris took it now. Dr. Harris organized the nurses, and Helen had always done that. Everything that had been hers was now his.[26]

From the beginning there was almost continual tension between the two doctors that more than once culminated in bitter controversy. On one occasion Harris arbitrarily fired Roseveare's chauffeur on the grounds that he had used the van without permission. She was furious that Harris had fired him without consulting her.

WEC missionaries were scheduled for furloughs every seven years, but due to ill health she returned home in 1958 after only five years on the field. She was disillusioned with missionary work and, according to her biographer, "feeling that it was unlikely she would ever return to Congo."[27] But she became convinced that her real problem was her singleness. If she had a doctor-husband who would work with her and stand by her during the difficult times, she reasoned, everything would be all right.

Once her mind was made up, Roseveare did not vacillate. In the words of a missionary colleague, "she couldn't drag everybody after her at her speed. You can't keep pace. You're walking stride for stride and suddenly she's a hundred yards ahead. And just when you're catching up, she's off two hundred yards in another direction."[28] In her desire for a husband, she went full speed ahead, planning and scheming. While taking additional medical training she met a young doctor who, she became convinced, was right for her. She bought new clothes, permed her hair, and even resigned from the mission in an effort to win him, but the plan did not work. It was a very trying time for her, as she later confessed:

Helen Roseveare, missionary doctor to the Congo.

> The Lord spoke very clearly during my furlough that he was able to satisfy me.... I wasn't interested in a spiritualized husband. I wanted a husband with a couple of arms. Well, in the end I jolly near mucked up the whole furlough.... I couldn't find a husband in the mission, so I got out of the mission. God let me go a long way, and I made an awful mess. Then God graciously pulled me back and the mission graciously accepted me back.[29]

Roseveare's return to the Congo in 1960 coincided with that country's long-sought independence. It was an uneasy time for whites, and many missionaries believed the risks were too high. Some left with their families immediately. Helen, however, had no intention of turning around and going home. If God had truly called her back to the Congo, she was convinced he would protect her. Her stand made it difficult for the men. How would it look if they slunk away while the women bravely stayed on, and who would protect the women if they were gone? But in Helen's mind, such reasoning had no merit and was, in her biographer's words, "pure male chauvinism." The very fact that most of the men were married made their circumstances different. And as to protection, there was little a male missionary could do.

Roseveare's decision to stay offered her tremendous opportunities for service. Harris and his wife were on furlough, and she was once again in charge of the medical center at Nebobongo. Much was accomplished in the three years that followed, despite the political uneasiness as the Simba Rebels gained strength in their opposition to the new government. Reports came periodically of attacks against missionaries elsewhere, including reports of missionary women who had "suffered" at the hands of the rebels—an act so degrading and humiliating it could not even be named. Roseveare herself endured a burglary and an attempted poisoning, but always in her mind the situation was improving—and even if it was not, too many people depended on her. She had to stay.

By the summer of 1964 the Congo was in the throes of a bloody civil war as the Simba Rebels violently took control of village after village. On August 15, the mission compound at Nebobongo was occupied by soldiers, and for the next five months Roseveare was in captivity, though she remained at the compound, living in her own house until November. Brutal atrocities were committed in the name of black nationalism, and few whites escaped the violence and bloodshed. Helen was no exception. On the night of October 29, while the compound was under rebel occupation, she was overpowered by a black rebel soldier in her little bungalow. It was a night of terror. She tried to escape, but it was useless: "They found me, dragged me to my feet, struck me over head and shoulders, flung me on the ground, kicked me, dragged me to my feet only to strike me again—the sickening, searing pain of a broken tooth, a mouth full of sticky blood, my glasses gone. Beyond sense, numb with horror and unknown fear, driven, dragged, pushed back to my own house—yelled at, insulted, cursed."

Once in the house, it was all over in a few minutes. According to her biographer, the soldier "forced her backwards on the bed, falling on top of her. . . . The will to resist and fight had been knocked out of her. But she screamed over and over again. . . . The brutal act of rape was accomplished with animal vigor and without mercy."[30]

"My God, my God, why have you forsaken me?" rang over and over again through her numbed consciousness. Though she never could have understood it at the time, that terrible violation allowed her to have a ministry to others. One young Italian nun on the verge of a mental collapse, having been repeatedly raped, was convinced she had lost her purity and thus her salvation. The Mother Superior had tried in vain to reason with her and only reluctantly sought out Roseveare, whose frankness about her own experience and her spiritual insights brought consolation. It was a cathartic time for both of them—a time that helped prepare Helen for more sexual brutality that she would endure before her release.

Though she never could have understood it at the time, the brutal act allowed Roseveare to have a ministry to others.

Her rescue came on the last day of 1964. For months Roseveare had faced the almost daily threat of death; she hardly knew how to deal with her newfound freedom and the rude shock of suddenly being back home. There was a sense of joy and relief but also a sense of great sorrow as she listened to horror stories of the martyrdom of some of her dearest friends and colleagues. Initially, the prospect of returning to Africa seemed remote. But as the Congo political situation improved and as heartrending letters from African coworkers and friends arrived, the pull to Africa became intense. She was needed now more than ever.

Roseveare returned to Africa in March of 1966. Arriving at the devastated mission compound, she was greeted with jubilation, but she soon discovered that life in the Congo had irrevocably changed since her first term in the 1950s. Things would never be the same. The new spirit of independence and nationalism had penetrated every area of society, including the church, and no longer was there an automatic feeling of respect and admiration—especially from the younger generation—for the lady doctor who had sacrificed so much for the Congo.

Had Roseveare simply been caring for the sick, her work might have been more appreciated, but as it was, her seven-year term was filled with turmoil and disappointment. Africans were now in control, and as a white woman, she was denied the authority she needed as a teacher. Students challenged her in the classroom and resented her demands for excellence. Their careless work habits clashed with her drive and dictatorial ways.

Despite her remarkable sacrifice and great accomplishments during those seven years, Roseveare left Africa in 1973 broken in spirit. Students had rebelled against her authority, and even her colleagues questioned her leadership ability. It was a tragedy, at least in human terms, that her twenty years of service in Africa ended in such a way. Her own words tell the story best:

> When I knew I was coming home from the field and a young medical couple were taking my place at the college and an African colleague was taking over the directorship of the hospital, I organized a big day. It was to be a welcome to the two new doctors, a handover to my colleague, graduation day for the students in the college, and my farewell. A big choir had been practicing for five months. I got lots of cassettes to record everything and films to snap everything. Then at the last moment the whole thing fell to bits. The student body went on strike. I ended up having to resign the college where I'd been the director twenty years.[31]

Roseveare returned home to face a "very, very lonely period" in her life. But instead of bitterness there was a new spirit of humility and a new appreciation for Christ's death on the cross. She was not prepared for what would follow—an even greater ministry than her ministry in Africa. In the following decades, Alan Burgess wrote her biography, she wrote several autobiographical books, and the film *Mama Luka* featured her work in Africa. She became a much-sought-after, internationally known speaker for missions—hailed for her honest reflections on her own failures—a breath of fresh air in a profession that for too long was stifled by an image of super-sainthood.

Jackie Pullinger

Another English woman whose missionary outreach has gained the attention of the broader public is Jackie Pullinger, whose work in the Walled City has been the subject of books and several television documentaries. Like Mother Teresa, her mission was to the "poorest of the poor"—in this case in a walled, drug-infested area of Hong Kong. She arrived in the Walled City, the area called Hak Nam (which in Chinese means "darkness") in 1966. "Behind these tawdry shops rose the ramshackle skyscrapers," writes Pullinger, telling of her first visit. "We squeezed through a narrow gap between the shops and started walking down a slime-covered passageway. I will never forget the smell and the darkness, a fetid smell of rotten foodstuffs, excrement, offal and general rubbish." The narrow alleys, filled with opium and gambling dens and drug-ravaged prostitutes were dark even at midday, except for occasional shafts of sunlight. It was a lawless six-acre cesspool of humanity—tens of thousands—where police rarely ventured. Such a place seemed impossible in the midst of the wealth of Hong Kong, but there was a reason, as Pullinger explained, writing in 1980:

> How can such a place exist inside the British Crown Colony of Hong Kong? Over eighty years ago when Britain apportioned to herself not only the Chinese island of Hong Kong, but also the mainland Peninsula of Kowloon, and the Chinese territories behind it, one exception was made.
>
> The old wall village of Kowloon was to remain under Chinese Imperial Administration.... The Chinese magistrate died—he was never succeeded by either Chinese or British, and lawlessness inside the Walled City came to stay. It became a haven for gold smuggling, drug smuggling, illegal gambling dens and every kind of vice.[32]

In an era when community and mission teams were being emphasized, Pullinger was the ultimate example of individualism—a true "lone-ranger." But she defended her decision to go alone with neither a partner nor mission board support: "Abraham was willing to leave his country and follow Jehovah to a promised land without knowing where he was going," she argued. "In the same way thousands of years later Gladys Aylward journeyed in faith to China."[33]

Born a twin in a family of four daughters, she had sensed a call to missions at a young age. After graduating from the Royal College of Music, "the missionary idea came back," she later recalled. "So I wrote to Africa (that's where missionaries go to) to schools, to societies, to broadcasting companies. And they all wrote back, no—they did not want me." But after a dream in which she saw Hong Kong in the middle of a map of Africa, she decided to venture out on her own. The advice of a minister launched her on her journey: "If I were you, I would go out and buy a ticket for a boat going on the longest journey you can find and pray to know where to get off." That advice, combined with her dream, brought her to Hong Kong.[34]

Pullinger was able to make connections with others who were ministering in the Walled City, and she began teaching classes part-time in singing, percussion band, and English at a mission-run school. But her primary concern was a youth club that she organized and conducted with occasional volunteer help. To those who wondered what kind of work she actually did, she had a ready reply: "I'm doing unstructured Youth work."[35]

Initially, Pullinger saw very little success in her ministry. She struggled with the language, and most of those who showed interest turned out to be "rice Christians"—expecting money or something else from what they perceived to be a rich English woman. But then, quite suddenly, things began to change, as young men made decisions that took hold. She credits "speaking in tongues"—the power of the Holy Spirit—for turning things around. "As I continued praying in the Spirit," she testifies, "the results became apparent when more boys like Christopher made decisions to become Christians."[36]

Christopher was going through initiation to become one of the Triads, a Mafia-like organization that had its roots in the early nineteenth century. By the time Pullinger became familiar with them they had "degenerated into hundreds of separate Triad societies all claiming to be part of the Triad tradition." Yet they still had power by the very fact that they "inspired terror" both inside and outside the Walled City. Christopher had attended the Youth Club but then dropped out and avoided Pullinger—until one day when he was cornered in a narrow passageway—she carrying her accordion and blocking the way so that he was unable to pass by. "I asked him to carry the instrument for me to the repair shop." Through that encounter and her "praying in the Spirit," he severed his connections with the Triads, got a legitimate job, turned his life around, and began helping out in the Youth Club.[37]

Standard evangelism tactics did not work for Pullinger in her ministry to people in the Walled City. Rather than "insisting that new young Christians join the church," she writes, "I expanded our Bible study group; we met several times a week and were now open on Sunday mornings also. . . . We had raucous singing sessions and ping pong. If I insisted on a prayer, most of them would go outside and hoot in a friendly fashion in the alley till I had got it over with. Then back they swarmed." She justified her lack of emphasis on Christian literature, after an experience with a young man who expressed interest in becoming a Christian. She talked with him and then gave him a gospel of John. With that he left and she did not see him again for two years. When she unexpectedly encountered him one day, she asked why he had stayed away for so long. He responded: "I wanted to know Jesus and you gave me a library." That response set the stage for a new direction in her thinking: "I re-examined some of my concepts about studying the word of God. The early Christians certainly had no Bibles; they must have learned another way."[38] She was determined to focus on personal interaction and not insist that *reading* be a required aspect of Christian devotion.

Standard evangelism tactics did not work for Pullinger in her ministry to people in the Walled City.

Despite her best efforts, Pullinger faced setbacks in her work. The more influence she had, the more threatening her work became, and there were some who wanted her out of the Walled City. After a break-in and a night of vandalism that could have destroyed her Youth Club, she determinedly cleaned up the mess and repaired the damage. After that, she was given unsolicited protection from a notorious gang leader whom she referred to as "Big Brother." But she never had enough help to accomplish what needed to be done: "Many people came to me and asked to help in the club. It sounded romantic and exciting to work in the Walled City, but few stuck it [out] more than a few weeks." Her solution? "I learned how to cat-nap, sleeping on busses and ferries."[39]

Her most effective coworkers were those whose home was the Walled City and who had been converted through her ministry. Through their outreach, the work continued to expand and adjust to change—including the destruction of her "mission field." In 1993 work began on the demolition of the Walled City.

In its place a park was built. For many people the adjustment was difficult, and Pullinger was there in the transition. In the years since, the work has continued to focus on drug rehabilitation and evangelism, and there are centers and camps not only in Hong Kong but elsewhere around the world—in India, Sri Lanka, the Philippines, Indonesia, Malaysia, and Europe.

Reflecting back over her early years of ministry, Pullinger writes: "It was a time of learning and of growing up: often I was in awful confusion."[40] But those years laid the foundation for a worldwide ministry of bringing hope to society's most hopeless. The secret of her effective ministry may have been her perspective—her attitude toward her surroundings—that stayed with her through the decades, even after the Walled City was no more:

> I loved this dark place. I hated what was happening in it but I wanted to be nowhere else. It was almost as if I could already see another city in its place and that city was ablaze with light. It was my dream. There was no more crying, no more death or pain. . . . I had no idea how to bring this about but with "visionary zeal" imagined introducing the Walled City people to the one who could change it all: Jesus.[41]

Don Richardson

One of the bestselling mission books of the twentieth century was Don Richardson's *Peace Child*, which sold hundreds of thousands of copies, became a *Reader's Digest* Book-of-the-Month selection, and was made into a film. His book *Lords of the Earth* was also a bestseller. Richardson put missiological issues in story form that caught the attention of laypeople. His principle of Redemptive Analogy—"the application to local custom of spiritual truth"—generated debate in missiological circles after he first introduced the concept in a seminar at Dallas Theological Seminary in 1973.

Don Richardson, missionary to Irian Jaya and author of Peace Child.

It was in a chapel service at Prairie Bible Institute in 1955 that Richardson, then twenty years old, responded to the call to foreign missions. For him it was a very specific call to the headhunting tribes of Netherlands New Guinea. Among the students who also heard the call that day was Carol Soderstrom, who would become his wife five years later. In 1962, after completing a course with the

Summer Institute of Linguistics and awaiting the birth of their first child, the Richardsons sailed for New Guinea to work with the Regions Beyond Missionary Union among the Sawi, known for cannibalism and headhunting. The setting was quickly captured by Richardson's colorful writing:

> The brooding jungle stood tall against the sky, walling in the overgrown clearing as if to create an arena for an impending contest. . . . The wildness of the locale seemed to taunt me. Something in the mood of the place seemed to say mockingly, "I am not like your tame, manageable Canadian homeland. I am tangled. I am too dense to walk through. I am hot and steamy and drenched with rain. I am hip-deep mud and six-inch sago thorns. I am death adders and taipans and leeches and crocodiles. I am malaria and dysentery and filariasis and hepatitis."[42]

If fear of treachery and disease weighed heavily on their conscious and subconscious thinking, fear of never coming to grips with the language was a very conscious struggle. The nineteen tenses of each verb and the complex vocabulary was mind boggling. "In English you open your eyes, your heart, a door, a tin can or someone's understanding, all with one humdrum verb 'open.' But in Sawi you *fagadon* your eyes, *anahagkon* your heart, *tagavon* a door, *tarifan* a tin can, and *dargamon* a listener's understanding."[43] Though he frequently felt as though his "brain circuits would get shorted," he maintained an eight- to ten-hour-day language learning schedule and soon became proficient enough to communicate in Sawi. He viewed the task as a "great adventure": "I often felt like a mathematician must feel as he tackles problems and breaks through into new formulas which work like magic."[44]

IRIAN JAYA

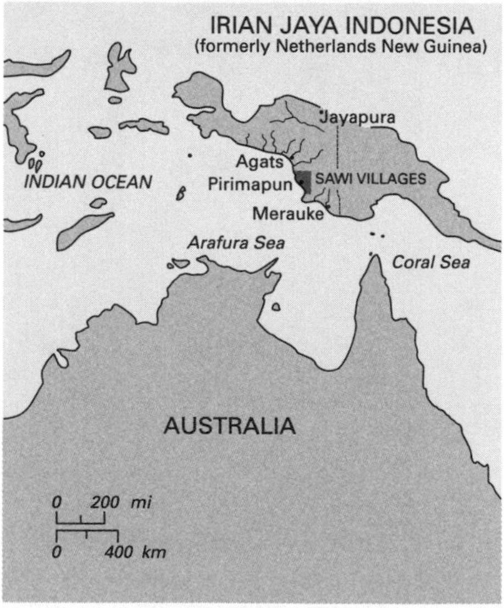

As he learned the language and lived with the people, he became more aware of the gulf that separated his Christian worldview from the worldview of the Sawi: "In their eyes Judas, not Jesus, was the hero of the Gospels, Jesus was just the dupe to be laughed at."[45] Eventually Richardson discovered what he referred to as a Redemptive Analogy that pointed to the Incarnate Christ far more clearly than any biblical passage alone could have done. What he discovered was the Sawi concept of the Peace Child.

The warlike nature of the Sawi was a factor that had greatly troubled him from the earliest days of his residence among them. Despite his best efforts, he could not prevent the tribal wars among the three villages in the vicinity of their work. He blamed himself: "I concluded . . . that Carol and I had unintentionally deprived Haenam, Kamur and Yohwi [the three villages] of the mutual isolation they needed to survive in relative peace by drawing them together into one community. It followed that for the good of the people, we ought to leave them. It would be a bitter pill to swallow, but I knew without us, they would scatter to their deep jungle homes and be at peace."[46]

So distressed were the Sawi on hearing of his proposed departure that they met in a special tribal session and then announced to him that the following day they were going to make peace. Encouraged by this turn of events, he anxiously awaited the next morning. Not long after dawn, the Sawi peace ritual began. The diplomatic process, though rarely exercised, was a deeply emotional experience. Young children from each of the warring villages were to be exchanged. As long as any of those children lived, the peace would continue. The decision as to whose child would be given up was a wrenching ordeal. Mothers with little children were filled with apprehension when they realized what was happening. Finally, a young man grabbed his only child, rushed toward the enemy camp, and literally gave his son to one of his enemies. A child was given in return for his, and peace was established. It was a peace based on trust—an element that had seemed to Richardson to be nonexistent in the Sawi culture. But in their own way the Sawi "had found a way to prove sincerity and establish peace. . . . Among the Sawi every demonstration of friendship was suspect except one. *If a man would actually give his own son to his enemies, that man could be trusted!*"[47] It was that analogy, then, that he used to point the Sawi to God sacrificing his Son on the cross.

> *"If a man would actually give his own son to his enemies, that man could be trusted!" It was that analogy that Richardson used to point the Sawi to God sacrificing his Son on the cross.*

The Peace Child analogy alone did not solve all the communication barriers. Other analogies were also to be discovered, and for the Richardsons there were many more trying experiences to endure. But through their patient toil, the Sawi gradually began to turn to Christianity, which better prepared them to withstand the "cultural disorientation" soon to be unleashed on them by the influx of oil, logging, mining, and immigration from other islands of Indonesia. As a nurse, Carol treated some two thousand patients a month, while at the same time teaching basic hygiene and other preventive care. Together they translated the New Testament and taught the Sawi to read.

By 1972, after a decade of ministry among the Sawi, much had changed. The meeting house used for Christian gatherings was enlarged twice and then replaced by a "Sawidome" that seated a thousand people. It was to be a "house of peace in which former enemies" could "sit down together at the Lord's table, and a house of prayer for the tribes without God's Word." The building was dedicated in the summer of 1972 and was believed to be the world's largest circular building made entirely of unmilled poles.[48]

After completing the translation of the New Testament, the Richardsons left the Sawi under the care of their own church elders and another missionary couple. They moved on to work with another missionary couple in analyzing the Auyy language. Then, in 1976, the Richardsons returned to North America, and he began teaching at the U.S. Center for World Mission in Pasadena, where he became the Director of Tribal Peoples' Studies. Here his emphasis on "Redemptive Analogies" found ready acceptance, and others joined him in similar efforts to develop more effective means to communicate the gospel among tribal peoples.

Redemptive analogies, Richardson insists, are not new. They are as old as Scripture itself and as applicable today as the commission to go to "the uttermost part of the earth." It is perhaps noteworthy that his rediscovery of these timeless methods and principles occurred in what must truly be considered the uttermost part of the world—Irian Jaya.

SELECT BIBLIOGRAPHY

Brother Andrew. *Battle for Africa.* Old Tappan, NJ: Fleming H. Revell, 1977.

______. *God's Smuggler.* Old Tappan, NJ: Fleming H. Revell, 1967.

Burgess, Alan. *Daylight Must Come: The Story of a Courageous Woman Doctor in the Congo.* New York: Dell, 1975.

Dunker, Marilee Pierce. *Man of Vision, Woman of Prayer.* Nashville: Thomas Nelson, 1980.

Egan, Eileen. *Such a Vision of the Street: Mother Teresa—the Spirit and the Work.* New York: Doubleday, 1985.

Le Joly, Edward, S.J., *Mother Teresa of Calcutta: A Biography.* San Francisco: Harper & Row, 1983.

Muggeridge, Malcolm. *Something Beautiful for God.* Garden City, NY: Image Books, 1971.

Olson, Bruce. *Bruchko.* Carol Stream, IL: Creation House, 1978.

Pullinger, Jackie, with Andrew Quicke. *Chasing the Dragon.* Ann Arbor, MI: Servant Books, 1980.

Pullinger, Jackie. *Crack in the Wall: Life and Death in Kowloon Walled City.* London: Hodder & Stoughton, 1989.

Richardson, Don. *Peace Child.* Glendale, CA: Regal, 1974.

Roseveare, Helen. *Give Me This Mountain.* London: Inter-Varsity Press, 1966.

______. *He Gave Us a Valley.* Downers Grove, IL: InterVarsity Press, 1976.

Sebba, Anne. *Mother Teresa: Beyond the Image.* New York: Doubleday, 1998.

Postscript

In retrospect, the most striking aspect of the Christian world mission has been the vast numbers of men and women who, against all odds, left family and homeland to endure the privations and the frustrations of cross-cultural evangelism to follow God's call. It was that nebulous and indefinable "missionary call" that impelled them to move out. If ministries in the homeland could be pursued without a "call," foreign missions could not. The stakes were too high. And it was that sense of calling, more than anything else, that was the staying power. Of course, there were those who went but did not stay, and who were relegated to the role of missionary "returnee." But at least they went out, and in many cases made significant contributions. Many who remained might have been far happier staying home. Yet they stayed on, decade after decade, prodded on by their sense of calling.

Who were these who were afflicted by such a high calling? Were they men and women especially fitted for that calling? Probably not—at least no more than earnest believers in any other segment of the Christian church. The history both of humankind and of missions is a saga checkered by shortcomings, failures, and setbacks.

After centuries of less-than-spectacular growth, the "Great Century" dawned, only to launch the "father of modern missions" with an unwilling wife and an associate of questionable character. The domestic unhappiness represented by even that famous missionary was hardly an ideal example; and later on, the bitter strife between junior and senior missionaries at the Serampore mission station in India further damaged the testimony Christianity was supposed to demonstrate.

But it was not just in India that the name of Christ was besmirched. In China, Christianity was indelibly linked to opium smuggling. In Africa, it was associated with racism and exploitation. In the Pacific islands, there were instances of sexual immorality among the missionaries. And on virtually every mission field in the world, moreover, there was embarrassing and amateurish understanding of cultural traditions, and the Western institutionalized church was taken for granted as the only way converts could follow the Lord.

Many modern scholars investigating the history of missions concede that often the failures were incidental and, in some cases, excusable; they were only ripples on the surface of a powerful groundswell of grace that flooded the earth. Yet it is no wonder that the critics have had a heyday with Christian missions. The very humanity of the missionaries themselves provided all the fuel that was needed. Why should we be surprised at their mistakes and sins and follies? Missionaries were neither the super-saints their admirers have created nor the unlearned and zealous misfits their detractors have described. But they were somehow called by God, and they made significant sacrifices to follow that call.

The spread of Christianity into the non-Western world, principally as a missionary achievement, is one of the great success stories of all history. After moving forward in the Middle Ages and the Reformation era and gaining momentum in the Evangelical Awakening, after escaping the vigorous counterforces of rationalism and secularism, and after surviving the French Revolution and Napoleonic wars, the Christian movement suddenly expanded to become a vibrant, universal religion passionately adhered to by people from every corner of the globe. True to form, this massive extension has been a working faith. No other cause in history has fostered such far-reaching humanitarian efforts of goodwill as has Christianity.

The very fact that this incredible worldwide expansion was carried out by frail and sinful human beings, backed by only a minority of Christians back home, only enhances the glory that must be given to God alone. Nevertheless, it is difficult from a human perspective not to admire and idealize those who were willing to go—those who so willingly sacrificed their own ambitions to make whatever contribution they could to a far greater cause. There were Henry Martyns and Helen Roseveares on every field—those who relinquished what surely would have been brilliant careers in their homeland and gave up the joys of marriage and family only to suffer pain and humiliation—all in obedience to God's call.

Far less attention has been paid to those who stayed behind and who may have been no less obedient to the heavenly vision. Countless individuals heard the same call and had good intentions of making the same kind of sacrifice but never went. Were they less spiritual? Were they less committed to God? Indeed, there may be only a fine line that separates those who went from those who stayed home.

It has been said that for every missionary who goes to the foreign mission field there are at least fifty individuals who at one time or another committed their lives to missions but never carried through with their commitment. Was their call to missions unrealized? In many cases it was. Their commitment was forgotten. In other instances, however, they played an indispensable role on the home front. Where would missions be today without these "stay-at-homes"?

Of the one hundred thousand student volunteers who signed the "Princeton Pledge," twenty thousand actually went abroad as foreign missionaries—but how could that army of volunteers have endured on the front lines without the powerful backup support network at home? During those years, monetary giving to missions more than quadrupled. There was a similar support system behind the vast movement of women that poured into cross-cultural missions beginning in the late nineteenth century. For every woman who went out, there were a dozen or more wholly committed female mission supporters on the home front—among them many who had felt called to go but never went.

In recent decades another student movement was launched, largely by devoted missionary-minded "stay-at-homes." C. Stacey Woods intended to go to India in 1934, but he ended up staying in America to develop and direct InterVarsity Christian Fellowship—a student organization involved in promoting missions on university campuses. InterVarsity is also known for its triennial Urbana Missionary Conferences—attracting thousands of students from campuses around the world. Dawson Trotman, who also stayed home, played a crucial role in missionary outreach through his founding of the Navigators. Trotman caught a vision for missions while in Paris in 1948, and since that time the Navigators have spread out across the globe with a zeal to disciple others in the Christian faith.

Campus Crusade for Christ, founded by Bill Bright, was initially focused on reaching students with the gospel, but by the 1980s it had thousands of staff members involved in evangelism in more than one hundred fifty countries around the world. Few areas of the world have remained untouched by that organization's "Here's Life" campaigns and the *Jesus* film, which has been translated into dozens of languages.

There is a growing consensus among many of today's leaders in missions that less distinction should be made between the career *foreign* missionary and the one who promotes missions from the home front or the one who serves as a mission consultant or a short-term missionary. Individuals such as George Verwer of Operation Mobilization and Loren Cunningham of Youth with a Mission have dedicated their lives to challenging young adults to commit themselves to missions—be it short-term or lifetime careers and be it at home or abroad.

So what about those who did not go overseas? How should their lives be evaluated? Are they any less a part of the Great Commission? Is their "missionary call" any less valid? Each one must answer that question individually before God—and perhaps reevaluate the very nature of the missionary "call." Indeed, what often seems to be so plainly a geographic call to a foreign field might better be described as a call to join in completing the unfinished task of world evangelism.

The story of those who served in overseas mission is a thrilling drama—far more exciting, no doubt, than the story of those who stayed home. Yet those who stayed behind also have a story that needs to be told, and sometimes it closely resembles the story of those who went out.

One of those stories began in the 1950s in a farming community in northern Wisconsin. The setting was a summer Bible camp where missionary Delmer Smith of the Christian and Missionary Alliance was the featured speaker. There in the rustic pavilion, under his moving messages, a thirteen-year-old farm girl caught a vision for missions, and at the closing meeting she stood to commit her life to God as a foreign missionary. Through her high school years that followed, foreign missions was her life's goal. Nothing, she vowed, would ever deter her.

Following high school graduation her life was busy and eventful. Bible college, Christian liberal arts college, university, marriage, family, teaching career. One followed on another. But as the years slipped by, the prospect of embarking on an overseas missions career became less and less a reality.

Only three miles away from her childhood home another young farm girl was growing up—her cousin, Valerie Stellrecht. They attended the same schools and the same little country church. Valerie too felt called to foreign missions. She too enrolled at the St. Paul Bible College to prepare for her life's calling. And she too longed for marriage and family. But her sense of calling to the foreign field came first. Valerie graduated from Bible college and soon thereafter bade farewell to her family and loved ones and set out alone for Ecuador, where she continues to serve today with the Christian and Missionary Alliance.

Two young women whose lives paralleled each other's in so many respects. Two young women who felt called to foreign missions. Valerie went. I stayed home.

NOTES

PART 1

THE IRRESISTIBLE ADVANCE

1. Ramsay MacMullen, *Christianizing the Roman Empire (A.D. 100-400)* (New Haven: Yale University Press, 1984), viii.
2. Ibid., 2.
3. Ibid.
4. Ralph D. Winter, "The Kingdom Strikes Back: The Ten Epochs of Redemptive History," in *Perspectives on the World Christian Movement,* ed. Ralph D. Winter and Steven C. Hawthorne (Pasadena: William Carey, 1981), 150.
5. J. Herbert Kane, *A Concise History of the Christian World Mission: A Panoramic View of Missions from Pentecost to the Present* (Grand Rapids: Baker, 1978), 43.
6. Winter, "The Kingdom Strikes Back," 148.
7. Philip Schaff, *The Middle Ages,* vol. 5 of *History of the Christian Church* (Grand Rapids: Eerdmans, 1979), 588–89.

1
THE EARLY CENTURIES: EVANGELIZING THE ROMAN EMPIRE

1. David Bosch, *Transforming Mission: Paradigm Shifts in Theology of Mission* (Maryknoll, NY: Orbis, 1991), 16.
2. J. Herbert Kane, *A Concise History of the Christian World Mission: A Panoramic View of Missions from Pentecost to the Present* (Grand Rapids: Baker, 1978), 7.
3. Stephen Neill, *A History of Christian Missions* (New York: Penguin, 1964), 24.
4. Milton L. Rudnick, *Speaking the Gospel through the Ages: A History of Evangelism* (St. Louis: Concordia, 1984), 14.
5. Ramsay MacMullen, *Christianizing the Roman Empire (A.D. 100–400)* (New Haven, CT: Yale University Press, 1984), 109–10, 150.
6. Eusebius, *Ecclesiastical History:* quoted in Neill, *History of Christian Missions,* 39–40.
7. John Foxe, *Foxe's Christian Martyrs of the World* (Chicago: Moody Press, n.d.), 41.
8. Quoted in Neill, *History of Christian Missions,* 45.
9. Ibid., 42.
10. Ibid., 43.
11. Quoted in F. F. Bruce, *The Spreading Flame: The Rise and Progress of Christianity from Its First Beginnings to the Conversion of the English* (Grand Rapids: Eerdmans, 1979), 170.

12. Ibid., 171.
13. Eusebius, *Ecclesiastical History,* 257–59.
14. Rudnick, *Speaking the Gospel,* 23.
15. Frederick W. Weidmann, *Polycarp and John* (Notre Dame, IN: University of Notre Dame Press, 1999), 60, 64, 72.
16. Kenneth Scott Latourette, *The First Five Centuries,* vol. 1 of *A History of the Expansion of Christianity* (Grand Rapids: Zondervan, 1970), 80.
17. N. T. Wright, *What Saint Paul Really Said* (Grand Rapids: Eerdmans, 1997), 37.
18. Roland Allen, *Missionary Methods: St. Paul's or Ours?* (Chicago: Moody Press, 1956), 3–4.
19. Ibid., 6–7.
20. Ben Witherington III, *The Renewed Search for the Jew of Tarsus* (Downers Grove, IL: InterVarsity, 1998), 128.
21. Michael Duncan, "The Other Side of Paul," *On Being* (June 1991): 21–23.
22. Bosch, *Transforming Mission,* 124.
23. Cited in John Mark Terry, "The History of Missions in the Early Church," in *Missiology: An Introduction to the Foundations, History, and Strategies of World Missions,* ed. John Mark Terry, Ebbie C. Smith, and Justice Anderson (Nashville: Broadman, 1998), 167.
24. Bruce, *The Spreading Flame,* 174.
25. W. H. C. Frend, *Martyrdom and Persecution in the Early Church* (Oxford: Blackwell, 1965), 241, 189.
26. Bruce, *The Spreading Flame,* 260.
27. Philip Schaff, *Ante-Nicene Christianity,* vol. 2 of *History of the Christian Church* (Grand Rapids: Eerdmans, 1979), 666.
28. Weidmann, *Polycarp and John,* passim.
29. Schaff, *Ante-Nicene Christianity,* 2:667.
30. Jack N. Sparks, *St. Irenaios: The Preaching of the Apostles.* See www.goarch.org/en/resources/fathers/contents.html (February 6, 2004).
31. Elliott Wright, *Holy Company: Christian Heroes and Heroines* (New York: Macmillan, 1980), 80.
32. Weidmann, *Polycarp and John,* 81.
33. Bruce, *The Spreading Flame,* 174.
34. Edith Deen, *Great Women of the Christian Faith* (New York: Harper & Row, 1959), 3.
35. Wright, *Holy Company,* 234.
36. Ibid., 235.
37. Deen, *Great Women,* 5.
38. Sherwood Wirt, "God's Darling," *Moody Monthly* (February 1977): 58.
39. Joyce E. Salisbury, *Perpetua's Passion: The Death and Memory of a Young Roman Woman* (New York: Routledge, 1997), 92.
40. Wright, *Holy Company,* 236.
41. Deen, *Great Women,* 6.
42. Wirt, "God's Darling," 60.
43. Latourette, *First Five Centuries,* 213.

44. Neill, *History of Christian Missions,* 55; V. Raymond Edman, *The Light in Dark Ages* (Wheaton, IL: Van Kampen, 1949), 91.
45. Neill, *History of Christian Missions,* 55n.
46. Latourette, *First Five Centuries,* 214.
47. Philostorgius, *History of the Church,* quoted in *Eerdmans' Handbook to the History of Christianity* (Grand Rapids: Erdmans, 1977), 180.
48. Edman, *Light in Dark Ages,* 93.
49. David Plotz, "St. Patrick: No snakes. No shamrocks. Just the facts," March 17, 2000, http://slate.msn.com/id/77427/.
50. Thomas O'Loughlin, *St. Patrick: The Man and His Works* (London: Society for Promoting Christian Knowledge, 1999), 1.
51. Bruce, *The Spreading Flame,* 373.
52. Ibid.
53. Ibid., 374.
54. O'Loughlin, *St. Patrick,* 43.
55. Bruce, *The Spreading Flame,* 376–77.
56. J. Herbert Kane, "Saint Patrick—Evangelical Missionary to Ireland," *Eternity* 23, no. 7 (July 1972): 34.
57. Latourette, *First Five Centuries,* 219.
58. Quoted in Bruce, *The Spreading Flame,* 381.
59. Edman, *Light in Dark Ages,* 145.
60. E. H. Broadbent, *The Pilgrim Church* (London: Pickering & Inglis, 1974), 34–35.
61. Will Durant, *The Age of Faith,* vol. 4 of *The Story of Civilization* (New York: Simon & Schuster, 1950), 532.
62. Kenneth Scott Latourette, *The Thousand Years of Uncertainty,* vol. 2 of *A History of the Expansion of Christianity* (Grand Rapids: Zondervan, 1970), 54.

2
ROMAN CATHOLIC MISSIONS: BAPTIZING THE MASSES

1. Philip Hughes, *A Popular History of the Reformation* (New York: Doubleday, 1960), 19.
2. Christopher Dawson, *Religion and the Rise of Western Culture* (rep., New York: Doubleday/Image Books, 1991), 34–35.
3. Bruce L. Shelley, *Church History in Plain Language* (Waco: Word, 1982), 176.
4. Stephen Neill, *A History of Christian Missions* (New York: Penguin, 1979), 67.
5. Quoted in ibid., 68–69.
6. John Stewart, *The Nestorian Missionary Enterprise: A Church on Fire* (Edinburgh: Clarke, 1923), 198, 29, 18.
7. Neill, *History of Christian Missions,* 74; Kenneth Scott Latourette, *The Thousand Years of Uncertainty,* vol. 2 of *A History of the Expansion of Christianity* (Grand Rapids: Zondervan, 1970), 85; Christopher Dawson, *The Making of Europe* (New York: New American Library, 1956), as quoted in Neill, *History of Christian Missions,* 74.
8. V. Raymond Edman, *The Light in Dark Ages* (Wheaton, IL: Van Kampen, 1949), 192.

9. John Cyril Sladden, *Boniface of Devon: Apostle of Germany* (Exeter, England: Paternoster Press, 1980), 33.
10. Latourette, *Thousand Years of Uncertainty,* 96.
11. George William Greenaway, *Saint Boniface* (London: Adam & Charles Black, 1955), 28.
12. Philip Schaff, *Medieval Christianity,* vol. 4 of *History of the Christian Church* (Grand Rapids: Eerdmans, 1979), 94.
13. C. H. Talbot, "St. Boniface and the German Mission," in *The Mission of the Church and the Propagation of the Faith,* ed. G. J. Cuming (Cambridge: Cambridge University Press, 1970), 49.
14. Latourette, *Thousand Years of Uncertainty,* 95.
15. Eleanor McLaughlin, "Women, Power and the Pursuit of Holiness in Medieval Christianity," in *Women of Spirit: Female Leaders in the Jewish and Christian Traditions,* ed. Rosemary Ruether and Eleanor McLaughlin (New York: Simon & Schuster, 1979), 105.
16. Norman F. Cantor, *Medieval History: The Life and Death of Civilization,* 2d ed. (New York: Macmillan, 1975), 186.
17. Ibid., 187.
18. Schaff, *Medieval Christianity,* 98.
19. Neill, *History of Christian Missions,* 76.
20. Latourette, *Thousand Years of Uncertainty,* 103.
21. Ibid., 117.
22. Schaff, *Medieval Christianity,* 114.
23. Latourette, *Thousand Years of Uncertainty,* 155.
24. Ibid., 161.
25. J. Herbert Kane, *A Concise History of the Christian World Mission,* rev. ed. (Grand Rapids: Baker, 1980), 49–50.
26. Samuel M. Zwemer, *Raymond Lull: First Missionary to the Moslems* (New York: Funk & Wagnalls, 1902), 26.
27. Ibid., 34, 36.
28. Quoted in ibid., 52–53.
29. Ibid., 64.
30. Ibid., 63–64.
31. Ibid., 81–82.
32. Ibid., 83.
33. Ibid., 94.
34. Ibid., 108–11.
35. Ibid., 141.
36. Ibid., 142–43.
37. Neill, *History of Christian Missions,* 169.
38. Gustavo Gutierrez, *Las Casas: In Search of the Poor of Jesus Christ*, trans. Robert R. Barr (Maryknoll, NY: Orbis, 1993), 47–48.
39. Quoted in Neill, *History of Christian Missions,* 171.
40. Kenneth Scott Latourette, *Three Centuries of Advance,* vol. 3 of *A History of the Expansion of Christianity* (Grand Rapids: Zondervan, 1978), 96.

41. Neill, *History of Christian Missions,* 148.
42. Quoted in Will Durant, *The Reformation,* vol. 6 of The *Story of Civilization* (New York: Simon & Schuster, 1957), 914.
43. Quoted in James Brodrick, *Saint Francis Xavier* (New York: Wicklow, 1952), 204.
44. Ibid., 174.
45. Ibid., 145.
46. Ibid., 144.
47. Quoted in Neill, *History of Christian Missions,* 150.
48. Francis Xavier, *The Letters and Instructions of Francis Xavier,* trans. M. Joseph Costelloe (St. Louis: Institute of Jesuit Sources, 1992), 130.
49. Neill, *History of Christian Missions,* 154.
50. Ibid., 156.
51. F. A. Rouleau, "Matteo Ricci," in *The New Catholic Encyclopedia,* ed. William J. McDonald (New York: McGraw-Hill, 1967), 12:472.
52. Vincent Cronin, *The Wise Man from the West* (New York: Dutton, 1955), 31.
53. Jonathan Spence, *The Memory Palace of Matteo Ricci* (New York: Viking, 1984), 220.
54. A. J. Broomhall, *Hudson Taylor and China's Open Century* (London: Hodder & Stoughton, 1981), 74.
55. Ibid., 64.
56. Quoted in Rouleau, "Matteo Ricci," 471.
57. "The Journal of Matthew Ricci," in *Classics of Christian Missions,* ed. Francis M. Dubose (Nashville: Broadman, 1979), 172–73.
58. Broomhall, *Hudson Taylor,* 75.

3
AMERICAN INDIAN MISSIONS: SEEKING THE "NOBLE SAVAGE"

1. Henry Warner Bowden, *American Indians and Christian Missions: Studies in Cultural Conflict* (Chicago: University of Chicago Press, 1981), 45–46.
2. Ibid., 48–49.
3. Ibid., 80.
4. Ibid., 87.
5. Quoted in Daniel Scalberg and Joy Cordell, "A Savage With the Savages," *Moody Magazine* (April 1987): 56.
6. Ibid., 55.
7. Ibid., 55–57.
8. Ibid., 57.
9. Ola Elisabeth Winslow, *John Eliot, "Apostle to the Indians"* (Boston: Houghton Mifflin, 1968), 96.
10. Ibid., 110.
11. Ibid., 113.
12. Neville B. Cryer, "John Eliot," in *Five Pioneer Missionaries* (London: Banner of Truth, 1965), 212.
13. Winslow, *John Eliot,* 179.

14. Elisabeth D. Dodds, *Marriage to a Difficult Man: The "Uncommon Union" of Jonathan and Sarah Edwards* (Philadelphia: Westminster, 1971), 118.
15. David Wynbeek, *David Brainerd: Beloved Yankee* (Grand Rapids: Eerdmans, 1961), 60.
16. Quoted in ibid., 60–61.
17. Ibid., 79.
18. Ibid., 113.
19. William R. Hutchinson, *Errand to the World: American Protestant Thought and Foreign Missions* (Chicago: University of Chicago Press, 1987), 30.
20. Ibid., 30–31.
21. Ibid., 32.
22. Jonathan Edwards, ed., *The Life and Diary of David Brainerd* (Chicago: Moody Press, 1949), 141, 146.
23. R. Pierce Beaver, *Pioneers in Mission: The Early Missionary Ordination Sermons, Charges, and Instructions* (Grand Rapids: Eerdmans, 1966), 211–12.
24. Quoted in Earl P. Olmstead, *David Zeisberger: A Life among the Indians* (Kent, OH: Kent State University Press, 1997), 334, 333.
25. Quoted in Robert F. Berkhofer Jr., *Salvation and the Savage: An Analysis of Protestant Missions and American Indian Response, 1787–1862* (Louisville: University of Kentucky Press, 1965), 101.
26. Quoted in John Ehle, *Trail of Tears: The Rise and Fall of the Cherokee Nation* (New York: Doubleday, 1988), 361.
27. R. Pierce Beaver, *Church, State, and the American Indians* (St. Louis: Concordia, 1966), 100.
28. Nard Jones, *The Great Command: The Story of Marcus and Narcissa Whitman and the Oregon Country Pioneers* (Boston: Little, Brown, 1959), 125.
29. Ibid., 202, 229.
30. Julie Roy Jeffrey, *Converting the West: A Biography of Narcissa Whitman* (Norman: University of Oklahoma Press, 1991), 138.
31. Jones, *The Great Command,* 219–20.
32. Jeffrey, *Converting the West,* 146.
33. Ibid., 151.
34. Don Pedro Casaldaliga, "Mass of the Land without Evil," cited in ibid., 222.
35. Leecy Barnett, "Hundreds of Pious Women: Presbyterian Women Missionaries to the American Indians, 1833–1893" (master's thesis, Trinity Evangelical Divinity School, 1985), 114–15.

4
THE MORAVIAN ADVANCE: DAWN OF PROTESTANT MISSIONS

1. William J. Danker, *Profit for the Lord* (Grand Rapids: Eerdmans, 1971), 73.
2. A. Skevington Wood, "Count von Zinzendorf," in *Eerdmans' Handbook to the History of Christianity* (Grand Rapids: Eerdmans, 1977), 477.
3. John R. Weinlick, *Count Zinzendorf* (Nashville: Abingdon, 1956), 225.
4. Ibid., 200.

5. Ibid., 205.
6. J. C. S. Mason, *The Moravian Church and the Missionary Awakening in England, 1760–1800* (Woodbridge, UK: Boydell Press, 2001), 9.
7. Quoted in ibid., 9–10.
8. Louis Bobé, *Hans Egede: Colonizer and Missionary to Greenland* (Copenhagen: Rosenkilde & Bagger, 1952), 22.
9. Ibid., 23.
10. Ibid., 29.
11. Ibid., 82.
12. Stephen Neill, *A History of Christian Missions* (New York: Penguin, 1964), 237.
13. Bobé, *Hans Egede,* 155.
14. Ibid., 162.
15. Ibid., 158.
16. Bernard Kruger, *The Pear Tree Blossoms: A History of the Moravian Mission Stations in South Africa, 1737–1869* (South Africa: Genadendal Printing Works, 1967), 19.
17. Ibid., 31.
18. Mason, *The Moravian Church*, 144.

PART 2

THE "GREAT CENTURY"

1. Stephen Neill, *A History of Christian Missions* (New York: Penguin, 1964), 243.
2. Martin E. Marty, *A Short History of Christianity* (New York: Meridian, 1959), 318.
3. Kenneth Scott Latourette, *The Great Century: North Africa and Asia,* vol. 6 of *A History of the Expansion of Christianity* (Grand Rapids: Zondervan, 1970), 445.
4. Marty, *A Short History of Christianity*, 273.
5. Harold Cook, *Highlights of Christian Missions: A History and Survey* (Chicago: Moody Press, 1967), 54.
6. Latourette, *The Great Century,* 443.
7. Neill, *History of Christian Missions,* 252.
8. Robert Hall Glover and J. Herbert Kane, *The Progress of Worldwide Missions* (New York: Harper & Brothers, 1960), 58.
9. A. F. Walls, "Outposts of Empire," in *Eerdmans' Handbook to the History of Christianity* (Grand Rapids: Eerdmans, 1977), 556.
10. Ralph D. Winter, "The Kingdom Strikes Back: The Ten Epochs of Redemptive History," in *Perspectives on the World Christian Movement,* ed. Ralph D. Winter and Steven C. Hawthorne (Pasadena: William Carey, 1981), 154.
11. Neill, *History of Christian Missions,* 259.

5

SOUTH CENTRAL ASIA: CONFRONTING ANCIENT CREEDS

1. Mary Drewery, *William Carey: A Biography* (Grand Rapids: Zondervan, 1979), 63.

2. George Smith, *Life of William Carey: Shoemaker and Missionary* (New York: E. P. Dutton, 1922), 98–99.
3. Christopher Smith, "The Legacy of William Carey," *International Bulletin of Missionary Research* (January 1992), 2.
4. Drewery, *William Carey,* 25.
5. J. Herbert Kane, *A Concise History of the Christian World Mission* (Grand Rapids: Baker, 1978), 85.
6. Drewery, *William Carey,* 70.
7. James R. Beck, *Dorothy Carey: The Tragic and Untold Story of Mrs. William Carey* (Grand Rapids: Baker, 1992), 109.
8. Ibid., 114.
9. Ibid., 116–17.
10. Drewery, *William Carey,* 89.
11. Smith, "Legacy," 2.
12. Timothy George, *Faithful Witness: The Life and Mission of William Carey* (Birmingham: New Hope, 1991), 97.
13. Drewery, *William Carey,* 69, 111.
14. Ibid., 102.
15. Ibid., 115.
16. Ibid., 146.
17. Beck, *Dorothy Carey,* 129.
18. Drewery, *William Carey,* 183, 185.
19. George, *Faithful Witness,* 128.
20. Drewery, *William Carey,* 173.
21. Ibid., 166.
22. Courtney Anderson, *To the Golden Shore: The Life of Adoniram Judson* (Grand Rapids: Zondervan, 1972), 509.
23. Ibid., 50.
24. Alan Neely, "Samuel John Mills Jr.," in *Biographical Dictionary of Christian Missions,* ed. Gerald Anderson (Grand Rapids: Eerdmans, 1998), 460.
25. Anderson, *To the Golden Shore,* 84.
26. Ibid., 181.
27. Ibid., 362.
28. Ibid., 391.
29. Ibid., 398.
30. Ibid., 478.
31. Wendy Tha Nyein, "How My Forefathers Helped Adoniram Judson Bring the Gospel to Burma," *Christian Mission* (March/April 1989), 3–5.
32. John Seamands, *Pioneers of the Younger Churches* (Nashville: Abingdon, 1969), 22.
33. Anderson, *To the Golden Shore,* 416.
34. William Paton, *Alexander Duff: Pioneer of Missionary Education* (New York: Doran, 1922), 150.
35. Ibid., 220.
36. A. T. Pierson quoted in Robert H. Glover and J. Herbert Kane, *The Progress of World-Wide Missions* (New York: Harper, 1960), 72.

37. Frederick S. Downs, "John Everett Clough," in Gerald H. Anderson, ed., *Biographical Dictionary of Christian Missions* (Grand Rapids: Eerdmans, 1998), 139.
38. Sherwood Eddy, *Pathfinders of the World Missionary Crusade* (Nashville: Abingdon-Cokesbury Press, 1945), 84.
39. Ibid., 93.
40. James M. Thoburn, *Life of Isabella Thoburn* (New York: Eaton and Mains, 1903), 148–49.
41. Gerald H. Anderson, "James Mills Thoburn," in *Biographical Dictionary of Christian Missions,* 665.
42. Thoburn, *Life of Isabella Thoburn*, 192.
43. Eddy, *Pathfinders*, 94.
44. Ibid.
45. Thoburn, *Life of Isabella Thoburn*, 360–62.
46. W. F. Oldham, *Thoburn—Called of God* (New York: Methodist Book Concern, 1918), 70.
47. Ruth M. Armstrong, "Judson's Successors in the Heyday of Burma Missions," *Missiology* (January 1995): 61–63.

6
BLACK AFRICA: "THE WHITE MAN'S GRAVEYARD"

1. Andrew Walls, *The Cross-Cultural Process in Christian History: Studies in the Transmission and Appropriation of Faith* (Maryknoll, NY: Orbis, 2002), 85.
2. Jon Bonk, "'All Things to All Persons,'—The Missionary as a Racist-Imperialist, 1860–1918," *Missiology* (July 1980): 300.
3. Ibid., 393–94.
4. Lamin Sanneh, "Africa," in *Toward the Twenty-first Century in Christian Mission,* ed. James M. Phillips and Robert T. Coote (Grand Rapids: Eerdmans, 1993), 91.
5. Cecil Northcott, *Robert Moffat: Pioneer in Africa, 1817–1870* (London: Lutterworth, 1961), 22.
6. Ibid., 34.
7. Adrian Hastings, *The Church in Africa, 1450–1950* (New York: Oxford University Press, 1994), 208.
8. Edith Deen, *Great Women of the Christian Faith* (New York: Harper & Row, 1959), 187.
9. J. H. Morrison, *The Missionary Heroes of Africa* (New York: Doran, 1922), 38.
10. Deen, *Great Women,* 188.
11. Northcott, *Robert Moffat,* 129.
12. Geoffrey Moorhouse, *The Missionaries* (New York: Lippincott, 1973), 111.
13. Oliver Ransford, *David Livingstone: The Dark Interior* (New York: St. Martin's, 1978), 14.
14. Ibid., 23.
15. Ibid., 38.
16. Deen, *Great Women,* 192.
17. Northcott, *Robert Moffat,* 189.

18. Ransford, *David Livingstone,* 39.
19. Deen, *Great Women,* 193–94.
20. Ibid., 193–94; Ransford, *David Livingstone,* 118.
21. Moorhouse, *The Missionaries,* 256.
22. James and Marti Hefley, *By Their Blood: Christian Martyrs of the 20th Century* (Milford, MI: Mott, 1979), 343.
23. Meriel Buxton, *David Livingstone* (New York: St. Martin's Press, 2001), 175.
24. Morrison, *Missionary Heroes,* 201.
25. Ibid., 206.
26. Ibid., 208.
27. Pagan Kennedy, *Black Livingstone: A True Tale of Adventure in the Nineteenth-Century Congo* (New York: Viking, 2002), 45.
28. Ibid., 51.
29. Ibid., 46.
30. Morrison, *Missionary Heroes,* 216.
31. Adam Hochschild, *King Leopold's Ghost: A Story of Greed, Terror, and Heroism in Colonial Africa* (Boston: Houghton Mifflin, 1999), 114.
32. Ibid., 153.
33. Ibid., 154.
34. Kennedy, *Black Livingstone,* 79.
35. Hochschild, *King Leopold's Ghost,* 155.
36. Ibid., 157.
37. Kennedy, *Black Livingstone,* 143.
38. Quoted in Hochschild, *King Leopold's Ghost,* 264.
39. Robert H. Glover and J. Herbert Kane, *The Progress of World-Wide Missions* (New York: Harper & Row, 1960), 329.
40. Edwin Bliss, ed., *Encyclopedia of Missions* (New York: Funk & Wagnalls, 1891), 2.
41. Hastings, *The Church in Africa,* 254, 375.
42. Ibid., 470.
43. Georgiana A. Gollock, *Sons of Africa* (New York: Friendship Press, 1920), 173.
44. Ibid., 178.
45. Hastings, *The Church in Africa,* 470.
46. Carol Christian and Gladys Plummer, *God and One Redhead: Mary Slessor of Calabar* (Grand Rapids: Zondervan, 1970), 34.
47. W. P. Livingstone, *Mary Slessor of Calabar: Pioneer Missionary* (London: Hodder & Stoughton, 1915), 51.
48. James Buchan, *The Expendable Mary Slessor* (New York: Seabury Press, 1981), 91, 95.
49. Quoted in Livingstone, *Mary Slessor of Calabar,* 142–43.
50. Christian and Plummer, *God and One Redhead,* 177.

7
CHINA: "BARBARIANS NOT WELCOME"

1. A. J. Broomhall, *Hudson Taylor and China's Open Century,* Book One: *Barbarians at the Gates* (London: Hodder & Stoughton, 1918), 267.

2. Sherwood Eddy, *Pathfinders of the World Missionary Crusade* (New York: Abingdon-Cokesbury, 1945), 34.
3. Ibid.
4. Marshall Broomhall, *Robert Morrison: A Master-builder* (New York: Doran, 1924), 59.
5. Ibid., 61, 131.
6. Ibid., 72.
7. A. J. Broomhall, *Barbarians at the Gates,* 127
8. Quoted in J. Barton Starr, "The Legacy of Robert Morrison," *International Bulletin of Missionary Research* (April 1998), 75.
9. A. J. Broomhall, *Barbarians at the Gates,* 207.
10. Ibid., 137–38.
11. Jonathan D. Spence, *God's Chinese Son: The Taiping Heavenly Kingdom and Hong Xiuquan* (New York: W. W. Norton, 1996), 16–17.
12. Ibid., 17.
13. Ibid., 18.
14. A. J. Broomhall, *Barbarians at the Gates,* 224.
15. Stephen Neill, *A History of Christian Missions* (New York: Penguin, 1964), 285.
16. J. C. Pollock, *Hudson Taylor and Maria: Pioneers in China* (Grand Rapids: Zondervan, 1976), 17.
17. Ibid., 20.
18. Ibid., 19.
19. Ibid., 29.
20. Dr. and Mrs. Howard Taylor, *J. Hudson Taylor: God's Man in China* (Chicago: Moody Press, 1978), 76.
21. Ibid., 70.
22. Pollock, *Hudson Taylor,* 31–32.
23. Taylor, *J. Hudson Taylor,* 100.
24. Pollock, *Hudson Taylor,* 49–50.
25. Ibid., 33.
26. Ibid., 81–82.
27. Ibid., 84–85.
28. Ibid., 89–91.
29. Ibid.
30. Ibid., 95.
31. Ibid., 97–98.
32. Ibid., 140.
33. Ibid., 147.
34. Ibid., 189.
35. Ibid., 193.
36. Ibid., 196–97.
37. Pat Barr, *To China with Love: The Lives and Times of Protestant Missionaries in China 1860–1900* (Garden City, NY: Doubleday, 1973), 50–51.
38. Alvyn Austin, "No Solicitation: The China Inland Mission and Money," in *More Money, More Ministry: Money and Evangelicals in Recent North American History*, ed. Larry Eskridge and Mark A. Noll (Grand Rapids: Eerdmans, 2000), 212.

39. Ibid., 222.
40. Taylor, *J. Hudson Taylor,* 272.
41. Kenneth Scott Latourette, *The Great Century: North Africa and Asia,* vol. 6 of *A History of the Expansion of Christianity* (Grand Rapids: Zondervan, 1970), 329.
42. Ralph D. Winter and Steven C. Hawthorne, eds. *Perspectives on the World Christian Movement* (Pasadena: William Carey, 1981), 172.
43. Rosalind Goforth, *Goforth of China* (Grand Rapids: Zondervan, 1937), 29.
44. Ibid., 48.
45. Ibid., 54–55.
46. Ibid., 119.
47. Ibid., 157–58.
48. Ibid., 189.
49. Ibid., 162.
50. Ibid., 214.
51. Mildred Cable and Francesca French, *Something Happened* (London: Hodder & Stoughton, 1934), 122.
52. Phyllis Thompson, *Desert Pilgrim* (Lincoln, NE: Back to the Bible, 1957), 14.
53. Cable and French, *Something Happened,* 142.
54. Ibid., 126–27.
55. Eileen Crossman, *Mountain Rain: A New Biography of James O. Fraser* (Southampton, UK: Overseas Missionary Fellowship, 1982), 101–2.

8
THE PACIFIC ISLANDS: PREACHING IN "PARADISE"

1. Robert H. Glover and J. Herbert Kane, *The Progress of World-Wide Missions* (New York: Harper & Row, 1960), 433.
2. Neil Gunson, *Messengers of Grace: Evangelical Missionaries in the South Seas, 1797–1860* (New York: Oxford, 1978), 178.
3. Graeme Kent, *Company of Heaven: Early Missionaries in the South Seas* (New York: Thomas Nelson, 1972), 83.
4. Stephen Neill, *A History of Christian Missions* (New York: Penguin, 1964), 297.
5. Kent, *Company of Heaven,* 33.
6. Ibid., 35.
7. Ibid., 45.
8. Gunson, *Messengers of Grace,* 202.
9. Ibid., 164–65.
10. Ibid., 153.
11. Kent, *Company of Heaven,* 57.
12. Ibid., 57.
13. Bradford Smith, *Yankees in Paradise: The New England Impact on Hawaii* (New York: Lippincott, 1956), 10.
14. Ibid., 164.
15. Ibid., 190.
16. Ibid., 191–92.

17. Ibid., 199.
18. Ibid., 205.
19. Ibid., 234.
20. John Gutch, *Beyond the Reefs: The Life of John Williams, Missionary* (London: McDonald, 1974), 18.
21. Ibid., 20.
22. Ibid., 33–34.
23. Ibid., 46.
24. Ibid., 47.
25. Kent, *Company of Heaven,* 79; Gutch, *Beyond the Reefs,* 87.
26. Neill, *History of Christian Missions,* 298–99.
27. Gutch, *Beyond the Reefs,* 109.
28. Kent, *Company of Heaven,* 82–83.
29. Ralph Bell, *John G. Paton: Apostle to the New Hebrides* (Butler, IN: Higley, 1957), 42–43.
30. John G. Paton, *The Story of Dr. John G. Paton's Thirty Years with South Sea Cannibals* (New York: Doran, 1923), 33.
31. Ibid., 36.
32. Kent, *Company of Heaven,* 118–19; Paton, *The Story,* 130.
33. Bell, *John G. Paton,* 157.
34. Paton, *The Story,* 180.
35. Bell, *John G. Paton,* 237–38.
36. Alan R. Tippett, *People Movements in Southern Polynesia: Studies in the Dynamics of Church-planting and Growth in Tahiti, New Zealand, Tonga, and Samoa* (Chicago: Moody Press, 1971), 59.
37. Ibid., 61.
38. Ibid., 66.
39. Delavan L. Pierson, *The Pacific Islanders: From Savages to Saints* (New York: Funk & Wagnalls, 1906), 173.
40. Kent, *Company of Heaven,* 147.
41. William R. Hutchinson, *Errand to the World: American Protestant Thought and Foreign Missions* (Chicago: University of Chicago Press, 1987), 74.

9
THE MUSLIM WORLD: MISSION FIELD IN THE DESERT

1. Stephen Neill, *A History of Christian Missions* (New York: Penguin, 1986), 310.
2. John Mark Terry, "Approaches to the Evangelization of Muslims," *Evangelical Missions Quarterly* (April 1996).
3. Ibid.
4. Ibid.
5. J. Dudley Woodbury, "Islam, Muslim," in A. Scott Moreau, *Evangelical Dictionary of World Missions* (Grand Rapids: Baker, 2000), 506.
6. Clinton Bennett, "Victorian Images of Islam," *International Bulletin of Missionary Research* (July 1991): 117.

7. Ibid.
8. Ibid., 118.
9. Ibid., 116.
10. Clinton Bennett, "The Legacy of Henry Martyn," *International Bulletin of Missionary Research* (January 1992): 12, 13.
11. David Bentley-Taylor, *My Love Must Wait: The Story of Henry Martyn* (Downers Grove, IL: InterVarsity, 1975), 26.
12. Richard T. France, "Henry Martyn" in *Five Pioneer Missionaries* (London: Banner of Truth, 1965), 255–56.
13. Bentley-Taylor, *My Love Must Wait,* 35.
14. Quoted in Kenneth Cragg, *Troubled by Truth* (Cleveland: Pilgrim Press, 1992), 18.
15. Ibid., 24.
16. Ibid., 21, 23.
17. Ibid.
18. Bennett, "The Legacy," 12.
19. J. Christy Wilson, *The Apostle to Islam: A Biography of Samuel M. Zwemer* (Grand Rapids: Baker, 1952), 23.
20. Ibid., 47.
21. Ibid., 43.
22. Ibid., 234.
23. Ibid., 81.
24. Alan Neely, "Samuel Marinus Zwemer," in Gerald H. Anderson, ed., *Biographical Dictionary of Christian Missions* (Grand Rapids: Eerdmans, 1998), 763.
25. Constance E. Padwick, *Temple Gairdner of Cairo* (London: Society for Promoting Christian Knowledge, 1930), 29.
26. Ibid., 38, 48.
27. Ibid., 93.
28. Ibid., 95.
29. Ibid., 125.
30. James A. Tebbe, "Kenneth Cragg in Perspective: A Comparison with Temple Gairdner and Wilfred Cantwell Smith," *International Bulletin of Missionary Research* (January 2002): 16–17.
31. Padwick, *Temple Gairdner,* 158, 260.
32. Ibid., 218.
33. Ibid., 267, 264.
34. Ibid., 220–22.
35. William Richey Hogg, *Ecumenical Foundations: A History of the International Missionary Council and Its Nineteenth Century Background* (New York: Harper, 1952), 325.
36. Gordon Hewitt, *The Problems of Success: A History of the Church Missionary Society, 1910–1942* (London: SCM Press, 1971), 314–16.
37. Constance Padwick, "North African Reverie," *International Review of Missions* 17 (1938): 351.
38. Agnes De Selincourt, "Signs of Progress in India," in Annie Van Sommer and Samuel Zwemer, *Daylight in the Harem: A New Era for Moslem Women* (New York: Fleming H. Revell, 1911), 57–58.

39. Constance Padwick, *Call to Istanbul* (London: Longmans, Green, 1958), ix.
40. Constance Padwick, "Lilias Trotter of Algiers," *International Review of Missions* XXI (1932): 124–25.
41. Louise Walker, "Lillian Trasher: Mother to Thousands in Egypt," Unpublished manuscript (Springfield, MO, 1986), 1.
42. Evelyn Stenbock, *"Miss Terri": The Story of Maude Cary, Pioneer GMU Missionary in Morocco* (Lincoln, NB: Good News Broadcasting, 1970), 30.
43. Ibid., 35–36.
44. Ibid., 46.
45. Isobel Kuhn, *By Searching* (Chicago: Moody Press, 1959), 120; Helen Roseveare, *Give Me This Mountain* (London: Inter-Varsity Press, 1966).
46. Stenbock, *"Miss Terri,"* 60.
47. Ibid., 71.
48. Ibid., 103.
49. Ibid., 139.

10
KOREA AND JAPAN: A CONTRAST IN RECEPTIVITY

1. Everett N. Hunt Jr., *Protestant Pioneers in Korea* (Maryknoll, NY: Orbis, 1980), 46, 51.
2. Ibid., 82.
3. Donald Richardson, *Eternity in Their Hearts* (Ventura, CA: Regal Books, 1984), 68.
4. Samuel Hugh Moffett, *The Christians of Korea* (New York: Friendship Press, 1962), 34.
5. Roy E. Shearer, *Wildfire: Church Growth in Korea* (Grand Rapids: Eerdmans, 1966), 39–40.
6. Wi Jo Kang, "The Legacy of Horace Newton Allen," *International Bulletin of Missionary Research* (July 1996): 126.
7. Hunt Jr., *Protestant Pioneers,* 37.
8. Ibid., 19.
9. Ibid., 20, 34, 35.
10. Kang, "Legacy," 126.
11. Ibid., 127.
12. Ibid., 128.
13. Ibid.
14. Hunt Jr., *Protestant Pioneers,* 43.
15. Ibid.
16. Ibid., 24.
17. Edward W. Poitras, "The Legacy of Henry G. Appenzeller," *International Bulletin of Missionary Research* (October 1994): 177, 179.
18. Ibid., 178.
19. Daniel M. Davies, *The Life and Thought of Henry Gerhard Appenzeller (1858–1902)* (Lewiston, NY: Edwin Mellen, 1988), 150.
20. Poitras, "Legacy," 178, 179.

21. Hunt Jr., *Protestant Pioneers,* 69, 70.
22. Davies, *Life and Thought of Appenzeller,* 299.
23. Ibid., 301.
24. Poitras, "Legacy," 177.
25. Davies, *Life and Thought of Appenzeller,* 327.
26. Ibid.
27. Hunt Jr., *Protestant Pioneers,* 44.
28. Ibid., 65.
29. Horace Grant Underwood, *The Call of Korea* (New York: Revell, 1908), 106–7.
30. Hunt Jr., *Protestant Pioneers,* 73.
31. Shearer, *Wildfire,* 43.
32. Ibid., 44.
33. Hunt Jr., *Protestant Pioneers,* 74.
34. Winifred Mathews, *Dauntless Women: Stories of Pioneer Wives* (Freeport, NY: Books for Libraries Press, 1970), 158.
35. Everett N. Hunt Jr., "The Legacy of John Livingston Nevius," *International Bulletin of Missionary Research* (July 1991): 120.
36. Ibid.
37. Quoted in Francis M. Dubose, ed., *Classics of Christian Missions* (Nashville: Broadman, 1979), 259.
38. Charles Allen Clark, *The Korean Church and the Nevius Methods* (New York: Fleming H. Revell, 1928), 241–42.
39. Alan Neely, "Samuel Austin Moffet," in Gerald H. Anderson, ed., *Biographical Dictionary of Christian Missions* (Grand Rapids: Eerdmans, 1998), 465.
40. Shearer, *Wildfire,* 49.
41. Ibid., 63.
42. Ibid., 65–66.
43. Stephen Neill, *A History of Christian Missions* (New York: Penguin, 1986), 375.
44. Quoted in ibid., 376–77.
45. David Mitchell, "William Smith Clark," in J. D. Douglas, ed., *The New International Dictionary of the Christian Church* (Grand Rapids: Zondervan), 230.
46. Andrew F. Walls, "The American Dimension in the History of the Missionary Movement," in Joel A. Carpenter and Wilbert R. Shenk, eds., *Earthen Vessels: American Evangelicals and Foreign Missions, 1880–1980* (Grand Rapids: Eerdmans, 1990), 1–2.
47. Chung Jun Ki, *Social Criticism of Uchimura Kanzo and Kim Kyo-Shin* (Seoul: UBF Press, 1988), 40.
48. Ibid., 41.
49. Ibid., 91–92.
50. Ibid., 94–95.
51. Ibid., 70–71.
52. Kanzo Uchimura, "Can Americans Teach Japanese in Religion?" *Japan Christian Intelligencer* 1 (1926): 357–61, cited in Walls, "The American Dimension," 2.
53. B. H. Pearson, *The Vision Lives: A Profile of Mrs. Charles E. Cowman* (Grand Rapids: Zondervan, 1961), 33.

54. B. H. Pearson, *The Vision Lives: The Life Story of Mrs. Charles E. Cowman* (Fort Washington, PA: Christian Literature Crusade, 1961), 36–37.
55. Lettie B. Cowman, *Charles E. Cowman: Missionary—Warrior* (Los Angeles: Oriental Missionary Society, 1939), 95.
56. Pearson, *The Vision Lives,* 39.
57. Ibid., 53–55, 99.
58. Ibid., 148.
59. Cowman, *Charles E. Cowman*, 227.
60. Pearson, *The Vision Lives*, 52.
61. Ibid., 51.
62. Ibid., 55.
63. Ibid., 94, 95, 97.
64. Ibid., 154.
65. Mabel Francis, *One Shall Chase a Thousand* (Harrisburg, PA: Christian Publications, 1968), 48.
66. Ibid., 89.
67. Ibid., 59–60.
68. Ibid., 46.
69. Robert L. Niklaus et al., *All for Jesus: God at Work in the Christian and Missionary Alliance Over One Hundred Years* (Camp Hill, PA: Christian Publications, 1986), 201.

PART 3
THE EXPANDING INVOLVEMENT

1. Stephen Neill, *A History of Christian Missions* (New York: Penguin, 1964), 243.
2. Ibid., 452.
3. Ibid., 451.
4. Robert D. Linder, "Introduction: The Christian Centuries," in *Eerdmans' Handbook to the History of Christianity* (Grand Rapids: Eerdmans, 1977), xxii.
5. Ibid.
6. Winthrop S. Hudson, *Religion in America: An Historical Account of the Development of American Religious Life* (New York: Scribner, 1973), 318.
7. Ibid.
8. Arthur J. Brown, *The Why and How of Foreign Missions* (New York: Missionary Education Movement, 1921), 127.

11
SINGLE WOMEN MISSIONARIES: "SECOND-CLASS CITIZENS"

1. R. Pierce Beaver, *American Protestant Women in World Mission* (Grand Rapids: Eerdmans, 1969), 59.
2. Glenn D. Kittler, *The Woman God Loved* (Garden City, NY: Hanover House, 1959), 225.

3. Helen Barnett Montgomery, *Western Women in Eastern Lands* (New York: Macmillan, 1910), 243–44.
4. Nancy A. Hardesty, *Great Women of Faith* (Grand Rapids: Baker, 1980), 104; Marlys Taege, *And God Gave Women Talents!* (St. Louis: Concordia, 1978), 90.
5. Dana Robert, *American Women in Mission: A Social History of Their Thought and Practice* (Macon, GA: Mercer University Press, 1996), 136.
6. Leonard Warren, *Adele Marion Fielde: Feminist, Social Activist, Scientist* (New York: Routledge, 2002), 9, 14.
7. Quoted in ibid., 16–20.
8. Quoted in ibid., 23.
9. Ibid., 24, 33.
10. Ibid., 33, 35.
11. Ibid., 35.
12. Ibid., 39.
13. Ibid., 41.
14. Ibid., 54.
15. Ibid., 61–62, 65, 67.
16. Helen N. Stevens, *Memorial Biography of Adele M. Fielde: Humanitarian* (New York: Fielde Memorial Committee, 1918), 115.
17. Warren, *Adele Marion Fielde,* 70.
18. Ibid., 139, 143.
19. Frederick B. Hoyt, "'When a Field Was Found Too Difficult for a Man, a Woman Should Be Sent': Adele M. Fielde in Asia, 1865–1890," *The Historian* 44 (May 1982): 334.
20. Quoted in Catherine Allen, *The New Lottie Moon Story* (Nashville: Broadman, 1980), 136.
21. Alan Neely, "Saints Who Sometimes Were: Utilizing Missionary Hagiography," *Missiology* (October 1999): 447.
22. Irwin Hyatt, *Our Ordered Lives Confess: Three Nineteenth-Century American Missionaries in East Shantung* (Cambridge, MA: Harvard University Press, 1976), 95.
23. Ibid., 96.
24. Ibid., 98.
25. Ibid., 99.
26. Catherine B. Allen, "The Legacy of Lottie Moon," *International Bulletin of Missionary Research* (October 1993):148.
27. Hyatt, *Our Ordered Lives,* 104–5
28. Ibid.
29. Ibid., 106.
30. Ibid., 115, 117.
31. Ibid., 113; Allen, *The New Lottie Moon,* 212–13.
32. Hyatt, *Our Ordered Lives,* 114.
33. Neely, "Saints Who Sometimes Were," 452.
34. Allen, *The New Lottie Moon,* 114.
35. Sherwood Eddy, *Pathfinders of the World Missionary Crusade* (New York: Abingdon-Cokesbury, 1945), 125.

36. Frank Houghton, *Amy Carmichael of Dohnavur* (London: Society for the Propagation of Christian Knowledge, 1954), 61, 73.
37. Ibid., 78.
38. Ibid., 213.
39. Ibid., 62.
40. Amy Carmichael, *Things as They Are: Missionary Work in Southern India* (New York: Fleming H. Revell, 1903), 158.
41. Elisabeth Elliot, *A Chance to Die: The Life and Legacy of Amy Carmichael* (Old Tappan, NJ: Fleming H. Revell, 1987), 142, 338.
42. Ibid., 119.
43. Ibid., 297, 170.
44. Ibid., 230, 126.
45. Ibid., 121–22, 155–56.
46. Ibid., 198, 201.
47. Amy Carmichael, *Gold Cord: The Story of a Fellowship* (London: Society for Promoting Christian Knowledge, 1932), 37, 179, 182.
48. Elliot, *A Chance to Die,* 268.
49. Ibid., 268, 270.
50. Stephen Neill, *God's Apprentice: The Autobiography of Stephen Neill* (London: Hodder & Stoughton, 1991), 95.
51. Eliot, *A Chance to Die,* 267–69.
52. Neill, *God's Apprentice,* 45.
53. Quoted in Henry Beets, *Johanna of Nigeria: Life and Labors of Johanna Veenstra* (Grand Rapids: Grand Rapids Printing Company, 1937), 90, 129.
54. Johanna Veenstra, *Pioneering for Christ in the Sudan* (Grand Rapids: Smitter Book, 1926), 165.
55. Ibid., 210.
56. Beets, *Johanna of Nigeria,* 205.
57. Phyllis Thompson, *A Transparent Woman: The Compelling Story of Gladys Aylward* (Grand Rapids: Zondervan, 1971), 20.
58. Alan Burgess, *The Small Woman* (New York: Dutton, 1957), 29.
59. Thompson, *A Transparent Woman,* 183.

12
STUDENT VOLUNTEERS: FORSAKING WEALTH AND PRESTIGE

1. J. Herbert Kane, *A Concise History of the Christian World Mission* (Grand Rapids: Baker, 1978), 103.
2. Harold R. Cook, *Highlights of Christian Missions: A History and Survey* (Chicago: Moody Press, 1967), 69.
3. Quoted in James and Marti Hefley, *By Their Blood: Christian Martyrs of the 20th Century* (Milford, MI: Mott, 1979), 76.
4. Sherwood Eddy, *Pathfinders of the World Missionary Crusade* (New York: Abingdon-Cokesbury, 1945), 5–6.

5. Norman P. Grubb, *C. T. Studd: Cricketer and Pioneer* (Fort Washington, PA: Christian Literature Crusade, 1969), 17.
6. J. Herbert Kane, "C. T. Studd: A Gambler for God," *Eternity* (December 1972): 39.
7. Grubb, *C. T. Studd,* 87.
8. Kane, "C. T. Studd," 40.
9. Grubb, *C. T. Studd,* 121.
10. Norman P. Grubb, *Once Caught, No Escape: My Life Story* (Fort Washington, PA: Christian Literature Crusade, 1969), 78.
11. Ibid.
12. Ibid., 81.
13. Ibid., 97.
14. Ibid., 99, 102.
15. Grubb, *C. T. Studd,* 205.
16. John R. Mott, *The Larger Evangelism* (Nashville: Abingdon-Cokesbury, 1944), 11.
17. C. Howard Hopkins, *John R. Mott, 1865–1955: A Biography* (Grand Rapids: Eerdmans, 1979), 19.
18. Mott, *The Larger Evangelism,* 36.
19. Ibid.
20. Hopkins, *John R. Mott,* 568.
21. Quoted in ibid., 276.
22. Quoted in Terry Hurlbert, *World Mission Today* (Wheaton, IL: Evangelical Teacher Training Association), 29.
23. W. Reginald Wheeler, *A Man Sent from God: A Biography of Robert E. Speer* (London: Revell, 1956), 53.
24. Eddy, *Pathfinders,* 263.
25. Quoted in Arthur P. Johnston, *The Battle for World Evangelism* (Wheaton, IL: Tyndale, 1978), 32.
26. Wheeler, *A Man Sent from God,* 219.
27. Ibid., 163.
28. Ibid., 166.
29. Ibid., 15.
30. Eddy, *Pathfinders,* 53.
31. Ibid., 202.
32. Quoted in ibid., 202.
33. Quoted in ibid., 207.
34. Quoted in ibid., 206.
35. Quoted in ibid.
36. E. Stanley Jones, *Along the Indian Road* (New York: Abingdon, 1939), 19–29.
37. E. Stanley Jones, *The Christ of the Indian Road* (New York: Abingdon, 1925), 19–20.
38. Ibid., 8.
39. Ibid., 49.
40. Chester E. Tulga, *The Case Against Modernism in Foreign Missions* (Chicago: Conservative Baptist, 1950), 44.
40. Quoted in John R. W. Stott, *Christian Mission in the Modern World* (Downers Grove, IL: InterVarsity Press, 1975), 76.

42. Jones, *Along the Indian Road,* 183–84.
43. Eddy, *Pathfinders,* 270; Robert H. Glover and J. Herbert Kane, *The Progress of World-Wide Missions* (New York: Harper, 1960), 185.
44. Jones, *Along the Indian Road,* 166.
45. Jones, *Christ of the Indian Road,* 212–13.

13
"FAITH" MISSIONARIES: DEPENDING ON GOD ALONE

1. Elisabeth Elliot, *Through Gates of Splendor* (New York: Harper & Row, 1958), 176.
2. J. Herbert Kane, *A Concise History of the Christian World Mission* (Grand Rapids: Baker, 1978), 102.
3. J. Herbert Kane, *Faith Mighty Faith: A Handbook of the Interdenominational Foreign Mission Association* (New York: Interdenominational Foreign Mission Association, 1956), 88.
4. A. E. Thompson, *The Life of A. B. Simpson* (New York: Christian Alliance Publishing, 1920), 65.
5. Ibid., 120.
6. Ibid., 121.
7. Ibid., 120.
8. A. W. Tozer, *Wingspread: A. B. Simpson: A Study in Spiritual Altitude* (Harrisburg: Christian Publications, 1943), 87.
9. Thompson, *Life of A. B. Simpson,* 227.
10. Tozer, *Wingspread,* 71.
11. Ibid., 72.
12. Edvard Torjesen, "The Legacy of Fredrik Franson," *International Bulletin of Missionary Research* (July 1991): 127.
13. Edvard Torjesen, *Fredrik Franson: A Model for Worldwide Evangelism* (Pasadena: William Carey Library, 1883), 73.
14. Fredrik Franson, "Prophesying Daughters," Unpublished paper (Stockholm, Sweden, 1897), 2.
15. J. H. Hunter, *A Flame of Fire: The Life and Work of R. V. Bingham* (Scarborough, ON: Sudan Interior Mission, 1961), 56.
16. Ibid., 50.
17. Quoted in ibid., 65.
18. Ibid., 67.
19. Ibid., 78.
20. Ibid., 79.
21. Ibid., 82.
22. Ibid., 111.
23. Ibid., 211.
24. Raymond Davis, *Fire on the Mountains: The Story of a Miracle—The Church in Ethiopia* (Grand Rapids: Zondervan, 1975), 88.
25. Ibid., 107.
26. Ibid.

27. Ibid., 115, 246–47.
28. This is not the Sudan of the 1890s but rather a portion of that great region that became known as the Anglo-Egyptian Sudan. With independence it became known as the Republic of the Sudan or simply Sudan.
29. Kenneth Richardson, *Garden of Miracle: The Story of the Africa Inland Mission* (London: AIM, 1976), 70.
30. James and Marti Hefley, *By Their Blood: Christian Martyrs of the 20th Century* (Milford, MI: Mott, 1979), 422–23.
31. Mildred W. Spain, *"And in Samaria": A Story of More Than Sixty Years' Missionary Witness in Central America, 1890–1954* (Dallas: Central American Mission, 1954), 8.
32. Robert H. Glover and J. Herbert Kane, *The Progress of World-Wide Missions* (New York: Harper, 1960), 356.
33. Harold R. Cook, *Highlights of Christian Missions: A History and Survey* (Chicago: Moody Press, 1967), 211–12.
34. Stephen Neill, *A History of Christian Missions* (New York: Penguin, 1986), 328.
35. Quoted in Cook, *Highlights of Christian Missions,* 214.
36. Jean Dye Johnson, *God Planted Five Seeds* (Woodworth, WI.: New Tribes Mission, 1966), 12, 23, 26.
37. Ibid., 84, 73.
38. Elliot, *Through Gates of Splendor,* 152–53.
39. Russell T. Hitt, *Jungle Pilot: The Life and Witness of Nate Saint* (Grand Rapids: Zondervan, 1973), 244.
40. *Diary of Pete Fleming,* December 6, 1953.
41. Elliot, *Through Gates of Splendor,* 146, 159; Hitt, *Jungle Pilot,* 241.
42. Hitt, *Jungle Pilot,* 252.
43. Elliot, *Through Gates of Splendor,* 104.
44. Ibid., 172, 176.
45. *Diary of Pete Fleming,* December 27, 1955.
46. Elliot, *Through Gates of Splendor,* 180.
47. Ibid., 196–97.
48. James C. Hefley, "The Auca Massacre and Beyond," *Power for Living* (April 19, 1981), 5.
49. Hitt, *Jungle Pilot,* 258.
50. Elisabeth Elliot, "Thirty Years Later: The Auca Massacre," *Christian Life* (April 1986): 28.
51. Elliott Wright, *Holy Company: Christian Heroes and Heroines* (New York: Macmillan, 1980), 93–94.
52. Lorry Lutz, *Born to Lose, Bound to Win: The Amazing Journey of Mother Eliza George* (Irvine, CA: Harvest House, 1980), 33.
53. Ibid., 37.
54. Ibid., 46–47.
55. Ibid., 54, 56, 61.
56. Ibid., 71, 77.
57. Ibid., 122.
58. Ibid., 137–38.

14
INNOVATION AND INGENUITY: THE CALL FOR SPECIALIZATION

1. Winthrop S. Hudson, *Religion in America: An Historical Account of the Development of American Religious Life* (New York: Scribner, 1956), 371–72.
2. Ibid., 383.
3. Sherwood Eddy, *Pathfinders of the World Missionary Crusade* (New York: Abingdon-Cokesbury, 1945), 225.
4. J. Lennox Kerr, *Wilfred Grenfell: His Life and Work* (New York: Dodd, 1959), 85.
5. Dorothy Clarke Wilson, *Dr. Ida: The Story of Dr. Ida Scudder of Vellore* (New York: McGraw-Hill, 1959), 5.
6. Eddy, *Pathfinders,* 131.
7. Wilson, *Dr. Ida,* 273.
8. Ibid., 286.
9. Ibid., 297.
10. Ibid., 321.
11. Ibid., 243.
12. Viggo Olsen, *Daktar: Diplomat in Bangladesh* (Chicago: Moody Press, 1973), 32.
13. William J. Peterson, *Another Hand on Mine: The Story of Dr. Carl K. Becker of Africa Inland Mission* (New York: McGraw-Hill, 1967), 40.
14. Ibid., 54.
15. Ibid., 89.
16. Ibid., 127.
17. Ibid., 154.
18. Ibid., 144.
19. Ibid., 127.
20. Jamie Buckingham, *Into the Glory* (Plainfield, NJ: Logos, 1974), 21.
21. Hugh Steven, *Wycliffe in the Making: The Memoirs of W. Cameron Townsend, 1920–1933* (Wheaton, IL: Harold Shaw, 1995), 111, 153–54.
22. James and Marti Hefley, *Uncle Cam: The Story of William Cameron Townsend, Founder of the Wycliffe Bible Translators and the Summer Institute of Linguistics* (Waco, TX: Word, 1974), 99.
23. Ibid., 200.
24. Ibid., 243.
25. Ibid., 173.
26. Clarence W. Hall, "Two Thousand Tongues to Go" in *Adventurers for God* (New York: Harper & Brothers, 1959), 119–20.
27. Ibid., 119.
28. Hefley, *Uncle Cam,* 96.
29. Ibid., 244.
30. Ibid., 182.
31. April 1982 Bulletin of Wycliffe Bible Translators on the death of William Cameron Townsend.
32. Ethel E. Wallis and Mary A. Bennett, *Two Thousand Tongues to Go* (New York: Harper & Brothers, 1959), 51.

33. Eunice V. Pike, *Ken Pike: Scholar and Christian* (Dallas: Summer Institute of Linguistics, 1981), 131.
34. Ibid., 179.
35. Barry Siedell, *Gospel Radio: A 20th-Century Tool for a 20th-Century Challenge* (Lincoln, NE: Good News Broadcasting, 1971), 132, 145.
36. Lois Neely, *Come Up to This Mountain: The Miracle of Clarence W. Jones and HCJB* (Wheaton, IL: Tyndale, 1980), 53.
37. Ibid., 54.
38. Ibid., 56.
39. Ibid., 67.
40. Ibid., 73.
41. Ibid., 108.
42. Ibid., 111.
43. Ibid., 140.
44. Gleason H. Ledyard, *Sky Waves: The Incredible Far East Broadcasting Company Story* (Chicago: Moody Press, 1968), 38.
45. Paul E. Freed, *Towers to Eternity* (Nashville: Sceptre, 1979), 63–64.
46. Lee Roddy, *On Wings of Love: Stories from Mission Aviation Fellowship* (Nashville: Nelson, 1981), 17.
47. Mary Wade, "On a Wing and a Prayer," *Saturday Evening Post* (April 1980): 105.
48. "Miss Betty Greene: First Lady of MAF," *Christian Times* (January 15, 1967): 3.
49. Russell T. Hitt, *Jungle Pilot: The Life and Witness of Nate Saint* (Grand Rapids: Zondervan, 1973), 99.
50. Dietrich G. Buss and Arthur F. Glasser, *Giving Wings to the Gospel: The Remarkable Story of Mission Aviation Fellowship* (Grand Rapids: Baker, 1995), 106–7, 110.
51. Hitt, *Jungle Pilot*, 203.
52. Ibid., 206, 226–27.
53. Gleason H. Ledyard, *And to the Eskimos* (Chicago: Moody Press, 1958), 91.
54. Ibid., 237.

PART 4

THE ERA OF THE NEW MILLENNIUM

1. Ralph D. Winter, *The Twenty-five Unbelievable Years, 1945–1969* (Pasadena, CA: William Carey, 1970), 13.
2. John R. W. Stott, "The Bible in World Evangelism," in *Perspectives on the World Christian Movement,* ed. Ralph D. Winter and Steven C. Hawthorne (Pasadena, CA: William Carey, 1981), 7.
3. A. Scott Moreau, "World Consultation on World Evangelization," *Evangelical Dictionary of World Misisons,* ed. by A. Scott Moreau (Grand Rapids: Baker, 2000), 1024.
4. Robert Clouse, "Pentecostal Churches," in *The New International Dictionary of the Christian Church,* ed. J. D. Douglas (Grand Rapids: Zondervan, 1978), 764.
5. Robert T. Coote, "The Uneven Growth of Conservative Evangelical Missions," *International Bulletin of Missionary Research* (July 1982): 118.

6. J. Herbert Kane, "The Saints Keep Marching ON," *Wherever* (Fall 1979): 2.
7. J. Herbert Kane, *Understanding Christian Missions* (Grand Rapids: Baker, 1975), 405.

15
TWENTIETH-CENTURY MARTYRS: "YANKEE, GO HOME"

1. Quoted in Hugh Steven, "Who Was Chet Bitterman?" *In Other Words* (April 1981): 5.
2. Vernon J. Sterk, "You Can Help the Persecuted Church: Lessons from Chiapas, Mexico," *IBMR* (January 1999): 15, 17.
3. Geoffrey Moorhouse, *The Missionaries* (London: Eyre Methuen, 1973), 175–78.
4. Ted Olsen, "Did Martin Die Needlessly?" *Christianity Today* (June 2003): 34.
5. Paul Marshall, *Their Blood Cries Out: The Untold Story of Persecution against Christians in the Modern World* (Dallas: Word, 1997), 4.
6. James and Marti Hefley, *By Their Blood: Christian Martyrs of the 20th Century* (Milford, MI: Mott, 1979), 46.
7. Leslie Lyall, *A Passion for the Impossible: The China Inland Mission, 1865–1965* (Chicago: Moody Press, 1965), 108–9.
8. Mrs. Howard Taylor, *The Triumph of John and Betty Stam* (Philadelphia: China Inland Mission, 1960), 51–52.
9. Quoted in ibid., 54–55.
10. Ibid., 92.
11. Quoted in ibid., 102.
12. Hefley, *By Their Blood*, 66.
13. Lois Carlson, *Monganga Paul: The Congo Ministry and Martyrdom of Paul Carlson, M.D.* (New York: Harper & Row, 1966), 34.
14. Ibid., 50.
15. Ibid., 53.
16. Homer E. Dowdy, *Out of the Jaws of the Lion: Christian Martyrdom in the Congo* (New York: Harper & Row, 1965), 186–87.
17. Ibid., 193.
18. John 15:13 NIV.
19. James and Marti Hefley, *No Time for Tombstones: Life and Death in the Vietnamese Jungle* (Wheaton, IL: Tyndale, 1976), 3.
20. Quoted in Hefley, *By Their Blood*, 126.
21. Hefley, *No Time,* 87.
22. Ibid., 91.
23. Hefley, *By Their Blood*, 95, 131.
24. *Time* (August 10, 1981): 41.
25. Betty Blair and Phil Landrum, "Chet Bitterman—Kidnappers' Choice," *In Other Words* (April 1981): 2.
26. Ibid.
27. Quoted in ibid., 3.
28. Molly Ekstrom, "Chet Bitterman: God's Special Envoy to Colombia," *In Other Words* (Summer 1981, Jubilee Edition): 19.

29. Blair and Landrum, "Chet Bitterman," 2.
30. Jeanne Pugh, "Death of Bible Translators Sparks Expansion of Work," *St. Petersburg Times* (April 4, 1981).
31. Harry Waterhouse, "We Gave Our Son to God," *In Other Words* (April 1981): 4.
32. Charles Partee, *Adventure in Africa: The Story of Don McClure* (Grand Rapids: Zondervan, 1990), 422.
33. Ibid., 280.
34. Don McClure, "Unpublished Letters," cited in Ruth A. Tucker, *Stories of Faith* (Grand Rapids: Zondervan, 1989), 147.
35. Ibid., 52.
36. Ibid., 64.
37. Ibid., 90–93.
38. Ibid., 97.
39. Ibid., 197–98.

16
THIRD WORLD MISSIONS: YOUNGER CHURCHES REACH OUT

1. Lawrence E. Keyes, *The Last Age of Missions: A Study of Third World Missionary Societies* (Pasadena: William Carey Library, 1983), 3.
2. Ibid., 9.
3. Theodore Williams, "Introduction: Missions within a Context of Poverty," in Luis Bush, *Funding Third World Missions* (Wheaton, IL: World Evangelical Fellowship Missions Commission, 1990), 5.
4. Luis Bush, *Funding Third World Missions* (Wheaton, IL: World Evangelical Fellowship Missions Commission, 1990), 9.
5. Luis Bush, "The State of Missions," *Christianity Today* (June 23, 2003): 19.
6. Pandita Ramabai, *The High Caste Hindu Woman* (London: George Bell and Sons, 1888), xxi.
7. Helen S. Dyler, *Pandita Ramabai: Her Vision, Her Mission and Her Triumph of Faith* (London: Pickering & Inglis, n.d.), 24.
8. John T. Seamands, *Pioneers of the Younger Churches* (Nashville: Abingdon, 1967), 102–3.
9. Shamsundar Manohar Adhav, *Pandita Ramabai* (Madras: Christian Literature Society, 1979), 131.
10. Ibid., 141–42.
11. Ibid., 142.
12. Pandita Ramabai, "Telling Others," as reported at www.born-again-christian.info/mukti.mission.htm (June 18, 2004).
13. Dyler, *Pandita Ramabai,* 71.
14. Colin Melbourne, "Pandita Ramabai," http://born-again-christian.info/mukti.mission.htm.
15. Gary B. McGee, "'Baptism of the Holy Ghost & Fire!' The Mission Legacy of Minnie F. Abrams," *Missiology* (October 1999): 517.
16. Seamands, *Pioneers of the Younger Churches,* 111.

17. Susan Billington Harper, *In the Shadow of the Mahatma: Bishop V. S. Azariah and the Travails of Christianity in British India* (Grand Rapids: Eerdmans, 2000), 1, 67.
18. David A. Shank, "The Legacy of William Wade Harris," *IBMR* (October 1986): 170.
19. Ibid., 171.
20. Ibid.
21. Ibid., 172, 176.
22. Ibid., 174.
23. Quoted in ibid., 175.
24. Adrian Hastings, *The Church in Africa, 1450–1950* (New York: Oxford University Press, 1994), 445.
25. Allan K. Davidson, "Semisi Nau—A Pacific Islander Missionary," *Missiology* (October 1999): 482.
26. Ibid., 493.
27. Ibid., 483.
28. Ibid.
29. Seamands, *Pioneers of the Younger Churches*, 88.
30. Ibid., 92–93.
31. William E. Schubert, *I Remember John Sung* (Singapore: Far Eastern Bible College Press, 1976), 42.
32. David Smithers, "John Sung: The Apostle of Revival," www.watchword.org/smithers/ww51a.html (June 18, 2004).
33. Homer Dowdy, *Christ's Witchdoctor* (Grand Rapids: Zondervan, 1973), 42.
34. Ibid., 103–4.
35. Ibid., 107, 113, 115, 124, 129.
36. Ibid., 148–49.
37. Ibid., 200.
38. Ibid., 211.
39. Ibid., 215, 217, 224.
40. Ibid., 229.

17
New Methods and Strategy: Reaching Tomorrow's World

1. Geoffrey Wainwright, *Lesslie Newbigin: A Theological Life* (New York: Oxford University Press, 2000), 222.
2. Charles Henry Long, "Roland Allen," in Gerald H. Anderson, ed., *Biographical Dictionary of Christian Missions* (Grand Rapids: Eerdmans, 1998), 12.
3. Roland Allen, *Missionary Methods: St. Paul's or Ours?* (1912; reprint, Grand Rapids: Eerdmans, 1962), 99–100.
4. J. van den Berg, "Johan Herman Bavinck," in Gerald H. Anderson, ed., *Mission Legacies: Biographical Studies of Leaders of the Modern Missionary Movement* (Maryknoll, NY: Orbis, 1994), 432.
5. J. Verkuyl, *Contemporary Missiology: An Introduction* (Grand Rapids: Eerdmans, 1978), 36.

6. J. H. Bavinck, *Faith and Its Difficulties* (N.p.: n.d.), 11–12.
7. W. Dayton Roberts, *Revolution in Evangelism: The Story of Evangelism-in-Depth in Latin America* (Chicago: Moody Press, 1976), 6.
8. Ibid., 17–18.
9. Ibid., 18.
10. Elisabeth Elliot, *Who Shall Ascend: The Life of R. Kenneth Strachan of Costa Rica* (New York: Harper & Row, 1968), 21.
11. Ibid., 73.
12. W. Dayton Roberts, *Strachan of Costa Rica: Missionary Insights and Strategies* (Grand Rapids: Eerdmans, 1971), 63.
13. Ibid., 108.
14. Ibid., 99.
15. Ibid., 83.
16. Ibid., 95.
17. Quoted in ibid., 96.
18. Roberts, *Revolution in Evangelism*, 60.
19. Ibid., 60, 64.
20. Charles Troutman, *Everything You Want to Know About the Mission Field, But Are Afraid You Won't Learn Until You Get There* (Downers Grove, IL: InterVarsity, 1976), 26.
21. Quoted in Samuel Escobar, "The Legacy of Orlando Costas," *IBMR* (April 2001): 50.
22. Ibid., 51.
23. Ibid., 52.
24. Ibid., 54.
25. Arthur Glasser, "Introducing Donald McGavran," *HIS* (December 1973): 19.
26. A. R. Tippet, ed. *God, Man and Church Growth* (Grand Rapids: Eerdmans, 1973), ix.
27. Ibid., 18.
28. C. Peter Wagner, "Concepts of Evangelism Have Changed Over the Years," *Evangelical Missions Quarterly* (January 1974): 43.
29. Ibid., 44.
30. Donald A. McGavran, "The Bridge of God," in *Perspectives on the World Christian Movement*, eds. Ralph D. Winter and Steven C. Hawthorne (Pasadena: William Carey, 1982), 282.
31. Ibid., 288–89.
32. C. Peter Wagner, *Our Kind of People: The Ethical Dimensions of Church Growth in America* (Atlanta: Knox, 1979), 21, 100.
33. Quoted in ibid., 101.
34. Quoted in ibid., 23.
35. Tippet, *Church Growth*, 35.
36. Glasser, "Donald McGavran," 18.
37. Tim Stafford, "The Father of Church Growth," *Christianity Today* (February 21, 1986): 20.

38. Gordon Aeschliman, "United States Center for World Mission," *World Christian* (March/April 1983): 20.
39. John Maust, "Ralph Winter's Mission Center Forges Ahead; Money Still Tight," *Christianity Today* (January 21, 1983): 34.
40. David Bryant, "Concerts of Prayer: Waking Up for a New Missions Thrust," *Mission Frontiers* (March/April 1983): 31.
41. Doris Haley, "Ralph and Roberta Winter: A Wartime Life-Style," *Family Life Today* (March 1983): 31.
42. Ralph Winter, "Welcome to the U.S. Center for World Mission," publicity material.
43. Lesslie Newbigin, *Unfinished Agenda* (London: Society for Promoting Christian Knowledge, 1993), 11–12.
44. Ibid., 12, 55.
45. Wainwright, *Lesslie Newbigin*, 75.
46. Ibid., 190–91.
47. Tim Stafford, "God's Missionary to Us," *Christianity Today* (December 9, 1996): 25.
48. Ibid., 26.
49. Wainwright, *Lesslie Newbigin*, 58.
50. Stafford, "God's Missionary to Us," 28.
51. George R. Hunsberger, *Bearing the Witness of the Spirit: Lesslie Newbigin's Theology of Cultural Plurality* (Grand Rapids: Eerdmans, 1998), 83–89.
52. Wainwright, *Lesslie Newbigin*, 388.

18
SAINTS AND CELEBRITIES: APPEALING TO THE MASSES

1. Quoted in Joan Jacobs Brumberg, *Mission for Life: The Story of the Family of Adoniram Judson* (New York: Macmillan, 1980), 7.
2. Ibid., 13.
3. Norman Grubb, *C. T. Studd: Cricketer and Pioneer* (Fort Washington, PA: Christian Literature Crusade, 1972), cover.
4. Anne Sebba, *Mother Teresa: Beyond the Image* (New York: Doubleday, 1998), xviii, 84.
5. Alan Neely, "Saints Who Sometimes Were: Utilizing Missionary Hagiography," *Missiology* (October 1999): 443.
6. Ibid., 448.
7. Marilee Pierce Dunker, *Man of Vision, Woman of Prayer* (Nashville, TN: Thomas Nelson, 1980), 179.
8. Ibid., 193–94.
9. Bruce Olson, *Bruchko* (Carol Stream, IL: Creation House, 1978), back cover.
10. Sebba, *Mother Teresa,* xiii.
11. Edward Le Joly, S.J., *Mother Teresa of Calcutta: A Biography* (San Francisco: Harper & Row, 1983), 8.
12. Sebba, *Mother Teresa,* 46.
13. Ibid., 36.

14. Eileen Egan, *Such a Vision of the Street: Mother Teresa—the Spirit and the Work* (New York: Doubleday, 1985), 90–91.
15. Sebba, *Mother Teresa,* 72.
16. Malcolm Muggeridge, *Something Beautiful for God* (Garden City, NY: Image Books, 1971), 37.
17. Egan, *Such a Vision*, 357.
18. Dee Jepson, *Women Beyond Equal Rights* (Waco, TX: Word Books, 1984), 52.
19. Brother Andrew, *God's Smuggler* (Old Tappan, NJ: Revell, 1967), 26.
20. Ibid., 108.
21. Brother Andrew, *Battle for Africa* (Old Tappan, NJ: Revell, 1977), 23–26.
22. Russ Hoyle, "Risky Rendezvous at Swatow," *Time,* (October 19, 1981): 109; "Bible Shipment to China," *Charisma* (February 1982): 14.
23. Brother Andrew, *The Ethics of Smuggling* (Wheaton, IL: Tyndale House, 1974), 136–37.
24. Hoyle, "Risky Rendezvous at Swatow," 109.
25. Brother Andrew, "God's Smuggler Confesses," *Christianity Today* (December 11, 1995): 46.
26. Alan Burgess, *Daylight Must Come: The Story of a Courageous Woman Doctor in the Congo* (New York: Dell, 1975), 135.
27. Ibid., 149.
28. Ibid., 95.
29. "A HIS Interview with Helen Roseveare," *HIS* (January 1977): 18.
30. Burgess, *Daylight Must Come*, 45.
31. "A HIS Interview," 19.
32. Jackie Pullinger with Andrew Quicke, *Chasing the Dragon* (Ann Arbor, MI: Servant Books, 1980), 36.
33. Ibid., 31.
34. Ibid., 28, 31.
35. Ibid., 84.
36. Ibid., 69.
37. Ibid., 67–69.
38. Ibid., 77.
39. Ibid., 84–86.
40. Ibid., 133.
41. Jackie Pullinger, *Crack in the Wall: Life and Death in Kowloon Walled City* (London: Hodder & Stoughton, 1989), 16.
42. Don Richardson, *Peace Child* (Glendale, CA: Regal, 1974), 96.
43. Ibid., 172.
44. Ibid.
45. "How to Reach the Hidden People: An Interview with Don Richardson by Robert Walker," *Christian Life* (July 1981): 52.
46. Richardson, *Peace Child*, 191.
47. Ibid., 206.
48. Ibid., 277, 283.

General Bibliography

Anderson, Gerald H., ed. *Biographical Dictionary of Christian Missions.* Grand Rapids: Eerdmans, 1998.

Barker, William P. *Who's Who in Church History.* Old Tappan, NJ: Revell, 1969.

Beaver, R. Pierce. *American Protestant Women in World Mission.* Grand Rapids: Eerdmans, 1968.

______. *Pioneers in Missions: The Early Missionary Ordination Sermons, Charges, and Instruction.* Grand Rapids: Eerdmans, 1966.

Bliss, Edwin, ed. *Encyclopedia of Missions.* 2 vols. New York: Funk & Wagnalls, 1891.

Bosch, David J. *Transforming Mission: Paradigm Shifts in Theology of Mission.* Maryknoll, NY: Orbis Books, 1991.

Broadbent, E. H. *The Pilgrim Church.* London: Pickering & Inglis, 1978.

Coggins, Wade T. *So That's What Missions Is All About.* Chicago: Moody Press, 1975.

Coggins, Wade T., and E. L. Frizen Jr. *Evangelical Missions Tomorrow.* Pasadena: William Carey, 1977.

Cook, Harold R. *Highlights of Christian Missions: A History and Survey.* Chicago: Moody Press, 1967.

Deen, Edith. *Great Women of the Christian Faith.* New York: Harper & Row, 1959.

Douglas, James D., ed. *The New International Dictionary of the Christian Church.* Grand Rapids: Zondervan, 1974.

DuBose, Francis M., ed. *Classics of Christian Missions.* Nashville: Broadman, 1979

Eddy, Sherwood. *Pathfinders of the World Missionary Crusade.* New York: Abingdon-Cokesbury, 1945.

Glover, Robert H., and Herbert J. Kane. *The Progress of World-Wide Missions.* New York: Harper & Brothers, 1960.

Harrison, Eugene Myers. *Giants of the Missionary Trail.* Chicago: Scripture Press, 1954.

Hastings, Adrian. *The Church in Africa, 1450–1950.* New York: Oxford University Press, 1994.

Hefley, James, and Marti Hefley. *By Their Blood: Christian Martyrs of the 20th Century.* Milford, MI: Mott Media, 1979.

Hulbert, Terry C. *World Missions Today.* Wheaton, IL: Evangelical Teacher Training Association, 1979.

Hutchinson, William R. *Errand to the World: American Protestant Thought and Foreign Missions.* Chicago: University of Chicago Press, 1987.

Kane, J. Herbert. *A Concise History of the Christian World Mission*. Grand Rapids: Baker, 1978.

______. *A Global View of Christian Missions*. Grand Rapids: Baker, 1971.

______. *Life and Work on the Mission Field,* Grand Rapids: Baker, 1980.

Latourette, Kenneth Scott. *A History of the Expansion of Christianity*. 7 vols. Grand Rapids: Zondervan, 1970.

Marshall, Paul. *Their Blood Cries Out: The Untold Story of Persecution against Christians in the Modern World*. Dallas: Word Books, 1997.

Moreau, A. Scott, ed. *Evangelical Dictionary of World Missions*. Grand Rapids: Baker, 2000.

Neill, Stephen. *A History of Christian Missions*. New York: Penguin, 1964.

Neill, Stephen, et al. *A Concise Dictionary of the Christian World Mission*. New York: Abingdon, 1971.

Robert, Dana. *American Women in Mission: A Social History of Their Thought and Practice*. Macon, GA: Mercer University Press, 1996.

Rudnick, Milton L. *Speaking the Gospel through the Ages: A History of Evangelism*. St. Louis: Concordia, 1984.

Seamands, John T. *Pioneers of the Younger Churches*. Nashville: Abingdon, 1967.

Schubert, William E. *I Remember John*. Singapore: Far Eastern Bible College Press, 1976

Thiessen, John C. *A Survey of World Missions*. Chicago: Moody Press, 1961.

Tucker, Ruth A. *Guardians of the Great Commission: The Story of Women in Modern Missions*. Grand Rapids: Zondervan, 1988.

Winter, Ralph D. *The Twenty-five Unbelievable Years, 1945 to 1969*. Pasadena: William Carey, 1970.

Winter, Ralph D., and Steven C. Hawthorne, eds. *Perspectives on the World Christian Movement*. Pasadena: William Carey, 1981.

Wright, Elliott. *Holy Company: Christian Heroes and Heroines*. New York: Macmillan, 1980.

Illustration Index

General Index